American Economists of the Late Twentieth Century

American Economists of the Late Twentieth Century

Edited by

Warren J. Samuels
Michigan State University, US

Edward Elgar
Cheltenham, UK • Brookfield, US

Published by
Edward Elgar Publishing Limited
8 Lansdown Place
Cheltenham
Glos GL50 2HU
UK

Edward Elgar Publishing Company
Old Post Road
Brookfield
Vermont 05036
US

British Library Cataloguing in Publication Data
American economists of the late twentieth century
    1. Economists – United States 2. Economists – United States –
    History – 20th century
    I. Samuels, Warren J. (Warren Joseph), 1933–
    330'.0922

Library of Congress Cataloguing in Publication Data
American economists of the late twentieth century / edited by Warren
  J. Samuels
    A collection of 19 original essays written by American economists
of varied schools of thought.
    "This collection is a sequel to my New horizons in economic
thought: appraisals of leading economists, published in 1992 by
Edward Elgar"—Introd.
    1. Economists—United States—Biography. I. Samuels, Warren J.,
1933– . II. New horizons in economic thought.
HB119.A3A42 1996
330'.0973'09045—dc20   95–51767
                                               CIP

ISBN 1 85278 876 3

Printed and bound in Great Britain by
Hartnolls Limited, Bodmin, Cornwall

For Paul Yarck

Contents

Contributors

Randall Bausor: Department of Economics, University of Massachusetts, Amherst.

Jeff E. Biddle: Department of Economics, Michigan State University.

Kathleen Brook: Department of Economics, New Mexico State University.

Fred Carstensen: Department of Economics, University of Connecticut.

Avinash Dixit: Department of Economics, Princeton University.

John E. Elliott: Department of Economics, University of Southern California.

Jerry Evensky: Department of Economics, Syracuse University.

Alexander J. Field: Department of Economics, Santa Clara University.

Edward M. Graham: Institute for International Economics, Washington, DC.

Geoffrey M. Hodgson: The Judge Institute of Management Studies, University of Cambridge.

R. Mark Isaac: Department of Economics, University of Arizona.

George F. Loewenstein: Department of Social and Decision Sciences, Carnegie Mellon University.

Scott E. Masten: School of Business Administration, University of Michigan.

Elaine McCrate: Department of Economics, University of Vermont.

James Peach: Department of Economics, New Mexico State University.

Robert Pollin: Department of Economics, University of California, Riverside.

Matthew Rabin: Department of Economics, University of California, Berkeley.

Roy J. Rotheim: Department of Economics, Skidmore College.

A. Allan Schmid: Department of Agricultural Economics, Michigan State University.

Janet A. Seiz: Department of Economics, Grinnell College.

Richard Zeckhauser: John F. Kennedy School of Government, Harvard University.

Introduction

The original essays collected in this book summarize, place in perspective and appraise the work of important accomplished scholars whose writings represent – though by no means exhaust – the best, the most promising and the most innovative in contemporary economics in the United States, work undertaken from a variety of perspectives. This collection is a sequel to my *New Horizons in Economic Thought: Appraisals of Leading Economists*, published in 1992 by Edward Elgar, which in turn was a sequel to the two-volume collection, *Contemporary Economists in Perspective*, co-edited with Henry W. Spiegel and published in 1984 by JAI Press.

As indicated in *New Horizons*, a principal purpose of these collections is to display and applaud the diversity of work in economics undertaken in the US. Therein I also describe twentieth-century economics as comprised of a heterogeneous neoclassical mainstream and a heterogeneous array of heterodox schools, each one of which is itself heterogeneous. This is not the place to consider the rhetorical and heuristic value of disaggregating economics as a whole into separate schools of thought, though certainly it is not altogether incorrect to do so and many, if not most, economists, identify themselves more or less as members of particular schools.

Yet it is important to recognize that individual scholars are each more or less *sui generis*. Each scholar, however comfortably (or, for that matter, uncomfortably) writing within the paradigm or research program of a particular school, gives effect in his or her research and writing to his or her own version of the work of that school. The aforementioned heterogeneity arises from and is best evidenced by the work of individual scholars. Thus many – though by no means all – of the writers whose work is discussed in these essays work within neoclassical economics. Compared to the work of scholars from other schools, their work *is* clearly within the ambit of neoclassicism. But the work of these nominal neoclassicists is remarkably different and, what is more, in many cases these scholars *consider* their own work as either in conflict with or going beyond the mainstream of neoclassicism. The conclusions are inescapable, therefore, that designation by schools is not entirely conclusively representative of what economics is all about, or how economics is being done, and that the history of economic thought must also be sought in the details, rather than solely in grand, overarching generalizations – which is, after all, what designations of 'schools' amount to. Indeed, every such school in the history of the discipline – including classical, historical, Austrian, neoclassical, Marxian, institutionalist, social, Keynesian, and so on schools – displays enormous heterogeneity. This is so far true that particular doctrines considered fundamental by some adherents, and also used by historians of economic thought to generalize the position of the school as a whole, are contradicted and denied by other members of each school.

What I have just been saying relates to the various ways in which the historian of economic thought, and the general practitioner of economics, can characterize the intellectual history and composition of the discipline. One does not have to be a doctrinaire methodological individualist to appreciate that both the history of economic thought and contemporary economics ultimately reduces to the work of particular individuals. And the intertemporal sequence which comprises that disciplinary history is a function of how later economists both use and transform the work of earlier economists. From this perspective, it follows that the meaning of a particular school is always in a process of *becoming*; each school could evolve along several different lines, the different lines having certain things in common yet varying in other arguably important respects. But in every case that history is the history of the work of particular individuals. It is largely by virtue of a generalizing hindsight that we are able to identify and erect schools on the basis of the self-perceptions of participants and the somewhat more removed, though not necessarily more independent and objective, historians of thought. In each case, identification of schools, and the attribution of membership of a particular writer to a particular school, are matters of selective perception.

In any event, the scholars represented in this book stand on their own feet. They work in quite varied ways and on different subjects, each economist often working in several fields or topics, the identification and attribution of which are both often arbitrary. These include: the psychology of economic behavior (Robert Frank, Thomas Schelling, Vernon Smith, Richard Thaler, Amos Tversky and David Kahneman); technology (Nathan Rosenberg, Robert Solo); economic growth and development (Robert Heilbroner, Mancur Olson, Nathan Rosenberg, Robert Solo); system dynamics (Richard R. Nelson and Sidney Winter); monetary and macroeconomics (Paul Davidson); capitalism as a system (Samuel Bowles and Herbert Gintis, Robert Heilbroner, William Lazonick, Mancur Olson, Robert Solo); the history of economic thought as a subfield within economics (Robert Heilbroner, Nathan Rosenberg, Nancy Folbre); labor economics (Samuel Bowles and Herbert Gintis, Gregg Lewis);

feminist economics (Nancy Folbre); economic history (Robert Heilbroner, Nathan Rosenberg, Nancy Folbre); economics as a rhetorical or discursive enterprise (Nancy Folbre); collective action/institutions (William Lazonick, Mancur Olson, Vernon Smith, Robert Solo, Oliver Williamson); the economy as a series of power and games (Thomas Schelling, Vernon Smith, Nancy Folbre); international economics (Paul Davidson, Paul Krugman); micro-economics (Joseph Stiglitz), and so on. Several of these scholars – especially Heilbroner, Krugman, Stiglitz and Thurow – are among the leading generalists of our time, though their views of the economy and about how to do economics vary enormously.

One interesting intellectual and disciplinary question raised by the work of several of these subjects concerns the degree to which they are neoclassical. From one perspective, often their own, they seriously depart from the neoclassical mainstream. From another perspective, their departures are incremental, perhaps minimal, insofar as it is perceived that they retain fundamental elements of the neoclassical paradigm and mode of normal science. Perhaps the key lessons are that neoclassicism has never been entirely homogeneous, that it too changes at the margin, and that incremental changes may seem to be greater/lesser (they are at the margin) than they are in relation to the totality of the paradigm.

Let us take a glimpse at the variety of topics and themes on which these individual scholars have worked – with due regard to the fact that different readers will be interested in different aspects of their work and indeed would emphasize quite different themes.

Samuel Bowles and *Herbert Gintis* raise questions which most other economists ignore and answer them in a quite different context. The context is that of an economy structured by power relationships and in which all significant, and many minor, arrangements are neither given nor fundamentally harmonious but are, rather, contested territory. Bowles and Gintis examine the formation of preferences, life styles and identities (including personality characteristics) as part of the social reproduction of the socioeconomic system and its class and power structures. They examine labor and capital, including money, markets are operating to both give effect to and reproduce hierarchy; production, investment and government are seen as domains of power characterized by unequal decision-making participation. Topics, such as transaction costs, efficiency wages and rent seeking, are given quite different interpretations in their analyses. In her concluding paragraphs, Elaine McCrate points to Bowles and Gintis's idealism. They have no monopoly of idealism: the perspectives and analyses of most if not all other economists, including the straightforward neoclassicist, are replete with their own idealized versions of what the regnant economy is all about. What is interesting is not only the differences between the idealized systems but the differences between the accompanying respective portrayals of what the extant economy is 'really' all about.

Paul Davidson is a Post Keynesian macroeconomic and monetary economist and as such has views on a number of topics that are significantly different from mainstream economists. He is concerned with the nonneutrality of money, that is how the supply of money and monetary institutions perform and have an effect on aggregate real variables, such as output and employment. He is fundamentally concerned with uncertainty and its underlying radical indeterminacy and how stochastic processes thereby affect real output and employment. He is concerned with both structural and what are at bottom psychological variables, the latter having to do with the decisions people make with regard to the management of assets and disposition of income, in part with regard to how they treat monetary variables, such as the price level. His work is in the tradition of such economists as Wesley Mitchell in its concentration on the organization and operation of an essentially pecuniary economy.

Nancy Folbre is one of a group of female economists who have both questioned the stories told about households in general and women in particular on the basis of neoclassical, and also Marxian, theory and developed alternative lines of research and reasoning. A founder of feminist economics, Folbre has analyzed the preconceptions underlying important concepts and lines of reasoning, thereby contributing to the study of the rhetoric of economics. She has both identified and questioned gender bias in economic theory; examined the household as an arena of both cooperation and conflict; provided explanations for phenomena – such as the household division of labor, fertility and decision making – which, in her view, do not merely reinforce existing power relations; raised questions about gender-related and -impacting public policy; analyzed the structure and process of power within the family and its implications for economic performance; and, *inter alia*, explored the history of gender-related institutions.

Robert Frank is concerned with how people choose. He considers the importance of choice of reference group as a foundation for preferences and choices; and, therefore, the role of status emulation, or of positional conflicts. He also examines the role of commitment and of inducing commitment; individual and group identity, conscience and reward. His work gives effect to the recognition that in the real world one encounters both narrow utility maximization (whatever that may mean) and non-cognitive committed and other behavior. Like several other subjects, Frank's work attacks the problem of how it is that people come to have the preferences and make the choices they do.

Robert Heilbroner is, together with Milton Friedman, John Kenneth Galbraith and Paul Samuelson, among the small group of economists who are widely known to both educated people and the general public. He is best known for *The World Philosophers*, a study of important contributors to the history of economic thought that is both magisterial and readable. He has written on the complex historical origins of the modern economic system; the human prospect; the status of Marxism; various topics in broader social and narrower economic theory; and the history of economic thought. He is a leading critic of the mode of institutionalization of the Western capitalist economy and of Western, neoclassical economics. He is also a leading interpreter of the predicament of mankind in matters of growth and welfare (broadly and philosophically, as well as psychologically, understood). He is a leading interpreter of the ideas of Adam Smith and of Karl Marx. He himself is unequivocally of the 'left' and devotes himself to compatible subjects, including power in many of its subtle manifestations. He is an economist with a consciously developed 'vision' in the sense of Joseph Schumpeter. He displays the fruits of his insights regarding the critical importance of government.

Daniel Kahneman and *Amos Tversky* are psychologists serious and bold enough to consider how in fact individuals in an organized economy actually behave. This is remarkable because they are pursuing the psychological foundations of economic behavior, whereas mainstream economists have largely been uninterested in the reality of behavior, preferring to assume 'rationality' in one or another formulation. The rationality assumption has generated implications which have been important to economists working in both positive and normative economics. Kahneman and Tversky's work is all the more remarkable, however, because they have been listened to by economists. Their work is serious, conceptually and experimentally well designed, and sensibly specified and interpreted. Their work should permit a more realistic, richer, and a more finely textured and more subtle – as well as less presumptuous and less tautological – treatment of the psychology of economic life. Like the work of Thomas Schelling, these psychologists focus on how people make choices given the alternatives open to them and how they confront uncertainty. Among their insights are the importance of heuristic principles and strategies; the role of biases in perception and choice; how learning takes place; the effects of framing, context and reference points; preference reversals; the differential treatment of gains and losses; and so on. Because of their work, and that of others, such as Robert Frank and Richard

Thaler, the psychology of economics will never be the same as it was for centuries.

Paul Krugman works in the areas of international trade and general economic policy. He has concentrated on structural – including industrial organization – and systemic as well as distributional considerations. His work addresses some of the major theoretical and policy subjects of our time, especially those having to do with the structure of the international economy and the respective economic policy systems of leading countries, especially Japan. He combines mastery of technique with attention to institutional developments and fundamental policy issues.

William Lazonick, working in part in the tradition of Joseph Schumpeter, among others, believes that the story told by neoclassical economics fails to capture the organizational transformations of capitalism which have taken place. As Fred Carstensen interprets him, Lazonick focuses on endogenous and path-dependent organizational form and technology; organizational responses to high fixed costs; and combinations of intrafirm and external coordination, participation and planning, including new forms of governmental activism. Together these have resulted in a transformation of managerial capitalism, which had replaced individual entrepreneurial capitalism, by collective capitalism. Lazonick's analysis depends strongly on his studies in economic history and of the modern Japanese economy. Throughout, markets take second place to systems of organization and control. If Lazonick is correct, then the general theory of both the modern economy and of economic policy needs to be severely reconstructed.

Gregg Lewis was a major figure in the development of post-World War Two labor economics through both his research and his teaching; contemporary labor economics is conducted along the lines he developed. He combined neoclassical economic theory and careful statistical testing in considering some of the most fundamental, and also politically and ideologically controversial, questions in labor economics. These questions included the effect of unions on relative wages, the issue of labor 'monopoly', the employment effect of unionism, the labor/leisure tradeoff, and so on. He was also attentive to questions of the nature and limits of statistical tests.

Richard Nelson and *Sidney Winter* have established themselves as the foremost analysts of economic evolution since Thorstein Veblen, John R. Commons and Joseph A. Schumpeter. They have worked at the levels of methodology and concept formation to undergird their principal contributions which have been in the areas of long-run change, technology and institutions and, especially, the cumulative results of their interactions. Among other things, they have focused on selection mechanisms within firms and on the habits and routines which embody received knowledge and skills. They have applied analogies and metaphors from evolutionary biology to the study of organizations in order to explore adjustment, adaptation and transmission phenomena. As the essay on them indicates, their work has made them the foremost economic analysts of how economic organization, operation and performance is driven and constrained by *knowledge*.

Mancur Olson is the author of one of the most seminal books of the last third of the twentieth century, *The Logic of Collective Action*. In this and other works, he explored the variables which affect how groups work or fail to work together for purposes generated by the group. He is concerned with the relative benefits and costs of collective action and their respective distribution. Among the variables his work encompasses are group size, transaction costs, asymmetry, public goods and externalities, free ridership, methods and limits of organizing collective action, and so on. His work applies to the formation and operation of both narrow and broad interest-group organizations, including both professional/industrial associations and treaty organizations, and has engendered insights both novel and important. His work also applies to such other questions as development, trade integration, inequality and the firm.

Nathan Rosenberg has contributed to at least three fields in economics: the history of economic thought, economic growth, and technology, in all three using the materials of economic history. His work on Adam Smith on institutions, including government, has contributed to the most sophisticated, as opposed to ideological, understanding of the work of this most seminal and important writer. Rosenberg's work has emphasized the system of social control necessary for a market economy, as understood by Smith himself, thereby rendering vacuous the conventional noninterventionist interpretation of both Smith and the economic role of government in general; *laissez-faire*, if it is to signify anything analytically meaningful, must mean something quite different and more subtle than it is usually held to say. His work on Smith and other writings, including that on Mandeville and Marx but also on such substantive topics as machine tools, has contributed to our understanding of economic growth, including the role of invention. His work on the relationships between growth and technology is among the most subtle and sophisticated in the discipline.

Thomas Schelling pursues economics as a discipline studying the logic of choice. He focuses on strategic thinking and choice in a huge variety of circumstances. His game-theoretic reasoning supplements the standard rationality assumption by examining the formation and perception of alternatives by economic agents. His work was central to the management of US relations with the former Soviet Union, contributing to the successful (avoidance of nuclear war and Western survival) conduct of the Cold War. Schelling's work in matters of economic theory concerns the situation in which choice is economically important, namely, where, unlike in the perfectly competitive case, how and which choices are made has demonstrable effect.

Vernon Smith is a, probably the leading, founder of the field of experimental economics, undertaking in economics a type of research long undertaken in psychology and other disciplines, including political science. Smith pays close attention to the research protocols governing his experiments and is deeply cognizant that these protocols govern both the content and the meaningfulness, as well as limits, of his work. He appreciates both the interconnections and mutual influences between research design and technique and substantive economic analysis and that the stories produced by the techniques he employs are derived from their methodological protocols. Perhaps the substantive conclusion derived from his work of the most wide-ranging and deepest significance is the critical role of institutions – including property right systems – in forming markets and generating economic performance. Given the necessity of some possibility of mutual beneficial gains, how those gains are generated, structured and distributed, as well as the underlying behavior, is governed by institutional arrangements. This view inevitably is in conflict with that version of neoclassical economics which posits that all adjustments are merely responses to changes in price. Both individual psychology and institutions are important.

Robert A. Solo is truly a *political* economist. He is interested in how the economic system is embedded in the social system and the consequences of that embeddedness. He is interested in social change and the manifold ways in which it originates and proceeds, especially at the systemic level. He is interested in general economic systems and particular organizations not as simple units but as structures of beliefs, roles, and power. He is interested in the methodology and language on the basis of which and/or with which one analyzes the economy. He is a leading critic of neoclassical economics, especially insofar as it fails to deal with the institutional, organizational, and power-structure nature of the actual economy. But above all he is interested in the economy as a *political* economy, as a complex system in which the state, contrary to the dominant ideology, is important in many and variegated ways. He offers his theory of the state as both a descriptive and prescriptive account.

Joseph E. Stiglitz is one of the most prolific and wide-ranging writers in economics. Yet the core of his work consists of the analysis of how people deal with information and risk in the real world. His work has provided insights into how institutions (relationships, contracts, and so on) are formed and operate in a world of incomplete and asymmetrical information and risk. He deals with moral hazard, principal–agent relations, incomplete and imperfect markets, market structures, organizations, search and screening, notions and limits of 'market failures', risk aversion, credit rationing, efficiency wages, and so on.

Richard Thaler is another economist who is interested in delving deeply into the psychological foundations and elements of economic behavior. He desires to enrich the treatment of actual economic behavior by both looking to the discipline of psychology for insights and taking up directly certain significant anomalies left hanging by the traditional theory of rational behavior. He, too, sees that economic decision making, even under the rubric of rational choice, is not only far more complex and richer than the traditional theory provides for, but is capable of being researched in various respectable and meaningfully productive ways. He provides, for example, roles for beliefs, nonsymmetric attitudes towards losses and gains and towards different income sources, non-monolithic personal identities, and other factors which enter into actual decision making.

Lester Thurow has made major contributions to several fields of economics, notably, income distribution, labor, public finance and macroeconomics. He has focused on the Smithian question of productivity, the institutionalist and Post Keynesian question of how labor markets actually work, the stochastic nature of economic life in the face of radical indeterminacy (uncertainty), the limits of econometric models and techniques, the necessity of choice consequent to scarcity and in the presence of conflicts, and the hegemonic growth of the international economy. On every topic his analysis carries implications for how the economic role of government can usefully be analyzed. Thurow is a theorist who has his feet firmly planted on the institutional and systemic ground.

Oliver Williamson uses the concept of transaction costs to examine the formation and operation of institutions. His analysis deals with uncertainty; adjustment to change; the construction of organizational governance, especially but not solely in the firm; the role of relationship-specific assets; human cognition and behavior; and so on. His is an approach to the theory of the firm, to the division of labor between firm and market, and to the design of markets. He is most fundamentally interested in the logic and psychology of choice, how people relate to one another, and the unpacking of such organizations as the firm and of technology.

Several themes, some explicit and others implicit, pervade these essays, at least as I read them (my finding them is hardly surprising, as it was I who chose the subjects to be included!): (1) Great attention to the nature, complexity and psychology of choice, at the very least greatly enriching the neoclassical treatment of rationality, self-interest and preference formation. (2) The richness and fertility of the history of economic thought as a subfield in the discipline. (3) The continued attention to uncertainty (radical indeterminacy) as a central problem in economics, one that should not be trivialized through assumptions that finesse the problem. (4) The importance of institutional and systemic history as, *inter alia*, influencing cultural options and path dependency. (5) Increasing attention to the organization and operation of economic agents, such as firms and governments. (6) Attention to the analysis of the evolving economic system as such. And so on.

To return to an earlier theme, these developments can be seen in at least two ways. They can be understood as further enriching the neoclassical mainstream of economics, making it more complex and modifying it but permitting its continuity, albeit revised in important ways. Or they can be understood as providing the basis for some new, future systematization, perhaps some new 'school', a systemization which will represent a new age, a new corpus of Kuhnian 'normal science' for the discipline. What seems to be clear is that the diversity represented in this collection treats fundamentally important topics, and points to both the multiplicity and open-ended future of economics, a discipline which is always being socially (re)constructed.

It is clear that the authors of these commissioned essays like their subjects; in some cases there has been a professor–student relation and in some a co-authoring relation. Ceremonial lionization of subjects has nonetheless been held, I believe, to a respectable minimum. But more important, the subjects have been shown to be bright, vital, dedicated human beings.

A complex, sensitive subject must be discussed. I was unable to commission and/or secure essays on several authors. Although the possibility is open for including essays on them in a subsequent collection(s), I am disappointed. Three of the subjects were males. For one, I was unable to find an author. For the second, the author, a male, did not produce the agreed-upon essay. For the third, the female author failed to produce the commissioned essay. A female author of a fourth essay (on a male) also did not come through, though I was able to secure a substitute (male) author. A female author of a commissioned essay on a female subject – the only female subject – did produce her essay. Another female author did produce her contribution.

The proportion of women originally included in the project was substantial: four as author, plus one co-author, and one as subject. The proportion of those who actually participate is, alas, much lower: two authors, one co-author, and one subject. A much smaller proportion of commissioned male authors did not contribute. I am disappointed and hope to do better next time.

Apropos the theme of diversity, attention should be called to *Foundations of Research in Economics: How Do Economists Do Economics?*, edited by Steven G. Medema and myself, and also published by Edward Elgar Publishing Ltd. That collection explores diverse ways and problems of doing economics and, together with the present collection, conclusively demonstrates (if more demonstration is needed) the heterogeneity of the practice of economics. If economics is what economists do, then economists do a great variety of things, using a variety of theoretical formulations and lines of reasoning, and do so in a great variety of ways.

Enormous appreciation is due to the contributors. The creation of essays such as these is often a daunting task for economists whose work typically is of a quite different nature. Very few of our authors are specialized historians of economic thought. For the most part they prepared their essays in a timely manner and all were responsive to editorial suggestions for improvement. More important, they produced essays which bring out the nature, depth and importance of the work of their subjects. I am very thankful to them as well as to the staff of Edward Elgar Publishing Ltd.

Warren J. Samuels

1. Samuel Bowles and Herbert Gintis

Elaine McCrate

For most of the twentieth century, economists schooled in the Walrasian tradition have been content to assume that economic relationships are fully specified by contract. Market exchanges have been characterized as a simple *quid pro quo* in which the parties freely exchange money for consumer goods, money for labor, money now for more money in the future, and so on. Accordingly, in a Walrasian world, people get the things they effectively demand at the going prices, but they do not bargain, monitor, discipline, coerce, evade or resist in the process. As a result, markets are simply allocational devices, and economics is what we were all told in our principles classes: the study of the allocation of scarce resources to competing uses.

We were also all taught that preferences are exogenous, or may safely be assumed so in most important economic situations. Those agents who do not bargain, coerce, and so forth, also are not influenced or changed in any fundamental way by their economic activities.

The late twentieth century has ushered in considerable skepticism concerning these assumptions. Samuel Bowles and Herbert Gintis in particular have challenged this view of the economy. First, they have rejected the notion that contracts fully characterize most important economic interactions: rather, in labor, credit and other important markets, one party cannot get what he/she wants without some means to enforce his/her claims. The labor contract alone cannot ensure the employer that work will be done at the speed and of the type which he/she desires; thus, in Marx's words, labor must be extracted from labor power. Similarly, the banker cannot be sure that the loan will be repaid; the borrower's risk taking must be regulated by noncontractual means. Such exchanges are, in Bowles and Gintis's terms, contested. The result, as will be discussed below, is that markets – as well as many other social institutions, such as schools – are characterized by the pervasive exercise of power. Markets do not just allocate; they also discipline.

Not only do markets come out of this analysis looking quite different from their representation in the Walrasian model; so do the agents. In Bowles and

1

Gintis's reformulation, their preferences are shaped by daily experience in markets, firms, schools, families and communities. In other words, economic actors are endogenous, both with respect to their individual preferences and with respect to the social norms which they observe.

Bowles and Gintis's joint work has developed over nearly three decades in three stages, around which this chapter is organized. In the first stage, spanning the late 1960s and early 1970s, they explored the relationship between class, schooling and economic opportunity, culminating in their book *Schooling in Capitalist America* (1976). They argued that schools were institutions which facilitated the extraction of labor from labor power by imparting behaviors and attitudes consonant with students' future positions in the work hierarchy. In the second stage, from the mid-1970s to the mid-1980s, Bowles and Gintis turned their attention to broader·questions about liberal and Marxian political and economic theory, asserting that neither was adequate to understand the democratic politics which animated most important recent social movements in the US. The major work from this period was *Democracy and Capitalism* (1986). Finally, in their most recent papers, Bowles and Gintis have developed microtheoretic models of several markets in which claims are enforced endogenously, and they have argued that what seemed to constitute the uniqueness of labor markets – the absence of costlessly observable behavior and of costlessly enforceable contracts – actually turns out to characterize a lot of other significant markets, among them credit, some consumer goods, and international financial markets. They have explored the implications of contested exchange for the quality of social institutions and norms – and conclude that a democratically organized economy would do better on both counts. This stage of their work will culminate in two books currently under way, *Property and Power: The Analytical Foundations of a Democratic Economy*, and *Contested Exchange: An Essay on the Microeconomic Foundations of Capitalism*.

SCHOOLING IN CAPITALIST AMERICA

Bowles and Gintis's work on education evolved in a curious period of intellectual history. Students all over the world were rebelling against repression in the schools, but economists were refining human capital theory, in which both the repression and rebellion were effaced. According to Bowles and Gintis, the problem with human capital theory is that it neglects the unique qualities of labor (the distinction between labor and labor power), thus obscuring the asymmetric relationship between capital and labor, and eliminating the concept of class from the economist's lexicon (Bowles and Gintis 1975). As a result, neoclassical theory is poorly suited to explaining the wage structure, the valuation of personal characteristics in the labor market, and the social relations of schooling.

The ability of their alternative theory to explain these phenomena hinged on the Marxian distinction between labor and labor power. Labor power is 'the maximum level of performance evincible from [the worker] by the capitalist'; in the employment relation the worker agrees to accept the employer's direction of his/her time, but the 'labor' or actual work done by the individual depends on control mechanisms embedded in the labor market and the social and political structure of the firm (ibid.). In the language of their most recent work, the labor process is a 'contested exchange' (Bowles and Gintis 1994).

Because of the political conflict between workers and owners over the extraction of labor from labor power, employers value ascriptive characteristics of workers, such as race, sex, age, demeanor and credentials. These can divide the workforce and inhibit the development of solidarity between workers. Educational credentials in particular legitimate inequality by 'providing an open, objective, and ostensibly meritocratic mechanism for assigning individuals to unequal occupational positions' (Bowles and Gintis 1975).

Bowles and Gintis further argued that the educational system fundamentally stratifies students according to their future positions in the workplace hierarchy, through the 'correspondence principle'. Schools do not just teach more or less; they teach different things to different people. In working-class schools, students are rewarded for rote learning and following the rules, while in the schools of professional/managerial families, students are rewarded for creativity and independent thought.[1] For most students, these behaviors will be necessary for secure employment in their adult occupational positions. The key political conclusion of the book follows from the correspondence principle: only a democratic transformation of the economy can provide the foundation for significant, sustainable educational reform.

Finally, Bowles and Gintis contended that the economic success associated with higher levels of schooling results not from the acquisition of cognitive skills but from the stratification process. Students do learn in school; but these skills are not scarce in the labor market.[2]

---

1. Regarding the question of how the classroom experience is different for children from working-class and professional/managerial families, see Chapter 5 of Carnoy and Levin 1985.
2. There has been quite a bit of discussion lately among labor economists concerning whether the return to skill has risen in the last decade or so. It is possible that Bowles and Gintis's argument was stronger in the 1960s, when their data was collected, than it is today. However, the last couple of

Bowles and Gintis have been charged with functionalism, and their book often seemed to suggest that the relations of schooling developed as they did because of the need of the capitalist class to fragment the workforce. However, Bowles and Gintis included three chapters detailing the historical process by which schooling came to be dominated by the capitalist class. In addition, their argument drew heavily on the work of Melvin Kohn and others, which showed that parents usually demand the type of education for their children which will teach behaviors rewarded in the parents' own experience of work (Kohn 1969). Thus professional/managerial parents stress independence and creativity, while more subordinate working-class families feel their children must learn to take orders.[3]

Bowles and Gintis supported their theory with extensive empirical work. First, in a paper in the *Journal of Political Economy*, Bowles disputed many sociological status attainment models and the nascent human capital model, which purported to show that earnings were not significantly related to socioeconomic background when the respondent's schooling was included in the regression equation. These studies typically measured the respondent's social background with father's education and occupation. Bowles argued that the importance of education was systematically overestimated and that of social class was underestimated in these models for two reasons: (1) the improper specification of socioeconomic background, in particular the omission of variables such as mother's education and occupation, parental income, wealth, and position in the work hierarchy; and (2) measurement errors, especially those arising from respondent reporting of father's occupation and education. Including a measure of parental income and deploying an errors-in-variables model, Bowles found that the partial relationship of schooling to income fell by 43 percent compared to the conventional model. He concluded that the contribution of education to income had indeed been overestimated and the intergenerational transmission of class had been underestimated in the conventional formulation (Bowles 1972).

Gintis (1971), Bowles and Nelson (1974), and Bowles, Gintis and Meyer (1975) explored the mechanism by which education affects earnings.[4] They found that the main contribution of schooling to earnings was not through its effect on cognitive achievement, but rather by inculcating personality traits

---

decades have also witnessed the rapid growth of inequality within schooling and experience groups. (See Levy and Murnane 1992.)

3.   For another re-evaluation of functionalism, see also Bowles and Gintis 1981.
4.   See also Edwards 1976.

necessary for work in a hierarchical environment. For example, Gintis compared pairs of earnings regressions where a measure of cognitive achievement was first excluded, then included in the model. He found that the reduction in the coefficient on schooling in earnings equations when achievement was included was typically well below 20 percent, supporting the view that schooling does not primarily contribute to higher earnings through the cognitive skills which it develops. Bowles and Nelson demonstrated that the distribution of income by education was virtually identical whether or not cognitive achievement was controlled for. Finally, they showed that the effect of socioeconomic background on economic success was very strong even for individuals with equal education and cognitive achievement.

Gintis also found evidence for the alternative interpretation of schooling, that it develops appropriate class-differentiated personality characteristics. For example, students' grade point averages were positively correlated with perseverance, suppression of aggression, and so on, and negatively correlated with independence, initiative, originality, and curiosity.

Another part of Bowles and Gintis's work on schooling was a response to the recently revived idea that class structure is explained by the distribution of heritable cognitive skills. In the early 1970s scholars were becoming aware of the failure of the human capital programs of the War on Poverty, and as at other times when educational reform had failed, there were many voices to attribute this defeat to the genetic deficiencies of the poor. At the time, these voices were led by Richard Herrnstein and Arthur Jensen. Most of the opposition to Herrnstein and Jensen had coalesced around the position that ability is not inherited; Bowles and Gintis's unique contribution was to show that cognitive ability is of much less economic importance than either the defenders or detractors of Herrnstein and Jensen supposed. They found that the distribution of income by socioeconomic background was just about as skewed for persons of equal childhood IQ as it was for persons of all IQ levels (Bowles and Nelson 1974; Bowles and Gintis 1972-73).

Bowles and Gintis's theoretical and empirical work on education demanded profound reconsideration of much of modern welfare economics. The normative basis of educational planning models, rate of return studies, and so on, requires that preferences be invariant to the schooling process. Yet Bowles and Gintis's work showed that the economic productivity of schooling resulted predominantly from its inculcation of the personality attributes needed for stable hierarchical relations at work – subordination to authority and inability to envision alternatives. Preferences, far from being exogenous, were systematically influenced by the structure of economic institutions: schools, workplaces and families (Gintis 1971, 1974).[5]

Twenty years have passed since the publication of *Schooling in Capitalist America*. The book keeps selling, and it has found a receptive audience in the more heterodox wing of the education and economics professions. Carnoy and Levin drew heavily on Bowles and Gintis's theory in the research included in their book (Carnoy and Levin 1985). Mark Blaug, a central figure in the economics of education, eventually incorporated Bowles and Gintis's views into his treatment of the screening hypothesis (Blaug 1987). Bowles's idea that errors in variables obscure the intergenerational transmission of class has experienced a mini-revival lately, with two important papers making similar arguments in the *American Economic Review* (Solon 1992; Zimmerman 1992). However, a quick perusal of leading labor journals such as the *Journal of Human Resources*, the *Journal of Labor Economics*, the *Industrial and Labor Relations Review*, and the *Economics of Education Review*, will establish the hegemony of human capital theory. The only fairly mainstream labor journal which still seems open to Bowles and Gintis's work on schooling is *Industrial Relations*.

DEMOCRACY AND CAPITALISM

During the 1960s and 1970s, radical social movements increasingly mobilized around the language of liberal democracy. Southern blacks marched for civil rights, women demanded the right to self-determination and an equal voice in the family, and workers began to articulate the goal of a democratic workplace. A deeply rooted commitment to individual rights and popular sovereignty provided the cultural tools to articulate the goals of these movements.

In *Democracy and Capitalism*, Bowles and Gintis argued that neither liberal nor Marxian social theory (the former including neoclassical economics) had much to say about these social movements, because neither satisfactorily addressed two of their central concerns, domination and identity.[6]

---

5. Gintis's work on endogenous preferences with respect to schooling suggested a larger problem with neoclassical theory and capitalist organization: society would have a materialist bias, because people could only improve by getting things, not by becoming better people. See Gintis (1972, 1971).

6. In this stage of their work, Bowles and Gintis began to move away from traditional Marxian formulations of economic problems, which they increasingly saw as insensitive to the priorities of modern social movements. Two papers document more of their transitional thinking, which tried to reformulate the labor theory of value to address their growing concerns about Marxism. These are Bowles and Gintis 1977, 1981.

First, both philosophies had highly restrictive views of domination. Liberalism had no conception of domination outside the sphere of physical coercion (predominantly, the state). Individual choice was the foundation of freedom, and found nearly full expression in markets. Indeed, 'democracy' was virtually equated with 'capitalism'. This perception, so clearly at variance with the historical record, was made possible by two partitions of social space. The first was the application of liberalism's basic terms – freedom, equality, democracy – to an arbitrarily demarcated public realm, which excluded families and workplaces. The second was the relegation of large groups of people to a category of learners, who are excluded for various reasons (ranging at times from age and incapacity to gender, race and propertylessness) from the sanctioned exercise of rights and freedoms.

Bowles and Gintis argued that the liberal rejection of popular sovereignty in the economy was inappropriately based on a characterization of the economy as private, that is, involving no socially consequential exercise of power (Bowles and Gintis 1983). They found three types of such power: capitalist control over the labor process, control of investment and disproportionate influence over state economic policy. Each of these was socially consequential in that they did not simply arise as a response to the competitive dictates of the market; a democratic reorganization of decision making concerning the labor process and the allocation of credit was feasible, and such reorganization would produce equivalent or greater output.

While Marxism did not share the propensity of liberal theory to declare the capitalist economy off-limits to democratic decision making, it contributed little else to the understanding of domination. Certainly, one of its great intellectual triumphs was demonstrating that owners may exploit workers in production, despite the absence of direct physical coercion in competitive labor markets. However, by remaining overly preoccupied with the unequal distribution of property, and the unequal distribution of the surplus to which this gave rise, Marxism expounded a one-dimensional view of oppression.[7] Not surprisingly, then, Marxism had little relevance for feminists who were greatly concerned with violence against women and the gender division of labor, and even for trade unionists who challenged the political, rather than just the distributional, dimension of exploitation.

---

7. This is the basis of Bowles and Gintis's debate with John Roemer. Roemer accepts the Walrasian assumption of clearing competitive markets, and abstracts from issues of agency and incentives, locating the primary source of capitalist power in the ownership of the means of production. See Roemer 1990.

Marxism was further limited in its comprehension of domination because the theory was generally hostile to the concepts of agency and freedom. If liberal theory misunderstood domination through its elevation of choice and freedom to the grand organizing principles of capitalism, Marxism had the same result by marginalizing the role of agency in the transformation of capitalism.

The second major shortcoming of both liberal and Marxist theories was their neglect of the politics of identity. In liberal social theory, the notion of 'identity' reduces to the exogenous interests of individuals. And despite the prominence of solidarity and class in Marxian social theory, Marxism also disregarded the process by which group identity and solidarity developed, trusting that these flowed automatically from membership in a class (and perhaps also race, gender or nationality). Both philosophies viewed institutions as means towards pregiven interests, rather than as profound influences on interests.

Thus, whatever their differences, Marxian and liberal theory shared two fundamental commitments: to a one-dimensional representation of power and to a notion of exogenous interests. Bowles and Gintis proposed that a democratic politics must come to grips with two fundamental realities: first, that oppression takes many forms operating under many different social rules, and second, that politics is as much about who we are to become as it is about what we get.

The Heterogeneity of Domination

Bowles and Gintis portrayed the immense diversity of forms of domination in their scheme of sites and practices. A site is a distinct set of social rules. Thus one site, the workplace, is structured around rules which (among other things) give the employer the right to decide investment strategies and determine layoffs. Another site, the family, is structured around rules which establish various divisions of labor and distributions of authority and goods among family members. Yet another site, the liberal democratic state, operates according to rules establishing civil liberties, elections, and so on.

Practices are interventions to change some aspect of social reality. They are of four types, distinguished by their objects: appropriative (transforming the physical world), distributive (changing the allocation of some social good), cultural (changing the tools of social discourse), and political (altering the rules of a social interaction). Bowles and Gintis asserted that forms of domination are generally not identified with any one site; rather, for example, gender inequality is reproduced through the interaction of the rules structuring wage work, families, and the state. Similarly, capitalism is reproduced not just at the workplace, but also in the state and family, much as Bowles and Gintis's earlier analysis of schooling had established. Furthermore, practices are often transported from one site to another as contesting groups seek to expand the range of applicability of practices which favor them.

Society is thus a 'mosaic' of structures and practices, interacting as a reproductive, but also potentially contradictory whole. Bowles and Gintis made extensive use of Marx's insight that social structures may contain the seeds of their own transformation. Certain sites tend to generate the kinds of practices which undermine one or more sites; for example, rapid expansion of the capitalist relations of production proletarianizes women and subjects them to capitalist domination at the same time that it mitigates male domination in the home. But in contrast to some passages of Marx, Bowles and Gintis did not regard the trajectory of fundamental social change as preordained by structure. Historically conjunctural social practices, with all their unpredictable, irreducibly human moments, profoundly influence what kind of institutional change will result from structural contradiction. In particular, the extent and forms of solidarity, which depend critically on how different oppressed groups articulate their priorities, determine the winners and losers of social change. And this depends on the ability of groups to shape communicative tools – such as the words 'freedom', 'right' and 'citizen' – in such a way that gives their diverse membership internal cohesion (Gintis 1980).

Bowles and Gintis analyzed the demise of the Keynesian accord in the 1970s using this framework (Bowles and Gintis 1982).[8] The accord, developed in the first several decades after 1930, set rules which attenuated a recurring clash between rights vested in persons by the liberal democratic state, and rights vested in property by the rules of capitalist production. Each set of rights has been characterized by an expansionary logic and history: capitalism has progressively encroached upon more and more spheres of social activity, while the language of rights has been increasingly transported to sites for which it was never intended by its original proponents. One such example is the 'right' to a safe workplace, which restricts the capitalist's 'right' to direct his/her workers and to invest his/her funds entirely as he/she sees fit.

Such clashes of property and personal rights escalated in the 1960s and 1970s. The labor, civil rights, anti-war, women's, environmental and occupational safety movements, all scored important successes by couching their demands in the culturally familiar and sanctioned language of liberal

---

8. See also Bowles, Gordon and Weisskopf 1983.

democratic rights, even though it challenged the traditional rights of capital. In the process, these movements increased workers' standard of living, about doubling average real income in a generation. They also gained for their constituents greater control over economic decision making, forcing dominant groups to spend ever more of their resources on enforcing the old but newly vulnerable social rules which buttressed their domination.

This was a structurally stable scenario only as long as the economy grew rapidly, permitting simultaneous growth of profits and workers' incomes, and increased expenditures on enforcing the rules of the game. The success of the Keynesian accord in attenuating conflict depended on the two to three percent growth in productivity which it was able to maintain from about the late 1940s to the late 1960s. However, the successful demand for greater rights by a broad range of groups undermined dominant groups' control, and contributed to the profit squeeze and attendant economic crisis of the late 1960s and 1970s.

Endogenous Interests: Learners and Choosers

Bowles and Gintis's work on schooling had shown that preferences are not independent of institutions. In *Democracy and Capitalism*, they argued that social action also changes the actors in economic conflicts. Marxism, they argued, only partially comprehended this phenomenon, because of the common assumption that actors' interests were preconstituted by class position. Liberal theory could not at all accommodate the process of learning through social participation, because learning lies outside the logic of choice. Most significantly, while agents may have a relatively great deal of freedom to choose consumer goods and even in many cases their occupational roles, they have far less liberty to influence the process by which wants are formed in the first place: to choose what kind of persons they want to be.

Thus liberal theory ensured that institutions were exempt from evaluation concerning their contribution to human development, and that hierarchical control was never scrutinized for its detraction from democratic culture. By sanctioning the complete ascendancy of 'exit' over 'voice', the theory rationalized the lack of participation which fosters personal growth. In addition, by identifying choice and freedom with the liberal state and with markets, liberal theory sanctioned the lack of participatory institutions (excepting the capitalist corporation) positioned in between the state and the individual.

MICROFOUNDATIONS OF POLITICAL ECONOMY

Missing from Bowles and Gintis's work to this point were persuasive answers to some key questions concerning power in the economy. How can capitalists dominate and exploit, when dissatisfied workers can simply walk away from their jobs, because labor markets clear in equilibrium? Why is there not a flourishing sector of democratically controlled firms in advanced capitalist economies if such organization is more efficient? In *Schooling in Capitalist America*, they had stressed that owners exercise power over workers through control over the labor process, and through educational practices which maintained capitalist domination. In *Democracy and Capitalism*, they also grappled further with the question of economic power, particularly in their discussion of why the capitalist economy is not private. In the third phase of their collaboration, they produced several rigorous models of what they called short-side power in the economy: the ability of agents with scarce resources (jobs, credit, and so on) to unilaterally sanction others (workers, democratic firms, and so on) by denying access to these resources.

Marx of course had developed the notion of a reserve army of unemployed labor, which was automatically replenished when profits began to fall. Unemployment reduced workers' bargaining power in the employment relationship and restored the surplus, in part by increasing the extraction of labor from labor power. This was the intuition behind short-side power. The first hint of how Bowles and Gintis would use it appeared in an early paper by Gintis (Gintis 1976). He suggested that the wage might be held above market-clearing levels, creating an excess supply of labor, and putting currently employed workers in the position where they could not walk away from their jobs, and would be motivated to submit to demands for greater work intensity. A decade later, they developed a full microtheoretic model around this idea, showing how an optimizing capitalist who cannot observe his/her workers nor enforce his/her labor contracts costlessly will choose a wage higher than the market-clearing level, in combination with worker surveillance, as a worker discipline device – producing unemployment, even when the labor market is in equilibrium (Bowles 1985; Gintis and Ishikawa 1987; Bowles and Gintis 1990, 1993).

The model works as follows. In order to elicit greater work effort, workers' gain from employment must exceed the value of their next best alternative. Thus, the credibility of the employer's threat of dismissal depends on what Bowles and Gintis call the 'employment rent' (or more broadly, the 'enforcement rent').[9] This is equal to the present value of the worker's earnings (taking into account the probability of dismissal) minus the present value of alternative sources of income. The employer can use some combination of employment rents (by varying the current wage) and costly monitoring to elicit greater work intensity. The worker will evaluate the marginal disutility of additional effort against its effect on the probability of dismissal, producing a 'labor extraction function'. If the magnitude of alternative income sources is exogenous, and the employer knows how workers react to variations in enforcement rents, the employer chooses a wage to maximize actual work done per unit of wages. This yields an equilibrium effort/wage configuration in which the worker is working at greater intensity than he/she would choose without the employment rent, but also receives a wage greater than the value of his/her fallback position. Because enforcement rents are positive, there is by definition involuntary unemployment. The employer has short-side power (the power of 'contingent renewal' of the employment relationship) because in equilibrium he/she supplies fewer jobs than are demanded.

But why do unemployed workers, or workers dissatisfied with the intensity of their labor under the direction of others, not start their own firms? The reason is that the capital market is also contested, much like the labor market (Bowles and Gintis 1992; Gintis 1989). Borrowers have an incentive to pursue high-risk high-expected-rate-of-return strategies because the cost of failure is borne by the lender. The lender in turn cannot collect debt obligations from a defunct borrower, so the lender will seek an enforcement mechanism. Monitoring a borrower's risk-taking behavior is extremely problematic, and the magnitude of the potential loss calls for some strategy in addition to contingent renewal to regulate the borrower's actions. The lender's optimizing strategy is to choose some combination of collateral and enforcement rents (in this case, interest rates below the level which makes the borrower indifferent to securing the loan).

The model of enforcement rents in credit markets works similarly to the model of enforcement rents in labor markets. The borrower's probability of default varies positively with the interest rate, because a higher rate lowers the value of the investment project for which the loan is being obtained, and reduces the magnitude of the enforcement rent. Assuming the lender knows the borrower's probability of default schedule, the lender chooses an optimal interest rate and amount of collateral to maximize his/her expected rate of

---

9. It was also called in some papers the cost of job loss. For an attempt to measure the magnitude of employment rents in the US economy, see Bowles and Schor 1987.

return, with several significant results. First, the optimal interest rate will be below the level at which the borrower is indifferent between securing and not securing the loan; that is, there will be positive enforcement rents. Second, because the interest rate is below that threshold, there will be capital-rationed agents, persons who would like to get a loan but cannot. Third, the borrower will choose less risky behavior than he/she would have without the enforcement rents.

The importance of collateral in the endogenous enforcement mechanism in credit markets explains why workers cannot just start their own firms. Because of the collateral requirement, they have to have money in order to borrow money. Thus wealth holders exercise power over more than the goods and services which they can purchase; they exercise power over people in a number of critical ways, including short-side power to deny credit and to withhold jobs.

The importance of wealth in endogenous enforcement situations also provides an answer to an old question raised by Bowles and Gintis's work on schooling: with human capital becoming more important in the advanced capitalist countries, why are the owners of human capital not as powerful as the owners of financial and physical capital? From Bowles and Gintis's analysis of short-side power, the answer is apparent: the transferral of human capital is not exogenously enforceable, and thus is not as attractive to potential lenders as physical capital.

Bowles and Gintis have most recently begun to explore the implications of endogenous enforcement for the evolution of social institutions and norms (Bowles and Gintis 1993). They argue that the evolution of social institutions depends not just on allocative efficiency but also on their relative effectiveness in enforcing claims. For example, exchange capital markets tend to penalize non-hierarchical firms because such organizations have more participants whose actions must be controlled to ensure a favorable outcome for the lender (Gintis 1989).[10] More obviously, the existence of involuntary unemployment and credit-rationed agents indicates substantial inefficiency in the economy.

Furthermore, because contested exchange involves personal, strategic interactions, rather than the anonymity of faceless contractors in the Walrasian model, there is far more opportunity and incentive to try to shape the values of those with whom an employer or lender interacts. The contested exchange economy is more like a series of repeated games, which are replicated over

---

10. Another example is that worker of ownership of the firm and control over enforcement strategies is more efficient than capitalist ownership and control: such a redistribution permits compensation to former owners while making workers better off. See Bowles and Gintis 1993.

time and across sites. Like any repeated game, there is ample opportunity for cooperation. However, because spot markets privilege 'exit' over 'voice', the potential for cooperation is severely curtailed by the Walrasian ideal of anonymous exchange. The favored modes of dealing with others become indifference, non-cooperation and opportunism, rather than reciprocity and solidarity.

Bowles and Gintis count themselves among a growing number of contemporary 'post-Walrasians' who recognize the importance of imperfect enforceability of contracts or the endogeneity of economic agents. The former include the school of transaction-cost economics (Williamson 1985; Aoki 1984) and efficiency-wage theorists (Shapiro and Stiglitz 1984). The latter include Amartya Sen. A very small number of economists have questioned both exogenous enforcement and exogenous agents, these including Douglass North (1981) and George Akerlof.

However, Bowles and Gintis's treatment of endogenous enforcement differs considerably from that of other post-Walrasians. The transaction-cost and efficiency-wage approaches treat a systematic propensity towards opportunism, and the disutility of labor with its attendant 'shirking', as human nature. Bowles and Gintis see these as the result of the organization of economic life, assisted by the Walrasian mode's representation of the ideal world as one of faceless, anonymous transactions.

The transaction-cost school (as well as Coase, and Alchian and Demsetz) also view the authoritarian structure of the firm as a transaction-cost minimizing, hence 'efficient' solution to these problems of human nature. In contrast, Bowles and Gintis have consistently emphasized the efficiency-enhancing characteristics of the democratic firm. Moreover, the transaction-cost economists tend to see the endogenous enforcement problem as bilateral, which flows from their somewhat different treatment of incomplete contracts. For them, contracts are incomplete in complex transactions governing future behavior because not all possible contingencies can be foreseen and addressed in the contract. Contract termination is costly because both parties have heavy relationship-specific investments. Hence each party is motivated to establish a governance structure to regulate the behavior of the other. In contrast, Bowles and Gintis regard the exercise of power as asymmetric: workers are hurt far more by separation from the firm than are their employers. When employers dismiss a worker, they only lose search and training costs for that one individual, while a worker who walks away from his/her job loses a major portion of his/her livelihood while imposing relatively minor costs on his/her employer.

CONCLUSION

Bowles and Gintis have done a lot to expand social scientists' views of conflict and power throughout the economy. In the process, they have also expanded social scientists' views of democracy in two ways. First, they have shown that democracy must be thought of as more than the registering of preferences (purchasing and voting); it ought also to concern the formation of preferences. Second, they have shown that the central terms of liberal democracy, freedom and sovereignty, ought not just apply to the state, but also to workplaces, schools, families and other sites.

Lest we be left with just a warm feeling in our hearts towards a couple of utopian idealists, it is important to remember that Bowles and Gintis have also been very outspoken on the need for progressive social movements to defend their projects with the language of technical and social feasibility. Not only is a democratic economy morally just; not only does it do a better job of fostering human development; it is also less wasteful and more rational, and promises greater prosperity for the vast majority of people. Their recent both popular and technical work on productivity-enhancing asset redistributions seeks to provide concreteness to these hopes (Bowles and Gintis 1993 and 1995).

BOWLES AND GINTIS'S MAJOR WRITINGS

Bowles, Samuel (1972), 'Schooling and Inequality from Generation to Generation', *Journal of Political Economy*, May/June, **80** (3), S219-S251.

Bowles, Samuel (1985), 'The Production Process in a Competitive Economy: Walrasian, Neo-Hobbesian, and Marxian Models', *American Economic Review*, **75** (1), March, 16-36.

Bowles, Samuel and Herbert Gintis (1972-73), 'IQ in the U.S. Class Structure', *Social Policy*, **3** (4-5), November/December, January/February, 1-27.

Bowles, Samuel and Herbert Gintis (1975), 'The Problem with Human Capital Theory – A Marxian Critique', *American Economic Review*, **65** (2), May, 74-82.

Bowles, Samuel and Herbert Gintis (1976), *Schooling in Capitalist America: Educational Reform and the Contradictions of Economic Life*, New York: Basic Books.

Bowles, Samuel and Herbert Gintis (1977), 'The Marxian Theory of Value and Heterogeneous Labor: A Critique and Reformulation', *Cambridge Journal of Economics*, **1** (2), June, 173-92.

Bowles, Samuel and Herbert Gintis (1981a), 'Structure and Practice in the Labor Theory of Value', *Review of Radical Political Economics*, **12** (4), Winter, 12-26.

Bowles, Samuel and Herbert Gintis (1981b), 'Education as a Site of Contradiction in Reproduction of the Capital–Labor Relationship', *Journal of Economic and Industrial Democracy*.

Bowles, Samuel and Herbert Gintis (1982), 'The Crisis of Liberal Democratic Capitalism', *Politics and Society*, **11**, 51-93.

Bowles, Samuel and Herbert Gintis (1983), 'The Power of Capital: On the Inadequacy of the Conception of the Capitalist Economy as "Private"', *The Philosophical Forum*, **14** (3-4), Spring–Summer, 225-45.

Bowles, Samuel and Herbert Gintis (1986), *Democracy and Capitalism: Property, Community, and the Contradictions of Modern Social Thought*, New York: Basic Books.

Bowles, Samuel and Herbert Gintis (1990), 'Contested Exchange: New Microfoundations of the Political Economy of Capitalism', *Politics and Society*, **18** (22), June, 165-222.

Bowles, Samuel and Herbert Gintis (1992), 'Power and Wealth in a Competitive Capitalist Economy', *Philosophy and Public Affairs*, **21** (4), Fall, 324-53.

Bowles, Samuel and Herbert Gintis (1993a), 'The Democratic Firm: An Agency-Theoretic Evaluation', in Samuel Bowles, Herbert Gintis and Bo Gustafsson (eds), *Democracy and Markets: Participation, Accountability, and Efficiency*, Cambridge: Cambridge University Press, 13-39.

Bowles, Samuel and Herbert Gintis (1993b), 'The Revenge of Homo Economicus: Contested Exchange and the Revival of Political Economy', *Journal of Economic Perspectives*, **7** (1), Winter, 83-102.

Bowles, Samuel and Herbert Gintis (1993c), 'Memo to Clinton: Economics', *Tikkun*, January, 16-20.

Bowles, Samuel and Herbert Gintis (1994), 'The Economics of Education Reconsidered: Implications of Recent Developments in Microeconomic Theory and Labor Economics', forthcoming in Martin Carnoy (ed.), *The International Encyclopedia of Economics of Education*, Oxford: Elsevier Science.

Bowles, Samuel and Herbert Gintis (1995), 'Escaping the Efficiency–Equity Tradeoff: Productivity-Enhancing Asset Redistributions', forthcoming in Gerald Epstein and Herbert Gintis (eds), *Macroeconomics after the Conservative Era: Studies in Savings, Investment, and Finance*, Cambridge: Cambridge University Press.

Bowles, Samuel, Herbert Gintis and Peter Meyer (1975), 'The Long Shadow of Work: Education, the Family, and the Reproduction of the Social Division of Labor', *Insurgent Sociologist*, Summer.

Bowles, Samuel, David Gordon and Thomas Weisskopf (1983), *Beyond the Waste Land: A Democratic Alternative to Economic Decline*, Garden City, New York: Doubleday.

Bowles, Samuel and Valerie I. Nelson (1974), 'The "Inheritance of IQ" and the Intergenerational Reproduction of Economic Inequality', *Review of Economics and Statistics*, **56** (1), February, 39-51.

Bowles, Samuel and Juliet Schor (1987), 'Employment Rents and the Incidence of Strikes', *Review of Economics and Statistics*, **64** (4), November, 584-91.

Gintis, Herbert (1971), 'Education, Technology, and the Characteristics of Worker Productivity', *American Economic Review*, **61** (2), May, 266-79.

Gintis, Herbert (1972), 'A Radical Analysis of Welfare Economics and Individual Development', *Quarterly Journal of Economics*, November.

Gintis, Herbert (1971), 'Consumer Behavior and the Concept of Sovereignty: Explanations of Social Decay', *American Economic Review*, May, 267-78.

Gintis, Herbert (1974), 'Welfare Criteria with Endogenous Preferences: The Economics of Education', *International Economic Review*, **15** (2), June.

Gintis, Herbert (1976), 'The Nature of the Labor Exchange and the Theory of Capitalist Production', *Review of Radical Political Economics*, **8** (2), Summer, 36-54.

Gintis, Herbert (1980), 'Communication and Politics: Marxism and the "Problem" of Liberal Democracy', *Socialist Review*, **10** (2-3), March-June, 189-232.

Gintis, Herbert (1989a), 'Financial Markets and the Political Structure of the Enterprise', *Journal of Economic Behavior and Organization*, **1**, 311-22.

Gintis, Herbert (1989b), 'The Principle of External Accountability in Financial Markets', in Masahiko Aoki, Bo Gustafsson and Oliver Williamson (eds), *The Firm as a Nexus of Treaties*, New York: Russell Sage, 289-302.

Gintis, Herbert and Tsuneo Ishikawa (1987), 'Wages, Work Discipline, and Unemployment', *Journal of Japanese and International Economics*, **1**, 195-228.

OTHER REFERENCES

Aoki, Masahiko (1984), *The Cooperative Game Theory of the Firm*, London: Clarendon.

Blaug, Mark (1987), 'Where Are We now in the Economics of Education?', in Mark Blaug (ed.), *The Economics of Education and the Education of an Economist*, New York: New York University Press, 129-40.

Carnoy, Martin and Henry M. Levin (1985), *Schooling and Work in the Democratic State*, Stanford, California: Stanford University Press.

Edwards, Richard C. (1976), 'Individual Traits and Organizational Incentives: What Makes a "Good Worker"?', *Journal of Human Resources*, Spring.

Kohn, Melvin (1969), *Class and Conformity: A Study in Values*, Homewood Illinois: Dorsey Press.

Levy, Frank and Richard Murnane (1992), 'U.S. Earnings Levels and Earnings Inequality: A Review of Recent Trends and Proposed Explanations', *Journal of Economic Literature*, **30**, September, 1333-81.

North, Douglass (1981), *Structure and Change in Economic History*, New York, Norton.

Roemer, John E. (1990), 'A Thin Thread: Comment on Bowles and Gintis's "Contested Exchange"', *Politics and Society*, **18** (2), 243-9.

Shapiro, Carl and Joseph E. Stiglitz (1984), 'Unemployment as a Worker Discipline Device', *American Economic Review*, **74** (3), June, 433-44.

Solon, Gary R. (1992), 'Intergenerational Income Mobility in the United States', *American Economic Review*, **82** (3), June, 393-408.

Williamson, Oliver E. (1985), *The Economic Institutions of Capitalism*, New York: The Free Press.

Zimmerman, David J. (1992), 'Regression Toward Mediocrity in Economic Stature', *American Economic Review*, **82** (3), June, 409-29.

2. Paul Davidson

Roy J. Rotheim

It is the synchronous existence of money as a unit of account and the presence of 'offer contracts' and 'debt contracts' which are denominated in money units which forms the core of a modern monetary production economy. Money is and must be the thing which is ubiquitously involved on one side or the other of all contracts if these contracts are to be enforceable in a viable monetary system. (Davidson 1972b, p. 149)

In a Post Keynesian world, time is an asymmetric variable, and the economy is moving irreversibly and unidirectionally (forward) through time. The past may be knowledge but the future is unknown – yet, economic decisions taken in the present will require actions which cannot be completed until some future day (or days). In such a world, economic decision makers are continuously involved in sequential decisions and actions which are coloured not only by their expectations of the unknowable future but also by the inherited stocks (which embody correct previous guesses as well as past errors) which they possess. Consequently decisions rarely if ever are made on a clean slate. (Davidson 1982, pp. 9-10)

Trust in the ability of money to be a stable store of generalized purchasing power over producible goods depends on people believing that no matter how far the current spot price for any producible be momentarily displaced by spot market conditions, the market price for the good at some future date is anchored in a forward price constrained by money flow-supply prices whose principal component is the money-wage rate. (Davidson 1994a, p. 6)

INTRODUCTORY REMARKS

Let me begin this essay with a personal reflection. My first encounter with Paul Davidson, in the beginning of the 1970s, occurred with the myth rather than the man. To give it some context, I need to recount my very first day in graduate school at Rutgers, sitting down with the then chair of the department, one of the many members of the faculty who over the years received their training at Columbia (then and still a farm team of Chicago), whose job it was to screen my class schedule for that fall term. Macro theory was not being offered because someone named Davidson was off in Cambridge writing a book on Keynes, or so I was told. Having the luxury of a blank in my schedule, I wrote down Economic Development, a new topic to someone whose undergraduate background had been limited to theory, labor economics and econometrics. I had gone to Rutgers to study labor economics with this chair and with another senior professor (whose PhD was from another Chicago farm team) and so I sat there calmly while he gave my schedule a condescending glare, crossed out the last entry, and asked me why I would ever want to take a course taught by an institutionalist? I agreed in typically obsequious graduate student style, even though I did not have a clue as to what an institutionalist might have been.

My relationship with this chair fizzled rather quickly after I withdrew from his course, the reason being that I had read, as an undergraduate, the two books he had chosen by Gary Becker, finding them displeasing to my tastes. Unfortunately, I was subsequently to find that my fellowship for the following year had been rescinded on the grounds that I had not worn a tie or jacket while I was a graduate teaching assistant ('What do you think this is: the English department?' he asked). My relationship with the other professor lasted not much longer when in class, after I made some disparaging remark about what I thought to be the innocuous empirical work that had been done on dead-weight loss, he asked: 'What's the matter? Don't you believe in downward-sloping demand curves either, Mr Rotheim?'. So there I was, penniless, and mentorless, trying to find a place in what had become a rather hostile environment for someone so new to the game.

Shortly after those incidents which severed me from the two persons with whom I had gone to Rutgers to study, I was mulling about in the department when I overheard the one saying to the other: 'Just received a letter from Davidson. You're not going to believe this, but he's become an *institutionalist*!'. Well that settled it. And in the spirit of 'I don't know art, but I know what I like', I decided that I was going to study with this Davidson person when he returned from England. And I did; and have never regretted it.

So what follows, then, is a somewhat one-sided assessment of Paul Davidson's economics. He once said to me that over time, I would find differences between my own views and his, just as that seemed to have happened between himself and his mentor. However, except for some flirtations with critical realism on my part that he has yet to embrace, I still find myself to be a Davidsonian hook, line and sinker. And what that means for the reader of this essay, is that criticisms of his work, of which some exist, will have to be found elsewhere.

A further qualification: Paul Davidson's contribution to the economics profession has been so profound and pervasive, covering fields as wide as natural resources, outdoor recreation, public finance, macroeconomic and monetary theory and policy (both domestic and international), income distribution, history of economic thought and methodology, that any article attempting to carefully assess and scrutinize his work in the detail that it deserves would span far beyond the limitations of this essay. As such, what I have set out to do, after a thumbnail sketch of the extent and breadth of his writings stretching over the last five decades, is to offer a clear statement on what appears to this writer as Davidson's principal contribution to the field of Post Keynesian economics, that being a theoretical foundation for a monetary production economy in which money and money contracts stand at the very heart of the system. This will be followed by a few additional personal comments.

THE SCOPE AND EXTENT OF PAUL DAVIDSON'S CONTRIBUTION TO ECONOMICS

First, some basic background information. Not unlike many of the other important persons in our discipline, Paul Davidson's route to Economics came after he had spent some time among the natural/pure sciences. Davidson took his undergraduate degree in Chemistry and Biology at Brooklyn College, proceeding on to the University of Pennsylvania in Biochemistry, getting as far as writing a dissertation on DNA and teaching in their Medical and Dental Schools. Having lost interest in this research program, he radically changed course, going on to the City University of New York to get an MBA, then returning to Penn, this time to do a PhD in Economics.

Davidson's doctoral dissertation, written under the supervision of Sidney Weintraub (defended in the summer of 1958), focused on a historical exegesis of aggregate income distribution, later published as Davidson (Davidson 1960a; see also 1959 and 1960b). After receiving his degree, he taught at Rutgers and Penn for a short while, but left academia to work as the Assistant Director of the Economics Division for the Continental Oil Company. He stayed in the corporate sector for only one year, returning to Penn for a few years, after which he took his principal position at Rutgers for the next 20 years. For the last eight years he has held the J.F. Holly Chair of Excellence in Political Economy at the University of Tennessee. In addition, Paul Davidson has been editor of the *Journal of Post Keynesian Economics*, since its inception in the Fall of 1978 (co-edited by Sidney Weintraub until the latter's death in 1983). And finally, above all else, he is considered to be the leading proponent and most highly respected member of what has come to be known, over these last 25 years, as Post Keynesian economics.

Let us begin, then, by identifying an ontological foundation for Paul Davidson's perspective on economics.[1] First appearing in *Money and the Real World* (Davidson 1972b, 1978) and reproduced in his *International Money and the Real World* (Davidson 1982, 1992), Davidson has constructed what he calls a 'Table of Political Economy'.[2] At the center of Davidson's 'Table of Political Economic Schools of Economic Thought' is, of course, the Keynes School itself: 'an exceedingly small group who have attempted to develop Keynes's original view on employment, growth and money, e.g., Harrod, Lerner, and Weintraub' (Davidson 1972b, p. 3).[3] In the second incarnation of this Tableau, ten years later, Davidson adds the names of Shackle, Minsky, Wells, Vickers and himself in this 'Keynes School of Political Economy' (Davidson 1982, p. 5).

To the right of the Keynes School are the Neoclassical/bastard Keynesians and the Monetarist/Neoclassical Schools; while to the left are the Neo-Keynesian and Socialist/Radical Schools. The seven categories Davidson employs to delineate these schools include: politics, money, wage rate and income distribution, capital theory, employment theory, inflation, and the role of government.

The politics of the Keynes School, Davidson describes as center;[4] monetary and real sectors are ubiquitously interrelated; the money-wage rate is

---

1. Davidson has consistently avoided any such philosophical notions in his writings, insisting that the most effective strategy is to beat one's opponents at their own game, using their turf and language as much as possible. I remember him saying that there is this hidden mechanism in his ear that automatically shuts off whenever phrases such as ontology and epistemology become the focus of attention. He once wrote to me: 'If you want to communicate with the mainstream who think mathematical terminology is the greatest thing since white bread, then you have to use the dialect of conventional math theory. ... One does not want to use fuzzy concepts that are easy for the mainstream to laugh off as mere hand waving'.
2. The 'table' is also reproduced in Davidson's exegetical entry on Post Keynesian Economics in (1980b).
3. The inclusion of Harrod among this group is somewhat contentious, as it was he who was one of the originators of the ISLM approach (along with Hicks and Meade). This would appear to situate him, therefore, more squarely in the school designated by Davidson as 'The Neoclassical/Bastard Keynesian School'.
4. I remember someone asking Davidson in our graduate Seminar on Monetary Theory, where we were working with an early draft of *Money and the Real World*, why he put *politics* at the top of his list. He responded by quipping that people always chose their politics before their economics. But when it came time to pinning down Davidson as to his own politics, the process became less precise. Once I asked him in his office, why he was not a socialist, given the direction that his economics tended to point. The only response I received was: 'Because I dislike parades'.

fundamental while income distribution is of lesser importance (to be compared with the neo-Keynesian School in which the money-wage rate is the linch-pin of the price level and income distribution is very important). Moreover, the Keynes school disavows both marginal productivity theories from the right and surplus approaches from the left in favor of what Davidson refers to as a *scarcity theory*, emphasizing the importance of quasi-rents. As such, Davidson identifies himself, in the main, as middle-of-the-road Keynesian. And although he would be averse to overly obtuse philosophical statements regarding methodology, it would be fair to say that Davidson would clearly adhere to the view that the crucial, non-ergodic nature of an economy in real historical time rules out theories and policies that exist only in the realm of logic, but not in the real world. And from this vantage point Davidson clearly concurs with Keynes in that the 'teaching [of orthodoxy] is misleading and disastrous if we attempt to apply it to the facts of experience' (Keynes 1936, p. 3).

Paul Davidson can be characterized as a second-generation Keynesian; but a first-generation Weintraubian, because it was from Weintraub that Davidson learned his Keynes. He once said that 'Sidney's masterpiece was a book that he'd written when I was a graduate student, *An Approach to the Theory of Income Distribution* (Weintraub 1958), which was his formative work. I understand Keynes from that book more than from Keynes. If you don't read that book, you don't really understand Keynes' (King 1994, p. 362). What Sidney Weintraub saw as essential to Keynes, emerging from both the *Treatise on Money* and *The General Theory* (to different extents) was the importance of the money-wage rate and the question of aggregate income distribution. In fact, two of Davidson's early significant contributions, his book with Eugene Smolensky on *Aggregate Supply and Demand Analysis* (Davidson and Smolensky 1964a) and his article on 'Keynes's Finance Motive' (Davidson 1965) received their impetus and in many ways followed directly from Weintraub's 1958 book. As Davidson observed, recently: 'Sidney's aggregate supply plus the finance motive was what broke the code of the *General Theory* for me. Those two things together were really what made me a post-Keynesian' (King 1994, p. 364).[5]

Among the many profound insights in Weintraub's book is the derivation of the demand curve for labor, not as the traditional marginal product of labor schedule, but rather as the loci of points of effective demand at different wage rates. Here what is important in determining the level of employment are both the supply-side phenomena (productivity questions) and aggregate demand (income

---

5.   See Weintraub (1958), Chapter 6: 'An Approach to the Theory of Wages', and Chapter 8: 'A Modified Liquidity-Preference Theory of Interest'.

effects) (Weintraub 1958, ch. 6). This Weintraubian construction clearly influenced Davidson's critique of Patinkin's so-called Keynesian theory of involuntary unemployment (Davidson 1965) and the critiques of Meltzer's, Weitzman's and Lucas's theories of labor supply and demand emanating from marginal productivity and choice phenomena in real-wage/labor space (Davidson 1983a, 1983b). As Davidson wrote in the latter piece: 'Until we get our theory of employment demand and supply logically correct, economists are unlikely to provide useful guidelines for employment policy' (Davidson, p. 106).

The finance motive, simply stated, involves a unique demand for money to finance business purchases, *before* those purchases are effected. Keynes neglects this demand decision from *The General Theory*, but rectified the omission a year later (Keynes 1937b), calling it the 'coping stone' of his liquidity preference theory. Weintraub gives brief reference to this motive in his 1958 book (Weintraub 1958, p. 153), but it is Davidson who truly elicits the profound nature of this motive. For in his 1965 article, what Davidson achieves is no less than a clear proof of the interdependence of the real and monetary sectors, vitiating the classical dichotomy of orthodoxy. Moreover, by focusing on the finance motive for demanding money, Davidson was able to show that the ISLM framework did not yield a unique equilibrium in output/interest rate space, because of the interdependence of the two functions (see also Davidson 1972b, ch. 7 and 1994a, ch. 8).

But it is in the two-year period 1968-69, that Davidson formulates a microfoundation for understanding money in an economic growth setting from the vantage point of the supply and demand price for capital, rather than from the neoclassical synthetic pretend Keynesian system (see Davidson 1968b, 1968c, 1969). There, Davidson's focus was, and continues to be, the construction of a path-dependent dynamical theory of money and value emanating from Keynes's *Treatise on Money* (1930) and Chapter 17 of *The General Theory* (1936). What is unique about those two sources is that in each, Keynes was attempting to juxtapose questions of stocks and flows in an environment in which the future was uncertain and in which the current stock of assets, both financial and capital, embodied those past decisions and stood as alternatives to the flow of new assets. Elaborating on this motif, Davidson makes a break from the more static aspects of the Weintraubian model under which he had been trained, in favor of a rich *open* framework in that the future unfolded from decisions made in the present, in light of the current stock of capital assets, which while embodying the successes and errors of the past, could not give probabilistic indications about what the future would bring. Within these two articles is embodied, in this writer's opinion, the most important theoretical contribution made by Paul Davidson to the discipline.

In the 1968 *Econometrica* article (1968b), Davidson takes aim at the *Keynesian* theory of money and economic growth expounded by James Tobin three years earlier (Tobin 1965; see also Davidson 1968c). He observes that Tobin's model only held true when Say's Law was operational, implying that money was redundant over the course of economic growth. In other words, there was no role for money in Tobin's model: 'Tobin simply assumes market clearance at full employment in a world of perfect certainty' (Davidson 1968b, p. 295).

As an alternative, Davidson constructs a stock-flow model of investment behavior, where the flow of investment is not a function either of the share of income that is saved by households or of the actual proceeds accruing to the stock of capital. Investment will occur, so long as the spot price of capital exceeds the forward price, a situation of normal backwardation.[6] To the extent that investment is financed externally, there is an outstanding stock of debt corresponding to the stock of capital, while the flow of new capital goods can be financed out of the flow of placements. However, 'the introduction of an exogenous money creating banking system allows investors to make investment decisions that can be incompatible with the public's portfolio preferences at the current rate of interest' (ibid., p. 312).

With some necessary overlap, Davidson developed these ideas in the following year, directed less at a criticism of Tobin, *per se*, but rather in a more constructive vein to establish what he called: 'a Keynesian view of the relationship between accumulation, money and the money wage-rate' (Davidson 1969). Again, he situates Keynes squarely in the capital accumulation decision, employing the same pathbreaking methodology formulated in the 1968 *Econometrica* article. In this sense he provided a theoretical foundation for what might be called a Chapter 17 Keynesianism. The motivation here is to show that real capital assets make poor stores of value, leaving that function to the only asset whose liquidity premium exceeds its carrying cost. And as a result of the unique properties of money defined by Keynes in Chapter 17 of *The General Theory*, real capital assets and money will never be substitutes such that only the latter can serve as a viable store of value in an uncertain world.

Moreover, Davidson constructs a model of investment based on his earlier stock-flow model which juxtaposes the relationship between the demand and supply prices of capital goods. In this way, he avoids the neoclassical approach to the topic which pits the marginal product of capital schedule (appropriately

---

6. Davidson observes in the interview with John King that, much to Davidson's disappointment, Tobin did not reply to this article, but instead published, one year later, his q-theory of investment, which in Davidson's opinion was exactly the same as his own stock-flow analysis: 'if you look at the q theory, that is exactly what it is: spot-forward, the existing price of capital (the spot price) versus the flow production price of capital' (1994a, p. 365).

discounted) against some real rate of interest.[7] Rather, it is the *money* rate of interest that is relevant. This money rate receives its uniqueness because 'the liquidity premium of money ... "rules the roost" in the long run, in the sense that it ultimately checks the output of capital by checking demand for capital goods' (Davidson 1969, p. 309). And such an outcome can occur, which of course can stop output before it reaches its full employment level, not because of some income constraint, but rather because of the two properties particular to money outlined by Keynes. This is what Davidson considers to be the source of Keynes's involuntary unemployment. Unlike capital goods, which had positive flow-supply schedules, such was not the case for money. The money rate of interest could never be negative, unlike capital goods (there could never be a contango[8] in the money market), and thus money would be the only asset in which wealth would ultimately be stored. If there were no assets which possessed those properties of money, that is that were not reproducible and which were not substitutable with real assets, then involuntary unemployment could not occur and the economy would be a non-monetary economy.

The argument did not end there, however. For the money rate of interest only had uniqueness so long as contracts denominated in money terms were equally unique:

> If money is to be designed as a store of value, then there must be a 'normal' expectation that the value of output in general will be more stable in terms of money than in terms of any other commodity. This does not necessarily require that wages be fixed in terms of money; rather what is necessary is that wages be relatively *sticky* in terms of money. ... [T]he stability of the exchange value of money is closely related with the stability of the money wage-rate. (ibid., p. 316)

As such, the precondition for stability in an economy in which capital accumulation is occurring is that there is confidence in the relative stability between flow supply prices and future spot prices, which in turn can be held with confidence to the extent that the money-wage rate (being the prime cost of production) is relatively sticky in both directions. [9]

---

7. Davidson's formulation of this model clearly predated Minsky's similar approach in (1975).

8. Contango is a situation where the demand for an asset is so low that its current spot price falls short of its flow supply price. In this case production will not occur until this relationship is inverted, when there occurs a deterioration of the existing stock of that asset so as to make it relatively scarcer.

9. Because of this analytical framework, Davidson concludes that it is more likely that price increases will occur because of changes in costs (primarily the money wage rate) rather than changes in demand: '[T]he money wage-rate is a ubiquitous component of the flow-supply prices of commodities and [thus] labour costs are uniquely related to short-run market prices' (p. 319). It is for this reason that Davidson indicates his preference for an incomes policy to regulate price increases.

I think it is fair to say that it was these three articles published in the two-year period 1968-69 that confirmed Paul Davidson's status as the leading young Post Keynesian economist of that time. In 1969-70, Davidson took leave from Rutgers to become Senior Visiting Scholar at the University of Cambridge, where he was to take his writings over the previous five years and compose them into a treatise on Post Keynesian economics. The final product appeared in 1972 under the title *Money and the Real World*. Space prevents retelling the amazing story of Davidson's year at Cambridge spent dodging Joan Robinson's attacks, assignments and aspersions. For this amusing account see Davidson's interview with John King (King 1994).

This immediate period saw two additional significant articles by Davidson: the first being his contribution among the critiques of Milton Friedman's 'Theoretical Framework for Monetary Analysis', in the *Journal of Political Economy* (Davidson 1972a); the second being his co-authored theoretical exegesis with Sidney Weintraub on 'Money as Cause and Effect' in *The Economic Journal* (Davidson and Weintraub 1973).

In the first, Davidson criticizes Friedman's theoretical framework as characteristic of an economy in which money is redundant and therefore inessential. Any consequent monetary policy to influence any variable, whether real or nominal, must be illusory. Instead, Davidson reiterates the Post Keynesian position that by this time he had well articulated. Money only mattered in a world of uncertainty, as opposed to risk, in which false trades and production were likely occurrences in the economy. But under such circumstances, the equilibrium path of real variables, independent of nominal magnitudes, lost all sense of credibility. The integration of the real and monetary sectors occurred because contracts to purchase and sell goods and resources were denominated in money terms. Moreover, Friedman's insistence that money was an exogenous variable in the system 'enter[ing] the system like manna from heaven, or dropped from the sky via a helicopter, or from the application of additional resources to the production process' (Davidson 1972a, p. 877), simply flew in the face of the nature of modern credit-money banking systems. Relying on his previous elaboration of Keynes's *finance motive*, Davidson identifies the *endogenous* nature of the money supply process in the form of income and portfolio change processes:

> In the first case ... an increased desire to buy more reproducible goods per period – the finance motive – induces individuals, firms, governments, or foreigners to enter into additional debt contracts with the banking system. If these contracts are accepted by the banking system, then additional private debts of banks are issued and used to accept additional offer contracts of producers and workers.
>
> In the second method ... the banking system removes assets which have a negligible elasticity of production (specifically securities) from the wealth holdings of the general public

by offering private bank-debt contracts as an alternative store of value at a rate of exchange which members of the public find very favourable. (ibid.)

Not surprisingly, Friedman saw little in Davidson's critique that would change his perception of the role of money and monetary policy in the economy. He chides Davidson for not recognizing that uncertainty played a crucial role in his own 'theoretical framework', although what he did not understand was that he was referring to situations of *risk* whereas Davidson was explicitly focusing on *uncertainty* (in the sense defined above). Adhering to a modal trend as the basis for theory and policy was, according to Friedman, a positivist methodology for which workable hypotheses could be formulated. Davidson's criticisms were perceived as a priori, according to Friedman, and therefore could be dismissed as 'armchair reasoning' (Friedman 1972, p. 925). Then Friedman outright rejects Davidson's contention that his was a non-monetary economy, and dismisses the second of Keynes's two properties of money (zero or negligible elasticity of substitution with reproducible assets) as a confusion on Keynes's part. Thus Friedman admits to accepting the very axiom of gross substitution which nullifies the existence of money as a store of value (on this see the expanded discussion of the three axioms of orthodoxy, below). And finally, with respect to the question of the endogeneity of money, Friedman accuses Davidson of confusing money with credit. Friedman has nothing else to say on the matter, leaving his case to be made by assertion rather than proof.

In the second contribution of this period, Davidson and Weintraub continue their attack on monetarism, this time focusing on the apparent lag between changes in the stock of money and changes in nominal income. Among the key issues raised in this article is that there is an important difference between the appearance, which monetarist researchers have correctly identified, and the reality of the money/income relation which in fact identifies money as the effect and not the cause of the process. Here Davidson and Weintraub employ the finance motive that they developed in their separate, earlier works to make their case (Weintraub 1958; Davidson 1965).

In the subsequent decade, Davidson honed his critique of neoclassical theory and policy, coming out with a second edition of *Money and the Real World* (Davidson 1972b/1978) and writing his extremely important follow-up to the critique of Friedman (Davidson 1977). He also devoted a great amount of time and energy to the formulation and initial construction of the *Journal of Post Keynesian Economics* with Sidney Weintraub.

The latter part of this period saw Davidson writing his extension of the 1972 book to the global realm, this time bearing the title *International Money and the Real World* (Davidson 1982). Here he was able to draw from his extensive understanding of international trade relations based on his studies of the oil industry, as well as his broad understanding of international finance both from his knowledge of Keynes's writings and from his own expertise in the subject. In the post-Breton Woods period, interest in flexible exchange rates as well as a possible return to a gold standard was pervasive. Both policies follow logically from a monetarist perspective in which the strict dichotomy between the real and monetary sectors called for money supplies at both domestic and international levels that grew at non-inflationary rates. Moreover, there was much talk during that period of neoclassical policies to stimulate global investment through increased savings and value-added taxes.

Not content to ever let things lie still, Davidson saw so much happen in the world economy over the period of the 1980s, that he set out to completely rewrite his book to bring it up to date, contemporaneous with the emergence of the European Union and the European Monetary System (Davidson 1982/1992). In this book, as well as in a series of articles (Davidson 1991, 1992-93, 1993), he set out to propose a revision of the world's monetary system. First he compared historical periods when exchange rates were fixed versus when they were flexible, clearly showing that all indicators were much more positive in the former regimes. From the lessons learned from Keynes's writings, Davidson suggested that '[w]hat is required is a *closed*, double-entry bookkeeping clearing institution to keep the payments score among the various trading regions plus some mutually agreed upon rules to create and reflux liquidity while maintaining the international purchasing power of the international currency' (see Davidson 1992-93, p. 158). This mechanism would be achieved by the creation of an international money clearing unit (IMCU), held only by central banks, in which central banks would assure convertibility between their domestic currencies and the IMCU in a fixed exchange rate environment. Moreover, seeing surplus nations as 'oversavers' who 'are creating a lack of global effective demand', leads Davidson to propose that 'deficit countries would no longer have to deflate their real economy merely to adjust their payment imbalance because others are oversaving. Instead, the system would seek to remedy the payment deficit by increasing opportunities for deficit nations to sell abroad' (ibid., p. 161). What Davidson has done in this proposal is to eschew the 'beggar thy neighbor' types of remedies for exchange rate imbalances, putting the issue into a global effective demand framework, consistent with a Post Keynesian perspective.

It is really impossible to end this survey of Davidson's writings as the flow continues without much let-up. About five years ago, I wrote to Jan Kregel suggesting that a group of Paul's former students honor him on his 60th birthday. Kregel balked at the idea remarking that Paul was as alive, well, and productive as ever, and that marking any milestones at this point would be premature.

Consequently, I feel no need to provide the reader with a sense of closure at this juncture. I have described what Paul Davidson has done to date; the reader can take it upon him/herself to continue to read what comes new from Davidson's pen in the coming years.

Instead, what I would like to do is focus on a taxonomical scheme devised by Davidson over the last decade which has enabled him to systematize his overall criticisms of orthodoxy as well as acting as a coherent vehicle for assessing his own contribution to the discipline. In this regard he has found it useful to define three axioms of orthodoxy: the axiom of substitutability, the axiom of reals (money neutrality), and the axiom of ergodicity. Using these three axioms, Davidson has been able to provide a theoretical foundation and policy framework for an entrepreneurial monetary economy, one in which there is a unique and viable institutional framework which helps to create the relative stability of prices and production operating in a world of fundamental uncertainty.

A POST KEYNESIAN VIEW OF THE THREE AXIOMS OF ORTHODOXY

The Axiom of Ergodicity

Probably the most important theoretical/empirical proposition for Paul Davidson is a recognition of the unique, path-dependent nature to the world in which we live, what Davidson is fond of calling the *real* world. The importance of the distinction between ergodic and nonergodic processes is foundational to an understanding of Keynes's and the Post Keynesian critique of the orthodox theory of capital accumulation, including the theory of the determination of investment and the theory of liquidity preference. Understanding the nature of ergodic and nonergodic processes, in turn, provides clarity to the distinction between a non-monetary or neutral economy, on the one hand, and a monetary economy, on the other. For in the latter, as Davidson has said in so many places, any framework 'which provides a model in which there is a presumption of a universe of discoverable stationary laws and regularities and therefore the neutrality of money is central, should appear to be a misleading analogy for developing policies for monetary, production economies where money matters, i.e., where money affects real production decisions in a world of unpredictable change' (Davidson 1982-83, p. 191).

Typical of most traditional analyses, certainly in all of those schools to the right of center of Davidson's table of political economy, is the positing of a dichotomy between some trend rate of growth of full employment – or more precisely, natural rate of employment – real output, which is independent of the ephemeral movements that exist about that trend. Belief in such a dichotomy has allowed orthodox economists to depict rational agents as recognizing this ephemeral nature of immediate data; what matters are the properties embodied in the long-term trend, properties to which every individual knows the current situation will gravitate. As such, one can be assured that there is some discernible probability distribution into which all current data fall. Such probability distributions define the natures of all data that enter into individuals' decision sets. Moreover, budget constraints, which define the discounted value of all future income streams, have built into them appropriate insurance contracts precisely calculated in reference to the probability distributions just described.

Taking the lead from Keynes, Davidson has always held that there is a significant difference between economic analyses based on a probabilistic future – defined in terms of the future being *risky* – and those in which the future is *uncertain*. For in the latter case, there is no sense in which one can posit a probability distribution about some normal trend, which means that individual decisions made today will be based not on a mathematically calculable probabilistically constructed income stream, but rather on the *expectation* of a stream of future income which may or may not accrue to the individual. Moreover, decisions made in such an uncertain environment may cause individuals to commit time and resources which once committed may alter the path of their expected course of action. Furthermore, the consequences of such decisions may have effects on the consequences of others' actions, affecting those paths as well.

Thus, once it is assumed that the future is uncertain, probability distributions regarding the future lose their meaning. Actions today become based on the expectation of future, uncertain streams of income, and the cumulative path taken by an economy becomes dependent upon, rather than being independent of, the totality of those very individual decisions at every moment in time. As such, the ontological presuppositions of the economy taken by those who follow the teaching of Keynes versus those to the right of these teachings, lead to diametrically divergent paths.

To know something requires more than axiomatically based conjectures (a priori reasoning); knowledge, at some juncture must be premised on an empirical foundation. Such scientifically based knowledge will come 'via statistical averages which have been calculated from past (and/or current) time series and/or cross-section data' (ibid., p. 331; see also Davidson 1994a, ch. 6). These two types of data are referred to by Davidson as time and space averages. Stationary stochastic processes where statistical time and space averages coincide in the limit are called ergodic processes. Therefore, either average can be inferred from a knowledge of the other.

From these definitional contexts, Davidson has concluded that 'the average expectation of future outcomes determined at any point in time will not be persistently different than the time average of future outcomes only if the stochastic process is ergodic' (Davidson 1982-83, p. 185). An ergodic process then is one where the two averages converge 'with the probability of unity as the number of observations increase' (Davidson 1988, p. 331). Here, what is known today is isomorphic to what has been known in the past and which can give us assurances about what to expect in the future. Davidson observes that in a logical sense, 'the future is merely a statistical reflection of the past' (ibid.). Historical events have no lasting effect on the time and space averages and economists may think of observable trends as law-like occurrences from which law-like inferences can be induced.

A nonergodic process, on the other hand, is one in which 'the underlying stochastic processes whose distribution functions are not independent of historical time, and if the rates of change in the distribution functions are also not independent of calendar time' (Davidson 1982-83, p. 187). Of course a nonergodic system need not be a stochastic process. When the economy is nonergodic, 'any estimated statistical average ... can be persistently and nonsystematically different from the future time averages actually occurring in the economy' (ibid.).

Davidson's original discussion of these issues occurs in *Money and the Real World* (Davidson 1972b), inspired by George Shackle's writings on uncertainty in economic analysis (Shackle 1955). There Davidson cites the distinction made by George Shackle between events that are divisible and those that are crucial. A divisible event is one which can be repeated an infinity of times under identical circumstances. In such cases, it is likely that an expected value of the outcome of such processes can be induced, given a probability distribution upon which any single estimate can rely. Crucial decisions, however, are those where the very act of committing those experiments changes the conditions under which the decisions can then be reperformed. As such, the single act has changed the experimentation circumstances and both assumptions for the establishment of a probability distribution have been violated. Repetition under the same circumstances is simply impossible. As Shackle stated: 'Napoleon could not repeat the battle of Waterloo a hundred times in the hope that, in a certain proportion of cases, the Prussians would arrive too late. ... Had he won, repetition would for a long time have been unnecessary; when he lost, repetition was impossible' (ibid., p. 25).

By the 1980s, Davidson was revising the language slightly: 'when agents make crucial decisions, they necessarily destroy any ergodic stochastic processes that may have existed at the point of time of the decision. ... In other words, crucial choice involves, by definition, situations where the very performance of choice destroys the existing distribution functions'; but the message is the same: 'if important decisions regarding the accumulation of wealth, the possession of liquidity, the commitment to a production process with significant set-up costs and gestation period, etc., are crucial, then the future waits, not for its contents to be discovered, but for the content to be originated' (Davidson 1982-83, p. 192).

Cruciality not only causes the objective functions to change over time, violating the stationarity assumptions of stochastic processes, but the recognition that decisions have crucial implications causes individuals to behave in fashions quite different from the postulates of rationality based on such stationary stochastic processes. In the latter case, we consistently hear Davidson referring to the necessity of individuals establishing institutional arrangements which can help them cope, to act 'sensibly' (in his words), in a nonergodic, crucial environment. Among these, Davidson notes, is the existence of hire and debt contracts both for the present and the future in money terms, since there is something about money wages (and money rates of interest) which cause a relative stickiness in future money prices relative to current money prices, thereby 'lulling the disquietude' possessed by individuals dealing in an uncertain world, and which provide the stability under the guise of uncertainty which allows them to commit their resources for a prolonged period of time, that is, to participate in the capital accumulation process which helps to explain the mechanism for economic growth. Here we find the theoretical elaboration on that set of conclusions articulated by Davidson in the late 1960s, as were described in an earlier portion of this chapter.

One last thing to note about the focus on a nonergodic economic process is that, as Davidson has long contended, uncertainty does not imply either nihilism or instability. In his interview with John King, Davidson tells of a communication between Joan Robinson and Keynes, where 'Joan is berating Keynes for using uncertainty because, if the world is uncertain, anything can happen. Keynes said to her, "You should not confuse uncertainty with instability. The fact that things are uncertain doesn't make them unstable"' (King 1994, p. 370). Clearly, such a perspective holds equally for Davidson as it did for Keynes. And, of course, for Davidson, that relative stability comes from the existence of institutional arrangements, especially forward contracts denominated in money terms, built upon a money-wage foundation which is sticky in all directions.

The Axiom of Gross Substitution

Among the most important foci of research for Paul Davidson has been an accurate assessment of the causes of what Keynes called *involuntary unemployment*. Such unemployment, beyond the control of labor as a whole, can be understood to the extent that Say's Law (there can never be an overproduction of goods in the aggregate) is or is not valid. This law will hold so long as all goods are interchangeable, substitutes, in the sense that appropriate fluctuations in relative prices will cause individuals to shift their income from one to another. A dollar not spent on consumption will automatically be stored in the purchase of a reproducible asset – saving always creating its own investment. In light of this, Davidson has remarked that

> if the gross substitution axiom is true, then even if savers attempt to use nonreproducible assets for storing their increments of wealth, this increase in demand will increase the price of nonproducibles. This relative price rise in nonproducibles will, under the gross substitution axiom, induce savers to substitute reproducible durables for nonproducibles in their wealth holding and therefore nonproducibles will not be the ultimate resting places for savings. The gross substitution axiom therefore restores Say's Law and denies the logical possibility of involuntary unemployment. (Davidson 1984, pp. 567-68; see also Davidson 1972b ,1977 and 1980a)

Involuntary unemployment, in this context, will not occur because of a constrained demand function for real goods and services, but rather because of an active demand function by resource providers for liquid assets that are not producible by labor and whose demand does not cause resources to flow into assets producible by labor: 'the desire to possess liquidity – liquid assets not producible by labour – is also an argument in any labour (factor owner) supply function' (Davidson 1984, p. 566). Or to put it another way:

> In the real world, planned spending need never be equal to, or constrained by, actual income as long as (a) agents who earn income by selling their labour (or goods produced by labour in the private sector) are not required to spend all of their earned income on goods produced by labour, and/or (b) agents who plan to spend on currently producible goods are not required to earn income (previously or concurrently) with their exercise of this demand (where by 'demand' we mean 'want' *plus the ability to pay*). (ibid., p. 567; see also Davidson 1977, 1982, 1983b and 1994)

The first part implies that unemployment can occur if savings do not find an outlet in reproducible assets: 'Workers can be involuntarily unemployed because the marginal propensity to spend (from income earned in the production process) on producible goods is less than one, and the income thus saved can be stored in nonreproducible assets such as money, bonds, collectibles, etc.' (Davidson 1982, p. 115; see also Davidson 1980a). But such a perspective, according to Davidson, requires that the *axiom of gross substitution* must be overthrown (see Davidson 1980a, pp. 303-5).[10]

And it is in this sense that Davidson has emphasized the importance of what Keynes referred to as the essential properties of money: that it has a zero or negligible elasticity of production (so that an increased demand for money does not call forth a diversion of resources into its production) and a zero or negligible elasticity of substitution between money and reproducible assets (so that the increased relative price of money when its demand increases does not cause demand to slough over to non-monetary reproducible assets). As a result of these unique properties, money has a store of value function which stands as the antithesis of the axiom of substitution, and more importantly, there exists a theoretical foundation for the existence of involuntary unemployment.

What is also clear by means of the rejection of the axiom of substitution is that involuntary unemployment is *not* a phenomenon directly caused by the assumption of sticky wages. True, money has its unique properties because of this assumption, but all that this implies is that the economy will not be wildly unstable, falling instead within a range of stability. However, within that range, there is no necessity that the level of output be one of full employment. Involuntary unemployment can exist regardless of whether money wages are sticky or flexible. Involuntary unemployment is not an occurrence following from some imperfection in some labor market; in fact, it does not follow from any concept of an aggregate labor market. Rather, it occurs because occasionally people demand an asset which is not reproducible nor that is substitutable for employment-generating assets, independent of the fixity of flexibility of money prices. (See the earlier discussion of the properties of money; Keynes ch. 17; and Davidson 1968a, 1968b, 1969, 1972a, pp. 874-5, 1972b, 1982, 1992, 1994.)

The Axiom of Reals

Now what does Davidson mean by the statement that planned spending need not be equal to, or constrained by actual income as long as agents who plan to spend on currently producibe goods are not required to earn income with their exercise of this demand? Does he mean that someone can spend today even if they do not have the current income? Or does he mean that current spending is not determined

---

10. Frank Hahn has reached a similar conclusion when he points out that 'any nonreproducible asset allows for a choice between employment-inducing and non-employment inducing demand' (1977, p. 39).

by current income, but by the expectation of future income? In fact, it means both, as Davidson clarifies in his explanation of what he calls the *axiom of reals*: 'The axiom of reals implies that money is a veil so that all economic decisions are made on the basis of real phenomena and relative prices alone. Money does not matter!' (Davidson 1984).

To reject the axiom of reals does not require the assumption that agents suffer from money illusion. It only means that 'money is not neutral'; money matters in both the short run and the long run, or as Keynes put it:

> the theory which I desiderate would deal ... with an economy in which money plays a part of its own and affects motives and decision, and is, in short, one of the operative factors in the situation, so that the course of events cannot be predicted in either the long period or in the short, without a knowledge of the behavior of money between the first state and the last. And it is this which we ought to mean when we speak of a *monetary economy*. (CW XIII, pp. 408-9, in Davidson 1984, p. 570)

What this implies is that contracts are made in money and not real terms. At the heart of Paul Davidson's research program has been the continuation and clarification of Keynes's profound insistence that 'money matters'. In fact, this insistence is revealed in the title of what is surely his *magnum opus, Money and the Real World* (Davidson 1972b). This statement is ironic, as Davidson has often indicated, in the sense that the phrase is normally attributed to the Neoclassical/Monetarist school of political economy (to employ Davidson's 'Tableau') who insist that the causes of fluctuations in the aggregate price level are directly attributable to previous changes in some measure of the money stock. However, as Keynes and Davidson have so often shown, a world in which the classical dichotomy is valid, is in fact one where at best money is neutral, but more precisely where money does not matter at all.

In each case, the operant notion focuses upon the requirements specifying knowledge of future events. For example, if all markets are assumed to clear, without false trades or false productions – more on this later – and if there are Debreu-type contingency contracts so that the entire future can be collapsed into the present and that appropriately discounted payment occurs today regardless of the future state of nature, then the necessity of having any object, either real or imaginary, serving the function of a medium of exchange or *numeraire*, let alone a store of value, is nugatory (to borrow a phrase Davidson is fond of using).

Now as we are quite aware, such theories provide us only with the determination of relative equilibrium prices, while saying nothing about the determination of absolute prices. These latter prices, we are told, find their identities linked to fluctuations in the stock of money. However, with such an admission, we are drawn all too quickly into discussions about the extent to which fluctuations in the stock of money have an effect on the real sector (violations of the classical dichotomy) or only on the monetary sector (confirmations of the classical dichotomy, even if only in the long run). But slow down. If the affirmation of a real sector equilibrium negates the existence of something satisfying the functions of money (to be distinguished from the *properties* of money, see below), then how can it be said that fluctuations in the aggregate price level are explained by fluctuations in something that does not exist in the first place? Surely such a 'things that go bump in the night' theory of inflation is theoretically infeasible, a conclusion that was clearly recognized by many writers, including Keynes and especially Davidson:

> It is difficult to understand therefore, from a Keynesian point of view, why the resources of so many economists have been wasted on Walrasian models in general, and quantity theory models in particular, where the latter make a fetish about the importance of the rate of growth of the quantity of money. If the Walrasian equations – which describe a barter economy ... – is the logical norm or trend around which Friedman believes the actual world fluctuates, then the quantity of money is indeed nugatory. (Davidson 1972a, p. 873)

In fact, looking at the issue in this fashion calls into question the veracity of the methodological imperative of the classical dichotomy, itself. For from this perspective, there is no dichotomy at all; rather there is a real sector equilibrium theory of value and distribution, and a fictitious (not monetary, because money has no theoretical justification once the real sector is identified as it has been) sector in which inflation is supposed to be explained.

Interestingly, if the idea of a classical dichotomy has no theoretical justification, then what can be said of the positive heuristic of those on the right of center of Davidson's 'Tableau', that is the Neoclassical/Bastard Keynesians and the Neoclassical/Monetarists, which embraces the rhetorical statement: 'What happens if there is a change in the money stock?'. All that can be said is that the statement, having no foundation in theory, is another attempt at a positivism which relies heavily on the assumptions of a closed system with constant conjunctions of events.

Since the time of Walras, attempts to integrate money into a general equilibrium framework have been less than satisfying. In all cases, the thrust has been to show that something is needed to be held in stock to minimize transactions costs or provide fluidity between the time of purchase and the time of sale. Walras, himself, trudged through this malaise by assuming that once the equilibrium in exchange, production and capital was struck, then people would hold stocks of things to allow each of these functions to be actualized (for example, firms need resources to begin production, shopkeepers need inventories to sell, individuals need stocks to save to be lent out, and so on). People held such stocks in inventory because they provided 'services of availability' for which people would be willing to pay a price (relative price, of course). Once these prices made their way into the complete nexus of relative prices in exchange, production and capital, all Walras had to do was to assume that these stocks were, instead, held in the form of money, and that people would be willing to pay a price for this latter object, depending upon the services of availability it provided. Davidson has always been fond of using the metaphor of the magician in such cases, where he points out that any rabbit pulled out of a hat (in this case, as justification for a relative price for money), must first have been put into the hat (the quantum leap from holding some stock of things to get the economy rolling, to having that thing be held as money). Needless to say, all such attempts are theoretically impossible – either the path occurring because of the process of time is meaningful or it is not; and in the case of general equilibrium it is not – which leaves theorists with the rather uneasy posture of assuming the existence of money, as if it fit naturally into the system from day one.

Even Keynes was guilty of such a solecism, when in the drafts of *The General Theory*, he correctly identifies what he calls 'classical' economics to be a real-exchange or non-monetary economy, and then characterizes a neutral economy as one identical to a real-exchange economy, except where money is used as a neutral medium of exchange. He continues this line of reasoning in Chapter 13 of *The General Theory* when he notes that if all future interest rates were known, then an individual could put in forward contracts for money to be synchronized with future equilibrium deliveries of goods and services, so that money would only serve the function of medium of circulation and not impinge on the real sector equilibrium (Keynes 1936, p.169). Again, we see it in the famous quote from his 1937 *Economic Journal* article 'The General Theory of Employment', where he says that 'in the classical world, only someone in a lunatic asylum would hold money as a store of value' (Keynes 1937a, pp. 115-16). But when all is said and done, Keynes does no more than anyone else thinking along traditional lines, when he makes the infinite leap between a real-exchange economy and a neutral money economy, by merely assuming the existence of money, without any theoretical justification for its presence.

Luckily for Keynes, his thought process did not end at this unnecessary, although interesting excursus, because the genuinely salient question, that is why would money exist at all, does get asked in *The General Theory*, although in such a form, and at such a juncture in the book to have been either incomprehensible to the reader looking for a sense of closure to 'the Keynesian model', or irrelevant. In that infamous and elusive Chapter 17, Keynes identifies the attributes possessed by all durable assets: a prospective yield, carrying cost and liquidity premium. Then, by means of a discussion of own-rates of interest, he shows how the essential properties of money assure that the asset whose liquidity premium exceeds its carrying cost will emerge as the monetary asset. Moreover, such an admission implies that it is the *money* rate of interest to which all other own-rates are compared, and that the money rate of interest takes on this unique character because of the fact that wages are bargained in *money*, not real terms – the existence of money, then, is contingent on the violation of the second postulate of classical economics.

To those who have seriously studied Keynes, it is clear that this chapter provides the Rosetta Stone to the theoretical foundation of Keynes's economics. However, to most, this chapter has been totally incomprehensible and therefore, all but ignored or dismissed as one of Keynes's many muddled musings that seem to permeate what was otherwise a clearly stated general equilibrium model of a macroeconomy. But, alas, such conclusions are, in fact, admissions of complete ignorance of Keynes's theoretical contribution and acceptance of what is clearly a poorly founded and potted version of 'Keynesian' economics, in the form of the ISLM framework. At the same time, I think it is fair to say that any clarity that has emerged from this foundational chapter has come to the discipline on account of the exegetical interpretations provided by Paul Davidson. In fact, the essential nature of Davidson's claim to providing a *Post* Keynesian economics, really centers on providing that clarity to the theoretical foundations of Keynes's own economics, which for reasons that are not at all clear to us, eluded Keynes's normal ability to convey things in a perspicuous manner.

The *axiom of reals* substantiates what is traditionally accepted to be the classical dichotomy between the real and monetary sectors, validating the principle of Say's Law. Neither money, nor monetary factors enter into real decision-making processes, and therefore all operant equilibrating mechanisms will always be stated in real terms: real wages clear labor markets, real rates of interest clear capital markets, and so on. Such relative price flexibility will assure that all markets clear including the markets for labor and capital implying full employment savings equal to investment. Money, if it exists at all, is, as Milton Friedman called it, a temporary abode of purchasing power, mediating exchange, but never factoring into the interstices of the exchange processes themselves. And when the axiom of reals is invoked, as Paul Davidson has so frequently pointed out, no exogenous change in the money supply can affect the real-exchange equilibrium; absolute prices are bid up in direct proportion to the increase in the stock of money.

SOME CONCLUDING REMARKS

Assessing the vastness of this taxonomical scheme as well as Davidson's overall theoretical framework described in these last two sections causes one to recognize that the profound nature of these contributions has yet to be embraced by the mainstream of the discipline. One explanation for this might be because conventional theoretical analyses (both Walrasian and game-theoretic) exist in the realm of flows, alone. Such analyses seek the existence of an equilibrium, somehow mediating this agglomeration of flows. Growth theory, by and large, traces out the path of successive equilibria, but in fact has little to say about the mechanisms which generate that path. Davidson's structure provides a framework by which the pricing, production, financing *and* investment decisions can be understood, not in law-like fashion such as is the case in orthodoxy, but rather in terms of motives and tendencies within a unique institutional setting. Paul Wells, reviewing *Money and the Real World*, in which this framework is refined and polished, characterized it as yielding a framework which is 'roughly right, instead of being precisely wrong' (Wells 1973, p. 1387). George Shackle, in his review of the book, spoke of Davidson's being 'content to study the directional or qualitative effects of various impacts or releases on first one and then another set of circumstances, that is, of propensities, policies, expectations and attitudes' (Shackle 1973, p. 533). However, precision (despite being wrong) is what the mainstream expects, and Davidson's rich heuristical open system simply does not do it for those in the mainstream. But despite this shunning by the mainstream – of which more in a moment – Davidson has still acquired an enormous sense of respect and admiration from scores of economists, albeit predominantly out of the mainstream.

The sad part here is that prominent figures such as Paul Davidson, have been denied access to those vehicles which contribute to success and recognition in the discipline. This has been a real problem in Economics in that those who control the means of communication (the journals) and the hiring, and the bases for retention (publication in the leading journals), cause there to be a process of natural selection which excludes all those who do not follow the fold of the main. How ironic it is that orthodox economists, who espouse a long-run market equilibrium process with freedom of exit and entry, have to resort to blocking coalitions to prevent entry into their market which might cause their own market share to be spoiled. In a sense, we have not come very far from the fifteenth-century inquisition, where heretics were burned at the stake for not believing the gospel truth as defined by the inquisitors.

Such, alas, has been the plight of Paul Davidson's career. Prior to 1965, when he was doing work primarily in natural resources and econometric macroeconomics, the pages of the *American Economic Review* were open to him. However, once he started seriously challenging orthodoxy, the doors closed as his work was considered no longer at the frontiers of theoretical knowledge, as they defined it. I cannot help but think that this blind exclusion of Paul from the mainstream channels of communication have been disheartening to him at one level, because he has been such an intellectual giant among economists and to do such profound and fundamental theoretical work and be rejected by the mainstream cannot be a happy experience. On the other hand, there surely has been an element of empowerment, as such exclusions, in the face of tremendous acceptance and almost reverence in other venues, must have persuaded him long ago that he was on to something important and that quitting his project would not be in his own or in the discipline's best interest. Still, one sometimes wonders what keeps him going in light of such blatant rejection by the mainstream.

The sociologists Peter Berger and Thomas Luckmann (1966), offer three reactions that people tend to exhibit to those who are different: they are either derogated, assimilated or annihilated. For the first, we can do no better than: 'Davidson's way with the English language ... does reflect the quality of the thinking conveyed in the book' (Yeager 1983, p. 126). In the case of the second, I think Davidson's insistence on keeping his terminology as close to the mainstream as possible, while partly a strategy to communicate, might also be a response to the human need to be accepted. And finally, the abuse that he and other Post Keynesians received by the Neoclassical droids on the Rutgers faculty, finally led to their moving on and out of that hostile environment. This is not a pretty picture, but it is more pervasive both in economics and in academia, in general, than we would like to admit. I suspect that it has been especially virulent in Davidson's case, because he is just simply that good, and opponents do not like their enemies to be good.

But let me end with a positive, personal note. I read with particular interest Davidson's telling John King, in his recent 'interview' that if one

> gets in a position of power, you've got to be very careful about what you say in print about other people. [One prominent member of the profession] likes to make jokes and josh a little bit, often facetiously but not always understandably so, particularly in the printed word. And I've learned from it: sometimes I do that and often regret it afterwards, and I try not to if I can – particularly with younger people. (King 1994, p. 363)

Of all my professors in graduate school, I do not remember anyone who fought harder to defend his beliefs than Paul Davidson. And yet for Davidson, none of that tenacity ever translated into an overinflated ego, or a need to address people in an *ad hominem way*. Davidson was only interested in the pursuit of knowledge; economics was a topic which had strong political overtones and needed confrontation and clarification because, at the end of the day, who was eating and who was not was an important issue to him.

This commitment to the pursuit of knowledge also tempered the way Davidson addressed his students. For many of them, Davidson was unapproachable. However, this was primarily their own doing, as his reputation caused many students to be nervous about visiting him in his office. And yet for those of us who did cross that threshold, what we found was someone who was warm and inviting, who had an almost childlike enthusiasm for knowledge and who thus shared the excitement of learning that many of us had. Davidson was one of the few professors to whom I could give something I had read and say: 'Here, read this; I think you're going to like it'. Those who were interested in Davidson's general research project were immediately embraced as colleagues, regardless of their rank or status. It was almost as if he were saying: 'Come on aboard; we have work to do'.

DAVIDSON'S MAJOR WRITINGS

(1959), 'A Clarification of the Ricardian Rent Share', *Canadian Journal of Economics and Political Science*, May, 190-95.

(1960a), *Theories of Aggregate Income Distribution*, New Brunswick: Rutgers University Press.

(1960b), 'Increasing Employment, Diminishing Returns, Relative Shares, and Ricardo', *Canadian Journal of Economics and Political Science*, February, 147-8.

(1962a), 'More on the Aggregate Supply Function', *Economic Journal*, June, 452-7.

(1962b), 'Employment and Income Multipliers, and the Price Level', *American Economic Review*, 743-9.

(1963), 'Public Policy Problems and the Domestic Crude Oil Industry', *American Economic Review*, March, 85-108.

(1964a) (with Eugene Smolensky), *Aggregate Supply and Demand Analysis*, New York: Harper and Row.

(1964b) (with Eugene Smolensky), 'Modigliani on the Interaction of Real and Monetary Phenomena', *Review of Economics and Statistics*, November, 429-31.

(1965), 'Keynes's Finance Motive', *Oxford Economic Papers*, March, 47-65.

(1967a), 'A Keynesian View of Patinkin's Theory of Employment', *Economic Journal*, September, 559-78.

(1967b), 'The Importance of the Demand for Finance', *Oxford Economic Papers*, July, 245-53.

(1967c), 'An Exploratory Study to Identify and Measure the Benefits Derived from the Scenic Enhancement of Federal-Aid Highways', Highway Research Record, No. 182.

(1968a), 'The Valuation of Public Goods', in M.G. Garnsey and J. Hibbs (eds), *Social Sciences and the Environment*, Boulder: University of Colorado Press.

(1968b), 'Money, Portfolio Balance, Capital Accumulation, and Economic Growth', *Econometrica*, April, 291-321.

(1968c), 'The Demand and Supply of Securities and Economic Growth and its Implications for the Kaldor–Pasinetti vs. Samuelson–Modigliani Controversy', *American Economic Review*, May, 252-69.

(1969), 'A Keynesian View of the Relationship between Accumulation, Money and the Money-Wage Rate', *Economic Journal*, June, 300-23.

(1972a), 'A Keynesian View of Friedman's Theoretical Framework for Monetary Analysis', *Journal of Political Economy*, October/November, 864-82.

(1972b), *Money and the Real World*, London: Macmillan. Second Edition, 1978.

(1973) (with Sidney Weintraub), 'Money as Cause and Effect', *Economic Journal*, December, 1117-32.

(1974), 'Market Disequilibrium Adjustments: Marshall Revisited', *Economic Inquiry*, June, 146-58.

(1974) (with L. Falk and H. Lee), 'Oil: Its Time Allocation and Project Independence', *Brookings Papers on Economic Activity*, 2, 411-48.

(1977), 'Money and General Equilibrium', *Economique Appliquée*, 30, 541-64.

(1980a), 'The Dual-Faceted Nature of the Keynesian Revolution: Money and Money Wages in Unemployment and Production Flow Prices', *Journal of Post Keynesian Economics*, Spring, 291-307.

(1980b), 'Post Keynesian Economics: Solving the Crisis in Economic Theory', in I. Kristol and D. Bell (eds), *The Crisis In Economic Theory*, New York: Basic Books, 151-73.

(1980) (with J.A. Kregel), 'Keynes's Paradigm: A Theoretical Framework for Monetary Analysis', in E.J. Nell, ed., *Growth, Property and Profits*, Cambridge: Cambridge University Press.

(1982), *International Money and the Real World*, London: Macmillan. Second Edition, 1992.

(1982-83), 'Rational Expectations: A Fallacious Foundation for Studying Crucial Decision-Making Processes', *Journal of Post Keynesian Economics*, Winter, 182-98.

(1983a), 'The Dubious Labour Market Analysis in Meltzer's Restatement', *Journal of Economic Literature*, 52-6.

(1983b), 'The Marginal Product Curve is not the Demand Curve for Labour and Lucas's Labour Supply Function is not the Supply Curve for Labour in the Real World', *Journal of Post Keynesian Economics*, Fall, 105-17.

(1984), 'Reviving Keynes's Revolution', *Journal of Post Keynesian Economics*, Summer, 561-75.

(1985), 'Sidney Weintraub – an Economist of the Real World', *Journal of Post Keynesian Economics*.

(1986-87), 'The Simple Macroeconomics of a Non-Ergodic Monetary Economy', *Journal of Post Keynesian Economics*, Winter, 212-25.

(1987-88), 'A Modest Set of Proposals for Solving the International Debt Problem', *Journal of Post Keynesian Economics*, Winter, 323-38.

(1988), 'A Technical Definition of Uncertainty and the Long-Run Non-Neutrality of Money', *Cambridge Journal of Economics*, September, 329-38.

(1988) (with Greg Davidson), *Economics for a Civilized Society*, New York: Norton.

(1991a), 'What International Payments Scheme Would Keynes Have Suggested for the Twenty-first Century?', in Davidson and Kregel (1991), 85-104.

(1991b), 'Is Probability Theory Relevant for Uncertainty? A Post Keynesian Perspective', *Journal of Economic Perspectives*, Winter, 129-43.

(1991c), *Controversies in Post Keynesian Economics*, Aldershot: Elgar.

(1991) (with J.A. Kregel), *Economic Problems in the 1990s*, Aldershot: Elgar.

(1992), 'Would Keynes be a New Keynesian?', *Eastern Economic Journal*, Fall, 449-63.

(1992-93), 'Reforming the World's Money', *Journal of Post Keynesian Economics*, Winter, 153-80.
(1993), 'The Global Dimension: It's Still the Economy, Mr. President', *The New Leader*, January 11.
(1994a), *Post Keynesian Macroeconomic Theory*, Aldershot: Elgar.
(1994b), 'Post Keynesian Thought Network', 30 November.

OTHER REFERENCES

Arthur, W. Brian (1989), 'Competing Technologies, Increasing Returns, and Lock-In by Historical Events', *Economic Journal*, March, 116-31.
Berger, Peter and Thomas Luckmann (1966), *The Social Construction of Reality*, Garden City: Doubleday.
Friedman, Milton (1972), 'Reply to My Critics', *Journal of Political Economy* October/November, 906-50.
Hahn, Frank (1977), 'Keynesian Economics and General Equilibrium Theory', in G.C. Harcourt (ed), *The Microfoundations of Macroeconomics*, London: Macmillan, 25-40.
Keynes, J.M. (1921), *A Treatise on Probability*, CW VI.
Keynes, J.M. (1930), *A Treatise on Money*, 2 volumes, CW.
Keynes, J.M. (1936), *The General Theory of Employment, Interest, and Money*. CW VII.
Keynes, J.M. (1937a), 'The General Theory of Employment', *Quarterly Journal of Economics*, February, 209-23; reprinted in CW XIV.
Keynes, J.M. (1937b), 'The Ex-Ante Theory of the Rate of Interest', *Economic Journal*, December, 663-9; reprinted in CW XIV.
Keynes, J.M. (1973a), *The General Theory and After: Preparation*, CW XIII.
Keynes, J.M. (1973b), *The General Theory and After: Defense and Development*, CW XIV.
Keynes, J.M. (1979), *The General Theory and After: Supplement*, CW XXIX.
King, John E. (1994), 'A Conversation with Paul Davidson', *Review of Political Economy*, July, 357-79.
Kregel, J.A. (1976), 'Economic Methodology in the Face of Uncertainty', *Economic Journal*, June, 209-25.
Minsky, Hyman (1975), *John Maynard Keynes*, New York: Columbia.
Shackle, G.L.S. (1955), *Uncertainty in Economics*, Cambridge: Cambridge University Press.
Shackle, G.L.S. (1973). 'Review of Davidson: *Money and the Real World*', *Economic Journal*, June, 532-3.
Tobin, James (1965), 'Money and Economic Growth', *Econometrica*, October, 671-84.
Wells, Paul (1973), 'Review of Davidson: *Money and the Real World*', *Journal of Economic Literature*, December, 1387-8.
Weintraub, Sidney (1958), *An Approach to the Theory of Income Distribution*, Philadelphia: Chilton.
Yeager, Leland (1983), 'Review of Davidson: *International Money and the Real World*', *Journal of Economic Literature*, March, 124-6.

3. Nancy Folbre

Janet A. Seiz

Nancy Folbre received a BA from the University of Texas in 1971, an MA in Latin American Studies from the same university in 1973, and a PhD in economics from the University of Massachusetts in 1979. She is best known for her theoretical work on the political economy of gender, and has made significant related contributions in economic history, economic development and demography, the history of economic thought and economic methodology. This essay will focus primarily upon Folbre's theoretical work on gender, giving briefer mention of her contributions to other fields.

In order to place Folbre's work in historical context, I begin by discussing the treatment of gender in neoclassical and Marxian economics up to the early 1980s when Folbre began research in this area. Then I survey her theoretical work on gender relations within and outside the household, including its applications to the theory of fertility and the transformation of households due to capitalist economic development. This is followed by a summary of her recent book. The essay concludes with shorter sections on Folbre's contributions to economic methodology, the history of economic thought and economic history.

I am most strongly interested in three related strands in Folbre's research:

1. Her examination of the operation of gender bias in economics, identifying ways in which economic arguments reflect distinctively masculine perspectives and/or serve distinctively masculine interests. Folbre has criticized (while also drawing upon) both neoclassical and Marxian economics, arguing that they have often served to legitimate and obscure gender inequality.
2. Her efforts to redress the gender bias in economic theory, particularly regarding economic analysis of the household. Much of Folbre's work has been devoted to seeing that the 'caring labor' performed by women receives proper recognition, and to arguing for changes in policies and in social norms so that this labor might be distributed more equitably.

3. Her assessment of neoclassical and Marxian economic methodologies, and her
    contributions to the development of new theoretical frameworks adequate for
    analysis of gender relations.

GENDER IN ECONOMIC THEORY PRIOR TO THE 1980s

Mainstream economists, as several feminist critics have noted, have historically
shown little interest in the economic experiences and problems of women.[1] From
Adam Smith to Alfred Marshall and beyond, classical and neoclassical economists
paid little attention to phenomena such as the gender division of labor and its
evolution over time; the distribution of tasks, consumption and authority within
the household; the occupational segregation of women and men; gender inequality
in earnings; or policies which might enhance the well-being of women in and
outside the labor force. The tendency has been, as Folbre and Hartmann (1988, p.
184) put it, to see gender relations as 'beyond the purview of economic analysis,
either in the realm of biological givens or sociological imponderables'. While
Marx and Engels and some of their followers showed more interest in women's
plight, their explanations and prescriptions had serious flaws (see below). By the
beginning of the 1980s, however, when Folbre started to write, questions about
gender had begun to receive some significant attention from both neoclassical and
Marxian economists.[2]

Gender in Neoclassical Labor Economics

The pioneers in neoclassical work on women were Jacob Mincer, Gary Becker
and Solomon Polachek, who collectively constructed a tight 'supply-side' account
in which the gender division of labor and male–female occupational and earnings
differentials could all be explained as the results of individual rational choice in
the household and the labor market. Mincer (1962) extended the standard labor–
leisure choice model to portray a tripartite decision problem for married women,
the allocation of time between market work, work at home and leisure. He argued

---

1. On this, see especially the pioneering study of classical and early neoclassical economics by Michele
    Pujol (1992). The problem is also mentioned by Marianne Ferber and Michelle Teiman (1981),
    Nancy Barrett (1981), and other feminist commentators. Pujol (1992) emphasizes that mainstream
    economists prior to the 1960s were not simply silent about women: she shows that in several
    instances prominent economists explicitly endorsed the view that women's place was in the home
    and actively opposed reforms meant to equalize economic opportunity.
2. For background on the variety of 'feminisms' existing in Britain and the US during this period, the
    reader may wish to consult Jaggar (1983).

that rising real wages for women had increased the opportunity costs of leisure and work at home, explaining the increase in married women's labor force participation in the twentieth-century US. Beginning in the mid-1960s, Gary Becker inaugurated a field of study soon dubbed the 'new home economics'.[3] Here the gender division of labor resulted from male–female differences in relative productivity in market and domestic work, which were seen as partly rooted in biology: men had comparative advantage in market work, and women in childrearing and housework. The story was completed by Mincer and Polachek (1974; see also Polachek 1981): given women's specialization in housework and childcare, they anticipated discontinuous employment in the labor market; they therefore invested less in market human capital than men, and chose occupations which had relatively low penalties for intermittent work, and their wages were accordingly lower.

In the eyes of its supporters, this account reveals the economic rationality underlying the gender division of labor and of rewards within and outside the household, and provides an analytical framework for investigating changes over time. In the eyes of many feminist critics, however, its main accomplishment is ideological: as Barbara Bergmann observes, such work 'explains, justifies, and even glorifies role differentiation by sex' (Bergmann 1987, p. 132), and presents a view of 'the inferior labor market position of women as something women have freely chosen, as a normal and generally benign adaptation to "their re-sponsibilities" for housework and childrearing' (Bergmann 1989, p. 43).

Many neoclassical economists found the Chicagoan account inadequate, and focused instead on the demand side of the labor market, arguing that discrimination against women was important in explaining occupational and wage differentials. This work required some modification to Becker's (1971) 'tastes' theory of discrimination, which had been devised to explain racial discrimination in the US, and rested upon the discriminating group's aversion to contact with members of the group discriminated against. Since men do not in general seek to avoid contact with women, those who discriminate against women in the workplace must be seen as averse not to contact with women *per se*, but to the placement of women in roles they see as socially inappropriate. In the application of discrimination theory to women, the work of Barbara Bergmann (1971, 1974) and Janice Madden (1973) was particularly significant.[4]

---

3.   See Becker (1965, 1973, 1974, 1976, 1981a, 1981b and 1985).
4.   For a survey of the literature on discrimination against women, see Blau (1984). Both the demand-side and supply-side approaches are discussed in Lloyd and Niemi (1979), Blau and Ferber (1992), and Bergmann (1986). A more recent book examining the literature on gender differentials is Jacobsen (1994).

Gender in Marxian Political Economy

In the writings of Marx and Engels, the historical evolution of the family and of gender relations was linked to changes in institutions and technology. In capitalist societies, according to Marx and Engels, women in bourgeois families were subordinated because they were economically dependent; in proletarian families, in contrast, since men were propertyless and women were likely to be wage earners, there was less inequality.[5] Later Marxian analysts, when they showed interest in gender relations at all, tended to view gender inequality as a sort of byproduct of capitalist class relations. In the 1970s, a series of articles later referred to as the 'domestic labor debates' sought to relate women's labor in the home to Marx's categories of value and surplus value and to show how gender inequality was 'functional' for capitalists.[6] Women's unwaged work in the home made it possible to sustain a family on lower wages than would otherwise be the case, increasing capitalists' profits. Women were also said to constitute a 'reserve army of labor' useful to capitalists, being available for wage labor if they were needed (e.g. in wartime) and easily ejected from the labor force when they were no longer required. The work of women in nurturing and socializing children was recognized as necessary work of 'social reproduction'. But the 'social relations of reproduction' still tended to be viewed as subordinate to the 'social relations of production', meaning that gender relations (within and outside the household) developed in accordance with the needs of the capitalist economy.

Many feminists viewed these Marxian accounts as seriously flawed: they failed to account for the noneconomic aspects of gender relations; they did not explain why inegalitarian gender relations existed in noncapitalist societies; and they failed to recognize ways in which noncapitalist men benefited from gender inequality. The innovative 'dual systems theory' of Heidi Hartmann (1981a) sought to remedy these problems, and to put class relations and gender relations on a more equal footing. Capitalism and 'patriarchy', Hartmann suggested, constituted two separate and semiautonomous systems; the oppression of women was not just a product of capitalist class relations. Capitalists benefited from the subordination of women, but so did 'men' as a group. For instance, the exclusion of women from large parts of the labor market made men's wages higher than they would otherwise be; guaranteed men the benefit of women's household services; and allowed men to enjoy parenthood while exempting them from most of the actual

---

5. For a history of Marxian work on 'the woman question', see Vogel (1983).
6. Several of the key articles in this debate are collected in Malos ((ed.) 1980).

labor of childcare and housework.[7] The two beneficiary groups, capitalists and men, might be seen as having a mutual interest in maintaining women's subordination.

FOLBRE ON THE POLITICAL ECONOMY OF GENDER

In a 1981 essay written with Ann Ferguson, Folbre endorsed Hartmann's choice to view capitalism and patriarchy as separate systems, but argued that the relationship between the two might be at least in part an antagonistic one, rather than simply one of mutual reinforcement. Capitalist employers and individual men in households might, for example, be viewed as competing for the labor time of women. Ferguson and Folbre called for further research on the historical interaction of gender interests and class interests, and for a closer analysis of women's labor in and outside the home. They defined a new category of work, 'sex-affective production', which included the bearing and rearing of children and the provision of affection, nurturance and sexual satisfaction to adults. Some of this work (which may be paid or unpaid) was performed by men, but most was done by women, who were 'socialized toward an "ideal mother" personality which keeps them willing to give more than they receive from men in nurturance and sexual satisfaction' (Ferguson and Folbre 1981, p. 319). As a result of their socialization and of restrictions on their choices regarding work outside the home, women had a 'longer working day with less material and emotional rewards than men, less control over family decisions, and less sexual freedom combined with less sexual satisfaction' (ibid., p. 319). The beneficiaries of women's subordination included men and children as well as employers.

Folbre continued to explore and extend the Marxian conceptual framework in 'A patriarchal mode of production' (1987a). 'Patriarchy' and 'capitalism', she suggested here, might be viewed as two 'modes of production' in Marx's sense. The mode of production concept was useful because it focused analysis on 'systematic consideration of the way in which economic surpluses are extracted' and on the question 'Who benefits materially from a given set of social relations of ownership and control, and who is hurt?' (1987a, p. 329). She urged researchers to investigate 'patriarchal exploitation' (the appropriation of women's surplus labor time by men) and the ways in which gender relations in the household changed over time. She wrote again of a 'patriarchal mode of production' in an article (1987b) on the evolution of gender relations in Zimbabwe: here she

---

7.   Other important contributions to the Marxist–feminist literature during this period included Barrett (1980), Beneria (1979), Hartmann (1976, 1981b) and Kuhn and Wolpe (1978).

explored how gender relations in Zimbabwean communities were affected by British colonialism and why women's disadvantaged status persisted after independence.

Gender Relations in the Household

In several papers published in the mid-1980s, Folbre criticized the ways in which both neoclassical and Marxian economists dealt with the household. Neoclassical work on a variety of topics (including consumption and saving, fertility and labor supply) took 'the household' as the relevant decision-making unit, and portrayed it as seeking to maximize a unitary household utility function. Although it was acknowledged that this aggregation of individuals' preference-orderings was methodologically quite problematic in light of Arrow's (1951) Impossibility Theorem, economists continued to use the formulation because of its simplicity. Most posited a household utility function without discussing how it was derived; others might cite the ingenious solution offered by Gary Becker's 'Rotten Kid Theorem' (1976, 1981a, 1981b), in which the utility function maximized by the household was that of an altruistic household head. The head used contingent transfers of wealth to induce other household members to maximize his utility function: this was a dictatorship, but a benevolent one, because the head's utility was a positive function of other members' well-being. In Marxian political economy, with its focus on class conflicts in the workplace and the political sphere, the household played a relatively minor role, and Marxists were even less inclined than neoclassical economists to explore the household's internal dynamics.

In 'Hearts and Spades' (1986a) and other essays, including one co-authored with Heidi Hartmann (Folbre and Hartmann 1988), Folbre noted the striking fact that despite the many sharp conflicts between Marxian and neoclassical economics, they had 'remarkably similar theories of the household. Economists of both persuasions tend to treat the household as though it were an almost wholly cooperative, altruistic unit' (1986a, p. 245). Both groups seemed 'wedded to a rosy picture of the household as "home, sweet home"' (1986a, p. 246), and both were '"silent" on the issue of inequality within the home' (1986a, p. 247). Neoclassical economics presented a paradox in 'the juxtaposition of naked self-interest, which presumably motivates efficient allocation of resources through the market, with a fully clothed altruism that presumably motivates efficient allocation of resources within the family' (1988, p. 252). The association of selfishness with the market (seen as men's preserve) and of altruism with the home (seen as women's sphere) reinforced gender stereotypes and misrepresented the complex motivational dynamics in both sites. Becker's 'benevolent dictatorship' model also served to idealize inegalitarian gender relations in the family: 'This explanation of the joint utility function assumes that the only power holders in the family are altruists and the only rotten family members are those who wield no effective power' (1986a, p. 248). Analogously, 'Marxist economists confine the concept of exploitation to the capitalist firm and use the rhetoric of class solidarity to avoid the possibility of exploitation in the home' (Folbre and Hartmann 1988, pp. 190-91). Marxists assumed that individuals' only significant interests were class interests, and that members of families had the same class membership and interests as those of the male household head (ibid., p. 191). Thus, 'within the neoclassical tradition, the assumption of a joint utility function has obscured the possibility of conflicts between individuals in the family. Within the Marxian tradition, the assumption that class interests are primary has obscured the possibility of conflicts between individuals within the same class. As a result, both paradigms idealize the family' (ibid., p. 185).

These misrepresentations were, Folbre suggested, no accident: portrayals of the household as a sphere free of conflict, in which altruism prevailed and decisions were equitable, served the interests of men who benefited from the restriction of women's choices. 'The economic individualism so central to neoclassical economic theory could better be termed male individualism. Most of the progenitors of economic theory defined women as wives or mothers, not as individuals. ... A strict rhetorical boundary between the impersonal world of men and the personal world of women has helped protect the marketplace from moral criticism and insulated gender relations from economic scrutiny' (ibid., p. 186). In other words, 'economic self-interest has influenced the way economists think about the concept of self-interest' (ibid., p. 185). Women appeared in economists' portrayals as relatively 'noneconomic creatures', selfless rather than self-interested, innately predisposed to devote their energies to others' well-being. And '[t]elling women that caring for others is part of their nature, rather than an important form of work, is one way of lowering the cost of getting such care' (ibid., p. 196).

Folbre and Hartmann argued that the household should be seen as an arena of both altruism and selfishness, both cooperation and conflict. The gender division of responsibilities and rewards was neither equitable nor strictly ordained by 'nature'. Women's and men's preferences (themselves the products of socialization) might tend to differ, causing women to receive satisfaction from their work in the home that they would not receive through market work. But the gender division of labor also had clearly nonvoluntary aspects: 'Women's commitment to family is not necessarily a function of their preferences or their productivity. It is often constrained by the reluctance of other family members to help with housework and child care responsibilities' (ibid., p. 195).

What was required, Folbre and Hartmann emphasized, was not a simple reversal of the image of the household, to portray it as governed wholly by selfishness; rather, economists needed a more complex theory of human motivation, one that included altruism, selfishness and reciprocity, both in the household and in the workplace.

Another question Folbre raised in these articles was one that had otherwise been associated primarily with antifeminist rhetoric. At present, she noted, women are socialized to be better altruists than men, to put others' interests ahead of their own; but one must wonder, '[a]s women begin to spend less time working within the home, and more time in the capitalist marketplace, will their traditional altruism diminish?' (1986a, p. 252). This question regarding who will perform women's traditional 'caring labor' as women are drawn more and more into market work arises again in Folbre's 1994 book, as will be seen below.

In contrast to the rosy view of the household offered by economists, Folbre argued, there was much evidence of intrahousehold inequality in both highly industrialized and less industrialized countries. In 'Cleaning House' (1986b), she surveyed numerous studies which showed women working longer hours than men and faring poorly relative to men on measures of nutrition, health, education, and so on. Such inequality might of course be explained in terms of women's stronger 'tastes' for altruism or proclivities for voluntary sacrifice. Alternatively, she suggested, one could explore the possibility that intrahousehold allocations had something to do with household members' 'bargaining power'.

> Observed differences in the economic welfare of men, women and children may shed some doubt on the assumption of perfect altruism in the family, but they do not, in and of themselves, establish the importance of intrafamily conflict. Unless and until inequalities within the family can be systematically linked to differences in bargaining power, it can be argued that they represent voluntary choices, collective decisions, or simple cultural prejudices. (1986b, p. 24)

Thus the problems posed for researchers were urgent ones: 'Is this inequality related to systematic differences in the economic bargaining power of family members? What are the components and determinants of economic bargaining power within the family? And ... how are both relative bargaining power and inequality affected by the process of capitalist development?' (1988, p. 255).

The Nash bargaining models that a few neoclassical economists had begun to apply to the household had much promise, in Folbre's view: they focused attention on the conflictual aspects of households as well as their cooperative dimensions, and they served to 'redirect attention from the purely microeconomic level to the economy-wide factors that determine relative bargaining power'

(1986a, p. 250).[8] And yet the formal bargaining models were unlikely to be adequate by themselves. In the Nash model, the household's utility function is in effect a weighted average of the individual utility functions of its adult members; the weight given each person's preferences depends upon his/her bargaining power, which is essentially determined by his/her 'threat point', or level of well-being if cooperation should cease. These threat points, in turn, are defined in terms of individual access to assets, employment opportunities and support from the state. The implication is that if something occurs which improves a married woman's threat point – for example, if her potential wages rise or if new social programs are created to support divorced mothers – then she will get a better 'deal' in the household than she did previously. Folbre suggested that these economic factors were unlikely to be the sole determinants of bargaining power, which might be 'significantly affected simply by the cultural and political implications of membership in certain demographic groups' (1987c, p. 257). Social norms would strongly affect household decisions about work and consumption. As a result, one should not expect increases in resources available to women outside the household to necessarily or immediately lead to changes in their position within the household, as the Nash models would predict (1986b, pp. 20-21).

Folbre also argued that investigation of the determinants of bargaining power would require methodological pluralism: one would expect that bargaining power would undergo shifts over time because of changes in social and economic institutions, and these would not be amenable to traditional neoclassical analysis. Marxist-feminist work exploring the structural factors that provided family members very different social and economic options according to gender and age would be important in order to complete the stories. Thus neoclassical-style optimization modeling and Marxist-style historical-structural accounts might be viewed as complementary for feminist purposes, rather than as strictly competing and mutually exclusive approaches (1986a).

Folbre explored intrahousehold inequality within a Marxian analytical framework in 'Exploitation Comes Home' (1982). Marxists had failed to analyze exploitation within the household, she suggested, partly because of their adherence to an interpretation of Marx's labor theory of value (LTV) which held that the LTV was not applicable outside capitalist commodity production because of the absence of competition to force down producers' labor time to that which was socially necessary. Marxists had defined the 'value of labor power' as the socially

---

8.   The pioneering applications of Nash bargaining models to the household were McElroy and Horney (1981) and Manser and Brown (1980). Readers interested in feminist assessments of such models might see Seiz (1991, 1995) and Kabeer (1994, ch. 5).

necessary labor time embodied in the goods and services the worker and his family consumed, but they had paid no attention to the relationship between the value of goods and services transferred by the worker to family members, and the value of goods and services produced by the family for the worker. Using the terminology Marx had developed to characterize class relations, Folbre proposed, one could study whether this 'exchange' was an equivalent or an exploitative one. And if the exchanges appeared typically to be unequal, one could then inquire into the structural differences in bargaining power that led to inegalitarian distribution of goods and leisure within the household.

In Folbre's model, the family has one wage earner, and its other members produce goods and services only as unwaged labor. Each person consumes some share of the products of both waged and unwaged work, and one can calculate for each person the labor hours worked and the labor hours embodied in what is consumed. Then one can compare the ratios of 'hours worked' to 'hours consumed' for all members, to see how the 'burden of exploitation' (of the wage worker) is shared. 'The wage worker may exchange labor equally with family members, in which case he is exploited, but they are not. The wage worker may recoup the surplus value relinquished to the capitalist through unequal exchange with the family, in which case family members may be exploited but he is not. Alternatively, if [the ratios of hours worked to hours consumed are the same for all family members] the burden of exploitation is shared equally' (1982, p. 323).

Folbre acknowledged that to compare these ratios, hours worked in household labor must be commensurable with hours of wage work in terms of abstract socially necessary labor time. This presented problems, but the problems were not qualitatively different from those faced in applying the LTV to the market economy: 'Despite the fact that household workers do not produce for the market [we may reasonably assume that] they choose the most efficient means possible to perform their tasks. Their work may differ in skill and intensity, their fixed capital may differ in cost and depreciation, and they may engage in joint production, but none of these factors significantly distinguishes their work from that of wage workers' (1982, p. 323). Thus in principle one might seek to test whether unequal exchange takes place within families, using data on individual time allocation and consumption.

Folbre noted that transfers of value between household members were not necessarily exploitative, but 'may reflect purely voluntary material sacrifices ... related perhaps to the intangible and emotional aspects of family life' (1982, p. 323). But exploitation appeared quite possible: if women or children lacked independent means of livelihood, they would be compelled to cooperate within the patriarchal family despite its inequalities. And 'where men participate in the formation and enforcement of laws, institutions and social practices which weaken women's and children's potential for economic independence, where men enjoy substantially greater bargaining power than women and children, and where men's rate of exploitation is much lower than that of other family members, one can make a strong case that they are indeed exploiters' (1982, p. 324).

Capitalist Economic Development, the Family and Fertility

In several case studies of very different settings, Folbre extended the bargaining approach to explain changes in family size and structure over the course of capitalist economic development: changes in technology, the distribution of assets, and other institutions, she suggested, change the relative bargaining power of men and women, and of parents and children. These changes affect the intrahousehold distribution of goods, services, tasks and leisure; they also affect the costs and benefits of children, and therefore change fertility behavior.

In pre-capitalist Europe and the colonial US, for example (Folbre 1980, 1983), children made substantial contributions to family production, and the male family head exercised considerable control over the labor of his children and his wife. Families tended to be large, and women had heavy childbearing and childrearing responsibilities. There was little alternative to marriage for women, since they lacked property sufficient to provide independent livelihoods, and there were severe restrictions on their sexual-reproductive behavior. The links between adult men's control over women and over their children were clear: 'when and if children are economically advantageous to the male head of household, there is a particularly strong motive to channel women's productive efforts into childbearing and related forms of sex-affective production' (Ferguson and Folbre 1981, p. 322).

With the transition to capitalism, however, the family lost viability as a production unit. The individual patriarch lost control over the means of production to the capitalist class, thereby losing control over his children's labor power. Capitalists and patriarchs then competed for the labor time of women and children. Children's economic contributions to parents became smaller, and as a result family size was reduced. Women's labor force participation increased, and individual male household heads' power over women was weakened.[9]

---

9. Folbre notes that capitalist development need not always weaken precapitalist 'traditional' inequalities. In some instances, a 'complementarity' might be established between the new class relations brought by capitalism and preexisting forms of stratification (1986b, p. 28). The histories of gender and intergenerational relations in Europe and the US are explored in much greater detail in Folbre (1994).

In 'Household production in the Philippines' (1984a), Folbre used the bargaining framework to interpret empirical data on rural households in the Philippines. Neoclassical interpretations, positing a joint household utility function, emphasized that the cost of children depended heavily on the cost of the mother's time; this explained why the number of children varied positively with children's wages and negatively with mothers' wages. As economic development proceeded, technological change and increased education tended to raise the wages available to women; this made children more expensive and thus led to fertility decline.

Folbre proposed an alternative account of the same phenomena, centered on changes in relative bargaining power within the household, both between men and women and between adults and children. The intergenerational story focused upon how much children contributed to family income while living with their parents and after leaving home. As in the histories of Europe and the US discussed above, these transfers would depend in part on parental wealth. In the Philippines, parents clearly relied on their children's support in their old age. But there was considerable evidence that 'economic development is associated with a decline in the magnitude and reliability of children's contributions to parental income' (1984a, p. 311). This could be explained in terms of changes in bargaining power: 'If the process of decision making in the family is pictured as a bargaining process in which relative individual endowments determine distributional outcomes, changes in income flows between the generations can be seen as the result of changes in patterns of ownership and control of wealth and access to income' (1984a, p. 311). The capitalist development process was associated with a decline in the number of households which owned and farmed their own land, and with an increase in wage labor. 'Increasing landlessness ... diminishes the relative value of parental assets, while the potential for market employment ... makes many children less economically dependent on inheritance of parental assets' (1984a, p. 311). Income flows from adult children to parents thus declined, and families reduced their fertility: 'By asserting their economic independence, children raise their own "price"' (1984a, p. 311).

Folbre also argued that the observed gender inequalities in total time worked and consumption were not well explained by neoclassical accounts. The Philippine data clearly showed that girls and women worked more hours than boys and men, and received less in consumption. The main difference in work time was due to mothers' work in childcare, which seemed to come mostly from sacrifice of leisure, not reduction in other sorts of work. Again Folbre acknowledged that there might be differences in the intensity of women's work and/or its pleasurability that compensated them for longer hours and lower consumption. But the inequalities might equally well be viewed as a sign that women's preferences were receiving less weight than men's in the household's utility function, in accordance with the bargaining model: women's threat points were less favorable than men's because their wages in the market were much lower. Wealth might also be an important factor: in case of divorce, a Filipino woman's legal share of the household property was virtually the same as the man's. Consistent with this analysis, the observed gender differences in labor time were much smaller for wealthier families than for poorer ones.

Folbre noted that there were important policy implications of this story: to reduce labor market discrimination and other institutional inequalities (such as laws disadvantaging women) would likely increase women's bargaining power in the household and lead to more equitable distribution of tasks and consumption.

Folbre again applied the bargaining framework in a 'Comment' (1984b) on an article by Rosenzweig and Schultz. Rosenzweig and Schultz (1982) had argued that sex differences in infant mortality rates in India resulted from rational (if painful) resource allocation choices on the part of households: since males would make larger contributions to family income than females, poor households would rationally allocate their scarce resources preferentially to sons to ensure their survival. They hypothesized that sex differences in infant mortality should be smaller where female labor force participation rates were higher, since having higher potential earnings would increase the value of female children to the household; their empirical results were consistent with this account. Folbre suggested an alternative story, however, which was equally consistent with the data: mothers benefited more from female child survival than did fathers, because daughters helped with mothers' work. Expanded market opportunities for women would increase adult women's bargaining power, giving their preferences greater weight in the household utility function; and this would lead to greater resource flows to daughters.

Folbre has continued to explore the effects of economic change on household structure in recent studies (1991a, 1993a) that compare data on women, household headship and social security programs in countries of both North and South.

Gender and Public Policy

As noted above, making bargaining power central in household analysis focuses attention on the structural factors, including those shaped by state policy, that determine individual threat points. Men's bargaining power is increased, for example, by laws that enable husbands to prevent their wives from working outside the home or give them control over their wives' earnings; by 'protective' legislation restricting women's employment opportunities; by state actions that prevent women from owning or controlling property; and by policies denying public support to women with children who lack access to a husband's income.

In 'The pauperization of motherhood' (1984c), Folbre examined the effects of policies in the US on the distribution of the costs and benefits of children between men and women. She concluded that 'State policies toward motherhood in the US have consistently benefited men and disadvantaged women and children' (1984c, p. 73).

She began her story in the latter part of the nineteenth century, when desired family size was falling because of social and economic changes which reduced the economic benefits of children to parents. Whereas family law in the US had earlier served to reinforce a 'coercive pronatalism' (1984c, p. 75), now divorce laws were liberalized, and child custody became the responsibility of mothers rather than the automatic right of fathers. Throughout most of the twentieth century, governments limited women's reproductive freedom (restricting access to contraceptives and abortion, for example, at the same time that many black women in southern states were pressured to accept sterilization). Governments further disadvantaged women by failing to enforce fathers' child support responsibilities and providing very low levels of public assistance for female heads of households. These policies were complemented by labor market policies which added to women's difficulties: 'Women's work as mothers has always constrained their participation in wage labor. Public policies could serve to make these limitations less binding, but they have seldom done so, largely because this would entail transferring more of the costs of children to employers and/or taxpayers' (1984c, p. 78). Governments provided little support for daycare and refused to require employers to provide parental leave benefits. Thus mothers remained 'uniquely disadvantaged members of the labor force' (1984c, p. 81).

Women were also disadvantaged by the Social Security system, which in effect made children 'public goods' while enabling nonparents and many fathers to 'free ride'. 'When the state takes control over intergenerational transfers, the economic benefits of children become "public" benefits. The Social Security system distributes the earnings of the younger generation to the older generation largely on the basis of wages, without taking the unpaid labor of childrearing into account' (1984c, pp. 74-5). A male wage earner who divorced his wife and made a negligible contribution to the expenses of raising his children would receive far more from Social Security than would a single mother who was unemployed or employed at low wages because she devoted her time to childcare. 'Recognition of childrearing as highly productive labor', Folbre argued, 'would currently entail considerable redistribution of income from wage earners to home workers and from men to women' (1984c, p. 75). In summary,

Children no longer provide significant economic benefits to parents, but they do provide significant economic benefits to the elder generation as a whole. Mothers, single mothers in particular, pay a disproportionate share of the costs of rearing the next generation, and public policies exacerbate this inequality. Patriarchy has gone 'public' in the sense that employers and the state have proved as reluctant, if not more reluctant, than individual fathers to help out with the kids. (1984c, p. 85)[10]

Gender and the Structures of Constraint

Folbre's recent book, *Who Pays for the Kids? Gender and the Structures of Constraint* (1994), brings together her concerns with gender relations in the household, institutions and policies outside the household, and economic methodology. The principal objectives of the book are twofold:

1. to remedy economists' neglect of the 'costs of social reproduction' by addressing the question, 'How are the costs of caring for ourselves, our children, and other dependents distributed among members of society?' (1994, p. 1);
2. to develop a conceptual framework adequate for analyzing group differences in economic experiences, applicable not only to gender relations but also to other systems of inequality such as race and age, and giving a central role to collective action.

Part I of the book constructs the theoretical foundations for the analysis (as discussed below). Part II applies the framework to comparative histories of social reproduction in Northwest Europe, the United States, and Latin America and the Caribbean, and offers suggestions for policy.

The costs of social reproduction, as conceptualized here by Folbre, include the material resources and time devoted to the care of children, the sick, the disabled and the elderly ('dependents') and to the daily maintenance of working adults. In industrialized capitalist economies, much of this work is done in the home, and some is done for pay in the service sector (e.g. education, health care, child care and elder care). In both the home and the market, most of the providers of care are women, and in both sites, this labor is 'undervalued'. The distribution of the costs of social reproduction between women and men, adults and children, individual families and the public sector, shifts with capitalist economic development and is significantly shaped by collective action.

---

10. Folbre observes elsewhere that providing only low levels of public support for mothers and children is consistent with a 'strategy of rapid capital accumulation, but biases economic growth toward the accumulation of physical rather than human capital' (1986b, p. 29).

Capitalist economic development (as has been discussed above) destabilizes many aspects of traditional patriarchal structures of constraint, creating greater freedom for women and youth. But it also increases the cost of children, as well as weakening implicit familial contracts which earlier provided women and children some degree of economic security. Because of the persistence of the gender division of labor in the home, children tend to reduce women's income and consumption, and increase women's work time, more than men's. The result is a 'crisis of social reproduction': women suffer from low earnings, a rising risk of poverty, and a lack of leisure time, and children, the sick and the elderly receive less care than they should.

To analyze these complex historical processes, Folbre develops a new theoretical framework which draws upon neoclassical, Marxian and institutional economics, and seeks to provide a broader analytical scope without any unnecessary sacrifice of rigor. Individual preferences and choices are given roles to play, as are structural asymmetries in the distribution of assets and op-portunities; rules enforced by states are prominent, and so are social norms and other institutions. Folbre defines 'structures of constraint' as sets of asset distributions, political rules, cultural norms and personal preferences which produce different economic experiences for individuals according to their group memberships. These structures 'place individuals in similar circumstances and create similar realms of choice' (1994, p. 54) and 'empower given social groups' (1994, p. 51). Folbre discusses structures of constraint based on gender, age, class, race, nationality and sexual preference. Her historical studies of the US, Northwestern Europe and Latin America and the Caribbean emphasize the ways in which groups engage in collective action to shape these structures in their own favor. For example, working men and employers in the US at times acted jointly to exclude women from employment in many trades; African-Americans organized to change laws that prevented them from voting and obtaining education; colonial administrators in Latin America denied inheritance rights to children of 'mixed' marriages; and heterosexuals in industrialized countries act to oppose legal reforms which would extend to lesbians and gay men the benefits of marriage.

The policy implications of Folbre's analysis of social reproduction are powerful ones. The multiple asymmetries between women's and men's economic lives are not encompassed by the prevailing notion of 'equality of opportunity', which, she argues, 'reflects a male standpoint that pictures society in terms of adult males engaged in competitive sport' (1994, p. 61). To adequately address these problems, 'the concept of equal rights ... should be accompanied by a concept of equal obligations to children and other dependents. ... Women cannot compete fairly with men if they are saddled with greater responsibilities.

Furthermore, if these responsibilities are not redistributed, they may go unfulfilled' (1994, pp. 61-2). The 'structures of constraint' framework highlights the multiplicity of reforms that are necessary if women and men are to enjoy equality: whereas social scientists and policy makers have tended to focus narrowly on whether formal social rules (laws) are neutral in their impact on different groups, Folbre's framework suggests that not nearly enough attention has been paid to how asset distributions, cultural norms and discriminatory personal preferences function as sources of advantage and disadvantage (1994, pp. 62-63).

As Folbre summarizes the transformation that is required,

> We need an economy based on equal opportunity that enforces equal responsibilities as well as rights. We need to reorient our economic goals away from increasing Gross National Product and toward improving social welfare. We need to provide greater recognition and support for labor devoted to the care and nurturance of children, the sick and the elderly. (1994, pp. 252-3)

Towards these ends, she calls for a number of changes in policies, business practices and social norms; among them are:

a. 'equal sharing of the costs of family labor between men and women', which requires strengthening and enforcing laws regarding the financial obligations of parents, and changing social norms to encourage men to do a greater share of childcare work (1994, p. 258);
b. 'public compensation for the value of family labor', which could take the form of family allowances or tax credits for those performing direct care of children and other dependents (1994, p. 258);
c. 'equal childcare and educational opportunities', through publicly-subsidized, high-quality childcare services and educational institutions (1994, p. 258); and
d. 'workplace rules that encourage men and women to combine family work and market work', such as shorter average workdays, flexible schedules and family leave benefits (1994, p. 259).

METHODOLOGY AND FEMINIST ECONOMICS

What conceptual framework is best suited for explanation of the economic experiences of women? Can neoclassical language, which has so often served to rationalize gender inequality, be used just as well to tell feminist stories? Some feminist economists answer this latter question in the affirmative; but others have suggested that a variety of problems with the analytical framework of neoclassical economics render it inadequate for understanding gender relations.[11] For instance, Isabel Sawhill (1977) points out that economists' emphasis on individual choice might be misleading, given the strong shaping of preferences by social norms. Seiz (1992) argues that neoclassical economists overemphasize individual agency, pay too little attention to systematic differences in the options individuals face, and have no theory of economic/social 'power'. Feiner and Roberts (1990) observe that the neoclassical general equilibrium framework conveys a false sense of inevitability, seriously misrepresenting the complex institutional settings and open-ended conflictual processes that determine distributional outcomes. In Julie Nelson's (1990, p. 17) concise formulation, 'Analyzing phenomena fraught with connection to others (e.g. responsibility for children), tradition (e.g. the division of household tasks), and relations of domination (e.g. labor market discrimination) with only the language of individual agency, markets and choice is very likely to create a feeling of distortion, a feeling that what is most important has been left out'.

Folbre has been unusual among economists in drawing upon (while also criticizing) a variety of economic paradigms, and she has made powerful contributions to discussions of feminist economic methodology. She has criticized neoclassical theory for overemphasizing individual agency and neglecting structures and the social construction of 'preferences'; at the same time, she has argued, while Marxists do emphasize structures, they focus too narrowly on class relations and asset distributions, neglecting other dimensions and sources of inequality.

Folbre has consistently sought to construct an analytical framework which can encompass both structure and agency, first in her work with the bargaining framework and more recently in her writing on 'structures of constraint'. She argues that economists should retain a notion of purposeful (if not necessarily 'rational') choice, but should employ a much more complex view of human subjectivity which recognizes:

a. the mix of altruism and selfishness that characterizes many actions,
b. the social construction of desires and aspirations, associated with membership in groups defined by gender, class, race, nationality, and so on; and
c. the central importance of collective action.

In addition, she notes that any individual will belong to multiple groups, so that one's 'interests' may not always be clear.

---

11. For more discussion of these methodological issues, see Seiz (1992), Nelson (1992), and several of the essays in the excellent compilation by Marianne Ferber and Julie Nelson ((eds) 1993).

Institutions, she suggests, are also due for more nuanced treatment by economists. Institutions are created partly in the context of collective problem-solving (as emphasized by 'neoinstitutional' economists), as groups seek 'efficient solutions to coordination problems'. But they also reflect conflict between social groups and the pursuit of economic 'rents' and group aggrandizement (1994, p. 2). For example, the gender division of labor that assigns women responsibility for 'caring labor' is obviously in many ways an 'efficient' solution to the social problem of dependents' need for care. But 'this does not imply that all aspects of the family are functional, or that all its members benefit equally from it' (1994, p. 48); the structure disadvantages women in many ways, and therefore requires reform.

HISTORY OF ECONOMIC THOUGHT AND ECONOMIC HISTORY

With a few very recent exceptions, historians of economic thought have paid woefully little attention to how gender issues have been treated in economic discourse (Seiz 1993). Folbre has made several insightful and provocative contributions in this area.

Folbre (1992) traces the treatment of sexuality by Adam Smith, Thomas Malthus, Jeremy Bentham and several other classical writers, discussing their attitudes towards contraception and the sexual 'double standard'. Folbre (1993b) compares the stances on gender relations of nineteenth-century Marxist and non-Marxist socialist thinkers (e.g., Robert Owen and William Thompson), finding the latter in some cases more progressive (and no less 'scientific') than the former. Folbre (1993c) examines the feminist critiques of 'science' and of economics, and suggests that investigators of gender bias in economic discourse should pay more attention to the ways in which economic inequality and other structural constraints outside the academy have helped determine who would be represented in the scientific community and whose interests would be served by that community's products. And several of Folbre's essays on the measurement of women's economic activity (discussed below) include material on the participation of economists in the debates on this subject in the US and Britain.

As many feminists have argued, economists' definitions of employment and production are strongly gender-biased, and the resulting mismeasurements are an obstacle to understanding women's economic lives. As Folbre observed in a 1986 article, 'much of the observed variation in women's labor force participation within as well as across countries is largely an artifact of arbitrary definitions of economic activity that significantly understate women's contributions' (1986b, p. 14). 'Why', she asked, 'should cooking and serving food be considered less economic than growing and gathering food? Why should caring for childen be considered less productive than caring for livestock?' (1986b, p. 14).

Folbre has done a great deal of work both to trace the development of gender-biased measures of economic activity, and to use improved measures to revise the historical record on women's lives in the nineteenth-century United States. Folbre and Abel (1989) provide a fascinating history of the US Census Bureau's treatment of women's employment and of family 'headship'. Folbre (1991b) examines the treatment of women's household labor in the US and British Census in the nineteenth century, showing how women doing family work at home, who were initially recognized as 'productively employed', later came to be categorized as 'dependents'. Abel and Folbre (1990) dispute US Census data that suggest that there was only a very slow increase in married women's participation in the market economy between 1880 and 1930, relative to the dramatic upswing between 1940 and 1985. Census data in the earlier period, they argue, undercounted women's market-oriented economic activity, in the same way in which women's work is undercounted in contemporary less-industrialized countries. The data were based on subjects' self-descriptions, and women asked to specify only one occupation for themselves are likely to say they are keeping house, even if they are also working for wages and/or producing goods and services at home for sale on markets. This 'self-representation bias' is accompanied by 'enumerator bias'. Folbre and Abel provide new estimates of women's participation in market activity – defined to include industrial homework, work on family farms, and taking in boarders – for two towns in Western Massachusetts in 1880. Their revised market-activity participation rates for married women are dramatically higher than the Census labor force participation rates. Folbre (1993d) finds that as women's wage employment (formally recognized as employment by the Census) increased in the late nineteenth-century US, opportunities dwindled for industrial homework, boarding and participation in family farms or other businesses. Thus what changed was more the nature of women's involvement in the market economy than its extent. 'Women did not simply move from the household into the labor market. Rather, the early expansion of wage employment was accompanied by a reduction in forms of work that would, if performed by men, probably be termed "self-employment"' (1993d, p. 136). She estimates married women's market participation for five Massachusetts towns between 1880 and 1910, finding that the increase in Census-measured labor force participation was 'more than countervailed by declines in the percent engaged in only informal market work. ... In a time when single women were gaining economic independence, married women may have become more dependent on their husbands for market income' (1993d, p. 155). Folbre (1991c) shows 'that women's early participation in wage labor was accompanied by significant increases in female residential independence' (1991, p. 87). Large numbers of women began living away from home, as boarders, lodgers and domestic servants. These trends would have produced important conflicts of interest between wage-earning women and those dependent on their husbands' earnings, for example in debates over the payment of a 'family wage' to men. And, Folbre warns, one should not look only at the low number of 'female headed households' in the strict sense and conclude that household structures were stable over the late nineteenth century. Folbre and Wagman (1993) extend the critique to measures of national product, noting that after 1940, a consensus emerged among national income accountants that 'affirmed the qualitative importance of nonmarket household labor but largely disregarded its quantitative dimensions' (Folbre and Wagman 1993, p. 277). They estimate participation rates for nonenslaved men in market work, and for women in market and nonmarket work, for the US by decade from 1800 to 1860, then estimate the value of nonmarket production and compare the growth of market and total output over the period.

CONCLUSION

Nancy Folbre has been a pioneer on many fronts:

- documenting ways in which neoclassical and Marxian economics have both reflected and contributed to social ideologies legitimating gender inequality;
- pressing economists to recognize the household as an important economic site and to recognize women's work in the home as essential and productive;
- helping to revise the historical record to make it better reflect women's economic lives in many parts of the world; and
- contributing to the development of new analytical frameworks for feminist economic theory.

Her efforts have been characterized by an open-mindedness and eschewal of dogma that are rare among economists. She has urged Marxists to learn from neoclassical rational choice theory, and neoclassical economists to learn from Marxist and institutionalist accounts of how institutions develop; she exhorts all economists to pay attention to feminists, and feminists to pay attention to sociobiology and the fears of conservatives. Her contributions to feminist economic theory and methodology promise to continue to be influential; and this reader looks forward enormously to Folbre's innovations and provocations still to come.

FOLBRE'S MAJOR WRITINGS

(1980), 'Patriarchy in colonial New England', *Review of Radical Political Economics*, **12** (2), Summer, 4-13.

(1981) (with Ann Ferguson), 'The unhappy marriage of patriarchy and capitalism', in Lydia Sargent (ed.), *Women and Revolution*, Boston: South End Press.

(1982), 'Exploitation comes home: A critique of the Marxian theory of family labor', *Cambridge Journal of Economics*, **6** (4), December, 317-29.

(1983), 'Of patriarchy born: The political economy of fertility decisions', *Feminist Studies*, **9** (2), June, 261-84.

(1984a), 'Household production in the Philippines: A non-neoclassical approach', *Economic Development and Cultural Change*, **32** (2), January, 303-30.

(1984b), 'Market opportunities, genetic endowments, and intrafamily resource distribution: Comment', *American Economic Review*, **74** (3), June, 518-20.

(1984c), 'The pauperization of motherhood: Patriarchy and public policy in the United States', *Review of Radical Political Economics* **16** (4), Fall, 72-88.

(1986a), 'Hearts and spades: Paradigms of household economics', *World Development* **14** (2), February, 245-55.

(1986b), 'Cleaning house: New perspectives on households and economic development', *Journal of Development Economics*, **22**, Spring, 5-40.

(1987a), 'A patriarchal mode of production', in Randy Albelda, Christopher Gunn and William Weller (eds), *Alternatives to Economic Orthodoxy: A Reader in Political Economy*, Armonk, New York: M.E. Sharpe, Inc.

(1987b), 'Patriarchal social formations in Zimbabwe', in Sharon Stichter and Jane Parpart (eds), *Patriarchy and Class in Africa*, New York: Sage Publications.

(1988), 'The black four of hearts: Toward a new paradigm of household economics', in Daisy Dwyer and Judith Bruce (eds), *A Home Divided: Women and Income in the Third World*, Stanford: Stanford University Press.

(1988) (with Heidi Hartmann), 'The rhetoric of self-interest: Ideology and gender in economic theory', in Arjo Klamer, Donald McCloskey and Robert Solow, (eds), *The Consequences of Economic Rhetoric*, Cambridge: Cambridge University Press.

(1989) (with Marjorie Abel), 'Women's work and women's households: Gender bias in the U.S. Census', *Social Research*, **56** (3), Autumn, 545-69.

(1990) (with Marjorie Abel), 'A methodology for revising estimates: Female market participation in the U.S. before 1940', *Historical Methods*, **23** (4), Fall, 167-76.

(1991a), 'Women on their own: Global patterns of female headship', in Rita S. Gallin and Anne Ferguson (eds), *The Women and International Development Annual*, vol. 2, Boulder: Westview Press.

(1991b), 'The unproductive housewife: Her evolution in nineteenth-century economic thought', *Signs: Journal of Women in Culture and Society*, **16** (3), Spring, 463-84.

(1991c), 'Women on their own: Residential independence in Massachusetts in 1880', *Continuity and Change*, **6** (1), 87-105.
(1992), '"The improper arts": Sex in classical political economy', *Population and Development Review* **18** (1), March 105-21.
(1993a), 'Women and social security in Latin America, the Caribbean and Sub-Saharan Africa', *IDP Women Working Papers No. 5*, Geneva: International Labour Office.
(1993b), 'Socialism, feminist and scientific', in Marianne Ferber and Julie Nelson (eds), *Beyond Economic Man: Feminist Theory and Economics*, Chicago and London: University of Chicago Press.
(1993c), 'How does she know? Feminist theories of gender bias in economics', *History of Political Economy*, **25** (1), Spring, 167-84.
(1993d), 'Women's informal market work in Massachusetts 1875-1920', *Social Science History*, **17** (1), Spring, 135-60.
(1993e), 'Micro, macro, choice and structure', in Paula England (ed.), *Theory on Gender/Feminism on Theory*, New York: Aldine Publishers.
(1993) (with Barnet Wagman), 'Counting housework: New estimates of real product in the United States, 1800-1860', *Journal of Economic History*, **53** (2), June, 275-88.
(1994), *Who Pays for the Kids? Gender and the Structures of Constraint*, London and New York: Routledge.

OTHER REFERENCES

Arrow, Kenneth (1951), *Social Choice and Individual Values*, New York: Wiley. Second edition, 1963.
Barrett, Michele (1980), *Woman's Oppression Today: Problems in Marxist Feminist Analysis*, London: Verso. Second edition, 1988.
Barrett, Nancy S. (1981), 'How the study of women has restructured the discipline of economics', in Elizabeth Langland and Walter Grove (eds), *A Feminist Perspective in the Academy: The Difference it Makes*, Chicago: University of Chicago Press.
Becker, Gary S. (1965), 'A Theory of the Allocation of Time', *The Economic Journal* **75**, 493-517.
Becker, Gary S. (1971), *The Economics of Discrimination*, second edition, Chicago: University of Chicago Press.
Becker, Gary S. (1973), 'A theory of marriage, part I', *Journal of Political Economy*, **81**, July-August, 813-46.
Becker, Gary S. (1974), 'A theory of marriage, part II', *Journal of Political Economy*, **82**, March-April, S11-S26.
Becker, Gary S. (1976), 'Altruism, egotism and genetic fitness: Economics and sociobiology', *Journal of Economic Literature*, **14**, September, 817-26.
Becker, Gary S. (1981a), *A Treatise on the Family*, Cambridge, Mass.: Harvard University Press.
Becker, Gary S. (1981b), 'Altruism in the family and selfishness in the market place', *Economica*, **48** (1), February 1-15.
Becker, Gary S. (1985), 'Human capital, effort, and the sexual division of labor', *Journal of Labor Economics*, **3**, S33-58.

Beneria, Lourdes (1979), 'Reproduction, production, and the sexual division of labour', *Cambridge Journal of Economics*, **3**.

Bergmann, Barbara R. (1971), 'The effect on white incomes of discrimination in employment', *Journal of Political Economy*, **79**.

Bergmann, Barbara R. (1974), 'Occupational segregation, wages and profits when employers discriminate by race or sex', *Eastern Economic Journal*, **1** (2), April-July, 103-10.

Bergmann, Barbara R. (1986), *The Economic Emergence of Women*, New York: Basic Books.

Bergmann, Barbara R. (1987), 'The task of a feminist economics: A more equitable future', in Christie Farnham (ed.), *The Impact of Feminist Research in the Academy*, Bloomington, Indiana: Indiana University Press..

Bergmann, Barbara R. (1989), 'Does the market for women's labor need fixing?', *Journal of Economic Perspectives*, **3**, Winter, 43-60..

Blau, Francine D. (1984), 'Discrimination against women: Theory and evidence', in William Darity, Jr. (ed.), *Labor Economics: Modern Views*, Boston: Kluwer Nijhoff.

Blau, Francine D. and Marianne Ferber (1992), *The Economics of Women, Men and Work*, second edition, Englewood Cliffs, NJ: Prentice-Hall.

Feiner, Susan and Bruce Roberts (1990), 'Hidden by the invisible hand: Neoclassical economic theory and the textbook treatment of race and gender', *Gender and Society*, **4** (2), June, 159-81.

Ferber, Marianne A. and Bonnie G. Birnbaum (1977), 'The "new home economics": Retrospects and prospects', *Journal of Consumer Research*, **4** , June, 19-28.

Ferber, Marianne A. and Julie A. Nelson (eds) (1993), *Beyond Economic Man: Feminist Theory and Economics*, Chicago: University of Chicago Press.

Ferber, Marianne A. and Michelle L. Teiman (1981), 'The oldest, the most established, the most quantitative of the social sciences – and the most dominated by men: The impact of feminism on economics', in Dale Spender (ed.), *Men's Studies Modified: The Impact of Feminism on the Academic Disciplines*, New York: Pergamon Press.

Hartmann, Heidi (1976), 'Capitalism, patriarchy and job segregation by sex', *Signs: Journal of Women in Culture and Society*, **1** (3 pt. 2), Spring, 137-69.

Hartmann, Heidi (1981a), 'The unhappy marriage of Marxism and feminism', in Lydia Sargent (ed.), *Women and Revolution*, Boston: South End Press.

Hartmann, Heidi (1981b), 'The family as the locus of gender, class and political struggle: The example of housework', *Signs: Journal of Women in Culture and Society*, **6** (3), Spring, 366-94.

Jacobsen, Joyce P. (1994), *The Economics of Gender*, Cambridge, Mass. and Oxford, UK: Blackwell.

Jaggar, Alison (1983), *Feminist Politics and Human Nature*, Totowa, New Jersey: Rowman & Allenheld.

Kabeer, Naila (1994), *Reversed Realities: Gender Hierarchies in Development Thought*, New York and London: Verso.

Kuhn, Annette and AnnMarie Wolpe (1978), *Feminism and Materialism: Women and Modes of Production*, Boston and London: Routledge & Kegan Paul.

Lloyd, Cynthia B. and Beth T. Niemi (1979), *The Economics of Sex Differentials*, New York: Columbia University Press.

Madden, Janice (1973), *The Economics of Sex Discrimination*. Lexington, Mass.: Lexington Books.

Malos, Ellen (ed.) (1980), *The Politics of Housework*, London: Alison & Busby.

Manser, Marilyn and Murray Brown (1980), 'Marriage and household decisionmaking: A bargaining analysis', *International Economic Review*, **21** (1), February, 31-44.

McElroy, Marjorie B. and Mary Jean Horney (1981), 'Nash-bargained household decisions: Toward a generalization of the theory of demand', *International Economic Review*, **22** (2), June, 333-49.

Mincer, Jacob (1962), 'Labor Force Participation of Married Women', in H. Gregg Lewis (ed.), *Aspects of Labor Economics*, Princeton: Princeton University Press.

Mincer, Jacob and Solomon Polachek (1974), 'Family Investments in Human Capital: Earnings of Women', *Journal of Political Economy*, **82** (part 2), March-April, S76-108.

Nelson, Julie A. (1992), 'Gender, metaphor and the definition of economics', *Economics and Philosophy*, **8** (1), 103-25.

Polachek, Solomon (1981), 'Occupational self-selection: A human capital approach to sex differences in occupational structure', *Review of Economics and Statistics*, **63** (1), February, 60-69.

Pujol, Michele (1992), *Feminism and Anti-feminism in Early Economic Thought*, Brookfield, Vermont: Edward Elgar.

Rosenzweig, Mark and T. Paul Schultz (1982), 'Market opportunities, genetic endowments and intrafamily resource distribution: Child survival in rural India', *American Economic Review*, **72**, 803-15.

Sawhill, Isabel (1977), 'Economic perspectives on the family', *Daedalus*, **106**, 115-25.

Seiz, Janet A. (1991), 'The bargaining approach and feminist methodology', *Review of Radical Political Economics*, **23** (1&2), Spring, 22-9.

Seiz, Janet A. (1992), 'Gender and economic research', in Neil de Marchi (ed.), *Post-Popperian Methodology of Economics: Recovering Practice*, Boston: Kluwer.

Seiz, Janet A. (1993), 'Feminism and the history of economic thought', *History of Political Economy*, **25** (1).

Seiz, Janet A. (1995), 'Bargaining models, feminism, and institutionalism', *Journal of Economic Issues*, **29** (2), June, 609-18.

Vogel, Lise (1983), *Marxism and the Oppression of Women: Toward a Unitary Theory*, New Brunswick, New Jersey: Rutgers University Press.

4. Robert H. Frank

A. Allan Schmid

Robert Frank writes the kind of meaty books that reviewers hate. It simply takes longer to come to grips with the deep ideas than is usually allotted to reviews. His titles are works of art that contain the essence: *Choosing the Right Pond* (1985) and *Passions Within Reason* (1988). Most would sell their souls to the devil for those pregnant titles.

Choosing the right pond is a metaphor for a fundamental choice that has been largely overlooked in economics. Most have focused on maximizing utility by choice of goods, but Frank argues that choice of one's reference group is even more fundamental. He begins not with assumptions, but with empirical observation. People value relative standing in a society. And like other goods, status has costs and is the subject of economizing.

Can one write a whole book on the quest for status? It turns out that the valuation of status explains a great many economic phenomena that conventional theory has explained poorly or not at all. Why are wage rates among co-workers more egalitarian than predicted by standard theories of the labor market? Why do most countries have redistributive tax programs? Would unions, occupational safety and health regulations, minimum wage laws and overtime laws play useful roles even in perfectly competitive markets? Would forced savings be beneficial even if people had perfect foresight and self-discipline? Why do many societies impose ethical sanctions against the sale of organs, babies and sex? The quest for status is involved in all of these instances and it causes individually independent choice to go wrong. Individuals cannot get what they want acting alone. Yes, this is a book about the economics of collective action. This book will pique the libertarian at the same time that it gives little comfort to liberals.

Near and dear to the minds of conventional theorists is the assertion that labor is paid the value of its marginal product. Not so, says Frank. But it is not because labor is exploited in non-competitive markets. It is because of people's concern for relative standing. Since people differ greatly in their natural abilities, marginal productivity theory predicts that wages will differ greatly for an occupational class. But in fact pay schedules are quite egalitarian and piece-rates are seldom found even when transaction costs do not make them impractible to implement (cf. chapter on Williamson in this book).

People care as much or more for their relative standing among local associates as for absolute income. Frank takes a lesson from Thomas Schelling, who has called attention to the mathematical phenomenon of reciprocal relationships. In this case, one person's high status requires someone else in a lower status. (See the chapter on Schelling in this book.) Since people have the right to choose their own pond (coworkers), you cannot get something for nothing. The person who accepts lower status provides a valued product to the person honored with higher status, and this must be paid for in wages higher than marginal product for the lowly and less than marginal product for the honoree. This behavior is consistent with the facts of compressed wage structures (Frank 1985, ch. 4).

Without payment, the lowly would form ponds (firms) of like skilled workers and avoid low-status pain. The high-output workers would be left alone in other firms with their high pay but no local status honor. Frank derives a number of corollaries. Occupations where work routines involve close contact with coworkers should have more compressed wage structures than their opposite. Indeed, car salespersons have more egalitarian wage structures than real estate brokers who work more independently out of the office. Wage structures are also more egalitarian in unionized firms where job tenure allows more interaction among workers and in the military where people are more likely to interact socially with fellow employees. Even college professors appear to be partly paid in status rather than the full value of extra grant resources they produce. Competitive firms cannot bid the more productive workers away to new ponds if workers value relative standing.

The concern for relative position affects not only private transactions, but is the basis for collective action to achieve individual purposes. While local status is most highly prized, status in the broader society is also valuable. People can individually and privately sort themselves into firms offering the preferred mix of income and status. But paying for the preferred society presents problems for private choice because the result is a high-exclusion cost good plagued with free riders. And therein lies Frank's answer to why many societies utilize redistributed taxation.

Persons who individually purchase status by paying lower productivity persons to stay in their society thereby purchase a good available to all others desiring the status conferred by the presence of these lower-status people. As Frank (1985, p. 106) puts it, 'If people value both status and material goods, and if they are free to form societies with whomever they wish, then transfer payments (which are equivalent to a redistributive income tax schedule) are necessary for the achievement of the most-preferred social structure. Hardly a burden on the high-ranking members of various societies, redistributive taxes are rather the means without which these members would be unable to achieve their favored positions' (p. 106).

Frank thus offers an alternative to John Rawls, who takes pain to avoid consideration of relative standing to justify greater equality. The alternative also constitutes a critique of Milton Friedman's and Robert Nozick's justification of inequality. At this point, Frank employs a feature of institutionalist thought, namely a two-sided transaction as the unit of analysis. Yes, the requirement that all pay a redistributive tax reduces the freedom of the wealthy who do not care about status and do not mind the departure of the lower-status people. But the retention of this opportunity reduces the freedom of those wealthy who do care about relative status. Opportunities conflict and appeal to freedom in general is not dispositive of the issue. As Frank puts it, 'Whenever one group's demands conflict with another's and neither side has decisive moral arguments in its favor, practical guidelines are needed to reach a compromise' (p. 115). For those with a taste for deterministic policy models, the call for compromise will not appeal, but so be it. Frank argues that if people 'cannot escape compromise in the labor market, where they have complete freedom to choose their associates, then why should they be protected by the state from having to make similar compromises outside the labor market?' (p. 115).

Just as skilled people working alongside the less skilled will together produce more than the sum of what each would produce alone, there are efficiency gains from larger groupings. The provision of marginal cost equal to zero goods such as national defense is but one example. The average cost is less for larger nations. Fragmentation is costly. But who pays to keep us together?

INDIVIDUAL VS. COLLECTIVE RATIONALITY

A less inventive author might have entitled this book 'The Economics of Collective Action', but choosing the right pond is not only more colorful but captures the operative point. The quest for status puts one on a positional treadmill. As each person struggles to gain utility, the mathematical reciprocity of interdependence means that in the aggregate few or none can succeed. After others follow suit and after the expenditure of many resources, it is possible that the positional hierarchy remains unchanged. Frank notes the parallel to the classic problem of the prisoners' dilemma. The dilemma is characterized by the existence of a dominant strategy which when followed produces a result that is favored by neither party. While each one makes the best choice available at the margin, no one likes the result. This is not a problem of the individual vs. the collective. It is a problem where individuals with identical preferences may prefer collective solutions in order to obtain their individual preferences. Optimality requires collective action. How does this insight help us better understand why societies choose safety regulations, group pensions and minimum wages?

In competitive markets, workers may trade off safe working conditions for income. Libertarians insist on the individual freedom to make this choice. Frank argues that people with the freedom to choose their own reference group would nevertheless freely choose to limit their choices if coordinated with the choices of others. Frank's favorite method is to first present a thought experiment and then generalize to a theoretical proposition and then confront it with evidence. Imagine a person who does not find the income differential in the risky work environment worth the cost. Yet in the quest for status both for him/herself and his/her children he/she is tempted to go for the extra income. He/she may realize that when other workers see his/her behavior, they too will be tempted to accept the risky environment. Soon they are all engaged in a contest to see who can accept the most risk which is not unlike other prisoners' dilemma situations such as the arms race.

The only way off the treadmill is to join with others in some agreed-upon restraint. This can take the form of a regulation that all workplaces must meet some standard level of safety. Out of context this may appear as a forced limit to freedom, but in the interdependent world of concern for relative standing it is the only way for individuals to get what they want. In Frank's words, 'When everyone's parents work in the unsafe mine, the advantage each parent sought to provide for the next generation serves only to protect against falling behind in the contest' (p. 130). Resources are expended, but no extra utility is created. Frank emphasizes that the problem can arise in competitive markets with perfect information and no failure of telescopic vision. You do not need a theory of exploitation to justify safety regulations. People can exploit themselves in the interdependent quest for status.

The concern for relative standing means that work-place safety is worth more to workers than they are observed to pay for it in forgone wages if they took a safer lower-pay job. This constitutes a fundamental challenge to a widely held theoretical tenet of revealed preferences. In the context of interdependent choice (including that of positional and high-exclusion cost goods), behavior does not reveal a person's preferences. It may only reveal that persons are making the best out of a treadmill that they would like to stop and get off of. In Frank's colorful and surprising twists on convention, 'It does not follow that we always learn more by watching what people do than by listening to what they say' (p. 191).

Both minimum wages and upper limits to wages (such as forced vacations) can be responses to positional demand. The low skilled are paid more than they are worth even if it decreases the demand for their services in order to keep them in the positional hierarchy. And the aggressive workaholic is held in check to prevent the outbreak of unconstrained emulation that defeats the promise the first mover had in mind. Frank argues that without collective self-imposed limits, people in their attempt to keep up with the Joneses in spending for positional goods will consume more of them than they actually want. It is a race that neither they nor the Joneses can win.

Nowhere is the contrast between conventional theory and Frank more clear than with respect to lifetime savings behavior. Traditional theory requires that high-income families save the same fraction of their incomes as low-income families in order to smooth the consumption stream over one's lifetime. Careful surveys of the literature do not support the life-cycle hypothesis. While the facts contradict this theory, alternative theories such as that of Duesenberry (1949) have been relegated to the footnotes in most texts, again demonstrating the power of a priori beliefs. Frank explains the facts not by assuming irrationality, but by a rational seeking of relative standing. People are tempted to consume more of their income during the period of high income in an attempt to gain positional advantage and this temptation is stronger for the lower-income people. Veblen's conspicuous consumption is just that – conspicuous – while one's saving for old age is not (until it is too late). A relatively few dollars of extra spending is more conspicuous for lower-income people than for the rich.

Once we have a theory that fits the facts it sheds a different light on public policy. National savings and pension plans are ways for people to step off the positional treadmill and satisfy their preferences, rather than violations of consumer sovereignty. One might ask why self-aware people cannot step off by themselves. In addition to the disadvantage of losing the positional contest (which no one can win), Frank notes that, 'We process information with our brains, not computer hardware' (p. 141). Frank's work is carefully grounded in behavioral science. He is consistent with Herbert Simon's conception of bounded rationality. Frank says, 'We do the best we can to promote our purposes with the neurological capacities we have. Yet most people are either unable, or find it not worth the effort, to base all of their judgments on strictly cognitive considerations' (p. 141). In such contexts we seek the help of our fellows to design some cultural and political institutions to economize on our scarce cognitive resources.

The perspective of the quest for relative standing has implications for recalibrating the now tiresome arguments between critics and defenders of capitalism. Critics from the left point out some undesirable feature such as worker alienation and claim it occurs because of unequal power. Supporters from the right claim that there is no issue of power and that people are entitled to freely make their own decisions. If people accept fragmented work situations, they must regard the compensation as adequate. However, Frank concludes that 'The real difficulty here does not lie in the power of firms to exploit people. Instead, it stems from our tendency to engage in unproductive competitions among ourselves' (p. 177).

The market enthusiast cannot see any good reason for laws against the use of markets for fingers, kidneys, babies and sex. Frank can. Because of inter-dependence caused by positional concern, people may be tempted to sell more of these goods than they otherwise would. Frank says, 'The payoffs facing each potential seller are misleadingly attractive' (p. 185). The libertarian asks how can anyone object if people willingly buy and sell? Frank finds that the notion of victimless crime requires tunnel vision. He cannot find any moral reason to categorically reject the problem arising from the externality of a person's behavior offending the sensibility of another while accepting as legitimate the problem arising from the externality of industrial waste on environmentalists. He might accept the following revision of a familiar refrain, 'Sticks and stones only hurt my bones, but some words and behaviors destroy my peace of mind'. And it is, of course, in our minds where utility lies.

I believe that Frank would agree with Guido Calabresi (1985) who argues that cost is not a matter of physics, but a matter of ineluctable collective choice of what interdependent interests are to be regarded as reasonable. If a person's concerns are not reasonable, then any violation of them is not a cost which others must consider. J.S. Mill's dictum that no one's freedom can be abridged unless the action causes harm to others cannot dispose of conflicts. Harm to others must be socially defined. Does a person having an abortion harm other mothers? It does if concern for the unborn counts. It does if the pain of having to make a conscious decision which otherwise would be circumscribed in habitual practices counts. Frank says, 'The right not to be offended is just as worthy of our respect as the right not to be restricted' (p. 224). Again, this is a matter to be compromised and worked out, not something to derive from some deterministic model.

While Frank has a place for moral choices, he would like to avoid such choices where possible. He offers the following: 'decision rules for collective action should be sought that mimic as closely as possible the decisions that citizens would reach themselves if they could negotiate costlessly with one another in a hypothetical unrestricted environment' (p. 225). He is more optimistic that this can be implemented than this commentator. He observes that there are important economies of scale in a society and economy. This 'scale surplus' is the glue which can hold a people together. This presents a familiar economizing problem of how to constitute the rules of society so that enough people can be kept in to achieve the scale economies. Frank hopes that we all give up some of our first-preference choices in order to get the scale surplus. He proposes that we substitute more opportunities for trade for the more usual all-or-nothing allowances or prohibitions. Thus the first test for a collective rule would be to see if what Group 1 is willing to pay for the rule exceeds what Group 2 would be willing to pay to avoid it.

The next test would be to ask if the rule imposes major costs on anyone and if that group can be identified and compensation paid. He offers the example of a blasphemer who would desist for $10 and a devout who would pay $50 for the desistance (p. 213). If the scale surplus is greater than ten, Frank concludes that the parties would 'gladly' participate since both are better off with the devout paying ten. But in another context, Frank observes that quarrels over distribution of the surplus often preclude its realization. The devout may be willing to forgo the realization of any of the surplus in order to avoid paying anything to someone they regard as unworthy (having unreasonable preferences). Frank raises practical objections to implementing his proposal but uses its thrust to argue that we use taxes more than prohibitions. Good idea. But the equivalent of the devout may insist on a tax that approaches prohibition and the taxpayers may begrudge the payment for what they consider an unreasonable demand. It is clear that the destruction of homes and bridges does not achieve the scale surplus or any other in Bosnia. An appeal to cost–benefit does not settle the question of righting past wrongs or the utility of getting even at any cost. Even if it could be determined that the devout would pay 50 to avoid the blasphemy, it may not impress them that they should pay anything, let alone the lion's share of any joint surplus. Willingness to pay does not exist in an institutional vacuum. It depends on other rights which produce income which may be begrudged by the other party. In this case, a moral principle of certain human rights and limitations is the only way to compromise out of the literal arms race. A Pareto-better opportunity without some respect if not love is no guarantee of its success.

In the end, Frank does not find any logical fault with the decision-making procedures found in many countries. He feels his contribution is mainly to show that these procedures are compatible with the existence of powerful individual rights (p. 226). The US is now racked with taxpayer revolts. Those taxpayers on one side of their brain realize that the loss of their first choices is the cost of getting other things they want but could not have apart from the community. But on the other side they have more vivid impressions of these losses and convince themselves that government is an impersonal thing running over their freedoms. Would that Frank's message could get through to restore the balance. If it does not, the present world trend towards fragmentation and tribal warfare will continue.

To complete his book, Frank springs another juxtapositional trap that rivals those of Gary Larson's 'Farside' cartoons. His last chapter is entitled, 'The Libertarian Welfare State'. Before Frank, that would have been an oxymoron.

Frank turns the usual public finance dictum on its head. 'Instead of being one in which we try to minimize the distortions we *create* through tax policy, it becomes one in which we employ tax policy to *remove* existing distortions' (p. 232). He advocates taxing specific categories of consumption to diminish the tendencies people have to save too little, take too many safety risks, or patronize large firms and thus have too little sociability from small firms.

As to welfare policy itself, Frank finds much to recommend the negative income tax and much to object to in price controls. But he recognizes that psychologically people do not like to give direct transfers even if economists find them efficient. Frank summarizes that 'A prudently designed mix of cash and in-kind transfers, together with an offer of publicly sponsored employment at low wages, would eliminate many of the perverse incentives inherent in our traditional array of welfare programs' (p. 242). Frank demonstrates that redistributive taxation and regulation of the labor contract are features that could be part of perfectly voluntary societies that could form and dissolve costlessly at will. He acknowledges that his libertarian welfare state would contain ineluctable tensions, tradeoffs and disputes. His concluding words are worth full quotation and he deserves the last word: 'Where individually rational and collectively rational choices point in opposite directions for many people, such disputes, we have seen are often more practical than moral in flavor. Having provided safeguards for fundamental constitutional liberties, a system that attempts to sift through the preferences of the opposing camps in such disputes will generally outperform one that chooses aimlessly between conflicting moral platitudes' (p. 249).

Frank has demonstrated that choosing the right pond, friends, firm and reference group are important for human welfare and that this boundary choice is subject to the same economizing discipline that has been developed for goods and services. This economizing often requires collective action. He has provided a framework for the analysis of interdependent choice. He has applied it to interdependences originating from a concern for position, but it is equally applicable to other sources of interdependence.

PASSIONS WITHIN REASON

Passions within reason? Another oxymoron? Not after reading Frank's 1988 book. He argues that passion rather than being the opposite of reason is one of the ways humans cope with the commitment problem and achieve their reasoned purposes. The commitment problem 'arises when it is in a person's interest to make a binding commitment to behave in a way that will later seem contrary to self-interest' (1988, p. 47). In his 1985 book he noted that the human concern for position put people onto a treadmill-like prisoners' dilemma (PD) problem. In that book he urged us not to condemn collective solutions to the status quest. But in this book he takes up the problem of how to solve PD problems of all types. How do we actually get off the treadmill even if we realize that getting off does not imply a loss of individual freedom? PD is characterized by a dominant strategy facing each of the interdependent parties which when chosen results in outcomes which neither party prefers.

In his typical fashion, Frank confronts conventional theory with the facts and then creates a new theory more consistent with those facts. The self-interest model in economics is useful. It is the foundation of the path-breaking work of Mancur Olson (see the chapter on Olson in this book) who extended the self-interest model to argue that high-exclusion cost goods can only be provided by some outside coercion or by being tied to the provision of low-exclusion cost goods. So following Olson, economists have felt the model confirmed by observing that many people do not bother to vote or free ride rather than voluntarily contributing to a high-exclusion cost good like broadcast television. But there is simply more of this behavior than Olson predicts.

Frank points to behavior ranging from leaving a tip on a one-time visit to an out-of-town restaurant, anonymous gifts to public television, and voting. The point is not that all people do these things all the time, but that they exist at a significant level above that predicted by the narrow selfish utility-maximization model. To complement this self-interest model, Frank proposes what he calls the 'commitment model'. The distinguishing feature of the commitment model is that seemingly irrational behavior is sometimes explained by non-cognitive emotional predispositions. The calculating person chooses the dominant strategy in the PD case. The emotional person simply behaves in a manner which is consistent with the individually preferred outcome of interdependent choice with others.

The essence of Frank's commitment model has been well stated by Alan Hamlin, 'First, rational pursuit of material interests is potentially self-defeating. ... Second, appropriate emotional predispositions might overcome the commitment problem in at least some cases. Third, humans have acquired an in-built, or hard-wired, ability to internalize emotions of certain types – although the precise content of the emotional package may depend on cultural and other factors. Fourth, humans have also acquired an in-built, but imperfect, means of displaying or signaling their emotional makeup' (1991, p. 411). The emotions then prevent us from succumbing to the temptation of opportunistic behavior in the case at hand in order to fulfil our preferences over time.

But, do not nice guys finish last? Will not the non-opportunistic person lose out? The competitive model deduces that persons who do not press their advantage will be eliminated by others who do. Following an evolutionary trajectory, the self-interest theory can be employed to imagine that if as a result of random mutation, caring persons exist but do not press their advantage over others, the randomly existing calculators will soon bankrupt them. In this model the caring persons are well advised to abandon their values lamenting that they cannot afford to follow their preferences. Such was the conclusion of Bertold Brecht's 'Good Woman of Sichuan' who was charitable by day and ran an exploitative and secretive sweat shop by night.

Still, the trustworthy person who will not be opportunistic will be sought by business partners. Instead of being competed away, he/she will be solicited and rewarded. If that is the case, then would not calculating individuals simply be good when it pays and then defect when it does not? A calculating person may observe that honesty and good reputation pay. In this case there is no need for emotions (non-calculating non-cognitive behavior).

We can go a long way to achieve cooperative behavior by arranging incentives appropriately. A current literature in economics is referred to as designing incentive compatible institutions. But in the PD problem the parties know that cooperation is preferable but they cannot easily solve the commitment problem by arranging case-specific incentives. They are tempted to cheat and know the other person has the same temptation. Bringing the future consequences of the breakdown to bear is not always possible. Knowing that the other person is predisposed to cooperation is economically valuable and is the condition for each party to participate.

Another example of the commitment problem is deterrence. In many cases contract monitoring costs are too high and overwhelm any scale advantage. Just having a legal right to expected behavior of others is worthless if it costs too much to enforce it. Transaction-cost economics focuses on these situations and predicts that the parties will choose relationships to economize on transaction costs (see Williamson in this book). The hierarchical firm may economize on transaction costs, but still in many cases, opportunities for cooperation are lost. However, the temptation to be opportunistic may be reduced if the person considering defection calculates that the other person may act to punish the defection even if it constitutes a net loss to the enforcer. A person who acts as a matter of principle even if the net gains are negative is often referred to as emotional. This emotional non-calculating response to defection is a deterrence to the calculating would-be defector.

Joint ventures are the occasion for bargaining over surpluses. People know that in a series of exchanges they may be occasionally in a weak position and may be bluffed and taken advantage of. This category is related to what game theorists call the 'chicken game'. Some theorists assume that people will play the game as long as it is Pareto-better, even if the other parties extract the lion's share. Not

Frank. From the perspective of his earlier work, he observes that some Pareto-better exchanges do not occur because of feared unfair changes in the relative standing of the parties. The threat of an emotional rejection of the short end of an otherwise Pareto-better exchange gives incentives to the calculating defector to avoid defection. This probable emotional non-calculating response to defection may prevent some people from rejecting profitable ventures which offer the possibility of future bargaining advantage upsetting the predicted and hoped-for status maintenance.

The problem of immobile assets is another category of commitment problem which Frank observes. As Oliver Williamson notes, use of specialized immobile and transaction-specific capital may lower per unit production costs, but exposes its user to possible capital losses if trading partners desert before the capital is recovered. Williamson predicts that industries and firms with transaction-specific assets will be characterized by binding contracts and hierarchical relationships between the parties. Where this is not possible, the parties will have to forgo the advantage of the cheaper immobile technologies. Frank might predict that there will be more ventures utilizing unprotected immobile assets than transaction-cost theory would expect. The commitment problem is solved not only by contracts and hierarchies, but also by emotions functioning as incentives. The persons who exhibit trustworthiness will be sought when the other commitment instruments are not available.

In Frank's colorful language, this category is illustrated with bargaining between marriage partners, but its implications for business are obvious. Williamson describes the 'fundamental transformation' from competition to bilateral monopoly occasioned by immobile assets and transaction costs. In the context of marriage, Frank (1988, p. 195) finds a parallel, 'Because search is costly, it is rational to settle on a partner before having examined all potential candidates. Once a partner is chosen, however, the relevant circumstances will often change'. If the commitment problem cannot be solved, joint investments that would otherwise be profitable will not be realized.

The place for emotions also depends on fundamental trustworthiness being observable and not something that the calculating person can turn off and on. The preservation of the truly trustworthy depends on others not being able to deceive the person seeking a non-opportunistic partner. The linkage does not depend on complete predictive accuracy, but only statistical regularity.

To confirm this linkage, Frank turns to the biological and behavioral science literature. Committed people experience emotions such as sympathy, guilt, anger, envy and love. These emotions emit signals which others can observe and can be used to select partners for joint ventures. We all know, for example, that blushing reveals something about the person which is not fully controlled by calculation.

'Extensive research has identified a multitude of statistically reliable clues to the emotions that people feel' (p. 132). Frank makes much use of the type of experiments pioneered by those like Vernon Smith (see chapter in this book). In a PD-type game, two-thirds of formerly unacquainted people who have time to get acquainted rejected the dominant strategy. The game was structured to ensure that promises could not be enforced and there could be no fear of reprisal. Again, the self-interest model fails and the subjects were remarkably accurate in their predictions of who would default (Frank, Gilovich and Regan 1993).

At this point, reviewer Alan Hamlin (1991, pp. 411-12) asks whether 'emotion trumps reason and forces a particular action' or whether 'emotions do not act as constraints but are simply additional arguments that enter into the rational calculus'. All subjects did not follow a single strategy. Emotion does not dominate no matter what, but may be cued (framed, in the language of Tversky and Kahneman, see chapter in this book). The response to the cue may be cognitive or not. One cue is the expected behavior of one's partner. Over 80 percent of the subjects who predicted their partner would cooperate also cooperated themselves. They were not opportunistic though they could have got away with it. Why? Is it because they have developed rapport and sympathy and social closeness with their partner and calculate that they gain more warm glow utility by cooperation? And, does this calculation overcome any predisposition to cooperate when the partner is expected to defect? Over 80 percent who predicted defection also defected.

Can we separate the effects of group identity, conscience and material reward? A series of experiments were designed by Dawes, van de Kragt and Orbell (1990) to do just that. The work is entitled, 'Cooperation for the Benefit of Us – Not Me, or My Conscience'. How do these people find all the great titles? Space does not allow description of the experiment but the authors concluded that discussion (getting to know each other) has a powerful effect. In the absence of discussion, the cooperators said they acted in order to do the right thing (conscience). With discussion, they emphasized concern for group welfare. The defectors emphasized personal material payoff. For Dawes et al., the key point is that group identity matters. The key point for the commitment model is that emotion, whether warm glow seeking, altruistic, conscience satisfying, or whatever, saves a person from making case-by-case calculation of material advantage and thereby defeating that person's more aggregative material preferences. Perhaps the meaning of emotion is to describe behavior which does not respond linearly to changes in relative prices. It is sticky. Not frozen, but sticky.

It is not Frank's purpose to persuade anyone that biological forces play the primary role in human choice, but 'to establish that even if biological forces were the only ones that influenced behavior, it would still be possible for unopportunistic behavior to emerge' (Frank 1988, p. 45) He is searching for a coherent role for cultural reinforcement. 'If people inherit anything at all, it is a receptiveness to training about the attitudes that are likely to serve them in life. Virtually every culture invests heavily in the moral training of its young. If people who successfully internalize these teachings are observably different from those who don't, it is no puzzle that parents cooperate enthusiastically in the training process' (p. 93). Parents who want their children to succeed want them to internalize some behaviors so that they will exhibit emotional signals of trustworthiness to others and not be tempted by opportunities to defect. Concern for material advantage can lead parents to insist on moral training as much as on mathematics and chemistry.

The best way to exhibit sought-for character is to actually have that character. How does character evolve? This story would require at least a book of its own. Emotion is conditionable but within limits. Frank quarrels with the strict behavioralists because he observes that not all experienced feedback acts as reinforcement.

Fairness and love are not woolly notions in Frank's theory and observations. He offers the following testable hypothesis: 'People will sometimes reject transactions in which the other party gets the lion's share of the surplus, even though the price at which the product sells may compare favorably with their own reservation price' (p. 167). Various experiments confirm this.

The domain of Frank's analysis can be seen by contrasting it to situations of repeated play. Robert Axelrod's experiments show that in repeated games, people obtain higher payoffs by adopting tit-for-tat strategies than any other (Axelrod and Hodgson 1994). The next encounter must be important enough to make defection an unprofitable strategy. For the cooperation to get started, there must be some clustering of individuals who use strategies involving cooperation on the first move and who discriminate between those who respond to cooperation from those who do not. Tit-for-tat cannot beat a player who defaults on the first move and stays with it. Cooperation can emerge without the parties being knowledgeable since via evolution successful strategies can survive even if the players do not know why; there is no necessity for words, trust, altruism or central authority. This is consistent with a narrow calculation of material self-interest without any need for the emotions. This is great as far as it goes. But it is precisely in situations where no tit can follow tat that such calculations fail. These are situations where the game cannot be repeated, the tatter against which one might direct one's tit cannot be identified; exclusion, monitoring and transaction costs are high; players are not forgiving; in a word – commitment problems.

What are the policy implications of Frank's model? It expands our policy options in those cases where material incentives are difficult to apply. Some of the implications for business are the following: take advantage of workers' concern for relative standing; hire workers who feel bad when they shirk; create a work environment that fosters closer personal ties between coworkers (such as practised by the Japanese); encourage the emotions that support cooperation. These suggestions are supported by hard-headed business motives as well as humanitarian concerns.

What has Frank accomplished? He has given us an expanded agenda and a research program. If Douglass North's work can be summarized by saying economic development is the history of reducing transaction costs, Frank's work may lead to an amendment saying that development is the history of solving the commitment problem. North (1990, p. 140) states, 'One gets efficient institutions by a polity that has built-in incentives to create and enforce efficient property rights. But it is hard – maybe impossible – to model such a polity with wealth-maximizing actors unconstrained by other considerations. ... We need to know much more about culturally derived norms of behavior'. Frank has made a big step along these lines.

North and others have emphasized the importance of stable property rights for development. Where does this stability come from? In a democracy it comes from widespread support for a given distribution of rights. Frank's perspective suggests that such support will come from meeting people's concerns about relative standing. Distribution cannot be divorced from support for the institutions that facilitate development. So in the context of the former communist nations, Frank suggests that 'the emerging market economies of Eastern Europe would be much better advised to eschew the regulatory approach adopted by most Western countries in favor of the alternative of taxing positional consumption' (Frank 1993, p. 280). Stable democracy and stable rights must go together and reflect an emotive concern with fairness.

The commitment model challenges the self-interest model on its own ground. It accepts the premise that material incentives govern behavior. 'Its point of departure is the observation that persons directly motivated to pursue self-interest are often for that very reason doomed to fail. They fail because they are unable to solve commitment problems' (Frank 1988, p. 258). Passion has its reasons. That reason applies both at the level of the isolated individual and the collective level where the individual seeks the help of others to achieve individual ends. It is in the reasoned interest of the most opportunistic to nevertheless train its progeny to internalize trustworthiness so that its presence will be signaled to others seeking joint ventures.

It is also in the reasoned interest of the individual to seek collective action to further reinforce emotions to support certain behaviors. Institutions are much more than constraints. They are enabling and allow individuals to obtain things they cannot obtain alone. It is not unknown for an individual to support collective action directed to a class of actions which makes some joint ventures possible and still be tempted to defect and rail against the sanctions applied to the case at hand. We can see cycles in political action as we swing between the vividness of these points. It is only the broad perspective offered by such as Frank that keeps this swing in check. Collective institutions have their reasons. The emotions preempt reason in some contexts and in others, the emotions serve material interests. All important dimensions of evolution are both dependent and independent variables.

It is perhaps the human destiny to be both served and bedeviled by emotion. The emotional content appropriate in a certain previous environment may become dysfunctional in another. The very tenacity of emotion is both its safeguard against temporary desertion and its armor against change of outmoded emotional reactions.

To say that emotions can be exploited and their supply enhanced to serve materialist purposes is not to say that materialism is everything. It is only to say that hard-nosed materialists as well as humanists have a stake in the emotions and if that forms the basis for some joint ventures and reduced conflicts, that will not be all bad.

Robert H. Frank, born 1945, was a high school mathematics teacher for the Peace Corps before pursuing his PhD in economics at the University of California. He has spent his career in the Department of Economics at Cornell except for a tour as Alfred Kahn's chief economist at the Civil Aeronautics Board. Frank's association with Richard Thaler (see chapter in this book) in the Cornell Graduate School of Management seems to have been mutually stimulating and the two of them, along with Tversky and Kahneman, have set the pace for an economics firmly based on empirical behavioral science. Frank's own behavior gives evidence to a strong commitment to teaching and the responsibility it contains for affecting the behavior of students. His own conduct seems to reflect the idea that 'our beliefs about human nature help shape human nature itself' as well as human nature shaping behavior (1988, p. 237). This is a hallmark of certain institutionalists who see key variables as both dependent and independent. After observing that economics students were more opportunistic in prisoners' dilemma type games than were students in other disciplines (1993a), he committed himself to writing an intermediate text book, *Microeconomics and Behavior* (1991), that would acknowledge that humans are capable of both calculated narrow utility maximization and non-cognitive, emotive committed behavior. The book contains a masterful summary of behavioral regularities which have implications for economics. (Needless to say, it gives an alternative to the lifetime savings hypothesis.) Frank has shown that it is not necessary to abandon the insights of the self-interest model even if amendments are in order. Humans in certain contexts exhibit elements of such behavior. And when they are in the planner part of their brain they can set self-limits and shape the direction of their emotions especially in cooperation with others to save themselves from interdependent treadmills. The conception is consistent with a brain of multiple and somewhat independent compartments rather than a completely unified brain. People learn, and they can in part affect what they learn. Frank appears to care deeply what we learn.

FRANK'S MAJOR WRITINGS

Books

(1978) (with Richard T. Freeman), *The Distributional Consequences of Direct Foreign Investment*, New York: Academic Press.

(1985), *Choosing the Right Pond: Human Behavior and the Quest for Status*, New York: Oxford University Press.

(1988), *Passions Within Reason: The Strategic Role of the Emotions*, New York: W.W. Norton.

(1991), *Microeconomics and Behavior*, New York: McGraw-Hill.

Selected Articles and Chapters

(1975) (with Philip Cook), 'The Effect of Unemployment Dispersion on the Rate of Wage Inflation', *Journal of Monetary Economics*, **1**, April.

(1977), 'Lifeline Proposals and Economic Efficiency Requirements', *Public Utilities Fortnightly*, May 26.

(1978), 'How Long Is a Spell of Unemployment?', *Econometrica*, **46**, March.

(1978), 'Why Women Earn Less: The Theory and Estimation of Differential Overqualification', *American Economic Review*, **68**, June.

(1978), 'Family Location Constraints and the Geographic Distribution of Female Professionals', *Journal of Political Economy*, **86**, February.

(1978) (with R. Freeman), 'The Distribution of the Unemployment Burden: Do the Last Hired Leave First?', *Review of Economics and Statistics*, **LX**, August.

(1983), 'When Are Price Differentials Discriminatory?' *Journal of Policy Analysis and Management*, **2**, Winter.

(1984), 'Are Workers Paid Their Marginal Products?' *American Economic Review*, **74**, September.

(1984), 'Interdependent Preferences and the Competitive Wage Structure', *The Rand Journal of Economics*, Winter.

(1985), 'The Demand for Unobservable and Other Nonpositional Goods', *American Economic Review*, **75**, March.

(1987), 'If *Homo Economicus* Could Choose His Own Utility Function, Would He Want One with a Conscience?', *American Economic Review*, **77**, September.

(1987), 'Shrewdly Irrational', *Sociological Forum*, **2**, Winter.

(1988), 'Bureaucratic Turfbuilding in a Rational World', *European Journal of Political Economy*, **4**, Supplementary Issue.

(1989), 'Honesty as an Evolutionarily Stable Strategy', *Behavioral and Brain Sciences*, **12**, December.

(1989), 'If *Homo Economicus* Could Choose His Own Utility Function, Would He Want One with a Conscience? Reply to Harrington', *American Economic Review*, **79**, June.

(1989), 'Frames of Reference and the Quality of Life', *American Economic Review*, **79**, *Papers and Proceedings*, May.

(1989), 'Beyond Self-Interest?', *Challenge*, March.

(1990), 'Rethinking Rational Choice', in Roger Friedland and A.W. Robertson (eds), *Beyond the Marketplace: Rethinking Economy and Society*, Hawthorne, NY: Aldine de Gruyter.

(1990), 'A Theory of Moral Sentiments', in Jane Mansbridge (ed.), *Beyond Self-Interest*, Chicago: University of Chicago Press.

(1991), 'Positional Externalities', in Richard Zeckhauser (ed.), *Strategy and Choice: Essays in Honor of Thomas C. Schelling*, Cambridge, MA: MIT Press.

(1991), 'Social Forces in the Workplace', in Kenneth G. Koford and Jeffrey Miller (eds.), *Social Norms and Economic Institutions*, Ann Arbor: University of Michigan Press.

(1992), 'The Differences Between Gifts and Exchange: Comment on Carol Rose', *Florida Law Review*, July.

(1992), 'Melding Sociology and Economics: James Coleman's *Foundations of Social Theory*', *Journal of Economic Literature*, **30**, March.

(1992), 'Toward a Theory of the Sense of Justice', in Margaret Gruter and Michael McGuire (eds.), *The Sense of Justice*, Newbury Park, CA: Sage.

(1993), 'The Strategic Role of the Emotions: Reconciling Over- and Undersocialized Accounts of Behavior', *Rationality and Society*, **5** (April).

(1993), 'A New Contractarian View of Tax and Regulatory Policy in the Emerging Market Economies', *Social Philosophy and Policy* **10** (2) Summer.

(1993), 'The Role of Moral Sentiments in the Theory of Intertemporal Choice', in Jon Elster and George Loewenstein (eds), *Choice Over Time*, New York: Russell Sage.

(1993), 'Frames of Reference and the Intertemporal Wage Profile', in Jon Elster and George Loewenstein (eds), *Choice Over Time*, New York: Russell Sage.

(1993a) (with Thomas Gilovich and Dennis Regan), 'Does Studying Economics Inhibit Cooperation?', *Journal of Economic Perspectives*, **7** (2).

(1993) (with Thomas Gilovich and Dennis Regan), 'The Evolution of One-Shot Cooperation', *Ethology and Sociobiology*, **14**, July.

(1993) (with Robert M. Hutchens), 'Wages, Seniority, and the Demand for Rising Consumption Profiles', *Journal of Economic Behavior and Organization*, **21**.

(1993) (with Philip Cook), 'The Growing Concentration of Top Students at Elite Schools', in Charles Clotfelter and Michael Rothschild (eds), *Studies of Supply and Demand in Higher Education*, Chicago: NBER-University of Chicago Press.

OTHER REFERENCES

Axelrod, Robert and Geoffrey Hodgson (1994), 'The Evolution of Cooperation' in Geoffrey Hodgson, Warren J. Samuels and Marc Tool (eds), *Institutional and Evolutionary Economics*, Aldershot: Edward Elgar.

Calabresi, Guido (1985), *Ideals, Beliefs, Attitudes and the Law*, Syracuse: Syracuse University Press.

Dawes, Robyn, Alphons van de Kragt and John Orbell (1990), 'Cooperation for the Benefit of Us – Not Me, or My Conscience', in Jane Mansbridge (ed.), *Beyond Self Interest*, Chicago: University of Chicago Press.

Duesenberry, James (1949), *Income, Saving, and the Theory of Consumer Behavior*, Cambridge, Mass.: Harvard University Press.

Hamlin, Alan (1991), 'Review of Passions Within Reason', *Ethics*, **101** (2).

North, Douglass (1990), *Institutions, Institutional Change and Economic Performance*, Cambridge: University of Cambridge Press.

5. Robert Heilbroner

Jerry Evensky and Robert Pollin

In the mid-1950s, Robert Heilbroner wrote to his revered mentor and colleague Adolph Lowe, 'If I had been born as an atom of humanity in Africa, Asia, or South America, the chances are very great that I would be a communist'.

Instead, Heilbroner's fate was to be born in New York City in 1919, an atom of humanity in a wealthy German Jewish family. His father, Louis Heilbroner, founded Weber and Heilbroner, one of the best known men's clothing businesses of the inter-war period. Robert's secondary education was at Horace Mann School, at that time an adjunct to Columbia University's Teachers' College and a way-station toward an Ivy League university education.

Living amid privilege, Heilbroner nevertheless developed a strong concern for social justice as he grew up. His father died when he was only five. Afterwards, his family's chauffeur, Willy Gerkin, became a surrogate father to him. But the young Heilbroner also sensed the indignity of Mr Gerkin's position – a family intimate yet a subordinate, set apart even through the formal driver's uniform that he wore. Looking back, Heilbroner explains that his lifelong social conscience springs from feelings of indignation when he realized that his mother could give orders to 'William' only because his beloved 'Willy' needed the money and she had it.

Heilbroner went on to Harvard in the fall of 1936: his timing could not have been more propitious. Keynes's *General Theory* had just been published that year. The Harvard Economics Department, which was to evolve into the leading center of Keynesian thought by the decade's end, was locked in battle over the book's message, particularly as it pertained to combating the economic depression then ravaging the country. Heilbroner was initially oblivious to the swirl of controversy. But in his sophomore year, he took a course in which his tutor was Paul Sweezy, at that time a leading young Keynesian and soon to develop into the foremost US Marxist economist of the post World War Two period. The class was learning about the rate of interest as the reward for abstinence. But Sweezy assigned Veblen's *The Theory of The Leisure Class* as supplemental reading, and then asked Heilbroner, 'What do you think Veblen would have thought of abstinence?'

'I still remember a light going on', Heilbroner remembers. Sweezy's engagement with the social dimensions of economics thus provided an analytic underpinning to Heilbroner's already strong social concerns. The overall Harvard experience also forged a lifelong attachment to the Keynesian project of engaging the power of government to fight mass unemployment and allied afflictions of free market capitalism.

But Heilbroner's full flowering as an economist was to come some years later, after having served in World War Two and briefly afterward in business. Working as a freelance writer in New York in 1946, Heilbroner once again wandered into an economics class that was to shape his life. This time it was Adolph Lowe's course on the history of economic thought at the New School for Social Research. Heilbroner 'fell under the spell' of Professor Lowe:

> What Lowe conveyed was the idea of the economic process as a force imposing a powerful order-bestowing shape and impetus to the material activities of society. Classical political economy could thus be seen as a succession of attempts to explicate this process from (roughly) the mid-eighteenth to the mid-nineteenth centuries. Of special interest to myself, as a burgeoning student of the history of economic thought, was the way in which the investigators of different periods fastened on, or interpreted, different aspects of society as strategic for its evolution. (1992, p. 242)

This course became the incubator for Heilbroner's classic 1953 book, *The Worldly Philosophers*, and, thereby, the launching pad for Heilbroner's 40 years of unique accomplishment as a professional economist.

The term 'unique' – meaning 'single, sole, alone of its kind' according to the *Oxford English Dictionary* – is normally debased in modern usage, deployed most often as a synonym for 'uncommon'. But for describing Heilbroner's career, the precise meaning of the term actually fits: he is one of a kind. For despite the numerous professional honors he has received and his status, according to *Business Week* magazine as 'perhaps the best selling economics author of all time' (9/30/72, p. 58), Heilbroner has always stood apart from the mainstream of the profession.

The most obvious feature distinguishing Heilbroner from his professional colleagues is his masterful, often magisterial, prose. Incomprehensibility is the hallmark of the overwhelming mass of economics writing, and is often regarded, in fact, as a measure of an author's perspicacity. But Heilbroner is not simply a great stylist. The most striking feature of his writing is his ability to lead readers on searching journeys through complex questions of political economy and public policy. That is why, even beyond the boundaries of the economics profession,

Heilbroner is among the great public intellectuals of the post-World War Two period.

Heilbroner also stands apart from the profession as a person of the left. Being the atom of humanity from New York's privileged enclaves rather than the third world, Heilbroner was never a communist. But his sympathies, extending back to his childhood bond with his chauffeur, have been consistent throughout his career. Having been appointed Norman Thomas Professor of Economics at the New School in 1963 and holding that position until his retirement thirty years later, Heilbroner is almost surely the only economist in the US whose endowed chair was named for a socialist political leader. And, more to the point, while the worldwide celebration of capitalism reached unprecedented levels in the 1980s, including within the economics profession, Heilbroner published a series of works in those years which built upon much of the Marxian method and critique of capitalism. Perhaps even more contrary to customary modes of thought, Heilbroner has advanced a perspective on Adam Smith which shows Smith to be not only an inspired champion of *laissez-faire*, but also a deep critic of many features of market economies.

More broadly, Heilbroner has never accepted the fundamental project of modern mainstream economics: to develop elaborate mathematical and statistical techniques which bring far greater precision to economic reasoning than existed in previous periods. Indeed, Heilbroner largely regards this project with disdain – as having generated, in one of his most memorable turns of phrase, 'rigor, but, alas, also mortis'. For Heilbroner, what is enervating about most modern economics is its refusal even to attempt the grand-scale projects characteristic of the classical economists: the 'wide-searching beacons' rather than the 'pinpoint beams' through which the historical dynamics of a civilization become discernible via its system of material provisioning. Throughout his career, Heilbroner has insisted on throwing out such wide-searching beacons. This is evident from the very titles of his books: *An Inquiry into the Human Prospect, The Nature and Logic of Capitalism, Marxism: For and Against, Between Capitalism and Socialism, 21st Century Capitalism, The Future as History*, as well as, of course, *The Worldly Philosophers*.

Heilbroner, finally, is a Cassandra in a profession of Panglossians. He is unflinching in describing the afflictions of contemporary societies – the environmental crisis, virulent nationalism, economic stagnation, the decline of a democratic socialist ethos – as well as, perhaps most troubling, the demons embedded in human nature itself. He thus returned to the theme of his 1950s letter to Adolph Lowe with another letter 25 years later. He wrote that he would still be drawn to communism were he, like most of the world's population, a poor person living in a poor country. But he had changed his assessment of the prospects for such revolutionary movements to improve life significantly. 'I am' he told Lowe, 'much more struck now by the properties of inertia in the human personality'.[1]

And yet, Heilbroner is the pessimist who cannot truly believe his most disturbing assessments. He could not otherwise write so powerfully of the need for reason, creative scholarship, an ethical imperative and progressive political change. 'Pessimism of the mind; optimism of the will', as the Italian Marxist Antonio Gramsci put it: this is the tension that is palpable in Heilbroner's work.

EXPLORATIONS IN THE WORLDLY PHILOSOPHY

The Worldly Philosophers, published in 1953 while Heilbroner was still a New School graduate student, was a stunning achievement. It told the story of the history of economic thought in a way that had not been previously attempted. Beautifully written and abundant in its presentation of illuminating history and biography, it was accessible and entertaining. Now translated into two dozen languages, it maintains a wide readership throughout the world, ranging from high school students to professional economists.

But *The Worldly Philosophers* diverges in substance as well as style from standard treatments. Most scholarly research in the history of thought consists of detailed and agnostic considerations of some aspect of the work of a major economic thinker. Standard textbooks then attempt to judiciously synthesize the perspectives on the major authors developed in the professional literature. The unifying thread in most such works is that the great books of the past are no more than prolegomena to the present. As Heilbroner himself has argued, the point of such standard fare is to evaluate the economists of previous epochs by the degree to which they anticipate the present, with evaluations rising the closer one approximates the prevailing state of mainstream understanding (see Heilbroner 1979).

The Worldly Philosophers makes no pretense of encyclopedic coverage or even-handedness. For example, the original edition included no mention of Alfred Marshall. Though this gap was filled by the second edition, the coverage of Marshall, even in the latest 1986 edition, is barely half that given to the 'utopian socialists', Robert Owen, Charles Fourier and Count Henri de Rouvroy de Saint-Simon, authors who would receive perhaps a footnote in most texts.

Why the Utopian Socialists over Marshall? What becomes evident is that Heilbroner is inspired by the thinkers who excavated beneath the surface of market

---

1. Heilbroner describes these two letters to Lowe in a profile in the *Chronicle of Higher Education*, 10/16/78, p. 4.

exchange relations under capitalism, even if, as with the utopian socialists, their explorations never yielded deep insights. He is far less interested in those offering ever greater refinements of the market economy's surface features, Marshall being, in Heilbroner's view, a prototype of this latter category of thinkers.

Of course, Smith is the first great hero of the story. Heilbroner is careful to recognize that Smith was not the first to unlock the secret of a market economy: how the forces of selfishness and competition operating in an unregulated environment could yield a coherent, and even efficient and dynamic, social order. Others, including Locke, Steuart, Mandeville, Petty, Cantillion, Turgot, Quesnay and Hume preceded Smith in this intellectual project, and Smith learned from them. However, as Heilbroner writes:

> Smith was the first to understand the full philosophy of action that such a conception demanded, the first to formulate the entire scheme in a wide and systematic fashion. He was the man who made England, and then the whole Western world, understand just how the market kept society together, and the first to build an edifice of social order on the understanding he achieved. (1986, pp. 72-3)

Smith, then, sets the standard for the enterprise of worldly philosophy. His successors may reject Smith's vision, but to be worthy of him, they had to emulate his ambition: to explain not simply the functioning of a market economy, but also the concatenations between market relations, social relations, politics and culture.

Heilbroner also honors Smith in another way: beyond *The Worldly Philosophers*, he is the one economist about whom Heilbroner has written in the standard format of the professional historian of thought. For example, in 'The Socialization of the Individual in Adam Smith' (1982), Heilbroner pursues an issue in Smith that, as we will explore later, has deep ramifications in his own work, namely the formation of individual motivation within a market society. For Heilbroner, the individual in Smith is, at root, neither a mere pleasure-seeking machine nor a simple byproduct of a given social environment. Individuals are rather endowed with a basic set of ethical standards to which, under most circumstances, they will cleave. However, Heilbroner argues that Smith's first great book, *The Theory of Moral Sentiments* describes the 'transformation of what I shall call "primal human nature" into socialized man' (Heilbroner 1982, p. 419). The persons that emerge from the pages of *The Theory of Moral Sentiments* have learned to be both acquisitive of wealth and deferential to the wealthy. This provides the engine that drives the market system and the gyroscope that maintains stability of a highly stratified class society. Such a socialization process then sets the stage for the drama of the market itself that Smith describes in *The Wealth of Nations*. Heilbroner explains:

> Whereas *The Theory of Moral Sentiments* covers the socio-psychological process of the
> individual, *The Wealth of Nations* explores the socio-economic consequences brought about
> by socialized man. ... The 'problem' in Smith's socialization of the individual is that social
> cohesion is achieved at the price of social compassion. ... A stratified and class-oriented society
> has been set into motion and kept in stable order by the passions of mankind, unknowingly
> harnessed. (1982, pp. 434, 439)

Heilbroner's work on Smith clearly places him among the most distinguished
contemporary Smith scholars. At the same time, it is likely that Smith's
conception of the individual is not the one that Heilbroner describes. Heilbroner
suggests a sequential social logic from *The Theory of Moral Sentiments* to *The
Wealth of Nations*, in that the dynamics of the market described in the *Wealth* are
ultimately responsible for eroding the social ethics with which the individual of
The Theory of Moral Sentiments is naturally endowed. An alternative interpretation of this relationship is that the individuals who populate both books are
one and the same. From this perspective, Smith's point is that the maturation of
the self-seeking individual of the *Wealth* must be accompanied by the growth of
the individual's ethical standards, as described in *The Theory of Moral Sentiments*.
From this perspective, what Smith is arguing is that only the simultaneous
development of society's ethical standards will prevent a market-dominated
society – driven as it is by self-interest and competition – from degenerating into
a Hobbesian war of all against all.[2]

Returning to *The Worldly Philosophers*, Heilbroner moves from the 'wonderful
world' of Smith to the 'gloomy presentiments' of Ricardo and Malthus. But Marx
is clearly the next great epoch-defining thinker in Heilbroner's narrative. He is
also the economist, along with Smith, who has most influenced Heilbroner's own
work, a relationship we explore in some detail below.

John Stuart Mill also receives a place of honor. Heilbroner portrays Mill as the
great champion of the utopian socialist tradition, 'with them in heart but whose
head [was] somewhat more firmly attached to his shoulders' (1986, p. 127). But
Mill was also a transitional figure, for after Mill, Heilbroner's narrative reaches
a fork. On the one hand, a distinct orthodox tradition of professors of 'Economics'
emerges (the term having replaced 'Political Economy' in the standard lexicon).
This tradition includes Marshall, but also Edgeworth, Jevons, Walras and others.
Heilbroner describes them as 'elucidators', those who would 'examine the
workings of the system in great detail, but not men who would express doubts as
to its basic merits or make troublesome prognostications as to its eventual fate'
(1986, p. 173).

---

2.   See Evensky (1992) for a further development of this view.

A major feature of their redefining the discipline was their systematic incorporation of mathematics into their work. Heilbroner is hostile to this endeavor from its beginnings, describing Edgeworth's model of 'mathematical psychics' as an abandonment of 'that tension-fraught world of the earlier economists' and an effort to 'dehumanize political economy'.

But Heilbroner's greatest objection to the new mainstream professorate was not the use of mathematics *per se*, but their abandonment of a historical perspective. With Marshall, for example, time was an abstraction, 'not the irreversible flow of historic time'. This enabled him and his colleagues to detach their investigations from the ongoing upheavals of their epoch, and neglect those authors who were still committed to examining economic questions within the optic of contemporary history. Heilbroner regards this development as 'an intellectual tragedy of the first order' (1986, p. 211).

But an underground of economics flourished alongside the professorate, and Heilbroner embraces them. Thus, Heilbroner describes the work of Henry George, whose amazingly popular 1889 book *Progress and Poverty* developed, on the basis of Ricardo's theory of rent, a broad social critique as well as the famous proposal for a single tax on land. Heilbroner also gives serious attention to John Hobson, author of *Imperialism*, which explored the relationship between the highly unequal income distribution characteristic of capitalist economies, the underconsumptionist tendencies of these economies, and the nineteenth-century impulse towards imperial conquests.

But the most important underground figure of this epoch was actually a professor, namely the American Thorstein Veblen. Veblen, however, was anything but an ordinary academic, and Heilbroner shifts into high comedic mode in describing the life of this wildly idiosyncratic figure. But Heilbroner shifts again before the reader is allowed to judge Veblen a mere fount of anecdotes, making clear by the end of his narrative that he places Veblen among the great figures of economic thought:

> After Veblen's savage description of the mores of daily life, the neoclassical picture of society as a well-mannered tea party became increasingly difficult to maintain. ... He highlighted the emptiness of trying to understand the actions of modern man in terms that derived from an incomplete and outmoded set of preconceptions. Man, said Veblen, is not to be comprehended in terms of sophisticated 'economic laws' in which both his innate ferocity and creativity are smothered under a cloak of rationalization. He is better dealt with in the less flattering but more fundamental vocabulary of the anthropologist or the psychologist. Leave aside the flattering fictions, he asked of the economists, and find out why man actually behaves the way he does. (1986, p. 247)

After Veblen, the last two figures presented in *The Worldly Philosophers* are John Maynard Keynes and Joseph Schumpeter. Both, of course, spent their careers at the very pinnacles of academic prestige. And yet, in Heilbroner's view, the wellsprings of their creative genius were not their academic milieus, but two shared features of their characters: passionate commitments to their political and social visions; and a willingness to ask overarching questions about the nature of capitalist economies, even though, by the time Keynes and Schumpeter had reached academic ascendancy, such modes of thinking had long been relegated to the underworld.

In the *General Theory*, Keynes acknowledged his debt to the underworld tradition: the term economic 'underworld' was itself coined in those pages. But Keynes pushed forward from that dissident foundation, and in the process broke from the tradition in which he was molded by Marshall, his own teacher. The result was an economic theory capable of grappling with the overwhelming problems of his time. Heilbroner tells the story with verve:

> Marshall lacked the necessary iconoclasm to give his economics deep social penetration. Keynes came closer: the Bloomsbury attitude of 'nothing sacred' spilled over into the sacred precincts of economic orthodoxy; once again the world was put into focus by a man not so blind as to fail to see its sickness, and not so emotionally and intellectually dispossessed as to wish not to cure it. If he was an economic sophisticate, he was politically devout, and it is in this curious combination of an engineering mind and a hopeful heart that his greatness lies. (1986, p. 287)

Schumpeter was a highly complex figure, and Heilbroner's chapter on him is appropriately titled 'The Contradictions of Joseph Schumpeter'. An ardent defender of capitalism, Schumpeter still drew his greatest intellectual inspiration from Marx. Indeed, Schumpeter's driving ambition was to follow Marx's model and construct a full analytic edifice of capitalism that would stand as the conservative answer to Marx. As Heilbroner points out, this vast project yielded an array of insights – for example, on the source of profits in capitalist economies, the nature of the bourgeois family, imperialism, and the prospects for socialism (which Schumpeter assessed – to the surprise and consternation of his conservative colleagues – as favorable).

The area of Schumpeter's work that has most influenced Heilbroner, however, is his discussion of the underlying roots of economic analysis. In his monumental *History of Economic Analysis*, which Schumpeter was completing at the time of his death in 1950, he argued that 'preanalytic vision' precedes any analytic enterprise. For Heilbroner, indeed, Schumpeter's notion of 'vision' lies at the center of Schumpeter's *History*:

Analysis may be the great glory of economics, but analysis does not spring full-blown from the mind of an economist, any more than Minerva from the brow of Jupiter. There is a 'preanalytic' process that precedes our logical scenarios, a process from which we cannot escape, and which is inescapably colored with our innermost values and preferences. (1986, p. 309)

But what is the relationship between analysis and vision? Schumpeter never attempted a careful answer, and thus Heilbroner's discussion of the question in *The Worldly Philosophers* ends with a question about Schumpeter himself: was Schumpeter, with his vast domain of interests, as well as his concern with economic 'visions', really practising economics as that term has come to be understood? Heilbroner's answer is agnostic. He regards Schumpeter as part theorist, part visionary, and it was precisely through that combination that Schumpeter not only contributed to economics but also demonstrated the limitations of the field.

With Schumpeter, Heilbroner ends his exploration through the pantheon of worldly philosophers. However, in the last chapter of the most recent edition (1986) of the book, Heilbroner is clearly still gnawing at the question of analysis and vision. It is not surprising, therefore, that a good share of Heilbroner's scholarly writing since then has taken up this Schumpeterian question.

Thus, in 'Vision and Ideology', the concluding chapter of the 1988 book *Behind the Veil of Economics*, Heilbroner presents his fellow economists with the following question and challenge:

What lies behind the veil of economics? Vision and ideology. ... If, as I deeply believe, there is no escape from the influence of visions and ideologies, we then must learn to live with them – not by abandoning all hope of examining society in a dispassionate and penetrative manner, or by resigning ourselves to becoming mere lackeys of interest and slaves of unexamined promptings, but by taking the measure of these hidden forces as best we can. (1988, p. 185)

But how does one 'take the measure of these hidden forces' in as scientific a manner as possible? Heilbroner considers two solutions. The first is a set of what he calls 'defensive measures'. One possible defensive measure is to formulate techniques that can separate truth from wishful thinking. However, he rejects this approach because he considers it unlikely to succeed. A second is to simply recognize that ideological influences will color one's analysis, and move forward from there. But he considers this solution to be irresponsible.

Heilbroner's alternative to such 'defensive measures' is to first of all abandon the notion that vision and ideology are infections against which the serious economist must be inoculated. They are rather 'psychologically indispensable' elements of any analytic enterprise. Given that, one must be willing both to acknowledge one's vision and to submit the research questions that emerge out of it to the standards of rigorous analysis. But how then does one establish such standards of rigorous analysis? There is no obvious answer to this question, as Heilbroner makes clear in, among other places, his discussions of dialectical and positivistic reasoning. Economic reasoning, in other words, is left with an inescapable residue of ambiguity. For Heilbroner, however, this is the price to be paid for acknowledging the truth that vision and ideology are ubiquitous features of the economics enterprise.[3]

THE HEILBRONERIAN VISION

What is the vision of capitalism that Heilbroner has himself projected? Characteristically, in the book *The Nature and Logic of Capitalism* (1985), he first poses an overarching question: What is capitalism? The question hits the reader with a jolt. It is, on the one hand, a perfectly logical place to begin such an investigation. Yet it is unlikely that more than a handful of contemporary economists have ever pondered the issue at all.

To pursue the matter, Heilbroner proposes to examine capitalism not as a mere 'economic system' but as a 'regime', since he is 'seeking to conjure up political and psychological implications' that are not conveyed by the notion of an economic system. What are these political and psychological dimensions?

First, following Marx, Heilbroner is clear that 'capital' itself is not a mere assemblage of factories, machines, financial securities or any other set of physical entities. Capital, rather, is a social relation. There are two defining characteristics of this social relation: the forms under which wealth is held and the ways that wealth is deployed.

Heilbroner argues that a substantial surplus of production existed in feudal and other traditional or command social systems, and this surplus is what constituted these systems' wealth. In these pre-capitalist systems, the social surplus took the form of prestige or luxury goods, and social status was conferred on people according to how opulent a level of consumption they could maintain. The ruling classes of such societies were therefore easily identifiable as those who had amassed the overwhelming share of prestige goods through their control of society's surplus. Heilbroner then shifts his focus to capitalism. At one level, he argues that wealth serves a similar function in capitalist societies. As Veblen had made clear, there is no shortage of prestige goods that may be conspicuously

---

3.   Heilbroner's position on vision and analysis in economics is developed in depth in (1990) and (1993b), as well as the 1988 volume.

consumed by those receiving a capitalist society's surplus. At the same time, what is distinctive about capitalism is that ownership and display of prestige goods is not the primary way that wealth is either held or deployed.

Under capitalism, wealth is primarily held in the form of means of production. That is, the capitalist ruling classes acquire their status through their ownership of the instruments necessary to generate society's material provisions. Heilbroner argues that a unique source of power flows from such ownership: 'the right accorded [the owners of the means of production] to *withhold* their property from the use of society if they wish' (1988, p. 38; emphasis in original).

It is through this power, in turn, that the capitalist class as a whole receives profits. This is because the capacity to withhold means of production confers a decisive bargaining advantage to capitalists over workers in the labor market, enabling capitalists to extract for themselves the preponderance of society's surplus. In the absence of this unequal bargaining power for capitalists, Heilbroner argues that, in the aggregate, competition among capitalists would drive profits to zero: no profits could exist for the system as a whole if capitalists did not exercise unequal bargaining power over workers.

This argument, of course, constitutes the core of Marx's theory of surplus value, and Heilbroner regards this formulation as one of Marx's greatest achievements. Correspondingly, Heilbroner argues that one of the great failures of orthodox economics is that, for all its technical virtuosity and attention to detail, it has no explanation for the existence of profits in capitalism.

> The theory of surplus value provides an explanation for a problem that has always been the Achilles' heel of economics, namely, the source of profits. Unwilling to attribute profits to the transfer of wealth from one class to another, bourgeois economists have struggled in vain to explain profits, not as a transient monopoly return or an evanescent technological advantage, but as a persistent, central feature of the system of capitalism. (1980, p. 114)

Heilbroner argues that two further fundamental insights flow from Marx's theory of surplus value; and with these as well, the illuminating force of the Marxian perspective appears intensified relative to the obtuseness of orthodoxy.

The first is that the 'factors of production' – land, labor and capital – cannot be regarded as comparable entities acting in concert to produce society's wealth. Capital (i.e., plants and equipment) and land can produce wealth only to the extent that workers act upon them. Moreover, as Heilbroner notes, the returns to land and capital are actually expressions of social relationships, 'namely the right accorded to the owners of land and capital to exert a claim on production on behalf of the contribution to output made by "their" resources or capital goods' (1980, p. 103). Because orthodox economists fail to recognize these underlying social relationships, Heilbroner, following Marx, says that 'land, labor and capital then appear only as things that "cooperate" to create social wealth, each contributing its measurable share, for which each is properly rewarded. The antagonisms and conflicts apparent in the view of these same things as social relationships ... is effectively screened from view' (1980, p. 105).

Marx's second basic insight here is his understanding of the nature of commodities, and his famous formulation of 'commodity fetishism'. This follows from his analysis of the sources of capitalists' power and profits. As Heilbroner puts it, Marx sees the commodity 'as the carrier and encapsulation of the social history of capitalism', because it 'contains within itself the disguised elements of the class struggle' (1980, p. 103). Heilbroner regards this as a transcendent achievement: 'one of the most remarkable and illuminating acts of intellectual penetration of which we have record, truly meriting the comparison ... with Plato and Freud' (1980, p. 137). By contrast, orthodox economists overwhelmingly concern themselves only with the question of how commodities exchange, in particular the process through which their relative prices are established via market activity. For Marx, this approach 'fethishizes' commodities because it perceives a relationship among people – the class struggle underlying the production of commodities – as a relationship between things.

Marx clearly exerts a formidable influence on Heilbroner. This influence has also increased over the course of Heilbroner's career, in part, as he generously acknowledges, through the influence of his New School colleagues and students.[4] At the same time, Heilbroner's understanding of the nature and logic of capitalism departs from Marxism in significant ways.

The first is over the treatment of the state. One of Marx's most famous pronouncements is that in capitalist societies, 'the state is the executive committee of the bourgeoisie'. Heilbroner's deviation from this view is subtle but fundamental. According to Heilbroner, one of the most distinctive features of the rise of capitalism was the emergence of capitalists as holders of social power which was independent of the state's control over the means of violence. Under feudalism, as well as all other regimes which operated according to tradition or command, the state essentially monopolized both political and economic power. But with the development of a merchant capitalist class in the interstices of the feudal order – primarily in the independent towns – property rights were slowly established, initially to protect the assets of merchants from being seized by kings. This created a formal bifurcation of power as capitalism developed, with the state still controlling the means of violence but the capitalists now controlling the means of production.

---

4.   Heilbroner dedicated *Marxism For and Against* to his 'colleagues and students' because the book 'evolved from a long dialogue with them' (1980, p. 11).

But Marx argued that this bifurcation is a matter of appearances only: the bourgeoisie is actually able to control the state apparatus via the economic power it exercises through owning the means of production. This is the sense in which the state is merely the capitalists' executive committee, pursuing capital's agenda at one step's remove.

Heilbroner acknowledges the strong convergence of interests between these two nodes of power in capitalism; that, for example, the state's means of violence are almost always employed to protect the rights of capital over those of workers. At the same time – and this is the crucial point – Heilbroner argues against Marx that the formal bifurcation between governmental and economic power in capitalism is not merely, or even largely, an illusion. Rather, it has been decisive in allowing political and economic freedom to emerge and be sustained in some capitalist societies.

'Unquestionably', Heilbroner writes, 'the greatest attainments of human liberty thus far attained in organized society have been achieved in certain advanced capitalist societies'. The only plausible explanation for this historically unique outcome is that 'the two realms of capitalism are conducive to certain important kinds of freedom, and that a sphere of market (or other non-state) ties may be necessary for the prevention of excessive state power'. Among other things, such limits on state power create space for political dissidents to speak critically of the government while still being capable of earning a living outside the reaches of the state. At the same time, Heilbroner is fully aware that the mere presence of capitalist economic relations is not a sufficient condition for political freedom, 'as the most cursory survey of modern history will confirm'.[5]

The second major way that Heilbroner's vision departs substantially from that of Marx concerns the role of psychological factors in determining the possibilities for progressive political change. As we have seen, Heilbroner agrees with Marx that one crucial distinction between capitalism and previous modes of production is that under capitalism, the drive for wealth takes the peculiar form of the accumulation of capital.

But then Heilbroner wants to push the analysis deeper and pose the question: what drives capitalists to accumulate? At one level, Marx's answer is sufficient for Heilbroner: capitalists must accumulate or lose their market position to competitors. But this answer does not explain a further question: why, to begin with, do capitalists care obsessively about winning the competitive battle?

Heilbroner argues that the drive to accumulate means of production in capitalism is ultimately a manifestation of the same underlying craving for power and prestige that occurs in other social formations; such desires, indeed, are a

---

5. Quotations in this paragraph are from (1988), pp. 45-6.

transcendent feature of all social formations. This is true, in Heilbroner's view, despite the important differences that he himself underscores between capitalist accumulation and the desire for prestige goods in non-capitalist societies.

Heilbroner, in other words, follows Freud in arguing that a universal drive for power and domination exists in human nature, and therefore will be present in all social settings, regardless of the institutional particulars through which such drives are manifested. This is because the drive for power and domination – and its concomitant, the need for acquiescence and subordination – derive from the universal experience of prolonged infantile dependency:

> Infancy is thus the great readying experience that prepares us for the adult condition of sub- and superordination – an experience that appears so 'natural' that few inquire as to the origin or nature of the desire to impose one's will, or the pleasure that is derived from its imposition, or the obverse, the impulse to acquiesce in, or even to identify sympathetically with, the imposition of another's will over oneself. Infancy is the condition from which we must all escape, and as such, the source of the emancipatory thrust that is also part of the human drama; but it is as well a condition to which we all to some degree wish to return, the prototype of the existential security that we also seek. (1985, p. 49)

In other words, the universal experience of infancy encodes all people with a natural predisposition towards hierarchy – some seeking a dominant, and others a submissive role within that hierarchy. And because Heilbroner sees these drives as fundamental to human nature, their social and political implications are dramatic – namely that the universal drive for hierarchy establishes enormous obstacles to the kind of egalitarian transformation of society sought by socialists. As Heilbroner writes:

> The personality, as the partial product of these givens, cannot be altered as rapidly or thoroughly as would be the case were it solely the product of social conditioning. In turn, this admission drastically limits the Marxist expectations for social change, because it must recognize the persistence of latent human traits, however dramatic may be the alteration in manifest activity. (1980, p. 165)

For Heilbroner then, the most daunting problem for a socialist movement is not whether it can develop economic policies that effectively support both the priority of equality and the need for efficiency. Rather, the greatest difficulty – indeed as he puts it, the 'Achilles' heel of socialism' – is that a socialist society will reproduce the same psychological drives for dominance and submission that are found in capitalism and all other social formations. These drives, moreover, are likely to take especially pathological forms in a socialist society – for example, dictatorial politicians standing as spokespersons for egalitarianism – precisely because they will take root in an inhospitable social and ideological terrain.

Heilbroner clearly attaches fundamental importance to his psychoanalytic critique of Marxism and socialist politics more generally, even while retaining sympathy with both Marxism and socialism. Is his critique sustainable?

It is broadly true that the Marxist tradition does not accept the notion of human nature. Even such an open-minded Marxian thinker as Antonio Gramsci held that, 'The fundamental innovation introduced by Marxism into the science of politics and history is the proof that there does not exist an abstract, fixed, and immutable "human nature" ... but that human nature is the totality of historically determined social relations' (cited in Chomsky 1975, p. 128).

However, this interpretation of the relationship between Marxism and the notion of human nature is not universally accepted. Freud, for one, wrote late in his life that he needed to reverse his earlier judgement of Marxism since neither Marx nor Engels 'had denied the influence of ideas and super-ego factors' (cited in Jacoby 1975, p. 84). This position of Freud is consistent with most of the Western Marxist tradition, especially authors associated with the Frankfurt School, including Eric Fromm, Herbert Marcuse and Theodor Adorno, and those building from that literature.

Moreover, authors within this perspective recognize that to accept a notion of human nature means acknowledging the existence of ineradicable drives towards domination, submission, violence and the death instinct. Nevertheless, this tradition is more optimistic than Heilbroner as to the ability of a more egalitarian social order to mitigate such tendencies. Thus, for example, Martin Jay, in *The Dialectical Imagination*, his history of the Frankfurt School, summarizes Marcuse's understanding of the death instinct as follows:

> The real aim of the death instinct was not aggression but the end of the tension that was life. It was grounded in the so-called Nirvana principle, which expressed a yearning for the tranquility of inorganic nature. In this desire, it was surprisingly similar to the life instinct: both sought gratification and the end of desire itself. If the goal of the death instinct was the reduction of tension, then it would cease to be very powerful once the tension of life was reduced. (1973, p. 110)

While the writings of Freud himself are ambiguous on this question, there is certainly a large body of his thought which supports the view that psychological drives are substantially shaped by social environments. A telling passage from *The Future of an Illusion* is representative of much of his writing on this question:

> If a culture has not got beyond a point at which the satisfaction of one portion of its participants depends upon the suppression of another, and perhaps larger, portion – and this

is the case in all present-day cultures – it is understandable that the suppressed people should develop an intense hostility towards a culture whose existence they make possible by their work, but in whose wealth they have too small a share. (1971, p. 12)

The work of Noam Chomsky represents another, non-psychoanalytic, strand of radical thought that both embraces the concept of human nature and contends that such an idea is present in Marx, most explicitly in his *Economic and Philosophical Manuscripts of 1844*. Chomksy's own view of human nature comes out of the rationalist tradition of Rousseau, Descartes and von Humboldt, as well as his studies of linguistics. Chomsky's position is that human nature is essentially a biological phenomenon, deriving from the enormous potential for complex creative thought and action that is embedded in the human brain. He argues that the evidence for this capacity for creative activity is the ability of virtually all humans to succeed in the enormously complex task of acquiring language. For almost all people, Chomsky holds, this creative potential is never given adequate opportunities to flourish; it lies dormant or is repressed as a result of poverty and extreme social inequality. Dramatic changes in social institutions could therefore create the space for a flowering of human potential.[6]

For at least the foreseeable future, it is unimaginable that a scientific consensus will form around any single conception of human nature. Given this uncertainty, we can at least suggest that Heilbroner's view that human nature 'drastically limits' the Marxist expectations for egalitarian social change represents a decidedly pessimistic perspective on what remains an open question. A more balanced view may be similar to that which the late Communist Chinese leader Zhou Enlai expressed in assessing the consequences for the modern world of the French Revolution: 'It's too soon to tell'.

CRITIQUE OF NEOCLASSICAL ECONOMICS

Whatever Heilbroner's differences with Marx, these pale by comparison with the attack on mainstream economics that emerges from his work. It will be useful here to pull together the main strands of his critique, asking again why he contends that the mainstream's rigor has also yielded mortis.

For Heilbroner, the most basic weakness of modern orthodoxy is its failure to consider what he regards as the central objective of economics, namely, 'the identification and explication of hidden problems in society's process of material self-reproduction' (1979, p. 194). The key phrase here is 'hidden problems'. By

6.   Chomsky's position is developed in (1975), ch. 3 and (1987) Part 3, among other places.

this Heilbroner means that 'economics studies the reproduction process only insofar as it gives rise to outcomes that are not immediately apparent or inherent in the physical or social processes of production' (1979, p. 194).

Why has orthodoxy failed to address, or even, for the most part, apprehend these subterranean questions? This is due to its underlying vision, of an economic system composed of an agglomeration of discrete individuals engaged in maximizing activities. Heilbroner, by contrast, sees economic activity as unavoidably a social and relational process. Individual motivations are therefore comprehensible in the orthodox framework, but the social processes that shape these motivations are obscure. Heilbroner sees these deficiencies emerging even within the simplest concepts of mainstream thinking:

> Virtually the first act the individual is called on to perform – in a hundred textbooks, not in life – is the rational, maximizing allocation of his or her income. What is the problem here? It is that *income* is intrinsically a social concept, whereas 'individual' is intrinsically a nonsocial one. There can be no 'income' in a Robinson Crusoe economy of a single individual. No doubt a solitary person can apportion his energies as he wishes, including in a rational and maximizing fashion, but energies are not 'income' – if they were, all energetic individuals would be rich without further ado. (1988, p. 190)

Heilbroner accepts that orthodox economics has been quite ambitious and, in many instances, successful, in seeking to explain what he considers 'social movements in the small, such as the dynamics of market prices, the response of production to these prices, the multiplicative possibilities of bank credit, the dependency of consumers' expenditures on the level of national income, the etiology and course of various kinds of crises; and a great deal more' (1985, p. 192). One may argue with Heilbroner as to the degree of success actually attained by orthodoxy in grappling with what is really a quite extensive list of 'social movements in the small'. For example, mainstream perspectives on 'the multiplicative possibilities of bank credit' have almost completely overlooked the capacity of financial market participants to generate credit independently of the one-way link flowing from central banks to private banks. As a result, orthodox monetary theory has become almost completely useless as a guide to policy.[7]

Still, Heilbroner's broader point is that, despite the undeniable prodigies of technique which mainstream economists have developed during his career, they have nevertheless failed at explaining 'social relations in the large'. Heilbroner argues that the profession has been unable to anticipate *any* of the large-scale economic events over the past 40 years, including the advent of the multinational

---

7.   Benjamin Friedman is among the most forthright mainstream economists in recognizing this. See for example (1988).

corporation, the rise of Japan as a major economic power, the emergence of inflation as a chronic problem associated with mixed capitalist economies, the decline of productivity growth among the advanced economies since the early 1970s, and most egregiously, the collapse of the Soviet Union (see Heilbroner 1993a, p. 19). For Heilbroner, the basic failure of mainstream economics does not derive from the techniques it has devoted so much effort at developing. The problem is rather its constricted vision, which ultimately has prevented the mainstream from deploying their techniques to illuminate the most basic questions of social existence.

THE NATURE AND LOGIC OF PUBLIC POLICY ANALYSIS

Professor Heilbroner clearly does not fit the standard profile of a policy economist. He is no policy maven, does not crunch numbers, and his political views are substantially to the left of mainstream policy circles. Nevertheless, he is among the most widely read writers on economic policy of his generation. What makes his policy writing distinctive and compelling is his insistence on locating any given policy issue within its broader historical and political framework. Heilbroner himself explained his approach to policy analysis as follows:

> I find a central thread missing from the endless discussions about what we should be doing – namely an absence of any historical appreciation of the nature of the system. ... One of the reasons I shy away from too exclusive an emphasis on policy is that it assumes that the underlying process is basically all right – it has just been turned aside or thwarted because of some poorly conceived operation on the part of government. (1988, pp. 66-7)

Probably his best-known policy-oriented work is the 1974 book *An Inquiry Into the Human Prospect*, which, as its title makes clear, eschews the pinpoint beams of standard policy literature to send out a characteristically wide-searching beacon. And yet, despite its breadth, *An Inquiry* is no mere compendium of armchair reflections. It is a careful consideration of a set of concrete issues – population growth, nationalism and nuclear proliferation among third world countries, and environmental degradation – that had not been previously conceptualized within a unified framework. Heilbroner understood these developments as genuine threats to the continuation of the human species. Heilbroner almost invites the mockery of sophisticates with the book's opening question, 'Is there hope for man?'. But as his argument gathers force, it is clear that the question deserved to be asked, and that Heilbroner forces his readers to consider that the answer is not necessarily in the affirmative.

As Heilbroner has recognized in more recent editions of the book, the urgency associated with some of his initial concerns, like population growth, has receded. Other problems, the environmental crisis in particular, have worsened, but at least the alarm Heilbroner and others sounded twenty years ago has been heard. By 1994, environmental degradation is almost universally recognized as a severe problem resulting from the very process of economic growth. Thus the dilemma that Heilbroner posed so starkly in *An Inquiry*: 'Even more disturbing than the possibility of a serious deterioration in the quality of life if growth comes to an end is the awareness of a possibly disastrous decline in the material conditions of existence if growth does not come to an end' (1991, p. 17).

What is the solution Heilbroner offers to the environmental crisis? Typically, he provides no agenda for political action. However, also typically, he pursues the problem to its root, and concludes that addressing the environmental crisis means controlling the very accumulation process that is the heart and soul of capitalism. He thereby links environmental policies with broader concerns about the nature of capital accumulation, and the role of the public sector in defining the contours of the growth process.

This then leads us to the overarching theme of Heilbroner's policy writings: the case for an extensive, and perhaps predominant, public sector presence within the US and other advanced capitalist economies. He has developed this perspective around a range of issues. For example, as noted earlier, he has long been a proponent of Keynesian macroeconomic management policies, and in that context has contributed extensively to the public debate around the federal debt and deficit.

His intervention on this issue began auspiciously in 1963, when he published *A Primer on Government Spending* along with Peter Bernstein. This book presented briefly and with exceptional clarity the Keynesian defense of deficit spending. Though the majority of the economics profession at that time supported the Keynesian arguments, mainstream public opinion – or more precisely the 'opinion leaders' at the *New York Times*, in Congress, and the like – did not. Despite this, *A Primer* sold well and was widely appreciated, even by President Kennedy, who read it in manuscript form shortly before his assassination. Heilbroner has frequently returned to the subject, including in a 1989 book, again with Bernstein, *The Debt and the Deficit*. This volume also embraces a Keynesian perspective on the deficit, though, by this time, Heilbroner and Bernstein faced a hostile professional as well as general audience.

One striking feature of both books was that, despite their accessible style, neither were simply popularizations of either Keynes's own thinking or a consensus Keynesian position. Consider, for example, Heilbroner and Bernstein's significant departure from Keynes around the issue of debt-financed public investment. Keynes, of course, went to great pains to emphasize the salutary effects of countercyclical deficit spending, *regardless of how the money was spent*: his proposal to raise employment and output via money-burying and retrieving projects was only partially tongue-in-cheek. But even in the 1963 book, Heilbroner and Bernstein stressed that it did indeed matter, even for employment policies, what the government purchased with its borrowed funds. In particular, they argued that borrowed funds used to enhance the economy's long-term productive capacity – through increased spending on infrastructure, research and development or education, for example – are ultimately self-financing, because they will generate increases in income over the long run to cover the debt. Correspondingly, deficit spending that finances mainly operating expenses or increases in consumption should be seen as burdensome.

Following this logic Heilbroner has argued in these books and several other forums that the federal government should establish a capital account, following the practice of business accounting, to clarify the extent to which deficit spending was creating self-financing assets. In Heilbroner's view, this portion of the government debt should not be considered as part of the operating deficit at all. The political implication of this argument is striking: it means that, absent a capital-accounting framework, the officially measured deficit figures, and the regular political outcries surrounding them, are without intellectual foundations.

Many questions can be raised about this argument. For one, the officially measured deficit should provide a reasonable measure of the short-term stimulus effect of deficits, if not its long-term consequences for productivity. Thus, focusing just on such short-term issues, it should be a genuine matter of concern that deficits in the 1990s do not generate a short-term boost to output equivalent to that of, say, the 1960s.[8]

But technical questions aside, the broader issue Heilbroner raises is, again, the very legitimacy of a large-scale public sector. The mainstream notion that the federal deficit 'crowds out' private spending presupposes that the government deserves a lower priority than business in allocating the economy's financial resources. But Heilbroner argues that much of government spending is crucial to economic well-being, while much of private spending is wasteful. Should government borrowing for education and infrastructure be 'crowded out' to make room for corporate takeovers and buyouts?

---

8.   See Pollin (1993) for further discussion on this question.

> The issue [write Heilbroner and Bernstein] turns out to have little to do with deficit spending but a great deal to do with how we feel about the role of government in a capitalist economy. For at its core, crowding out boils down to the relative size of private and public spending. It is as simple – and as complex – as that. (1989, pp. 110-11)

Given Heilbroner's commitment to a large public sector, it is not surprising that he has expressed increasing apprehension over the accelerated rate at which the world economy is becoming integrated, and in particular at the rate whereby large-scale corporations are spreading their production processes throughout the globe. For what globalization makes clear, as Heilbroner puts it, is that 'the economic reach of capital is immeasurably longer than the political reach of the national entities from which it emanates' (1993a, p. 80).

We need to recall here that Heilbroner believes the genuine bifurcation of power between the economy and the state has been indispensable to capitalism's successful functioning. But with transportation and communication technologies bringing dramatic increases in the ability of transnational firms to be mobile, the firms have been able to gain bargaining power relative to any given government entity. Thus, before choosing where to locate their production sites, the firms are increasingly able to extract concessions on wage rates, taxes, environmental standards and their own freedom of movement. Compliant politicians flourish in such an environment while defiant ones are forced on the defensive. As Heilbroner says,

> What emerges in this increasingly globalized pattern of production is a challenge to the traditional relationship between the economy and the state. The globalized market system stretches beyond the political authority of any single government. Faced with a network of connections that escape their powers of surveillance or regulation, national governments have become increasingly unequal to providing the legal, monetary or protective functions that are their contributions to a well-working economy. (1993a, p. 81)

Heilbroner considers possible denouements to this trend. The obvious one is the ever-greater domination of transnational capital over the political as well as economic destinies of most of the world's population. A second, equally unsettling scenario is the emergence of strong nationalist movements that seek to defy the logic of modern economics and reassert the independent authority of the state. Heilbroner implies that such nationalist movements could easily resemble the configurations that emerged on the ashes of the former Yugoslavia. But is that the only option?

Here we must finally return to the issue of democratic socialism, a theme which has been at the forefront of Heilbroner's thinking throughout his career. Reading Heilbroner, one can easily conclude that the prospects for democratic socialism are dim. There is, of course, the Soviet experience to explain. It is clear that Heilbroner does not regard the Soviet system as simply a betrayal of socialism's high ideals. Rather, its history is explicable once one takes full measure of the importance of separate political and economic domains under capitalism, and the fact that the Soviets collapsed these two domains into one. For Heilbroner then, the single, dictatorial political sphere in the Soviet system provided unrestrained opportunities for the psychological drama of domination and subordination to flourish in public life.

But while the collapse of this system was 'everywhere hailed as a victory for human freedom', Heilbroner still contends that it was also a 'defeat ... for human aspiration' (1993a, p. 150) Free market capitalism, in his view, 'is clearly inadequate to resolve the most pressing problems of our coming century – namely, the internationalization of production and the globalization of our ecological encounter. One cannot contemplate this catalogue of deficiencies and expect the order as a whole to make the passage through the 21st century unscathed' (1993a, p. 161).

For Heilbroner, therefore, human aspiration is still best expressed through democratic socialism, or what he frequently calls 'slightly imaginary Sweden'. This is a society that remains within 'the force field' of liberal democratic capitalism simply because humanity does not yet have the self-knowledge or wherewithal to organize itself otherwise. However, slightly imaginary Sweden would push the institutions of liberal capitalism to their limit in allowing democratic politics and egalitarian goals to gain ascendance over acquisitiveness. This is what Heilbroner prefers to call a movement forward, rather than a movement to either the right or left. Downward movements point towards Yugoslavia.

In view of globalization, the ecological crisis, the prospects for virulent nationalism and the millstone of human nature itself, Heilbroner obviously regards the challenge of constructing slightly imaginary Sweden as daunting. Yet it is just such a challenge that this consummate 'pessimist of the mind but optimist of the will' urges upon his fellow economists: 'Too often a vehicle for mystification, economics can best become an instrument for enlightenment if we see it as the means by which we strive to make a workable science out of morality' (1988, p. 199).

ACKNOWLEDGMENTS

Robert Pollin would like to thank Russell Jacoby for his guidance on the question of Marxism and psychology, and especially Robert Heilbroner for a long, illuminating conversation in January 1994 about his life and work.

HEILBRONER'S MAJOR WRITINGS

(1963) (with Peter L. Bernstein), *A Primer on Government Spending*, New York: Random House.

(1979), 'Modern Economics as a Chapter in the History of Economic Thought', *History of Political Economy*, **11** (2), 192-8.

(1980), *Marxism: For and Against*, New York: W.W. Norton & Co.

(1982), 'The Socialization of the Individual in Adam Smith', *History of Political Economy*, **14** (3), 427-39.

(1985), *The Nature and Logic of Capitalism*, New York: W.W. Norton & Co.

(1986), *The Worldly Philosophers*, New York: Simon & Schuster.

(1988), *Behind the Veil of Economics*, New York: W.W. Norton & Co.

(1989) (with Peter L. Bernstein), *The Debt and the Deficit: False Alarms, Real Possibilities*, New York: W.W. Norton & Co.

(1990), 'Analysis and Vision in the History of Modern Economic Thought', *Journal of Economic Literature*, September, 1097-114.

(1991), *An Inquiry into the Human Prospect: Looked At Again for the 1990s*, New York: W.W. Norton & Co.

(1992), Untitled autobiographical entry in Phillip Arestis and Malcolm Sawyer (eds), *A Biographical Dictionary of Dissenting Economists*, Brookfield, VT: Edward Elgar, 241-8.

(1993a), *21st Century Capitalism*, New York: W.W. Norton & Co.

(1993b), 'Was Schumpeter Right After All', *Journal of Economic Perspectives*, **3**, Summer, 87-96.

OTHER REFERENCES

Chomsky, Noam (1975), *Reflections on Language*, New York: Random House.

Chomsky, Noam (1987), *The Chomsky Reader*, New York: Pantheon.

Evensky, Jerry (1992), 'Ethics and the Invisible Hand', *Journal of Economic Perspectives*, **1**, Spring, 197-205.

Freud, Sigmund (1971), *The Complete Psychological Works of Sigmund Freud, Volume XXI: The Future of an Illusion, Civilization and its Discontents and Other Works*, London: The Hogarth Press.

Friedman, Benjamin (1988), 'Lessons of Monetary Policy from the 1980s', *Journal of Economic Perspectives*, **2**, Summer, 51-72.

Jacoby, Russell (1975), *Social Amnesia: A Critique of Conformist Psychology from Adler to Laing*, Boston: Beacon Press.

Jay, Martin (1973), *The Dialectical Imagination: A History of the Frankfurt School and the Institute of Social Research 1923-1950*, Boston: Little Brown & Company.

Pollin, Robert (1993), 'Budget Deficits and the U.S. Economy: Considerations in a Heilbronerian Mode', in Ronald Blackwell, Jaspal Chatha and Edward J. Nell (eds), *Economics as Worldly Philosophy: Essays in Political and Historical Economics in Honour of Robert L. Heilbroner*, New York: St. Martin's Press, 107-45.

6. Daniel Kahneman and Amos Tversky

Matthew Rabin

INTRODUCTION

More than any other social science, economics systematically explores the social implications of precise assumptions about individual beliefs and behavior. More than any other social science, psychology systematically explores the nature of individual beliefs and behavior. Presumably, therefore, a greater awareness of psychological research by economists might enhance the descriptive realism of economics. The research by psychologists Daniel Kahneman and Amos Tversky is especially relevant for economics because of its subject matter and its high quality. Furthermore, because they are able and willing to address economists in standard economic language and venues, their research has over the last couple of decades become more influential in economics than that of any other psychologists.

In the next three sections, I outline some of Kahneman and Tversky's main findings that seem most relevant for economics.[1] In the next section, I discuss their research on heuristics and biases in judgement under uncertainty. This research identifies the shortcuts in reasoning (heuristics) people use in decision-making, and identifies broad classes of situations where such shortcuts lead to systematically erroneous judgements (biases). The third section presents research on framing effects, preference reversals and related phenomena that illustrate the surprisingly strong ways in which the details of the phrasing or structure of a decision problem can affect choices made. Even more than the research on heuristics and biases, this research raises fundamental questions about whether

---

1. Much of the specific research and broader issues I discuss below reflect the contributions of other researchers in addition to Kahneman and Tversky, and I shall not in this essay worry excessively about precise attributions of credit. I shall, for instance, discuss much research that has grown out of themes hit upon in Kahneman and Tversky's collaborative efforts, but has been conducted either by them separately or by others. Also, some of Kahneman and Tversky's research I discuss builds from research conducted by others or is related to research conducted in parallel by others.

people's choices reflect their underlying preferences, and about the very existence of stable, context-free preferences. The fourth section presents research by Kahneman and Tversky and others on how a person's status quo and other reference points strongly influences his/her tastes and choices, with an emphasis on research demonstrating that people seem very averse to even small losses relative to their reference points.

Economists have in recent years begun to pay more heed to Kahneman and Tversky's and related research. Their papers have been published in prominent economics journals such as *Econometrica, American Economic Review*, and *Journal of Political Economy*, and many of their insights have been related to economists through Richard Thaler's 'Anomalies' column in the *Journal of Economic Perspectives*. Kahneman and Tversky have been active participants in the increasingly influential movements such as behavioral economics and experimental economics. Cursory familiarity with, and vague tolerance of, their research is now fairly common among mainstream economists.

As it stands in 1994, however, the direct influence on economics of research conducted by Kahneman and Tversky and other psychologists remains limited. This neglect is in large part because most of Kahneman and Tversky's research centers on the existence and nature of departures from rationality as traditionally conceived by economists, and thus it raises some broad challenges to the content and methodology of mainstream economics, and these challenges have induced an array of arguments by economists for neglecting their research. In the final section, I consider some of these standard arguments for dismissing Kahneman and Tversky's research, as well as some of Kahneman and Tversky's rebuttals. I also discuss some of the ways that Kahneman and Tversky's research is currently being incorporated into economics, and the potential for its increased use in the future.

HEURISTICS AND BIASES

How do people make decisions in situations of uncertainty? Economists have traditionally assumed that decision makers are approximately rational – economic actors are assumed to maximize their expected utility given their subjective probabilistic assessments of the consequences of their choices, where these assessments are derived correctly according to the laws of probability. The most influential part of Kahneman and Tversky's research to date has been their documentation of departures from rationality in judgement and decision making under uncertainty.

This research is reflected in a volume of research (co-edited with Paul Slovic) published in 1982 called *Judgment under Uncertainty: Heuristics and Biases*. This volume contains many of the main contributions by Kahneman and Tversky and other researchers on heuristics and biases, and it serves as a bible of sorts for research in the descriptive theory of judgement under uncertainty. A feel for what this research is about is well expressed in Kahneman and Tversky's introduction to one of their articles, which Kahneman, Slovic and Tversky also use as a de facto introduction to their volume:

> How do people assess the probability of an uncertain event or the value of an uncertain quantity? This article shows that people rely on a limited number of heuristic principles which reduce the complex tasks of assessing probabilities and predicting values to simpler judgmental operations. In general, these heuristics are quite useful, but sometimes they lead to severe and systematic errors.
>
> The subjective assessment of probability resembles the subjective assessment of physical quantities such as distance or size. These judgments are all based on data of limited validity, which are processed according to heuristic rules. For example, the apparent distance of an object is determined in part by its clarity. The more sharply the object is seen, the closer it appears to be. This rule has some validity, because in any given scene the more distant objects are seen less sharply than nearer objects. However, the reliance on this rule leads to systematic errors in the estimation of distance. Specifically, distances are often overestimated when visibility is poor because the contours of objects are blurred. On the other hand, distances are often underestimated when visibility is good because the objects are seen sharply. Thus, the reliance on clarity as an indication of distance leads to common biases. Such biases are also found in the intuitive judgment of probability. This article describes three heuristics that are employed to assess probabilities and to predict values. Biases to which these heuristics lead are enumerated, and the applied and theoretical implications of these observations are discussed. (Tversky and Kahneman 1974)

In this passage, the word 'error' does not appear without the word 'systematic'. By systematic, Kahneman and Tversky mean not so much the frequency of errors as their predictable nature. We learn from Kahneman and Tversky's research not merely that people are not perfectly rational, but rather we learn some of the patterns of *how* judgement under uncertainty departs from our standard model. I now describe some of the heuristics and biases that Kahneman and Tversky have identified in their research.

One of the most widely studied patterns of judgement under uncertainty identified by Kahneman and Tversky is what they call the *representativeness heuristic*. Both probability theory and intuition tell us that a person is more likely to be a member of some group if that person is similar to the typical member of that group. If one person looks or behaves more like a criminal than a second person, then we naturally predict that the first is more likely to be a criminal than the second.

However, research by Kahneman and Tversky demonstrates that the degree to which people use representativeness as a determinant in assessing probabilities is far too great. Whereas Bayes' Law tells us that our assessment of likelihoods should be heavily influenced by base rates, Kahneman and Tversky demonstrate that people tend to underweight base-rate information in forming their judgements. If we see somebody who looks like a criminal, our assessment of the probability that he/she is a criminal tends to under-use his/her knowledge of what percentage of people are criminals. To illustrate the representativeness heuristic, consider the following example, originally explored in Kahneman and Tversky (1973):

> Subjects were shown brief personality descriptions of several individuals, allegedly sampled at random from a group of 100 professionals – engineers and lawyers. The subjects were asked to assess, for each description, the probability that it belonged to an engineer rather than to a lawyer. In one experimental condition, subjects were told that the group from which the descriptions had been drawn consisted of 70 engineers and 30 lawyers. In another condition, subjects were told that the group consisted of 30 engineers and 70 lawyers. The odds that any particular description belongs to an engineer rather than to a lawyer should be higher in the first condition, where there is a majority of engineers, than in the second condition, where there is a majority of lawyers. Specifically, it can be shown by applying Bayes' rule that the ratio of these odds should be $(.7/.3)^2$, or 5.44, for each description. In a sharp violation of Bayes' rule, the subjects in the two conditions produced essentially the same probability judgments. Apparently, subjects evaluated the likelihood that a particular description belonged to an engineer rather than to a lawyer by the degree to which this description was representative of the two stereotypes, with little or no regard for the prior probabilities of the categories. (Tversky and Kahneman 1974)

In the situation considered in the above passage, the perceived probability that a person matching various descriptions was an engineer reflected overwhelmingly their subjective probability that a given description was typical of an engineer rather than a lawyer. There was a statistically significant effect of the population proportions, but this effect was minuscule in comparison to the magnitude demanded by Bayes' Law.

The problem does not appear to be that subjects somehow do not register the population proportions. Kahneman and Tversky (1973) show, for instance, that when given no description at all of an individual chosen randomly from the population, subjects chose the obvious probabilities corresponding to the base population. Rather than any inability *per se* to process information contained in the base rates, subjects apparently did not feel these base rates were of fundamental importance in assessing probabilistic beliefs when they had alternative evidence. Kahneman and Tversky (1973) provide a more striking example of the under-use of base-rate probabilities: when provided with a description of a man that is totally uninformative about whether he is an engineer or a lawyer, people guessed that the probability that the man was an engineer was approximately 50 percent, *irrespective* of whether the population was comprised of 70 percent or 30 percent engineers. By assessing the odds at 50 percent, subjects clearly found the description uninformative about whether the person was a lawyer or an engineer; but once they got the information, they ignored the information contained in the population base rates. Tversky and Kahneman (1982b, p. 159) report that subsequent experiments did not support this extreme conclusion, but summarized the literature as indicating that 'the base rate was not discarded but rather diluted by nondiagnostic evidence about the case at hand'.

Perhaps the most striking illustration of the representativeness heuristic is the observed violation of the conjunction rule, a fundamental axiom of probability theory: The probability that somebody belongs to *both* categories A and B is no greater than, and almost always less than, the probability that he/she belongs to category B alone. Tversky and Kahneman (1982a) demonstrate what they call the *conjunction effect*: when a description is representative of a person in category A but not of a person in category B, people often judge it more likely that the description matches somebody who falls into *both* categories A and B than in category B alone. As one illustration of this effect, they provided subjects with the following description of a person:

> Linda is 31 years old, single, outspoken, and very bright. She majored in philosophy. As a student, she was deeply concerned with issues of discrimination and social justice, and also participated in anti-nuclear demonstrations. (Tversky and Kahneman 1982a)

Subjects were then asked to rate the relative likelihood that eight different statements about Linda were true. Two statements on the list were 'Linda is a bank teller' and 'Linda is a bank teller and is active in the feminist movement'. Clearly it is more likely that Linda is a bank teller than that she is both a bank teller *and* a feminist. Yet over 85 percent of subjects judged it more likely that Linda was both a bank teller and a feminist. This ranking reflected the fact that the description of Linda made her seem like a feminist, so that being a bank teller and a feminist seems a more natural description, and more 'representative', of Linda than simply being a bank teller.

Connected with their research on the representativeness heuristic, Kahneman and Tversky have provided many examples of what they call 'the law of small numbers'. Briefly stated, people think that the makeup of even a small group will closely resemble that of the parent population or underlying probability distribution that generates the group.[2] This is an example of the representativeness heuristic because people assume that even small groups will be representative of the parent population from which they are drawn. If we believe that a financial analyst is insightful, for instance, we are overconfident that his/her next few predictions will turn out correct, and if they are incorrect we are too suspicious that he/she is no longer insightful.

The most basic example of the law of small numbers is that people seem to expect the same probabilistic distribution of average values in small groups as they do in large groups. Thus, while the laws of probability tell us that the probability that at least 80 percent of 20 coin flips will come up heads is much lower than for at least 80 percent of 5 coin flips to come up heads, people tend to view these as comparably likely. As an illustration of this error, Kahneman and Tversky (1972) asked undergraduates the following question:

> A certain town is served by two hospitals. In the larger hospital about 45 babies are born each day, and in the smaller hospital about 15 babies are born each day. As you know, about 50 percent of all babies are boys. However, the exact percentage varies from day to day. Sometimes it may be higher than 50 percent, sometimes lower.
>
> For a period of 1 year, each hospital recorded the days on which more than 60 percent of the babies born were boys. Which hospital do you think recorded more such days?

Twenty-one of the subjects said that they thought that it was more likely that the larger hospital recorded more such days, and 53 said that they thought the number of days would be about the same. Only 21 subjects answered correctly that the smaller hospital would report more such days. This is the same number as guessed exactly wrong. Apparently, the subjects simply did not see the relevance of the number of child births per day in determining the likely proportions of boys and girls.

Perhaps the most important cases of the law of small numbers are in the predictions regarding sequences of random events. For instance, people exaggerate the likelihood that a short sequence of flips of a fair coin will yield roughly the same number of heads as tails. What is commonly known as 'the gambler's fallacy' is a manifestation of this bias: if a fair coin has not (say) come up tails for a while, then it is 'due' for a tails, because a sequence of flips of a fair coin ought to include about as many tails as heads. The law of small numbers also has important implications when people are not certain about the true underlying probability distribution generating observed sequences. Belief in the law of small numbers leads people, in such situations, to over-infer the underlying probability

---

2.   For research related to the law of small numbers, see for example Kahneman and Tversky (1972) and Tversky and Kahneman (1971, 1982a, 1982b).

distribution from short sequences. Because people exaggerate how often a fair coin tossed three times will turn up at least one head, they will exaggerate the likelihood that a coin is biased if they observe a coin coming up tails three times in a row.

An important related phenomenon is misperception of regression to the mean. Because we read too much into patterns that depart from the norm, we do not expect that further observations will look more normal. To consider an example that Kahneman and Tversky have studied, because we exaggerate the extent to which exceptionally good or exceptionally bad performance on a test is a sign of exceptionally good or exceptionally bad aptitude, we do not expect students' exceptional performances to be followed by unexceptional performances as often as they are. Examples of this regression fallacy abound, and Kahneman and Tversky (1973) provide interesting illustrations of how misunderstanding regression to the mean leads people to offer spurious explanations for regression; these spurious explanations in turn can lead to people to alter their behavior in ways that have important economic consequences.

In various papers, Kahneman and Tversky have identified other heuristics that they perceive as important, such as the *availability heuristic* and *anchoring and adjustment*. Tversky and Kahneman (1973) propose that '[a] person is said to employ the availability heuristic whenever he estimates frequency or probability by the ease with which instances or associations could be brought to mind'. As with the representativeness and other heuristics, availability is clearly an appropriate criterion for individuals to use in making probabilistic judgements. But as with other heuristics, availability becomes a bias by its over-use in identifiable classes of situations. Probably the most important instances of the availability heuristic are where individuals exaggerate the likelihood of events because of their *salience*, even in situations where they have available other sources of information. For instance, our assessment of the dangerousness of a given city is likely to be overly influenced by whether we personally know somebody who has been assaulted, even if we are also familiar with general statistics. Likewise, dramatic stories by people we know about difficulties with a brand of car are likely to be overly influential even if we are familiar, via *Consumer Reports*, with general statistics of the reliability of different brands. In both these cases, the more salient information should have virtually no influence on our beliefs.

In formulating their theory of anchoring and adjustment, Kahneman and Tversky demonstrate that numerical estimates of uncertain quantities can be very sensitive to numbers on people's minds at the time they make those estimates. In particular, they follow Slovic and Lichtenstein (1971) in noting that adjustments in assessments away from initial values are typically too small. Tversky and Kahneman (1974) provide the following striking example, where subjects were influenced in making an assessment by a manifestly random number they were exposed to before making that assessment:

> In a demonstration of the anchoring effect, subjects were asked to estimate various quantities, stated in percentages (for example, the percentage of African countries in the United Nations). For each quantity, a number between 0 and 100 was determined by spinning a wheel of fortune in the subjects' presence. The subjects were instructed to indicate first whether that number was higher or lower than the value of the quantity, and then to estimate the value of the quantity by moving upward or downward from the given number. Different groups were given different numbers for each quantity, and these arbitrary numbers had a marked effect on estimates. For example, the median estimates of the percentage of African countries in the United Nations were 25 and 45 for groups that received 10 and 65, respectively, as starting points. Payoffs for accuracy did not reduce the anchoring effect.

Kahneman and Tversky point out that anchoring can occur as part of the assessment process itself. To use one of their examples, if we ask an individual to construct a probability distribution for the level of the Dow Jones, his/her likely beginning point will be to estimate a median level. This value will likely then serve as an anchor in his/her further probability assessments. By contrast, if he/she is asked by somebody to construct the probability assessments by stating the likelihood of the Dow Jones exceeding a pre-specified value, he/she is likely to anchor on this value. The two procedures, therefore, are likely to lead to different predictions, with the first procedure yielding a probability distribution more concentrated around the median than the second.

It is of interest, of course, to understand the effects of learning and experience on heuristics and biases. Indeed, the conjecture that experience helps overcome biases has often led economists to doubt the relevance of laboratory evidence based on the performance of inexperienced subjects. Especially if much activity in the economy is performed by specialists and experts, it is argued, the rationality assumption fares much better than psychological evidence indicates.

Yet research by psychologists does not overall support strong versions of the experts-get-things-right and in-the-real-world-people-learn hypotheses. Griffin and Tversky (1992), for instance, discuss the evidence about whether learning or expertise will eliminate the well-established general tendency for people to be overconfident in the quality of their predictions. They point out first that when certain forms of predictability are high, experts tend to have a pretty good sense of how accurate their predictions are. In such cases, experts not only know more, but are more realistic than laypersons about how much they know. But experts are quite often *more* susceptible to overconfidence than are laypersons. Griffin and Tversky (1992) provide the following examples:

When predictability is reasonably high, experts are generally better calibrated than lay people. ... When predictability is very low, however, experts may be more prone to overconfidence than novices. If the future state of a mental patient, the Russian economy, or the stock market cannot be predicted from present data, then experts who have rich models of the system in question are more likely to exhibit overconfidence than lay people who have a very limited understanding of these systems. Studies of clinical psychologists (e.g., Oskamp 1965) and stock market analysts (e.g., Yates 1990) are consistent with this hypothesis.

Griffin and Tversky also find support in their experiments for a pattern that has been found frequently by other researchers: even when people *do* understand the limits in their abilities to predict events accurately, they tend not to apply this general knowledge in calibrating the appropriate confidence in individual cases. This form of non-learning implies that even if people *do* learn the relevant statistical truths of their environment, they may continue to make errors in their judgements and decision making in individual cases. Redelmeier and Tversky (1990, p. 1163) illustrate the difference between a person's behavior in individual cases and his/her beliefs about what is the right response on average using field data on decision making by experts:

results indicate that physicians make different decisions when evaluating an individual patient than when considering a group of comparable patients. ... From the individual as compared with the aggregate perspective, physicians are more likely to order an additional test, expend time directly assessing a patient, avoid raising some troubling issues, and recommend a therapy with a high probability of success but the chance of an adverse outcome. The discrepancy between the aggregate and individual perspectives demonstrated in these experiments cannot be attributed to differences in either medical information or economic incentives; hence it is difficult to explain on normative grounds.

More generally, many people who know general principles do not apply those principles in particular situations. Kahneman and Tversky (1982, p. 495) call such errors *errors of applications*: 'A failure in a particular problem is called an error of application if there is evidence that people know and accept a rule that they did not apply'.

FRAMING EFFECTS, PREFERENCE REVERSALS AND CONTEXT EFFECTS

The heuristics and biases reviewed in the previous section obviously involve departures from full rationality, and research presented later demonstrates further departures from expected-utility maximization. But probably the most striking and problematic departures from rationality identified by Kahneman and Tversky are what they call *framing effects*: many examples have been produced in which people prefer some option A to B when the choice is presented to them one way, but prefer B to A when the choice is presented another way. Examples of framing effects typically involve differing frames whose logical equivalence is neither totally transparent *nor* terribly obscure, and the ways in which decisions are influenced is typically predictable by the features emphasized by the different frames. Tversky and Kahneman (1986, pp. S254-5) give the following striking example of framing effects, taken from a study of medical decisions by McNeil, Pauker, Sox and Tversky (1982):

Respondents were given statistical information about the outcomes of two treatments of lung cancer. The same statistics were presented to some respondents in terms of mortality rates and to others in terms of survival rates. The respondents then indicated their preferred treatment. The information was presented [exactly] as follows.

Problem 1 (Survival frame)
   Surgery: Of 100 people having surgery 90 live through the post-operative period, 68 are alive at the end of the first year and 34 are alive at the end of five years.
   Radiation Therapy: Of 100 people having radiation therapy all live through the treatment, 77 are alive at the end of one year and 22 are alive at the end of five years.

Problem 1 (Mortality frame)
   Surgery: Of 100 people having surgery 10 die during surgery or the post-operative period, 32 die by the end of the first year and 66 die by the end of five years.
   Radiation Therapy: Of 100 people having radiation therapy, none die during treatment, 23 die by the end of one year and 78 die by the end of five years.

The inconsequential difference in formulation produced a marked effect. The overall percentage of respondents who favored radiation therapy rose from 18% in the survival frame (N = 247) to 44% in the mortality frame (N = 336). The advantage of radiation therapy over surgery evidently looms larger when stated as a reduction of the risk of immediate death from 10% to 0% rather than as an increase from 90% to 100% in the rate of survival. The framing effect was not smaller for experienced physicians or for statistically sophisticated business students than for a group of clinic patients.

This question is hypothetical, of course, and one might imagine that real stakes could substantially change the level of care which subjects give to the problem. For obvious reasons, controlled real-world field tests of the issues above would be problematic. But the fact that experienced physicians make the same mistakes suggests that similarly significant patterns might play out in the real world. Moreover, similar framing effects were found in choices over lotteries with real stakes, and Tversky and Kahneman (1986, S261-2) cite some important real-world examples of framing effects:[3]

> Thaler (1980) drew attention to the effect of labeling a difference between two prices as a surcharge or a discount. It is easier to forgo a discount than to accept a surcharge because the same price difference is valued as a gain in the former case and as a loss in the latter. Indeed, the credit card lobby is said to insist that any price difference between cash and card purchases should be labeled a cash discount rather than a credit surcharge. ... Schelling (1981) has described a striking framing effect in a context of tax policy. He points out that the tax table can be constructed by using as a default case either the childless family (as is in fact done) or, say, the modal two-child family. The tax difference between a childless family and a two-child family is naturally framed as an exemption (for the two-child family) in the first frame and as a tax premium (on the childless family) in the second frame. This seemingly innocuous difference has a large effect on judgments of the desired relation between income, family size, and tax. Schelling reported that his students rejected the idea of granting the rich a larger exemption than the poor in the first frame but favored a larger tax premium on the childless rich than on the childless poor in the second frame. Because the exemption and the premium are alternative labels for the same tax differences in the two cases, the judgments violate invariance. Framing the consequences of public policy in positive or in negative terms can greatly alter its appeal. ... Bazerman (1983) has documented framing effects in experimental studies of bargaining. He compared the performance of experimental subjects when the outcomes of bargaining were formulated as gains or as losses. Subjects who bargained over the allocation of losses more often failed to reach agreement and more often failed to discover a Pareto-optimal solution.

While many examples of framing effects seem to be mere confusion by subjects who have well-defined preferences, further research raises the possibility that preferences are themselves influenced by the framing and structure of the decision problem. Indeed, the related phenomena of *preference reversals* and *context effects* raise even more fundamental doubts than do framing effects about economists' assumption that choices reflect stable, well-defined preferences. Tversky and Thaler (1990, p. 209) quote approvingly the following conclusion by two economists who experimentally confronted and failed to refute evidence on preference reversals:

> Taken at face value the data [showing preference reversals] are simply inconsistent with preference theory and have broad implications about research priorities within economics. The inconsistency is deeper than the mere lack of transitivity or even stochastic transitivity. It suggests that no optimization principles of any sort lie behind the simplest of human choices and that the uniformities in human choice behavior which lie behind market behavior may

---

3. Many of these examples of framing effects reflect the fact that losses resonate with people much more than gains. I discuss this phenomenon of *loss aversion* in the next section.

result from principles which are of a completely different sort from those generally accepted. (Grether and Plott 1979, p. 623).

Tversky and Thaler (1990) conclude their paper with an even stronger statement about an approach to economics implied by much of the research outlined below:

First, people do not possess a set of pre-defined preferences for every contingency. Rather, preferences are constructed in the process of making a choice or judgment. Second, the context and procedures involved in making choices or judgments influence the preferences that are implied by the elicited responses. In practical terms, this implies that behavior is likely to vary across situations that economists consider identical. For example, alternative auction mechanisms which are equivalent in theory might produce different outcomes if the auction procedures themselves influence bidding behavior.

The discussion of the meaning of preference and the status of value may be illuminated by the well-known exchange among three baseball umpires. 'I call them as I see them', said the first. 'I call them as they are', claimed the second. The third disagreed, 'They ain't nothing till I call them.' Analogously, we can describe three different views regarding the nature of values. First, values exist – like body temperature – and people perceive and report them as best they can, possibly with bias (I call them as I see them). Second, people know their values and preferences directly – as they know the multiplication table (I call them as they are). Third, values or preferences are commonly constructed in the process of elicitation (they ain't nothing till I call them). The research reviewed in this article is most compatible with the third view of preference as a constructive, context-dependent process.

Tversky and Thaler (1990, pp. 202-3) review research by both economists and psychologists in recent years regarding what has come to be called *preference reversals*:

For almost two decades, economists and psychologists have been intrigued by [an] inconsistency involving risky prospects. Subjects are first asked to choose between two gambles with nearly the same expected values. One gamble, called the *H* bet (for high chance of winning) has a high chance of winning a relatively small prize (say, 8/9 chance of win $4), while the other gamble, the *L* bet, offers a lower chance to win a larger prize (say, a 1/9 chance to win $40). Most subjects choose the *H* bet. Subjects are then asked to price each of the gambles. Specifically, they are asked to state the lowest price at which they would be willing to sell each gamble if they owned it. Surprisingly, most subjects put a higher price on the *L* bet. (In a recent study that used this particular pair of bets, for example, 71 percent of the subjects chose the *H* bet, while 67 percent priced *L* above *H*.) This pattern is called a *preference reversal*. Sarah Lichtenstein and Paul Slovic (1971, 1973) first demonstrated such reversals in a series of studies, one of which was conducted for real money with gamblers on the floor of the Four Queens Casino in Las Vegas.

Lichtenstein and Slovic did not come upon this result by chance. In an earlier study (Slovic and Lichtenstein, 1968), they observed that both buying and selling prices of gambles were more highly correlated with payoffs than with chances of winning, whereas choices between gambles (and ratings of their attractiveness) were more highly correlated with the probabilities of winning and losing than with the payoffs. The authors reasoned that if the method used to elicit preferences affected the weighting of the gamble's components, it should be possible to construct pairs of gambles such that the same individual would choose one member of the pair but set a higher price for the other. Experimental tests supported this conjecture.

Preference reversals provide an example where putative preferences are different in different decision contexts which economists have always treated as equivalent. Other psychological research likewise raises doubts regarding the standard assumption that there exist stable preferences independent of the menu of choices available to a decision maker. Simonson and Tversky (1992) provide examples where the addition of a new option to a set of choices may actually decrease the proportion of consumers who choose one of the existing options.

The more general principle that an unattractive option can enhance the attractiveness of other options is folk wisdom among salespersons. Simonson and Tversky (1992, p. 287) ran an experiment that illustrates this idea particularly well:

> [Subjects] were informed that some of them, selected randomly, would receive $6. They were further told that the winners would have the option of trading the $6 for a pen. Subjects were asked to examine the available pens and indicate whether they would like to trade the $6 for a pen. Later 10% of the participants received either $6 or the pen they had chosen.
>
> In one version of the questionnaire, subjects were presented an elegant Cross pen. In the other version, subjects were given an additional option – a lesser known brand name that was selected specifically for its unattractiveness. ... Though [only 2% of the] subjects selected the less attractive pen, its inclusion in the offered set increased the percentage of respondents who preferred the more attractive Cross pen from 36% to 46% ($t = 1.5, p < .10$). This observation suggests that the tendency to pay cash for a good can be increased by the introduction of an inferior alternative.

Recent research by Tversky and others suggests that many of the phenomena discussed in this section can be attributed to the desire by decision makers to have *reasons* for their decisions. Shafir, Simonson and Tversky (forthcoming, pp. 3-6) present this research program as follows:

> [one traditional approach to decision making] characterizes choice as the maximization of value. ... An alternative tradition in the study of decision making, characteristic of scholarship in history and the law, and typical of political and business discourse, employs an informal, reason-based analysis. This approach identifies various reasons and arguments that are purported to enter into and influence decision, and explains choice in terms of the balance of reasons for and against the various alternatives. ...
>
> Despite its limitations, a reason-based conception of choice has several attractive features. First, a focus on reasons seems closer to the way we normally think and talk about choices.

When facing a difficult choice (e.g., between schools, or jobs) we try to come up with reasons for and against each option – we do not normally attempt to estimate their overall values. Second, thinking of choice as guided by reasons provides a natural way to understand the conflict that characterizes the making of decisions. From the perspective of reason-based choice, conflict arises when the decision maker has good reasons for and against each option, or conflicting reasons for competing options. Unlike numerical values, which are easy to compare, conflicting reasons may be hard to reconcile. An analysis based on reasons can also accommodate framing effects (Tversky & Kahneman 1986) and elicitation effects (Tversky, Sattath, & Slovic 1988), which show that preferences are sensitive to the ways in which options are described (e.g., in terms of gains or losses), and to the methods through which preferences are elicited (e.g., pricing versus choice). These findings, which are puzzling from the perspective of value maximization, are easier to interpret if we assume that different frames and elicitation procedures highlight different aspects of the options and thus bring forth different reasons to guide decision. Finally, a conception of choice based on reasons may incorporate comparative considerations (such as relative advantages, or anticipated regret) that typically remain outside the purview of value maximization.

As noted in this passage, framing effects and 'elicitation effects' can be understood to some degree in terms of the influence of different choice contexts on the decision maker's notion of when he/she has a 'reason' to choose one option over another. Some recent research establishes even more dramatically the role of reasons in decision making. For instance, Tversky and Shafir (1992b) demonstrate that people do not merely search to find a high-value option – as assumed in conventional search theory – but also seem to search to acquire a menu of choices for which they feel there is a reason for selecting one choice over others. Tversky and Shafir (1992a) provide an interesting twist on the role of reasons in decision making, showing that people are likely to delay decisions until they learn information, even if the information will not in the end affect their *decision*, but will affect the *reason* for that decision. As with the search example, people choose to defer decisions in part so as to make a later decision that involves a more clear-cut reason.

GAINS, LOSSES AND REFERENCE POINTS

Building from earlier research, Kahneman and Tversky have emphasized that much of human decision making is influenced more by how anticipated consumption differs from some reference level than by the absolute level of consumption itself. While they focus on the realm of consumption and income, Kahneman and Tversky (1979, p. 277) stress that the salience of changes from reference points is a basic feature of human beings:

An essential feature of the present theory is that the carriers of value are changes in wealth or welfare, rather than final states. This assumption is compatible with basic principles of perception and judgment. Our perceptual apparatus is attuned to the evaluation of changes or differences rather than to the evaluation of absolute magnitudes. When we respond to attributes such as brightness, loudness, or temperature, the past and present context of experience defines an adaptation level, or reference point, and stimuli are perceived in relation to this reference point (Helson (1964)). Thus, an object at a given temperature may be experienced as hot or cold to the touch depending on the temperature to which one has adapted. The same principle applies to non-sensory attributes such as health, prestige, and wealth. The same level of wealth, for example, may imply abject poverty for one person and great riches for another – depending on their current assets.

The general notion that a person's sense of well-being is heavily influenced by past consumption, past experiences, expectations and other reference points, is a major fact about human beings, and is gradually being incorporated into economic modeling. Kahneman and Tversky have, however, documented that reference points influence behavior in ways that economists will find surprising and problematic.[4]

Kahneman and Tversky first introduced the idea of *loss aversion* in the context of risky choice, and showed that relative to their reference level, losses resonate with people much more than do comparable gains. The notion that the pain associated with a loss is greater than the pleasure of a same-sized gain is, of course, also implied by the standard assumption of a concave utility function. Besides the assumption of reference-dependence, what distinguishes loss aversion from the conventional notion of risk aversion is that the value function exhibits an *abrupt* and significant change in slope at the reference level, so that people are significantly risk averse even for small amounts of money. While such 'first-order' risk aversion is widely observed, it is ruled out by the standard concave-utility function approach to risk aversion, which implies that people are approximately risk-neutral for small stakes.

The idea of loss aversion helps explain the phenomenon of the *endowment effect* identified by Thaler (1980, 1985). It appears that, typically, once a person comes to possess a good, he/she almost immediately attaches more value to it. Tversky and Kahneman (1991, pp. 1041-2) succinctly describe an experiment that nicely illustrates this phenomenon:

Kahneman, Knetsch, and Thaler [1990] tested the endowment effect in a series of experiments, conducted in a classroom setting. In one of these experiments a decorated mug (retail value of

---

4. Examples of papers by Kahneman and Tversky that hit on this theme include Kahneman, Knetsch and Thaler (1986a, 1986b, 1990, 1991), Kahneman and Tversky (1979), and Tversky and Kahneman (1991, 1992).

about $5) was placed in front of one third of the seats after students had chosen their places. All participants received a questionnaire. The form given to the recipients of a mug (the 'sellers') indicated that 'You now own the object in your possession. You have the option of selling it if a price, which will be determined later, is acceptable to you. For each of the possible prices below indicate whether you wish to (x) Sell your object and receive this price; (y) Keep your object and take it home with you. ...' The subjects indicated their decision for prices ranging from $0.50 to $9.50 in steps of 50 cents. Some of the students who had not received a mug (the 'choosers') were given a similar questionnaire, informing them that they would have the option of receiving either a mug or a sum of money to be determined later. They indicated their preference between a mug and sums of money ranging from $0.50 to $9.50.

The choosers and the sellers face precisely the same decision problem, but their reference states differ. ... [The choosers] face a positive choice between two options that dominate [their reference state] ... The sellers ... must choose between retaining the status quo (the mug) or giving up the mug in exchange for money. Thus, the mug is evaluated as a gain by the choosers, and as a loss by the sellers. Loss aversion entails that the rate of exchange of the mug against money will be different in the two cases. Indeed, the median value of the mug was $7.12 for the sellers and $3.12 for the choosers in one experiment, $7.00 and $3.50 in another. The difference between these values reflects an endowment effect which is produced, apparently instantaneously, by giving an individual property rights over a consumption good.

Despite the riskless context and the involvement of a non-monetary good, this is well conceptualized as a case of loss aversion: Individuals who are given mugs treat the mugs as part of their endowment, and consider not having a mug to be a loss, whereas individuals without the mugs to begin with do not consider this to be a loss.

As established by Knetsch and Sinden (1984), Samuelson and Zeckhauser (1988), and Knetsch (1990), a comparable phenomenon holds for choices that involve trading off two goods or attributes of goods against each other. Here, loss aversion implies that an individual's willingness to forgo one object for the other depends on which object he/she begins with – forgoing something that is part of his/her reference point is a loss, whereas forgoing something that is not part of his/her reference point is merely not a gain. There is, therefore, a *status quo bias* whereby individuals tend to prefer the status quo to changes that involve losses in some dimensions even with gains in other dimensions.

Research establishing the endowment effect and the status quo bias is in some ways very similar to models developed by economists such as Becker and Murphy (1988) (in the context of addictive goods) and Ryder and Heal (1973) (in the context of macroeconomics). But it is worth re-emphasizing the nature of the situations and the scale of the effects being considered by Kahneman and Tversky and others. Kahneman, Knetsch and Thaler (1990, p. 1342) note, for instance, that

The evidence presented in this paper supports what may be called an instant endowment effect: the value that an individual assigns to such objects as mugs, pens, binoculars, and chocolate bars appears to increase substantially as soon as that individual is given the object. ... While long-term endowment effects could be explained by sentimental attachment ... the differences in preference or taste demonstrated by more than 700 participants in the experiments reported in this paper cannot be explained in this fashion.

More than the general idea that decisions and experienced well-being can depend on past consumption and other reference points, economists should learn from this research that people's reference points can be formed strikingly quickly, and that they can influence decision making in situations that involve consumer goods which are non-addictive and seemingly sentiment free.

Loss aversion, the endowment effect and the status quo bias seem to be pervasive features of human attitudes. These phenomena are indeed becoming a more active part of research in economics and policy analysis; Kahneman and Tversky (forthcoming) consider the role that loss aversion plays in conflict resolution; Kahneman and Thaler (1991) hypothesize about some of the implications of loss aversion and reference dependence for welfare policy; Cohen and Knetsch (1990) consider the role of the status quo bias in judicial decision making; Hartman, Doane and Woo (1991) find empirical evidence for the existence of a status quo bias in consumer demand for electrical utilities. More generally, Thaler (1980) and Kahneman, Knetsch and Thaler (1986a,1986b) demonstrate that loss aversion plays a very strong role in people's notion of fairness. Finally, many of the economic examples regarding framing effects cited earlier revolved around loss aversion, in that consumer preferences were strongly influenced by whether a choice was framed in ways that make losses more salient or less salient.

In addition to loss aversion, another feature of how people value departures from their reference point is *diminishing sensitivity* – the marginal change in perceived well-being is greater for changes that are close to one's reference level than for changes that are further away. As with loss aversion, diminishing sensitivity is a reflection of a more fundamental feature of human cognition and motivation. Kahneman and Tversky (1979, p. 278) note the following:

> Many sensory and perceptual dimensions share the property that the psychological response is a concave function of the magnitude of physical change. For example, it is easier to discriminate between a change of $3°$ and a change of $6°$ in room temperature, than it is to discriminate between a change of $13°$ and a change of $16°$. We propose that this principle applies in particular to the evaluation of monetary changes. Thus, the difference between a gain of 100 and a gain of 200 appears to be greater than the difference between a gain of 1,100 and a gain of 1,200. Similarly, the difference between a loss of 100 and a loss of 200 appears greater than the difference between a loss of 1,100 and a loss of 1,200, unless the larger loss is intolerable. Thus, we hypothesize that the value function for changes of wealth is normally

concave above the reference point ... and often convex below it. ... That is, the marginal value of both gains and losses generally decreases with their magnitude.

Kahneman and Tverky's original exposition of loss aversion was in the context of preferences over uncertain monetary outcomes. In this context, of course, diminishing sensitivity implies that while people are likely to be risk averse over gains, they are often risk *loving* over losses. For instance, Kahneman and Tversky (1979) found that 70 percent of subjects report that they would prefer a 3/4 probability of losing nothing and 1/4 probability of losing $6,000 to a 2/4 probability of losing nothing and 1/4 probability each of losing $4,000 or $2,000. The preferred lottery here is a mean-preserving spread of the less preferred lottery, so that the responses of 70 percent of the subjects are inconsistent with the standard assumption of concave utility functions.[5]

The question arises as to whether loss aversion, diminishing sensitivity and other reference effects should be deemed rational or irrational. Tversky and Kahneman (1991, pp. 1057-8) address the issue as follows:

Is loss aversion irrational? This question raises a number of difficult normative issues. Questioning the values that decision makers assign to outcomes requires a criterion for the evaluation of preferences. ... The effects of reference levels on decisions can only be justified by corresponding effects of these reference levels on the experience of consequences. For example, a bias in favor of the status quo can be justified if the disadvantages of any change will be experienced more keenly than its advantages. However, some reference levels that are naturally adopted in the context of decision are irrelevant to the subsequent experience of outcomes, and the impact of such reference levels on decisions is normatively dubious. In evaluating a decision that has long-term consequences, for example, the initial response to

---

5. Another element of their multi-faceted *prospect theory*, introduced in Kahneman and Tversky (1979), is the fact that individuals depart from expected-utility maximization when choosing under uncertainty by using *decision weights* that systematically depart from the probabilities in the situation at hand. In parallel to other researchers in non-expected utility theory, Kahneman and Tversky have explored some systematic ways in which choices diverge from the linear use of probabilities implied by expected-utility theory. (See, e.g., Kahneman and Tversky 1979 and Tversky and Kahneman 1992. For reviews of this literature, see Machina 1989 and Camerer 1992.) One of the main behavioral implications of this research in non-expected utility is that people will exhibit behavior like that found in the so-called *Allais paradox*, a widely replicated behavioral regularity in choice under uncertainty first observed in Allais (1953). In this and other implications, Kahneman and Tversky's experimental research on the nature of the non-linearity of choice under uncertainty is similar in broad terms to the results from other researchers in non-expected utility. But in their original paper on prospect theory (Kahneman and Tversky 1979) and in their recent modifications (Tversky and Kahneman 1992), they have emphasized more than other researchers the interaction of decision weights with the differential attitudes towards gains and losses. In particular, Tversky and Kahneman (1992, p. 297) conclude that decision weights and the value function described in the previous section combine to imply 'a distinctive fourfold pattern of risk attitudes: risk aversion for gains and risk seeking for losses of high probability; risk seeking for gains and risk aversion for losses of low probability'.

these consequences may be relatively unimportant, if adaptation eventually induces a shift of reference. We conclude that there is no general answer to the question about the normative status of loss aversion or of other reference effects, but there is a principled way of examining the normative status of these effects in particular cases.

Indeed, recent research by Kahneman and co-authors establishes that, even if people correctly perceive the physical outcomes of their decisions, there are identifiable, systematic departures from full rationality in decision making because people have misperceptions of what will be their well-being from such outcomes. Kahneman (1994, p. 10) notes, for instance, that 'radical changes of circumstances produce adaptations and changes of experienced utility that violate common expectations', and cites a classical study by Brickman, Coates, and Janoff-Bulman (1978), which 'showed that most paraplegics adapt far better than most people would predict, and that lottery winners are generally less happy in the long run than the common fascination with lotteries might suggest'.

Of course, one major source of predicted utility from future experiences is the recollected utility from comparable experiences in the past. One might conjecture, in fact, that people's predictions about their utility from familiar experiences will be fairly accurate. But some recent research, summarized in Kahneman (1994), gives dramatic evidence that there may be some systematic differences in people's experienced utility of episodes and their recollections of those episodes. This research adds to the doubts about the degree to which people's choice reflects the maximization of experienced well-being, even when decision makers have a very concrete and correct perception of the physical consequences of their choices.

IS THIS RESEARCH RELEVANT FOR ECONOMICS?

Both the methods and the content of the research conducted by Kahneman and Tversky and other psychologists are gaining increased acceptance by mainstream economists. Nonetheless, many reasons and rationalizations for dismissing their research continue to be expressed. These reasons can be usefully classified into three categories. First, their research is dismissed on the *psychological grounds* that their claimed results do not well capture real-world individual behavior. Second, it is dismissed on the *economic grounds* that the types of behavior they identify are not likely to matter economically because of the effects of competitive markets or other economic mechanisms. Finally, their research is sometimes dismissed on the *methodological grounds* that their findings are not – irrespective of their validity and potential economic implications – readily incorporatable into economic analysis.

The psychological grounds for dismissing Kahneman and Tversky's research stem largely from the fact that little of the evidence presented by Kahneman and Tversky to support their hypotheses comes from the type of non-laboratory empirical evidence traditionally studied by economists. As such, one major objection to their research reflects prevalent attitudes among economists that survey and experimental evidence are not very good indicators of people's behavior in the 'real world'. Economists worry that people who are asked to reveal how they would behave in hypothetical situations may not correctly predict, or truthfully reveal, their own behavior. Even when evidence is garnered from experiments involving real choices, economists worry that subjects may not pay close attention to their decisions because of the low stakes involved, and that minor considerations may influence people's behavior to a degree that they would not in the real world. Finally, economists worry that the environment created in the laboratory is too artificial and too unfamiliar to subjects to allow us to make strong inferences about real-world behavior.

These worries have some merit. It is proper to be skeptical of many reports given by people in the laboratory, especially when there are clear psychological incentives for subjects to make self-serving reports. And certainly many experiments seem too artificial in their attempts to replicate analogous real-world situations to confidently infer real-world behavior from these experiments. Indeed, it seems clear that the levels of stakes and experience inherent in some economic situations are impossible to replicate in the laboratory.

But using these criticisms as a justification for maintaining 'standard' assumptions is highly problematic, and begs the question of whether standard economic assumptions are themselves supported by conclusive evidence. It is weird to argue that research identifying alternative behavioral hypotheses has no scientific standing when the standard assumptions this research challenges are rarely based on more than casual intuitions.

Some worries expressed by economists, however, are based on very reasonable intuitions that laboratory experiments will yield less rational behavior than would be observed in other contexts. One common critique of Kahneman and Tversky's findings (and psychology and experimental economics more generally) is that participants in these experiments are amateurs at the tasks they face, and are not given ample opportunity to learn more rational behavior. If most important economic activity involves people experienced with the decisions they face, then the heavy reliance by psychologists on relatively inexperienced subjects is problematic. As reviewed earlier, however, psychological research on the real-world effects of incentives, learning and expertise does not support the hypothesis that these factors will eliminate nearly all biases.

Perhaps the most frequent worry expressed by economists about experimental results is that the stakes involved are too small to infer real-world behavior from. The role of stake size is an important unanswered question that raises questions about how much to infer from some of the experiments discussed above, and it is probably fair to say that psychologists (including Kahneman and Tversky) *were* in general under-curious about how well their results carried over when stakes are sizeable, and that economists (especially experimentalists) have contributed to improving the psychological evidence because of their greater attentiveness to experimental incentives. But while it is surely true that people are, on average, more rational when stakes are large rather than small, this does not mean that they are nearly perfectly rational. Yet when there is direct evidence for how people behave when stakes are small, but none when stakes are large, economists' tendency to maintain our familiar assumptions rather than extrapolate from small-stakes experimental evidence seems questionable. Until we gather more substantial evidence supporting or contradicting economists' presumptions about what people do when stakes are large, taking seriously the evidence when stakes are small seems to be warranted.

Many economists argue that, even if real, departures from our standard model of rationality will have few important economic implications because of economic incentives and feedback mechanisms. The most pervasive conjecture along these lines is that perfectly competitive markets will generally eliminate the effects of departures from rationality. This argument is problematic on many grounds. Akerlof and Yellen (1985), Conlisk (1980) and others have pointed out that markets need not correct irrationalities. Haltiwanger and Waldman (1985) begin to explore what types of markets are most likely to reduce irrationalities, *and* which are likely to *exacerbate* them. The conclusion we can draw from such papers is that there is no general rule that markets will correct irrationalities, nor even that rational participants will always mitigate rather than magnify the effects of non-rational market participants. Recent empirical and experimental investigations of the markets-negate-irrationalities hypothesis likewise cast doubt on the validity of the assertion. An imagined general principle that rational participants will nearly eliminate the effects of non-rational participants has been repeatedly asserted but never coherently explained.

As is perfect competition, so too learning and incentives are often invoked as reasons why departures from pure rationality will be mitigated. The psychological case against the learning-eliminates-irrationalities hypothesis was discussed earlier. But even if it *were* true that sufficient learning eliminates irrationalities, the economic implications of this fact are not clear. While economists seem frequently (if selectively) to assert that most important decisions are made repeatedly, this claim has not been explored with any care.

A third category of skepticism about Kahneman and Tversky's research includes a set of concerns that their insights, however valid, are not readily incorporatable into economics. Probably the major objection by economists to basing assumptions more directly on psychological evidence is that such assumptions would often be complicated and context specific, and complicated and context-specific assumptions are much harder to work with than simple and general assumptions. The lower emphasis on 'parsimony' and 'tractability' often makes it difficult to incorporate psychological research into economics. If economists exaggerate these factors, psychologists seem simply to underestimate the need by economists for workably simple, rigorous and general assumptions about human behavior. While they understand economists' attachment to simplifying and general assumptions more than most psychologists, Kahneman and Tversky themselves sometimes underestimate its importance, and at times they make claims that economic assumptions are 'inadequate' simply because the simplifications economists make share the feature of all simplifications that they are false if interpreted literally.

Of course, Kahneman and Tversky are not economists, and it is not clear that it makes scientific sense to insist that they fully develop the economic implications of their research, or even that they develop just the right mix of simplifying assumptions and behavioral accuracy. And it seems clear that Kahneman and Tversky and other psychologists have accumulated enough seemingly relevant, general and tractable insights to make it worthwhile to begin to integrate these insights into economics.

In order to do so, some counterproductive methodological attitudes need to be overcome. For instance, a particularly seductive methodological roadblock is the view that we should maintain the rationality assumption until somebody comes up with a single better assumption which can, in one fell swoop, replace it. That is, until we find an alternative general theory, we should maintain our current general theory. This requirement is especially unconducive to real progress if alternative general theories are asked to be as simple as the current general theory, or are asked to 'deliver the goods' immediately in terms of making strong and precise predictions. It is certainly appropriate to judge the value of alternative behavioral hypotheses in part in terms of their generality, simplicity and likely economic implications. But it is counterproductive to demand that explorations of alternatives immediately rank as high in these factors as does the current theory, which has been fleshed out and worked over for decades. Even if we insist that we must have a parsimonious general theory – a goal that is likely overvalued by economists – it will probably take a while to build one up. And while no alternative model is likely to be as parsimonious as our current models, the systematic patterns that Kahneman and Tversky identify can help economists develop models that gain much in realism with minimal loss in tractability.

Despite all the obstacles and resistances, there are strong signs that Kahneman and Tversky's research, and psychological findings more generally, will play an increasing role in economics. It is rarer nowadays to hear blanket dismissals by economists of psychological research, and many mainstream economists quite clearly feel that adding this type of research to the economics discipline is (in principle) a healthy development. Even among skeptics, a common response these days is more often the demand for clearer statements of what specifically we learn from behavioral research, rather than insisting a priori that we learn nothing.

Their research is likely to serve many different productive roles for economics. Sometimes the main lesson of their research is simply the destructive one of telling us not to put much faith in insights derived from our traditional assumptions. Their research can also contribute on a constructive but *ad hoc* basis. For instance, money illusion is an example of a phenomenon believed by many economists yet not part of our standard reportoire of assumptions. Perhaps the fact that money illusion can be framed as part of this more general phenomenon of framing effects – different inflation rates imply different 'frames' on the same real choices that people make – can facilitate research. Patterns identified by Kahneman and Tversky, for instance, suggest likely implications of the framing generated by inflation (for example, inflation allows real cuts in wages to in part appear as gains rather than losses). More generally, their conceptualization of framing effects can legitimize and provide structure for investigation of such issues as money illusion.[6]

A final use of Kahneman and Tversky's research is to replace some of the current assumptions in economics with assumptions built from the systematic patterns of behavior identified by their research. That is, we can use Kahneman and Tversky's research to make the inputs into our models more empirically sound. Whatever the advantages and disadvantages of the method of rigorously deriving conclusions from formally stated assumptions, our conclusions are likely to be more behaviorally realistic if the assumptions we make have a better empirical base. Kahneman, Knetsch and Thaler (1991, p. 205) speculate on such an example where behavioral findings can be usefully integrated into mainstream methods:

> It is in the nature of economic anomalies that they violate standard theory. The next question is what to do about it. In many cases there is no obvious way to amend the theory to fit the facts, either because too little is known, or because the changes would greatly increase the

---

6. For preliminary research on the topic of framing and money illusion, see Shafir, Diamond and Tversky (1994).

complexity of the theory and reduce its predictive yield. The anomalies that we have described under the labels of the endowment effect, the status quo bias and loss aversion may be an exceptional case, where the needed amendments in the theory are both obvious and tractable.

Tversky and Kahneman (1991) indeed articulate a model of reference-based utility and loss aversion that is wholly within the language and the spirit of standard economic analysis. While the influence of the reference point doubles the number of parameters needed for analyzing consumer behavior, such models well indicate that much of their research can be incorporated into mainstream modes of analysis.

Much of Kahneman and Tversky's research discussed above identifies behavior that departs more dramatically from standard notions of rationality; developing tractable and general formalizations of such research is likely to be more problematic. It should still be possible, however, and should in any event be perceived by economists as an important goal in improving the descriptive realism of our formal models. More generally, Kahneman and Tversky's research has already enriched economics. Whether incorporated into mainstream modes of analysis, or used to modify our approach to economic analysis, yet greater attentiveness to their research will surely improve the quality of economics even further.

KAHNEMAN AND TVERSKY'S MAJOR WRITINGS

Griffin, D. and A. Tversky (1992), 'The Weighing of Evidence and the Determinants of Confidence, *Cognitive Psychology*, **24**, 411-435.

Kahneman, D. (1994), 'New Challenges to the Rationality Assumption', *Journal of Institutional and Theoretical Economics*, March.

Kahneman, D., J. Knetsch and R. Thaler (1986a), 'Fairness and the Assumptions of Economics', *Journal of Business*, **59**, S285-S300.

Kahneman, D., J. Knetsch and R. Thaler (1986b), 'Fairness as a Constraint on Profit Seeking: Entitlements in the Market', *The American Economic Review*, **76**.

Kahneman, D., J. Knetsch and R. Thaler (1990), 'Experimental Tests of the Endowment Effect and the Coase Theorem', *Journal of Political Economy*, **98**, 1325-48.

Kahneman, D., J. Knetsch and R. Thaler (1991), 'The Endowment Effect, Loss Aversion, and Status Quo Bias', *Journal of Economic Perspectives*, **5**, 193-206.

Kahneman, D., P. Slovic and A. Tversky (eds) (1982), *Judgement under Uncertainty: Heuristics and Biases*, New York: Cambridge University Press.

Kahneman, D. and R. Thaler (1991), 'Economic Analysis and the Psychology of Utility: Applications to Compensation Policy', *The American Economic Review (Proceedings)*, **81**, 341-52.

Kahneman, D. and A. Tversky (1972), 'Subjective Probability: A Judgement of Representativeness', *Cognitive Psychology*, **3**, 430-54.

Kahneman, D. and A. Tversky (1973), 'On the Psychology of Prediction', *Psychological Review*, **80**, 237-51.

Kahneman, D. and A. Tversky (1979), 'Prospect Theory: An Analysis of Decisions under Risk', *Econometrica*, **47**, 263-91.

Kahneman, D. and A. Tversky (1982), 'On the Study of Statistical Intuitions', *Cognition*, **11**, 123-41.

Kahneman, D. and A. Tversky (forthcoming), 'Conflict Resolution: A Cognitive Perspective', in K. Arrow et al. (eds), *Barriers to Conflict Resolution*, New York: Norton.

McNeil, B., S. Pauker, H. Sox Jr. and A. Tversky (1982), 'On the Elicitation of Preferences for Alternative Therapies', *New England Journal of Medicine*, **306**, 1259-62.

Redelmeier, D.A. and A. Tversky (1990), 'Discrepancy between Medical Decisions for Individual Patients and for Groups', *New England Journal of Medicine*, **322**, 1162-4.

Shafir, E., P. Diamond and A. Tversky (1994), 'On Money Illusion', working draft, MIT, February.

Shafir, E., I. Simonson and A. Tversky (forthcoming), 'Reason-Based Choice', *Cognition*.

Simonson, Itamar and A. Tversky (1992), 'Choice in Context: Tradeoff Contrast and Extremeness Aversion', *Journal of Marketing Research*, **29**, August, 281-95.

Tversky, A. and D. Kahneman (1971), 'Belief in the Law of Small Numbers', *Psychological Bulletin*, **76**, 105-10.

Tversky, A. and D. Kahneman (1973), 'Availability: A Heuristic for Judging Frequency and Probability', *Cognitive Psychology*, **5**, 207-32.

Tversky, A. and D. Kahneman (1974), 'Judgement under Uncertainty: Heuristics and Biases', *Science*, **185**, 1124-31.

Tversky, A. and D. Kahneman (1982a), 'Judgments of and by Representativeness', in Kahneman, D., P. Slovic and A. Tversky (eds) (1982), *Judgement under Uncertainty: Heuristics and Biases*, New York: Cambridge University Press, 84-98.

Tversky, A. and D. Kahneman (1982b), 'Evidential Impact of Base Rates', in Kahneman, D., P. Slovic and A. Tversky (eds), *Judgement under Uncertainty: Heuristics and Biases*, New York: Cambridge University Press, 153-60.

Tversky, A. and D. Kahneman (1986), 'Rational Choice and the Framing of Decisions', *Journal of Business*, **59**, S251-S278.

Tversky, A. and D. Kahneman (1991), 'Loss Aversion in Riskless Choice: A Reference-Dependent Model', *Quarterly Journal of Economics*, November, 1039-61.

Tversky, A. and D. Kahneman (1992), 'Advances in Prospect Theory: Cumulative Representation of Uncertainty', *Journal of Risk and Uncertainty*, **5**, November, 297-323.

Tversky, A., S. Sattath and P. Slovic (1988), 'Contingent Weighting in Judgment and Choice', *Psychological Review*, **95** (3), 371-84.

Tversky, A. and E. Shafir (1992a), 'The Disjunction Effect in Choice under Uncertainty', *Psychological Science*, **3** (5), 305-9.

Tversky, A. and E. Shafir (1992b), 'Choice under Conflict: The Dynamics of Deferred Decision', *Psychological Science*, **3** (6), 358-61.

Tversky, A. and R. Thaler (1990), 'Anomalies: Preference Reversals', *Journal of Economic Perspectives*, **4** (2), 201-11.

OTHER REFERENCES

Akerlof, George and Janet Yellen (1985), 'Can Small Deviations from Rationality Make Significant Differences to Economic Equilibria?' *American Economic Review*, **75**, 708-20.

Allais, M. (1953), 'Le Comportement de L'homme Rationel Devant le Risque, Critique des Postulates et Axiomes de L'école Américaine', *Econometrica*, **21**, 503-26.

Bazerman, M.H. (1983), 'Negotiator Judgment', *American Behavioral Scientist*, **27**, 211-28.

Becker, G. and K.M. Murphy (1988), 'A Theory of Rational Addiction', *Journal of Political Economy*, **96**, 675-700.

Brickman, P., D. Coates and R. Janoff-Bulman (1978), 'Lottery Winners and Accident Victims: Is Happiness Relative?', *Journal of Personality and Social Psychology*, **36** (8), 917-27.

Camerer, Colin (1992), 'Recent Tests of Generalizations of Expected Utility Theory', in W. Edwards (ed.), *Utility Theories: Measurements and Applications*, Boston: Kluwer Academic Publishers.

Cohen, D. and J. Knetsch (1990), 'Judicial Choice and Disparities Between Measures of Economic Values', Simon Fraser University Working Paper.

Conlisk, John (1980), 'Costly Optimizers Versus Cheap Imitators', *Journal of Economic Behavior and Organization*, **1**, 275-93.

Grether, David M. and Charles R. Plott (1979), 'Economic Theory of Choice and the Preference Reversal Phenomena', *American Economic Review*, **69**, 623-38.

Haltiwanger, J. and M. Waldman (1985), 'Rational Expectations and the Limits of Rationality: An Analysis of Heterogeneity', *American Economic Review*, **75**, 326-40.

Hartman, R., M.J. Doane and C.-K. Woo (1991), *The Quarterly Journal of Economics*, February, 141-62.

Helson, H. (1964), *Adaptation-Level Theory*, New York: Harper.

Knetsch, Jack L. (1990), 'The Endowment Effect and Evidence of Nonreversible Indifference Curves', *American Economic Review*, **79**, 1277-84.

Knetsch, J.L. and J.A. Sinden (1984), 'Willingness to Pay and Compensation Demanded: Experimental Evidence of an Unexpected Disparity in Measures of Value', *Quarterly Journal of Economics*, **99**, August, 507-21.

Lichtenstein, Sarah and Paul Slovic (1971), 'Reversals of Preference Between Bids and Choices in Gambling Decisions', *Journal of Experimental Psychology*, **89**, January, 46-55.

Lichtenstein, Sarah and Paul Slovic (1973), 'Response-Induced Reversals of Preference in Gambling: An Extended Replication in Las Vegas', *Journal of Experimental Psychology*, **101**, November, 16-20.

Machina, Mark (1989), 'Dynamic Consistency and Non-Expected Utility Models of Choice Under Uncertainty', *Journal of Economic Literature*, **32**, December 1622-68.

Oskamp, Stuart (1965), 'Overconfidence in Case-Study Judgments', *The Journal of Consulting Psychology*, **29**, 261-5.

Ryder, H.E. and G.M. Heal (1973), 'Optimal Growth with Intertemporally Dependent Preferences', *Review of Economic Studies*, **40**, 1-33.

Samuelson, W. and R. Zeckhauser (1988), 'Status Quo Bias in Decision Making', *Journal of Risk and Uncertainty*, **1**, 7-59.

Schelling, Thomas (1981), 'Economic Reasoning and the Ethics of Policy', *Public Interest*, **63**, 37-61.

Slovic, Paul and Sarah Lichtenstein (1968), 'The Relative Importance of Probabilities and Payoffs in Risk-Taking', *Journal of Experimental Psychology Monograph Supplement*, **78**, Part 2, November, 1-18.

Slovic, Paul and Sarah Lichtenstein (1971), 'Comparison of Bayesian and Regression Approaches to the Study of Information Processing in Judgment', *Organizational Behavior and Human Performance*, **6**, 649-744.

Thaler, R. (1980), 'Toward a Positive Theory of Consumer Choice', *Journal of Economic Behavior and Organization*, **1**, 39-60.

Thaler, R. (1985), 'Mental Accounting and Consumer Choice', *Marketing Science*, **4**, Summer, 199-214.

Yates, J.F. (1990), *Judgment and Decision Making*, Englewood Cliffs, NJ: Prentice-Hall.

Zeckhauser, Richard (1987), 'Comments: Behavioral versus Rational Economics: What You See Is What You Conquer', in Robin Hogarth and Melvin Reder (eds) (1987), *Rational Choice: The Contrast Between Economics and Psychology*, Chicago: University of Chicago Press, 251-66.

7. Paul Krugman

Edward M. Graham

Criticizing the economic reasoning of some of the highest level economic advisors to the Clinton Administration in an article appearing in *Foreign Affairs*, Paul Krugman entitles his final section 'Advisers with no Clothes'.[1] The content of the article is no less provocative than the title of this last section and, to keep things jumping, Krugman mentions the names of those advisors to Clinton he feels are inept. In a subsequent issue of *Foreign Affairs*, several leading defenders of 'Clintonomics' (or, if not that, critics of Krugman) attempt counterattacks, to which Krugman replies.[2] The verdict: Krugman 5, the counterattackers 0. All of this should be a delight to those of a Republican bent; after all, Krugman is essentially trashing an activist microeconomic policy designed to enhance US 'competitiveness', a policy that is anathema to economic conservatives. But, for the Republicans, there is ultimately no joy. Krugman is, at heart and soul, a liberal Democrat who ruthlessly (and effectively) dismisses the 'supply siders' of the Reagan–Bush era as sellers of snake oil in his popular book *Peddling Prosperity* (1994c).

In the meantime, the *Foreign Affairs* article spawns a series of commentary on both sides of the issue. *Washington Post* business page columnist Michael Schrage intones 'Alternating between statistical scalpels and macroeconomic machetes, Krugman bloodily eviscerates "competitiveness" as a policy doctrine without any kind of economic validity. ... His numbers would command respect even without his impeccable credentials'.[3] But *Harvard Business Review* contributing editor and former Senate staffer Charles W. McMillion writes of the same article 'Paul Krugman is blatantly preposterous and seeking any available public forum as he attempts to smear others in a childish and misguided fit of

---

1. Krugman 1994a.
2. Prestowitz et al. 1994; Krugman 1994b.
3. Schrage 1994.

pique. ... We can only hope that Krugman does less damage to rigorous and important economic policy analysis than Rollins did to race relations'.[4]

In a quote in an article on rejections by refereed journals of articles now seen as classics, Krugman indicates 'I don't know what other people's experience is, but I would estimate that 60% of my papers sent to refereed journals have been rejected on the first try'.[5] Among this 60 percent, however, are many of the papers that earned him the John Bates Clark medal, considered by many to be a more significant honor than the Nobel Prize in economics (because the Clark medal is given only every two years, and then to a young economist). Krugman's experience with refereed journals, of course, is not atypical; a substantial number of what are now considered the pathbreaking articles in modern economics have been rejected upon first submission to refereed journals.

So, one might reasonably ask, who is Paul Krugman? Is he the economics profession's equivalent of Wolfgang Amadeus Mozart, a young genius whose talents were so great but social graces so deplorable that he became both a pariah and a legend in his own time? We might note that Mozart had the misfortune to die young, a fate that even Paul Krugman's worst detractors would not wish upon him (or, at least, one hopes not!). We ask, would Mozart have mellowed had he lived past his middle thirties? If Krugman is a twentieth-century *doppelganger* of Mozart cleverly disguised as an economist, we now know that Mozart likely would not have become particularly mellow any time soon after 1791. Krugman is, as of the time of this writing, 41 years old, six years older than Mozart at the time of the latter's death. According to Schrage, Krugman is 'one of the country's most brilliant young economists ... with a reputation for intellectual honesty and a cruel tongue'.

At the age of 41, of course, there is time for mellowing yet. But then, too, 'young' is a relative concept. Forty-one is quite a mature age, if not completely over the hill, if one happens to be a professional football player. By contrast, forty-seven is considered very young if one happens to be President of the United States. Economists seem to pass out of the 'young' category at some point in their forties and, as a 'brilliant young' economist, Krugman's days are numbered. It remains to be seen, of course, whether he will make the grade as a brilliant old economist.

---

4. McMillion 1994; it is alleged that Edward Rollins, formerly an advisor to President Ronald Reagan, in managing the successful Republican campaign for the New Jersey governorship, tried to discourage black voters (who tend to vote for the Democratic Party) from going to the polls by paying ministers of predominantly black churches to denounce the incumbent Democratic governor (who was running for reelection).

5. Gans and Shepherd 1994.

If to describe Paul Krugman as 'young' is rapidly becoming obsolete, to describe him as being in any sense 'cruel' would reflect a complete misunderstanding of his character. Although he doubtlessly does have a cruel tongue (or, perhaps more to the point, a cruel word processor), this is about the only cruel thing about him. Rather, he is by nature quite gentle and kind. He is a rather shy person. But he hides his shyness well, especially when he is speaking before a large audience. He has a soft spot for children and (especially) cats. While he is fascinated by military strategy – he is, among other things, a Civil War buff – he is horrified by the prospect of an actual war or, indeed, any form of human suffering.

He has a wry sense of humor but an uncanny ability to make humorous remarks that go over the heads of many people, including ones considered to be highly intelligent. More than once this has got him into deep water. One notable incident took place at the now-infamous 'shootout at Jackson Hole' during the summer of 1991 (the 'shootout' is otherwise known as the summer workshop of the Federal Reserve Bank of Kansas City). At that time he offered a throw-away line to the effect that 'we now know that the Japanese never have been the enemy; rather all along it has been the French'. This was meant to be funny in an ironic and rather absurd sort of way – something that Lewis Carroll might have penned or, at least, found amusing. But rather than finding the statement to be funny, one very prominent former director of the International Monetary Fund of French nationality took serious umbrage. Krugman was accused of being anti-European or worse. What started as a joke turned almost into an international incident.

Indeed, to get a sense of where Krugman is coming from when he makes statements such as this, it helps if one is a fan of 'Mighty Mouse' or 'Dilbert'. To get oneself into the proper frame of mind before reading *Peddling Prosperity*, one might first want to read any of the anthologies of 'Dilbert'. With 'Dilbert' firmly in mind, one is much better placed to understand Krugman.

During his four undergraduate years at Yale University, Krugman majored not in economics, or in mathematics or physics, the undergraduate fields of choice of many economists today, but rather in history. Two things ensue: his thinking is not constrained by the limitations of higher mathematics, and he has a broader understanding of the nature of human society than do most technical economists. A qualification must be added to this last statement: he has no lack of aptitude for mathematics. And while he takes pride in developing models that are more insightful than mathematical, he has over the decade and a half since receiving his PhD delved into increasingly sophisticated mathematical subject areas, especially with regard to his recent work in economic geography.

This notwithstanding, the accomplishments that Krugman is best known for are indeed more characterized by insight than by mathematical erudition. The lack of higher mathematics in his major articles has earned him criticism from some of the more technically-oriented members of the profession. The most valid of these criticisms is that certain of his best-known models are built on special-case assumptions that are not readily generalized. The rejoinder is that the insights gained via these special-case models have often survived efforts by others to build less restrictive models covering the same territory.[6]

In economics, Paul Krugman has been nothing if not a pioneer, and it is often the fate of pioneers to see their early efforts refined, improved, and even corrected. To take an example from another discipline, the general theory of relativity is generally considered to be the crowning achievement of another wry and quirky pioneer, Albert Einstein, whose thinking often exceeded his ability to express it in polished mathematics. This theory, in the version that is known to contemporary physicists, is the product of much mathematical refinement by Sir Arthur Eddington and others. Nonetheless, it is still widely known as 'Einstein's theory'.

It is also almost always the case that intellectual pioneers do not work in a vacuum; rather, they build upon works left by others. To return to Einstein, his special theory of relativity builds heavily on Lorentz's transform for electromagnetic fields. Indeed, historians of science know that Einstein's thinking was heavily shaped by many others of his contemporaries, most of whose names are no longer remembered except when attached – e.g., the Fitzgerald contraction – to elements of what is now thought of as Einstein's theory. In the area that Krugman is probably best known professionally, the 'new' theory of international trade, he has hardly worked alone and certainly has not been the source of all of the bright new ideas even in their early, unrefined versions. And many of Krugman's best ideas were, indeed, anticipated by others. But his thinking probably has done more to shape this new theory than has that of any other single individual, and it is his good fortune that a short history of any endeavor – the sort of history that is consumed by the nonspecialist audience – will tend to overstate the contributions of the leading pioneers to the detriment of lesser-known figures whose contributions were, nonetheless, substantial or even seminal.

The following two sections of this biographical sketch detail some of the professional accomplishments of Paul Krugman. The first section deals with contributions to the theory of international economics (including, but not limited to, the new trade theory), and the second with contributions to economic policy making. This second domain is one that many contemporary academic economists tend to ignore.[7] But these are important and, indeed, have the potential to define

---

6. On these same points, see Dixit (1993) as well as Krugman (1993a).
7. Including, I might note, Avinash Dixit in his recent review of Paul Krugman's professional contributions (Dixit 1993).

the life and work of an important figure at least as much as the more abstract contributions. Of course, it can be difficult at times to separate these two sets, contributions to theory and contributions to policy, because their intersection clearly is nonempty. But I shall try, and where the separation is impossible, I shall simply bow to that reality.

KRUGMAN'S MAJOR CONTRIBUTIONS TO THE THEORY OF INTERNATIONAL ECONOMICS

The first thing to say about Krugman's contributions to international economic theory is that they have been many. Indeed, it is probably too restrictive to confine this discussion to the domain of 'international' economics; he has made significant contributions to other subfields as well. However, because Krugman is known as an 'international economist' and because others who suffer from also being members of this obscure professional category tend to take some pride in the fame that Krugman has brought to their subprofession, I shall stick with this classification. And, because this professional biography is article length rather than book length and some subjects are treated in moderate depth, the treatment here is necessarily somewhat selective.

Krugman first garnered wide attention with an article that extended the preexisting Dixit–Stiglitz model of monopolistic competition into the domain of international trade (Krugman 1979).[8] To condense this article into a single sentence, it provided a theoretical explanation of the by-then well-documented intraindustry trade in differentiated products among advanced nations, a type of trade not well explained by traditional Heckscher–Ohlin models of comparative advantage in international trade. That intraindustry trade could be occasioned by product differentiation – one of the insights of Krugman 1979 – had already been suggested by two European economists, Jacques Drèze and Staffan Linder; the latter is acknowledged by Krugman but he seems to have been unaware of the earlier effort by the former.[9] That economies of scale might play a role in

---

8. Krugman (1979) is reprinted in Krugman (1990) along with several related papers. This paper is one that Krugman had difficulty in placing. Indeed, as the story goes, it was published in the *Journal of International Economics* by then-editor Jagdish Bhagwati over negative recommendations by two referees. Bhagwati himself in fact has expressed some reservations about his decision, largely because the 'new' trade theory has given some comfort to protectionists (see discussion later in the text). Even so, Krugman (1979) is now considered one of the early classics of the new international trade theory (see Gans and Shepherd 1994).
9. See Drèze 1960 and Linder 1961. I am grateful to Charles Kindleberger and Raymond Vernon for pointing out to me the former.

intraindustry trade in differentiated products – another of the insights – was explored by, *inter alia*, Bela Balassa, Herbert Grubel and Irving Kravis.[10] Krugman's contribution was to create a plausible model that formalized this earlier, but often imprecise, thinking.

As noted, Krugman's basic model was built on the results of Avinash Dixit and Joseph Stiglitz.[11] These results provide a formal treatment of Edward Chamberlain's model of monopolistic competition wherein a series of producers each monopolize production of one variant of the same product. In this model, every producer is operating in a range of the relevant cost function where returns to scale are increasing. The products are sufficiently differentiated so that each producer perceives that he or she faces a downward-sloping demand curve; however, there are no barriers to entry to new producers of additional varieties of the product, and there is sufficient substitutability among the varieties that all monopolistic profits in equilibrium are bid away. The Dixit–Stiglitz formulation of monopolistic competition relies on an assumption that each firm produces at constant marginal costs but with a fixed cost (the model is static, so there is no issue of the time frame in which the cost is fixed), so that average costs can be represented by a rectangular hyperbola in cost/output space. The advantage of this is that the profit-maximizing price for the ith product can be written as a simple function of its marginal cost and elasticity of demand ϵ_i:

$$p_i = \frac{\epsilon_i}{\epsilon_i - 1} c_i.$$ (1)

One should note that the only difference between this and the standard relationship for monopoly pricing is that in equation (1) marginal cost is constant; the elasticity of demand remains a function of quantity produced and cannot be determined from equation (1).

Dixit and Stiglitz further assume that all consumers maximize the same utility function and that it is symmetric in the differentiated product; if q_i is a representative individual consumer's demand for the ith product (remember, this is produced by only the ith firm) this consumer's utility is given by:

$$U = \sum_{i=1}^{n} v(q_i).$$ (2)

The function $v(q_i)$ is the same for all q_i (an unrealistic assumption) and must be concave and twice differentiable. Thus, the utility function is 'additive' so that the

---

10. See Grubel 1970 and Kravis 1971.
11. Dixit and Stiglitz 1977. However, the results presented here follow Krugman's minor reformulation of the Dixit–Stiglitz model.

marginal utility of an extra unit of consumption of the ith product is unaffected by the consumption of any of the other variants of the product. This is of course unrealistic: one would expect for differentiated products that this marginal utility would decline as Σq_j, $i \neq j$, increases. The model is sensitive to this assumption.

Concavity requires that $v'' < 0$, whereas for a consumer's income constraint to be binding it must be that $v' > 0$. From the first-order conditions for the solution of the consumer's budget constrained utility maximization, $v'(q_i) = \lambda p_i$ (where λ is the shadow price of income) and an additional assumption that no firm's output decision affects significantly consumer income (so that $\partial \lambda / \partial q_i = 0 \ \forall i$), then, for the ith firm,

$$\epsilon_i = -\frac{v_{q_i}}{v_{q_i q_i} q_i}. \tag{2a}$$

The condition of no profits is

$$p_i x_i - \alpha w - c_i x_i = 0 \tag{3}$$

where α is the fixed labor input for the ith product $(\forall i)^{12}$, w is the wage rate (common to all workers) and x_i is the total amount of this product produced; because the same utility function applies to all consumers (there are L of these, equal also to the number of workers), $x_i = Lq_i$. If β is the unit input of labor for the ith product $\forall i$, then $\beta w = c_i$. The no-profit condition and equation (1) can then be rewritten as

$$\frac{p_i}{w} = \beta + \frac{\alpha}{x_i} = \beta + \frac{\alpha}{Lq_i} \tag{3a}$$

and

$$\frac{p_i}{w} = \frac{\beta \epsilon_i}{\epsilon_i - 1}. \tag{1a}$$

Equations (1a) and (3a) jointly determine the demand faced by the ith firm. From these and the assumption of factor exhaustion,[13] the number of products N can be determined as

12. This fixed labor input could be likened to a fixed capital cost.
13. There is only one factor, labor, that is exhausted. Neither Dixit and Stiglitz nor Krugman comment on whether or not the labor exhaustion violates any labor laws!

$$N = \frac{L}{\alpha + \beta x} = \frac{L}{\alpha + \beta L q} \qquad (4)$$

where now the subscripts on q and x are dropped because the symmetry of the utility function (2) ensures that all products that are produced are consumed (and hence produced) in equal quantities.

The model as described thus far is, as already indicated, largely that of Dixit and Stiglitz rather than Krugman. It is easy to find fault with the model. For example, what is the source of the fixed-cost element in the individual firm's cost functions upon which the model's functioning depends? Is it R&D? If so, would not the fixed cost of a new variant be less than that of the original product? Treatment of product differentiation is, to say the least, a bit bare-bones. There is no detail of how and why products are differentiated, and thus potential richness is lost. Some element of reality might be captured by assigning different marginal and/or fixed costs to different variants of the product, but the cost would be considerably more involved calculations with no real gain in insight. The additivity of the utility function has already been noted as problematic.

Despite its shortcomings, the model is useful because it is tractable. The shortcomings largely arise from the usual tradeoff between that which is tractable and that which describes fully the real world.

Krugman's major contribution was to extend the model to explain international trade in the differentiated goods. The basic argument is that if two markets, each previously closed to producers located in the other, are suddenly opened to trade (which is assumed to be free of transport and other transactions costs), the effect is as though in each market the labor supply were augmented. Thus, the relevant analysis pertains to labor supply augmentation. If labor supply augmentation leads to new varieties of the product being produced, then because every consumer in both markets would consume the same bundle of product variants but each firm would still specialize in the production of one variant, the end result would be trade between the two markets.

That labor supply augmentation does in fact lead to new product varieties being introduced is in principle straightforward; the assumption of diminishing marginal utility ($V_{qq} < 0$) in each product variety virtually ensures it. Nonetheless, it is messy to show it analytically. Krugman in fact makes the case diagrammatically, without resort to algebra. The algebraic case can be made by differentiating both sides of equation (4) with respect to L (and noting that $q = q(L)$) to get

$$\frac{dN}{dL} = \frac{\alpha - \beta L^2 \dfrac{dq}{dL}}{(\alpha + \beta q L)^2}. \qquad (5)$$

Thus, if $dq/dL \leq 0$, the result is unambiguous that an increase in L would lead to an increase in N.

To determine the sign of dq/dL, one can solve simultaneously equations (1a), (2a) and (3a) (and recalling that the own price elasticity of a commodity is signed positive by convention but in fact is negative) to obtain

$$L = \frac{\alpha}{\beta} \frac{v_q + q v_{qq}}{q^2 v_{qq}}.$$

Differentiating this, we get the following

$$\frac{dL}{dq} = -\frac{\alpha}{(\beta q^2 v_{qq})^2}(q^2 + 2q)(v_q v_{qqq}). \tag{6}$$

If v_{qqq} is zero (which holds if utility is quadratic), the condition $dq/dL \leq 0$ is met and Krugman's result holds. Otherwise, the condition $v_{qqq} > 0$ would seem to be necessary. This holds for a number of functions that have the desired properties ($v_q > 0$ and $v_{qq} > 0$), e.g., a hyperbolic function $v = 1 - 1/q$, $q > 1$. I do not know of any general theorem to the effect that a utility function must be such that $v_{qqq} \geq 0$, however.

What about welfare and distributional effects? Krugman explores these in a later article (Krugman 1981) which, in the view of this author at least, represents half a step backwards combined with a full step forwards. The reason for the step backwards is that Krugman moves away from the (fairly) general utility function as specified above and uses a more restrictive form. To explore distributional issues, he also introduces two classes of products, each of which is differentiated and is characterized by specialized labor factors. Indeed, the labor is so specialized that there is no labor mobility at all between the two industries. No effort is made here to go through the analytics. The key results regarding distributional effects are: (i) both types of worker gain if there is a lot of product differentiation but one factor might lose relative to the other if differentiation is slight; (ii) both types gain if factor endowments in the two trading partners are sufficiently similar, but one type might lose if factor endowments are dissimilar. The key effect regarding welfare gains is that, because the number of products increases, there must be a gain. But this result is (or should be) evident from the model presented above; given constant income of an individual and the properties of the utility function of equation (2) above (specifically, diminishing marginal utility for the ith product), if $N_1 > N_2$, it is clear that when both sides of the equation are subject to the same income constraint and the prices of the N_1 or N_2 products are all the same, then

$$U_1 = \sum_{i=1}^{N_1} v(q_i) > U_2 = \sum_{i=1}^{N_2} v(q_i).$$

Also in the same genre as the 1979 article is a 1983 article written with James Brander (Brander and Krugman 1983) in which two rival firms might engage in 'reciprocal dumping', that is, each sells in the other's market at below the price charged in the home market in the absence of imports. The model is based upon imperfect (in this case, duopoly) competition rather than scale economies.[14] Each of two firms produces at constant average and marginal cost c, but incurs a transport cost to service the foreign market such that the cost in that market is c/g, $0 > g > 1$. It is easily worked out that under a Cournot conjecture there are demand curves in the two markets such that both firms will sell in both markets; Brander and Krugman show that the same result can be obtained with conjectures other than a Cournot conjecture. Pure waste is generated by the reciprocal dumping, because each firm could in principle supply its home market at the price with trade. But neither firm would choose to do so (rather, in the absence of trade, each would sell at the monopoly price). Thus, there are gains as the result of increased competition. Brander and Krugman demonstrate that the gains from increased competition outweigh the costs of unnecessary transport if the latter are not too high (i.e., g is close to 1).

Krugman's contribution in the 1979 and related articles was to introduce scale economies and, later, imperfect competition into a tractable model of international trade and, in particular, models of intraindustry trade. As already noted, intraindustry trade among industrial economies constitutes an anomaly if international trade is caused by differences in factor proportions (as predicted by the Heckscher–Ohlin model), and this anomaly had, well before Krugman, been scrutinized by economists. Likewise, that scale economies or imperfect competition might play some role in the determination of international trade had long been considered by economists but whatever these roles might be, they had largely defied efforts at formal modeling. Krugman's contribution was thus something of a 'twofer', incorporation of scale economies and imperfect competition into models that were tractable and provided plausible explanations of intraindustry trade. Again, it cannot be emphasized enough that Krugman in this regard did not work in a vacuum and that a number of other researchers were pursuing similar lines of inquiry. Nonetheless, Krugman's work tends to stand out for its elegance, clarity, and simplicity.

---

14. The basic logic is developed in an earlier article by James Brander (Brander 1981).

What might be Krugman's most controversial article (or at least not counting the one in *Foreign Affairs* cited in the introduction of this essay) is a 1984 piece in which he develops a model wherein, by granting protection to an industry subject to increasing returns *and* oligopolistic competition, the result is that the exports of the industry expand. The key assumption is that *marginal* costs decline with output; in the 1979 article, marginal costs were constant but average costs declined with output, because of the existence of a fixed cost. The logic of the 1984 model then becomes very straightforward. By granting protection in the form of, say, a tariff, the government raises the costs of the foreign rival exporting to its home market. Price in that market goes up as a simple consequence of the dynamics of the Cournot conjecture on which the model is based, but also the home firm is able to expand output and thereby reduce marginal costs. These reduced costs are reflected in their costs in the export market; their price will decline and its market share will increase. Krugman works through three cases that appear to be different but in fact are all similar in term of the analytics: where the economies of scale are static (marginal cost depends upon current rate of output), where marginal costs are constant with respect to output but decline with a prior investment in R&D, and where the economies of scale are dynamic (marginal costs decline with cumulative output – also termed 'learning effects'). For the latter two cases, Krugman is dependent upon analytics developed by Michael Spence (Spence 1981).

The reason why this article is controversial is because perhaps to a greater extent than any other it has provided fodder to neomercantilists who argue that the competitiveness of an industry can be enhanced via the granting of trade protection. Thus, it has been argued that Krugman's logic vindicates the policies allegedly followed by the Japanese Ministry of Trade and Industry to enhance the competitiveness of Japanese industries by closing these industries to foreign competition and who argue that the United States should do likewise, especially in the light of the 'Japanese challenge'.[15] Krugman himself rejects the idea (see, e.g., Krugman 1982b as well as Krugman 1994a), but mostly on empirical grounds. These are examined in the section that follows.

Krugman has made additional contributions to international trade theory, for example, by introducing elements from the new 'endogenous growth theory' (Krugman 1990), two graduate level textbooks co-authored by Elhanan Helpman (Helpman and Krugman 1985 and 1989), and many other works too numerous to

---

15. Another line of reasoning often cited by the same neomercantilists is that presented in Brander and Spencer (1985); often this second line of reasoning is attributed to Krugman (see e.g., Prestowitz in Prestowitz et. al. 1994).

list here. Helpman and Krugman (1985) is considered by many to be something of a 'bible' of the new trade theory of the late 1970s and early 1980s.

Although not as numerous nor as influential as his contributions to international trade, Krugman has also made a number of important contributions to international money and finance. Most of these were written during the second half of the 1980s, a period when Krugman by his own testimony took a hiatus from working in the new trade theory. Almost all of these works were inspired by issues that were, at the time at least, of immediate policy relevance. The best of these articles are collected in Krugman (1992a). Here I take a look at two of the better of this collection of the best, one of which is simplicity itself, while the other relies on moderately advanced techniques of analysis.

Simplicity itself is the essence of Krugman (1989), where he examines the then very extant question of whether the decline in the US dollar was leading to a 'fire sale' on US assets. At the time, the United States was experiencing an unprecedented wave of inward direct investment, and many persons were concerned that US assets were being somehow picked up on the cheap by foreign investors. It later proved to be true that some of the most controversial sales of US assets to foreigners were cases where the foreign investor overpaid for the assets (I return to this issue in the section following), but this was not evident to many in 1989. Krugman's contribution was essentially to make two very simple points. First, if US assets are grossly undervalued, this would be apparent to many potential investors (domestic as well as foreign) and the resulting demand for these assets would bid prices up. Second, if an undervalued dollar does depress, in foreign currency prices, the price of a US asset, it equally depresses the flow of earnings to that asset (because this flow would be in those undervalued dollars). Thus, unless the foreign investor held some asymmetric information (i.e., not held by domestic investors) about future appreciation of the dollar, the asset would have equal value to foreign and domestic investors.

Not so simple is Krugman (1991a), an article long in the making. In this article, Krugman uses stochastic calculus-based techniques to examine the behavior of exchange rates within 'target zones'. A 'target zone' is a prespecified range within which monetary authorities will let an exchange rate vary but beyond which they will intervene to return the rate to the range. Although target zones were at the basis of the 'snake in tunnel' arrangements of the early (late 1970s) version of European monetary union, they first received serious analytic attention in Bergsten and Williamson (1983) and Williamson (1985). The main analytic conclusion derived from Krugman's model is that the existence of a target zone has a stabilizing effect on the exchange rate, in the sense that shocks in the velocity of money have a smaller effect on exchange rates than would be the case under a free float.

This is, of course, an interesting conclusion, but is it correct? As noted, the model depends upon the techniques of stochastic calculus. The velocity of money v in the model, in particular, is assumed to follow a continuous random walk (a 'Gauss–Wiener process'), such that $dv = \sigma dz$, where dz is a continuous random variable defined on a filtration $\mathscr{F}_t$ on a probability space such that z ($= z(t)$) is normally distributed with zero mean and unit variance. Use of Gauss–Wiener processes to model economic phenomena dates from the late 1960s and early 1970s, and the Black–Scholes–Merton valuation of call options on common stocks, where the logarithm of the price of a stock is assumed to follow a Gauss–Wiener process, has been enormously successful. However, Gauss–Wiener processes possess some properties that are very peculiar; their realizations are continuous but nondifferentiable (the latter because 'cusps' are dense in any subset of a realization, 'dense' used here in the topological sense), with the consequence that they are of unbounded variation.[16] (One property of these processes is that because they are nondifferentiable, one cannot write $dz(t) = (dz/dt)\ dt$, and hence, if f is a function of z and t, one cannot use the normal chain rule to derive df. A more complex rule, Ito's lemma, involving higher-order terms of the Taylor expansion of a function of z, must be employed. Most of the successful applications of stochastic calculus to economics have involved creative applications of Ito's lemma.) The only physical phenomenon that comes close to resembling a Gauss–Wiener process is the primordial white noise left over from the 'Big Bang' at the origin of the physical universe; even Brownian motion – the description of which led to early developments of stochastic calculus – is only approximately a Gauss–Wiener process. Whether any economic process is reasonably well modeled by such a process is a foundational issue that is not well explored, although there are efforts in this direction. To the extent that economic processes are well modeled by Gauss–Wiener processes, these would have to be ones wherein the underlying variable is subject to constant change; securities prices do in fact seem to be reasonably well modeled by a lognormally distributed random walk (but, in fact, a discrete process would clearly be a better model than a continuous one). Exchange rates, by contrast, seem to be mean reverting; a continuous mean-reverting random process (e.g., an Ornstein–Uhlenbeck process)

---

16. Unbounded variation means that the Lebesgue–Stieljes integral of the process (yielding the 'length' of the trajectory of 'z' as it evolves over time) is infinite for *any* t_1 and t_2, no matter how close these two points in time might be:

$$\forall t_1 < t_2,\ \int_A |dz(t)| = \infty \qquad A = [z_{t_1}, z_{t_2}]$$

It has been noted that if transactions costs are associated with any economic process of unbounded variation, no matter how small these costs, their total will be infinite!

is not subject to the simple tools of stochastic calculus used by Krugman.[17] Further, whether even such a process takes us close enough to the reality of exchange rate movement is open to question for the reasons touched upon here.

Following 1990, Krugman has moved back into the domain of his original work and with something of a vengeance. His new work, in the field of economic geography, asks in more general terms than the 'new trade theory' articles why certain economic activities tend to be clustered in regions (or, indeed, in cities) rather than spread more or less uniformly over geographic space. The new emphasis is on localized external economies of scale – that is, advantages of scale that are common to any of several producers so long as these producers are located in close geographic proximity to one another. The first of his published works in this vein (Krugman 1991b), is an easy read with many of the characteristics of his early work: simplicity, clarity and elegance. However, later extensions have entered into increasingly more sophisticated territory, involving models wherein equilibria undergo bifurcations of the sort found in the new theory of deterministic chaos. As indicated in the introduction of this article, Krugman is, as a result of this work, finding himself in a world of great mathematical complexity. Bifurcation theory is at the frontier of mathematics (note: it is at the frontier of *modern* mathematics, not the advanced applied mathematics that defines the frontier of most economics but in fact is at least a century old!). At the moment, Krugman's efforts are increasingly driven by the mathematics and, in contrast to his earlier work, the economic rationale for some of the models is often missing. What Krugman is hoping to do is to create something like a 'general theory of economic geography', out of which (perhaps) the earlier 'new trade theory' will emerge as a set of special cases. Will he make it? My own sense is that he is not there yet. But, of course, only time will tell the final result.

CONTRIBUTIONS TO ECONOMIC POLICY

Any discussion of Krugman's contributions to economic policy must begin where the last section left off with respect to Krugman (1984). This article, as noted earlier, has fortified greatly the intellectual arsenal of those who would use trade policy as a tool of industrial policy. Krugman's own rejection of such a neomercantilist approach is based largely on empirical studies that show small gains (or, in some cases, losses) to be had to nations that employ such policies,

---

17. Krugman in fact admits all of this; he notes first that 'There is no good economic reason for assuming a random walk on v' and, subsequently, notes that 'target zone models with some inherent autoregression' would be more realistic (but require the use of numerical methods).

combined with a sense that losses of the classical gains from trade would be great.[18] It is incumbent upon those who argue otherwise, that the 'new trade theory' does in fact warrant a new trade policy, to show that the empirical studies are wrong.

Krugman's own major contribution to the empirical literature is a study of the 16K dynamic random access memory (DRAM) microchip, conducted with Richard Baldwin (Baldwin and Krugman 1988). The major objective was to explore whether Japan gained by (allegedly) closing its borders to imports of these chips during the late 1970s. The main conclusion of the study was that Japan not only did not gain from market closure, but actually suffered net losses from pursuing this policy. This conclusion is contrary to those of a number of analysts who have studied Japan's Very Large Scale Integrated Circuit (VLSI) program in somewhat greater detail in terms of the actual events that took place but without utilizing the sophisticated empirical methodologies of Baldwin and Krugman (see, e.g., Borrus et al. 1983 and Tyson and Yoffie 1993). My own reaction is that while Baldwin and Krugman (1988) is a very thoughtful and creative piece of research (it has made me think about a number of things in ways that I had never done before), it leaves untouched a sufficient number of loose ends that one can reasonably question the main conclusions. Indeed, it strikes me that the critics of Krugman would not have lost the *Foreign Affairs* debate by so lopsided a score (see the introduction to this chapter) if they simply had gone after the loose ends in Baldwin and Krugman (1988). Indeed, the irony of it is that Baldwin and Krugman made it easy for the critics, for all (or at least most) of the loose ends are acknowledged in the introduction to their article!

Baldwin and Krugman (1988) in fact displays much of the virtuosity that has come to be associated with the works of Krugman and a number of the vices as well. The approach taken is to simulate the world 16K DRAM industry in a model that attempts to capture some important characteristics of the industry as it was in the late 1970s, for example, that production was subject to strong economies of learning, that the industry was oligopolistic in structure (but with upwards of ten major producers), that demand was fast growing, and that the market share of US producers in Japan was much lower than elsewhere, implying some sort of barriers to imports in Japan. Underlying the methodology used to simulate economies of learning is a result developed by Michael Spence (Spence 1981): that if product life expectancies are sufficiently short, so that future profits are not discounted, a

---

18. In this regard, it is important to note that in rejecting neomercantilist *trade* policies, Krugman does not necessarily reject all policy instruments contemplated in the 'new' trade theory. He has advocated, for example, greater government support for commercial research and development. Krugman's own views on neomercantilist trade policy are well summarized in Krugman (1992c).

producer can maximize profits over the life of a product by setting something that looks like marginal revenue equal something that looks like a marginal cost; this turns a potentially difficult dynamic optimization problem into a relatively simple static optimization. The result depends upon additional simplifying assumptions, for example, that demand is stationary with respect to time.[19] But, whereas Spence's original model postulates that there is a component of variable cost that declines as a function of total cumulative output of the product, Baldwin and Krugman specify a fixed capacity per producer (set at the beginning of the process) that yields a certain number of 'batches' of output. The key point is that each 'batch' yields only a certain percentage of nondefective DRAMs (and increasing yields indeed seems to be the right story for this product!) and that this percentage increases with cumulative output. Thus, over time, as yield increases, so does total supply, so that price is driven down.[20] The problem for the individual producer is thus to set capacity at the beginning of the period so as to maximize profit, taking into account the actions of other producers. To accomplish this last, Baldwin and Krugman introduce into their marginal revenue function a conjectural variant, and calibrate this so that, given exogenous estimates of the price elasticity of demand and of the slope of the yield curve and subject to a no-profit condition (so that there is no incentive for either entry or exit from the industry), the number of firms given by the model is equal to the number actually observed in the industry.[21] The authors admit that the conjectural variations approach leaves much to be desired, but it is retained for reasons of tractability.

To make their model computable, Baldwin and Krugman make additional simplifying assumptions, for example, that demand in both Japan and the rest of the world (treated as an aggregate) can be specified by a constant elasticity demand function and that the elasticity is the same both in Japan and outside of it. This is a weak assumption both because of the specificity of the demand curve and of the use of the same elasticity figure in both markets; indeed, I would

---

19. Spence demonstrated his result using the classical calculus of variations, an accomplishment to which I take off my hat. The problem can be tackled, of course, using Pontryagin's principle, which enables more formidable versions of the problem to be explored, such as discounting and nonstationary demand. Solutions to these versions generally depend, however, upon specification of specific functional forms for demand and cost, whereas Spence's result holds for a quite general class of functional forms. Also, as is well known from optimal control theory, the solutions usually are not of closed form, and hence must be approximated by numerical techniques. The simplifying assumptions of no discounting and stationary demand result in separability of the time and state variables so that closed form solutions are possible.

20. In contrast, Spence's result is that, to maximize profits, the producer sets marginal revenue equal to marginal cost of the last unit of product sold, implying a constant price (and constant rate of output) across the whole product life cycle.

21. Baldwin and Krugman assume that products of different producers are perfect substitutes and that the only transactions costs are associated with export.

question whether the implicit assumption of a time-stationary demand function is appropriate for this industry.

Overall, then, there is much scope for criticism of the Baldwin and Krugman methodology. But at the same time it must be acknowledged that, for all of the simplification and weaknesses, it does capture important aspects of the industry that are intrinsically difficult to handle in a formal model. Furthermore, and importantly, whatever error in the results of the simulations as a result of the simplifications does not necessarily bias the results in an identifiable direction, that is, improvements in the model might as easily show additional losses to Japan as gains.

Why then did Krugman's critics miss the boat by not criticizing the model? The reason has little to do with possible errors made by Baldwin and Krugman in measuring what they set out to measure, but rather in what they did not try to measure. As they themselves acknowledge, much of the gains to Japan might have been exogenous to the production of 16K DRAMs, for example, gains that came in the form of some sort of externality or of knowhow that spills over from one generation of DRAM to another (or that spills over into the production of a different category of integrated circuit). The latter type of gain almost surely existed – manufacturing knowhow generated by the production of 16K DRAMs almost surely gave its holders some sort of competitive edge in the production of 64K DRAMs – and Baldwin and Krugman's model would not pick up any resulting benefits to Japan. Whether there were any external benefits (that is, ones captured by parties other than producers or users of the product) is, at root, unknowable. But if there were any of these, they too would not be picked up by the model. The reason why these potential benefits are omitted is because they cannot be accurately measured. However, their omission clearly biases the results: any such benefits are an unmitigated blessing, untempered by any offsetting costs.

Having said this, I hasten to note that Baldwin and Krugman's finding that import protection for 16K DRAMs did not yield net benefits to the Japanese economy is consistent with other empirical research on the costs and benefits of 'strategic trade policies'. (See, for example, the other articles in Feenstra (ed.) 1988). Indeed, the empirical evidence is sufficiently robust (and consistent) against the benefits of neomercantilist policies that the onus surely must rest with those who would have the United States adopt such policies to show that positive externalities will be generated in magnitudes sufficient to offset the measurable net costs. Thus, while Krugman's critics might have scored points by raising the weaknesses in the empirical studies, they probably could not thus have actually won the debate.

Krugman's contribution to economic policy goes beyond work related to the competitiveness issue. His 1989 co-authored book *Foreign Direct Investment in the United States* (Graham and Krugman 1989) surely did much to add a rational note to what was becoming a hysterical debate over foreign-controlled firms operating in the United States, although for obvious reasons it is presumptuous of me to claim this. His writings in the field of international finance have largely been motivated by issues of immediate policy concern, as noted above, and these writings have often provided policy makers with clear and pertinent advice with respect to murky problems. One of the best of these works from a policy perspective (Krugman 1991c), was also one of his last in this area. This was a synthesis of evidence on whether the process of trade adjustment to exchange rate movements actually works along the lines of neoclassical analysis (it does!).

His 1991 *The Age of Diminished Expectations*, by contrast, asked interesting questions but provided little in the way of answers (why has productivity slowed down? We do not really know, but it is nonetheless one of the central issues of our time). Nonetheless, this book played a role both as a guide to little understood issues that greatly affect our times and as a clear exposition of what economics is about. Work done by Krugman during the 1992 election campaign on the growing disparities in the distribution of income was flawed, as he himself has acknowledged (the underlying data were not adjusted for cyclical effects). Krugman's analysis nonetheless received wide publicity (largely courtesy of Sylvia Nasar of *The New York Times*), including a sympathetic hearing before the Joint Economic Committee of Congress, and undeniably gave Bill Clinton one of his more potent campaign issues. There are those who would argue that the vehemence with which Krugman has written about (i.e., mostly against) Clinton's economic philosophies reflects the fact that Clinton never paid back the favor. But, while there may be some merit to this argument, I must note that Krugman really does object to aspects of these philosophies. And, although Krugman's analysis was undeniably flawed, I am told by experts in the field of income distribution that his conclusions were nonetheless right.

A FEW ADDITIONAL NOTES

Paul Krugman has for most of his professional career been on the faculty of the Department of Economics at MIT, where he also received his doctorate. He did spend a few years as an assistant professor at Yale, and he took leave of absence from MIT during the early 1980s to spend one year as Senior Economist on the staff of the President's Council of Economic Advisors and a second leave of absence in 1992 to spend one year at the Harvard Business School. In January 1994 he took leave of absence for a third time to spend a semester at the Stanford Business School but, this time, the leave was to prove permanent. Beginning in

July 1994 – only one month earlier than the date of this writing – he joined the Stanford University economics department on a full-time, long-term basis.

The clear question for Paul Krugman is, having been anointed before attaining the age of forty by no less an institution than *The Economist* as the 'most influential economist of his time', can he keep up the pace he has maintained for a decade and a half for another three decades or so? The record of intellectuals who have reached superstardom at an early age is, alas, not encouraging. Albert Einstein spent most of his last forty years on largely fruitless efforts to develop a 'unified field theory'. This theory was never developed. Norbert Wiener's evident brilliance did not diminish with age, but his creative output did. Beethoven went deaf and could not even hear the works he continued to produce. And, as noted in the introduction, Mozart died young, thus avoiding the issue altogether.

Along these lines, I must note that the record of Stanford itself is not wholly inspiring. Stanford has managed to lure numerous scholars at the top of their fields to its beautiful and sunny campus, but a number of these have chosen to spend their days hiking in the lovely hills and valleys to the immediate south and west of the campus to the detriment of scholarly output. After all, how can one work in a place where it never freezes but where the temperature never gets much above 80 degrees, where the air is clear and dry, and where the smell of fragrant eucalyptus trees is pervasive?

In spite of these handicaps, however, a lot of good work does get done at Stanford. And my own feeling about Paul is that he will be one of those who continue to produce insightful research. After all, how many big name economists have actually increased the level of mathematical content in their work as they aged? Paul has; one of his latest articles is to be published in the *Journal of Economic Theory*, a first for him at the age of forty-one. My impression is that most persons who publish in this journal do so during their late twenties and early thirties and then go off to do more useful (but less elegant) things.

Whatever it is that drives Paul, I must admit I do not know. But whatever it is, he clearly is not yet satisfied with himself. My guess is that he will continue to drive himself and hence that there is more to come.

KRUGMAN'S MAJOR WRITINGS

(1979), 'Increasing Returns, Monopolistic Competition, and International Trade', *Journal of International Economics*, 9, 469-79.
(1980), 'Scale Economies, Product Differentiation, and the Pattern of Trade', *American Economic Review*, 70, 950-9.

(1981), 'Intraindustry Specialization and the Gains from Trade', *Journal of Political Economy*, **89**, 959-74.

(1983) (with James A. Brander), 'A Reciprocal Dumping Model of International Trade', *Journal of International Economics*, **15**, 313-21.

(1984), 'Import Protection as Export Promotion: International Competition in the Presence of Oligopoly and Economies of Scale', in H. Kierzkoushi (ed.), *Monopolistic Competition in International Trade*, Oxford and New York: Oxford University Press.

(1985) (with Elhanan Helpman),*Market Structure and Foreign Trade*, Cambridge, Mass.: The MIT Press.

(1988) (with Richard E. Baldwin), 'Market Access and International Competition: A Simulation Study of 16K Random Access Memories', in Robert Feenstra (ed.), *Empirical Research in International Trade*, Cambridge, Mass.: The MIT Press.

(1989), 'The J-Curve, the Fire Sale, and the Hard Landing', *American Economic Review*, Papers and Proceedings issue, **79**, 31-5.

(1989) (with Edward M. Graham), *Foreign Direct Investment in the United States*, Washington, DC: The Institute for International Economics; third edition, 1994

(1989) (with Elhanan Helpman), *Trade Policy and Market Structure*, Cambridge, Mass.: The MIT Press.

(1990), 'Endogenous Innovation, International Trade, and Growth', in Krugman (ed.), *Rethinking International Trade*, Cambridge, Mass.: The MIT Press.

(1991a), 'Target Zones and Exchange Rate Dynamics', *Journal of Political Economy*, **56**, 669-82.

(1991b), *Geography and Trade*, Cambridge, Mass.: The MIT Press.

(1991c), *Has the Adjustment Process Worked?*, Washington, DC: The Institute for International Economics.

(1992a), *Currencies and Crises*, Cambridge, Mass.: The MIT Press.

(1992b), 'Does the New Trade Theory Require a New Trade Policy', *The World Economy*, **15**, 423-42.

(1993a), 'How I Work', *The American Economist*, **37**, 25-31.

(1994a), 'Competitiveness: A Dangerous Obsession', *Foreign Affairs*, **73**, 28-44.

(1994b), 'Proving My Point', *Foreign Affairs*, **73**, 198-203.

OTHER REFERENCES

Balassa, Bela (1967), *Trade Liberalization Among Industrial Countries: Objectives and Alternatives*, New York: McGraw Hill.

Bergsten, C. Fred and John Williamson (1983), 'Exchange Rates and Trade Policy', in William R. Cline (ed.), *Trade Policy in the 1980s*, Washington, DC: Institute for International Economics.

Borrus, Michael, James Millstein and John Zysman (1983), 'US–Japanese Competition in the Semiconductor Industry', University of California (Berkeley) Institute for International Studies, *Policy Papers in International Affairs*, **17**.

Brander, James A. (1981), 'Intra-industry Trade in Identical Commodities', *Journal of International Economics*, **11**, 1-14.

Brander, James A. and Barbara J. Spencer (1985), 'Export Subsidies and International Market Share Rivalry', *Journal of International Economics*, **18**, 83-100.

Dixit, Avinash K. (1993), 'In Honor of Paul Krugman: Winner of the John Bates Clark Medal', *Journal of Economic Perspectives*, **7**, 173-88.

Dixit, Avinash K. and Joseph E. Stiglitz (1977), 'Monopolistic Competition and Optimum Product Diversity', *American Economic Review*, **67**, 297-308.

Drèze, Jacques (1960), 'Quelques Reflections Sereines sur l'Adaptation de l'Industrie Belge au Marché Commun Européen', *Comptes Rendus des Travaux de la Société Royale d'Economie Politique de Belgique*, December.

Feenstra, Robert (ed.) (1988), *Empirical Research in International Trade*, Cambridge, Mass.: The MIT Press.

Gans, Joshua S. and George B. Shepherd (1994), 'How Are the Mighty Fallen: Rejected Classic Articles by Leading Economists', *Journal of Economic Perspectives*, **8**, 165-9.

Grubel, Herbert G. (1970), 'The Theory of Intra-industry Trade', in I.A. McDougall and R.H. Snape (eds), *Studies in International Economics*, Amsterdam: North Holland.

Kravis, Irving (1971), 'The Current Case for Import Limitations', Commission on International Trade and Investment Policy, *United States Economic Policy in an Interdependent World*, Washington, DC: US Government Printing Office.

Linder, Staffan (1961), *An Essay on Trade and Transformation*, Stockholm: Almquist & Wiksell.

McMillion, Charles W. (1994), 'Paul Krugman Does a Rollins', MBG Information Services (newsletter).

Prestowitz, Clyde V. Jr., Lester C. Thurow, Rudolph Scharping, Stephen S. Cohen and Benn Steil (1994), 'The Fight Over Competitiveness: A Zero-Sum Debate?', *Foreign Affairs*, **73**, 186-97.

Schrage, Michael (1994), 'To an MIT Maven, "Competitiveness" is Just Clinton's Voodoo Economics', *The Washington Post*, March 11, D3.

Spence, A. Michael (1981), 'The Learning Curve and Competition', *Bell Journal of Economics*, **12**, 49-70.

Tyson, Laura d'Andrea and David B. Yoffie (1993), 'Semi-conductors: From Manipulated to Managed Trade', in David B. Yoffie (ed.), *Beyond Free Trade: Firms, Governments, and Global Competition*, Boston, Mass.: Harvard Business School Press.

8. William Lazonick

Fred Carstensen

The 1993 Nobel Prize in Economic Science went to two economic historians, Robert Fogel and Douglass North. The work that won the prize for both Fogel and North fits firmly and comfortably within the neoclassical paradigm that has dominated economic scholarship for at least the last fifty years. Even so, the award must have surprised most economists; economic history has largely ceased to be a part of the required or expected training of an economist, and many would suggest that economic history has little to offer economic theory. The work of William Lazonick, brought together in three recent books (Lazonick 1990, 1991a 1992), offers a vigorous, voluminous, articulate dissent to that view. Lazonick combines a telling critique of the narrowness of much contemporary economic analysis with a compellingly nuanced history of the shifts in competitive advantage in the late nineteenth- and early twentieth-century cotton-spinning industry to construct a sweeping argument about the critical importance of institutional constraints and social relationships in determining national competitive capabilities over time. He proposes to explain why 'those national economies that had gained international dominance on the basis of one mode of economic coordination ... have had difficulty responding to new competition based on more highly organized institutional structures'. He promises to offer 'a theory of the innovative business organization that provides the foundations for explaining shifts in international industrial leadership and changes in the wealth of capitalist nations'. In Hegelian (Marxian) style, he argues forcefully that there is a clear, unambiguous answer: 'history shows this changing institutional reality is characterized by the growing importance of planned coordination within the business organization and the growing dominance of the business organization over the determination of economic outcomes' (Lazonick 1991a, pp. 15-17). This is heady stuff; Lazonick deserves serious attention precisely because he, unlike most economists, is willing to ask – and answer – the Smithian question: what contexts create and sustain those innovative processes that generate the wealth of a nation? That the answer he gives neither flows comfortably from his own historical research nor builds on the recognition that the market as it functions in the real world – as opposed to the caricature central to neoclassical analysis – is itself a social construct, underlines the need for more economists to join and thus enlarge this dialogue.

Lazonick's disaffection from mainstream, neoclassical analysis began early, as an undergraduate at the University of Toronto. By 1969, after stints as a graduate student at the London School of Economics and the University of Geneva, he 'had come to the realization that understanding economics and understanding the economy were not necessarily the same endeavors'. Indeed, he declared to 'anyone who would listen that "the price system" had to be studied as a set of social relationships'; he came to the central belief that 'to comprehend why and how a modern economy is successful, economists must be able to tell a story of the impact of social relationships on economic outcomes' (Lazonick 1991b, pp. 3-5). In particular, the neoclassical 'idealization of an economy that gives free vent to individualistic behavior' leaves neoclassical theory with 'no way of comprehending why, in a so-called market economy, a business organization that brings together thousands and tens of thousands of people could be anything but a burdensome market imperfection, much less an institution that is central to the process of economic development'. More broadly, he charges that the 'methodological obsession with static equilibrium means that economists normally lack the training to analyze the process of economic development'; that they have 'a trained incapacity to understand the central features of a modern economy'. He found particularly offensive the picture of 'passive and powerless business firms portrayed in the many courses in microeconomics' he took during his studies (Lazonick 1991b, pp. 1-5). Critically, 'mainstream economics contains no theory of innovation and no theory of competitive advantage', it lacks 'a theory of how business organization and technological change interact dynamically to develop the economy' (Lazonick 1991a, pp. 17, 312). As a result, 'economists concerned with estimating differential rates of economic growth ... define the "residual" as everything that commonsense tells them is important but, for lack' of such a theory, 'they can neither measure nor understand' (Lazonick 1992, p. 121). Despite such forceful statements, and in spite of his lengthy, even distracting critiques of specific neoclassical economists such as Chamberlin and Coase, Lazonick carries his general critique of neoclassical analysis no further (ignoring even such invitingly easy and rhetorically significant targets as Pareto optimality). He simply declares his intention to fill that theoretical void, laying down 'a theory of the innovative business organization that provides the foundations for explaining shifts in international industrial leadership and changes in the wealth of capitalist nations' (Lazonick 1991a, p. 16).

For Lazonick, such a theory must be 'historically relevant' (Lazonick 1992, p. vi), and thus necessarily approached through historical study. Specifically, it must explain that most challenging of economic phenomena often (remarkably) overlooked by economists: the extraordinary disparities in national economic performance and the changes in international economic leadership over the past hundred years – from Britain to the United States to Japan. Historical analysis should lay bare the mechanisms that conferred competitive advantage on one industry, permitting it to surpass competitors. He undertakes precisely such a study to reveal why the Lancashire cotton textile industry lost its competitive position, with American firms adopting superior technology before World War One, and then the Japanese becoming the world leaders by the 1930s. Identifying the institutional constraints that shaped the shop-floor relationships between managers, workers, and choice of process technology (that is, production technique as opposed to say product design or system of distribution) leads Lazonick to insist that such relationships underlie not just industry performance, but also national competitiveness. More than that, he argues, government plays a fundamental role in shaping both the context in which the business organization functions and how that organization structures itself. Thus, he maintains that 'the institutions of planned coordination that have been responsible for Japan's rise to international industrial leadership ... represent[s] not so much a departure from U.S. experience as a more thoroughgoing elaboration of the institutions of planned coordination that had previously brought leadership to the U.S.' (Lazonick 1991a, p. 12).

Lazonick's central argument has five parts, in which one can see intersections with Karl Marx, Joseph Schumpeter, Alfred Chandler and Alfred Marshall. First, organizational form, particularly the structure of the relationship between managers and workers, is a prime determinant of performance, with the form itself flowing from the historical process. As a result, the organization form is both path dependent and frames the production function that it faces; the function is not exogenous. Second, technological choice and innovative processes are endogenous; managers and workers, in the proper context, determine the rate and direction of innovation. Third, the dominant and dynamic sector of the economy, and therefore the sector that accounts for economic growth, has high fixed costs, which can only be sustained by high-volume production. This in turn requires creation of a large, stable, hierarchical organization that can both effectively maintain a dominant or at least large market share and search out appropriate production processes and product innovations to preserve that position over time. Fourth, over time planned coordination and constructive participation by employees within large organizations and between legally distinct but closely linked firms has increasing advantages in generating technological change, raising productivity, and thus generating economic growth compared to the un-coordinated, rivalrous conduct found in neoclassical markets. This participation progressively embraces both a larger proportion of employees, including blue-collar workers, and a wider array of distinct firms, which shifts competitive advantage from the 'managerial capitalism' of the United States to the 'collective capitalism' of Japan. Fifth, government plays a central role in shaping the organizational forms available to enterprise and by defining internal employment relationships. Taken collectively, Lazonick's focus on innovation, productivity growth and economic development occurring within an economic environment structured by government and organizational form argues that equilibrium is neither the normal state of markets nor even the state towards which markets gravitate. Indeed, Lazonick essentially eliminates the very concept of equilibrium, so central to neoclassical thought, as a relevant analytic concept. In its place, he articulates another theory of convergence, convergence in terms of organizational form.

Lazonick's most persuasive work is his historical studies of production relations, choice of technique, and labor productivity. He argues that the 'critical issue in analyzing British decline was not whether British managers optimized subject to constraints but whether the constraints that they faced in the British environment discouraged them from making investments in advanced technology'. The scholarly challenge is 'to identify the constraints on technological change' and thus explain 'why, as economic actors, British industrialists would not or could not overcome the constraints' (Lazonick 1992, p. viii). Probably his best single essay offers a compelling answer to this challenge, offering an explanation of why the Lancashire cotton-spinning industry evolved along a path that limited firms to adaptive responses within the existing mule-spinning technology, leaving their economic environment essentially unchanged, while Fall River (US) firms followed an innovative path that led to quick adoption of ring-spinners and changed their environment.

Lazonick opens his study by drawing on 'Marx's crucial contribution to the analysis of economic development ... the integration of a theory of production relations into a theory of market economy', with its 'emphasis on conflict and compromise' in the contest between managers and workers to control wages and working conditions (Lazonick 1981, p. 491). The outcome of that contest determines not just wages, but more critically 'factor proportions and factor productivity' of 'a given industrial process at any point in time'. Thus, even when using the same capital equipment – mule-spinners – production functions in different regions (or firms) will be different if industrial relations are different (Lazonick 1981, p. 499).

In Lancashire, the Amalgamated Association of Operative Cotton-Spinners and Twiners, organized in 1869, quickly became one of 'the best-organized and best-financed unions in Britain', controlling the availability of minders for self-acting mules and effectively enforcing industry-wide piece-rate wage lists. Critically, the minders controlled both an inside contracting system in which they hired and paid their assistants (usually two) and the maintenance, repair and technical adjustment of the mules that they supervised. This set of relationships meant that managers could not re-organize work along functional, specialized lines, had incomplete information about the internal structure of costs in the production process, and could not capture the benefits of introducing better machinery. The only variable that they had immediate, direct control over was the quality of the cotton fiber supplied to the minders, the cost of which ran from 45 to 80 percent of total spinning costs (Lazonick 1981, pp. 494, 501). As international competition increased in the 1880s, Lancashire managers bought a larger proportion of cheaper (i.e., shorter staple) grades of cotton. This resulted in more breakage during spinning, and in 1892 an industry-wide agreement set up a grievance procedure to settle disputes over 'bad spinning' but also limited cyclical wage fluctuations of the minders (Lazonick 1981, pp. 495, 501).

More productive ring-spinners later became available, but they put much higher tension on the fibers during spinning. This, in turn, required the use of costly higher-grade (longer staple) cotton fiber. But with the structure of industrial relations then in place, switching to ring-spinners and buying the high-grade fiber would not deliver higher profits to the Lancashire firms; virtually all benefit of improved productivity would flow to the minders through higher wages. As a result, Lancashire firms were slow to adopt the ring-spinner.

In Fall River, a comparative scarcity of labor (created in significant measure by the wide range of alternative employment opportunities available in America) led to high wages for minders, but it also led to managers dividing spinning-room work into much more highly specialized activities, including a separate cadre of mechanics to handle repair and technical adjustment. Thus American spinners, though highly paid, never established themselves at the top of a labor hierarchy, did not control critical information about production activities or cost, and influenced working conditions only through moving to a new job. Critically, American cotton managers had control over more variables of production and could capture a significant share of the benefit that flowed from the higher productivity that using higher-quality fiber inputs generated, but were still, in their treatment of workers, disciplined by the external environment of a highly competitive market for labor. Thus Lazonick argues that 'production relations in Lancashire encouraged the use of inferior cotton, [and the] production relations in New England encouraged [both] the use of higher quality cotton' and better working conditions. Fall River found adoption of ring-spinners easy, which pushed the technology of the American textile industry well ahead of the British (Lazonick 1981, pp. 509-10).

Though Lazonick does not use the terminology of power, the attempt to identify where workers and managers had the capacity to shape their own environment – i.e., where they had power – defines more clearly his distaste for the neoclassical framework. After all, central to the neoclassical conceptualization of the competitive market is the powerlessness of all actors – everyone becomes a price taker and must function in a purely reactive mode within the 'dictates' of the market. By definition no participant is able to influence the price at which a transaction takes place. This elimination of power from the analytical framework is fundamental to constructing models with predictable (stable) outcomes. The use of power, the action of unpredictable and indeterminate human will, fundamentally destabilizes model-based analysis. That we almost never observe competitive markets of the type the neoclassicists envision (and that good enterprise management often means avoiding such a competitive context) highlights the deficiency of that neoclassical model and underlines the validity of Lazonick's approach that takes power seriously.

Lazonick closes his comparative Lancashire–Fall River analysis with a devastating critique of the limitations of neoclassical analysis that assumes a single-production function with different factor intensities reflecting merely different relative factor prices. He shows that they had different isoquants, a difference which arose from different labor relations. Thus no industry necessarily has a purely 'technically determined' production isoquant: analysis must incorporate the human component of the nature of the relationship between management and labor (Lazonick 1981, pp. 511-12). There has been much argument between economic historians about the validity of Lazonick's analysis of the Lancashire and Fall River experiences, but this central analytical insight is fundamentally, pervasively valid: humans and the specific institutional context in which humans conduct their affairs matter. (For Lazonick's own assessment of the debate, see Lazonick 1992, pp. 83-133).

In collaboration with Bernard Elbaum, Lazonick expands this analysis to explain why 'the British economy, once the workshop of the world, seems to have become a victim to some century-long affliction' (Lazonick 1992, p. 3). The affliction has its roots, they argue, in

> the rigid persistence of economic and social institutions from the nineteenth-century era of relatively atomistic competition. In such countries as the United States, Germany, and Japan, successful twentieth-century economic development has been based on mass production methods and corporate forms of managerial coordination. But in Britain adoption of these modern technological and organizational innovations was impeded by inherited socioeconomic constraints at the levels of the enterprise, industry, and society. Entrenched institutional structures – including the structures of industrial relations, industrial organization, educational systems, financial intermediation, international trade, and state-enterprise relations –

constrained the ability of individuals, groups, or corporate entities to transform the productive system. (Lazonick 1992, p. 4)

Here again Lazonick (with Elbaum) presses the central argument that the issue is not the economic rationality of individual British managers or enterprises; they probably did act coherently within the economic environment they confronted, satisfying the requirements of constrained optimization. The critical issue, Lazonick insists, is the Schumpeterian concept of fundamentally transforming the existing environment, for 'the process of economic development is about how constraints on technological choices are overcome' (Lazonick 1992, p. ix). Lazonick has thus made a compelling – and fundamentally correct – case that there never was historically (and by inference there can never be) a neoclassical market, that every real 'market'– for specific goods, for different kinds of labor within specific industries or even firms, and so on – is *sui generis*. Every market in the real world is shaped and constrained by a staggering array of institutions, from the details of property, contract and tort law to the mechanisms of legal interpretation and enforcement, from the institutions that formulate public policy to the forms of industrial relations, from what constitutes legally permissible forms of advertising to requirements for financial disclosure and the organization of financial markets. But if this is the case, then any 'national' characteristics of the sort Elbaum and Lazonick have identified (largely correctly) must be linked to the specific context of particular industries. Oddly, Lazonick ignores the implications of this line of argument, which would fulfil his own declaration that markets are social relationships and must be studied as such.

Lazonick recognizes that the neoclassical conception of the market as a universal, standardized form of exchange is an abstraction, even caricature, of economic reality (that the neoclassical market is, thus, a myth), one that can at best describe only marginal or adaptive changes in a given economy but can never penetrate its fundamental characteristics or understand its institutional constraints. Even so, he resurrects the neoclassical concept to characterize the British economy as an archetypal market:

> when challenged by international competition based on textile technologies capable of achieving much higher levels of throughput than the traditional technologies used in Britain, the market-coordinate British industry had great difficulty in reorganizing itself through horizontal and vertical integration to permit the adoption of [these] technologies. (Lazonick 1992, p. ix)

Thus British failure is at one and the same time the result of institutional rigidity and excessive reliance on atomistic market processes. That Lazonick had earlier explained the capacity of those Fall River cotton managers to re-order their economic environment in part because of the vitality of the American labor market – that is, an efficient market process in neoclassical terms that facilitated Schumpeterian innovation – only underlines the logical tension within this analysis and suggests that Lazonick himself sometimes believes in the myth.

Lazonick acknowledges that the insights gained from the comparative study of British and American cotton spinning are insufficient to explain the emergence of the next dominant participant in world textile markets, the Japanese. Indeed, the Americans functioned behind a significant tariff barrier and played little role in export markets. Japanese success had been typically ascribed to cheap labor, but Lazonick recognizes that this argument by itself is untenable. India and other Asian countries offered labor even cheaper than in Japan, so there had to be a broader foundation to Japanese success. In developing this analysis, Lazonick adds two critical components to his broad argument. First, the Japanese firms, while utilizing a large number of comparatively short-term, low-skill female workers, began to invest in developing the capabilities of their core cadre of male production workers, a strategy that made sense when linked with the corporate commitment to lifetime employment for these workers. Thus the cotton manufacturing firms began the process of integrating shop-floor workers into the firm as respected, contributing members of the corporate family. Second, he argues that managed coordination between vertically related activities – here spinning and weaving – has inherent superiority to market coordination. Only such planned coordination could exploit the technological advantages of ring-spinning and the automatic loom. Seen in its context, then, the firm is not simply an efficient response to 'market failure', it is an organization for achieving that which 'markets' cannot achieve: the accumulation of competitive capabilities and generation of critical productivity-enhancing technological change. Summarizing the Japanese experience, Lazonick concludes:

> In the first two decades of this century, the larger employers, particularly in heavy industry, were pursuing policies to integrate skilled or 'key' workers into their organizations, in part to reduce labor mobility and in part to fend off the union organizers. ... Because Japanese employers were not engaged in a battle to obliterate craft control and, what is the other side of the same coin, because they were willing to develop the skills of their shop-floor workers in whatever manner could best serve the needs of production, they tied pay increases directly to length of service with the company as well as life-cycle needs and individual merit. Japanese management did not insist, as was the case in the United States both during and after the nonunion era, on paying for the job rather than for the worker. (Lazonick 1990, pp. 295-6)

By the mid-1980s, Lazonick recognizes that he needs to 'extricate' himself from the narrow study of the cotton industry if he was 'to advance [his] larger project of constructing a historically relevant theory of capitalist development'.

Two years as a research fellow at Harvard Business School (1984-86) gives him 'the opportunity and the stimulus to expand the scope of [his] research agenda'. This shift produces two substantial books: in 1990 *Competitive Advantage on the Shop Floor*; in 1991 *Business Organization and the Myth of the Market Economy*. The first uses his work on the cotton industry as a foundation for a broad comparison of 'the general evolution of shop-floor organization and technology in Britain, United States, and Japan' (Lazonick 1992, p. x). The second builds on this comparison to make 'a full-blown argument concerning the increasingly important role of managerial coordination at the level of the business enterprise for successful capitalist development'. Lazonick then adds an 'extended analysis of how and why Anglo-American economists have ... clung to the myth of the market economy' as the source of economic prosperity (Lazonick 1992, pp. x-xi). In 1992, Lazonick brings together his most significant writings of the previous dozen years, prefaced with a reflective review of his own evolution, in *Organization and Technology in Capitalist Development.*

Competitive Advantage generalizes the insights gained from the study of the spinning industry. Lazonick argues that, 'since the late nineteenth century, U.S. industrial employers have been obsessed with taking skills off the shop floor in an attempt to make any individual worker dispensable' (Lazonick 1990, p. 306). Indeed, 'American ideology has it that the shop-floor worker is a dispensable cog in the productive machine' (Lazonick 1992, p. 271). This also deprived workers of the ability to influence the relationship 'between effort and pay'. It meant that American firms 'failed to develop the capabilities among shop-floor workers that can enable them to utilize flexible machine technologies', technologies critical to late twentieth-century competitive success (Lazonick 1990, p. 306). But then, with the rise of industrial unionism in the 1930s, workers acquired seniority rights, thus transforming themselves into permanent employees while remaining, from management perspective, hourly workers. So American management ended up with the liabilities of permanent shop-floor employees, giving up 'substantial control over the organization of work and the allocation of workers', yet losing the benefits of a mutually accepted, long-term commitment, which had been established with salaried employees. Thus, 'rather than maintaining flexible control over the development and utilization of the human resources that had become attached to the firm, U.S. management became entrapped in the elaboration of a structure of job classifications and work rules that became increasingly difficult to change' (Lazonick 1990, p. 294).

In contrast, generalizing from the specific study of treatment of male textile workers and alluding to the later, and better known, lifetime employment in automotive and other industrial enterprises, Lazonick concludes that Japanese managers 'never questioned the importance of creating a structure of labor relations that permitted the skills of the Japanese worker to be developed and utilized' (Lazonick 1990, p. 297). This 'ability of Japanese enterprises to include shop-floor workers in the process of planned coordination without losing control over the pursuit of organization goals' found 'its basis in the historical willingness of Japanese employers to develop skills on the shop floor' (Lazonick 1990, p. 306). Lazonick observes that the

> foundation for cooperative labor–management relations is not merely the sharing-out of the value gains at a point in time but also the long-term commitment of the enterprise to do so – a commitment that is manifested by employment security, rising incomes, and better work conditions. In return for this commitment from the enterprise, workers supply sufficiently high levels of effort to the value-creation process to enable the firm to secure and maintain its dominant competitive position, and hence enable it to afford to live up to its commitments to them. (Lazonick 1990, p. 321)

Thus, the

> historical record of advanced capitalist development ... strongly suggests that capitalists enterprises ... willing and able to make use of effort-saving technological change to fashion cooperative labor–management relations have ... through the consequent development and utilization of their organizations's productive resources, been able to gain sustained competitive advantage. (Lazonick 1990, p. 321)

Thus Lazonick finds the core of national competitive advantage *in general* on the shop floor and in the nature of the relationship between management and production workers. He summarizes the comparative history, declaring that 'whereas Japanese managers have sought to put skills on the shop floor and American managers to take skills off the shop floor, British industrial employers, for lack of developed managerial structures, have simply left skills on the shop floor, thereby giving workers effective control over the flow of work, and hence over the utilization of the firm's investments' (Lazonick 1990, p. 307).

Such an argument does not simply appeal to the common (American) belief (fear) of the 1980s and early 1990s that the Japanese had, using their unique and thus non-reproducible culture and history, created a form of national economic organization and coordination that gave them a permanent, unassailable superiority over America, but directly attacks the theoretical legitimacy of competitive labor markets.

> Contrary to the policy implication of efficiency wage models, then, effort-saving technological change means that capitalist firms do not have to rely on the flexibility of the labor market to enforce discipline on their workers. Organization commitment manifests an alternative labor-relations strategy with far more powerful value-creating potential. In the conventional

economic models, in which effort-saving technological change in particular and economic development in general play no role, *labor market inflexibility is the source of the economic problem*; the firm looks to unemployment as the way to get reluctant workers to supply effort. In my model, with its central focus on effort-saving technology in the process of economic development, *labor market inflexibility is the solution to the economic problem*; the firm builds organizational commitment that makes possible the development and utilization of effort-saving technological change. (Lazonick 1990, pp. 321-2)

Two lines of argument animate *Business Organization*: Lazonick sustains his attack on the utility of traditional, neoclasscial, 'market-based' analysis; he extends and enrichs his argument supporting the centrality and criticality of business organization. Lazonick frames his discussion in terms of the 'proprietary capitalism' of Britain, overtaken by the 'managerial capitalism' of America, in turn supplanted by the 'collective capitalism' of Japan. 'Over the long run, these [Japanese] organizations have outperformed, and in my view will continue to outperform, their U.S. counterparts because of organizational integration that extends beyond the limits of the planned coordination of the specialized division of labor as practiced under U.S. managerial capitalism' (Lazonick 1991a, p. 37). Lazonick sees that 'the institutions of planned coordination that have been responsible for Japan's rise to international industrial leadership ... represent not so much a departure from U.S. experience as a more thorough-going elaboration of the institutions of planned coordination that had ... brought leadership to the US' (Lazonick 1991a, p. 12). Lazonick thus incorporates Chandler's powerful assessment of the historical importance of the rise of the large, hierarchical, managerial firm to enlarge his own argument from the relationship with shop-floor workers to the importance of the overall organization.

Organizational capabilities represent the power of planned and coordinated, specialized divisions of labor to achieve organizational goals. Through planned coordination, the specialized productive activities of masses of individuals can coalesce into a coherent collective force. Through planned coordination, organizations can integrate the various types of knowledge needed to develop new products and processes. Through planned coordination, organizations can speed the flow of work from purchased inputs to sold outputs, thereby enabling the enterprise to achieve lower unit costs. (Lazonick 1992, p. 265)

The Japanese have gone further than the Americans are able to, because they are not constrained by the long history of acrimonious labor relations, the problem of skill-controlling craft guilds on the factory floor, and the misguided 'ideology that individual property rights provide the only foundation for economic activity', an ideology which 'finds its intellectual expression in neoclassical economic theory' (Lazonick 1991a, p. 315).

The strength of Japanese enterprise derives from organizational integration that extends beyond the limits of the planned coordination of the specialized division of labor as practiced under U.S. managerial capitalism. First, organizational integration in Japan extends across horizontally and vertically related *firms* to a much greater extent than in the United States (where such integration is indeed often illegal) so that planned coordination spans units of financial control to encompass multifirm business organizations. Second, within dominant Japanese enterprises, organizational integration extends further down the organizational hierarchy, beyond the managerial structure itself, to include male blue-collar workers. (Lazonick 1992, pp. 27-77)

Lazonick emphasizes how this 'ability to organize cooperative investment strategies *across* enterprises is enhanced by the structure of managerial decision making *within* enterprises. Consensus decision making – the *ringi* system – emphasizes the two-way flow of ideas and information up and down the corporate hierarchy' (Lazonick 1991a, p. 39). These 'extensions of organization integration', Lazonick concludes, 'significantly enhance the organizational capability available to Japanese enterprises' (Lazonick 1991a, p. 37).

Critically, this enhanced organizational capability – which translates into the ability to maintain high rates of innovation – 'significantly' increases the competitive pressure on American competitors, who would have to 'make huge investments in facilities and personnel ... to remain competitive'. Yet even that seems unlikely to restore the American position:

Confronted by an international economy that they no longer dominate, many major U.S. enterprises have sought to adapt on the basis of the past successes, thereby reaping the returns on their prior investments without committing sufficient resources to ensure their future prosperity. Short-run adaptive responses inevitably lead to the erosion of organizational capabilities as the business enterprise can no longer maintain the incentives for key employees to remain committed to the organization – even if, as is increasingly less likely to be the case, these employees have the training and the physical facilities available that are necessary to enable the enterprise to remain at the forefront of innovation. (Lazonick 1992, pp. 276-7)

Lazonick concludes his analysis of the three forms of capitalism:

If there is one lesson to be learned from the comparative history of three industrial revolutions, it is that, now more than ever, industrial innovation requires the long-term commitment of resources to organizations that can plan and coordinate the development and utilization of productive capabilities. In developed capitalist economics, however, those who control wealth can choose to live off the past rather than invest in the future. A necessary condition for continued investment in innovation is that such adaptive behavior be constrained. A sufficient condition is that the economic uncertainty inherent in innovative investment be reduced by means of policies that educate the labor force, mobilize committed financial resources, and coordinate interdependent innovative efforts.

> If, in a particular social environment, private enterprise cannot itself create organizational conditions for the appropriate education, mobilization, and coordination to occur, then public intervention is required. Proprietary capitalism has long since vanished, and managerial capitalism can no longer compete. ... Anyone interested in understanding the nature and causes of the wealth of capitalist nations in the late twentieth century must grasp the enormous, and apparently growing, economic power of collective capitalism. (Lazonick 1991a, pp. 57-8)

The only hint that Lazonick may recast his analysis to give America more competitive hope is in his suggestive work with Louis Ferleger. They study the linkages in the United States between the highly dynamic, publicly funded agricultural research structure, which began to take shape in the late nineteenth century, and the long-term, sustained productivity growth, flexibility, and world-class competitive capability of the American farm sector. The study supports Lazonick's broad argument about the importance of the role of the state in structuring the economic environment, but it is unclear whether he believes it offers any hope for what he sees as America's failing industrial sector (Ferleger and Lazonick 1993).

The excitement in Lazonick's work lies in his attempt to break away from the narrowness of neoclassical analysis, which lacks a coherent sense of human psychology, of organizations, of the source of innovations, of the role of the state. The corpus of his work thus finds its principal strength in its response to these deficiencies, in his insistence on the importance of understanding the organizational context for innovation (and hence economic growth), and in his analysis that puts the role of organizational capabilities in a holistic sense – from the shop floor to government policy makers – at the center of dynamic economic growth. He thus attempts to bring within a single framework the ideas of Schumpeter, Chandler, Marx, and even Marshall. He seeks to restore the psychological importance of work – taken presumably from Thorstein Veblen as well as Marx – to a central place in understanding economic behavior. He accepts Schumpeter's focus on innovation and economic evolution, but modifies it by drawing on Chandler. Thus Lazonick finds that it is the stability of the organizational form of collective capitalism, with its remarkable capacity for coordination and motivation, which provides the crucible that contains the 'perennial gale of creative destruction'. He then extends his conceptual meaning of organizational coordination to embrace the Marshallian industrial district. As imaginative as this is, Lazonick has inverted Chandler, whose argument is primarily one based on material conditions and who rejects explicitly the significance of both state policy and labor relations. Lazonick also eliminates one of Schumpeter's critical forms of innovation – new organizational forms; he makes the Marshallian conception so sweeping that it is unclear what is left of any competitive market. Like Marx, he seems to think of 'collective capitalism' as the third and last historical stage of business and economic evolution.

The primary challenges to Lazonick are threefold. First, his analysis, while often conceptually appealing, has no solid foundation in quantitative analysis or a clear model of how national economies operate. Thus, for instance, he does not demonstrate that the specific industrial sectors he analyzes – which tend to be mature or even declining sectors such as textiles and automobiles – are representative of industrial activity generally. And he does not demonstrate why industrial activity is *the* critical sector that drives economic growth, why union restrictions are of current significance when unions play such a diminished role in the American labor market, or why, in spite of apparent Japanese superiority in specific industrial sectors, it has achieved only about 70 percent of America's aggregate productivity. Second, he needs to engage more explicitly the relevant surrounding literatures. He gives scant attention to organization theory, its discussion of innovation, and the literature on learning (for example, Richard Langlois, A. Michael Spence, Joseph Stiglitz). He makes no distinction between innovation in process and in product. He calls on neither the useful distinction of Herbert Simon (Simon 1976, 1978) between functional rationality and process rationality nor the particularly insightful framework of Joseph Berliner (Berliner 1976), which identifies the price system, incentive system, decision rules and institutional framework as the basic elements that shape innovative behavior. Neoclassical economics collapses all four elements into the specialized, single-function firm operating through competitive markets with the defined objective (incentive) of maximizing profit. If Lazonick engaged this literature more fully, it would both enrich his analysis and build a clearer and more sympathetic scholarly context. Third, he offers neither a clear conceptual framework delineating the role(s) of the state in shaping markets nor an acknowledgement of the real power of market competition and the flexibility of American enterprise. Kodak and IBM, which Lazonick holds up as models of good American management, have undergone brutal downsizing when their organizations proved unable to identify and respond to changing demand for their products; the NUMMI factory in Fremont, California, fully incorporated Japanese management/labor relations principles, and built virtually defect-free Chevrolet Novas – which few wished to buy. American firms, led by Nucor, have reclaimed world leadership in virtually every phase of steel production. And in the last ten years, American industrial unions have been willing to negotiate a host of innovative contracts that attempt to respond to the new imperatives of world competition.

Lazonick deserves more serious attention – and response – than he has so far received, for only in such a scholarly dialogue will economics enlarge its vision of human and social potential, capacity and opportunity.

LAZONICK'S MAJOR WRITINGS

(1981), 'Production Relations, Labor Productivity, and Choice of Technique: British and U.S. Choice of Technique', *Journal of Economic History*, **41** (3), September.

(1990), *Competitive Advantage on the Shop Floor*, Cambridge, Mass.: Harvard University Press.

(1991a), *Business Organization and the Myth of the Market Economy*, Cambridge: Cambridge University Press.

(1991b), 'Business History and Economics', *Business and Economic History*, second series, **20**.

(1992), *Organization and Technology in Capitalist Development*, Aldershot: Edward Elgar.

(1993) (with Louis Ferleger), 'The Managerial Revolution and the Developmental State: The Case of U.S. Agriculture', Business History Conference.

OTHER REFERENCES

Berliner, Joseph (1976), *The Innovation Decision in Soviet Industry*, Cambridge, Mass.: Harvard University Press.

Simon, Herbert A. (1976), 'From Substantive to Procedural Rationality', in Sprio J. Latsis (ed.), *Method and Appraisal in Economics*, Cambridge: Cambridge University Press.

Simon, Herbert A. (1978), 'Rationality as Process and as Product of Thought', *American Economic Review*, **68** (2), 4.

9. H. Gregg Lewis

Jeff E. Biddle

On at least three occasions, colleagues and former students of H. Gregg Lewis have reflected formally on his personal qualities and his contributions to economics. In 1976 the *Journal of Political Economy* published a special issue in Lewis's honor to commemorate his retirement from the University of Chicago. This collection of research papers by fellow labor economists was prefaced by Gary Becker's one-page appreciation and a longer essay on Lewis by Albert Rees. In 1982 a brief tribute appeared in the *American Economic Review* to mark Lewis's selection as a distinguished fellow of the American Economic Association. In 1994 *The Journal of Labor Economics* published a collection of memorial essays composed shortly after Lewis's death in 1992.[1]

One takes away from these various pieces a consistent picture of Lewis as a person and as an economist. The authors present Lewis as a man of remarkable integrity both in his personal life and in his scholarly work. He had a strong sense of duty – duty to his department, to his students, to his fellow economists, and to the ideal of the careful and impartial scholar. As an economist, statistical theory and neoclassical economics were his tools, and he applied them meticulously and masterfully to both theoretical and empirical questions. His empirical work was especially noteworthy, marked by an intimate knowledge and judicious handling of the relevant data, and a commitment to draw only those conclusions fully warranted by statistical and theoretical considerations, regardless of their ideological or political implications.

The essayists note that at a time when labor economics was dominated by institutionalist and eclectic approaches, Lewis looked at the field through a neoclassical lens, sometimes bringing a fresh perspective to traditional topics, but more often taking up neglected questions upon which the neoclassical approach might shed light. Lewis's own published output was rather small, a fact that the authors attributed to an excessive perfectionism. He produced a few articles or

---

1. The relevant references are Becker 1976, Rees 1976, American Economic Association 1982, Ashenfelter 1994, Freeman 1994, McElroy 1994 and Rosen 1994.

book chapters each decade, in addition to the 1963 classic *Unionism and Relative Wages in the United States* and its 1986 sequel *Union Relative Wage Effects: A Survey*. Other potentially influential papers were circulated among friends but never published; and colleagues speak of profiting greatly from Lewis's comments in conversations, letters and referee reports.

For the most part, however, Lewis's research program was carried on in the work of his graduate students at the University of Chicago, and it is through these students that Lewis had his greatest influence on the field of labor economics. He was a member of close to a hundred doctoral committees and chairman of some thirty during his years at Chicago and Duke. He set high standards, but gave more than generously of his time to help students meet them. Under Lewis's guidance, his students applied the tools of neoclassical economics to topics including labor market discrimination, labor force participation and labor supply, the economic impact of unionism, and the economic returns to education; they continued such work on their own after receiving their degrees. Albert Rees's essay on Lewis speaks of the transformation of labor economics by Lewis's colleagues, students, and the students of his students, 'his intellectual brothers, children and grandchildren'. Rees is not alone in this sentiment. In 1976 Becker referred to Lewis as the 'founder of the "Chicago School" of labor economics'; in the 1994 memorials Orley Ashenfelter echoed the American Economic Association's 1982 tribute, calling Lewis the 'father of modern labor economics'.[2]

The essays in which one finds these assessments of Lewis are commemorative in nature, and for that reason might be expected to present his character and his work in the best possible light. My own examination of Lewis's published writings and of his papers and correspondence (held by the Duke University Library)[3] have led me to the conclusion that the picture of Lewis presented in the existing commemorative essays is essentially correct. The bulk of this essay serves simply to flesh out and substantiate that picture, looking at Lewis the man, at the nature of his work as an economic researcher, and at his relationships with students and colleagues – relationships through which his particular approach to labor economics may have become an exemplar for many in the field. The question of the extent to which labor economics was transformed in the sixties and seventies, and the role Lewis played in that transformation, is something I have neither the space nor the historical perspective to address adequately here, but I do offer some speculations on the matter in the final section.

2. Reder's 1982 essay on Chicago economics also refers to the transformation of the field of labor economics by Lewis and his students.
3. The Lewis papers are currently uncatalogued. All material cited herein is in Boxes 1&2, accession #92-059, H.G. Lewis papers.

I

Harold Gregg Lewis was born in Homer, Michigan in 1914, a son of two college-educated school teachers.[4] He received his primary and secondary education in public schools, and upon completing high school enrolled in Port Huron Community College to study engineering. A faculty member there was impressed by Lewis's mathematical prowess, and encouraged him to attend the University of Chicago. Chicago had no engineering school, but the professor felt that Lewis's skills could be put to good use in the Department of Economics. Lewis acted on the man's advice, and received both an AB (1936) and a PhD (1947) in economics from Chicago.

Lewis was recognized early at Chicago as a precocious student, part of a select group of undergraduates (including also Paul Samuelson and Herbert Simon) permitted to enrol in graduate classes.[5] He took courses from such Chicago luminaries as Jacob Viner, Frank Knight and Henry Simons, all of whom made a lasting impression on him. He was also influenced by Henry Schultz, for whom he served as a research assistant. Paul Douglas, who made it a practice to offer promising students co-authorship opportunities, asked Lewis to join him in preparing a study of income elasticities based on a large cross-section sample of family budgets.[6]

An important early association for Lewis was with Chicago statistics professor T.O. Yntema. Lewis had been an outstanding student in one of Yntema's classes, and early in 1939 Yntema invited Lewis to join US Steel's Special Economic Research Section, a group being formed to prepare material relevant to a pending Congressional investigation of the steel industry.[7] The assignment lasted less than a year but was an intense experience for Lewis. The group worked with the most advanced tools of statistics and economic theory, and although the subject of the work was highly controversial and of considerable policy importance, Yntema

---

4. The information in this and the next section, unless otherwise noted, was obtained from Lewis's vita and from interviews with his wife Julia Lewis in December 1994.
5. Rosen (1994) reports Allen Wallis's recollection of Lewis as an exceptional student; Martin Bronfenbrenner, like Wallis a graduate student during Lewis's undergraduate years, shares Wallis's recollection (personal communication). A 1939 memorial to Henry Schultz by Harold Hotelling, then at Columbia University, lists Lewis as one of Schultz's promising students.
6. This joint work ultimately led to two publications (Douglas and Lewis 1939, 1947).
7. US Steel was preparing to testify before Congress's Temporary National Economic Committee, formed in 1938 to investigate concentration in the US economy. The TNEC's interest in the steel industry was expected to center on industry-pricing policies, in particular the basing-point pricing system and US Steel's role as coordinator of an industry-wide program to maintain 'stable prices'. With regard to the latter, US Steel hoped to produce information on the elasticity of demand for steel that would quantify the extent to which steel price inflexibility contributed to instability in the employment of steel workers.

insisted upon maintaining an atmosphere of scientific impartiality. So much did Lewis enjoy this project that when the assignment ended, he abandoned his partially completed doctoral thesis and began a new one summarizing and building upon the work the group had done on the elasticity of demand for steel.[8] The completion of this new dissertation was delayed by the war, during which Lewis spent two years with the War Labor Board and six months with the Army Air Force. He finally received his PhD in 1947.

By this time Lewis had already been a member of the Chicago economics faculty for eight years. The death of Henry Schultz in an automobile accident in 1938 had left the department with several courses uncovered, including an advanced statistics course. The department was divided over the question of a successor to Schultz (as it was over so many issues during this period). The idea of appointing Lewis to the position emerged as an acceptable compromise, satisfying in particular both Paul Douglas and Henry Simons.[9] Douglas informed Lewis of the appointment on the day of Lewis's wedding to Julia Elliot, a fellow economics student and Douglas's research assistant. Lewis took over Schultz's courses in 1939, and until 1943 was the department's 'sole representative of econometrics and of quantitative economics generally' (Patinkin 1981, p. 10).

When Lewis joined the Chicago faculty he was the youngest member of the department by more than ten years, and there was a tendency among other faculty members to burden him with administrative chores. He was appointed permanent scribe at departmental meetings, and become the unofficial 'vice chairman', performing administrative duties left behind when the actual chairman was temporarily away. In 1945 he was named departmental counselor, a job entailing administrative responsibility for both undergraduate and graduate students and programs. He quickly earned a reputation as a helpful and accessible advisor to graduate students (Patinkin 1981, pp. 10-11), and for the first time in the department's history developed a set of standardized rules for determining when doctoral candidates had actually completed their degree requirements. He retained responsibility for the department's graduate program until leaving Chicago in 1975.[10]

---

8. Mrs Lewis does not recall the topic of the abandoned dissertation, but it was related either to the income elasticity work with Douglas or to the theoretical foundations of producer price indices (see Lewis and Court 1942). At the close of the dissertation on steel, Lewis comments on the importance for economists of working on topics with policy relevance (Lewis 1947, p. 151, Box 1, Lewis papers).

9. The ongoing conflicts in the Chicago economics department beginning in the mid-thirties are described in Reder (1982) pp. 10-11.

10. In 1964, Lewis's title was upgraded to Director of the Graduate Program. In 1967, as a condition of continuing in that role, he requested that his departmental duties be narrowed and formally defined, protesting against the attitude of 'let Gregg do it' that had prevailed for over twenty years

Lewis reluctantly accepted additional departmental responsibilities in the mid-fifties, when the University of Chicago, with funding from USAID, began a program designed to upgrade the teaching of economics in Latin America. Chilean students were to come to the University of Chicago for graduate training in economics, then return to join and revamp the faculties of economics in their own and neighboring countries. Lewis agreed to serve as coordinator of this program in 1956, and soon found that the job went beyond routine paper-shuffling, requiring service as an academic and sometimes personal advisor to the Chilean students. Lewis's official ties to Chicago's Latin American program ended in 1967, but the experience left him with strong and lasting relationships with a number of former students who rose to prominent positions in teaching and government in Latin America.

II

Lewis is remembered as a labor economist, but there is little evidence in his published work prior to 1950 of an interest in labor-related matters. After 1950, however, almost all of his own work and the bulk of the doctoral theses he supervised dealt with topics now considered part of labor economics. The reason for Lewis's change in focus is not clear, but it may be due in part to his relationship with Henry Simons. In the years following Lewis's appointment to the faculty, the teacher–student relationship between Lewis and Simons developed into a closer collegial and personal one. In terms of professional styles, however, the two men could hardly have been more different. Simons was a polemicist, outlining and defending policy proposals that grew out of a libertarian philosophy; employing vigorous prose and (sometimes loose) neoclassical reasoning to defend the free market, discredit government interventions, and attack 'monopoly' in all its forms. Everything Simons wrote, Lewis once noted, was a tract (Lewis 1946). Lewis, on the other hand, pursued the ideal of the detached, objective social scientist, using precise mathematical and statistical techniques to explore narrowly defined problems of theory and estimation. Although indications are that Lewis agreed with Simons politically, he also believed in maintaining a clear distinction between the positive and the normative, and preferred to stick with positive analysis.

Lewis was profoundly affected when Simons took his own life in 1946. He penned a tribute to Simons for the *American Economic Review* (Lewis 1946), and

(Lewis to Harberger, April 1967, Lewis papers, box 2).

it seems likely that Lewis's work on unions grew out of a resolution to find a way to carry on Simons's work in his own research.[11] The strongest piece of evidence for this view is the article published in 1951, 'The Labor-Monopoly Problem: A Positive Program', Lewis's first on a labor topic. The article's title evoked that of Simons's 1936 book *A Positive Program for Laissez Faire*, in which Simons had identified labor unionism as one of the many manifestations of monopoly that should not be tolerated in a free society. Lewis began by noting that Simons had never outlined a policy for dealing with the problem of labor monopoly; Lewis's purpose was to fill that void. He proposed that the geographical extent of collective bargaining units be limited by law. The probable effects of the proposal were explained, and arguments were made to demonstrate its superiority over a number of then commonly-discussed alternatives.

But designing and defending policy proposals, however dispassionately, must not have fit Lewis's style or tastes, as the 1951 article was Lewis's first and last foray into explicitly normative economics. The notion of building on Simons's work, though, did not end. In his indictment of unionism Simons had identified several of its deleterious effects: the misallocation of resources resulting from the distortion of the price of labor; the increase in inequality as the unionists raised their wages at the expense of non-union workers; the unemployment effects of high union wages; the tendency for unions to become autocratic, and so on. These, Lewis realized, were things that could be comprehended and analyzed within the neoclassical model; what is more, they were in principle capable of being measured statistically. In particular, under certain circumstances the severity of the 'labor monopoly problem' could be proxied by the size of the difference between the wages of unionized workers and similar non-union workers.

Here was a set of tasks more in keeping with Lewis's talents and his conception of what economic research should be: the rigorous theoretical analysis and the empirical measurement of the impact of unionism. By 1950 he had already served on the thesis committees of two graduate students investigating the effects of unions on wages, and within a few years he was teaching a graduate course in labor economics (Rees 1976). More Chicago dissertations on the effects of unions on wages followed, and an additional intellectual problem caught Lewis's attention: the several different studies of union wage effects produced widely divergent estimates. In 1955 Lewis set for himself the task of attempting to reconcile these estimates (Lewis 1963, p. vii). It was not an unfamiliar type of

---

11. This suggestion comes from Mrs Lewis, who is fairly confident in its accuracy. She recalls her husband expressing other reasons for his turn to labor, but cannot recall what they were. The opinion of Reder (1982) that Lewis's interest in labor economics grew out of his association with Paul Douglas is less convincing, given that his work with Douglas had little to do with labor economics and the timing of Lewis's change in research interests towards the labor field.

project for Lewis; much of his doctoral dissertation had been devoted to reconciling or explaining the variation in previous estimates of the elasticity of demand for steel. In 1956 Lewis sought and received funding from the American Enterprise Association for research on 'The Relative Wage Effects of Unionism'.[12] Work on the project continued for six years, culminating in the 1963 book *Unionism and Relative Wages in the United States*.

The book surveyed and synthesized twenty studies of the relative effects of unionism on wages, that is, how much unionism raised the wage of unionized workers relative to those of non-union workers. (Lewis noted that the separate effects of unionism on the wages of union and non-union workers could not be inferred from existing data.) The centerpiece of these studies was generally a regression of the average wages of a group of workers on the proportion of the group that was unionized, using either time-series data on a single group of workers or cross-section observations of several comparable groups of workers. Such regressions would yield unbiased measures of the effect of unionism on wages only to the extent that other forces affecting wages across time or across groups were held equal, and operationalizing this *ceteris paribus* assumption was often the most troublesome aspect of the studies. Prior to running regressions the average wage figures had to be adjusted to account for differences across observations in the composition of the group and underlying supply and demand conditions. Lewis's critiques of the studies often focused on the way authors had handled this aspect of the empirical work, and he sometimes provided his own corrections and re-analysis of other authors' data. He also produced new estimates of the relative wage effect of unions based on carefully constructed time series of average wages and the extent of unionism for the economy as a whole.

Lewis concluded that unionized workers earned on average 10-15 percent more than similar non-union workers, although this gap varied through time and across the labor force. It was unusual for a group of unionized workers to earn over 25 percent more than their non-union counterparts; in most industries the gap was under 5 percent. High inflation tended to lower the gap, rapid deflation to raise it. Over the period covered by the studies, the relative wage gap had been highest in the early thirties and had declined to near zero by the late forties before increasing again in the fifties.

During the period when the book was being written, Lewis also produced studies of the employment effect of unionism (Lewis 1964) and the impact of unions on interindustry wage differentials, one indicator of the effect of unions on inequality (Lewis 1962). A published lecture on 'Competitive and Monopoly Unionism' presented a rigorous theoretical analysis of the union phenomenon,

---

12. Contract between Lewis and the American Enterprise Association, 4/23/56, Lewis papers, box 2.

with attention to the empirical implications of the analysis. The first lines of the article stated succinctly the guiding thrust of all Lewis's union research:

> many of the differences among economists in the positions they hold regarding public policy towards trade unions, as well as in their assessments of the importance of unionism as a labor market factor, stem from disagreement on the answer to this question: What is the impact of unionism on relative real wages? If we knew the answer to this question, we would surely know much about the extent to which unionism is monopolistic, the conditions that strengthen or weaken monopoly unionism, and the consequences of unionism for the distribution of wage and salary income and for the allocation of labor and other resources among uses. (Lewis 1959, p. 181)[13]

Whatever impetus Lewis might have received in the late forties from Simons's concerns with monopoly unionism, by the mid-fifties Lewis had redefined the problem and made it his own. Rather than inveighing against the union monopoly problem he was taking its measure with what he considered to be the tools of an impartial scientist, a step that in his mind was logically prior to that of discussing policy. His goal became the establishment of propositions about unionism that were consistent with neoclassical theory and the existing data, regardless of their relationship with any explicitly ideological or political position on unionism.[14]

For example, Lewis's theoretical analyses of unionism led him to conclude that, *contra* Simons, unions themselves were not necessarily inconsistent with competition, and that neoclassical theory did not imply that concentration in product markets would facilitate the growth of monopoly power in the labor market (Lewis 1959). A repeated theme in his empirical work was the difficulty of making any confident assertions at all about the economic impact of unions given the existing data, and the conclusions that he was willing to draw did not cleave to any ideological line. Lewis (1962) argued that any impact of unionism on wage inequality was likely to be small. In his 1963 book he carefully examined and ultimately rejected the finding of Friedman and Kuznets (1945), famous in the lore of Chicago economics, that physicians' earnings were kept artificially high by the monopolistic practices of the American Medical Association. The American Enterprise Association, having partially funded Lewis's research into the relative wage effects of unionism and having agreed to publish a non-technical summary of his work, persistently prodded him to include material about the

---

13. One hears in this passage echoes of fellow Chicago economist Milton Friedman's assertion that most disagreements between economists on policy matters could be resolved through the pursuit of positive economics.

14. Reder (1982) speaks generally of the shift in Chicago labor economics during the fifties and sixties from 'normative condemnation to positive analysis'; the work of Lewis and his students is cited as an important part of this shift.

inflationary impact of union wage increases. In a long correspondence with American Enterprise Association board member Gottfried Haberler, Lewis patiently explained why his results on the relative wage effects of unionism had no implications for the effect of unions on the general price level. 'It is my very sincere desire that my paper be neutral on the issue of wages and inflation', Lewis insisted in one letter; in another, 'in my judgement, the evidence to date is too meager to support any strong empirical assertions on this matter'.[15]

Indeed, it pained Lewis to think that his results would be viewed as anything but the work of an impartial investigator. During the early sixties a series of articles in the *Journal of Political Economy* and elsewhere debated the question of whether there was a 'Chicago School' of economics with a distinctive ideological program.[16] In 1967 Lewis received a letter questioning some of the results reported in his 1963 book, and commenting in passing that 'the Chicago School' tended to 'belittle' the effect of unions by concentrating on particular periods in history. Lewis gave characteristically clinical responses to the writer's questions, but lashed out angrily at his reference to the 'Chicago School':

> you show the utmost contempt for not only me but also my colleagues. In effect you are telling me that I am guilty of error not because of mistakes in my book ... but because I am a member of the faculty of the University of Chicago, all of whose members you label the 'Chicago School' with the clear intention that the label be derogatory.[17]

The fifties saw Lewis developing an interest in labor topics beyond the impact of unionism, due perhaps to his teaching of the graduate labor course or his participation in the department's labor economics workshop. Lewis pursued these interests for the most part in the context of his role as an advisor or supervisor to students writing doctoral theses. In the 1956 paper 'Hours of Work and Hours of Leisure', Lewis used the neoclassical model of the consumer's demand for leisure as a vehicle for explaining the secular decline in the average work week and for understanding other empirical regularities in labor supply behavior. The paper was presented as part of ongoing work with two Chicago graduate students. Over the next ten years, Lewis supervised or was involved with several other dissertations, all with significant empirical content, which examined labor force participation and hours of work decisions in the context of the neoclassical model (Rees 1976, pp. s6-s7). Gary Becker's famous neoclassical analysis of discrimination began

---

15. Box 2, Lewis papers: Lewis to Haberler 12/7/62; Lewis to Haberler 11/2/62. The American Enterprise Association was also concerned with Lewis's minimization of the effect of unions on inequality.
16. See, e.g., Miller (1962) and Bronfenbrenner (1962).
17. Lewis to Paul Anderson, 5/4/67, box 2, Lewis papers.

as a thesis written under Lewis's supervision; according to Becker's acknowledgement, Lewis 'influenced every page' of the work (Becker 1957, p. 4). Other Chicago labor theses of the fifties and sixties looked at black–white differentials in income and earnings, rates of return to education, and factors affecting the demand for labor (Rees 1976).

Lewis left the University of Chicago in 1975 to join the faculty of Duke University. His departure from Chicago was not motivated by any dissatisfaction with the department, he told friends, but by the desire of himself and his wife to put down roots in a warmer climate in which they could eventually retire.[18] At Duke he once again became deeply involved in departmental matters, supervised several dissertations, and began writing a second book on the effect of unions on wages, *Union Relative Wage Effects: A Survey*.

While Lewis's first book synthesized the findings of twenty studies, the second, published in 1986, covered almost 200. The two decades following the appearance of Lewis's first book had seen the development of new data sets that allowed comparisons between the earnings of individual union and non-union workers, controlling for a number of other relevant individual characteristics; a few of the data sets were longitudinal, following the same groups of workers as they moved between union and non-union jobs. The new data sets provided the raw material for a host of studies re-examining Lewis's 1963 conclusions, often with the aid of recently developed econometric techniques.

The majority of the studies surveyed by Lewis in the 1986 book were based on ordinary least squares, cross-section regressions of the wages of individual workers on a variable indicating whether or not they belonged to a union along with several variables meant to control for demographic and productivity differences across workers. Lewis concluded that this 'OLS–CS' approach to estimating the relative wage effect of unionism (now termed the 'union/non-union wage gap') eliminated many of the problems associated with the comparisons between average wages of groups of workers that formed the basis of his 1963 book. A problem remained, however. One could not observe all of the factors that made one worker different from another, and some of these factors might be correlated with union status, biasing the estimated effect of union status on wages. Researchers had attempted to circumvent the problem by using more complex statistical techniques or by taking advantage of longitudinal data, but Lewis did not believe that they had succeeded. He found that the estimates produced by more elaborate statistical methods were sensitive to arbitrary changes in the economic and statistical assumptions underlying the estimation procedure. Estimates based on longitudinal data were more sensitive to measurement error than those based

---

18. Letter from Lewis to G. Becker, 2/17/75, Lewis papers, box 2; also McElroy (1994).

on cross-section data, and Lewis had evidence that the level of measurement error in the longitudinal data was sufficiently high to render the estimates unreliable. Though flawed, then, the OLS–CS estimates provided the best available basis for Lewis's synthesis.

After careful adjustment across studies for differences in things such as sample composition and lists of control variables, Lewis produced year by year averages of the union/non-union wage gap from 1967 to 1978, and concluded that over this period the gap had remained in the neighborhood of 15 percent. The studies of the sixties and seventies also allowed Lewis to look more carefully at variations in the wage gap across the labor force. They supported the hypothesis that the wage gap was lower for workers with more human capital, but not the broader hypothesis that unions raised relative wages for low-wage groups more than for high-wage groups.

The 1986 book was Lewis's last major research effort, appearing two years after his retirement from Duke. He remained professionally active, however, until close to his death in 1992.[19]

III

From his doctoral dissertation to his final book on unionism and relative wages, three features mark Lewis's work as an economist. The first is a thoroughgoing mathematical neoclassicism: discussions of economic phenomena invariably take place within confines of a mathematical neoclassical model. The second is Lewis's empiricism, a commitment to exploring and measuring the empirical content of neoclassical theory. The third is the craftsmanlike quality of Lewis's work – careful, precise, thorough, complete – which previous writers have emphasized.[20]

Lewis's uncompromising neoclassicism should not be surprising, given his exposure at Chicago to the likes of Viner, Simons, Knight and Henry Schultz, but Lewis's overall research style most closely resembled that of Schultz. Of the four of Lewis's teachers just mentioned, only Schultz was an enthusiastic advocate of the mathematization of theory and of the possibilities of developing, through the use of the most sophisticated statistical tools, an empirical adjunct to neoclassical

19. Freeman (1994) provides a more thorough discussion and comparison of the two union books; McElroy (1994) chronicles Lewis's years at Duke.
20. Freeman (1994) invokes the craftsman metaphor in describing Lewis, but it also appears much earlier in a letter to Lewis from Armen Alchian (1/19/59, box 2, Lewis papers) who comments that after having read Lewis's comments on Alchian's work he understands Reuben Kessel's description of Lewis as a 'craftsman'.

theory (Reder 1982). Schultz's econometric program has been described in Morgan (1990), but for our purposes it is sufficient to note that the goal of Schultz's work was to measure statistically the real-world manifestations of the parameters identified by neoclassical theory (for example, supply and demand elasticities), taking the existence and significance of those parameters as unproblematic. Of course, the preponderance of the empirical work with which Lewis is associated is in the same vein: the attempt to estimate the elasticity of demand for steel, the quest for the most reliable measures of the effect of unions on wages, and the Lewis-inspired work of estimating the income and wage elasticities of the neoclassical demand for leisure model. Also, Schultz was known for his meticulous, orderly approach to research (Reder 1982). Shortly after Schultz's death in 1938, Lewis wrote of his teacher in words that could easily be mistaken for a description of Lewis by one of his own students:

> Whether in economics or statistics he began by building a mathematical or logical foundation of a theory – a model to serve as a frame of reference for further analysis ... he impressed upon students the necessity for thoroughly understanding all the premises upon which the model was built.
>
> But he did not stop with the strict logical pattern; he proceeded to show us how we could test the assumptions underlying it, first by a priori reasoning ... and then by statistical techniques.[21]

The first step for Lewis in dealing with any research problem was to conceptualize it within a neoclassical model, to express it in the language of utility and production functions, costs and prices, competition or monopoly, and so on. The models were laid out mathematically, and were in most instances drawn from or patterned after those found in R.G.D. Allen's *Mathematics for Economists*.[22] Lewis's technique for presenting theoretical results through logarithmic differentiation of his model allowed him to express the key relationships between variables largely in terms of elasticities, cost shares and factor ratios – entities that

---

21. Lewis quoted in Hotelling 1939, p. 101. Reder (1982, p. 3) has argued that Lewis's work represents a continuation of the tradition of Paul Douglas at Chicago. This is a plausible claim, given Douglas's program of estimating the parameters of the Cobb–Douglas production function (a mathematically expressed neoclassical relationship), his work with Lewis on estimation of income elasticities, and his interest in labor topics. However, when interviewed, Mrs Lewis expressed the strong opinion that while Douglas provided encouragement to Lewis, it was Schultz (and T.O. Yntema) who left the greatest mark on Lewis's research style. In particular, she felt, Lewis was attracted by the care and thoroughness with which Schultz went about both his empirical and theoretical work.

22. Freeman (1994) correctly notes Lewis's tendency to think about problems using the neoclassical theory of factor demand as developed in his graduate lectures on labor demand. These lectures, in turn, were based on Allen's book (Lewis to Katz 12/30/70, box 2, Lewis papers).

lent themselves to measurement, and whose magnitudes economists could meaningfully discuss even in the absence of hard statistical evidence.

Lewis explored his models thoroughly. Where others might implicitly assume that certain functions were perfectly elastic, or that a production function was homothetic and linear homogenous, or that all relevant markets were competitive, Lewis would make these assumptions explicit, discuss their plausibility, and determine consequences of their failure.[23] Never questioned, however, were the fundamental neoclassical assumptions such as profit maximization or utility maximization.

For Lewis, theorizing was almost always intended as an (essential) component of a larger empirical project. Sometimes the theory served to provide interpretation of an existing empirical observation (e.g., Lewis 1956), but more often the purpose of theorizing was to identify important empirical relationships to be measured and to suggest strategies for measuring them. For example, in his doctoral dissertation Lewis used neoclassical theory to establish the link between the elasticity of demand for steel and the probable impact of policies designed to increase the flexibility of steel prices. Following attempts to measure the elasticity directly (using multiple regression equations grounded in a theoretical model), Lewis turned to theory again to propose an indirect means of establishing an upper bound for the value of the elasticity of demand for steel from two other quantities of less uncertain magnitude: the elasticity of demand for products made from steel, and the share of steel in the total cost of those products. Likewise, alongside his attempts to measure directly the union wage effect (the importance of which followed from neoclassical theory) Lewis developed theoretical models intended to identify proxy variables from which the wage effect could be indirectly inferred (Lewis 1959, p. 182).

Many of Lewis's empirical conclusions rested on estimates produced by himself or others using ordinary least squares regression techniques, and his work evidences a thorough understanding of the statistical theory underlying those techniques. The apparatus of hypothesis testing that has come to be associated with the use of regression analysis in economics is not common in Lewis's work; discussions of standard errors and issues of statistical significance seldom appear. This is in part because of the tasks Lewis set for himself – he was engaged in measurement, not theory testing. The magnitude of an empirical entity itself was of interest, not whether it differed from some hypothesized value. Also, as a synthesizer of the results of others, the basic unit of observation for Lewis was

---

23. A contribution in this vein is Lewis (1975), which explores in the context of a generic two-sector general equilibrium model the conditions under which the results of partial equilibrium analysis will provide a good approximation to the conclusions of general equilibrium analysis.

often the estimate, and the variation of interest was the variation across estimates produced by different researchers, rather than the sampling variation of a single estimate with which the textbook theory of inference and the procedure of hypothesis testing are concerned.

Lewis's discussions of possible bias in the estimates he produced or assessed were those of a researcher dealing with a concrete problem, and went well beyond considerations of the properties of an estimator calculated from a hypothesized random sample of generic X's and Y's. With the same precise attention to detail that marked his theoretical work, he considered the representativeness of the sample, the correspondence between theoretical concepts and empirical variables, the reliability of the data, and the likelihood of misspecification. Suspicion that another author's estimate suffered from bias because of these or other considerations might lead to an adjustment of the author's data, or even a re-analysis of the data with alternative statistical models.

A distinctive feature of Lewis's empirical work is that the evidence produced by standard statistical techniques is often coupled with, checked by, indeed sometimes subordinated to, evidence of another sort: Lewis's 'hunches' or judgements regarding the values of critical parameters of the relevant theoretical model. One example of this has already been mentioned – Lewis's attempt to infer a range of values for the steel elasticity from reasonable guesses about the magnitudes of other model parameters. A more thorough example of Lewis's 'back of the envelope' style of empiricism is found in Lewis's comment on a study of the impact of the payroll tax provisions of the Black Lung Benefits program (Lewis 1976; Goldstein and Smith 1976). The study had used regression techniques to estimate the probable effect of the program on prices, employment and output in the coal industry. Lewis checked the estimates by setting up a partial equilibrium model of the coal industry, deriving theoretical expressions relating prices, output and employment to payroll taxes, then assigning values to the parameters of those expressions based on published sources and intuition. Lewis's answers were very close to those of the original study, but he suggested that the regression estimates were less precise than their standard errors might indicate, in part because of the sensitivity of his own estimates to changes in the values he had assumed for parameters!

These instances are just two of many in which Lewis was equally if not more willing to rely on his theory-plus-judgement estimates than on those produced by statistical techniques. And it is interesting that while Lewis's diffidence towards estimates of the latter sort was usually solidly based on considerations of statistical theory or data quality, his frequent reliance on the theory-plus-judgement estimators required an acceptance of the neoclassical model as a description of reality, an acceptance that was uncharacteristically uncritical.

A final, somewhat innovative, feature of Lewis's economics was his use of statistical theory not only as a guide to the process of estimation and measurement, but also as an adjunct to his theorizing. This probably stemmed from his desire to take neoclassical models seriously, to discover exactly what, granting a set of conventional neoclassical assumptions, one could or could not infer about observable behavior.[24] As a labor economist Lewis made considerable use of neoclassical models of individual choice: the labor supply decision, the labor force participation decision, the decision of whether or not to support a union, and so on. The empirical measures these models were designed to explain, generated through the use of standard statistical techniques, were of the nature of averages, pertaining to groups rather than individuals (for example, labor force participation rates and average weekly hours of work for various demographic groups). Only under rather narrow circumstances could the empirical measures be expected to correspond exactly to the theoretical parameters of individualistic models, but in Lewis's day such a correspondence was often taken for granted implicitly. Lewis, however, was not willing to do so, and he turned to statistical theory as a means of building a rigorous bridge between the implications of the theory regarding the behavior of an individual and the implications of that theory regarding group or market-level phenomena.

The Lewis approach was the now familiar one of defining the model for an individual, then capturing the possibility of heterogeneity in the group by assuming certain crucial parameters of the individualistic model to be random variables with a well-defined distribution in the group. Lewis used this strategy in his 1959 essay to determine whether what he called 'competitive unionism', devoid of monopoly power, could give rise to a union wage effect, and it is used by Becker in his dissertation where he explores the consequences of allowing 'tastes for discrimination' to differ across agents in the economy. Perhaps the archetypical application is found in Lewis's unpublished but well-circulated 1967 paper 'On Income and Substitution Effects in Labor Force Participation'. He begins with a recognition of the difference between the entities identified by theory (elasticities defined by individual utility function parameters) and the entities being measured (partial correlation coefficients between variables defined over groups). By introducing explicit assumptions about the distributions across the group of the parameters of individual utility functions, Lewis derives

---

24. It might be tempting to link Lewis's introduction of statistical theory (i.e., probabilism) into neoclassical models to his association with the Cowles Commission during the Commission's time at Chicago. I see no other evidence to substantiate such a link, however. Lewis understood the significance of the econometric theoretical research going on at Cowles (see Lewis 1947, pp. 129-30) but his approach to statistical modeling, his notation, and so on, do not resemble the better-known Cowles Commission work.

propositions about the relationships between these distributions and empirical estimates of labor force participation and labor supply elasticities.[25]

IV

All who have written on Lewis have singled out as his most important contribution to economics his activities as a mentor and teacher, noting both his extraordinary devotion of time and effort to these aspects of his professional life and the impact he had on the profession as a result of them. This impact, according to Rosen, was 'much greater ... than the most ambitious economists can imagine' (1994, p. 143). On Lewis's dedication to his role as a teacher there is ample evidence beyond the reflections found in the memorial essays. Despite his position at a major research university, it was Lewis's expressed opinion that the primary purpose of being on a university faculty was to teach. In his twenty-plus years as Department Counselor, his office hours for students were nine to five, five days a week. On several occasions he spent weekends with graduate students, helping them to iron out difficulties in their dissertations. Both the University of Chicago and Duke University honored him with teaching awards.[26]

In the Lewis papers one finds half a dozen unsolicited letters from former students, thanking him many years after the fact for his guidance and crucial assistance.[27] There are also letters from colleagues, written when Lewis announced his decision to leave Chicago. George Stigler opined that Lewis 'deserved a statue', as 'the Chicago miracle of turning out innumerable well trained economists' was due to him more than any other person. Harry Johnson thanked Lewis for teaching him of his 'responsibility in looking after and caring for the students and the department', while Ted Schultz noted that many of Schultz's best students had 'learned to be precise in their thinking and their work' from Lewis.[28]

The assertion that Lewis's devotion to teaching allowed him to have a large impact on the profession is more difficult to substantiate. The nature of the field of labor economics does appear to have changed during the sixties and seventies; to the testimony on this point by practitioners such as Rees and Rosen, one can add Ramstad's (1981) demonstration of the relative decline in the number of

---

25. See also Lewis (1974), the early and influential exposition of the problem of sample selection bias in the estimation of labor supply equations.
26. Interview, Julia Lewis.
27. Cooper to Lewis 1/18/71; Cook to Lewis, 8/3/71; Cain to Lewis, 8/25/76; Herrick to Lewis, 8/26/76; Keat to Lewis, 9/3/79. Lewis wrote in response to one such expression of gratitude 'The greatest rewards we have come from our students' (Lewis to Lurie, 5/28/75). All in box 2, Lewis papers.
28. Stigler to Lewis, 1/3/75; Johnson to Lewis, 2/7/75; Schultz to Lewis, 1/21/75. Box 2, Lewis papers.

institutionalist-style articles and the corresponding rise in the number of neoclassical articles in the journal literature of labor economics between the mid-fifties and the end of the sixties. The contributions to neoclassical labor economics over this period of Lewis's 'intellectual children and grandchildren', to use Rees's phrase, have been discussed in the commemorative essays, which also point out that a great deal of empirical research on labor supply and the economic impact of unions continues to be devoted to answering questions framed by Lewis in the fifties and sixties.

The remarkable impact on economics of Lewis's best-known student, Gary Becker, need not be recounted here. Although it is impossible to gauge the extent to which the nature and content of Becker's influential research was shaped by his association with Lewis, one can point to Becker's own acknowledgement of Lewis's influence on his seminal dissertation on discrimination in labor markets, and see in Becker's neoclassical modeling of family interactions, crime, and so on a reflection of Lewis's program of applying neoclassical concepts to areas of labor economics not previously comprehended in neoclasscial terms. Another Lewis student, Sherwin Rosen, has produced a much-cited body of theoretical literature on the employment relationship. Like Lewis, Rosen works within a neoclassical framework, exploring the consequences of relaxing certain conventional assumptions (such as those concerning the way in which labor enters the production function), and using constructs from statistical theory to build a bridge from models of individual optimization to characterizations of equilibrium in markets with heterogeneous agents.[29]

It is not only through research, however, that Lewis and his students might have influenced the direction of labor economics. Lewis himself had a strong and rather exclusive vision of what constituted good research in economics, with his own empirical neoclassical work reflecting this vision. In published writings he never denigrated alternative approaches to economics; indeed, he never acknowledged their existence.[30] In classes or discussions with colleagues, however, Lewis would occasionally reveal his opinion that non-neoclassical approaches to economic questions were not properly considered as economics at all.[31] Lewis frequently served as a referee for *The Journal of Political Economy* and other prestigious journals (many of his reports can be found in the Lewis papers), and in the later

---

29. The Lewis papers contain a long and interesting correspondence between Rosen and Lewis dealing with some of the theoretical issues later dealt with by Rosen in his seminal paper on implicit markets (Rosen 1974).

30. On at least one occasion Lewis's own approach to labor economics was publicly attacked by John Dunlop (1962), who questioned the value of and motives behind the Chicago research program on the impact of unions. Lewis never responded to this attack in print.

31. For example, in a graduate labor economics class in which I was a student, Lewis remarked that most labor economics in the fifties was 'not really economics at all'.

decades of his career, was often consulted when other departments were considering candidates for hiring or promotion in the field of labor economics. Not surprisingly, he used his own views on what constituted good economics as a means of judging the work of others. When hiring and promotion decisions were made by the Chicago economics department in the sixties, Lewis's general opinion on the appropriate approach to economic research was probably not a source of contention. At Duke, Lewis found less agreement on this matter. He did, however, have a notable impact on the department's hiring and promotion decisions, basing his arguments for or against particular candidates on remarkably detailed reviews of their records.[32] As a result, the Duke economics department had developed a noticeable 'Chicago' flavor by the early eighties.

Those of Lewis's students who moved into academic positions likewise came in their time to serve as referees, to participate in hiring decisions, and to supervise PhD students. It would be wrong to suggest that Lewis's students behaved just as Lewis would have, or that they all carried into their non-research professional responsibilities Lewis's strong commitment to promoting a particular style of neoclassical research. Given what we know about the attention which Lewis gave to his duties as a guide and advisor to graduate students, however, it would not be out of line to speculate that the intellectual affinities between Lewis and his students might be stronger than those between the typical economist and his or her advisor; or that when choosing colleagues or advising journal editors, Lewis's students have probably tended to make decisions that would have pleased their mentor. And through those decisions, they, like Lewis, have contributed to the increasingly neoclassical tone characterizing labor economics since the sixties.

LEWIS'S MAJOR WRITINGS

(1939) (with Paul Douglas), 'Some Problems in the Measurement of Income Elasticities', *Econometrica*, **7**, April, 208-20.

(1942) (with L.M. Court), 'Production Cost Indices', *Review of Economic Studies*, **10** (1), 28-42.

(1946), 'Henry Calvert Simons', *American Economic Review*, **36** (4), 668-9.

(1947), 'Studies in the Elasticity of Demand for Steel'. Unpublished Doctoral Dissertation, University of Chicago.

(1947) (with Paul Douglas), *Studies in Consumer Expenditures*, Chicago: University of Chicago Press.

(1951), 'The Labor-Monopoly Problem: A Positive Program', *Journal of Political Economy*, **54** (4), 277-87.

---

32. Personal communication with Duke faculty member Craufurd Goodwin.

(1956), 'Hours of Work and Hours of Leisure', *Proceedings of the Ninth Annual Meeting*, Industrial Relations Research Association, 1-11.

(1959), 'Competitive and Monopoly Unionism', in Philip Bradley (ed.), *The Public Stake in Union Power*, Charlottesville: University of Virginia Press.

(1962), 'The Effects of Unions on Industrial Wage Differentials', in H.G. Lewis (ed.), *Aspects of Labor Economics*, Princeton: Princeton University Press.

(1963), *Unionism and Relative Wages in the United States: An Empirical Inquiry*. Chicago: University of Chicago Press.

(1964), 'Relative Employment Effects of Unionism', *American Economic Review*, **54** (3), 123-32.

(1967), 'On Income and Substitution Effects in Labor Force Participation', mimeo, University of Chicago.

(1974), 'Comments on Selectivity Biases in Wage Comparisons', *Journal of Political Economy*, **82** (6), 1145-57.

(1975), 'Notes on Partial Equilibrium Analysis', Working Paper No. 69, Industrial Relations Section, Princeton University.

(1976), 'Discussion', in O. Ashenfelter and J. Blum (eds), *Evaluating the Labor Market Effects of Social Programs*, Princeton: Industrial Relations Section, Princeton University.

(1986), *Union Relative Wage Effects: A Survey*, Chicago: University of Chicago Press.

OTHER REFERENCES

Allen, R.G.D. (1938), *Mathematical Analysis for Economists*, London: MacMillan and Co.

American Economic Association (1982), 'H. Gregg Lewis', *American Economic Review*, **72** (4).

Ashenfelter, Orley (1994), 'Introduction', *Journal of Labor Economics*, **12** (1), 138.

Becker, Gary (1957), *The Economics of Discrimination*, Chicago: University of Chicago Press.

Becker, Gary (1976), 'Prefatory Note', *Journal of Political Economy*, **84** (4), pt. 2, s2.

Bronfenbrenner, Martin (1962), 'Observation on the "Chicago School(s)"', *Journal of Political Economy*, **70** (1), 72-5.

Dunlop, John (1962), 'Comment', in H.G. Lewis (ed.), *Aspects of Labor Economics*, Princeton: Princeton University Press.

Freeman, Richard (1994), 'H.G. Lewis and the Study of Union Wage Effects', *Journal of Labor Economics*, **12** (1), 143-9.

Friedman, Milton and Simon Kuznets (1945), *Income from Independent Professional Practice*, New York: National Bureau of Economic Research.

Goldstein, Morris and Robert S. Smith (1976), 'The Predicted Impact of the Black Lung Benefits Program on the Coal Industry', in O. Ashenfelter and J. Blum (eds), *Evaluating the Labor Market Effects of Social Programs*, Princeton: Industrial Relations Section, Princeton University.

Hotelling, Harold (1939), 'The Work of Henry Schultz', *Econometrica*, 7, April, 97-103.

McElroy, Marjorie B. (1994), 'H. Gregg Lewis – Duke Days: 1975-1992 – The Mellow Years', *Journal of Labor Economics*, **12** (1), 149-54.

Miller, Henry (1962), 'On the "Chicago School of Economics"', *Journal of Political Economy*, **70** (1), 64-9.

Morgan, Mary S. (1990), *The History of Econometric Ideas*, Cambridge: Cambridge University Press.

Patinkin, Don (1981), *Essays on and in the Chicago Tradition*, Durham NC: Duke University Press.

Ramstad, Yngve (1981), 'Institutional Economics: How Prevalent in the Labor Literature?', *Journal of Economic Issues*, **15** (1), 339-50.

Reder, Melvin (1982), 'Chicago Economics: Permanence and Change', *Journal of Economic Literature*, **20** (1), 1-38.

Rees, Albert (1976), 'H. Gregg Lewis and the Development of Analytical Labor Economics', *Journal of Political Economy*, **84** (4), pt. 2, s3-s8.

Rosen, Sherwin (1974), 'Hedonic Prices and Implicit Markets: Product Differentiation in Pure Competition', *Journal of Political Economy*, **82** (1), 34-55.

Rosen, Sherwin (1994), 'H.G. Lewis and Modern Labor Economics', *Journal of Labor Economics*, **12** (1), 139-43.

Simons, Henry (1936), *A Positive Program for Laissez Faire: Some Proposals for a Liberal Economic Policy*, Chicago: University of Chicago Press.

10. Richard R. Nelson and Sidney G. Winter

Geoffrey M. Hodgson

The names of Richard Nelson and Sidney G. Winter Jr are linked together because of their pathbreaking joint work on economic evolution and their 1982 book *An Evolutionary Theory of Economic Change*. Nelson is known independently for his extensive writing on industry and technical change and Winter has made a number of additional and noted contributions to economic theory. The first section of this essay gives some biographical details of both authors. The second section discusses Winter's important critique of Friedman's often-cited 1953 paper. This leads appropriately to the third section which evaluates their joint 1982 book. The final section discusses other work in the 1980s and 1990s by both authors.

BIOGRAPHICAL ESSENTIALS

Richard Nelson was born in 1930 in New York City. He obtained his first degree in 1952 in Oberlin College, and moved on to Yale University where he obtained his PhD in 1956. He returned to Oberlin College as an Assistant Professor but shortly afterwards he was appointed as an economist to RAND Corporation. In 1960 he served for a year as an Associate Professor at Carnegie Institute of Technology, followed by a two-year period as a Senior Staff Member on the Council of National Advisors. After returning to the RAND Corporation for four more years, in 1968 he became a Professor of Economics at Yale University. He moved to Columbia University in 1986.

The underlying theme in Nelson's work is on the process of long-run economic change, with emphasis on the processes of technological development and the transformation of economic institutions. One of his first major publications was on Harrod-type growth models, in the *Economic Journal* in 1961. A series of subsequent publications on production functions appeared in 1964 and 1965 in the

American Economic Review, the *Quarterly Journal of Economics* and *The Review of Economics and Statistics*. In the late 1960s Nelson published works on full employment policy, technological diffusion and productivity growth. This early work established Nelson's reputation as a leading industrial economist by the age of 40, before his joint work on economic evolution with Sidney Winter.

Sidney G. Winter Jr was born in 1935 in Iowa City. He obtained his BA in Economics from Swarthmore College in 1956. At Yale University he received his MA in 1957 and PhD in 1964. From 1959 to 1962 he served alongside Richard Nelson, first as a Research Economist at the RAND Corporation and then as a Staff Member on the Council of Economic Advisors. From 1963 to 1966 he taught economics at the University of California at Berkeley. The next two years found him as a Research Economist at the RAND Corporation, crossing paths once more with Nelson. From 1968 he served as a Professor of Economics at the University of Michigan, but in 1976 he joined Nelson as a Professor at Yale University, where he was employed until 1989. He subsequently took up a post as Chief Economist at the US General Accounting Office in Washington DC.

In 1964 Winter published his major essay 'Economic "Natural Selection" and the Theory of the Firm'. This was essentially his PhD thesis, and is discussed in the next section. Some of these early ideas were developed in Winter's 1971 *Quarterly Journal of Economics* article and they became an important ingredient in the evolutionary theory of economic change developed jointly with Nelson. Early joint articles announcing the fruits of this collaboration appeared in the *American Economic Review* in 1973 and in the *Economic Journal* in 1974.

WINTER'S CRITIQUE OF FRIEDMAN

In his 1964 article in *Yale Economic Essays*, Winter made a milestone contribution to the long debate about the objectives of the firm. This debate had started a quarter of a century earlier when in 1939 the Oxford economists Robert Hall and Charles Hitch published empirical evidence concerning the behavior and apparent objectives of the firm. According to their evidence, the firms they studied did not attempt to maximize short-run profits or apply the $MC = MR$ rule. In fact, they did not have sufficient knowledge of their cost curves to find this optimum. Instead, the firms claimed that their aim was long-run profit maximization but they did not attempt to achieve this by finding out about and using the long-run costs curves. In fact they set prices according to the average-cost principle. That is, instead of trying to equate marginal revenue and marginal cost, prices were set to cover the average total cost plus a 'normal' profit margin in the order of 10 percent. Although subsequent empirical studies are not unanimous, they confirm that average-cost pricing is widely used.

Despite this and other corroborative evidence, a major debate followed on the objectives of the firm and the viability and appropriateness of the assumption that the firm is a profit maximizer (Hodgson 1994; Koutsoyiannis 1979, ch. 11). On the one hand, economists such as Robert A. Gordon (1948) argued that firms face a large number of complex or uncertain variables. It is implausible that firms could make marginal adjustments to all these variables simultaneously and thereby maximize profits, and they are thus forced to rely on established decision-making routines such as mark-up pricing. In reply, economists such as Fritz Machlup (1946) defended the profit-maximization hypotheses. He argued that what matters is the beliefs of firms as to what their *MC* and *MR* values are, not their objective values. If firms are maximizing they are doing so on the basis of their hunches and perceptions – which may or may not correspond to the real situation. The appeal to 'realism of assumptions' is thus misconceived and it is legitimate to assume that firms maximize profits.

In a classic article Armen Alchian (1950) turned the debate onto a novel theoretical terrain. He proposed that the assumption of overt maximizing behavior by business firms is not necessary for the scientific purposes of explanation and prediction. Indeed he goes further, arguing that because agents operate in a world of uncertainty and may react in different ways to given stimulii, individual behavior is not predictable. This seemed to concede key points to the institutionalists and others who opposed the maximization assumption.

However, Alchian argued that evolutionary processes ensure that patterns of development can be observed in the aggregate. Selective success, Alchian argued, depends on behavior and results, not motivations. If firms never actually attempted to maximize profits, 'evolutionary' processes of selection and imitation would ensure the survival of the more profitable enterprises. Thus Alchian saw the idea of evolutionary selection less as a buttress and more as an alternative to the assumption that individual firms are actually attempting to maximize their profits. Nevertheless, the more profitable firms are the ones more likely to survive.

Alchian's article was important for a number of reasons. First, it distinguished between the overt behavior and the actual decision rules of firms. Second, it re-introduced into economics the biological analogy which had lain dormant since the deaths of Alfred Marshall and Thorstein Veblen in the 1920s (Hodgson 1993). Years later, and principally for these reasons, Alchian's article provided a crucial inspiration for Nelson and Winter. However, at the time this work served more to support the neoclassical side in the marginalist controversy, as Alchian implied that the assumption of profit maximization for aggregate, industry-wide behavior was legitimate.

Crucially, the adoption of the evolutionary analogy was severely criticized by Edith Penrose (1952). She argued that the analogy with natural selection in biology is weak, in part because there is no economic equivalent to heritable traits. Such an equivalent and relatively durable element has to be found if such an evolutionary notion can be sustained. In addition, Penrose pointed out that biologists assume that behavior is determined by genetic disposition rather than intention, whereas economists in general and Alchian in particular retain the contradictory assumption that human behavior is calculative and purposeful. For these reasons Penrose cast doubt on the use of the biological analogy.

Penrose's riposte did not deter Milton Friedman. In his famous 1953 article on 'The Methodology of Positive Economics' he took the line that the realism of an assumption such as $MC = MR$ is not the key issue, as all theories are inevitably unrealistic. The main criterion for assessing a theory, he asserted, is not its realism but whether or not it makes correct predictions. On these grounds the profit-maximization hypothesis was supported. Following Alchian, and despite Penrose, Friedman briefly developed the 'evolutionary' line of argument, by seeing 'natural selection' as grounds for assuming that agents act 'as if' they maximize, whether or not firms and individuals actually do so. The relevant quotation is as follows:

> Let the apparent immediate determinant of business behaviour be anything at all – habitual reaction, random chance, or whatnot. Whenever this determinant happens to lead to behaviour consistent with rational and informed maximization of returns, the business will prosper and acquire resources with which to expand; whenever it does not, the business will tend to lose resources and can be kept in existence only by the addition of resources from outside. The process of 'natural selection' thus helps to validate the hypothesis – or, rather, given natural selection, acceptance of the hypothesis can be based largely on the judgement that it summarizes appropriately the conditions for survival. (Friedman 1953, p. 22)

In short, Friedman argued that competitive 'natural selection' between firms will ensure that the firms which are actually maximizing profits are the ones most likely to survive. Accordingly, firms do not have to *consciously* apply the $MC = MR$ rule for profit-maximizing behavior to emerge. Friedman thus argued that empirical evidence on the overt intentions and actions of firms – such as that supplied by Hall and Hitch – was irrelevant.

Friedman's argument was and remains highly influential. Partly as a result of his dismissal of the empirical studies, by the early 1950s this debate had swung in favor of those arguing for the retention of the profit-maximization hypothesis. This outcome was of enormous significance for economics in the United States, for it consolidated the supremacy of the rising neoclassical school over the lingering remnants of the formerly influential 'old' institutionalist tradition of Thorstein Veblen, John Commons and Wesley Mitchell. This tradition was pervasive among

American economists in the 1920s and 1930s. In the 1940s its ideas still infused the works of leading critics of the maximization hypothesis such as Robert Gordon, even if they claimed no more than a loose affiliation with that school.

Nevertheless, although the balance of forces had shifted dramatically, the debate did not end. In the 1950s Herbert Simon launched an attack on the assumption of maximizing behavior, including profit maximization by firms. In *Models of Man* (1957) and other works he argued that the assumption of 'global rationality' ignores the complexity and uncertainty involved in real-world decision making. Simon rejected the postulate that global maximization is possible but retained a qualified notion of 'bounded' rationality. Agents are generally unable to gather and process all the information required for reaching global maximization decisions but they can make a 'rational' decision within a small set of possibilities. It was suggested by Simon and his followers, such as Richard Cyert and James March in their book *A Behavioral Theory of the Firm* (1963) that firms and consumers do not maximize but 'satisfice' instead. 'Satisficing' was defined as attaining an acceptable level of attainment, or 'aspiration level'. Agents make use of given routines or 'rules of thumb' to determine when this aspiration level has been reached. An example of such a 'rule of thumb' is the average-cost pricing principle.

It is no accident that Simon (1979) has acknowledged that he has been influenced by the 'old' institutionalists, particularly Commons. Furthermore, Simon (1979, p. 499) goes on to say that 'the principal forerunner of a behavioural theory of the firm is usually called Institutionalism'. (In the context, the 'old' rather than the 'new' institutionalism is implied.) In effect, Simon developed and extended Veblen's (1919) earlier and radical critique of the maximization hypothesis. The major influence of Simon on their thinking is explicitly acknowledged by Nelson and Winter.

However, Simon did not directly attack Friedman's evolutionary argument, and the first major critique of this was by Winter in his *Yale Economic Papers* article. Winter points out that Friedman was vague about the mechanisms of selection and the nature of the evolutionary process. In particular, Friedman's 'natural selection' argument was imperfectly specified in that it did not show how maximizing behavior was replicated through time. For selection to work there must be some sustaining feature that ensures that the maximizers or near-maximizers that are 'selected' through competition will continue for some time in that mode of behavior. For instance, if firm behavior is random, then there is no reason to assume that a firm that happens to be maximizing will continue to do so in the next period. Further, such randomness could mean that a firm on the brink of bankruptcy at one instant could by chance be a good profit maximizer in the next.

Finally, even if 'habitual reaction' is the actual determinant of firm behavior, the selection of maximizers is not guaranteed.

As Penrose had pointed out earlier, for natural selection to work there must be heritable variation in fitness. The heritable element was missing from Friedman's account. For selection to operate consistently in favor of some characteristics rather than others, behavior cannot be purely accidental. There has to be some equivalent to the genetic constitution or genotype, such as the structural characteristics, routines or culture of the firm, which fixes, determines, moulds or constrains the phenotype in some way.

Winter pointed out that to presume that maximization emerges from an evolutionary process means that the organizational forms, habits or routines giving rise to such behavior are being selected through their superior capacity for survival. What is required is a degree of inertia in such routines to restrict change so that selection can operate effectively. Although they are not nearly as permanent as the gene, organizations nurture routines and patterns of thought and action which have self-reinforcing and durable qualities.

Winter suggested that routines in the firm have a relatively durable quality through time. They may help to retain skills and other forms of knowledge, and to some extent they have the capacity to replicate through imitation, personal mobility, takeovers and so on. Further, routines can change through managerial or other action when the firm's profits are below a satisfactory level. As he put it in a later article: 'The assumption that firms have decision rules, and retain or replace them according to the satisficing principle, provides both genetic stability and an endogenous mutation mechanism' (Winter 1971, p. 247).

Hence Winter's work was a partial answer to Penrose (1952) as well as a direct attack on Friedman (1953). Winter discovered in the routine an answer to Penrose's complaint that there the heritable mechanisms were not clearly specified in earlier presentations of the evolutionary analogy in economics. However, in identifying an economic analogue to the mechanism of heredity provided by the gene in biology, Winter argued that such an evolutionary process does not always result in a preponderance of profit-maximizing firms. As Winter (1964, p. 240) puts it:

> If the habitual reactions of some firms at a particular time are consistent with profit maximization, and if as a consequence these firms expand relative to other firms in the economy, this very fact will tend to alter the market price environment facing all firms. It is not clear why, in this altered environment, the same firms should continue to have the good fortune to be closer to maximizing behavior than their competitors ... the environment is changed by the dynamic process itself.

Here Winter exposed a central problem with Friedman's argument which can be illuminated by use of evolutionary concepts from modern biology. Indeed, Winter's suggestion that the 'environment is changed by the dynamic process itself' has its analogue in feedback effects between organisms and their environment, the full biological significance of which has been recognized in recent years.

In addition, the characteristics of new entrants to the industry have to be considered. In Winter (1964, p. 242) there is a brief suggestion that problems may arise if selection is thwarted by a 'disruptive entry of non-maximizers'. Winter also went on to consider the question of returns to scale. He argued that in the cases of decreasing and increasing returns the evolutionary selection of maximizers is likely to be thwarted.

Winter's early work is important not only for its penetrating critique of Friedman, but also for its pioneering development of evolutionary theory. Winter laid the basis for the re-application of the evolutionary analogy, but he had done so by asserting the importance of routine-driven rather than maximizing behavior. Furthermore, Winter had demonstrated that the use of the evolutionary metaphor does not drive analysis inexorably towards the kind of Panglossian and *laissez-faire* conclusions that Friedman had popularized.

In a subsequent article, Winter (1971) developed some of the arguments of his earlier paper. The link with the work of the behavioralists was emphasized, with the proposition that behavioral decision rules provide the required 'genetic' element in an evolutionary theory. Links were also declared with the work of Joseph Schumpeter.

THE MAKING OF A SCIENTIFIC REVOLUTION

By the late 1960s, Nelson had independently moved towards an evolutionary approach to economic theory. His original work on economic growth was broadly neoclassical, but the difficulties involved in explaining manifest productivity differences within the framework of the neoclassical production function led him to develop a new perspective. Nelson (1994b) writes: 'In 1964, I was basically a neoclassical growth theorist, albeit of a rather eclectic kind. By 1968 I was almost a full blown evolutionary theorist'. The stage was thus set for one of the most fruitful collaborations in modern economics.

As noted above, some of the basic ideas of *An Evolutionary Theory of Economic Change* (1982) were published jointly by Nelson and Winter in the early 1970s. To their joint venture, Nelson also brought his rich theoretical and empirical knowledge of industrial economics, and Winter carried the important theoretical innovations that he had made to reinstate in economics the evolutionary analogy from biology.

The inspiration provided by this analogy was crucial and explicit. The term 'evolutionary' was addressed by Nelson and Winter in biological terms: 'above all a signal that we have borrowed basic ideas from biology, thus exercising an option to which economists are entitled in perpetuity by virtue of the stimulus our predecessor Malthus provided to Darwin's thinking' (Nelson and Winter 1982, p. 9). Nelson and Winter were careful to point out the limitations and dangers of this analogy, and the fact that, in strict terms, socioeconomic evolution is more Lamarckian than Darwinian in character. But this qualification should not divert attention from the crucial inspirational role of the biological metaphor in their work. This is another important example of the creative potential of metaphor in the social and physical sciences (Hodgson 1993, ch. 2).

As evidenced throughout their joint and individual works since the mid-1960s, both authors have shared a deep anxiety about the theoretical, empirical and practical limitations of neoclassical economics. This uneasiness is so profound that it has led to a rejection of the core assumptions of neoclassical economic theory. The 'reliance on equilibrium analysis, even in its more flexible forms, still leads the discipline blind to phenomena associated with historical change'. Furthermore, 'although it is not literally appropriate to stigmatize orthodoxy as concerned only with hypothetical situations of perfect information and static equilibrium, the prevalence of analogous restrictions in advanced work lends a metaphorical validity to the complaint'. Finally, they rejected 'the assumption that economic actors are rational in the sense that they optimize' (Nelson and Winter 1982, p. 8).

Accordingly, Nelson and Winter developed an alternative theoretical framework to profit maximization for the analysis of the firm. Instead of such an optimizing procedure, they proposed an evolutionary model in which selection operates on the firm's internal routines. Routines include 'characteristics of firms that range from well-specified technical routines for producing things, through procedures for hiring and firing, ordering new inventory, or stepping up production of items in high demand, to policies regarding investment, research and development (R&D), or advertising, and business strategies about product diversification and overseas investment'. In their analysis 'these routines play the role that genes play in biological evolutionary theory' (p. 14).

Routines are not simply widespread and characteristic of much activity within organizations: they also have functional characteristics. Being concerned to show how technological skills are acquired and passed on within the economy, Nelson and Winter argued that habits and routines act as relatively durable repositories of knowledge and skills. In their words, routines are the 'organizational memory' (p.

99) of the firm. Furthermore, routines may have the capacity to replicate through imitation, personal mobility, and so on. Because of their relatively durable character and their capacity to replicate, routines act as the economic analogue of the gene in biology. They transmit information through time in a manner which is loosely analogous to the conservation and replication of information via the gene.

However, it is freely accepted that innovative activity is possible and much business behavior is not essentially routine. Such irregular and unpredictable behavior was accommodated in their evolutionary theory 'by recognizing that there are stochastic elements in the determination of decisions and decision outcomes' (p. 15). Here again there are clear parallels in the biological theory of evolution where stochastic variation is important in many evolutionary models.

Just as the routine is the analogue of the gene, Nelson and Winter borrowed a second key concept directly from evolutionary biology. They developed the concept of 'search' to encompass changes in the routines of firms: 'Our concept of search obviously is the counterpart of that of mutation in biological evolutionary theory' (p. 18). This concept was illustrated by the evolutionary model in Chapter 9 of their book. A threshold level of profitability was assumed. If firms are sufficiently profitable they attempt to maintain their existing routines and do no 'searching' at all. In some cases Nelson and Winter adopted Simon's 'satisficing' idea: agents attempt to gain a given 'aspiration level' rather than to optimize. However, if profitability falls below this level then 'firms are driven to consider alternatives ... under the pressure of adversity' (p. 211). They invest in R&D and attempt to discover new techniques so that profitability can be restored. In other models, instead of satisficing behavior, Nelson and Winter consider organizations that are 'always searching' for new and improved techniques.

Third, there is a clear analogue to the idea of economic 'natural selection': 'Market environments provide a definition of success for business firms, and that definition is very closely related to their ability to survive and grow' (p. 9). Clearly, this is the application of the analogy of market competition with the 'struggle for existence' in biology. In this third case, unlike the preceding two, there is much common ground with Alchian, Friedman and many others. However, unlike most of their predecessors, Nelson and Winter were careful not to endow market selection mechanisms or private ownership with the aura of a 'natural' order or the mantle of supreme efficiency (Nelson 1981b).

The adoption of these three crucial analogues completed the link between the Nelson–Winter concept of economic evolution and the corresponding idea in biology. In biology, evolution requires three essential components. First, there must be sustained variation among the members of a species or population. Variations may be blind, random or purposive in character, but without them, as

Darwin insisted, natural selection cannot operate. Second, there must be some principle of heredity or continuity through which offspring have to resemble their parents more than they resemble other members of their species. In other words, there has to be some mechanism through which individual characteristics are passed on through the generations. Third, natural selection itself operates either because better-adapted organisms leave increased numbers of offspring, or because the variations or gene combinations that are preserved are those bestowing advantage in struggling to survive. This is the principle of the struggle for existence. Nelson and Winter explicitly appropriated and amended these ideas from biology to build their evolutionary theory. This triad of ideas demarcates their 'evolutionary' approach from many different and contending uses of the term (Hodgson 1993, ch. 3).

However, while the theoretical approach of Nelson and Winter conformed to these three characteristics of evolutionary biology, they make it clear that it does not amount to an exact correspondence. We have already noted that while routines are relatively sturdy in socioeconomic terms they are not nearly as durable as the gene in biology. In addition, when routines change their new characteristics can be imitated and directly inherited by imitators or subsidiary firms. For this reason, as several evolutionary theorists have pointed out, in the socioeconomic sphere the inheritance of acquired characteristics is possible and thereby socioeconomic evolution has Lamarckian characteristics. It could also be classed as Lamarckian because – contrary to the gene-programmed behavior of Darwinism – there is a place for intentionality and novelty in human behavior (Hodgson 1993, ch. 14). As a result it is possible to overcome another objection to the use of the evolutionary analogy raised by Penrose in 1952.

The evolutionary metaphor provided the escape route from the rigidities of neoclassical orthodoxy. Despite many problems and dangers, modern biology is a rich source of ideas and approaches from which a revitalized economics may draw. In all, the application of an evolutionary approach to economics seems to involve a number of advantages and improvements over the orthodox and mechanistic paradigm. For instance, it enhances a concern with irreversible and ongoing processes in time, with long-run development rather than short-run marginal adjustments, with qualitative as well as quantitative change, with variation and diversity, with non-equilibrium as well as equilibrium situations, and with the possibility of persistent and systematic error-making and thereby non-optimizing behavior.

Indeed, as Nicolai Foss (1994) has argued at length, the characterization of the divergence between evolutionary and neoclassical thinking in economics is at root ontological. Evolutionary economics of the type developed by Giovanni Dosi, Richard Nelson, Sidney Winter, Ulrich Witt (see Dosi et al. 1988; Witt 1987) and others is concerned with 'the transformation of already existing structures and the emergence and possible spread of novelties' (Foss 1994, p. 21). Indeed, whereas evolutionary economics theorizes on the basis of a universe that is open, in the sense that the emergence of novelties is allowed, neoclassical economics addresses closed systems and suppresses novelty. In short, evolutionary and neoclassical economics start from very different ontological assumptions about the social world. In this manner, Foss forged links between evolutionary economics and the philosophical realism of Roy Bhaskar (1979) (see also Lawson 1989).

The linkage between evolutionary economics and philosophical realism is of particular significance. Although Nelson and Winter use formal methods and computer simulations, their work has a strong empirical orientation. 'The approach in much of the book is to lay out what the "stylized" facts seem to be, and then try to develop a theoretical explanation that explains these facts' (Nelson 1994b). Notably, in making a distinction between 'formal' and 'appreciative' theorizing, Nelson and Winter (1982, pp. 45-8) argue that formal modeling should play a significant but not a central role. Instead, as in appreciative theorizing, the overriding concern is with empirical grounding and richness. As Nelson (1994a, pp. 154-5) elaborates:

> Appreciative theorizing tends to be close to empirical work and provides both guidance and interpretation. Empirical findings seldom influence formal theorizing directly. Rather, in the first instance, they influence appreciative theory and, in turn, appreciative theory challenges formal theory to encompass these understandings in stylized form. The attempt to do so may identify gaps or inconsistencies in the verbal stories, or modelling may suggest new theoretical storylines to explore. In turn, the empirical research enterprise is reorientated.

Clearly the emphasis here is on the guidance and conceptual framing of empirical study, rather than the development of mathematical formalism itself.

The theoretical innovation brought about by Nelson and Winter is of enormous significance, being the most extensive and rigorous application of the evolutionary metaphor from biology in economics to date. This creative achievement was in part facilitated by Winter's earlier work, which rigorously examined the conditions under which the evolutionary analogy might apply. Nelson's key contribution was his rich knowledge of industrial organization and technological change. Their *Evolutionary Theory of Economic Change* is not only destined to be a classic of late-twentieth-century economics, it also is an archetypal and classical case of the way in which scientific creativity may result from the transfer of metaphor from one discipline to another, but generally only when there is already a rich theoretical and empirical knowledge of the home discipline.

There are additionally instructive aspects of the form, content and context of the work. For instance, although the authors effectively carried out a revolution in our way of thinking about economic change in general and the firm in particular, they sometimes understated their differences with the preceding orthodoxy. For instance, one feature of the Winter (1971) and Nelson and Winter (1982) works is that, despite their dynamic and evolutionary qualities, they are in part attempts to show that the Nelson–Winter type of theory subsumed neoclassical analysis as a special case. Thus they tried to reproduce neoclassical equilibria or production functions by tuning their parameter values, but on the basis of a broader theory which allegedly has greater 'behavioral realism'. Consequently, their work has been seen as occupying an uncomfortable no-man's-land between neoclassical theorists who do not care about empirical realism, on the one hand, and institutionalists and allies who reject neoclassical assumptions, on the other.

As a result, on the one hand, their work has had a limited positive reception amongst heterodox economists. Indeed, Philip Mirowski (1983) has strongly criticized *An Evolutionary Theory of Economic Change* in a review. He pointed out that in seemingly attempting to 'improve' Solow's (1957) production function analysis of growth, Nelson and Winter ignored the theoretical devastation wreaked on Solow's neoclassical theoretical constructions in the Cambridge capital controversy (Harcourt 1972). This criticism is apposite, for Nelson and Winter paid no attention to the devastating work of Piero Sraffa (1960) and his followers. But at the same time Mirowski underestimated the positive contribution and significance of Nelson and Winter's work.

On the other hand, the impact of their work on orthodoxy has not matched the scale of their own intellectual revolution. Casual inspection of the 1983-93 citations to *An Evolutionary Theory of Economic Change* in the Social Science Citations Index suggests that this work is cited much more frequently in management and business publications, rather than in the core theoretical journals of mainstream economics. Arguably the impact to date of the book on mainstream economic theory has been detectable but no more than marginal.

Nelson and Winter have often presented their work less as an intellectual revolution (clearly modesty, too, has a role here) and more as a result of cumulative development of mainstream thought. In casting their own theory in these terms they have many illustrious predecessors. In his famous study of 'scientific revolutions', Thomas Kuhn (1970, p. 139) noted the 'persistent tendency of science to look linear or cumulative, a tendency that even affects scientists looking back at their own research'. To illustrate, Kuhn (1970, pp. 139-40) notes the way in which Newton reinterpreted Galileo's theory to fit in the story about his own:

Newton wrote that Galileo had discovered that the constant force of gravity produces a motion proportional to the square of the time. ... But Galileo said nothing of the sort. His discussion of falling bodies rarely alludes to forces, much less to a uniform gravitational force that causes bodies to fall. By crediting to Galileo the answer to a question that Galileo's paradigms did not permit to be asked, Newton's account hides the effect of a small but revolutionary reformulation in the questions that scientists asked about motion as well as in the answers they felt able to accept.

In effect, by presenting his own work as merely a cumulative development of Galileo's, Newton ignored the conceptual innovations and paradigm shifts implicit in his own theory.

This and many other similar episodes in the history of science leads us to re-examine what Nelson and Winter write about their own intellectual antecedents. We are helped by a thoughtful and lengthy (Nelson and Winter 1982, pp. 33-45) section on this theme. The influence of the works of Simon and the behavioralists was acknowledged: 'We accept and absorb into our analysis many of the ideas of behavioral theorists' (pp. 35-6). There was apposite recognition of the importance for evolutionary theorizing of Armen Alchian's 1950 article, which 'stands out as a direct intellectual antecedent of the present work' (p. 41). And in particular, Schumpeter was singled out: 'The influence of Joseph Schumpeter is so pervasive in our work that it requires particular mention here' (p. 39).

Yet, apart from a brief mention of J.M. Clark and J.K. Galbraith (p. 38), one school is conspicuous by its absence – American institutionalism. There is no mention of Veblen, or of Commons, or of Mitchell in the entire book. Given the precedence of this school of thought in the United States in the interwar period, such an omission is strange, amounting perhaps to an implicit denial of the significance or relevance of the school to the project in hand.

While not being irrelevant, the invocation of Schumpeter by Nelson and Winter has a deep irony. Schumpeter frequently used the term 'evolution' but what he meant by this was the general idea of economic development, involving technological, structural and institutional change. Far from drawing inspiration from outside the social sciences, he persistently alleged that analogies with physics or biology were at best an irrelevant diversion and at worst completely misleading (Schumpeter 1954, pp. 17-18, 30, 119, 211, 537, 788-90).

In particular, and crucially, Schumpeter (1954, p. 789) clearly stated that in economics 'no appeal to biology would be of the slightest use'. Schumpeter's frequent use of the word 'evolution' should not mislead us into believing that his work was a precedent for the employment of a biological analogy. Indeed, we do not find in his work an emphasis on the three principles of evolutionary change (heritable traits, generation of variety, and selection) as discussed above. He occasionally uses a biological metaphor, but this goes against his own strictures and his thoroughly positivist view of science.

In contrast, as I have argued elsewhere (Hodgson 1992, 1993) Veblen stands out as the very first economist to apply the evolutionary analogy in the strict terms of the aforementioned three principles. For instance, we can find the notion of the relative durability of habits or routines and their role as heritable traits in the following passage:

> men's present habits of thought tend to persist indefinitely, except as circumstances enforce a change. These institutions which have so been handed down, these habits of thought, points of view, mental attitudes and aptitudes, or what not, are therefore themselves a conservative factor. This is the factor of social inertia, psychological inertia, conservatism. (Veblen 1899, pp. 190-91)

Likewise, Veblen (1914, pp. 86-9) recognized the role of creativity and novelty with his concept of 'idle curiosity'. Veblen's recognition of the open-endedness of the evolutionary process, is evidenced in his conception of 'change, realized to be self-continuing or self-propagating and to have no final term' (Veblen 1919, p. 37). Finally, Veblen, like Nelson and Winter – and without drawing Panglossian or *laissez-faire* conclusions – subscribed to a notion of evolutionary selection in the socioeconomic sphere:

> The life of man in society, just as the life of other species, is a struggle for existence, and therefore it is a process of selective adaptation. The evolution of social structure has been a process of natural selection of institutions. (Veblen 1899, p. 188)

Hence Nelson and Winter's idea of the 'natural selection' and quasi-genetic quality of institutions and routines also has a strong resonance in the earlier evolutionary economic theory of Veblen. Veblen is a unique precedent for the application of the principles of evolutionary change which Nelson and Winter themselves explicate.

Accordingly, although Nelson and Winter failed to acknowledge his influence, a much more appropriate precedent than Schumpeter for their rediscovery and development of the biological analogy was Veblen, as pointed out by Curtis Eaton (1984) in his review of their book. For these reasons, the work of Nelson and Winter is as much 'Veblenian' as 'Schumpeterian' in character.

Two important questions are raised immediately, but at this stage they cannot be answered fully. First, why did Nelson and Winter place so much emphasis on the inspiration of Schumpeter, but none at all on Veblen? Second, can any indirect traces of the influence of Veblen and the 'old' institutionalists be found in Nelson and Winter's work?

In answer to the first question it is obvious that in developing their ideas Nelson and Winter consulted Schumpeter's works much more often than Veblen's. But this answer is not sufficient, especially in two authors so careful about intellectual precedents and knowledgeable about the intellectual evolution of their own discipline. Clearly, something relating to the 'sociology' of the economics profession is relevant here. Perhaps it is in part due to the fact that the 'Schumpeterian' label is more acceptable to the orthodox economist than the allegedly discredited, defunct and more thoroughly anti-neoclassical work of Veblen and the 'old' institutionalists? The precise answer is not clear. But if scientific geniuses such as Sir Isaac Newton can misconceive of their own intellectual history it is no great disrespect even to innovative and intellectually courageous authors such as Nelson and Winter to suggest here that they may have committed the same error.

The second question is equally complex. We have noted the failure of Nelson and Winter to note the direct influence of known members of the institutional school other than J.M. Clark and J.K. Galbraith. Part of the problem is that the influence of the 'old' institutionalists in the United States in the interwar period was so pervasive that an entire generation of economists were strongly influenced by this school without necessarily declaring a formal or tribal allegiance to institutionalism.

Robert Gordon is a classic example. He was reluctant to declare himself to be an institutionalist, but in his first major monograph, on large corporations, Gordon (1945) made erudite references to the work of Veblen and cited extensively the seminal and institutionalist-inspired study of Adolf Berle and Gardiner Means (1932). Veblenian themes are also present in his famous critique of the maximization hypothesis (Gordon 1948). Gordon (1963) recognized the importance of institutions in economic life, and believed that since Veblen's time mainstream economics had partially absorbed some of the insights of the 'old' institutionalists, while the core theoretical idea of 'rational economic man' was unchanged and the prediliction for mathematical formalism had become much stronger. As is again clear in his presidential address to the American Economic Association, Gordon (1976) was deeply sympathetic to institutionalism, yet he seemed to believe in reforming mainstream economics from within.

It is this same Robert Gordon who Nelson and Winter (1982, p. 16n.) cited as a precursor, one who emphasized that 'many of the decisions with which economic theory is concerned ... are made by routinized procedures'. Likewise, Gordon's work shares with Nelson and Winter a strong and now unfashionable concern with 'big questions' in economics including 'where is the economic system going?' (Gordon 1976, p. 10). Gordon – who died in 1978 – was at

Berkeley from 1938 to 1976: the same university at which Winter taught for three years in the 1960s.

Gordon is not being singled out here as the only influence, nor even a major one, nor as a definitive demonstration that Nelson and Winter's work bore the hidden hallmarks of the 'old' institutionalism. Such a brief discussion does not close the matter. Nothing approaching a definitive history of the intellectual, institutional and sociological development of twentieth-century economics has yet been written. When it is, it will have to explain the all-too-hasty predilection of many leading mainstream US economists to write off and disregard such an important, influential and quite recent episode in their own intellectual history.

OTHER CONTRIBUTIONS IN THE 1980s AND 1990s

The challenge to mainstream economic theory in the works of Nelson and Winter is clearly manifest in several additional works. We shall confine ourselves to a few illustrative examples.

Neoclassical economics has a tendency to treat information and knowledge as resources which are scarce. They are regarded as 'out there' and obtainable by individuals like any other commodity, and at a price. In a series of works Nelson and Winter have argued against this view, rejecting the 'blueprint' view of knowledge 'out there' and seeing the acquisition of knowledge as a social process, deeply embedded in groups and institutions. Clearly this very different view of information and knowledge is related to their rejection of the rationality postulate of neoclassical theory, where agents choose the 'best' option from a number of *known* alternatives. By replacing the central concepts of optimization and equilibrium by an evolutionary picture of ceaseless change, Nelson and Winter have focused on the complex processes of learning, and on the generation and transmission of knowledge.

In an important article, Nelson (1980) criticized the orthodox treatment of information and knowledge – including technological knowledge – as codifiable and cumulative. He rejected the common idea that 'technological knowledge is in the form of codified how-to-do-it knowledge which provides sufficient guidance so that if one had access to the book one would be able to do it' (p. 63). Also discarded is the notion that such knowledge is easily or directly expanded by expenditure on research and development: 'If the salient elements of techniques involve special personal skills, or a personalized pattern of interaction and cooperation among a group of individuals in an important way, then one cannot easily infer how it would work from an experiment conducted elsewhere' (p. 67).

This conceptualization of human knowledge has important implications. It involves, so to speak, a unity of knowing and doing. Furthermore, knowledge may relate to the shared practices of the group, and not simply individuals. Winter has also insisted on the proposition that the knowledge within a corporation relates essentially to the organization and the group, rather than to the individuals composing them. He writes that: 'it is undeniable that large corporations are *as organisations* among society's most significant repositories of the productive knowledge that they exercise and not merely an economic contrivance of the individuals currently associated with them' (Winter 1988, p. 170).

> The coordination displayed in the performance of organizational routines is, like that displayed in the exercise of individual skills, the fruit of practice. What requires emphasis is that ... the learning experience is a shared experience of organization members ... Thus, even if the contents of the organizational memory are stored only in the form of memory traces in the memories of individual members, it is still an organizational knowledge in the sense that the fragment stored by each individual member is not fully meaningful or effective except in the context provided by the fragments stored by other members. (Winter 1982, p. 76)

Accordingly 'it is firms, not the people that work for firms, that know how to make gasoline, automobiles and computers' (ibid.). Clearly, the radical reconceptualization of the notion of knowledge by both Nelson and Winter is of enormous significance, as well as being a major departure from the treatment of knowledge and information problems in neoclassical theory.

Notably, these ideas also have strong and earlier precedents in the writings of the American pragmatists who influenced early American institutional economists such as Thorstein Veblen and John Commons. Furthermore, Veblen (1919, p. 186) himself argued that the 'great body of commonplace knowledge made use of in an industry is the product and heritage of the group'. 'These immaterial industrial expedients are necessarily a product of the community, the immaterial residue of the community's experience, past and present; which has no existence apart from the community's life, and can be transmitted only in the keeping of the community at large' (Veblen 1919, p. 348).

Nelson and Winter's arguments also have precursors in the economic writings of Edith Penrose (1959) and the philosophy of Michael Polanyi (1957). Contrary to the treatment of 'information problems' by neoclassical theorists, 'tacit' or 'unteachable' knowledge cannot be reduced simply to 'information' because it is partly embodied in habits and routines, and it cannot be reduced to, or transmitted in, a codified form.

In other articles, Nelson drew out a number of the implications of this general view. Because knowledge relates to the structures and routines of the firm, and is often in a non-codifiable form, 'management cannot effectively "choose" what is to be done in any detailed way, and has only broad control over what is done, and how well. Only a small portion of what people actually do on a job can be monitored in detail' (Nelson 1981b, p. 1038).

This important view of the role and distribution of knowledge in corporate organizations is a clear rival both to Frederick Winslow Taylor's *Scientific Management* (1911) and to Harry Braverman's Marxist analysis in *Labor and Monopoly Capital* (1974). Both involve the untenable idea that the worker has become 'an appendage to the machine'. The supposed 'separation of conception and execution' which is stressed by these theorists, where managers conceive and give orders, and workers carry them out, is implicitly denied by Nelson. He argued that the firm is a 'social system' and not 'a machine'.

In another paper, Nelson (1981a, p. 109) aimed to hammer 'on the point that the analysis contained in contemporary welfare economics provides an extremely shaky intellectual basis for the favorable views that most Western-trained economists apparently have for private enterprise'. It is not that private enterprise is without its virtues, but Nelson showed that the evaluation of the merits of private enterprise is far more complex than the mask of orthodox theorizing would suggest. Typically, the aim here was both to avoid all simplistic policy conclusions and to suggest a program for major renovation or even replacement of orthodox theory.

More recently, Nelson (1991) has extended his evolutionary analysis of the firm, arguing that the differences between real-world firms must be recognized by economic theory. Orthodox theory often ignores intraindustry firm differences, or denies that they are of any economic significance. In contrast, within an evolutionary approach, both the generation and function of corporate diversity is explicable.

Nelson ((ed.)1993) has also developed a pioneering analysis of 'national systems of innovation'. The argument here was that innovation and technical change are not simply matters for individual entrepreneurs, but also involve cultural and institutional features at the national level. As in all his studies, the aim was to help develop economics as an operational and empirically-enriched science, which can engage with real-world problems and avoid the dogmatic and simplistic policy pronouncements with which we are unfortunately all too familiar.

Winter's continuing willingness to expose the limitations of orthodox economics is evidenced in a forceful critique of neoclassical rationality (Winter 1986), demonstrating a tireless attack on this key proposition over several decades. He rejected the characterization of human agents as 'superoptimizers', asserting, the need for 'a fruitful relationship between theory and empiricism in economics' (p. S432). 'There is an important role for inquiry into the learning and adaptive processes of boundedly rational economic actors who are forced to act in a changing world they do not understand' (p. S433).

Against the prevailing individualism and mechanistic reductionism of mainstream economics, Nelson and Winter have both pioneered a new route of enquiry that promises to develop into the most significant challenge to the foundations of neoclassical orthodoxy for many years. Their work does not exhibit formalism for its own sake, but is a genuine attempt to rebuild economics as an operational and empirically enriched science.

It remains to be seen if and how this battle will be won: whether mainstream economics itself will change, or that the key developments will occur in business schools and elsewhere, and outside the economics departments which are generally increasingly dominated by a relatively closed and formalistic orthodoxy. Time will tell.

ACKNOWLEDGEMENTS

The author is extremely grateful to Richard Nelson and Warren Samuels for helpful comments on an earlier draft of this essay.

NELSON AND WINTER'S MAJOR WRITINGS

Dosi, Giovanni, Christopher Freeman, Richard Nelson, Gerald Silverberg and Luc Soete (eds) (1988), *Technical Change and Economic Theory*, London: Pinter.

Nelson, Richard R. (1980), 'Production Sets, Technological Knowledge and R&D: Fragile and Overworked Constructs for Analysis of Productivity Growth?', *American Economic Review (Papers and Proceedings)*, **70** (2), May, 62-67.

Nelson, Richard R. (1981a), 'Assessing Private Enterprise: An Exegesis of Tangled Doctrine', *Bell Journal of Economics*, **12** (1), 93-111.

Nelson, Richard R. (1981b), 'Research on Productivity Growth and Productivity Differences: Dead Ends and New Departures', *Journal of Economic Literature*, **29**, September, 1029-64.

Nelson, Richard R. (1987), *Understanding Technical Change as an Evolutionary Process*, Amsterdam: North-Holland.

Nelson, Richard R. (1991) 'Why Do Firms Differ, and How Does it Matter?', *Strategic Management Journal*, **12**, Special Issue, Winter, 61-74.

Nelson, Richard R. (ed.) (1993), *National Innovation Systems: A Comparative Analysis*, Oxford: Oxford University Press.

Nelson, Richard R. (1994a) 'The Coevolution of Technologies and Institutions', in Richard W. England (ed.) (1994), *Evolutionary Concepts in Contemporary Economics*, Ann Arbor: University of Michigan Press, 139-56.

Nelson, Richard R. (1994b), Personal communication to G. Hodgson, dated September 21, 1994.

Nelson, Richard R. and Sidney G. Winter (1973), 'Towards an Evolutionary Theory of Economic Capabilities', *American Economic Review (Papers and Proceedings)*, **63** (2), May, 440-9.

Nelson, Richard R. and Sidney G. Winter (1974), 'Neoclassical vs. Evolutionary Theories of Economic Growth: Critique and Prospectus', *Economic Journal*, **84** (4), December, 886-905. Reprinted in Christopher Freeman (ed.) (1990), *The Economics of Innovation*, Aldershot: Edward Elgar.

Nelson, Richard R. and Sidney G. Winter (1977), 'In Search of a Useful Theory of Innovation', *Research Policy*, **6**, 36-76.

Nelson, Richard R. and S.G. Winter (1982), *An Evolutionary Theory of Economic Change*, Cambridge, MA: Harvard University Press.

Winter, Sidney G. (1964), 'Economic "Natural Selection" and the Theory of the Firm', *Yale Economic Essays*, **4** (1), 225-72.

Winter, Sidney G. (1971), 'Satisfying, Selection and the Innovating Remnant', *Quarterly Journal of Economics*, **85** (2), May, 237-61. Reprinted in Ulrich Witt (ed.) (1993), *Evolutionary Economics*, Aldershot: Edward Elgar.

Winter, Sidney G. (1975), 'Optimization and Evolution in the Theory of the Firm', in R. H. Day and T. Groves (eds) (1975), *Adaptive Economic Models*, New York: Academic Press, 73-118.

Winter, Sidney G. (1982), 'An Essay on the Theory of Production', in S. H. Hymans (ed.) (1982), *Economics and the World Around It*, Ann Arbor, Michigan: University of Michigan Press, 55-91.

Winter, Sidney G. (1986), 'Comments on Arrow and Lucas', *Journal of Business*, **59** (4.2), S427-34. Reprinted in C. Freeman (ed.) (1990), *The Economics of Innovation*, Aldershot: Edward Elgar, and in R.M. Hogarth and M.W. Reder (eds) (1987), *Rational Choice: The Contrast Between Economics and Psychology*, Chicago, University of Chicago Press.

Winter, Sidney G. (1988), 'On Coase, Competence, and the Corporation', *Journal of Law, Economics, and Organization*, **4** (1), Spring, 163-80. Reprinted in Oliver E. Williamson and Sidney G. Winter (eds) (1991), *The Nature of the Firm: Origins, Evolution, and Development*, Oxford and New York: Oxford University Press.

OTHER REFERENCES

Alchian, Armen A. (1950), 'Uncertainty, Evolution and Economic Theory', *Journal of Political Economy*, **58**, June, 211-22. Reprinted in Ulrich Witt (ed.) (1993), *Evolutionary Economics*, Aldershot: Edward Elgar.

Berle, Adolf A. and Gardiner C. Means (1932), *The Modern Corporation and Private Property*, New York: Commerce Clearing House.

Bhaskar, Roy (1979), *The Possibility of Naturalism: A Philosophic Critique of the Contemporary Human Sciences*, Brighton: Harvester.

Braverman, Harry (1974), *Labor and Monopoly Capital: The Degradation of Work in the Twentieth Century*, New York: Monthly Review Press.

Cyert, Richard M. and James G. March (1963), *A Behavioral Theory of the Firm*, Engelwood Cliffs, NJ: Prentice-Hall.

Dyer, Alan W. (1984), 'The Habit of Work: A Theoretical Exploration', *Journal of Economic Issues*, **18** (2), June, 557-64.

Eaton, B. Curtis (1984), Review of *An Evolutionary Theory of Economic Change* by R.R. Nelson and S.G. Winter, *Canadian Journal of Economics*, **17** (4), November, 868-71.

Foss, Nicolai Juul (1994), 'Realism and Evolutionary Economics', *Journal of Social and Evolutionary Systems*, **17** (1), 21-40.

Friedman, Milton (1953), 'The Methodology of Positive Economics', in M. Friedman, *Essays in Positive Economics*, Chicago: University of Chicago Press. Reprinted in B.J. Caldwell (ed.) (1984), *Appraisal and Criticism In Economics: A Book of Readings*, Boston: Allen and Unwin.

Gordon, Robert A. (1945), *Business Leadership in the Large Corporation*, Washington, DC: Brookings Institution.

Gordon, Robert A. (1948), 'Short-Period Price Determination in Theory and Practice', *American Economic Review*, **38**, June, 265-88.

Gordon, Robert A. (1963), 'Institutional Elements in Contemporary Economics', in Clarence E. Ayres et al. (eds) (1963), *Institutional Economics, Veblen, Commons, and Mitchell Reconsidered*, Berkeley, CA: University of California Press, 123-47.

Gordon, Robert A. (1976), 'Rigor and Relevance in a Changing Institutional Setting', *American Economic Review*, **66** (1), March, 1-14. Reprinted in Warren J. Samuels (ed.) (1988), *Institutional Economics*, vol. 2, Aldershot: Edward Elgar.

Hall, Robert L. and Charles J. Hitch (1939), 'Price Theory and Business Behaviour', *Oxford Economic Papers*, **2**, 12-45. Reprinted in T. Wilson and Philip W.S. Andrews (eds) (1951), *Oxford Studies in the Price Mechanism*, Oxford: Clarendon Press.

Harcourt, Geoffrey C. (1972), *Some Cambridge Controversies in the Theory of Capital*, Cambridge: Cambridge University Press.

Hodgson, Geoffrey M. (1992), 'Thorstein Veblen and Post-Darwinian Economics', *Cambridge Journal of Economics*, **16** (3), 285-301.

Hodgson, Geoffrey M. (1993), *Economics and Evolution: Bringing Life Back Into Economics*, Cambridge, UK and Ann Arbor, MI: Polity Press and University of Michigan Press.

Hodgson, Geoffrey M. (1994), 'Optimisation and Evolution: Winter's Critique of Friedman Revisited', *Cambridge Journal of Economics*, **17** (4), August, 413-30.

Koutsoyiannis, A. (1979), *Modern Microeconomics*, London: Macmillan.

Kuhn, Thomas S. (1970), *The Structure of Scientific Revolutions*, 2nd edn., Chicago: University of Chicago Press.

Lawson, Antony (1989), 'Abstraction, Tendencies and Stylised Facts: A Realist Approach to Economic Analysis', *Cambridge Journal of Economics*, **13** (1), March, 59-78. Reprinted in Antony Lawson, J.G. Palma and J. Sender (eds) (1989), *Kaldor's Political Economy*, London: Academic Press.

Machlup, Fritz (1946), 'Marginal Analysis and Empirical Research', *American Economic Review*, **36** (3), September, 519-54.

Mirowski, Philip (1983), 'An Evolutionary Theory of Economic Change: A Review Article', *Journal of Economic Issues*, **17** (3), September, 757-68. Reprinted in Philip Mirowski (1988), *Against Mechanism: Protecting Economics from Science*, Totowa, NJ: Rowman and Littlefield.

Penrose, Edith T. (1952), 'Biological Analogies in the Theory of the Firm', *American Economic Review*, **42** (4), December, 804-19.

Penrose, Edith T. (1959), *The Theory of the Growth of the Firm*, Oxford: Basil Blackwell.

Polanyi, Michael (1957), *Personal Knowledge: Towards a Post-Critical Philosophy*, London: Routledge and Kegan Paul.

Schumpeter, Joseph A. (1954), *History of Economic Analysis*, New York: Oxford University Press.

Simon, Herbert A. (1957), *Models of Man: Social and Rational*, New York: Wiley.

Simon, Herbert A. (1979), 'Rational Decision Making in Business Organizations', *American Economic Review*, **69**, 493-513.

Solow, Robert M. (1957), 'Technical Change and the Aggregate Production Function', *Review of Economics and Statistics*, **39**, 312-20.

Sraffa, Piero (1960), *Production of Commodities by Means of Commodities: Prelude to a Critique of Economic Theory*, Cambridge: Cambridge University Press.

Taylor, Frederick Winslow (1911), *The Principles of Scientific Management*, New York: Harper.

Veblen, Thorstein B. (1899), *The Theory of the Leisure Class: An Economic Study of Institutions*, New York: Macmillan.

Veblen, Thorstein B. (1914), *The Instinct of Workmanship, and the State of the Industrial Arts*, New York: Augustus Kelley. Reprinted 1990 with a new introduction by M.G. Murphey and a 1964 introductory note by J. Dorfman, New Brunswick: Transaction Books.

Veblen, Thorstein B. (1919), *The Place of Science in Modern Civilisation and Other Essays*, New York: Huebsch. Reprinted 1990 with a new introduction by W.J. Samuels, New Brunswick: Transaction Books.

Witt, Ulrich (1987), *Individualistiche Grundlagen der evolutorischen Ökonomie*, Tübingen: Mohr.

11. Mancur Olson, Jr

A. Allan Schmid

New PhD's are well advised to publish something from their thesis. But, seldom has such a work been widely cited for the next 30 years or been the cause of a small industry trying to extend or refute its lines of thought in so many disciplines. Such is the case for Mancur Olson's, *The Logic of Collective Action* published in 1965.

When will rational, self-interested individuals not act to achieve their common or group interests? Olson distinguishes situations where the collectively rational outcome emerges automatically – Smith's famous invisible hand – from situations where it does not. Individuals acting independently in markets may not achieve a Pareto-better outcome when the good in question is such that if it is available to one person it is available to others. Olson calls these 'collective goods', but since whether they should or will be collectively provided is the question, they might better simply be called high-exclusion cost goods. If the good is provided by someone, others know they can benefit without helping provide the good. When the group of potential beneficiaries is large, Olson predicts that the good will not be provided unless there is coercion or selective incentives.

Olson has extended the neoclassical insight that while each firm would benefit from reduced output, in competitive markets it pays no one to reduce output. As firms try to maximize profit, the price drops to cost and the collective interest of some group of producers is lost to consumers. 'Just as it was not rational for a particular producer to restrict his output in order that there might be a higher price for the product of his industry, so it would not be rational for him to sacrifice his time and money to support a lobbying organization to obtain government assistance for the industry' (p. 11). Olson insists that individuals in markets are no different from individuals forming interest groups. He mocks the idea that there is any 'propensity to form and join associations' (p. 17).

The major themes of Olson's *Logic* are: (1) group size matters, (2) asymmetry of individual valuation of the good matters, (3) ability to coerce and offer selective incentives matter, and (4) many groups will remain latent, unserved and silent.

GROUP SIZE

The center of Olson's analysis and the theme he most ardently defends is the proposition that the likelihood of the collective good's provision is a function of group size. 'The larger the group, the farther it will fall short of providing an optimal amount of a collective good' (p. 35). And this turns essentially on how the character of the collective good affects the calculation of an individual. The individual has to perceive how his action affects a good's provision. In large groups the individual will not see the effect of his/her own contribution to the good's existence. Olson distinguishes three categories of groups – the privileged, intermediate and latent. The 'privileged group' has a member whose individual benefit from some amount of the good exceeds the total cost of its provision. Olson assumes that this person will act to provide the good regardless of the lack of participation by other beneficiaries.

The 'intermediate group' does not have one member with individual net benefits, but there is some relatively small group whose members can see the effect of their own non-participation. The outcome of this realization is indeterminate and subject to strategic action, but it is presumed there is a chance of success. On the other hand, the 'latent group' is large and likely composed of no one and no small subset who can see the effect of their non-contribution. As Olson puts it, 'an individual in a "latent" group, by definition, cannot make a noticeable contribution to any group effort, and since no one in the group will react if he makes no contribution, he has no incentive to contribute' (p. 50). Occasionally large federated groups comprised of small cells of socially interactive members may provide collective goods.

Olson argues that as the size of the group increases, any individual's share of the total benefit becomes smaller and therefore is likely to be less than cost. But as Todd Sandler (1994) points out, it is not the share that is critical, but the absolute size of the gain to an individual relative to cost. Sandler illustrates with a person who restores the town's monument because it is valuable to that person as a descendant to the person memorialized. In that case the number of people in town who also enjoy the monument is irrelevant to its provision.

The relationship of group size and transaction cost is also noted (p. 48). (Also see Williamson, in this book.) While there might be economies of scale in organization, larger groups are expected to be more costly to organize including identification of beneficiaries. In spite of his recognition of transaction costs as a reinforcing support for the pessimism about large groups, Olson takes pains to minimize it. In his foreword to Sandler's book, Olson distances himself from Coasian analysis which he says is sometimes expressed as saying that only transaction costs prevent collective action and the internalization of externalities.

He says that transaction costs 'are not applicable to sufficiently "large" or "latent" groups that would benefit from the provision of a collective good' (Sandler 1994, p. xv). 'If no two members, or no other small subset of the members of the group of potential beneficiaries of a collective good, would, in the aggregate, gain from bearing the costs of providing some amount of the collective good, then there is no incentive for individuals to interact strategically or even to bear the cost of communicating and bargaining'. Is this to say that if the gain to the individual is less than the cost, then the fact that transaction costs further widen the negative return is irrelevant? But, if individuals are capable of comparing their gain to total cost acting alone, surely they can imagine that if others were to share the costs, the individual might have a net gain (as their share of costs declines while individual benefit is constant). Even if your failure to contribute is not noticed, you may imagine all by yourself that if others were to share the costs, you could be better off. Transaction cost is the barrier to individuals seeking this potential Pareto improvement.

Group size matters and Olson's story is the touchstone. The quarrels come over the details. The theoretical literature survey by Sandler (1994, pp. 35-54) shows that the relationship between provision of a collective good is far from simple. It is affected by linearity in costs and benefits, whether the benefits of each person's provision are additive or whether dependent on the weakest link. In terms of game theory, the relation between size and outcome is different for assurance games, coordination games, chicken games, and so on. It is also complicated by different combinations of collective and selective goods. Olson dismisses the relevance of the prisoners' dilemma game where its limits to communication and contract enforcement can be removed (ibid. p. xii).

Rational ignorance is another deduction from *The Logic*. Just as it may not pay the individual to contribute to a collective good's provision, it may not pay to become informed about the public affairs. That which some might label a failure to perform over civic duty is rational behavior says Olson.

ASYMMETRY

Economists love counter-intuitive findings and Olson supplies the demand. 'Where small groups with common interests are concerned then, there is a systematic tendency for "exploitation" of the great by the small!' (p. 29). The individual or small group with benefits exceeding cost may provide all of the good that people with more modest demands want. Olson assumes that a person who stands to gain a great deal from going it alone will supply the good even if there are many free riders. This is the neoclassical assumption that since people prefer more to less they will always act consistently with its realization. In a companion work, Olson and Zeckhauser (1966) find that the larger members with more to lose in the NATO alliance contribute more per capita than the smaller and poorer nations. The subsequent theoretical literature shows that this result obtains only when goods have normal income elasticities, purchases rise with income and tastes are identical. Where tastes are widely different as in the Israeli–US military alliance, the poorer country spends more per capita (Sandler 1994, p. 11).

Olson appreciates but does not develop any broadening of the psychological basis for action beyond the simple preference for more over less. Thus, in the case of privileged or intermediate groups, Olson does not consider the possibility that the individuals with excess benefit may begrudge the free rider their ride. The free rider may not be regarded as a neutral party but an undeserving free loader. Free loaders evoke malevolence and the possibility that a party may reduce their own gain to prevent an undeserved gain to another. People reject a Pareto-better offer when it is regarded as unfair. This is demonstrated in experiments with ultimatum games where one party may propose a split of a pot to another who has the right to reject it and thereby the pot is lost. (See Frank, in this book). Olson may have been well advised to put the word 'exploitation' in quotes, since this is a judgemental term which evokes exceptional behavior.

EXCLUSIVE AND INCLUSIVE GROUPS

The characteristics of goods also affect whether a group wants to accept new members. Olson distinguishes exclusive and inclusive groups (pp. 36–43). The exclusive group is marked by interest in a high-exclusion cost good in fixed supply. Firms in an industry are not interested in having new entrants since they are rivals. At the same time, if the group is to effectively control output it requires the cooperation of all firms. One defector can ruin the efforts of all the rest. Olson pointed out that this leads to much strategic bargaining in small groups.

In contrast, the inclusive group values a high-exclusion cost good whose supply equals the number of users. Supply is measured in terms of number of users of a given physical quantity of the good. The group welcomes new members if they help pay for the good, and all users need not contribute for some level of physical good to be provided. Olson did not discuss the fact that while more members help reduce the per person cost, it increases the probability of disagreement over the quality of the commonly available good. Additional people help pay for national defense and do not increase its total cost, but do increase the quarrel over what type of force to deploy. This is the problem of building coalitions in a legislature.

As a political entrepreneur tries to add groups to a coalition it dilutes the ability of the originators to control the character of the program.

COERCION

Can the latent group ever succeed? Olson argues that their only options are selective incentives and coercion. He uses the case of labor unions to illustrate the role of coercion. The history of unions shows that they were first organized in small firms with relatively few employees, which supports Olson's thesis that small groups are more likely to provide collective goods. (Unions even in small firms do not track with the concept of a privileged group. A picket line does not require all workers to contribute, but a substantial proportion must participate or at least be sympathetic to obtain success.) Small size does mean that non-participation will be noticed.

A period of rapid gains in union membership from 1897 to 1904 was correlated with advances in compulsory membership. Like all correlations, causality is another matter. Did compulsion get members or did members get compulsion? The closed shop was achieved by bargaining supported by strikes. Olson does not ask where the solidarity necessary for the strikes to succeed in obtaining compulsory membership came from. If you can get your group together to bargain for compulsory membership it is then easier to build further membership.

Further proof of the role of compulsion is offered by Olson by reference to the 1935 Wagner Act which required employers to bargain collectively if a majority of workers voted for a union. This evidence, too, begs the question of how labor successfully lobbied for passage of the act (or why the tenor of the times resulted in the Supreme Court upholding its constitutionality). But, Olson's main point remains: compulsion of the closed shop was highly desired by unions and contributed to their success. However, a coevolutionary model where compulsion is both a dependent and independent variable might better fit the evidence.

Other examples of compulsion are noted in the provision of collective goods. Various professional associations including medicine and law act to limit practice to those who support the associations. In agriculture, promotion of generic products is financed by legally approved check-offs. But it must be asked how these groups obtained this legislation which is a collective good. Further, it must be asked why those opposing these collective actions themselves remained a latent group. Does it matter if your cause is regarded as just?

Does the closed shop and other compulsion reduce freedom in general? Olson says no. He says that to argue that it reduces freedom one would have to argue for voluntary support of all collective goods (something no nation has ever done). He draws an analogy between collective bargaining, military protection and basic government services. 'Compulsion is involved in all three and has to be' (p. 90). So he says the question is not whether we want more or less freedom in the abstract, but whether the goods that require compulsion are worth it (p. 89). Olson does not buy the classical liberal argument that abstract freedom is the supreme value independent of freedom to pursue the realization of certain kinds of goods. Thus the Virginia Public Choice School is at odds with the Maryland School.

The point could be made even stronger if Olson had followed up on his observation that the collective failure of an oligopoly to form is a success for the consumer (p. 15n). It is an ill market failure that does not blow someone a good. The person who wants the collective good compels the unwilling riders to join the union, or pay a tax for a good they do not want. But for symmetry it can be noted that the unwilling and would-be free rider also compels the person who wants the collective good to live without it. The scab is a thief from the view of the union supporter and a blessing for the employer and unsympathetic employee. Since Olson distances himself from the classical institutionalists like John R. Commons, it is perhaps relevant to quote Commons on the issue of compulsion raised by the Supreme Court in a 1917 case where the majority ruled that attempts to organize a union were an illegal conspiracy. Commons (1924, p. 297) said, 'If it is coercion to threaten to strike unless plaintiff consents to a closed union shop, it is coercion also to threaten not to give one employment unless the applicant will consent to a closed non-union shop'. The difference in Olson's and Commons's perspective can be summarized by saying that Olson asks if the provision of the good is worth the loss of freedom while Commons asks which party's freedom counts most as their freedoms conflict. Whether or not a closed shop or tax is passed, the interdependence of high-exclusion cost goods inevitably means that someone's freedom is another's non-freedom.

BYPRODUCT THEORY OF PRESSURE GROUPS

Political pressure groups generally provide a good which if available to one person is available to others in the same general category, such as farmer, environmentalist or manufacturer. Olson's survey of the characteristics of large groups that are successful in providing collective goods identified those who also provide low-exclusion cost, selective goods. Thus successful pressure groups offer a byproduct and mobilize a latent group with 'selective incentives often in combination with some form of compulsion' (p. 133). Olson argues 'that the main types of large economic lobbies – the labor unions, the farm organizations, and the professional organizations – obtain their support mainly because they perform some function besides lobbying' (p. 135).

The Farm Bureau sells insurance and farm supplies, and the American Medical Association sells advertizing in its journal and uses the profits for lobbying. While Olson (p. 137) argues that 'the political power of unions is a by-product of their nonpolitical activities', the picture is confusing. He cites as evidence the fact that the 1935 Wagner Act which made compulsory membership easier was passed before labor unions came to play an important role in politics (p. 136). The problem with the labor example is that ostensibly the main product of the union is wage and security benefits which are also collective goods. How then did the union get organized to achieve either its main product or its byproduct lobbying?

The byproduct theory fits many cases, but is incomplete. It begs the question of why entrepreneurs who can organize nonpolitical activities would want to divert profits to political action? Why would the manager not pocket the insurance profits and why would the members not want the profits returned as dividends which are selective rather than used for a collective good like lobbying? Could it be that these entrepreneurs and members are committed to a cause? Could it be that insurance offered by one's own organization is a different product from that offered by a strictly commercial company? When information costs are high, does trust give a competitive advantage?

Olson asks 'why no organization of college professors has acquired anything like the political power of the American Medical Association' (pp. 140-1). Answer – because the academic and political functions were separated into different organizations. (It also has something to do with the fact that doctors are the gatekeepers for the drug market while academics do not prescribe or use many commercial products.) But the next question is why did this occur? Are academics more stupid than farmers and so did not discover Olson's theory on their own? Are academics even more individualistic than farmers? Are they ideologically non-union? Is the demand less because academics were given more participation in management? These propositions are not easy to test.

The case of business lobbies is used by Olson to reinforce his small is beautiful theory and to show what happens when lobbies cannot utilize byproducts. 'The high degree of organization of business interests, and the power of these business interests, must be due in large part to the fact that the business community is divided into a series of (generally oligopolistic) "industries", each of which contains only a fairly small number of firms' (pp. 143-4). He observes that the most successful business lobbies are for industries with a small number of firms and thus constitute privileged or intermediate groups. He quotes a study finding that of 421 trade associations in the metal products industry, 153 have a membership of less that 20 and the median is between 24 and 50 (p. 144). He calls this his 'special interest theory' where the special interest is a variety of small. (His reference to oligopoly and other non-competitive situations puts him closer to Bowles and Gintis (see in this book) than those who insist that the American economy is essentially competitive.)

Where business as a whole tries to organize a large lobby representing all manufacturers such as the National Association of Manufacturers, it is little more successful than other large groups. Where selective incentives are not offered, its existence is made possible only by a small subset who find the organization a useful front for their interests and thus about 5 percent of the membership contribute about half the money. (It is still interesting to try to explain why the other half is contributed at all – which is not explained by Olson.)

Olson acknowledges that his theory is less useful for non-economic lobbies with social, political, religious or philanthropic objectives. He does not succumb to the temptation to regard all individual behavior as rational regardless of context. He refuses to regard gifts to a large national charity as a selective good in the form of an increase of self-worth or whatever (p. 160n). He says this would make all behavior the pursuit of selective goods and thus any theory untestable. Sandler reviews the deductive analysis of Booth (1985), who analyzed a situation where benefits are derived from a union wage which is non-rival and high exclusion cost and from reputation which is excludable (following the lead of a work by Akerlof). Booth finds that everyone would choose to join. Sandler says this is still consistent with Olson as reputation is a selective incentive. If Olson held true to his 1965 book, he would not take this way out of the problem. Or is it an out? The research implications of Booth/Akerlof while testable in the same way as Olson's are quite different from Olson's. Olson asks if the latent group can go into the insurance business. Booth/Akerlof ask if the group can go into the reputation/sentiment business. It may turn out that Olson was right about the similarity of the behavior in markets and pressure groups, but for the wrong reason. Business firms spend a great deal of effort to create loyalty on the part of their employees in part on the idea that there is a limit to management ability to directly monitor individual performance. Both business and collective bodies invest in 'non-economic' loyalty building.

While Olson does not deny a possible role for what he calls non-economic behaviors, one gets the impression from Olson's overall work that these behaviors are marginalized. For example, when he comes to explaining voting whose product is after all largely a collective good and the individual cannot perceive the difference one vote could make, Olson approvingly quotes a study which says voting is not typically motivated by ideological concerns or plain civic duty (p. 164n). He just says that the cost of voting is minimal. He sees a parallel between not being able to perceive the effects of one's contribution and not being able to see the costs of voting. He posits a 'threshold above which costs and returns influence a person's action, and below which they do not' (p. 164n). But why should low cost be a presumption for voting? What is the habitual action which perception of either cost or benefit must overcome in order to alter that action? The fact that more people vote than contribute to pressure groups could be due to the fact that voting is cheaper, or that the net benefit is positive, or that more people regard it as the right thing to do. Institutions have to do with what is perceived and what magnitudes are perceptible and capable of altering a patterned behavior. (See Kahneman and Tversky and Thaler, in this book.)

Olson would on the one hand like to say that when a person decides not to participate in output reduction in a competitive market he/she is using the same logic as when he/she defects from participation in provision of a collective good. On the other hand, Olson seems to presume that there is some habitual action which continues unless some cost is perceived. Could, then, a person have a habitual action to contribute to organizations that are regarded to have rightful claims on one's resources as long as nothing is perceived to alter that habit? Is the contribution to public TV, charities and unions all that different? One does it because one learns it is the right thing to do.

In the final analysis, Olson's analysis posits that substantial groups will remain latent and their needs unmet. 'Only when groups are small, or when they are fortunate enough to have an independent source of selective incentives, will they organize or act to achieve their objectives' (p. 167). Many are not going to be so fortunate. Is this a council of despair or just hard-headed realism? Are we to be satisfied by knowing that the majority free ride and a lot of groups will fail? Or are analysts to be challenged by the fact that significant numbers do not free ride, and formulate a research agenda on how their number might be increased? The percentage of people voting in different countries differs. It is hard to imagine that this is due to differences in the perception or reality of voting costs. If some can learn a given behavior is it possible that is a variable? If we depend only on *The Logic* we shall never know. Is our glass of social science knowledge half full or half empty? When we congratulate ourselves for explaining the half that it is empty (the free riders) a lot of this explanation will be owed to Olson. Or do we search for ways to expand the part that is filled with cooperative behavior, in which case Olson is of little help?

METHODOLOGY

Olson say he is a methodological individualist, though he insists he does not assume that people are always rational or self-interested (Swedburg interview

1990). He just asks what would a rational self-interested person do and then sees if that is what happens. Olson, like many other economists, has a preference for positing a certain type of rationality, predicting a behavior that follows, and then looking for confirmation. If the confirmation is there it is assumed that the theory was correct or at least one can stop searching for an alternative. This is much preferred to asking people why they did something and whether or not they made the calculation that was posited. Such analysts are content with 'as if' deductions. Since they do not trust people's stated reasons they prefer to make up their own reasons. It is then a matter of rhetoric and personal preference of why one set of reasons (say narrow self-interest) consistent with the evidence is to be preferred over another consistent set (say altruism or sense of doing the right thing). Olson dismisses the latter by saying that no country relies on patriotism to motivate voluntary donations to provide public services. Still we are left wondering why the early strikes to obtain a closed shop were successful. While the first unions may have started in small firms, it is hard to imagine that the leaders or those who manned the picket lines had benefits greater than total costs while non-participants did not. Of course, neither Olson's nor Booth/Akerloff's proposition is directly testable. The neoclassicist will think it is self-evident and others will look within themselves.

Olson focuses primarily on the characteristics of long-lived large groups and ignores bursts of mass collective action. Yet these bursts often establish policy directions and set paths that are long lasting even if the organizations that spawned them disappear. Such is the case of the Granger and other Populist movements which set the path for antitrust legislation. Note that we often use the term movements rather than associations to describe these behaviors. Much depends on the question asked.

OLSON IN HISTORICAL PERSPECTIVE

Like all good thesis writers, Olson learned to review the literature and contrast his contribution to that which went before. He paints his predecessors as pluralists who believed that interest alone was sufficient to motivate contribution to provision of collective goods and that the result was generally benign in the sense that power to affect action was proportionate (to some unnamed something). For example, Marx was interested in how different economic interests (classes) participated in the economy and he assumed people rationally pursued their interests. He made his mistake in not realizing that 'there are no individual economic incentives for class action' (p. 108). In this context Olson says 'a theory of irrational behavior leading to class action might in certain cases be of some interest' (p. 108). Olson observes that Marx 'gave little or no attention to the sociological and psychological processes by which an irrational, emotional class consciousness might develop' (p. 109). And of course, neither does Olson.

The institutionalists fare no better in Olson's mind. John R. Commons argued that representatives of pressure groups might better represent some interests than territorially elected legislatures. He also had no welfare economics and would not make arguments about what was good for the whole of society (p. 115). And for this, Olson paints Commons as a methodological pluralist who does not appreciate individual calculation of whether to be a part of a collective action or not (pp. 114-16).

But a broader reading of Commons is something quite different. Commons observed that 'The system of economic government is not idealistic nor even voluntary because it is not built upon an ideal of a perfect society of socially minded individuals' (1950, p. 268). He observed 'a conflict of inequality of power between great corporations and unorganized individuals' (p. 269). Did Commons appreciate the consequence of group size? 'Small cooperatives seem to work well, when all have similar interests and are fairly well acquainted with each other' (1934, p. 901). Speaking of farm cooperatives, 'They have yet to demonstrate that, on a large scale, they can elect their own leaders ... to deal with the big corporations' (p. 902). He understood with Olson that collective groups did not have full participation. Commons observed that 10 percent of union membership did the work (1950, p. 34) and that 'organization workers' got things done rather than the rank and file.

Olson (pp. 76-97) contrasts his analysis of the labor movement with that of Selig Perlman. Olson emphasizes that Perlman made a great deal out of worker 'job pessimism' as the cause of union formation and goals. Olson interprets Perlman as believing that this interest is sufficient to spontaneously motivate union participation and not appreciating that the closed shop was to provide the compulsion for membership rather than primarily to improve job security. But Perlman's analysis is more subtle. Perlman's (1928, pp. 162-3) language is in fact quite Olsonian: 'The overshadowing problem of the American labor movement has always been the problem of staying organized' and 'the lack of class cohesiveness' and 'lack of a spontaneous class solidarity'. So Perlman like Olson searched for a solution. Perlman believed he found it in a rationale/ideology based on the worker's most threatening experience – namely the consequences of losing one's job to someone willing to work for less. Perlman understood that people often justify a particular action in conformity to some general property rights principle. For some it is Lockean, and for labor it is that present workers own the jobs in a firm or industry. Is this automatic support for collective participation? Perlman says, 'There is, however, a practical limitation upon labor's solidarity' (p.

277). Not just any interest supports collective action. Leaders must be careful not to make their appeal stray too far from the rationale that evokes the strongest emotional response – namely job security. A portrayal of 'us vs. them' gets the emotions going especially if the 'them' is a recent immigrant. (There are plenty of modern parallels in immigration and foreign trade agreement clashes.) Thus Perlman's advice to union leaders was to constrain objectives to collective bargaining and avoid broad concern with social and political action (advice which has some Olsonian special interest features). Olson's advice is to try to get into the insurance business and hope that something permits access to compulsory membership.

Olson regards the concern with job pessimism as a variable thing (rather than an ever-present gut concern) so correlates job availability with union growth and finds little correlation (pp. 77-9). Periods of great demand for labor were periods of great union growth so Olson concludes that job pessimism was not driving people to create and join unions. In the end all models depend on construct validity and rhetoric. Why could individual workers not take the long view and use periods of high demand for labor as opportunities to improve their long-term security? When jobs are plentiful, a strike for union recognition and closed shops is more effective. Some prefer one story and some prefer another. And some may even prefer the co-evolutionary story where ideology, cognition, legislative approval of collective action and closed shops, and strikes to obtain them all evolve together. Compulsion is both an independent and dependent variable. Olson and Perlman can both be right.

In spite of his denial of any heritage from the institutionalists, Olson is consistent with some of its tenants. The prime one is that individuals acting independently in markets may not be able to provide themselves with certain goods. The resulting equilibrium may not be optimal for anyone. This is what unites Commons, Keynes, Galbraith, Schelling and Olson. Olson is neoclassical in knowing what the optimal outcome should have been without reference to the political process, though he understands that one person's market failure is another's success. In the end, however, for all of its brilliant insights, the limit to *The Logic* is that it is only logical and ignores that the human brain is more than a logic machine. This critique is blunted by a man who says that 'reality is so complex that very simple general principles can almost never apply (without exception) to all cases' (Sandler 1994, p. xvi).

RISE AND DECLINE OF NATIONS

The logic of collective action was extended by Olson to explain the rise and decline of nations in a 1982 book (*The Rise and Decline of Nations*). *The Logic* predicted that small, special interest groups would be more powerful than larger and more likely latent general interest groups. Olson reasons that general economic growth is a collective good and therefore in no one's rational interest to support. On the other hand plenty of special-interest groups can make selective goods out of redistributions of income in their favor. To this is added a time dimension which makes the divergence between the powers of special and latent groups a function of time to associate ('freedom of organization'). This leads to a number of suggestive deductions.

'There will be no countries that attain symmetrical organization of all groups with a common interest and thereby optimal outcomes through comprehensive bargaining' (p. 37); 'Stable societies with unchanged boundaries will do the worst and get worse over time' (p. 41); and, 'small groups will do increasingly better relative to latent groups over time' (p. 41). This is tied to development by hypothesizing that 'On balance, special-interest organizations and collusions reduce efficiency and aggregate income in the societies in which they operate and make political life more divisive' (p. 47).

These distributive coalitions make decisions slowly, slow technological adoption, are exclusive, and increase the complexity of regulation and government. The only offsetting tendency is 'encompassing organizations' which represent a large enough proportion of the population so that the group is more interested in general growth than redistribution. But, *The Logic* has already suggested that few of these can be expected.

A number of historical cases are described which are consistent with Olson's theory. Germany and Japan had many organizations destroyed by World War Two and thus got a fresh start which contributed to a postwar growth rate superior to much of the more mature and stable Western countries such as Great Britain, where the process of special interest organization could continue unabated. 'Britain has not suffered the institutional destruction, or the forcible replacement of elites, or the decimation of social classes, that its Continental counterparts have experienced' (p. 84).

The theory tends to suggest that the process of development is spontaneous and the only thing that stops it is redistributive inefficiencies. So positive collective actions such as labor-management codetermination and the role of banks in coordinating investments in Germany are not mentioned. These would be hard to explain with *The Logic*.

Postwar growth in Sweden had a different organizational context. Olson points to the role of 'encompassing groups'. Sweden has one large national labor union rather than being organized along firm or craft lines. There is also a national association of employers. These large groups can bargain with each other without breaking down into redistributive struggles within each group. Olson does not explain how these encompassing groups came about except to note that Sweden is a relatively homogeneous country, which is a somewhat *ad hoc* explanation.

The most extensive and systematic test that Olson provides of his theory is to correlate the growth rate of US states with the date of their founding (pp. 98-119). The confederate states organizations are considered upset by the Civil War and thus that date is used for them. Olson finds years since statehood is negatively correlated with growth in both per capita and total income from 1965 to 1978.

Olson equates years since statehood with stability in the representation of special-interest groups, and the conclusions follow from the theory without any need to actually measure state differences in policy related to growth. He does not measure stability directly such as dominance of one-party rule or political philosophy of the political leaders. No data on the actual length of life of interest groups is presented. Take the case of the Farm Bureau. It may be older in Illinois than in the South or West, but by 1965 is there any reason to think its effectiveness is a function of date of statehood? Would the same be true of the state medical societies and are they in fact less monopolistic in the South? Labor union membership is substantially lower in the South. Olson claims this is due to the Civil War. He finds a negative correlation between union membership by state and growth rates. 'Labor unions are the main organizations with negative effects on local growth' (p. 105). To be impartial he also correlated number of lawyers per capita with growth. He does not, however, inquire into why there are regional differences in public investment in education or how that might be related to regional differences in incomes. While the South has grown since 1965, it is not at all clear that it will ever catch up with the rest of the country with a collective decision to work for less.

Commentators on the Olsonian growth thesis have questioned whether cross-sectional models are appropriate for testing dynamic relationships. James Garland (1992, p. 480) found that 'The relationship between state age and economic growth is unstable and highly time dependent, with the inference drawn from cross-sectional tests of Olson's thesis shown to be a function of years utilized in one's analysis'. Similarly, Lester Thurow (1983, p. 10) points to the history of Massachusetts which was severely depressed in 1964 but growing in 1982. Contrary to Olson, he finds these changes not associated with any change in tariffs, unions, or size of local government.

TRADE INTEGRATION

A deeper excursion into economic history enables Olson to put a twist on the classical case for free trade. Beyond its efficiency gains from comparative advantage, there is a more dynamic source of productivity in freeing the general interest from the power of small groups who act to establish monopolies and cartels. Olson says that the usual case for customs unions is based on static comparative advantage. His concept of 'jurisdictional integration' is much broader (p. 121). It includes the rise of nation states out of feudal Europe as well as domestic market expansion to get rid of organizational brakes on productivity.

The rise of feudal guilds fits Olson's model. Small groups of craftsmen form to regulate quality and price. They are particularly effective with local town government and not successfully opposed by consumer interests. Only the power hunger of the nation-building kings could expose them to competition from outside the city state. Olson notes that it was not enlightened liberal arguments that eventually destroyed the guilds, but the individual ambition of centralizing monarchs (p. 141) He also observes that some kings let the guilds alone in exchange for taxes. In later writing Olson (1993) works out a revenue-maximization rationale for why rulers choose to simply tax what exists or enact other policies to enhance total output – this avoids any non-rational basis for the king's choices. Bringing the story to the present, Olson says, 'With free trade among independent countries there is no way the coercive power of governments can be used to enforce the output restriction that cartels require. There is also no way to obtain special-interest legislation over the whole set of countries because there is no common government' (p. 139). Some are now worried that the general interest in environmental protection may also not be served given the interests of international corporations whose mobility makes national environmental protection difficult. Here is a case where the broader interest requires a positive set of institutions rather than just the removal of constraints.

Olson's trade thesis is not without its critics. Lester Thurow (1983b, p. 9) notes that 'During the late nineteenth century, when the American economy overcame the lead of the British economy, the US was not more open to international trade than Great Britain'. Douglass North (1983, p. 164) argues that Olson has placed too much emphasis on interest groups and has ignored the role of the state. 'The characteristics of the state and the interests of its rulers have produced stagnation even when the distributional coalitions that are the heart of Olson's study have not evolved'.

It is at this point in the book that Olson is willing to speak of policy prescriptions. Is he in favor of instability and revolution in order to destroy special interest groups? He says that his 'theory here does shift the balance marginally in the revolutionary direction' (p. 140) He hopes that by tying revolution to the conservative argument for free trade that it is more palatable and the reader will stay for the end of the book.

INEQUALITY, DISCRIMINATION AND DEVELOPMENT

Theories which explain a host of phenomena are to be preferred to those which explain only a few, says Olson. So he extends his observations from Europe and the US, described above, to the non-Western world. In China, Japan and India he finds the same guild-like organizations that he described in Europe. And they act in similar fashion to establish monopolies and restrict trade. Something new is found in the castes of India, but it too is explained by *The Logic*. The Indian castes based on occupations, like other cartels, were exclusive groups and sought to limit membership. One technique that increased returns to present members was endogamy – members of the caste could only marry other members. What others might regard as irrational prejudice, Olson finds just another logical profit-maximizing strategy by members of small groups. 'Distributional coalitions, once big enough to succeed, are exclusive, and seek to limit the diversity of incomes and values of their membership' (p. 74). To speak of groups as actors is curious for a methodological individualist. The economics of a cartel is well understood. What Olson adds is an explanation of how a cartel can be created and sustained. While a privileged caste is a smaller group than those it dominates, this is not sufficient explanation for Olson. Thus he emphasizes that 'The promotion of prejudices about race, ethnicity, culture, and intergroup differences in lifestyle will also make the coalition work better' (p. 160). These variables add to realism, but are less a matter of *Logic* and more matters of cognition and emotion, which Olson usually regards as *ad hoc*.

A complete theory would have to explain why some individuals and groups refuse to use exclusionary cartels even when profitable – for surely it was no more profitable in India than other places without castes and with equally stable environments. Recall that Olson used the individual greed of the kings to expand their jurisdictions to explain the decline of European guilds. He only notes here that parochial rulers did not challenge the power of the castes. And he does not explain why the caste retained much of its power even after India overthrew the British.

The same economic logic is applied to apartheid in South Africa and it is found to be good business practice for the minority whites. Since the entrenchment of special interests can only get worse, how would Olson explain the eventual fall of apartheid? (And how would he explain the contrasting mass movement led by

Ghandi, which drove the British from India?) Olson's theory would have us look for a change in the basic economics. The fact that the blacks (a large group) were not an effective mass pressure group for change fits Olson's theory. But the subsequent change in policy of the ruling party does not. This appears to be more of a learning process and ideological change than calculation of economic advantage. Olson does not deny the role of ideological change, he just relegates it to the *ad hoc* category. The fact that individuals and governments around the world pressured South Africa for change is hard to explain by mere greed. Olson is careful to argue that it does not pay any individual to discriminate whether employer, employee or consumer (p. 164). Why then would anyone give up a high return on South African stocks or business just to obtain a high-exclusion cost good like knowing that the blacks were self-governing?

As Olson extends his analysis, he observes a large number of less-developed countries in Latin America, Africa, and elsewhere that have been persistently unstable. So at this point he modifies his general theme to say that instability is also inefficient. 'There is no inconsistency in this' (p. 165). 'On the whole, stable countries are more prosperous than unstable ones ... and other things being equal, the most rapid growth will occur in societies that have lately experienced upheaval but are expected nonetheless to be stable for the foreseeable future' (p. 165). True or not, this seems to destroy the simplicity of the theory and introduces the possibility of much *ad hoc* interpretation. Douglass North (1990) puts the emphasis on the other side and presents historical evidence of the role of stability in property rights so that entrepreneurs may invest with confidence.

STAGFLATION, UNEMPLOYMENT AND CYCLES

All of the extant theories of stagflation, unemployment and business cycles are found wanting by Olson. They lack a firm grounding in individual maximizing behavior of micro theory. Keynes's attention to sticky prices was well placed but their source was not explained. In the neoclassical tradition, Olson believes that all would be well if markets cleared. So he asks what prevents mutually advantageous labor exchange from happening and who has an interest in preventing it. The now familiar answer from Olson's logic is that privileged interest groups with high wages form coalitions to prevent the employment of those who would willingly work for less.

Informational asymmetry is rejected as an explanation of sticky prices because Olson cannot imagine that it could persist for as long as the Great Depression did. But in turn he argues that distributional coalitions have cluttered agendas which slow decision making on wage adjustments. By his own argument it seems difficult to imagine that agendas remain cluttered for so long. There are some research programs that differ from Olson's that are also consistent with micro economics, but with different policy implications. It is nice for economists to draw intersecting curves of marginal value product and marginal productivity of labor, but not so easy for employers. Joseph Stiglitz (1987) argues that because of information cost, employers do not accept offers from the unemployed to work for lower wages because they fear it will result in their selecting from a pool of workers of lower quality than before (the cost of an effective unit of labor will be higher even if the wage is lower). So a profit-maximizing employer sticks with prevailing wages for a long time even without urging from unions. Lester Thurow (1983a, ch. 7) points out that wages have not become more flexible as union membership has declined. Thurow argues for a behavioral approach in which wage structures and changes are a variable affecting marginal productivity. A self-interested employer does not want to accept offers to work for less if it reduces learning on the job and cooperation among workers.

In support of his hypothesis, Olson makes some cross-sectional comparisons of Japan, Germany and Taiwan, which have enjoyed relatively low unemployment during the 1970s as compared to the United States or the United Kingdom. All of the former supposedly had 'clean institutional slates'. But one can think of new nations and governments in Africa and Central Europe that have nevertheless experienced inflation and unemployment.

Collective action for Olson is usually conspiratorial and the policy recommendation is to destroy it. In Olson's view, there is no major problem with information or in human psychology such as mass hysteria and mutually enforcing expectations – just damnable coalitions. He concludes that the Keynesian policy of increasing aggregate demand can only help to offset the effects of special interests, but is only second best. The best policy is to remove barriers to market clearing. He advocates a tax on employers who raise wages above productivity. He advocates that we 'repeal all special-interest legislation or regulation and at the same time apply rigorous anti-trust laws to every type of cartel or collusion that used its power to obtain prices or wages above competitive levels' (p. 236).

Olson's argument trivializes politics by visualizing that there is a possibility of a 'clean slate' where each group automatically has 'symmetrical organization' and gets its just deserts. But individuals differ in their substantive view of what constitutes development. As they struggle to make the institutions that define growth fit their own view, they necessarily determine whose deserts count. Olson has made a path-breaking contribution to explaining why some groups count for more than others. Each of us may wish that some particular interest had done better. But to hope that it would do better if all groups were destroyed is unreal.

Olson expresses the hope that his work will serve as a basis for political reform. An academic reviewer cannot knock the role of economic education. But, even if one favors his policy advice, the thrust of Olson's argument is that knowledge of self-interest and sharing an interest are not enough for individuals to act from selfish motives and provide high-exclusion cost goods. Recall his argument for rational ignorance of public affairs. Many have read Olson as support for the superiority of rational choice models for explanation and prediction. But could it be that it contains an implicit argument that political reform depends more on ideology and emotion than on rational calculation? Historians of thought may find that Olson's greatest impact was the persuasiveness of his ideology. And the frequency of citations to his work is indeed testimony to his persuasiveness.

Mancur Olson is Distinguished Professor of Economics at the University of Maryland. He was born in 1932 in Grand Forks, North Dakota, of farmer parents. He was educated at North Dakota State University, Oxford (Rhodes Scholar), and received a Harvard PhD in 1963. He was assistant professor at Princeton from 1963-67 and then worked at the Department of Health, Education, and Welfare for two years where he helped write *Toward A Social Report*, which was the first governmental effort to move beyond the national income accounts to a broader social accounting. He received a major multiyear grant from the US Agency for International Development for a project on Institutional Reform and the Informal Sector in 1990. It was a recognition of the power of his theories of development. At the same time it is interesting to speculate just how US AID will utilize his logical pessimism of the possibility of internal reform. Will the US government use it to justify a withdrawal from foreign aid and leave reform and economic growth to the winds of revolution, changed national boundaries, and military defeat?

OLSON'S MAJOR WRITINGS

Books

(1963), *The Economics of the Wartime Shortage: A History of British Food Shortages in the Napoleonic War and World Wars I and II*, Durham, North Carolina: Duke University Press.

(1965), *The Logic of Collective Action: Public Goods and the Theory of Groups*, Harvard Economic Studies, Vol. 124, Cambridge, Mass.: Harvard University Press.

(1969) (with others), *Toward A Social Report*, U.S. Department of Health, Education, and Welfare, Washington, DC, US Government Printing Office.

(1982), *The Rise and Decline of Nations: Economic Growth, Stagflation, and Social Rigidities*, New Haven: Yale University Press.

Selected Articles

(1959) (with Curtis C. Harris, Jr), 'Free Trade in Corn: A Statistical Study of the Prices and Production of Wheat in Great Britain from 1873 to 1914', *Quarterly Journal of Economics*, **LXXIII**, February, 145-69.

(1966) (with Richard Zeckhauser), 'An Economic Theory of Alliances', *Review of Economics and Statistics*, **XLVII**, August, 266-79.

(1968), 'Economics, Sociology, and the Best of all Possible Worlds', *The Public Interest*, Summer, 96-118.

(1970) (with Richard Zeckhauser), 'The Efficient Production of External Economies', *American Economic Review*, **LX**, June, 512-17.

(1970), 'New Problems for Social Policy: The Rationale of Social Indicators and Social Reporting', *International Institute for Labour Studies Bulletin*, **7**, June, 18-39.

(1976), 'Cost-Benefit Analysis, Statistical Decision Theory, and Environmental Policy', *Philosophy of Science Association 1976 Proceedings*, Vol. II, 372-94.

(1980) (with Martin J. Bailey and Paul Wonnacott), 'The Marginal Utility of Income Does Not Increase: Borrowing, Lending, and Friedman–Savage Gambles', *American Economic Review*, **70** (3), June, 372-9.

(1981) (with Martin J. Bailey), 'Positive Time Preference', *Journal of Political Economy*, **89** (1), February, 1-25.

(1982), 'Environmental Indivisibilities and Information Costs: Fanaticism, Agnosticism, and Intellectual Progress', *American Economic Review, Papers and Proceedings*, **72** (2), May, 262-6.

(1984), 'Beyond Keynesianism and Monetarism', *Economic Inquiry*, **XXII**, July, 297-321.

(1986), 'An Appreciation of the Tests and Criticisms', *Scandinavian Political Studies*, **9** (1), 65-80.

(1986), 'Toward a More General Theory of Governmental Structure', *The American Economic Review, Papers and Proceedings*, **76** (2), May, 120-25.

(1988), 'The Productivity Slowdown, the Oil Shocks, and the Real Cycle', *Journal of Economic Perspectives*, **2** (4), Fall, 43-69.

(1988), 'The Treatment of Agriculture in Developing and Developed Countries', *Journal of Economic Growth*, **3** (2), November, 10-15.

(1988), 'Toward a New Social Report', *Public Opinion*, **11** (4), November/December, 2-4.

(1989), 'A Microeconomic Approach to Macroeconomic Policy', *The American Economic Review, Papers and Proceedings*, **79** (2), May, 377-81.

(1990), 'The Logic of Collective Action in Soviet-type Societies', *Journal of Soviet Nationalities*, **I** (2), Summer, 8-33.

(1991), 'A Collective-Choice and Microeconomic Approach to Macroeconomics: From Sticky Prices and Lags to Incentives', *Osaka Economic Papers*, **40** (3,4), March, 37-54.

(1993), 'Dictatorship, Democracy, and Development', *American Political Science Review*, **87** (87), 567-77.

Selected Book Chapters and Reviews

(1973), 'The Economics of Integrative Systems', in Bernhard Kulp and Wolfgang Stutzel (eds.), *Beitrage Zu Einer Theorie der Sozialpolitic, Festschrift für Elisabeth Leiffmann-Keil*, Berlin: Duncker & Humbolt, 31-42.

(1975), 'Preliminary Thoughts About the Causes of Harmony and Conflict', in Robert D. Leiter and Gerald Sirkin (eds), *Economics of Public Choice*, New York: City College of New York, Cyrco Press, 160-67.

(1976), 'On Boulding's Conception of Integrative Systems', in Martin Pfaff (ed.), *Frontiers in Social Thought: Essays in Honor of Kenneth E. Boulding*, Amsterdam: North-Holland Publishing Co.

(1978), 'Comment on James M. Buchanan and Richard E. Wagner "The Political Biases of Keynesian Economics"', in James M. Buchanan and Richard E. Wagner (eds), *Fiscal Responsibility in Constitutional Democracy*, Leiden/Boston: Martinus Nijhoff, 106-17.

(1984), 'Ideology and Economic Growth', in Charles R. Hulten and Isabel V. Sawhill (eds), *The Legacy of Reaganomics: Prospects for Long-Term Growth*, Washington, DC: The Urban Institute, 229-52.

(1984), 'Review of Thomas C. Schelling, *Choice and Consequence*, "How Rational Are We?"', *The New York Times Book Review*, July 1.

(1984), 'Review of Robert Axelrod, *The Evolution of Cooperation*', in *American Journal of Sociology*.

(1986), 'A Theory of Social Movements, Social Classes, and Castes', in Siegwart Lindenberg, James S. Coleman and Stefan Nowak (eds), *Approaches to Social Theory*, New York: Russell Sage Foundation.

(1986), 'Why Some Welfare-State Redistribution to the Poor is a Great Idea', in Charles K. Rowley (ed.), *Public Choice and Liberty, Essays in Honor of Gordon Tullock*, Oxford: Basil Blackwell.

(1987), 'Collective Action', in John Eatwell, Murray Milgate, and Peter Newman (eds), *The New Palgrave: A Dictionary of Economics*, Vol. 1, New York: Macmillan and The Stockton Press, 474-7.

(1989), 'How Ideas Affect Societies: Is Britain the Wave of the Future?', in *Ideas, Interests and Consequences*, London: Institute of Economic Affairs.

(1990), 'Interview', by Richard Swedberg, in *Economics and Sociology, Redefining their Boundaries: Conversations with Economists and Sociologists*, Princeton, NJ: Princeton University Press, 167-85.

(1990), 'Toward a Unified View of Economics and the Other Social Sciences', in James Alt and Kenneth A. Shepsle (eds), *Perspectives on Positive Political Economy*, Cambridge University Press.

(1991), 'The Role of Morals and Incentives in Society', in Joseph E. Earley (ed.), *Individuality and Cooperative Action*, Washington, DC: Georgetown University Press, 117-28.

(1992), 'The Hidden Path to a Successful Economy', in Christopher Clague and Gordon Rausser (eds), *The Transition to a Market Economy in Eastern Europe*, New York: Basil Blackwell, 55-75.

Anthologies or Symposia Devoted to Assessments and Extensions of Olson's *Rise and Decline of Nations*

(1983), *The Political Economy of Growth*, New Haven: Yale University Press, Dennis C. Mueller (ed.).

(1983), 'Symposium: Mancur Olson on the Rise and Decline of Nations', *International Studies Quarterly*, **27** (1), March.

(1986), *Scandinavian Political Studies*, **9** (1).

OTHER REFERENCES

Commons, John R. (1934), *Institutional Economics*, New York: Macmillan.

Commons, John R. (1950), *The Economics of Collective Action*, New York: Macmillan.

Garand, James C. (1992), 'Changing Patterns of Relative State Economic Growth Over Time', *Western Political Quarterly*, **45** (2), 469-84.

North, Douglass C. (1983), 'Review of Olson's Rise and Decline of Nations', *Science*, **219**, January 14.

North, Douglass C. (1990), *Institutions, Institutional Change and Economic Performance*, Cambridge: Cambridge University Press.

Perlman, Selig (1928, 1949), *A Theory of the Labor Movement*, New York: Augustus M. Kelley.

Sandler, Todd (1994), *Collective Action*, Ann Arbor: University of Michigan Press.

Stiglitz, Joseph (1987), 'The Causes and Consequences of the Dependence of Quality on Price', *Journal of Economic Literature*, 1-48.

Thurow, Lester (1983a), *Dangerous Currents*, New York: Random House.

Thurow, Lester (1983b), 'Review of Olson's Rise and Decline of Nations', *New York Review of Books*, March 3.

12. Nathan Rosenberg

Alexander J. Field

Nathan Rosenberg was born on November 22, 1927 in Passaic, New Jersey. After service in the US Armed Forces, he enrolled in Rutgers University in 1947, receiving his Bachelor of Arts degree *summa cum laude* in 1950. He began graduate study at the University of Wisconsin at Madison in 1950, and received his PhD in 1955, spending two years at Oxford University in England between 1952 and 1954. He served as an instructor at Indiana University between 1955 and 1957, assistant professor at the University of Pennsylvania between 1957 and 1961, and associate and full professor at Purdue between 1961 and 1967. After teaching as a visiting professor at Harvard for two years beginning in 1967, he joined the economics department at the University of Wisconsin in 1969. In 1974 he migrated westward to Stanford University, where in 1980 he was appointed the Fairleigh S. Dickinson Jr Professor of Public Policy.

Rosenberg's many writings have focused on a number of interconnected themes. Perhaps the most prominent has been a concern with the process of economic growth, which he has pursued through research in economic history and economic policy, as well as the history of economic thought. His writings have been empirical and historical but not by and large quantitative, in the sense that he has eschewed use of mathematical modeling or econometric tools.[1] His microeconomic research in economic history has had a particular focus on civil and mechanical engineering, with a heavy emphasis on construction and on the machine tool industry and applications in metal and woodworking. These micro-level studies also inform his excursions into the history of economic thought (and vice versa), as well as his treatments of twentieth-century science and technology policy issues and his more general analyses of the process of economic growth and development.

It is useful to think of Rosenberg's work as encompassing three intersecting circles. The largest of these, into which one can classify more than half of his

---

1. The only use of formal mathematical modeling notation occurs in joint work with Edward Ames (1963a, 1968b) and I am unable to locate a single regression in all of Rosenberg's published work.

publications, concerns new technologies, their commercialization and their transfer; science and engineering policy at the national level; and the impact of these factors on economic growth. A subsidiary circle consists of works explicitly in the history of economic thought. These articles focus on the writings of Adam Smith and Karl Marx – with an emphasis on the division of labor and its growth-enhancing or alienating qualities, the problem of individualism and social cohesion, the treatment of science and technology (principally in Marx) and the role of different institutional structures in creating incentives that foster growth (principally in Smith). A second subsidiary circle consists of industry or sectoral studies, with an emphasis on machine tools and civil engineering (construction) in the nineteenth century, and the airframe, chemical and electronic industries (semiconductors, computers, telecommunications) in the twentieth (1980, 1981, 1991, 1994). These three circles are interrelated, with a number of contributions arguably classifiable in two, and in a few cases all three of these categories.

ADAM SMITH AND THE EFFECT OF INSTITUTIONS ON ECONOMIC DEVELOPMENT

Thirteen of Rosenberg's publications can be clearly classified as contributions to the history of economic thought. The principal focus is on textual analysis of the writings of Adam Smith (1960c, 1965a, 1968a, 1974c, 1976c, 1978, 1990) and Karl Marx (1974b, 1976b). Rosenberg's portfolio in this area is rounded out with an article (1963c) on Bernard Mandeville (a precursor of Smith), an exploration of the economics of Charles Babbage (1992a), an appreciation of Joseph Schumpeter (1992b), and a retrospective (1993a) on George Stigler (certainly a follower of Smith). Although these inquiries are clearly motivated by an interest in what these writers can tell us about the process of economic growth, the articles are presented primarily as contributions in intellectual history.

Both Adam Smith and Karl Marx were broad thinkers with interests in philosophy as well as economics, primarily concerned, in Smith's case, with the institutional framework and governmental policies most conducive to economic growth, and in Marx's case, with the 'dynamics of capitalist development': the interactions of technological change with economic institutions in propelling history forward. Combining the general interests of these two classical economists gives one a pretty good guide to the themes Rosenberg has pursued in his studies in economic history, development and policy.

Rosenberg's 1960 article, 'Some Institutional Aspects of *The Wealth of Nations*', is one of his most original and subtle, and one in which many of the themes developed in subsequent articles are adumbrated. In this paper, Rosenberg rejects the notion that Smith envisioned a society that could be fueled purely by private interest, unconstrained by governmental rules (the anarchist/libertarian solution), as well as the proposition that solving the 'laissez faire problem' was simply a matter of appealing to a moral order that blocked antisocial venues for selfish endeavor. Rosenberg views as incomplete the notion that Smith simply advocated the elimination of interventionist policies associated with mercantilism. The absence of excessive restraints on the freedom of economic action was not enough to secure social harmony or economic growth. According to Rosenberg, Smith clearly saw, and was quite concerned, that self-interest could be pursued in antisocial ways, and that institutional mechanisms were needed to 'cut off all avenues' (he maintained there were many) along which wealth could be pursued without contributing to the progress of society. Different institutional structures should be judged, he maintained, not only according to how well they encouraged the pursuit of self-interest in socially beneficial ways, but also according to how well they frustrated avenues for enlarging wealth through antisocial means (Rosenberg 1960c, p. 560).

Smith believed, according to Rosenberg, that human behavior was governed by a conflict between a natural tendency towards indolence and sloth, and a desire for wealth, which was capable of eliciting the most sustained efforts. Wealth once attained, however, corrupted the impulse to put forth socially beneficial labor. Smith's opposition to high profits was that they reduced the motivation of proprietors to run their enterprises carefully and conduced to waste and prodigality. Smith opposed monopoly not just (or even principally) because it was allocatively inefficient, but because it channeled large flows of resources to individuals who would have weakened incentives to manage them prudently. He excoriated large enterprises and the joint stock mechanism for similar reasons: managers of large enterprise would simply not have the motivation to husband or deploy their resources with the same care as would be true in a society of small-scale individual proprietors.

In envisioning the good society, Smith did not appeal (or at least did not appeal exclusively) to a natural order of moral sentiments to restrain men's impulses to lie, cheat, or steal. It is not enough, argues Rosenberg, to make reference to the often neglected precursor to *The Wealth of Nations*, *The Theory of Moral Sentiments*, as explaining why a society fueled by individualism did not degenerate into a war of all against all. Explicit institutional mechanisms were needed to block anti-social outlets for self-serving impulses. The existence of these mechanisms could not be counted on, but depended on the wisdom of legislators in framing rules that would lead to an economically progressive society.

Rosenberg argues convincingly that Smith's case for a competitive market system, freed of governmentally sanctioned monopoly privileges, was based on more than the desirability of allocative efficiency. Beyond efficiency, Smith was acutely concerned with human motivation, believing that a social system that encouraged economic advance would offer incentives that were neither too low, as in slave systems, nor too high, in a fashion that, to use modern language, would result in a backward-bending labor supply curve. Rosenberg, however, may have excessively differentiated his interpretation from those who see Smith as 'solving' the Hobbesian problem through appeal to a system of moral sentiments developed according to 'natural' or 'God-given' principles. There are certainly grounds to suggest that Smith saw the two mechanisms as supplementing and reinforcing each other.

It is clear, in his concluding remarks, that Rosenberg is interested in Smith not purely from the standpoint of the history of economic thought, but also because Smith is a useful starting point for thinking about the effect of institutional structures on contemporary economic development. His reference to parallels between Smith's analysis of the incentive effects of different institutional arrangements and Albert Hirschman's work on economic development in Colombia, which addressed why Colombia's airlines were run efficiently and its railroads in a mediocre fashion, while its roads were allowed to deteriorate, shows Rosenberg's concern for the relevance of research in the history of thought for analysis of contemporary issues in economic development (Rosenberg 1960, p. 566).

The question of how best to solve the problem of social order also forms the backdrop for Rosenberg's (1963c) essay on Mandeville. Bernard Mandeville's *The Fable of the Bees* has often been identified as a key precursor to Smith's *laissez-faire* views, in particular Smith's emphasis on the paradox of virtue. Rosenberg's starting point is an observation by Jacob Viner that Mandeville had written that it was 'by the skillful Management of the clever Politician' that private vices could be made to serve the public good. According to Viner, this quotation shows that *The Fable of the Bees* cannot provide support for a pure *laissez-faire* view. Rosenberg, however, intends not to bury the Smithian concept of *laissez-faire*, but to save it, by arguing that Mandeville saw the role of government as limited to establishing rules such that society would 'run itself' without arbitrary intervention (Rosenberg 1963c, p. 190). The function of government, in Mandeville's (and Smith's framework), was to establish the basic rules of the game, and then allow individuals to operate within these rules as they best saw fit. Government had a responsibility to establish and maintain the rules, without necessarily trying to mandate each player's particular moves. This seems an eminently reasonable interpretation of what *laissez-faire* meant to Smith. Neither

Smith nor Mandeville believed in a world without government. Both recognized that bees managed to engage in apparently cooperative, coordinated activities without one, and that this metaphor might be useful in thinking about some aspects of human interaction. Neither believed that the metaphor carried forward in all its particulars to human affairs.

A second concern in Rosenberg's writings on the history of thought concerns what one might call the division of labor problem. This issue is addressed in 'Adam Smith and the Division of Labor: Two Views or One?' (1965a). In Part I of *The Wealth of Nations* Smith extolled the productivity enhancing features of the division of labor, whereas in Part V he talked about the psychologically deadening effects of mindless repetitive work, using this as justification for his support of expanded primary education as a possible palliative. Marx, of course, also wrote extensively about the 'alienating' features of labor in a capitalist society.

In this article Rosenberg asked if these 'two views' were in fact in conflict, and concluded that they were not, because (according to Smith) the debilitating effects of the division of labor were not uniformly spread throughout society. Agriculture was spared because the biological cycles of growth and germination put limits in that sector on the degree to which the division of labor could be pursued. Secondly, the upper reaches of the occupational distribution, in particular, professional and scientific personnel, were also spared. Indeed, the abilities of professional and scientific personnel to pursue speculative research were enhanced by the productivity improvements associated with the division of labor. Rosenberg concludes that, on balance, Smith had no fear that the increasing division of labor would cause the degree of creative energy in a society as a whole to deteriorate, and thus there was no conflict between the views expressed in Book I and Book V of *The Wealth of Nations*. (This analysis, particularly the emphasis on the beneficial effects of the division of labor among administrative as well as professional and scientific personnel, is developed further in Rosenberg's (1976c) communication, 'Another Advantage of the Division of Labor'.)

In 'Adam Smith, Consumer Tastes and Economic Growth' (1968a), Rosenberg explored how, in Smith's analysis, the availability of new commodities interacted with the preference structures of certain classes of consumers to affect household behavior in a manner that was favorable to economic development. In particular, he maintained that before the invention and increased availability of new categories of household durables, wealthy landowners had little incentive to do other with their agricultural surplus than sustain large armies of dependents who would then owe them loyalty. With new product and process innovations expanding the range and availability of consumer durables, landowners now had a motive for rationalizing their cultivation and improving its efficiency, which they did as consumption among the wealthy shifted from services to durable goods.

Both of these developments, according to Smith, were good from the standpoint of economic growth.

Why the former of these effects was desirable is self-evident, but why the latter should be beneficial is more puzzling. Rosenberg's analysis follows naturally from Smith's distinction between productive and unproductive labor (the latter perishing in the instance of its creation while the former fixes itself in vendible products). If consumption shifted towards durables, the stock of useful things was augmented. These goods continued to yield service flows after purchase and would eventually benefit even the lower orders of society as they were cast off by their superiors.

How can one make sense of this argument? Although our modern national accounts classify the purchase of long-lived consumer durables (vehicles, household appliances or furniture) as consumption, it is obvious that in important ways such purchases are closer to investment expenditures. Perhaps Smith's views make sense if we see a shift in spending from services to durables as ultimately augmenting the nation's aggregate saving or investment rate.

But modern economic theory also views a dollar spent on a service as yielding as much utility at the margin as a dollar spent on a good. Should we as a matter of public policy stigmatize the spending of $700 on an opera subscription series, yet laud the purchase of a television set of equivalent value? Indeed, Smith recognizes that the pleasure to be derived from accumulating objects can be overrated (and in fact usually is, he says). That psychological bias Smith nevertheless saw as desirable because it drove men to industry. But why is the desire to consume services necessarily any less a motivator to industry than the desire to acquire durables?

These issues are of more than strictly historical interest, because in subtle ways much of Rosenberg's work in economic history and policy is colored by Smith's (and Marx's) sympathies regarding productive and unproductive labor. Rosenberg's heavy emphasis on manufacturing, and the machine tool industry which was important for its growth in the nineteenth century, are at least consistent with the belief that, on a dollar-for-dollar basis, consumption and resources devoted to manufacturing are in some sense more 'productive' than equivalent value directed towards services (these issues are addressed in more detail below).

Rosenberg's (1974c) article, 'Adam Smith on Profits – Paradox Lost and Regained', explores in substantially greater detail a theme already introduced in his (1960c) article, namely the effect of high profits on the care with which merchants and capitalists husband their resources and manage their affairs. Put in other ways, as Rosenberg states at the end of the article, the concern is with the process whereby the accumulation of wealth corrupts the incentives leading to its generation (Rosenberg 1974c, p. 1189).

The paradox referred to in the title is that whereas Smith emphatically rejects the notion of a backward-bending labor supply curve for labor, he appears to embrace it with respect to capitalists. Smith took strong exception to the prevailing wisdom that the toiling masses had to be kept in poverty or they would cease to work. On the contrary, Smith enthusiastically supported high wages, first because he viewed them as testimony to the success of economic development, and second because he believed (at least within empirically relevant ranges) that higher wages would elicit more rather than less effort. Indeed, the social and managerial problem in a high-wage environment, far from being one of eliciting effort from labor, was to prevent individuals from overworking themselves and prematurely depleting their human capital.

Smith was much less optimistic (and sympathetic) when it came to capitalists. First of all, whereas high returns to labor and landlords were symptomatic of a progressive economy, high returns to capitalists were not. Rosenberg repeats the analysis developed in earlier (1960c and 1968a) contributions, but adds to it the proposition that by redirecting control over at least some of the surplus from agriculture to commerce, as landlords developed an interest in exchanging their surplus with manufactured products, large numbers of people developed a greater sense and reality of independence. This he viewed as an essential foundation for good government. Moreover, as feudalism decayed, crime would in fact go down: Smith argued at several points that dependency bred crime, irrespective of the number of policemen, whereas independence and self-reliance did the reverse. According to Rosenberg, Smith maintained that encouraging commerce and manufacture would reduce crime more effectively than would additional police.

Along similar lines, Smith argued that as commercial relations developed, probity and punctuality in the population would rise, partly because merchants' reputations and economic success depended on their behaving in these fashions. Smith viewed landlords as leading lives of indolence and ostentation, but believed all men aspired to such a life, and merchants would do the same if given half a chance. The merit of commercial capitalism was that it restrained so many from doing so. And by shifting control of the economic surplus to a group of individuals who were so constrained, the efficiency with which resources were allocated and the rate at which capital was accumulated would increase. If profits were high it meant that the economic system was not working properly, and capitalists had reduced incentives for frugality and careful management. Only the force of competition could ensure a low rate of profits, and keep capitalists from beginning to act like landowners. High profits would reduce the quality if not the amount of capitalist effort.

After a gap of more than a decade, Rosenberg returned to issues in the history of economic thought. 'Adam Smith and the Stock of Moral Capital' (1990), breaks a little new ground, but is largely derivative of ideas developed in earlier work. In his (1960c) article, Rosenberg differentiated his views to those who solved the *laissez-faire* problem by appealing to a natural order of moral sentiments developed in Smith's earlier writing. Rosenberg now revisits the issue of moral sentiments, suggesting that they could be viewed as akin to social overhead capital, and asks whether Smith believed on balance that commercial development depleted or strengthened such capital. Rosenberg argues that Smith believed that in certain ways development clearly depleted the stock. Returning to the division of labor problem, Rosenberg requotes the passage from Book V of *The Wealth of Nations* about how division of labor makes (at least some) workers stupid and ignorant, and thus presumably also less moral. He also develops Smith's analysis of how economic development weakens the family because the state can now guarantee physical security, one of the chief roles previously played by the extended family. This is important because the family is seen as one of the chief intergenerational conduits of moral sentiments.

Smith believed that although society was better off with a prevalence of mutual love and affection, this prevalence was not absolutely necessary for economic progress. What a society *had* to have in order to advance was the *absence* of a widespread sense of injustice. Commercial society, although more impersonal, increased respect for the rule of law, which, by implication, increased the frequency of behavior (honoring contracts, telling the truth) that an external observer would view as moral. This point had of course, been developed earlier by Rosenberg, and indeed, much of the remainder of the 1990 piece recapitulates the analysis developed in (1974c), which in turn built on ideas put forth in (1960c). The long block quote from Smith on pages 11-12 of the 1990 article is identically cited on pages 1185-6 of (1974c), and the long block quote on pages 16-17 of the 1990 article is identically cited on pages 1187-8 of (1974c). These quotes are certainly worth reading again, but they represent terrain already, in a sense, heavily traveled.

KARL MARX AND THE IMPACT OF SCIENCE AND INVENTION ON ECONOMIC GROWTH

It has frequently been remarked that Smith, who published *The Wealth of Nations* in 1776, had little to say about and perhaps relatively little direct experience of the forces typically associated with the Industrial Revolution. Steam power in mining, manufacturing and transportation, the revolution in the smelting and refining of iron, the dramatic productivity improvements in the spinning and weaving of cotton – none of these are touched on by Smith. His most famous manufacturing example, that of the pin-making establishment, is clearly a non-mechanized factory. If Rosenberg's starting point for considering the impact of legal and institutional structures on economic development can safely be said to have been Smith, his views on science and technology were heavily influenced by Karl Marx (and Friedrich Engels), who of course wrote later, during the height of the period in which new technologies in manufacturing and transportation transformed the economic face of Europe.

Rosenberg's two scholarly articles on Marx concern the latter's views on technology and the advance of scientific knowledge. 'Marx as a Student of Technology' (1976b), is particularly interesting in the light of Rosenberg's research in economic history, because of the emphasis placed on the special importance that Marx attached to the capital goods sector. Rosenberg's research in economic history focuses heavily on the machinery portion of the capital goods sector, and can be seem explicitly as an attempt to develop the implication of Marx's argument. In rereading this article, I was struck by Marx's emphasis on the growing importance of capital-saving innovation, both in the form of cheapening of the costs of constant capital (making machines and buildings less expensive relative to consumer goods) and in the form of increasing inventory turnover, and thus utilization rates. Rosenberg uses these materials to support his contention that Marx was a careful student of technology, and in several of his articles develops the implications of the former point, particularly with reference to experience-related reductions in the costs of producing equipment. Rosenberg does not systematically address the latter point involving inventory turnover and fixed capital utilization rates. As it happens, I have, although I found myself initially inspired by Alfred Chandler's emphasis on speed of throughput.[2] It was a surprise to find this line of analysis foreshadowed in Marx, and reflects the type of unexpected illumination one can get from reading or rereading Rosenberg's work.

Rosenberg's other article on Marx, 'Karl Marx on the Economic Role of Scientific Knowledge', (1974b) appeared in the same year as his *Economic Journal* article, 'Science, Invention and Economic Growth' (1974a), which was really an extended commentary by Rosenberg on Jacob Schmookler's 1966 work, *Invention and Economic Growth*. Schmookler had developed a demand-centered view of the inventive process, using patent data to establish, for example, that

---

2.   See my articles, 'Modern Business Enterprise as a Capital Saving Innovation' (1987) and 'The Magnetic Telegraph, Price and Quantity Data, and the New Management of Capital' (1992a), which develop these arguments.

when a sector's purchases of capital goods grew, so too (with a lag) did patenting (read inventive) activity. Thus, far from being exogenous, technological change in Schmookler's framework was induced by changes in incomes and relative prices which affected spending patterns.

Rosenberg begins his *Economic Journal* article in very general terms, talking about the degree to which economists have limited their attention to the consequences of technological change, a predilection for which he holds Schumpeter partly responsible. Rosenberg notes that after World War Two, several factors pushed economists to make technological change somewhat more endogenous. These factors included increased research and development spending, the large residual discovered in growth-accounting studies (which suggested problems with models of economic development that focused only on saving rates and physical capital accumulation) and the new interest in growth in less-developed regions. Of course, while the first of these developments does suggest the need for a more demand-focused analysis of technological change, the latter two developments speak only to the importance of such change, not whether it should be treated as endogenous.

Having begun in very general terms, Rosenberg then moves to an analysis and critique of Schmookler's framework, much of which Rosenberg accepts. The problem is where, and to what degree, to allow an autonomous role for science and technology. This is an important question because, as Rosenberg recognizes, if scientific and technological change is completely endogenous, its history is frankly of little ultimate interest to economists and economic historians. If technical change is entirely induced, there are other, presumably more fundamental factors changing the prices and incomes to which scientific and technological change responds.[3]

Rosenberg sees Schmookler as arguing that although demand influences the realm or commodity classes of inventive activity, supply-side progress in science and technology influences the characteristics of new invention: whether, for example, it exploits mechanical, electrical, chemical or biological principles. But Schmookler goes too far, according to Rosenberg, in claiming that scientific advance itself is also ultimately demand driven. If this is true, then the Schmookler thesis becomes irrefutable because it is tautological, particularly if demand is identified as equivalent to patents or inventive activity. Surely, says Rosenberg, there was a strong demand in the sixteenth and seventeenth centuries for advances in both navigation and medicine. But whereas the state of scientific knowledge in

---

3. The same argument applies to institutions: if they are completely endogenous, there is no particular reason for economists to study them, accept as illustrations of the way in which more fundamental forces work their will. See Field (1991).

mathematics and astronomy could support advances in navigation, the same was not true in medicine, and it is likely that the investment of no amount of resources in the seventeenth century could have changed that reality. In other words, the supply schedule for advances in medicine was completely inelastic at that point.

Science, says Rosenberg, has progressed from simpler to more complex problems. In antiquity, the greatest progress was made in mathematics, mechanics, astronomy and optics: fields that relied on direct human observation, with little need for instrumentation or complex experimental apparatus. Thus mechanics matured two centuries before basic chemistry, and inorganic chemistry decades before advances in the understanding of more complex organic chemistry. Scientific advances have always been easier in some areas than others, and, Rosenberg argues, it is hard to imagine that 'any plausible set of social or economic forces could have brought about a total reversal of that order' (Rosenberg 1974a, p. 100). Economic influences have some impact on the sequence of technological development, but even here, Rosenberg does not buy the Schmookler perspective in its entirety. The substitution of coal for charcoal in England took place first where it was technologically easiest to do so, in the evaporation of sea salt, for example. It took many years for the substitution to take place in glass making, the drying of malt, or in the smelting of iron. Arguably, the applications in which its economic payoff were highest came last. Similarly, the mechanization of spinning took place much more rapidly in cotton than in wool, because the cotton fibers were far more amenable to the application of the new techniques.

Rosenberg concludes by noting that Schmookler does not take into account the differential development of sciences (note the plural), but denies that this critique represents a return to technological determinism, since, as Rosenberg notes in a final footnote, if demand conditions are sufficiently strong, more costly innovations can precede less costly ones (Rosenberg 1974a, p. 108).

With this article as a backdrop, it is quite interesting to read Rosenberg's analysis of Marx's views on the economic role of science, published in the same year. One must of course recall that Marx has often been placed squarely in the supply-side (technological-determinist) camp – indeed that perspective has sometimes been seen as the hallmark of his approach. Rosenberg opens this article by painting Marx (and Engels) almost completely into the Schmookler (demand-based) camp. Marx, according to Rosenberg, did not view science as an independent variable, arguing to the contrary that the progress of scientific inquiry was socially determined. Egyptian astronomy developed out of the compelling need to control the Nile. The application of machinery in the seventeenth century created the incentive for mathematicians to understand mechanics. Scientific knowledge was acquired when a social need for that knowledge had been established.

But Rosenberg rescues a supply-side role for science in Marx by pointing out that Marx also argues that only centuries after capitalism was established did a marriage of science and industry take place. Yet surely the demand for this union existed earlier. The resolution of this apparent paradox is (according to Marx) that so long as production was controlled by hand workers, scientific principles could not be applied. Technological developments in the machine tool industry (a persisting Rosenberg focus) broke the log jam. Whereas the direction of scientific effort might be demand driven, the capacity to absorb fruits of scientific discovery was supply constrained by current levels of technology. Rosenberg goes on to find support in Marx for the view that scientific progress has proceeded sequentially and unevenly, and in ways which cannot be attributed to purely demand factors (this, of course, is the core of Rosenberg's critique of Schmookler).

Rosenberg concludes this article by noting, somewhat coyly, that Marx and Engels' qualifications to the demand view 'strike me as collectively more interesting than the original proposition'. The conclusion I draw is that Marx and Engels were not totally consistent in their arguments, and indeed, Rosenberg himself sometimes gives the impression of not being totally consistent. In a 1981 essay, 'How exogenous is science?' (1982, ch. 7), prepared for a celebration of Simon Kuznets's 80th birthday, Rosenberg gently criticized Kuznets for suggesting that in the modern era, science was an autonomous motor driving history. In fact, says Rosenberg, the challenges presented by technological search have frequently influenced the direction of scientific inquiry. Great technological progress has often been made initially with only the most imperfect understanding of the scientific principles underlying what was going on; much progress in pure science has emerged out of technological empiricism.

The question is not whether science is completely exogenous or completely endogenous with respect to market forces; as the title of this article suggests the question is one of degree, and Rosenberg wishes to get away from either/or propositions. Nevertheless, his positions are sufficiently nuanced that he does sometimes seem to be on both sides of the question, criticizing Schmookler (persuasively) for going too far in making technological change endogenous, at the same time criticizing economists or economic historians who have viewed technological change as autonomous, or have interpreted Marx as strictly within that tradition. Overall, however, he seems most consistently to argue against the extreme demand-side view of innovation, which has become quite popular among some economists.

Support for this interpretation is found in the (1979b) Mowery and Rosenberg survey of empirical studies purporting to demonstrate that market-demand forces 'govern' the innovation process. The two authors conclude that this hypothesis is simply not demonstrated by the empirical analyses that have claimed to support it. The authors accept the public policy implications of the demand-oriented scholars that government ought to take whatever steps it can to improve the efficiency of market processes. But they also argue that the production of new knowledge is very inadequately served by private markets, and a more activist public policy is needed. Breakthroughs in semiconductors, for example, represented the playing out of possibilities created by fundamental advances in solid state physics that had their own internal dynamic, and were not a simple response to market forces demanding cheap calculators and computers. The conclusions of this article are completely consistent with those of the (1974a) article criticizing Schmookler.

Nevertheless, when Rosenberg assembled a number of his papers in his 1982 collection, *Inside the Black Box*, he put this article within a section entitled 'Market Determinants of Technological Innovation', possibly leading inattentive browsers to conclude that Rosenberg was part of the trendy tendency to view innovation as almost entirely demand determined. And his short essay 'Does Science Shape Economic Progress – Or is it the Other Way Around?' (1993b) as well as some of the papers in his 1994 collection seem to tilt again towards a greater emphasis on demand.

Whatever Rosenberg's final conclusion on the precise balance between supply and demand forces in determining the direction of technological search, he insists that we dirty our fingernails with the details of engineering history, because it is the past historical evolution of technological capabilities, more fundamentally even than recent scientific breakthroughs or current market prices, that governs the direction of technological change. A great deal of productivity improvement comes from actual experience with a new process, a point made, perhaps most forcefully, in his essay 'Learning by Using' (1982, ch. 6).

The attempt to get beyond the black box in evaluating the balance between supply and demand forces is also evident in a related debate in economic history to which Rosenberg contributed. This debate involved whether factor scarcity influences the direction of technological search. J.R. Hicks had argued that as labor became relatively scarce as capital accumulated, more innovative efforts would be devoted to finding labor-saving innovations. A number of economic theorists responded that businessmen would pursue inventive effort wherever it was likely to save them the most dollars or pounds, regardless of its factor-saving bias. Rosenberg builds on this critique, rejecting, along with these theorists, the notion that aggregate factor scarcity has much influence on the direction of technological search. He adds to this critique, however, by introducing the concept of 'compulsive sequences'. Complex technologies create internal compulsions and pressures which initiate exploratory activity in particular directions. The idea is that many economic activities involve interdependent systems, and an innovation in one part of a system often cannot yield its full potential until advances are made elsewhere, in complementary aspects of that system. Rosenberg's analysis is an implicit rebuke to theorists who assume that we live in a world of infinite substitutability. Improved automobile engines lead to a demand for better brakes. Without the more powerful engines, the payoff to better brakes was low; without the better brakes, however, the full potential of the more powerful engines could not be realized.

Rosenberg develops this point persuasively using a number of concrete examples, illustrating why an interest in the details of engineering and technical systems is important to understanding technical progress. Once an innovation occurs that impacts a particular technological system, a compulsive sequence of technological search is initiated. There must, of course, still be demand for the output of that interdependent system, but wide variations in prices will have little impact on the specific character of technological search at that point. This argument is developed more generally in 'Factors Affecting the Diffusion of Technology' (1972b) and reinforced in 'Technological Interdependence in the American Economy' (1979a).[4]

The concept of compulsive sequence reappears, with a new label, in 'Path Dependent Aspects of Technological Change' (1994). If sequences are compulsive then the past compels or constrains: history matters. Like Molière's *Bourgeois Gentilhomme*, Rosenberg discovers that he has been saying path dependence all these years and just had not realized it. He reiterates arguments advanced earlier (e.g., 1982), suggesting that even an autonomous breakthrough in scientific knowledge may have relatively little impact on innovation opportunities, which are largely governed by the *technological* capabilities inherited from the past. Moreover, these technological capabilities powerfully influence the development of science itself by shaping its research agenda (1994, ch.1, p. 19), a phenomenon that is relevant even when the technological improvement (for example in instrumentation) occurs as a direct result of scientific inquiry itself (1992c).

---

4. In (1972b) Rosenberg reinterprets Douglass North's classic study of the contribution of organizational change to rising productivity in the ocean shipping industry. North concludes that invention played little role in productivity improvement. Rosenberg argues that North is actually saying, among other things, that the prevalence of piracy slowed the diffusion of new hull designs. Surely what North meant was that new design blueprints were not the proximate cause of innovation, and that when we search for causal explanation, we are typically trying to identify proximate causes. I do not find Rosenberg's criticism here, if it is intended as such, to be persuasive.

EARLY MACROECONOMIC INTERESTS: THE BRITISH CONSTRUCTION INDUSTRY; BUSINESS CYCLES

The research on the British construction industry in the immediate post-World War Two period (1958) – Rosenberg's earliest published work – is noteworthy because it displays an interest in macroeconomics and economic fluctuations largely absent from much of the later work. This research, which stemmed from his dissertation, involved the efforts of the Labour Government to smooth and control the cycles in construction building in England, given the enormous demands associated with repairing wartime bombing damage.

The only other contribution with an explicitly macroeconomic focus is J.R.T. Hughes and Rosenberg (1963b) 'The United States Business Cycle 1820-1860: Some Problems of Interpretation' and it perhaps reflects the longer-term interests of Hughes more than those of Rosenberg. This article objects to an older tradition interpreting nineteenth-century business fluctuations as reflecting fundamentally a moral problem involving episodes of 'overspeculation'. According to Hughes and Rosenberg, the expansion phases of nineteenth-century cycles were associated with real investment booms, particularly in infrastructure, and these booms were part and parcel of the process of capital accumulation and economic growth. The authors reject the view that the downturns were due to 'wild speculation' which was morally unsound. It remains a possibility, however, that the real investments in railroads, canals and infrastructure which the authors identify may not have been as carefully planned and located during the ebullient phase of the expansion, in part because they were poorly considered (and poorly evaluated by credit intermediaries). Consequently these investments may have been unable to generate the incremental service flows upon which the promises to pay that financed them were predicated. It would be a mistake to say that study of the real estate construction booms of the 1980s, and the savings and loan practices which facilitated them, should be devoid of any moral or ethical dimensions, just as surely as it would be a mistake to say that they can be understood entirely in such terms. The same is probably true of nineteenth-century fluctuations.[5]

---

5. See Field (1992b) for an application of this line of thinking to the Great Depression.

MACHINE TOOLS AND THE AMERICAN SYSTEM OF MANUFACTURES

In addition to his general analyses of the role of science and technology in economic growth, Rosenberg has made several specific contributions to economic and technological history (1960a, 1963d, 1967a, 1975a) and written important surveys of technological change in American economic development (1967b, 1971a, 1972a). These contributions focus heavily on the history of the machine tool industry and its applications in manufacturing in the United States, a focus also apparent in his introduction to the Wallis and Whitworth reports on the American system of manufactures (1969b). If one is interested in the history of the machine tool industry, and its technological impact in manufacturing, this body of work is an indispensable place to start.

CAPITAL GOODS, TECHNOLOGY AND ECONOMIC GROWTH

Why the sustained emphasis on the machine tool industry? The argument that an indigenous machine tool industry is critical to economic development is clearly stated in 'Neglected Dimensions in the Analysis of Economic Change' (1964), where Rosenberg describes how less-developed countries import their capital goods (read machines) from abroad. 'This expedient', he argues, 'deprives them of a learning experience in the production, improvement and adaptation of machinery which may be vital to economic growth' (1964, p. 100). The line of argument can be traced back even earlier, to his (1960b) contribution, 'Capital Formation in Underdeveloped Countries'. The historical interest in machine tools is also reflected, in the co-authored 1960 and 1961 articles in *The Patent Trademark and Copyright Journal of Research and Education* and in 'Technological Change in the Machine Tool Industry 1840-1910' (1963e). In 'The Direction of Technological Change: Inducement Mechanisms and Focusing Devices' (1969a), the rationale for this emphasis is reiterated: 'It can be argued that a responsive machinery producing industry has been the key to successful industrialization'. And in 'Economic Development and the Transfer of Technology' (1970) Rosenberg argues that a well-developed machinery industry 'produces an external economy for the rest of the economy, a dynamic learning process that transfers skills throughout an economy. ... Creating a capital goods industry is ... a major means of institutionalizing internal pressures for the adoption of new technology' (p. 564).

Although Rosenberg eschews the attempt 'to press the analysis of technology transfer in the last third of the 20th century onto a 19th century Procrustean bed', (1970, p. 552) and admits that the policy implications of his analysis are unclear, it follows from his argument that a developing country might consider subsidizing, or, through commercial policy, otherwise favoring, a machine tool sector. It is clear that he is not opposed on ideological grounds to some type of industrial policy for either developing or developed countries. As we enter the twenty-first century, would it be prudent to subsidize an indigenous machine tool industry? Rosenberg is not clear. In places he suggests that multinational corporations may now be able to substitute for the role played by the machine tool industry in the nineteenth century; elsewhere that the option of importing the capital goods is available to followers. But if the importation strategy is to be criticized for the nineteenth century, why should it be advocated for the twentieth?

This discussion should serve to indicate how tricky it is to sustain arguments that a particular sector is relatively 'more important' than the value added it generates. Throughout his work Rosenberg places enormous emphasis on the machinery portion of the physical capital stock, again and again referring to capital goods and machinery as coextensive. There are one or two occasions in the publication record in which the analysis is qualified to indicate that structural investment is ignored, and of course Rosenberg began his academic work with a study of the British construction industry.[6] Intellectual specialization is certainly desirable, and there may be reasons for advocating development policies placing special emphasis on equipment. Nevertheless, the grounds for such policies are not self-evident.

As noted, Rosenberg offers a dynamic microeconomic rationale for his focus on machinery, particularly machine tools. What is problematic, however, is the mixing of microeconomic arguments about learning by using and technical diffusion and transfer, with discussions of the macroeconomic requirements of physical capital accumulation.[7] This Rosenberg does on several occasions. Doing so fails to recognize the small claim made by machine tools in particular and equipment in general on a society's flows of savings.

---

6. This tendency first appears in his 'Population Changes and Economic Development' (1959). This article, an inconclusive discussion of the extent to which population growth may or may not pose an obstacle to economic development, several times, and without qualification, equates capital goods with machinery (e.g., p. 216).

7. Rosenberg argues that countries with indigenous machine tool industries experience capital-saving innovation which reduces the relative cost of equipment relative to consumer goods (1963d), and that developing countries without machine tool industries face additional obstacles to capital accumulation as a result. What is lacking in this argument is any attempt to estimate the empirical magnitude of this effect, or to explain why countries importing machine tools do not also benefit from the reduction in relative prices.

In almost all epochs and regions the requirements of accumulating structures: houses, commercial warehouses, port facilities, roads and railway terminals, airports, power-generating equipment and the public infrastructure of governmental, educational, medical and religious facilities completely dwarf the claim on saving flows represented by the acquisition of new equipment (Field 1985). To suggest otherwise, a common habit among economists reinforced by some of Rosenberg's writings, distorts the nature of the challenges associated with physical capital accumulation in both developing and developed country contexts.

In his historical and policy-oriented work Rosenberg also places a very strong emphasis on the manufacturing portion of GDP. Manufacturing currently employs about a seventh of the US labor force. Rosenberg reached maturity during a period of United States history in which the share of the civilian labor force employed in the sector hit its all-time peak (just under 32 percent, in 1944). Even more striking, perhaps, was the absolute growth in manufacturing employment from 6.9 million in the depths of the Depression in 1932 to 17.6 million in 1943.[8] The images and the reality of the United States on a wartime footing, more than doubling the size of its manufacturing sector in a little over a decade in a process that surely contributed to Allied victory, must have made a powerful impact on all who shared in that experience.

But the economic structure of the US economy during World War Two, and the role that manufacturing played in the extraordinary recovery from the Depression, turn out to have been profoundly anomalous. The share of the civilian labor force in manufacturing in the US today is barely 14 percent, about what it was in 1850. There has been no long-term trend for the share of the manufacturing sector in the United States to increase, and a balanced view of American economic history, both prospective and retrospective, requires an integrated analysis of commodity-producing and service-generating activities, particularly those in transport and communication.

In the introduction to the *Report on the American System of Manufactures* (1969b), Rosenberg correctly describes the large fraction of the British labor force that was then not employed in manufacturing ('In short, the proportion of the labour force which was directly engaged in productive operations involving the extensive use of power driven machinery was still small' 1969b, p. 3). Rosenberg also reminds us (1969b, p. 24), of Lebergott's estimate that only 15 percent of the labor force in 1850 was in manufacturing. But in (1972, p. 87) he characterizes the American manufacturing sector as one which was small at the start of the nineteenth century but grew at the end to be its largest. This proposition, which is

---

8. US Bureau of the Census, *Historical Statistics*. Series D-4, D-130; *Economic Report of the President* 1993, Series B-30, B-41.

supported by Gallman's data on *commodity* output, ignores the major contributions of transport, wholesale and retail trade, and other services in the GDP denominator, and is not sustainable. Both Smith and Marx made a distinction (using different definitions) between productive and unproductive labor, with only the former crystallizing itself in vendible material products. Although this perspective has been rejected by twentieth-century economics and our system of national income accounts, a bit of its aura continues to suffuse Rosenberg's work, and may help us understand its particular emphases.

CONCLUSIONS

These critical comments are intended to place achievements in perspective. Nathan Rosenberg has made important contributions to our understanding of the history of economic thought, particularly that of Adam Smith and Karl Marx, and to our understanding of the process of technological change and its role in economic history and development. He has brought to the discussion of science and technology policy an insistence that technology be approached in concrete, not simply abstract terms, and that debate be disciplined by knowledge of what the process actually involves and how it evolves. He has provided classic overviews of the role of technological change in economic development, and developed carefully nuanced treatments of the degree to which scientific and technological progress is autonomous or induced. For these and many other contributions, we should continue to honor his efforts by reading them.

ROSENBERG'S MAJOR WRITINGS

(1958), 'Government Economic Controls in the British Building Industry 1945-49', *The Canadian Journal of Economic and Political Science*, August.

(1959), 'Population Changes and Economic Development', *Orbis*, Summer.

(1960a) (with Murray Brown), 'Patents and Other Factors in the Machine Tool Industry', *The Patent, Trademark and Copyright Journal of Research and Education*, Spring.

(1960b), 'Capital Formation in Underdeveloped Countries', *American Economic Review*, September.

(1960c), 'Some Institutional Aspects of the *Wealth of Nations*', *Journal of Political Economy*, December.

(1961) (with Murray Brown), 'Patents, Research, and Technology in the Machine Tool Industry', *The Patent Trademark and Copyright Journal of Research and Education*, Spring.

(1963a) (with Edward Ames), 'Changing Technological Leadership and Economic Growth', *Economic Journal*, March.

(1963b) (with J.R.T. Hughes), 'The United States Business Cycle 1820-1860: Some Problems of Interpretation', *Economic History Review*, April.

(1963c), 'Mandeville and Laissez Faire', *Journal of the History of Ideas*, April.

(1963d), 'Capital Goods, Technology and Economic Growth', *Oxford Economic Papers*, November.

(1963e), 'Technological Change in the Machine Tool Industry 1840-1910', *Journal of Economic History*, December.

(1964), 'Neglected Dimensions in the Analysis of Economic Change', *Bulletin of the Oxford University Institute of Economics and Statistics*, February.

(1965a), Adam Smith on the Division of Labor: Two Views or One?', *Economica*, May.

(1965b) (with Edward Ames), 'The Progressive Division and Specialization of Industries', *Journal of Development Studies*, July.

(1967a), 'Anglo American Wage Differences in the 1820s', *Journal of Economic History*, June.

(1967b), 'Economic Consequences of Technological Change 1830-1880', in Melvin Kranzberg and Carrol W. Purcell (eds), *Technology in Western Culture*, Oxford University Press.

(1968a), 'Adam Smith, Consumer Tastes and Economic Growth', *Journal of Political Economy*, June.

(1968b) (with Edward Ames), 'The Enfield Arsenal in Theory and History', *Economic Journal*, December.

(1969a), 'The Direction of Technological Change: Inducement Mechanisms and Focusing Devices', *Economic Development and Cultural Change*, October.

(1969b), Introduction to *The American System of Manufactures*, Edinburgh University Press.

(1970), 'The International Transmission of Technology: Some Historical Perspectives', *Technology and Culture*, October.

(1971a), 'Technological Change', in Lance Davis et al., *American Economic Growth*, Harper and Row.

(1971b), 'Technology and the Environment: An Economic Explanation', *Technology and Culture*, October.

(1972a), *Technology and American Economic Growth*, Harper and Row.

(1972b), 'Factors Affecting the Diffusion of Technology', *Explorations in Economic History*, Fall.

(1973a), 'The Direction of Technological Change: A Reply', *Economic Development and Cultural Change*, January.

(1973b), 'Innovative Responses to Materials Shortages', *American Economic Review*, May.

(1974a), 'Science, Invention and Economic Growth', *Economic Journal*, March.

(1974b), 'Karl Marx on the Economic Role of Scientific Knowledge', *Journal of Political Economy*, July–August.

(1974c), 'Adam Smith on Profits – Paradox Lost and Regained', *Journal of Political Economy*, November–December.

(1975a), 'America's Rise to Woodworking Leadership', in Brooke Hindle (ed.), *America's Wooden Age*, Sleepy Hollow Restorations.

(1975b), 'Problems in the Economist's Conceptualization of Technological Innovation', *History of Political Economy*, December.

(1976a), 'Machine Tools', *Dictionary of American History*.

(1976b), 'Marx as a Student of Technology', *Monthly Review*, July–August.

(1976c), 'Another Advantage of the Division of Labor', *Journal of Political Economy*, August.

(1976d), 'On Technological Expectations', *Economic Journal*, September.

(1978), 'Adam Smith and Laissez Faire Revisited', in Gerald O'Driscoll, Jr (ed.), *Adam Smith and Modern Political Economy, Bicentennial Essays in the Wealth of Nations.*

(1979a), 'Technological Interdependence in the American Economy', *Technology and Culture*, January.

(1979b) (with David C. Mowery), 'The Influence of Market Demand Upon Innovation; A Critical Review of Some Recent Empirical Studies', *Research Policy*, April.

(1980) (with W. Edward Steinmueller), 'The Economic Implications of the VLSI Revolution', *Futures*, October; also in Rosenberg (1982), ch. 9.

(1981) (with David C. Mowery), 'Technical Change in the Commercial Aircraft Industry 1925-1975', *Technological Forecasting and Social Change*; also in Rosenberg (1982), ch. 8.

(1982), *Inside the Black Box: Technology and Economics*, Cambridge: Cambridge University Press.

(1986) (with L.E. Birdsell, Jr), *How the West Grew Rich*, Basic Books.

(1990), 'Adam Smith and the Stock of Moral Capital', *History of Political Economy*, Spring.

(1991) (with Ralph Landau), 'Innovation in the Chemical Processing Industries', in *Technology and Economics*, National Academy Press; also in Rosenberg (1994), ch. 10.

(1992a), 'Charles Babbage: Pioneer Economist', in Herbert Hax, Nathan Rosenberg and Karl Steinbuch, *Charles Babbage, Ein Pionier der Industriellen Organisation*, Dusseldorf; also in Rosenberg (1994), ch. 2.

(1992b), 'Joseph Schumpeter: Radical Economist', paper presented at meeting of Schumpeter Society in Kyoto, 1992; also in Rosenberg (1994), ch. 3.

(1992c), 'Scientific Instrumentation and University Research', *Research Policy*; also in Rosenberg (1994), ch. 13.

(1993a), 'George Stigler: Adam Smith's best friend', *Journal of Political Economy*, October.

(1993b), 'Does Science Shape Economic Progress – Or is it the Other Way Around?', in Donald McCloskey (ed.), *Second Thoughts*, Oxford: Oxford University Press.

(1994), *Exploring the Black Box: Technology, Economics, and History*, Cambridge: Cambridge University Press.

OTHER REFERENCES

Field, Alexander J. (1985), 'On the Unimportance of Machinery', *Explorations in Economic History*, October.

Field, Alexander J. (1987), 'Modern Business Enterprise as a Capital Saving Innovation', *Journal of Economic History*, June.

Field, Alexander J. (1991), 'Do Legal Systems Matter?', *Explorations in Economic History*, January.

Field, Alexander J. (1992a), 'The Magnetic Telegraph, Price and Quantity Data, and the New Management of Capital', *Journal of Economic History*, June.

Field, Alexander J. (1992b), 'Uncontrolled Land Development and the Duration of the Great Depression in the United States', *Journal of Economic History*, December.

Schmookler, Jacob (1966), *Invention and Economic Growth*, Cambridge, Mass.: Harvard University Press.

13. Thomas Schelling

Avinash Dixit and Richard Zeckhauser

Thomas Schelling cannot be confined. He strides across disciplinary boundaries, and makes his work accessible not just to economists but to anyone who is willing to think rigorously. He confronts an array of social situations that appear disparate, but he discerns salient patterns. The patterns speak; they predict outcomes, many of them surprising. Schelling then determines what minor adjustments in conditions will change outcomes. For example, even when racial preferences are very mild, a small change in a neighborhood's composition can set in motion a process of 'tipping' into complete segregation; unfortunately, there may be no way to 'tip' the neighborhood back. Throughout his work, as in this example, Schelling explains complicated situations through simple models, stripped of nearly all the specialized language of economics.

Often Schelling shows which changes in strategy will yield a superior outcome. A seller, for example, may improve his/her prospects by lowering his/her payoff for an outcome, say by staking his/her reputation so he/she would lose face should he/she accept a weakly favorable offer. This will induce a rational buyer to improve his/her offer. Indeed, Thomas Schelling's greatest contribution to economics has been to introduce strategic thinking to the analysis of a vast range of situations – mundane and profound, local and global.

Strategic thinking involves recognizing the influence of a participant's choices on the choices of others, and so ultimately on outcomes. The outcome cannot be foreseen simply by studying the decision of any one typical chooser, just as the properties of water as a liquid cannot be understood from studying the properties of a single H_2O molecule. Schelling has repeatedly identified surprising 'emergent properties' of social systems, important behaviors that appear in an aggregate of units albeit not in the units in isolation.[1]

Much of modern economics traces such patterns of interaction, often under the heading of game theory. Indeed, almost all of modern theoretical research in

---

1. The term 'emergent property', as say liquidity for water, comes from the currently fashionable science of complex theory. See Waldrop (1992, p. 82 et seq.).

industrial organization, international trade, political economy and several other areas is predominantly game-theoretic, and much of this work consists of mathematical models. The 1994 Nobel Memorial Prize in Economics was awarded to John Harsanyi, John Nash and Reinhard Selten for their work in game theory. All three are best known for mathematical work, in particular for establishing 'solution concepts', axiomatized procedures that identify outcomes for identifying outcomes in well-defined and formal games. Schelling has made seminal contributions to game theory and its application, but of a quite different sort. His mode of thinking is distinctive. With no compromise of logical rigor, he employs elegant language and parsimonious models as his primary tools for understanding analytic issues. He develops and applies the concepts of game theory extremely broadly, both within economics and beyond its borders. Inspired significantly by the work of Schelling, game theory has been applied effectively to industrial organization, international trade and labor markets, and in describing the behavior of governments, individuals and firms. A complementary strand of work recognizes the central role of information in markets for both goods and labor, and the potential for selectively revealing, concealing and unearthing it.

Since Thomas Schelling is blind to distinctions between disciplines and subject areas, he applies strategic thinking wherever it will provide insights. It is no surprise that he is widely cited in sociology and political science, and within economics in areas such as labor and industrial organization, on which he has written little.

BIOGRAPHICAL NOTES

Thomas Schelling joined the great classes of graduate students in economics at Harvard just after World War Two. His initial efforts looked like those of a conventional economist; his doctoral dissertation, which became his first book, was entitled *National Income Accounting*. His first four articles appeared in *Econometrica*, the *American Economic Review* (two), and the *Review of Economics and Statistics*. But many of his later writings only indirectly hint at economics in their titles, and a quick perusal of his works might suggest that he has left economics. No regressions appear on his pages; he regularly presents equations comprehensibly packaged as graphs and figures; terms like money supply and liquidity are infrequent. Though he writes of taxes and prices, he also talks of taboos and practices. Human society in general, not just the economy, is his stalking ground.

In fact, Schelling is a staunch and energetic economist (and we refer to more than his mountain climbing). Incentives frequent his pages; though often not dressed in dollar signs, they remain predominant influences on human behavior. He identifies implicit prices where others might miss them, or might assume that since they are not recorded in monetary amounts they do not count as prices. He cuts to the heart of non-economic situations – say the struggle to maintain one's weight – by recasting them in an economic framework. In this instance he writes of a divided self, one imposing negative externalities on the other. Midnight Snacker imposes costs on Morning Willpower, much as the upstream polluter imposes costs on the downstream firm.

A broad spectrum of policy concerns has provided the grist for Schelling's intellectual mill. From 1948-53 he served with the Marshall Plan in Europe, the White House, and the Executive Office of the President; international diplomacy and conflict have remained a concern throughout his career. The interplay among nations (or within nations that are dealing with other nations) is an ideal place to apply Schellingesque concepts such as threats, promises and tacit communication. Schelling was one of the United States' leading strategists of the nuclear age, helping intellectuals and policy makers understand how deterrence works and how it can be made more stable.

Schelling has also untangled an array of problems in the domestic arena. His approach to the problem of racial segregation and mixing well illustrates his abilities to extract the essence of a real-life phenomenon, and to capture it in a simple formulation. Consider Schelling's checkerboard exercise designed to explore and explain segregation:

> We place dimes and pennies on some of the squares, and suppose them to represent the members of two homogeneous groups – men and women, blacks and whites. ... And we can stipulate various decision rules, ... every dime wants at least half its neighbors to be dimes, every penny wants a third of its neighbors to be pennies, and any dime or penny whose immediate neighborhood does not meet these conditions gets up and moves.

From this simple model Schelling draws a powerful, policy-relevant conclusion: 'A moderate urge to avoid small-minority status may cause a nearly integrated pattern to unravel, and highly segregated neighborhoods to form'[2] (1978, p. 154).

In recent years, Schelling has been concerned about global warming. He is not an empiricist: he does not seek to unearth unknown facts. Rather, he tells us how to think about the problem, using information that is readily available to those who are willing to dig deeply and read without prejudice. He tells us how to organize our own thinking. Here is a snippet on bargaining, revealing the essence of the

---

2. Unless otherwise indicated, all references are to Schelling's work.

Schelling approach, drawn from his 1992 address as president of the American Economic Association:

> If the developed countries ever manage to act together toward the developing countries, their bargaining position is probably enhanced by the fact that cleaner fuels and more efficient fuel technologies bring a number of benefits other than reduced carbon, and recipients of greenhouse aid will be actively interested parties, not merely neutral agents attending to the global atmosphere. At the same time, large nations like India and China will be aware of the extortionate power that resides in ambitious coal-development projects. (1992, p. 13)

His policy investigations would assuredly be worthwhile even if they merely gave us greater insights into segregation, global warming, arms control or smoking – all areas to which Schelling has contributed. But they do much more; they inspire conceptual models that allow other researchers to address their own policy areas.

Three of Schelling's classic books, discussed below, reveal the depth and breadth of his thought. They cover a broad arena of strategic concerns, each addressing situations with a different number of participants – many, two or a few, and one.[3] These books have withstood the test of time. A tally starting in 1966 shows that each volume is increasingly cited in successive five-year periods.[4]

MICROMOTIVES AND MACROBEHAVIOR

When there are many players, and no central traffic cop (such as a price system or other coordinating mechanism), the outcome may be undesirable for everyone. Oceans are depleted of fish; segregation is more extreme than either blacks or whites would prefer. Or consider a community where a number of people have sexually transmitted diseases; the disease spreads because men snub condom use. The men might agree that all should wear condoms to diminish disease and raise acceptability, but given difficulties of monitoring, such an agreement would be difficult to enforce. (Schelling's original analysis related to the externalities of acceptance of the much more public activity of wearing hockey helmets.)

We illustrate this form of analysis with one of Schelling's examples. Consider a large population of people, each of whom must choose whether or not to own a citizen's band radio to communicate with friends in the population. Each will make this choice by balancing his or her own costs and benefits. The costs include

---

3. A volume written in honor of Thomas Schelling by his students and admirers was divided into three major sections titled by these books (Zeckhauser 1991).
4. Since 1966, the books have received more than 2,000 citations in the Social Sciences Citation Index.

the monetary cost of purchasing the radio, installing it in one's car, and so on; these are largely independent of how many others carry similar radios. But the benefits largely depend on the number of others who make a similar choice. If hardly anyone owns one, 'there is nobody to talk to; the externality benefits more the people who have sets than those who do not, though the latter get some benefits from the communication system ... if everybody has a set, you can save yourself the expense by dropping in on a friend and using his equipment or handing an emergency message to any passerby' (1978, p. 240).

The analysis is conducted using a very simple 'Schelling diagram' (Figure 1). The horizontal axis measures the number of others in the population who own the radios, and the vertical axis measures the benefit to a typical person. The straight line shows the benefit to a person who does not own a radio; it rises to the right because as more other people own radios, it becomes easier to use (or benefit from) someone else's, say in an emergency. The other curve shows the benefit to a person from owning his or her own set. This benefit is very low at the left-hand extreme, where almost no one else owns a radio (because there is no one to talk to) and rises as more people get sets. It flattens out toward the right-hand extreme, because there are diminishing returns to expanding one's circle of radio pals.

At the intersection of these two curves, the typical person is indifferent between owning and not owning the radio. Therefore there is no reason for an owner to switch to non-ownership or vice versa. The outcome is an equilibrium.

Figure 1

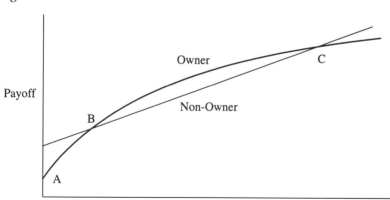

Number of Radio Owners

Given the shapes of the curves, there are two possible equilibria. There is one stable equilibrium at A, where no one owns a set, and another at C, where most people do. In the first case, few people choose to own radios because few others do, and in the second, most people own radios because most others do. Each equilibrium is sustained by the behaviors it engenders.[5] Yet all would prefer the 'most-are-owners' equilibrium.

A committee meeting, Schelling observes, has much the same structure: 'It is not worth going unless there is likely to be a quorum; over some numerical range, one's presence makes enough difference to make attendance worthwhile; and if the meeting is large enough, there is no need to give up the afternoon just to attend' (1978, p. 240). The intrigued reader might try the condom case, which lends itself well to a slightly more complex Schelling-diagram analysis, with condom acceptance, disease avoidance, and sexual pleasure determining the shapes of the curves. The technology-choice example can be enriched beautifully by allowing for heterogeneity in preferences among the population. Such heterogeneity was considered by Schelling in work on racial tipping. He examined what would happen in a white neighborhood where there were heterogeneous preferences towards integration. Say that 11 percent of the whites would depart if it turned 10 percent black, 21 percent of the original population would be gone if blacks comprised 20 percent, and so on. Then once the neighborhood turned 10 percent black a process would be set in motion whereby ultimately all the whites would leave, although a sizeable majority of whites would be happy with a 20 percent black neighborhood (1978, pp. 101-10).

Think now of the problem confronting the world of students and professors in their choices of information technologies. Say a superior word-processing system or spreadsheet comes along. True computer laggards, who regularly capitalize on friends to help them out when they run into a snag, would prefer not to adopt until 75 percent of their peers chose to do so. Extreme technology hobbyists might prefer to be the first in their neighborhood to innovate. Think now of the curve telling how many adopters there will be as a function of the number of current users. There will be an equilibrium wherever that curve hits the 45-degree line. If the curve lies everywhere above the 45-degree line, that is, if the population is sufficiently bold in adoption for any level of use, there will be rapid progress to full use of the technology throughout the population. But even if full use is an equilibrium, the population may get stuck in a low-level trap if, say, only 10 percent would choose the technology conditional on 20 percent use by others. Figure 2 shows a possible situation with 5 percent hobbyists and 30 percent laggards. There are stable equilibria at low-level D or complete-use E. Software producers have come to recognize the problems that arise when populations are

---

5. The equilibrium at B is unstable: a chance deviation to the right will drive the outcome to C and a slight deviation to the left will push it all the way back to the point where no one owns the radios.

heterogeneous and there are positive externalities in adoption. They often give significant discounts to early users of their products.[6]

Figure 2

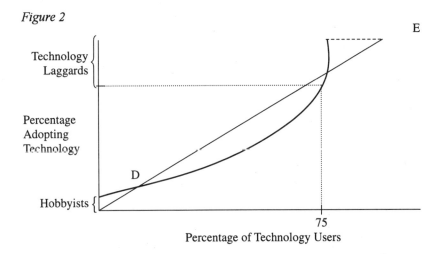

Another beautiful example of Schelling's work on externalities is the story of a common delay caused by accident perusal. Schelling writes:

> People slow down to enjoy a look at the wreckage on the other side of the divider. ... Even the driver who, when he arrives at the site, is ten minutes behind schedule is likely to feel that he's paid the price of admission and, though the highway is at least clear in front of him, will not resume speed until he's had his look, too. Eventually large numbers of commuters have spent an extra ten minutes driving for a ten-second look. (1978, p. 125)

Schelling generalizes, 'a person reacting, responding, and adapting to his surroundings fails to perceive, or doesn't care, how his actions combine with the actions of others to produce unanticipated results' (1978, back cover). In his work on tipping, Schelling showed the converse: it is not possible to infer the intentions of individual decision makers from observing the group outcomes. The system equilibrium has new, surprising 'emergent' properties that can only be understood by analyzing the strategic interaction and the equilibria it produces.

Much of the recent highly mathematical literature on issues such as product compatibility and strategic complementarities could be understood much more easily using a Schelling diagram. Schelling's expository triumph stems from his

6.   In essence, they are seeking to shift up the curve, particularly on the left-hand end. A significant advertizing budget may make widespread use seem likely, establishing a high-level equilibrium as a focal point.

constant search for a simpler, more unifying way to describe essential elements of superficially complex situations. He identifies the common factors that determine who wears hockey helmets, Clinton saxophone pins, and condoms.

THE STRATEGY OF CONFLICT

Schelling's uncanny ability to find simplicity in complex situations is well illustrated by *The Strategy of Conflict* (1960), his most widely known book. Though thirty-five years old, it reads like a refreshing breeze. The richness of its ideas, scope and illustrations do not diminish with many readings. Its contributions are too numerous to detail, but many stem from a basic observation about bargaining: it is *not* a zero-sum game. True, the players' interests are strictly opposed along the efficient frontier (that is, a move to a more favored solution for one would hurt the other's welfare). But disagreement is a logical possibility, and in comparing many points on the frontier with the disagreement alternative, the players' interests are aligned. Their joint interest in averting mutual disaster powerfully affects their attempts to resolve their conflict over where to land on the efficient frontier.

Perhaps the most important insight resulting from this observation is that 'what one player *can* do to avert mutual damage affects what another player *will* do to avert it' (1960, p. 81). This leads to several effects:

1. Commitment, which reduces one's own freedom of future action, acquires value. A committed player can show that he/she can make no further concession, leaving it to the other to concede. The idea of *strategic commitment* has been fruitful in many areas of economics and politics; oligopoly theory, the theory of macroeconomic policy, and various analyses of bargaining have all been enriched by these considerations.
2. Rather than committing to an inflexible position, players can commit to a *response rule*, which determines how the committed player will respond to various actions by the other player. Threats and promises are basic response rules. Such rules are found in a range of situations – parents dealing with children (*if* you behave well all day, you will get ice cream in the evening); the United States seeking to deter new nuclear nations (*if* you do not allow international inspection of your nuclear facilities, you will face a trade embargo); and firms promising not to raise the price of tie-in products (*if* you buy your computers from us, we will supply upgrades of system software at current prices for the next five years).
3. Commitments, threats, and promises must be credible; the position or rule must be truly fixed or irreversible, and one's adoption of it must be clearly

observable to the other player. These considerations lead to several new insights, of which we mention just two.

a. Credibility can be promoted through tactical devices. For example, one could use mandated negotiating agents who are not empowered to make concessions, such as trade union negotiators who are bound by the membership's instructions. A second approach would rely on seeming irrationality; if you are thought to be crazy enough to carry out threats no matter what the cost to yourself, then your threats will be more readily believed and therefore more effective. (But the price of creating an aura of irrationality may be excessive.)

The availability of devices that promote credibility depends on many features of the situation, including whether third parties would punish commitment breaking, and the ability to establish links to or precedents for seemingly unrelated negotiations. Such measures are usually ignored or poorly treated in formal models, which begin by specifying a limited repetoire of tactics, a particular strategy space, or at best a highly-structured situation such as the ability of a chain store to credibly threaten to persist through a disastrous price war at a single outlet, given the credibility externality that tough behavior will convey to its other outlets. Schelling approaches commitment from the opposite end; his players ask themselves, 'What tactics can I use to credibly make a threat or a promise to achieve my aim?'. This analysis, with its broader perspective and richer contextual detail, is both more relevant and more compelling, and should help a President who wants a worldwide audience to extrapolate from his demonstration of will in Haiti or Kuwait to his likely behavior in other arenas.

b. It is important to communicate a commitment truthfully and believably to the opponent, contradicting the naive view that each player must wish to conceal any relevant facts from an adversary. Thus, since the other player will not in general believe your unsupported statements, it may be desirable to allow his spies to observe your actions, or otherwise leak your intentions or capabilities deliberately and in a convincing manner.

4. A particular outcome on the efficient frontier may emerge if it is salient to both players. When each knows that the other knows (etc.) that the particular point has a special claim to attention, they may both choose it, and forgo any attempts to do better for themselves at the risk of failure. The possible outcome becomes a *focal point*. This can happen as a result of historical, cultural, or even purely coincidental factors. In seeking the essence of what makes for focal points, Schelling (1960, p. 70) talks in terms of 'the intrinsic magnetism of particular outcomes, especially those that enjoy prominence, uniqueness, simplicity,

precedent, or some rationale that makes them qualitatively differentiable from the continuum of possible alternatives'. Thus a 50-50 split serves as a focal point for a bargain even between asymmetrically situated parties; the single bridge over the river in a wilderness area may be the logical spot for two inadvertently separated hikers to meet, even though it is distant from one party, hence 'unfair', and though there are numerous road intersections that are closer to both. Such factors may have nothing to do with the formal descriptions of strategies and payoffs; thus, formal models of bargaining may miss essential features that can lead to a solution. Indeed, much of effective bargaining consists of trying to establish outcomes that are favorable to oneself as focal points, say by finding supporting relevant precedents and principles.[7]

More general lessons also flow from an understanding of convergent expectations, including the importance of ethical concerns such as fairness. In the ultimatum game, now widely studied experimentally, one player proposes a division of ten dollars (or some other amount), which the second player ends the game by either accepting, so that each gets his/her agreed share, or rejecting, in which case each gets nothing. Standard game theory would suggest that the first player offer one cent to the second player, who would have an incentive to accept rather than get nothing. But no student of Schelling would make such a proposal. It seems fair for each player to take five dollars, and in a community where fairness is an important norm a lopsided offer will likely be rejected. In such a community, as a number of game-playing experiments have illustrated, the rational proposal by the first player may well be an even division (Thaler 1988).

In modern game theory, few get far without displaying mathematical rigor. But Schelling foreshadowed important results using simpler methods that are accessible to a much broader audience. For example, his analysis of credibility captured the essence of 'subgame perfectness', the property requirement that as we proceed down a game tree no player will have an incentive to deviate from the equilibrium path. Using the matrix notation that was the norm of the 1950s, Schelling demonstrated credibility as the outcome that survives successive elimination of the dominated strategies of either player[8] (1960, pp. 150-59). We now know that this iterative process does indeed yield a subgame-perfect equilibrium in finite games of complete and perfect information (Kreps 1990, p.

---

7.   The role of conventions and focal points was explored by Schelling in a series of classroom experiments (1960, chs. 3, 6), and was later verified in many more detailed experiments (Roth 1987). Thus Schelling was incidentally also a pioneer of experimental economics.

8.   Deleting a dominated strategy of player 1 may render dominated a formerly active strategy of player 2.

424).[9] This example displays a rare Schelling trait: he can work informally, yet develop concepts that prove to have broad generality, and that are ultimately addressed in mathematically rigorous form by others.

In leading us through the strategic world, Schelling is like a master scientist revealing simple secrets of the universe. Consider some points about nuclear strategy: war should be thought of primarily as a nonzero-sum game. Arch-enemies have strong common interests; thus, the chess analogy, the work of Clausewitz, has been misleading. To deter a surprise attack, you must make sure that your opponent, not just you, has a secure second-strike capability. This will lessen his/her fear of your surprise attack, making it less attractive to him/her to launch a preemptive strike. Therefore 'Schemes to avert surprise attack have as their most immediate objective the safety of weapons rather than the safety of people' (1960, p. 233).

ARMS AND INFLUENCE

Schelling distilled his thinking about strategic games among two or a few parties and his deep knowledge of the nuclear balance between the superpowers in *Arms and Influence*. The book is full of new insights and illustrations; perhaps the most important is the concept of brinkmanship. We illustrate, as is so often best with Schelling, with a direct quote.

> [Brinkmanship] means exploiting the danger that somebody may inadvertently go over the brink, dragging the other with him. ... If the brink is clearly marked and provides a firm footing, ... [t]here is no danger in approaching it; and while either [of two climbers tied together] can deliberately jump off, he cannot credibly pretend that he is about to. Any attempt to intimidate or to deter the other climber depends on the threat of slipping or stumbling. (1966, p. 99)

> Deterrence has to be understood in relation to this uncertainty. ... The question is really: is the United States likely to do something that is fraught with the danger of war, something that could lead – through a compounding of actions and reactions, of calculations and miscalculations, of alarms and false alarms, of commitments and challenges – to a major war? ... A response that carries some risk of war can be plausible, even reasonable, at a time when a final, ultimate decision to *have* a general war would be implausible or unreasonable. (1966, pp. 97-8)

---

9. Formal game theorists usually credit Selten with the discovery of subgame perfectness, often citing entry deterrence in oligopoly theory as a triumph of this idea. Dixit (1980) and Spence (1977), authors of early papers in this area, report that they were inspired in their work by Schelling's discussion of credibility.

It cannot be said better. And here the quote also illustrates the clarity and force of Schelling's writing, and his ability to make general theoretical points through examples. Actually, brinkmanship is one idea that Schelling does develop using a formal model (1960, ch. 7), which should be read for its 'haiku' quality.

CHOICE AND CONSEQUENCE

After exploring situations with many players, and those with just a few, Schelling turned to games in which 'the enemy is us'. The well-developed theory of rational decision posits a stable set of preferences for bundles of goods and services. Schelling started from the basic observation that individuals frequently do not make choices that accord with this theory. Today's welfare is not judged absolutely, but in comparison to that of yesterday. Regret, remorse and anxiety significantly affect well-being, though they do not enter the economist's traditional framework. Individuals frequently make choices on the basis of principles; preferences may prove to be a secondary consideration.

Schelling also develops the metaphor of the divided self. It is the adulterous spouse who wishes to be faithful nearly all the time. It is the teenage smoker with little concern for the cancer and emphysema that may develop after many years.

A different class of inconsistencies arise in the arena of social policy. In his essay, 'The Life You Save May Be Your Own', Schelling observed that people are willing to spend much more to rescue particular individuals who are stranded, or to treat particular sufferers from a rare disease, rather than spend funds on general risk reduction or to make medical facilities available. He observes that 'We often know who died for lack of safety; we rarely know who lived because of it' (1984, p. 146). Hence, too little will be spent on safety, too much on rescues. This bold essay introduced the willingness-to-pay approach to life valuation and other touchy issues.

ASSESSING THOMAS SCHELLING

For more than forty years, Thomas Schelling has instructed us as he assessed everything from the play of children to the declarations of nuclear powers. His work shows a passion for simplicity and clarity, qualities that are facilitated by his elegant writing. Schelling assuredly will not simplify, however, if he must sacrifice the essence of a situation.

He looks at the world through the participants' eyes, be they dictators threatening annihilation, students procrastinating, or children subject to parental discipline. He always shows a keen concern for the way individuals can and do make decisions, and does not assume that what is rational is readily achieved. He is vitally concerned with the ability of individuals to commit themselves to their own long-term welfare. Bad habits, addictive behavior and myopia impinge on what economists commonly think of as effective choice.

In interactive situations, Schelling focuses on one person's ability to influence the choices of others. Often this is achieved through commitment, and commitment is usually achieved by reducing one's payoffs for particular outcomes. An apparently irrational act improves one's prospects.

More generally, when two or more parties are involved, Schelling shows us that no simplistic concept of rationality applies. For him, matters of trust and perception, experience and tacit communication play important roles. Though Schelling often abstracts a strategic situation into a matrix or a diagram, and is the author of many simple yet general models, he always delves into the factors that influence the numbers and the shapes of curves. For example, in Schelling's hands, with one matrix and set of termination rules, the outcome of a multi-play prisoners' dilemma may differ dramatically if the players are old competitors or experimental subjects, and whether a colleague will be kibitzing about the results. In a classroom, he might first develop the argument that in a sterile environment cooperation will unravel from the end, and then identify the circumstances that would likely promote reasonable cooperation in practice. He probably would illustrate with a flurry of specific examples, identifying their common and distinctive elements.

If one quality shines through Schelling's work and conversation, it is his ability to develop original insights having broad generality. Here are just two samples of what other eminent economists say about him.

James Tobin remarked, 'Tom was always several steps wider and a few layers deeper than the rest of us and our professors. He always perceived a new angle, a surprising implication, or a puzzling problem in arguments and propositions that satisfied most of us'.

Paul Samuelson remarked, 'Franz Schubert wrote hundreds of songs because melodies just bubbled out from inside of him. As a scientist, Tom Schelling is like that: he can't help having original ideas'.[10]

Some economists extend their discipline into unfamiliar realms because they are intellectual imperialists, others because their political views are best honed

---

10. The Tobin and Samuelson quotes, originally from personal communications, appeared in Zeckhauser 1989, pp. 156 and 157, respectively.

with concepts drawn from economics. Thomas Schelling merely ventures where his mind takes him, sometimes following a policy problem such as global warming, at other times explaining patterns of everyday life, such as how people cluster in auditoriums (away from the front rows) or lunchrooms (often by race). Given Schelling's intellectual generosity, it is not surprising that others often engage him in their problems, whether they are grappling to find a coherent theme for a doctoral dissertation or a foreign policy initiative. However far he ventures, Schelling thinks like an economist, a great compliment to our profession.

What lessons should one draw from Thomas Schelling's work? There are two primary lessons; the first of approach, the second of presentation. Economic reasoning should be simultaneously both deductive and inductive. Effective models are informed by close observation of the world, but are reduced to essential elements so they can make powerful predictions about a wide range of phenomena. Witness, for example, the remarkable insights afforded by Schelling's models of the threat, neighborhood tipping, and self-control.

Thomas Schelling's work exemplifies the symbiotic relationship between effective writing and clear thinking. Let us listen to him on market performance and market failure: 'Small children learn to trade stamps with an acumen that the real estate fraternity can only envy, but their parents can travel incommunicado behind a slow truck on a mountain grade without finding a way to make it worth the truck driver's while to pull off the road for fifteen seconds' (1971, p. 89).

High schoolers can understand what Schelling writes; university professors can debate his implications. Both can delight in his playful mind and elegant style. Thomas Schelling's writings offer an elixir for the mind, a distillation of essence in eloquence.

SCHELLING'S MAJOR WRITINGS

(1960), *The Strategy of Conflict*, Cambridge, MA: Harvard University Press.
(1966), *Arms and Influence*, New Haven, CT: Yale University Press.
(1971), 'On the Ecology of Micromotives', *Public Interest*, **25**, Fall, 59-98.
(1978), *Micromotives and Macrobehavior*, New York, NY: W.W. Norton.
(1984), *Choice and Consequence*, Cambridge, MA: Harvard University Press.
(1992), 'Some Economics of Global Warming', *American Economic Review*, **82**, 1-14.

OTHER REFERENCES

Dixit, Avinash (1980), 'The Role of Investment in Entry Deterrence', *Economic Journal*, **90**, 95-106.

Kreps, David (1990), *A Course in Microeconomic Theory*, Princeton, NJ: Princeton University Press.

Roth, Alvin (1987), 'Bargaining Phenomena and Bargaining Theory', in Alvin Roth (ed.), *Laboratory Experiments in Economics: Six Points of View*, New York: Cambridge University Press.

Social Sciences Citation Index (1966-1991), Philadelphia, PA: Institute for Scientific Information.

Spence, A. Michael (1977), 'Entry, Investment, and Oligopolistic Pricing', *Bell Journal of Economics*, **8**, 534-44.

Thaler, Richard (1988), 'The Ultimatum Game', *Journal of Economic Perspectives*, **2** (4), 195-206.

Waldrop, M. Mitchell (1992), *Complexity: The Emerging Science at the Edge of Order and Chaos*, New York: Simon and Schuster.

Zeckhauser, Richard (1989), 'Distinguished Fellow: Reflections on Thomas Schelling', *Journal of Economic Perspectives*, **3**, Spring, 153-64.

Zeckhauser, Richard (1991), 'The Strategy of Choice', in Richard J. Zeckhauser (ed.), *Strategy and Choice*, Cambridge, MA: MIT Press.

14. Vernon L. Smith

R. Mark Isaac

Whether meeting him in person or through his work, there is no doubt that Vernon Smith is a remarkable economist and scholar. In the course of this essay, we will confront, in the usual form, his scholarship. This will include, of course, Vernon Smith's revolutionary development of laboratory experimental economics. It will not be limited to that area but will also survey his work in such diverse areas as capital theory, natural resource economics and economic anthropology. But to learn about Vernon Smith only through the written output of his scholarship is to miss much, for colleagues of Vernon have long known that with him, the journey is as remarkable as the destination.

As must undoubtedly be the case with other great economists, the paradigmatic encounter with Vernon Smith is the lunchtime conversation. Vernon does not rule over these exchanges, nor is he interested in a carnival of ideas on an unlimited number of topics. But if we use having lunch as a metaphor for an introduction to Vernon's scholarship, we would come away with several realities with which to understand Vernon's scholarly work and the importance of his contributions to the economics profession.

First, Vernon Smith is, and always will be, at heart a Kansan. In such a land the long, hot summers and cold winters, endless horizons, blue skies, winter and summer clouds, and devastating other-worldly storms, suggest a curious mixture of practicality and idealism. Practicality because on the prairie it is impossible to escape the data of life. Whatever model one has about the nature of the universe must be disciplined by reality, both pleasant and unpleasant. Reality is that a tornado can carve a path of destruction in a matter of minutes. Reality is that it is possible to find places to look around and feel absolutely alone.

As for idealism, William Least Heat-Moon (1991) quotes Carl Becker (1910) as follows: 'Idealism must always prevail on the frontier, for the frontier, whether geographical or intellectual, offers little hope to those who see things as they are. To venture into the wilderness, one must see it, not as it is, but as it will be'.

I believe this combination of pragmatism and idealism defines Vernon Smith's scholarship. The pragmatic side comes in its discipline in realities of economic life. This does not mean at all that Vernon's work is primarily empirical: much of it is theoretical. The point is that, whether doing theory or empirical work (primarily laboratory experiments), Vernon always takes account of the tornados sweeping across the economic landscape. For example, consider his 1962 piece in the *Journal of Political Economy* – the first published of his experimental work. In the introductory description of hypotheses and institutions, he states the following: 'Since the organized stock, bond, and commodity exchanges would seem to have the best chance of fulfilling the conditions of an operational theory of supply and demand, most of these experiments have been designed to simulate, on a modest scale, the multilateral auction-trading process characteristic of these organized markets'. Now this is not necessarily the most appropriate design guideline for every economics experiment in every circumstance, but it was very appropriate here and demonstrated Vernon's sensitivity to a link between economic research programs and the ultimate reality of economic life. In addition, this paper, even as is the standard today, asked the question, 'How robust are these preliminary results to changes in institutional organization?'.

The idealism side of Vernon's work applies not so much to the work narrowly defined but to the intellectual program of scholarly inquiry behind it. It is striking that the Carl Becker quote above, which is about Kansas and the geographical frontier, specifically mentions the intellectual frontier as well. I can add nothing to that quote because, for me, it crystallizes my experience of Vernon's intellectual journey.

A second fact about Vernon Smith would become clear at lunch, which is that Vernon is the consummate educator, well educated himself, but who does not worship at the idols of conventional wisdom, within or without the academy. He knows the difference between education and learning. A look at Vernon's c.v. reveals great formal education: BSEE from Cal. Tech., MA from Kansas, and a PhD from Harvard. What this portrait does not get a chance to say is that, for a time, as a boy, Vernon attended a one-room schoolhouse in a small Kansas village. In conversation, Vernon has the ability to describe the pluses and the minuses of his own training in economics.

We can see this tension between Smith the formally educated, accomplished scientist and the Smith who knows that a great deal of learning takes place in one-room Kansas school houses in the two quotes chosen to introduce the 1982 'Microeconomic Systems' paper, his classic methodological explication of experimental economics. First, Smith quotes Louis Agassiz in saying, 'Study nature, not books'. Second, he cites the graffiti by an unknown student, as follows: 'After studying economics for six years I have reached the conclusion that there is no difference between discovery and creation'.

Again, over a hypothetical lunchtime conversation, something else one would discover about Vernon Smith is that he is interested in topics which span the entire range of human endeavor. His intellectual curiosity is almost unbounded. Within his publications one sees such areas as auction institutions, environmental economics, water deeds, psychology, property rights, primitive hunter culture, voting theory, philosophy of science and economic anthropology. The remarkable thing is that this wide range of topics has not meant a lack of focus. Indeed, all of his research has the same general themes: understanding the behavior of goal-directed, exchange-oriented human beings operating in a world of property rights, institutions and natural constraints.

Vernon frequently has reached into other subjects in order to improve the quality of economic research. In preparation for a study on alternatives to rate-of-return regulation of which I was a part, Vernon called all of the investigators together and spent several hours bringing us up to speed on the electrical engineering that we would need to know. Vernon believed, correctly as it it turned out, that if we were to be able to understand the existing institutions in the electric power industry (contracts, 'loop flows', and so on) then we had to understand how electricity is produced, how it is transmitted, and so forth. In a similar vein, discussions of the hunting patterns of early man are drawn into his work on the economic origins of humankind; breakthroughs in surface geology become models for the uses of theory and data in economics experiments, and so forth.

To this point, I have tried a give a glimpse of Vernon Smith, the person and the scholar. It is time to turn attention more specifically to a discussion of his research. This poses somewhat of a problem. What organizing principle should one use? A simple chronological procession will not do. Vernon has worked in many different traditional 'areas', at unequal chronological pace. The areas are neither evenly spaced throughout his career, nor are they bunched together, so that one cannot speak about his 'Blue Period'. Nor is it satisfactory to split his work apart in bundles based upon topic. This makes the research appear artificially disjointed. Further, there is the question of choice of topics. There is no doubt that Vernon would have a distinguished career on any one of his directions of inquiry: capital theory, natural resources, economic an-thropology, and so forth. But where is one to include experimental economics? The development of experimental economics is, also without a doubt, the hallmark of Vernon Smith's career. But where is it included? The methods of experimentation are a topic which can be talked of for their own sake. But most papers using experimental economics are not; they might be, for example, industrial organization (read: public economics, auction policy, game theory, and so on) using experimental methods just as other industrial organization (public economics, auction policy, game theory) papers use mathematical analysis or econometrics. Despite this, the fact remains that work *using* experimental economics in a developed discipline can also have the property of developing experimental economics itself. It is inevitable. Coursey, Isaac and Smith (1984) and Coursey, Isaac, Luke and Smith (1984) used experimental methods to investigate a conjecture (the contestable markets hypothesis) in industrial organization. But, beyond their contributions to IO, these papers teach much about issues in conducting experiments: When is it appropriate to simulate demand? What is the technology of creating a downward-sloping marginal cost curve? How can sunk costs be represented? and so forth.

With the preceding obstacles in mind, this essay will follow a different tack. I will examine, in turn, a series of articles important in the development of Vernon's corpus. The purpose of this approach is to use the papers as a series of anchors, to work through the development of Vernon Smith's scholarly career without having to work through article by article, and thus risk not seeing the forest for the trees. (This is a real danger, as Vernon has published, according to my count, over 140 articles and reviews and 10 authored or edited books.) Obviously, a great deal of the discussion will be devoted to the development of experimental economics, although some non-experimental papers will be included. I have included both early and recent papers, as well as papers that are singly authored as well as co-authored. Also included are historical events such as the founding of the Economic Science Association and the establishment of the Economic Science Laboratory. It is also worth noting that, because of the prominence of experimental articles, this will look like a history of experimental economics. It is not. It specifically is not because it would not, as a history, do justice to other pioneers such as Jim Friedman, Sidney Siegel and Charles Plott. Omission of their contributions, or those of others, in any of the discussion below is not meant to suggest exclusion from any larger discussing of the history of experiments.

Before beginning the section of the essay discussing Vernon's work, a bare-bones biography is probably useful to provide some structure. It has already been mentioned that Vernon's youth was spent in Kansas. His Cal. Tech. degree was in 1949, his Kansas MA in 1952, and his doctorate from Harvard in 1955. He has had three sustained professional appointments: Purdue (1955-67); University of Masssachusetts (1968-75); and Arizona (1975-present). However, he also has had an active career as a visiting faculty member or scholar, including the Cowles Foundation (Yale), Center for the Advanced Study in the Behavioral Sciences, and Cal. Tech. (Sherman Fairchild Distinguished Scholar). He has been on the editorial board of the *American Economic Review*, *Cato Journal*, and the *Journal of Economic Behavior and Organization*. He has been President or Vice-President of the Economic Science Association, the Public Choice Society, and the Western Economic Association. In recent years his travel overseas has been more, rather than less, frequent, often involving large-scale implementation questions such as the deregulation of electric power. His colleagues, most several years his junior, are in awe of his stamina. Lest all of this give the impression that Vernon spends all of his time in an experimental laboratory, it should be noted that he has no trouble keeping up his part of a conversation on new movies, Arizona Wildcat basketball, or the latest goings-on in Washington, Moscow or Somalia. He is not a dull boy.

Having thus quickly reviewed Vernon's *bona fides*, we turn to a discussion of Vernon's scholarship. As suggested above, this examination will proceed event by event, arranged to develop some of the intellectual themes of his work.

'AN EXPERIMENTAL STUDY ...' (1962)

This paper is transparently important because it is Vernon's first publication in experimental economics, the 'foundation stone' article as it were. The importance of this article is not just a matter of showing how experiments were done at that particular point in time and what evolution in those methods were underway. This is also a rich paper in terms of concepts of testing economic theory. And it also sets out the case for the competitive performance of the double auction-trading mechanism, a body of evidence which has replicated through to this day.

In order to place this paper more fully in a historical context, there are a couple of off-stage happenings which can profitably be discussed at this point. First, as discussed in his footnote 5, E.H. Chamberlin, at Harvard University, had conducted a type of proto-experiment as an instructional exercise. Vernon was around Harvard in that general time (although after Chamberlin's specific publication on the matter in 1948). The general result that Chamberlin's market did not equilibrate probably came as no shock to Chamberlin, to Vernon Smith, or to anyone else steeped in Harvard imperfect competition orthodoxy. Chamberlin apparently never pursued 'experimentation' as a research tool. Vernon opens the article with virtually no up-front explanation for what experimentation is all about, simply reporting that the purpose of the article is to report on 'a series of experimental games designed to study some of the hypotheses of neoclassical competitive market theory'.

What these experiments had in common with Chamberlin are a primitive concept of experimenter-induced valuation, which Vernon would later expand upon in his 1976 article, and the notion that players with induced valuation and a well-defined laboratory set of trading rules constitute a simple test of underlying conjectures of market behavior. The key to induced valuation is the creation of limit values. Instead of 'pretend you are a buyer' subjects are told they are buyers who value one of the objects in the market for up to X dollars (we will visit the issue of the saliency of these valuations shortly). Once the individual limit valuations are constructed, then the usual horizontal summation can produce a laboratory demand curve. A similar argument produces a laboratory supply curve from induced production costs on sellers.

After this one similarity, the differences between Vernon's experiments and Chamberlin's dominate. The key comes in another opening sentence: 'Since the organized stock, bond, and commodity exchanges would seem to have the best chance of fulfilling the conditions of an operational theory of supply and demand, most of these experiments have been designed to simulate, on a modest scale, the multilateral auction-trading process characteristic of these organized markets'. At one level, this observation anticipates the proposition that trading institutions matter, a proposition which would be confirmed in 30 plus years of economics experiments. At another level, the changes made put the research focus on the double auction and its competitive tendencies. Overall, the experimental markets as operationalized by Smith differed from those of Chamberlin in that (i) Smith used the organized double auction rather than the random meetings market of Chamberlin; (ii) Smith allowed for repetition, and hence learning, as compared with Chamberlin's one-shot occurrence.

The second historical reference of use in studying this paper is that, like Chamberlin, Vernon began this experimental research using hypothetical induced values. Neither buyers nor sellers were actually paid the amounts suggested by the rules of the markets. Vernon has often publicly credited psychologist Sidney Siegel, whom he met during a visit to Stanford (his 1961-62 visiting Professorship), with convincing him of the superiority of salient compensation. (Otherwise, how would we know that a buyer with a $2.00 demand value would actually behave in that regard? With saliency, that demand value is converted into a redemption value in which the experimenter agrees to buy the unit from the buyer for $2.00.) This apparently explains why the salient rewards do not appear until Experiments 4, 5A, and 5B in the paper (looking also at footnote 9).

In discussions with me about this period, Vernon said that Siegel gave him 'a good intellectual drubbing' while, at the same time, being curious that the issue of salient payoffs had not seemed to make much difference. By the time the 1962 paper was published, however, footnote 9 had identified one supply– demand configuration, the one shown in Vernon's Chart 4, in which the saliency of payoffs seemed to make a big difference. As Vernon told me, 'All of this meant that I would never again do experiments without money. I had been lucky, as was now made clear to me!'.

The two treatment dimensions in the paper are ones which will be replicated throughout future experimentation: changes in the supply–demand conditions, and changes in the form of the market-trading process. This also perfectly foreshadows how Vernon will organize the concept of a microeconomic experiment: the economic environment (including supply and demand conditions) and the economic institutions (including the market process).

In the primary context of the double auction, the fundamental conclusion of this paper is that, when there is the 'standard' condition of downward-sloping demand and upward-sloping supply, competitive predictions as to price and quantity obtain. This happens even in the presence of relatively small numbers of traders. The competitive comparative static predictions also perform well when supply and demand are shifted. Extreme supply and demand conditions, such as a perfectly horizontal supply curve, may not produce outcomes as closely corresponding to the competitive prediction (unless one pays the subjects real money – then competitive outcomes are achieved even here, see his footnote 9).

A second important conclusion from this paper is the idea that the relative success of the competitive model in predicting a market's performance may depend upon *how the market trading is organized*. In this paper, Vernon explored a switch from double auction to the 'seller only auction', in which only sellers were allowed to make offers.

Because we will repeatedly make reference to this as the 'first' experimental economics paper, it should be emphasized that this is not meant to overlook the parallel works on somewhat different tracks by J. Friedman and Siegel and Fouraker.

'... SEALED-BID AUCTION MARKETS' (1967)

This 1967 *Journal of Business* paper is, in some ways, quietly deceiving. It appears, on the surface, to be simply one of the extensions of the research program Vernon began with the 1962 paper. In this paper, the primary experimental treatment is the market institution – in this case, two different types of multiple unit, sealed-bid auctions. One type is the so-called discriminative auction (the highest bidders win the units, with each winning bidder paying his own bid). The other type is the so-called competitive auction (the highest bidders win the units, with each winning bidder paying a uniform competitive, or market-clearing, price, such as the highest losing bid). In the course of the primary research interest, comparing these two institutions along such dimensions as seller revenue, Smith conducts the two auctions in the context of several different supply and demand configurations.

In contrast to this rather unspectacular description, this paper is pathbreaking for two reasons. First, the paper was the precursor to auction experiments as a class. Such experiments have comprised an important group on through to today. Second, this paper is explicitly policy motivated, and serves as a forerunner of that category of experimental economics. Let us consider each of these, in reverse order.

Public Policy Experiments

The introduction to the paper explicitly motivates the research with the then ongoing debate over the design of auctions for US Treasury securities. This debate included both academic discussion and more lay-oriented writings by Milton Friedman. Friedman, among others, argued for changing the incumbent discriminative Treasury auctions to a competitive version as a way of enhancing government revenue (that is, generating interest savings).

It would be obvious today that laboratory experiments can be used to test the validity of the Friedman conjecture and to explore environments where it performed better or worse. Nevertheless, Smith downplayed, in the paper's introduction, the policy connection, arguing that the paper looked towards more general principles. He did, however, raise the policy debate several times in the article.

Although Vernon did not himself keep up an ongoing research program in T-bill auction experiments, he kept his interest in the topic even as it was pursued by others (for example, Miller and Plott 1985). One of the most interesting later examples was a series of field experiments by two Treasury officials. A preliminary report apparently existed (Tsao and Vignola 1977), and Vernon had scheduled a later version of the paper for one of his early experimental economics conferences. The paper was never presented because of internal opposition at the Treasury to getting the paper released. This served merely to increase interest in what the paper must show. Events of the past couple of years have vindicated those who continued the debate as to whether the Treasury might be advised to change the way it auctions securities.

Beyond this, experimental economics has a proven track record in conducting creative and informative experiments explicitly motivated by public policy issues. An excellent early example is that of Hong and Plott (1982). The topic areas include institutions for airport landing slots (Grether, Isaac and Plott 1989 and Rassenti, Smith and Bulfin 1982), evaluation of auctions for tradeable emissions permits (see, for example, Franciosi et al. 1993), new institutions for natural gas markets (McCabe et al. 1989) among many others. The evolution of experimental economics into a powerful public policy tool can be traced in surveys by Plott (1981) and Isaac (1983).

AUCTION EXPERIMENTS

Auctions are not limited to Treasury securities, nor are their forms limited to discriminative and competitive sealed-bid multiple unit auctions. Auctions are a ubiquitous form of resource allocation, with dozens of manifestations. Smith's 1967 paper served as one of the springboards for auction market experimentation, one of the most productive areas of experimental economics. The fraternity of experimental auction researchers includes James Cox, John Kagel, Dan Levin, Charles Plott and James Walker. Vernon remained active particularly in single unit auction experiments, with several co-authors including Cox, Bruce Roberson, and Walker. The importance of the Cox–Roberson–Smith–Walker line of research is the maturity of the experimental designs, the sophistication of the interaction of theory and data in the progressive research program, and the extent to which new projects are carefully built upon the results of those before (see, for example, Cox, Roberson and Smith 1982). Early experiments set the stage for later consideration of new bidding models. New experiments were run and the theory modified accordingly. Other new experiments were designed in the light of the newly modified theory, and so forth. Auction experiments are probably the best example in experimental economics of this type of progressive research program. Other researchers with parallel research programs sometimes had different interpretations, with resulting spirited discussion. But this is, after all, a normal part of the scientific enterprise.

In a different direction, there has been a renewal in interest in policy-specific auction experiments. One example is the Franciosi et al. (1993) examination of alternative auction mechanisms for acid rain emissions permits. When current public policy debates include auction design, we can almost take for granted that laboratory experimentation is, or could be, an accepted part of the policy analysis. This legitimation begins with the 1967 paper.

'AN EXPERIMENTAL EXAMINATION OF TWO EXCHANGE INSTITUTIONS' (1978)

This paper, co-authored with Charles Plott, also, appears deceptively simple. But it is also one of the landmark papers in the development of experimental economics. The paper notes a seeming inconsistency in previous experimental work by Smith and by F. Williams. Plott and Smith hypothesize that F. Williams had operationalized a new experimental trading institution, the posted bid (or posted offer), with differences from the oral-bid auction of Smith's previous works. Thus, they use the trading institution (posted bid, oral bid) as the treatment variable, half of the experiments using one, half using the other. The results clearly indicate that posted-bid trading prices are lower (posted-offer prices would be higher) than for institutions which converge to the competitive equilibrium. Behind this simple scenario are at least three achievements of this paper.

1. The paper is the opening salvo in research on the posted offer trading institution. While the trading system itself was used by F. Williams, it was this Plott and Smith paper which identified posted offer as a distinct trading institution and first identified its important properties. Because the posted-offer institution resembles naturally occurring markets in many retail and some wholesale settings, many of the important experimental economics papers in industrial organization use it. The broad-brush description about experimental posted-offer markets is that they have competitive tendencies, but convergence is slower than with the double auction, and out-of-equilibrium price paths tend to favor the seller (see Davis and Holt 1993, ch. 4).

2. Beyond the specific trading institutions examined, the paper strongly reinforces the point that market institutions can matter in market performance. This has implications in economics for everything from analyzing historical or existing market data to engaging in the process of market engineering: the systematic creation of new markets (for new products or for where markets were not previously allowed). Market engineering is occurring everywhere from the US (designing the process for spectrum auctions) to Eastern Europe. What this paper says is that this is not a needless task. Different market-trading institutions will have different performance properties. Of course, the logical extension of this proposition is that it is the process of laboratory economic experimentation which can reveal a great deal about how the market trading institutions differ. This establishes experimental economics as a key part of market engineering policy analysis.

3. This paper is co-authored with Charles Plott, another experimental economics pioneer, and hence it represents the fertile two-year period in which Vernon Smith was located at or near Cal. Tech. Following Vernon's move from Pasadena to Tucson, his activity level in experimental economics took off. Obviously, the two years that Plott and Smith spent together were extremely important intellectually, and it undoubtedly laid the foundation for Arizona and Cal. Tech. to become the two early leaders in experimental methods.

DEVELOPING METHODOLOGY

The first experimental papers by Vernon and others were not *about* experimental economics, they *were* experimental economics. For the most part, discerning the methodological developments and issues of laboratory experimentation required reconstructing them from the experimental economics papers themselves. An example, already discussed, is Vernon's transition from using hypothetical subject payments to using real subject payments, as discussed in the 1962 *Journal of Political Economy* paper. However, as the technology of experimentation progressed, as more papers were written, and, perhaps most importantly, as more people began conducting experiments, it was logical, even necessary, that important experimentalists (such as Smith and Plott) should begin to codify the methodological insights of experimentation.

Vernon's first methodological piece, in 1976, was narrowly focused, although it discussed a critical element of experimentation: how to control the supply and demand curves of the experimental market. The key lies in the process of 'induced valuation', which is the focus of the article. The experimenter would like Buyer #7 to have a reservation price (demand curve step) at $4.50. With an abstract hypothetical commodity and a hypothetical valuation process, there is still no reason that the buyer should behave as though his/her reservation value is $4.50. If he/she, for example, buys a unit of the commodity at $5.00, he/she incurs no actual loss, except whatever psychic pain he/she feels from trading above $4.50 (or from displeasing the experimenter). The alternative is to 'induce' the $4.50 value in the following way. Tell Buyer #7 that the experimenter will pay him/her $4.50 real US cash for purchasing one unit of the commodity and reselling it to the experimenter. Now the $4.50 amount is a real value. If a unit is purchased for less than $4.50, a real economic profit is generated. If the purchase price is greater than $4.50, an economic loss is incurred. The market price at which the buyer should be just indifferent between purchasing and not purchasing, the limit value, is $4.50. A mirror image argument creates limit selling values for sellers: they are given marginal production costs (for sale to order) for units which may be resold to the buyers. The possibility of mutually beneficial gains from exchange makes the market. By the use of multiple buyers and sellers (with multiple values), multiple step downward-sloping demand curves (upward-sloping supply curves) are created. The fundamental parametric structure of microeconomics can thus become a part of the controlled conditions of a microeconomics experiment.

The description above obviously bypasses some unexplored assumptions and hidden pitfalls in the process of creating and controlling the parts of a microeconomic system for purposes of experimentation. Smith's conceptual construct of the methodology of experimental economics took a quantum leap in his seminal article, 'Microeconomic Systems as an Experimental Science', which appeared as the lead article in the 1982 *American Economic Review*. The article is as much about economics broadly defined as it is about experimental economics. Smith draws upon prior work by Hurwicz and Reiter for the construction of a prototype of a microeconomic system. The microeconomic *environment* includes such things as the number and type of agents and conditions of supply and demand. The microeconomic *institution* reflects how the institutions of exchange are organized. The model also focuses upon what is *observable*. A part of the microeconomic institution is the language or message space available to each individual. In a naturally occurring economic system, the preferences or costs of economic agents are ultimately subjective and not directly observable. What one can observe are the messages sent by the agents. Economic models of behavior are attempts to predict those messages, which, through the rules of the institution, interact to determine the allocations of the economic system. Notice that in this construction, the emphasis is on issues of observability and upon the reality of market-trading institutions. These are essential in the world of ex-perimentation.

Experimental control is integral in any experiment, regardless of the discipline. This brings one immediately back to the structure of a micro-economic experiment above: environment and institution. In order to conduct a valid microeconomic experiment, to test a microeconomic model in a laboratory market, these must be controlled. The experimenter must spell out what the subjects are allowed to say and do and what the consequences of those actions are in terms of allocations and earnings. In other words, the very process of running an economic experiment means that the economic institution must be created and controlled in the laboratory.

Creating and controlling the economic environment is potentially more difficult. But inducing the conditions of supply and demand is exactly what Vernon Smith was describing in the 1976 paper. In the 'Microeconomic Systems' paper, he expands the discussion about successfully controlling the conditions of supply and demand. In doing so, Smith opened a formalized discussion on the practical details of conducting experiments.[1] This is in the form of five precepts, or sufficient conditions, for a valid microeconomics experiment. For example, with his *nonsatiation* and *saliency* condition, he brought to the table the key methodology issue of salient subject payments which Vernon faced in his very first paper. The *dominance* and *privacy* precepts speak to such practical issues as how instructions are written, how great must be the variation in payoffs for different subject actions, how complex tasks subjects can be asked to undertake,

---

1. Vernon clearly draws upon such earlier references as Kaplan (1964) and Wilde (1990).

and so forth. The *parallelism* precept has two faces. At one level, this precept is essentially a gestalt requirement that the regularities observed in experimental markets not be an artifact simply of the fact that they were observed in a laboratory, all other conditions being the same. At another level, the precept has put structure on discussions about the transferability of results from the laboratory to the field when conditions are not the same. For example, one arena has been that of subject pool differences. Does an experiment conducted largely with undergraduate college students have implications for markets where traders have a great deal of substantial trading experience? Several authors, including Smith, and Hong and Plott (1982), have shown that the answer is yes, but have also discussed the limits to such an extension. An interesting, related question, is when should the experimenter seek out well-trained, professional traders for laboratory experiments. The nature and scope of potential subject pool effects has been internalized by experimental economists as one of those ongoing topics for discussion in the art (not science) of scientific investigation (Beveridge 1950).

Smith's 1982 article holds a pivotal position in the evolution of experimental economics. We can denote the founding period as constituting Smith's pioneering early work. A second period begins with the Plott and Smith collaboration at Cal. Tech. and the entry into laboratory work by numerous other researchers. The 1982 article, together with the founding of the Economic Science Association which will be discussed below, signaled a transition of experimental economics from a period in which issues of design and methodology were discussed and transferred informally, almost as in a craft guild, to an era in which methodological issues were formally considered and certain practices were standardized and rationalized. The paper also, by appearing as a lead article, signaled the presence of experimental economics to those who only vaguely knew of its existence. What the paper also accomplished, and for which it may be less well known, was to demonstrate that laboratory experimentation is not simply a side-bar concept in economics but rather a step in the intellectual evolution of all of economics.

'MARKETS AS ECONOMIZERS OF INFORMATION ...' (1982)

Nowhere else does this synthesis among methodology, theory, economic structure, the institutions of contracting, and data come together better than Smith's paper on the Hayek hypothesis. The paper opens with a 'take no prisoners' discussion of the effectiveness (or lack thereof) of economics in the work of making public policy. He locks on to the disjointedness between economic theory and economic data, caricaturizing it 'as if economics had tried to do the work of classical physics by a shortcut that bypassed Galileo and Kepler and started "at the top" with the intellectually more interesting methods of Isaac Newton'.

The intellectual thread throughout the paper is the hypothesis of Hayek that the markets works well despite the fact that participants have little information on traders in the market other than themselves. Consideration of this hypothesis clearly fits into Vernon's paradigm, because it takes explicit account of the conditions of information in the market. Vernon evaluates the Hayek hypothesis through the presentation of several experimental data series. He reinterprets the numerous prior double auction experiments in the light of this information conjecture. The reason that the double auction experiments are particularly suitable is that buyers and sellers individually know *only* their own individual costs and valuations. The double auction is not, however, a price-taking institution. Buyers makes bids and accept offers; sellers make offers and accept bids. As the history of these double auction experiments has shown, despite the non-price-taking nature of the double auction, prices and quantities routinely converge to the competitive (fully efficient) equilibrium.

After the demonstration of the success of the Hayek hypothesis in one economic environment and institution, Vernon alters the economic en-vironment to put the hypothesis to a tougher test: demand conditions which change from period to period. Again, the convergence is cleanly towards the competitive predictions. Both the skeptical and the non-skeptical reader ought to be drawn, by this point, into the rhythm of all of laboratory experimental economics. 'What new economic conditions could I create that would, after all, cause the Hayek hypothesis to fail?' Or, 'If the Hayek Hypothesis can finally be found to fail, what will those conditions be and what other hypotheses might do a better job in replacing it?'. Whether they realize it or not, virtually all graduate students working with experimental economics inculcate some sense of this rhythm.

ORGANIZING THE PROFESSION

During the 1970s, Vernon hosted two small workshops in Tucson which brought together researchers interested in the now-expanding methodology of experimental economics. Some of those in attendance were themselves conducting laboratory experiments, others were theorists, others were doing field experiments, and so forth. These early conferences undoubtedly helped to build a nascent network of experimentalists. In the early 1980s, there was discussion around the University of Arizona about the possibility of a third conference. That idea leavened with early discussions about holding the annual meetings of the Public Choice Society, which were attracting a significant number of experimental papers, in Tucson. Unfortunately, the talks fizzled and the meetings (my memory recalls them as those of 1984) were scheduled for Phoenix. Not to be daunted, the Arizona department decided to hold a pre-conference meeting in Tucson aimed exclusively at experimental issues. The number of interested parties turned out to be higher than expected.

Seeing the interest in the experimental sessions, Arizona hosted subsequent meetings. Finally, seeing that the direction of the conferences was not far removed from the methodological issues of his 1982 article, Vernon presented the informal organization with a charge: the foundation of a new professional association dedicated to exploring the methodologies, research and discipline-wide issues of experimental economics. However, in his proposal, Vernon went out of his way to stress that this was not to be an 'experimental economics' club. While papers using experimental methodology would undoubtedly be prominent, the association was to actively recruit the participation of economic theorists, econometricians and representatives of the disciplines of law, finance, accounting and psychology. This was ac-complished by the organization of the group's government board into 'sections', whose head was to be a force for outreach to the areas listed above. Thus was the Economic Science Association formally born in 1986-87, with Vernon as founding president. It is an active organization today with one solo annual meeting, joint meetings with the Public Choice Society, and sponsored sessions at the winter ASSA meetings. It maintains the prominence of experimental economics as a common theme. Papers often present results of an economic investigation (into areas such as public goods, industrial organization or game theory) using laboratory experiments or papers on experimental methodology. A large number of participants every year are non-economists, with papers on finance, accounting or political science quite common. The association has matured to carry out such projects as dissertation prizes and discussions with publishers about journal activity. Even over the short period of its existence, it has evidenced the long-run stability characteristic of new generations of scholars coming into their own as authors and officers.

THE ONGOING ECONOMICS LABORATORY

In what we might call the entrepreneurial phase, the very first of Vernon's papers in experimental economics were sole authored. During his stay at Cal. Tech. and after his arrival at Arizona, Vernon began working with a number of co-authors, including Charles Plott, James Cox, Bruce Roberson, Arlington Williams, James

Walker, Don Coursey and myself. We might call this the 'cottage industry' phase of experimental economics: small groups of researchers working together with some economies of scope and specialization, but basically using refinements of the original (hand-run) technologies. Then, two things happened. First, there was the historical mating of experimental economics *per se* with computerized laboratory markets. The development of computerized laboratory experiments was pioneered by Arlington Williams, now at Indiana, who was a student of Vernon's at Arizona. Vernon recognized apace the potential for computerized markets. With a computerized version, of, say, a double auction experiment, more traders can be incorporated, instructions can be standardized, subject decision sets can be more robust, and more accurate records on parameter initialization and experimental data can be kept. It is also easier to conduct replications than with hand-run experiments .

The above discussion should not be interpreted as suggesting that computerized experiments are in every way superior to hand-run experiments, or that computerized experiments have supplanted hand-run experiments. Hand-run experiments maintain their own advantages. They do not have up-front programming costs. They can be more flexible in terms of design. In the early stages of a research program, I often prefer to work with pencil and paper technology in case I find out, in pilot experiments, that I have a mistake in my experimental design. An intermediate technology is the 'computer-assisted' experiment, in which the data aggregation and analysis portion of a pencil-and-paper experiment is handled by a PC or even a lap-top. Having said this, the computerized experimental revolution has become an irrevocable technological reality of laboratory market experimentation. Several uni-versities, both in the US and in Europe, have computerized experimental economics laboratories.

The second important innovation of this period was the use of laboratory experimental economics to investigate public policy questions which have combinatorial values or costs. A combinatorial value structure is one in which the agent values combinations of objects in a way other than just the same of valuations of individual objects (or smaller sets of objects). Thus a collector might value a set of three stamps different from the sum for owning each of the three stamps separately. Obviously, more complicated values are possible.

Experimental economic manifestations of the combinatorial problem evolved independently at Cal. Tech. and Arizona. The public policy issue that united them was the problem of allocating airport take-off and landing 'slots' (see Grether, Isaac and Plott 1989 and Rassenti, Smith and Bulfin 1982). At Arizona, Vernon teamed with Rassenti, a graduate student in Systems and Industrial Engineering, to merge a combinatorial auction market with a computerized optimization algorithm for dealing with the combinatorics.

These threads of computerization of experiments, combinatorial opti-mization and public policy application came together in the following circumstances. In the early 1980s, the State of Arizona allowed increased research funding to be requested through a type of competitive process at the university. The Economics Department was interested in developing a proposal around the experimental economics program. Vernon, meanwhile, believed that simply creating a bigger experimental economics lab (built on what I have called here the 'cottage industry' approach) was inadequate for the next generation of research. Instead, he envisioned that experimentation was going to need to be even more on the cutting edge of computerization than before. He believed that team research was going to be a way of life. He believed that experimental economics was going to face a stronger push to be involved in public policy issues, which require rapid submission of proposals and rapid production of results, all tied to external circumstances which have very little to do with the academic cycle. Vernon envisioned that this new phase required state-of-the-art physical resources plus a permanently available expert team whose appointments were outside the traditional faculty job description. The experimental economics lab would have to be a national and international resource, where graduate students and pre- and post-doctoral fellows would come to learn about experimental economics. The result of this vision was the creation of the University of Arizona's Economic Science Laboratory. More traditional experimentation can be supported at ESL, but its creation has opened up the possibility of research that could only have been dreamed of before. Now occupying its newly constructed second laboratory, ESL has grown to a maturity that few could have envisioned. Vernon, in his position as director, provided ESL with its defining vision.

An exciting example of the type of advanced policy-oriented research of ESL is work on computerized markets designed to replace centralized regulation of natural gas or electricity (see Rassenti and Smith 1994). The markets are complicated because of their network nature. Using the natural gas computerized market as an example, we see computerized markets with natural gas producers, pipeline owners and demanders (local service distributors). Because of the network, buyers can purchase from several producers, and gas can travel through different pipelines. Each of the economic agents submits a bid or offer to the market where an optimization program uses the revealed economic information (recall Vernon's emphasis on observability) to set an efficient allocation. The electric power version is similar except that it uses generators, transmission lines and demanders, and, obviously, different constraints regarding output flows. Work with these combinatorial network markets has not been, for the most part, primarily theory-testing in nature. Instead, it has been largely used to create a laboratory testbed for new economic institutions. There have been some actual policy successes, particularly in the worldwide interest in alternatives to state-owned electric power monopolies.

There has been an additional benefit to the creation of ESL. The team research atmosphere has brought a sense of camaraderie that is not necessarily at home in all academic settings. One particularly pleasant manifestation is the ESL pool party at the Smith residence, with Vernon holding court over his cowboy coffee and the lawn area engaged in games in which everyone from graduate students to faculty rugrats are welcome. If somewhere in this revelry the conversation turns to a new series of experiments, that is alright, too.

AUCTION EXPERIMENTS

Earlier on, I made reference to Vernon's role in a series of experiments designed to evaluate auction institutions, test existing auction market theories, and develop and refine those theories into new hypotheses. I wish to reiterate the importance of this research program. First, consider the diligence of Vernon and his co-authors in pursuing these questions. The Coppinger, Smith and Titus paper appeared at conferences in 1977 and appeared in print in 1980. This paper reported experiments comparing the English (oral-ascending) auction, Dutch (oral-descending or clock) auction, and the first- and second-price sealed-bid auctions. This comparison was extended, with extensive theoretical development of equilibrium-bid functions, in the Cox, Roberson and Smith paper of 1982. In these earlier papers, the experimental data generally did not support a theoretical isomorphism between the Dutch and first-price sealed-bid auctions. In Cox, Smith and Walker (1983), the authors report two models to explain this nonisomorphism, and use experimental data to discriminate between them. Another major stream of this research tracked the issue of heterogeneous versus homogeneous equilibrium-bid functions, with one proposed theory subjected to new experimental tests, followed by a reformulation of the theory in the light of the data, and so forth. This highly productive theory-experiment synthesis continued on, with new research being reported well into the 1990s.

What ought one to notice about this very productive research stream, beyond the fact that there is a lot of research there and that each paper, standing by itself, is interesting and of high quality? First, this work demonstrates that, in the vision that Vernon has developed, experimental economics is not anti-theoretical ultra-empiricism centered around experiments, narrowly defined. Rather, the experiments are a new tool to do economics, and part of doing economics is theory development (and testing). Over the decade or so of the auction market research, the various papers moved seamlessly between theory, experiments designed to test theory, interpretation of the theories in the light of the experimental data, the development of new or modified theories, the design of new experiments, and so forth.

A second important point about this auction research program is that its influence spread beyond the realm of the auctions we have defined here. For example, Vernon and co-authors such as Kevin McCabe and Stephen Rassenti began a separate but related investigation of multiple-unit versions of the English and Dutch auctions. Individual bid data from the first-price auction experiments opened a debate in the experimental economics community about the possibility or non-possibility of inducing not only values but also risk preferences upon experimental bidders.

There is no doubt that the auction experiments are an important research program in economics *broadly defined*. They ought to be familiar to anyone learning about auction theory. They obviously hold a similar position in experimental economics. While not written as pedagogical pieces, they can be used in a graduate seminar on the techniques of experimental economics.

A PERSONAL REFLECTION

There are three of Vernon's experimental papers to which I wish to turn for a moment: Coursey, Isaac and Smith (1984); Coursey, Isaac, Luke and Smith (1984); and Isaac and Smith (1985). They are important to me because they are the three experimental papers upon which Vernon and I have collaborated, and I thought they would be useful to organize some personal thoughts about working with Vernon. First, it is fairly obvious from looking at his vita that these papers form a large part of a fairly distinct subset of Vernon's research: experimental papers dealing with topics in industrial organization. The first two papers are concerned with the (then emerging) contestable markets hypothesis (cmh) of natural monopoly. The first paper looked at cmh in an environment designed to be quite favorable. The second added sunk costs, which were proposed as a possible barrier to contestability. Each of the two demonstrated the substantial robustness of the cmh. The third paper looked at the ever-present concept of 'predatory pricing'. Vernon and I were truly surprised by the data from the predation experiments as they were being conducted. We both had believed that our original design would yield predation, and that the rest of our research would be to look for ways to get rid of it. In fact, just the opposite happened. We were never able to capture an environment that produced predation (hence our title, 'In

Search of Predatory Pricing'). Instead of trying to get rid of predation, our most direct policy experiments showed that, under some circumstances, anti-predation public policies could make market performance worse. For both topics, contestability and predation, these were the first experimental papers in the area.

It is somewhat difficult to nail down a description of working with Vernon on these papers. He was extremely thorough and involved in every aspect of the experiment, even though Coursey, Luke and I were obviously the 'junior' researchers and might, in other sciences, have been relegated the 'grunt' work. In fact, because Vernon was just as involved in the 'grunt' work as we, working with at him at that level is comparable with other of my co-authors. Vernon and I together worried about how to assign subjects (who got to be the potential predator), about how to give sellers more units (should we use two computer screens), about designing the supply and demand conditions to capture as closely as possible what we believed was implied by the extensive industrial organization literature on predation. We wrote the instructions. We designed the experiments. All was careful and thoughtful, as one might expect.

The extraordinary part of working with Vernon occurred in a series of more discrete experiences. What would happen is that we would be in a routine series of discussions, usually on such topics as hypothesis development, data interpretation, treatment design, responding to referees, and so forth. Perhaps we were stuck about how to proceed. I could tell that some part of my contribution to whatever discussion we were having was meeting, not with resistance, but with a sense that something was going on elsewhere. Within a couple of days, Vernon would grab me, usually early in the morning, and would present some totally unexpected or radical way of looking at our problem. This often included a synthesis of what I had been saying but thought was lost. I usually ended up asking myself something like, 'How does he think of these things?' because what he came up with did exactly what we needed.

A final observation gained from personal interaction is that Vernon has absolute scholarly and intellectual integrity. He will not compromise his position just to get another journal article published or to please a potential grant referee. It took several rounds of reviewing to get his very first experimental article in the *Journal of Political Economy*. I do not know many who would have had such a level of persistence. It has appeared at times that Vernon has paid a short-term cost for this, but across a career the rewards to such a commitment to ideas has paid off. It is with such a picture of Vernon in my mind that I was immediately drawn to the prairie idealist presented at the beginning of these thoughts.

PROPERTY RIGHTS AND MARKETS

I have often heard the comment that Vernon would be a Chaired Professor even if every experimental economics paper disappeared from his vita. I believe that to be an accurate statement. Consider just one example, Vernon's work on capital and investment theory, which I have mentioned in passing. This is not some isolated paper. According to my count, Vernon has published at least *sixteen* papers on the topic, most of them in first-rate journals, many of them seminal works. A good example of the classics on this list is the 1972 paper on 'Default Risk, Scale and the Homemade Leverage Theorem'. (Actually, a colleague of mine once restated the opening premise of this paragraph: it would be possible to get tenure just with the ideas about capital and investment theory that Vernon had talked about but had never got around to writing up). When working on this commentary, I would mentally go over the question, 'How am I going to present Vernon's *other* papers?'. I finally came to the conclusion that this was the wrong approach to take. Although not themselves *experimental*, it would be a mistake to draw a line between this other work and the experimental work. Recall that the *first* part of Vernon's key methodological paper on microeconomic experiments begins not with techniques for experimentation but rather with a discussion about the nature of microeconomics *per se*. And, a key part of that discussion, as well as the closing discussion in the same paper, is the importance of recognizing in the microeconomic system the condition of property rights (to commodities, to information, and to messages in institutions) and the status of other institutional properties of markets. It is the importance of these conditions which is one of the key concepts underlying *all* of Vernon's work.

The key paper making this bridge, one we have already discussed, is the *Economic Inquiry* paper on the Hayek hypothesis (1982a). This paper puts flesh on the bones of the microeconomic systems paper from 1982. The Hayek hypothesis paper, as we saw above, combines experimental results with a respect for the process for creating hypotheses with the unambiguous supposition that theory and data ought to play a role in economic policy making. Because of its focus on the Hayek hypothesis, it is intimately concerned with the conditions of information in the economy and with the reality of market institutions.

Another place where the outcropping of these topics can be seen is in Vernon's work on the design of smart, networked market institutions. This has been one of the central areas of team research at the Economic Science Laboratory. In designing computerized 'smart' markets, one cannot escape from the issues of property rights, information and market institutions. Indeed this is what the process of market design is all about. Even the process of implementing a networked market is fraught with these issues. For example, setting a new market in operation has the potential of creating economic winners and losers (just ask the people of Eastern Europe). Political opposition to economic reform can, in some circumstances, be mitigated by appropriate transition property rights. Vernon has commented extensively on these problems, which reflects both his experimental economics expertise as well as his experience 'in the trenches' working to evaluate the possibilities for economic reform. He has been extensively involved, for example, in discussions of smart market approaches to privatization of electric power in both New Zealand and Australia. In this work, he is deliberately concerned with the property rights, contracting and market institution that must accompany any such major changes.

Viewed in this same light, one can see the pattern in many of Vernon's 'non-experimental' papers. He has written extensively on the creation of markets for water rights, with the issues of information, defining the property rights and constructing the nature of the institution being paramount. Vernon's several pieces on voting mechanisms (some of which are experimental examinations) focus upon the importance of unanimity – which represents a very important property rights structure. Even his environmental economics papers, such as his paper on pleistocene extinction (1975), draw upon this same paradigm.

Thus, although often overshadowed by his experimental work, these 'non-experimental papers' form an important part of the intellectual quilt behind his work. Looked at in this light, the experimental work ceases to look so much the merely methodological revolution that it might seem and instead becomes a necessary component of a complete research program guided by a particular view of microeconomics.

ECONOMIC MODELS OF HUMANKIND

Some of Vernon's most recent work is in the area of economic models of the evolution of humankind. I have found this to be one of Vernon's most interesting research topics, although it is among the ones about which I am the least knowledgeable. It is an illustration of Vernon's intense scientific and intellectual curiosity. At a time in a career when many of us would be justifiably resting on the laurels of a lifetime of discovery, Vernon is staking out a new area.

Actually, Vernon's work in an area that might be called economic anthropology is not entirely recent. It was, for example, an important theme in his pleistocene extinction paper, mentioned above. Vernon was addressing the extinction of large mammals. It is intriguing (in a politically correct world) to read Vernon's inquiry as to whether large mammal extinction might be explained by economically rational behavior of primitive hunters. Of course, as discussed above, the property rights structure of such a hunting culture plays a crucial role in the answer.

Vernon's most recent work (1992) takes off in a different direction. He is interested in the conditions for the switch of a culture from hunting–gathering to agriculture, and with the question of whether a culture could ever switch back (as is suggested by an economic view of the situation). His approach is not simply economic modeling but also a thorough understanding of the literature from anthropology – not simply a reading of what researchers in a different discipline are up to, but a chance to study their learning about culture for clues to property rights, trading structures, sources of changes in opportunity costs, and so on. Vernon and I have even had extensive discussions as to what can be learned on this topic from the Old Testament, something we would probably never agree upon on a theological level, but which is fascinating from our shared perspective on markets and property rights.

A sidelight to the work on the evolution of humankind comes from Vernon's recent undergraduate teaching. He has organized two seminar-type courses for general-background undergraduates. One course is a freshman colloquium on economics, with a substantial experimental economics component. A second course is a seminar organized to include many of the University of Arizona's Regents' Professors, of which Vernon is one. Taught as an honors course to lower-division undergraduates, the Regents' Professors are encouraged to talk about their most exciting frontier research: brain function, the formation of planets, and so forth. Vernon has used his two lectures not to talk about experimental economics, but rather to discuss economic models of humankind.

SOME PARTING REFLECTIONS

At this point in a typical scholarly article, the author is expected to provide a logical and structured reprise of the fundamental points which have been made. In this reflection, this might consist of a restatement of Vernon's most important scholarly contributions. Such a summary ought to be useful to the unfamiliar reader who could turn to it to get a coherent picture of Vernon's achievements. This is certainly an appropriate goal, but not easily done. There is no easy progression of Vernon's research in which one can start at one point and simply walk through all that follows. The obvious starting point in our journey was Vernon's 1962 *Journal of Political Economy* article, which essentially introduced laboratory experimental economics research. Following that were indeed a series of articles which seemed to build on the original paper. But the 1967 *Journal of Business* article also introduced fundamental ideas of auction processes. This paper not only provided a bridge to a later and much more advanced series on the theory and behavior of different types of auctions. It was also a prototypical policy paper. Walking through Vernon's research is like playing a video game in which one is always finding secret passages which lead from one chamber to another, a disconcerting circumstance because there is so much to find in the new hallway that it is not clear that one can or will want to return to where the process began.

We saw that it is not easy to classify Vernon's work by traditional subject boundaries. There is his defining record of scholarship in experimental economics. But, as Vernon insists, papers using experimental economics are not in the 'field' of experimental economics; they are in the field of industrial organization, or game theory, or labor economics, or environmental economics, and so forth. They use the methodology of experimentation just as papers using econometrics can be in a traditional field. Thus, even within the corpus of Vernon's 'experimental papers' (setting aside the purely methodo-logical papers) there are bodies of contributions in auction theory and design, in industrial organization, in game theory, in public goods provision, in public policy design and in other areas.

It really is not even possible to wall off Vernon's 'experimental' work from his 'non-experimental' work. Take, for example, the recent work of Vernon and several co-authors on the design of smart computer-assisted markets. The team of researchers working on this project has spent almost as much time travelling all over the world studying potential field applications of smart computerized markets (deregulation of electric power markets, for example) as they have running experiments (see 1994).

All of this interconnection is not some random accident. It is a reflection of the mind of Vernon Smith. Talk to him about public goods and he will tell you how that relates to early humankind. The original market experiments sprang from a curiosity about the performance of stock exchange mechanisms, a curiosity which has spanned decades and included his seminal work on the possibilities of bubbles and crashes in asset markets (see Smith et al. 1988). The experimental results, showing that bubbles and crashes could be found to exist in laboratory asset markets, led to other research on new ideas for asset-market trading rules. The research led to the practical public policy challenge of assisting in the opening of the Arizona Stock Exchange, a computerized stock market using a 'call' system of trading. This work was conducted as an Economic Science Laboratory team effort, illustrating the importance of the ESL team concept. From the running of the first double auction experiments to the implementation of the Arizona stock exchange more than thirty years have gone by. It is quite an achievement to follow one general research theme in such a focused program across such a long period of time. In following such a trail, Vernon did so across traditional methodologies, through the invention of a completely new methodology, through the reformulation of that new methodology several times to address new needs, ending up, years later, working on an actual 'real-world' implementation of the critical ideas. We see here Vernon Smith the scholar and methodological revolutionary who is both the pragmatist and the idealist, the man who has never lost his roots in the Kansas prairie.

ACKNOWLEDGEMENTS

I am particularly indebted to Prof. Warren Samuels for his very helpful editorial comments and to Prof. Vernon Smith who graciously critiqued an earlier draft. Of course, all remaining errors are strictly my own.

SMITH'S MAJOR WRITINGS

(1962), 'An Experimental Study of Competitive Market Behavior', *Journal of Political Economy*, **70**, 111-137.

(1967), 'Experimental Studies of Discrimination Versus Competition in Sealed-Bid Auction Markets', *Journal of Business*, **40**, 56-84.

(1972), 'Default Risk, Scale and the Homemade Leverage Theorem', *American Economic Review*, **62**, March, 66-76.

(1975), 'Economics of the Primitive Hunter Culture with Applications to Pleistocene Extinction and the Rise of Agriculture', *Journal of Political Economy*, **83**, July–August, 727-56.

(1976), 'Experimental Economics: Induced Value Theory', *American Economic Review*, **66**, May, 274-9.

(1978) (with C.R. Plott), 'An Experimental Examination of Two Exchange Institutions', *Review of Economic Studies*, **45**, February, 133-53.

(1980) (with V. Coppinger and J.Titus), 'Incentives and Behavior in English, Dutch, and Sealed-Bid Auctions', *Economic Inquiry*, **18**, January, 1-22.

(1982a), 'Markets as Economizers of Information: Experimental Examination of the "Hayek Hypothesis"', *Economic Inquiry*, **20**, 165-79.

(1982b), 'Microeconomic Systems as An Experimental Science', *American Economic Review*, **72**, 923-55.

(1982) (with J.C. Cox and B. Roberson), 'Theory and Behavior of Single Object Auctions', in V.L. Smith (ed.), *Research in Experimental Economics*, **Vol. 2**, Greenwich, Conn.: JAI Press, Inc.

(1982) (with S. Rassenti and R. Bulfin), 'A Combinatorial Auction Mechanism for Airport Time Slot Allocation', *Bell Journal of Economics*, **13**, Autumn, 402-17.

(1983) (with J.C. Cox and J.M. Walker), 'Tests of a Heterogeneous Bidders Theory of First Price Auctions', *Economic Letters*, **12**, 207-12.

(1984) (with D. Coursey and R.M. Isaac), 'Natural Monopoly and the Contestable Markets Hypothesis', *Journal of Law and Economics*, **27**, 91-114.

(1984) (with D. Coursey, R.M. Isaac and M. Luke), 'Market Contestability in the Presence of Sunk Entry Costs', *RAND Journal of Economics*, **15**, Spring, 69-84.
(1985) (with R.M. Isaac), 'In Search of Predatory Pricing', *Journal of Political Economy*, **93**, April, 320-45.
(1988) (with G. Suchanek and A. Williams), 'Bubbles, Crashes, and Endogenous Expectations', **56**, September, 1119-52.
(1989) (with K.A. McCabe and S.J. Rassenti), 'Designing "Smart" Computer Assisted Markets: An Experimental Auction for Gas Networks', *European Journal of Political Economy*, **5**, 259-83.
(1992), 'Economic Principles in the Emergence of Humankind', *Economic Inquiry*, **30**, January, 1-13.
(1994) (with S. Rassenti), 'Privatizing Electric Power in Australia: Proposed Experiments', mimeo, presented at the 1994 combined meetings of the Public Choice Society and the Economic Science Association, April 8-10, Austin, TX.

OTHER REFERENCES

Beveridge, W.I.B. (1950), *The Art of Scientific Investigation*, New York: Vintage.
Chamberlin, E.H. (1948), 'An Experimental Imperfect Market', *Journal of Political Economy*, **56**, April, 95-108.
Davis, D.D. and C.A. Holt (1993), *Experimental Economics*, Princeton: Princeton University Press.
Franciosi, R., R.M. Isaac, S.S. Reynolds and D.Pingry (1993), 'An Experimental Investigation of the Hahn–Noll Revenue Neutral Auction for Emissions Licenses', *Journal of Environmental Economics and Management*, **24**, 1-24.
Grether, D.M., R.M. Isaac and C.R. Plott (1989), *The Allocation of Scarce Resources: Experimental Economics and the Problem of Allocating Airport Slots*, Boulder, Co.: Westview Press.
Heat-Moon, W.L. (1991), *Prairy Earth*, Boston: Houghton-Mifflin.
Hong, J.T. and C.R. Plott (1982), 'Rate Filing Policies for Inland Water Transportation: An Experimental Approach', *Bell Journal of Economics*, **13**, Spring, 1-19.
Isaac, R.M. (1983), 'Laboratory Experimental Economics As A Tool in Public Policy Analysis', *Social Science Journal*, **20**, July, 45-58.
Kaplan, A. (1964), *The Conduct of Inquiry*, New York: Chandler Publishing.
Miller, G.J. and C.R. Plott (1985), 'Revenue Generating Properties of Sealed-Bid Auctions: An Experimental Analysis of One Price and Discriminative Processes', in V.L. Smith (ed.), *Research in Experimental Economics*, **Vol. III**, Greenwich, Conn.: JAI Press, Inc.
Plott, C.R. (1981), 'Experimental Methods in Political Economy: A Tool for Regulatory Research', in A.R. Ferguson (ed.), *Attacking Regulatory Problems: An Agenda for Research in the 1980s*, Cambridge, Mass.: Ballinger Pub. Co.
Wilde, L. (1980), 'On The Use of Laboratory Experiments in Economics', in J. Pitt (ed.), *The Philosophy of Economics*, Dordrecht: Reidel.

15. Robert A. Solo

John E. Elliott

INTRODUCTION

Like several creative and prominent American economists before him,[1] Robert A. Solo is an authentic midwest American original. Karl Popper once characterized Solo (1994, pp. 1-2) as 'a man who could not be taught but had to think out from the beginning whatever he knew'. Illustrations of this quality in Solo's work are provided in the first section, which examines his broad vision of social change (Solo 1974 et al.); the second section, on the scope, methodology and philosophy of economics (Solo 1991); and the third section, which considers *Economic Organizations and Social Systems* (Solo 1967; hereinafter EOSS), the closest approximation to a lifetime *magnum opus* and a brilliant, but unfortunately neglected, book.

In the remaining two sections of this paper, we shall discuss, first, Solo's critique of the content of neoclassical economic theory and his own movements, partly in unpublished manuscripts (e.g., 1968), in the direction of an alternative perspective on economic analysis between, but above and beyond, traditional micro- and macroeconomics (e.g., 1961, 1994a);[2] and finally, Solo's theory of the 'positive state' (e.g., 1982) and the challenges of public policy of such a state (e.g., 1991a).

In all of these, and related, works, we find, in addition to originality and creativity, an illuminating and persistent critique of orthodoxy. As Solo puts it (1994, p. 2):

---

1. Thorstein Veblen, John Rogers Commons and Wesley Claire Mitchell are good examples of such predecessors.
2. Stuart Holland (1987) aptly calls this terrain 'meso-economics'. Prominent examples are the economic analysis of regions, major sectors and organizations larger than those of individuals or relatively small firms, but smaller than the economy as a whole.

I prowl through the fields of establishment thought, to find and focus on one of its propositions or theories, questioning, wondering, searching for flaws, for I have in my mind that to upset a heaped cart of the sacred apples of science is the highest form of scientific achievement.

In his incisive review of EOSS, Kenneth Boulding has written (1967):

It may be that the real importance of Solo's book is as a demolition job. In Chapter 7, for instance, he demolishes in a few pages almost 200 years of capital theory, apparently with a single firecracker, but with astonishing thoroughness.

To this Solo adds (1994, p. 2) a characteristic postscript: 'Let them inscribe that on my tombstone!'.

Learning is a key, indeed defining, element in Solo's conceptualization of economics as a social and policy science. His own learning process included undergraduate study at Harvard (BS, 1938), where Edward Chamberlin and John Kenneth Galbraith were his tutors, graduate study at the American University (MA, 1941), and Cornell (PhD, 1953), all in economics, and the London School of Economics (1946-48), where he read economics with Lionel Robbins and philosophy with Karl Popper. His personal learning process also included several positions as a government economist in various federal agencies in the late 1930s and early 1940s, service in the United States Navy during World War Two, and several research and teaching positions in Europe, Canada and the United States before he finally settled down as tenured professor in the American heartland at Michigan State University, in 1966, where he mostly remained until assuming emeritus status in 1987.

All of these experiences left an imprint on Solo's subsequent thought and work. It was at Harvard that he was first introduced to the blend of economic theory, law and public policy, through the interdisciplinary discipline of industrial organization, in the lectures of Edward Mason, founder of that field.[3] At Harvard, also, he worked through Keynes's *General Theory* on his own. In 1939, Solo was employed by the Division of Industrial Economics of the Department of Commerce. The work of this Division 'was centered on Keynesian theory and practice, in which I devotedly believed' (Solo 1994, p. 10). But as a young maverick, Solo bucked the emerging new orthodoxy, which propounded increased government borrowing as a desirable alternative to higher taxation as a means to finance enlarged aggregate demand (Solo 1991b). Instead, he proposed a third

---

3. In his autobiographical statement (1994, p. 4), Solo reports that Chamberlin 'was dubious at my decision to try to make my way as an economist, given my total detachment from the mathematics which he saw as taking over the discipline'. This theme reappears in Solo's recent (1991, p. 97) study of the epistemological foundations of economics, wherein he excoriates the 'mathematization of empirico-judgmental discourse'.

alternative, of direct sales of non-interest- bearing government securities to the Federal Reserve System which, in his 1941 MA Thesis at the American University, he saw as another form of 'non-diversionary public spending' (Solo ND, pp. 91-3, 143-5). A bit more than a half-century later, he has restated this argument as a 'Modest Proposal' for expansionary policy which could circumvent the diversion of spending from the private sector through taxation, the potentially regressive redistribution of wealth and income to the rentier, and political opposition to expansion of the public debt (Solo 1994a).

If it was at Harvard that Solo became an economist, it was at the London School of Economics, after World War Two, particularly through his extensive reading and preparation of a (700+ page, ultimately aborted) dissertation on 'the presuppositions of economic theory' under the joint supervision of Robbins and Popper, that he became a methodologist and philosopher of economics. Popper had argued (1935/1959) that scientific hypotheses cannot be proved by any specific failure in predication, but can be disproved, that is, falsified. Hence, for Popper, a credible scientific theory is one that can be and is scientifically tested through prediction and has not yet been falsified. In his draft dissertation, Solo applied 'Popper's Rule' to economics. His conclusion: General theory in economics or any of the other social sciences can never be scientific in Popper's sense because, given the nature of its universe, it cannot be falsified by a specific prediction but must be accepted as credible or not based on a judgement of evidence both pro and con (Solo 1991, p. 10).

In 1950, Solo shifted to Cornell, where he returned to his starting point, so to speak, that is, industrial organization, which, in his particular variant thereof, would prove to be a life-long scholarly interest. His dissertation, on the synthetic rubber industry in the United States, became the basis for future studies, notably his 'classic' and 'definitive' book on this subject (1959), the 'first treatise published in the United States on science policy' (Solo 1994, p. 29). Altogether, Solo has published prolifically (14 books, more than 100 articles and chapters in books, and more than 20 reviews) in such fields as industrial organization and public utility regulation, corporations and the organizational economy, macroeconomics and public finance, economic theory, economic development, science and technology, the philosophy and methodology of economics (including structuralism), and the theory of the state and economic policy. We cannot review all of this vast body of literature in a relatively brief chapter, but shall draw on most of the books, several of the articles and chapters, and some unpublished manuscripts in elaborating the themes of the succeeding sections of this essay.

ON HISTORY AND SOCIAL CHANGE

Like Marx and Veblen before him, Solo has constructed an explicit conceptualization of social change over historical time. This interpretation of change, together with his analysis of the philosophy of economics, undergirds the analytical content both of his critique of orthodoxy and his own, alternative, economic (and political) theory. It contains three major di-mensions: (1) 'functional systems', or means and processes for organizing resolutions to various social or economic problems, such as resource employment, resource allocation, income distribution and economic growth; (2) 'ideologies', or 'ideas as to what is and ought to be with respect to a field of choice and action', such as liberalism, conservatism, or socialism; and (3) cognitive and cultural systems, that is, bodies of ideas to systematically process information and solve problems (e.g., science and technology) and sets of connected values to enable evaluation and choice (e.g., utilitarianism), respectively (Solo 1967, pp. 359, 362; 1982, pp. 4-5).

Solo distinguishes between mere 'flux without change', for instance, buying and selling of goods, adjustments in the income distributed to one individual as compared to another, and genuine or more fundamental 'change', for example, alterations in the bases of power, 'institutional structure', or 'the system and its objectives' (Solo 1974, p. 8).

An economy or culture thus changes as a result of significant alterations in one or more of the aforementioned basic structural elements of society. Because of the inertial force of 'social habit and the acceptance of precedence' (Solo 1967, p. 367), fundamental social 'change' is rooted in social tensions and psychic conflicts which become sufficiently powerful to overturn the basic unity rooted in congruence within and among functional systems, ideologies, and cultural and cognitive systems. In EOSS, Solo gives four prominent examples.

First, the cultural system may contain coexistent values, for example, rugged individualism and Christian charity, which imply 'contradictory responses'. If such contradictions engender tensions which are 'severe enough to expose the value substructure to conscious choice and reformulation', then the criteria for normative evaluation may change, and as a result, major reforms in institutional structure (e.g., establishment of a social security system) may be adopted (Solo 1967, p. 367).

Second, a society's cognitive system 'can be challenged as illogical or as inconsistent with observed phenomena and event' (Solo 1967, p. 368). If the incongruities become severe (e.g., neoclassical economics in the context of the Great Depression of the 1930s), the consequences may entail reconstruction of underlying values and policies as well as cognitive systems.

Third, when 'functional systems work badly', as, for instance, in the USSR in the 1980s, mounting 'dissatisfaction and tension' may become so great as to elicit a reexamination of the 'cultural content of functional organization', thereby 'permitting a reconstruction of values', as illustrated by programs for privatization and marketization, indeed even the collapse (the former Soviet Union) or overthrow (East Europe) of the state (Solo 1967, p. 368).

Fourth, when the roles implicit in a 'given functional organization impose upon those who play those roles' a divergent 'universe of experience', and when 'groups are fixed and immobile in those roles', then the dominating and dominated groups (e.g., bourgeoisie and proletariat in classical Marxian analysis) will acquire distinctively different 'outlook[s], skills, knowledge, and values'. The resulting social conflicts thus generated may elicit major reforms, even revolutions (Solo 1967, pp. 368-69).

Finally, at a deeper and higher level of abstraction, 'more fundamental, universal, and revolutionary change' occurs through the 'breakdown and transformation' of those 'cognitive–cultural structures' that 'contain and determine the spectrum of potential ideologies'. But, at a lower and more concrete level of abstraction, the 'process of ideological breakdown, transformation, replacement is the pivot of social change' (Solo 1982, p. 6).

Ideologies play this pivotal role in two major ways, each connected with what may be called an 'ideological lag', that is, a tendency for ideologies, notably those associated with the interests of dominant groups, to lag behind changes in other dynamic elements of the social system, such as science, technology, institutions and organizations, and to do so to a greater extent the more rapid the pace of such change.

First, when 'social need and crisis generate pressure for institutional change and those changes conflict with the dominant ideology', then ideology operates in a negative way, as a drag on social change. Reform proposals propounded by 'diverse, equivocal, and often conflicting' interests (what Solo calls 'composite' choices) are countered by critiques rooted in the dominant ideology and issued by 'authoritative' agencies, such as the Supreme Court in the United States. In such instances, ideologies are pivotal to social change by placing brakes upon it.

Second, eventually the distance between ideology ad experience is stretched to its limits. A turning point is reached, typically in a moment of great crisis, such as war or a severe depression. (The Great Depression of the 1930s is a notable example.) Ideology is then reconstructed in a more or less major way. Once the 'cohesive and resistive force' of the former dominant cognitive– cultural understructure is shattered and ideology is reconstituted in the light of accumulated changes in science, technology and institutions, opportunities are opened for 'pragmatic experiment and maneuver' (Solo 1974, p. 10; 1982, p. 8). New ideologies then play a positive role in guiding further social change. Thus,

> for any period of history, there is a shared and prevailing system of perception that gives form to and is reflected in the sciences, the arts, the literature and the politics of the time. And when that system of perception changes there occurs a series of revolutionary changes in the character of the sciences, the arts, and the politics of the time. ... The clue to the sequence of historical periods [is thus] the mode of conceptualizing and imaging the human creature. (Solo 1994, pp. 14, 31-32)

Over the last 500 years of Western history, there have been perhaps 'three such fundamental transformations in the cognitive–cultural understructure'. The first of these 'great mutations', associated with the Renaissance, marked the breaking away from the Age of Authority, from faith, church and tradition, to a World of Man, wherein 'unbridled self-interest and free-roaming reason of the individual formed a fundamentally new cognitive–cultural under-structure' (Solo 1982, pp. 8-9). Technologically, this transformation was characterized by a shift from 'craft' to 'shop', from the mysteries of the guilds to the use, organization and division of labor in factories. Economically, it meant a shift from tradition and status to market relations and private property. Politically, it was marked by the supersession of local fealties and allegiances by the emerging nation-state and centralized political authority. Ideologically, it was manifested by two great bodies of thought, Nationalism and Liberalism, which, through the mid-nineteenth century, were often progressive and democratizing. Intellectually, the evolution of this first great epoch in the modern history of 'being as nexus and integrating principle of the structures of thought', proceeded through three main phases in the conceptualization of 'autonomous Man': the passionate and 'Heroic Man' of the Renaissance; the ordered and 'Rational Man' of the Englightenment; and the 'Synthetic Man' of the nineteenth century, battered and propelled by 'forces that transcend the private volition', such as industrialization and internationalization of economic relationships (Solo NDa, p. 237).

The latter part of the nineteenth century marked the beginning of another 'fundamental transition in the nature of experienced reality', namely, transformation from the World of Man to the 'Universe of Systems', where the organization, especially the big corporation, but also labor unions and governments, becomes the 'key entity' and 'critical agency of decision and behavior'. Integral to the 'organizational revolution' are the following elements: (1) The uncertainties of quantum mechanics have replaced the certainties of classical Newtonian mechanics. (2) Technological creativity, through discovery, invention and innovation, is now purposefully organized and serves as the dominant cause of economic progress. (3) The economy is a system of power and politics, evidenced by 'negotiated relationships of gigantic corporations and trade unions'; these private organizations are 'arbitrary' in the sense that they are neither narrowly constrained by competitive 'market forces' nor are they accountable to the larger society through 'public participation in the processes of organizational policy formation'. (4) From the New Deal onward, Keynesian policies and the welfare state have (but only partially) grappled with the short-run dislocative consequences of these longer-term 'fundamental transitions' (see the last two sections, below). (5) During these generations of dramatic scientific, technological and organizational change, a 'lag' has occurred between 'ideologies–imageries' and 'this fundamental alteration of encountered reality', with ecalating 'crises' as a consequence (Solo 1983, pp. 49, 53; 1961, pp. 16-19).

THE PHILOSOPHY AND METHODOLOGY OF ECONOMICS

As noted earlier, Solo complements his perspectives on history and social change by a systematically thought-out philosophy and methodology of economics. This body of thinking ranges broadly over: the methods for testing–falsifying hypotheses; the nature of economics as a social and policy science; the mathematization of economic discourse; and the role and character of normative theory in economics.

According to Popper, we can never know truth with certainty. In science (classical mechanics is his paradigmatic model), the 'function of prediction is not to verify but to refute, not to establish truth but to eliminate falsehood'. Even in physics, however, the credibility of this canonical perspective raises two major problems. First, it requires 'a determinant world where all events in a closed system are predetermined with absolute precision'. Even in contemporary quantum mechanics, these conditions do not exist, and determinant falsifiability has been superseded by indeterminant probability distributions. But this is highly problematic because (1) any specification of a 'range of improbability' as equivalent to falsification is arbitrary; (2) it implies the same (unwarranted) privileged status for probability testing as for falsifiability testing. Second, as explicated persuasively by Kuhn (1962) and Foucault (1970), the falsifiability procedure does not accurately describe the actual operations of science (Solo 1991, pp. 26, 29-30, 32-3). It certainly does not do so in economics. Our discipline is replete with illustrations – mass unemployment and Keynesian theory, monopolistic competition, the overpowering role of technical change (as compared to capital accumulation) as the most compelling explanation of economic progress are paramount examples – of instances where substantial incongruities between theoretical predictions and experience led not to abandonment of refuted theories, but to their restatement or simply to their stubborn retention.

In contrast to the conditions implied by Popper's Rule, economics is both a policy science and a social science (Solo NDb). As a policy science, projections from the cognitive–cultural understructure, that is values, images and ideologies, invade and guide economic discourse. Consequently, economics is a 'moral philosophy' and a 'technology' as well as (or instead of) a 'science' in Popper's sense. As a social science, in economics, 'there can be no general theory or statement that is universally and invariably true'. Because human beings are free, heterogeneous, and open to learning, their actions are 'radically indeterminant, with neither constancy nor continuity in causal relationships nor in probability relationships'. Therefore, 'no failure of a specific prediction of event or of probability can conceivably falsify general theory or generalizing statement in the social sciences'. What economics actually searches for is 'essential' or 'fundamental' properties, that is, 'propensities' or 'tendencies'. Its discourse is 'empirico-judgmental'; that is, there is 'no other rational way' to proceed than to weigh the evidence pro and con and then to judge between contending theories. This 'system of social judgment' is more akin to 'the courts and their processes of counter-advocacy before judge and jurors' than it is to the physical science. In short, economics is as much a 'social philosophy' as it is a 'social science' (Solo 1953; 1991, pp. 69 ff., 87-9, 93-6).

As Solo observes, there have been 'two major methodological innovations in economics during the twentieth century, namely the mathematization of its language, and its anathema on value judgment'. The first of these innovations, Solo avers, has been a 'crippling aberration'. First, it 'fails its stated purpose'. In *The Foundations of Economic Analysis* (1947), Samuelson states that his intent in transforming the imprecise verbal and graphical language of economic theory into the precise language of mathematics was to enable thereby the testing and falsifying of economic 'laws' (or hypotheses) through specific empirical predictions. But, as observed above, what is problematic about testing economic theories pertains not to their (im)precision but to the fundamental 'empirico-judgmental' character of economics. Therefore, the 'transformation [into mathematical language] failed [in its] purpose. It did not work'. But mathematization was accepted nonetheless, partly for aesthetic reasons. The result has been 'unprecedented sterility', based at least in part on 'mathematizing the language' (Solo 1991, pp. 38, 97-8).

Second, Solo agrees with Nicholas Georgescu-Roegen's critique (1971) of strictly mathematical approaches to economics for their exclusion of 'qualitative difference, qualitative change, and novelty'. Such 'truly vital elements' of economics as 'process' (that is, wants, motivations, belief structures, and 'social organizations') are 'qualitatively variable', and 'not subject to cardinal measurement'. The economic process is historically 'irreversible'; and because its elements change form and character with the 'emergence of novelty', these qualitative aspects of economics cannot be 'encompassed by or accommodated to the symbolic structure of mathematics' (Solo 1991, pp. 98-9).

Third, when, as in classical Newtonian physics, the credibility of generalizations can be based on 'specific inferential prediction', mathematics is the preferred language of discourse. But in empirico-judgemental inquiry, as in economics, mathematization of generalizations 'collapses'. Although verbal language is equivocal and imprecise, it 'can do what mathematics can never do', that is, it can provide richly variegated images of the 'experienced reality' which is the object of communication. And when qualitative variance and transformation, and judgement rather than inferential prediction, 'counts for credibility', verbal language is the 'preferred instrument of com-munication'. Mathematical language 'perverts the process of judgment' in such discourse (Solo 1991, pp. 97, 101-4).

The second methodological innovation in the twentieth century was the proclamation, by John R. Hicks (1939), that (1) 'interpersonal comparisons' of utilities are 'unscientific', and (2) economists should eschew making judgements about the impact on welfare of changes in income distribution, but under the 'curious rule' of Pareto optimality, should instead restrict their analyses of welfare improvements to those in which income distribution remains given. But, first, there is nothing 'unscientific' about interpersonal comparisons. They are quite commonly made, for instance, in psychology and several disciplines in medical science, such as immunology. Second, to ban value judgements concerning income distribution and to restrict welfare judgements to Pareto optimality conditions constitutes a double value judgement, and therefore is an internal incongruity in Hicks's argument. If substitution of Hicks's indifference analysis for the old utilitarian arguments did not abolish either interpersonal comparisons or value judgement, it did conveniently serve other functions, namely, it provided an 'escape hatch' from such controversies, 'restored the discipline's ideological bias', and 'preserved the goodwill of its patrons'. Moreover, insofar as economics is a policy science, it is perforce, as noted, 'moral philosophy'. Value judgemental discourse is thus useful and, in any event, unavoidable (Solo 1991, pp. 108-11, 113-14).

ECONOMIC ORGANIZATIONS AND SOCIAL SYSTEMS

We have earlier characterized EOSS as the closest approximation to a lifetime *magnum opus*. We shall review briefly its purpose and overall structure and note some of its major novel features and connecting linkages with ideas discussed in other sections of this essay.

EOSS is written at three levels of abstraction and de facto constitutes three books. At the highest level of abstraction (Part I), EOSS compares three ideal type forms or systems for organizing economic activity. These are: decentralized market-directed economy; centralized politically-directed economy; organizational market-negotiated economy. Each of these economic forms is contrasted regarding: (1) allocative efficiency, distributive justice, instability and institutional costs; (2) technical change, productivity enhancement and economic progress; (3) ways of life, social environments and impacts on social values and human character.

Elements of intellectual novelty and innovation are immediately apparent even from this brief sketch. First, concerning the forms of economy, decentralized market-directed economy is the most familiar of the three models, based as it is on the ideas about competitive market processes of Marshall, Hicks and Keynes, with agriculture as its exemplar in practice; it requires no special comment here.

Solo's explication of his second model, that of the centralized politically-directed economy, incorporates several novel features. Foremost among these is clear specification, at the outset, that this form of economy is not only 'centralized' and focused on 'planning' in contrast to decentralized market processes, but also is subject to 'political direction'. First, in this system, 'the polity and the economy merge into one'. It is, by definition, a *political* economy. Here, the economy is 'a branch of government; it is one of the agencies of collective choice and political action'. Second, behind its choices stand 'the ultimate coercive power of the State. The limits upon the power of the planning authority are precisely the limits upon the power of the political authority' (Solo 1967, p. 10).

Solo's third form, that of organizational market-negotiation, is also a system of political economy. But in contrast to the centralized politically-directed economy, the state is one coparticipant among several powerful autonomous organizations, notably, gigantic corporations and, to some extent, trade unions, and functions as 'sovereign among the sovereignties'. Its power is limited by the countervailing power of autonomous private organizations, to some degree by the market negotiations of such organizations, and by constitutional and political constraints. In contrast to market-directed economy, where the state 'stands apart' from, and serves 'only to support the institutions of the competitive market', under this third form of economy, the state itself is an active coparticipant, serving to articulate collective needs, to regulate, and to mediate (Solo 1967, pp. 10, 15).

The organizational market-negotiated economy also contrasts with the market-directed economy in that 'the market is not master'. It is 'a forum for negotiations, a showcase for display, an area for maneuver by entities that find their analogue in rival nations'. Prices do not 'automatically reflect' simple demand and cost forces, but signify instead the politics of 'corporation or trade union policy or a negotiated relationship between autonomous powers' (Solo 1967, p. 13).

In contrast to both of the other forms of economy, autonomous organizations, especially the large corporation, are the loci of tremendous politico-economic power, partly independent of both market and the state. This is not simply a question of monopoly or oligopoly power, for a small proprietary firm under competitive market economy may be large relative to a small market, whereas a large corporation may be small relative to a large market. Organization itself is a source of power *vis-à-vis* individuals it confronts both externally and internally. When organizational power is compounded by market power (and by political influence), as in much of the manufacturing heartland, the dominance of big corporations is even more compellingly demonstrated. Conversely, the power of individuals is defined and enhanced by their positions and roles within or their relationships to large autonomous organizations. 'In the organizational economy individuals do not relate as subjects of a common political authority, nor as self-interested bargainers', but as colleagues, superiors or subordinants in managerial hierarchies, bargaining agents or representatives, or owners of financial assets (Solo 1967, p. 13).

Turning to the criteria for exposition and assessment of these three forms of economy, we also encounter several novel elements. First, by incorporating the criterion of institutional costs, as well as efficiency, equity and stability, Solo is able to cast his exposition in terms of systemic considerations; that is, discussion of resource allocation, income distribution and overall output and employment is enhanced by contrasting performance of these economic functions under alternative institutional conditions. This provides simul-taneously a richer and more variegated and a more concrete, institutionally specified, analysis.

Second, by separating out economic progress, and technical change and productivity increases as the paramount means to progress, Solo is able to set his contrasts of different forms of economy in a broader qualitative, dynamic and historical contest, and to link his *magnum opus* with his lifelong interest in science and technology. He is also able to provide sharper focus to his investigation of the organizational market-negotiated economy by incor-porating the unique role in that economy of competitive R&D by large, autonomous corporations.

Third, by expressly incorporating consideration of the effects of different modes of organizing economic activities upon ways of life and human values, he simultaneously broadens the scope of the discussion, provides a comparativist approach to these neglected aspects of contending forms of economy, and links EOSS with his methodological critique of standard economics. Solo's major critique of the organizational economy, for instance, is in the moral realm. His main indictment of large corporate organizations is the absence of any clear mechanism to render their politico-economic power publicly responsible. Decision makers in large autonomous organizations neither adapt to market processes beyond their control, as in a market-directed economy, nor stand directly accountable to the citizenry or political leadership, as in a politically-directed economy. Their exercise of power, in short, is amoral, if not immoral.

At an intermediary level of abstraction (Part II), EOSS examines the various forms of organizing production and consumption in the United States and studies economic policy in terms of the 'tensions and incongruities' arising out of interactions among four sectors: 'the enterprise economy, the political economy, the institutional economy, and the household economy'. In addition to market-directed and organizational market-negotiated economy, the enterprise sector includes the decentralized market-segmented sector (exemplars: wholesale and retail trade, construction and services) and price-regulated public utilities (exemplars: transportation and communication). The political economy in the United States organizes activities, especially the consumption of collective goods, by 'governmental policy or directive'. Its exemplars include military defense, science and technology, and transfers, such as social security and interest on the public debt. Its activities are partly market-oriented, as in publicly owned utility companies, but largely politically directed, as in space research, development of natural resources, and highway construction (Solo 1967, pp. v, 265).

The third sector in the national economy consists of institutions, such as schools, universities, churches and research institutes, which are neither profit-seeking nor politically directed. Instead, these institutions embody and are organized around internal core values or ways of life. Basic research and education exemplify this sector. A fourth sector is the household economy, which is devoted to the well-being of its constituent entities, notably families or individuals. Although its major economic activity is consumption (the largest component of GNP), it also organizes production on a substantial scale, exemplified by the education and rearing of children, most of which is not registered in the GNP.

Finally, in Chapter 29, one of the most enlightening chapters in EOSS, Solo aptly characterizes the national economy as a 'half-way house', consisting of a 'diversity of systems' (that is, enterprises, governments, non-profit in-stitutions and households). Because economic tasks are diverse and change over time, ways of life are also diverse and incorporate significant non-economic elements, and various forms of economy are 'cross-supporting', the blending of elements of a national economy conduces more fully to economic progress and human well-being than would a 'pure' system comprising only one sector. Yet, in practice, a 'single system and its derivative values tend to dominate the social outlook'. This is, of course, the enterprise economy, notably, the 'autonomous, market-negotiating form'. Diversity of organ-izational forms contains disadvantages as well as advantages, notably the tendency for the criteria from one sector to intrude inappropriately upon another, as when, for example, notions which are sensible concerning private debt are extended to debt in the public sector (Solo 1967, pp. v, 265).

At a still lower level of abstraction (Part III), Solo applies the basic ideas of EOSS (and elsewhere) to the challenging problem of economic development. Essentially, this turns his theory of history and social change (see the section on history and social change, above) into reverse gear. Having rooted past economic development in revolutionary transformations in cognitive–cultural understructures, it should come as no surprise that EOSS characterizes the task of scaling the heights of development as one of engineering such transformative changes. Central elements in developmental strategy and policy include: building a revolutionary leadership, fostering processes for transferring and assimilating science and technology, and constructing and expanding educational systems. These basic ideas are (re)stated theoretically, and tested by reference to developmental experiences in the USSR, Mexico and Puerto Rico.

FROM CRITIQUE OF NEOCLASSICISM TO POST-MODERNITY

In EOSS and other works, Solo challenges the presuppositions and content of neoclassical microeconomics and Keynesian macroeconomics. His critique of neoclassicism focuses on such items as the following. First, neoclassicism is based on methodological individualism, in two senses: on the one hand, it conceptualizes the 'social universe' as comprised of individual, 'independent decision makers', operating in 'splendid isolation'. On the other, it postulates the mind of the 'autonomous individual' as a 'perfect instrument of pleasure and pain'. These presuppositions rule out of account and fail to explain such vital phenomena as '(1) culture based differences in behavior, (2) significant variations in the level of economic performance, and, most important, (3) the process of individual, group, or social learning' (Solo 1975, p. 640).

Second, neoclassicism's equilibrium analysis constructs demand and supply functions strictly 'within the boundaries of *ceteris paribus*'. But movements along a demand or supply function typically entail significant changes which plausibly 'change the understructure upon which the form of the curve depends' and 'sets in motion forces that simultaneously change its entire shape'. The precision of demand and supply functions thus 'dissolves', and equilibrium theory is rendered 'inherently indeterminant' (Solo 1975, p. 636; 1968, pp. 59-62).

Third, neoclassical assumptions of pure and perfect competition also rule out the phenomenon of power. This is radically discordant with such experiential realities as market power (as in monopoly, oligopoly and monopolistic competition), organizational power (as in the large-scale corporation and trade unions), and countervailing power. Neoclassicism is an integral component of the 'ideological lag'. Paradoxically, at the very moments, in the late nineteenth and early twentieth centuries, when technological, institutional and organization change were generating large agglomerations of power, economists were busy evicting power from their argumentarium via models of perfect competition.

Fourth, one might argue that theories of pure-perfect competition are intended not as explanations of real-world experience, but as welfare norms. There is, no doubt, some truth to this. Entrepreneurs and industrialists, at the time of classical economic theory, were 'outsiders', who 'sought to escape the domination of an entrenched aristocracy', and 'pressed for a share in the temporal power'. By the late nineteenth century, they had become 'insiders' and were 'dominant and entrenched' as the 'prime possessor[s]' of power. Consequently, neoclassical theory 'developed as a defense of the status quo and of the policies of laissez-faire, became an apologia for capitalism' (Solo 1975, p. 628).

Moreover, perfect competition as a welfare norm is surely utopian. Segmented market economy, organizational economy and public utility enterprise are rooted in key economic forces which are probably ineradicable. In any event, the history of antitrust laws in the United States demonstrates that although the Supreme Court, as the agency of 'authoritative choice' (see the final section, below), was perfectly willing to prevent 'agreements between independent companies to fix prices, control output, or otherwise limit competition', the Court, for decades, *rejusted* to permit 'the dismemberment of large, going concerns on account of their alleged monopoly power'. Solo reasonably infers that the Court's underlying presupposition was that dissolution or divestiture 'must necessarily threaten the viability of technology and the effectiveness of organization' (Solo 1974, pp. 129, 131).

Even if pure-and-perfect competition were feasible, however, it would not thereby necessarily be desirable. Although the decentralized market-directed economy has its virtues, it also has 'peculiar vices'. Even setting aside effects upon economic progress and ways of life, it contains the 'following propensities for waste and malallocation':

> (1) an extreme and pervasive uncertainty; (2) extreme price instability with detrimental consequences for time-extended and contractual arrangements; (3) a maximum 'externalization' of the benefits and costs of choice with a consequent distortion in the allocation of resources; (4) a basic reliance on windfall profits and losses as the guide [to] the movement of resources with consequent inequities in the distribution of income and irrationalities in the recruitment of economic leadership; (5) property as the power base for the prejudice of a social class and the institutionalization of nepotism. (Solo 1968, pp. 194-5)

Solo's own alternative to neoclassicism has already been sketched in preceding sections of this chapter. A few connecting linkages, however, may be useful. First, Solo claims, economics has been in a state of 'epistemological crisis' for 70 years or more. This crisis is manifested by the domination of the discipline by underlying epistemological presuppositions, notably, those of logical positivism as found in the canonical statements of Karl Popper, and by the methodological innovations successfully introduced by some of its leading figures, for example, the 'sterile' mathematization of economics discourse (Samuelson) and the futile and misleading endeavors to make economics a *wertfrei* analytic (Hicks). These, and other, dubious methodological in-novations have been accepted by most economists 'blindly, without a critical and informed response, and with never an effort to test and evaluate effects'. What is now needed is a systematic 'epistemology for economics', that is, a thoughtful and considered inquiry into 'the conditions of coherence, the criteria of credibility, propriety of statement and boundaries of inquiry, and as to what economics must know about the character of knowing and the process of learning' (Solo 1975b, pp. 45, 47).

Drawing on the work of Jean Piaget in psychology, Kenneth Boulding (1968) in economics, and Michel Foucault in philosophy and methodology (Foucault 1970; Solo NDc) Solo proposes the epistemological perspective of 'structuralism' as a possible way out of this crisis.[4] On the one hand, structuralism 'postulates a distinctive cognitive structure as underlying, determining and setting boundaries upon observation, behavior, thought' and 'seeks to identify the constituent

---

4. 'I am a structuralist through and through. My work relates alternative forms of economic organization to their requisite cognitive structures; the pathways of economic transformations and economic revolutions to the topography of culture and cognition and the processes of ideological disintegration and creation to the formation of the law and of policy' (Solo 1975a, p. 621, 1967, 1974).

elements and integral form of cognitive structure'. The need for such an approach in economics is highlighted by the revolutionary shift to an economy, society and polity dominated by 'vast corporate and public organizations'. Human behavior in large organizations cannot be understood in terms of methodological individualism. Instead, the activities of many thousands of people need to be coordinated into patterns 'where coherence absolutely requires a mass perception and a shared commitment', defined in terms of 'shared cognition', and 'cognitive structure is the key to organizational form and behavior'. On the other hand, economics has an 'urgent need to understand the phenomenon of learning' as a 'sequential change in cognitive structures'. For instance, learning is 'at the heart' of overcoming 'endemic poverty' and accelerating and directing technological change because underdevelopment results from the 'failure of spontaneous social learning', development and technological improvements require processes of social learning, and R&D builds a part of the 'learning function into the operation of large corporate and public organizations' (Solo 1975a, p. 620; 1975b, pp. 42, 51).

FROM LIBERAL STATE THROUGH WELFARE STATE TO POSITIVE STATE

If Solo's critique of neoclassical microeconomics is rooted in his underlying epistemological perspective, his critical assessment of neoclassical and Keynesian macroeconomics is based on his theories of ideology, social change and the state.

We have noted earlier that Solo identifies Nationalism and Liberalism as the two paramount ideologies associated with the transformation from feudalism to capitalism. The 'nation' is united by an ideological commitment to its asserted right to 'collective autonomy' and to a 'sovereign power' exercised through the state. In extreme versions, the 'Nationalist State' and the 'Liberal State' are antithetical. The 'pure nationalist state' is both a maximal and a military state. Nineteenth-century Prussia is a classic example. Its 'power core' was a military elite. Its 'command center was dominated by the soldier with the statesman-diplomat at his elbow'. Its cultural virtues were those of 'patriotic obedience, discipline, and duty'. The Prussian State 'created a general system of education' and a 'literate population'. It 'systematically inculcated a range of industrial skills', 'managed an industrial revolution', and 'established the science–industrial linkage of R&D', all 'for the purpose of war' (Solo 1982, pp. 55-6, 58). The Communist state in the Soviet Union, to take a second example, largely 'retained the form it had had under the Czar[s]', but with an altered understructure of cognition and culture, namely, a commitment to industrialization and (some of) the 'moral goals of socialism: fair shares, universal education, and an egalitarian society' (Solo 1967, p. 405).

By contrast, the 'liberal state' is minimalist and juridical. Its paramount social values are personal liberty and autonomy, preserved by personal security and private property. The liberal state protects individual security and property, enforces rules for the exercise of 'property power', draws 'boundaries' in property rights, resolves conflicts among property owners, and enforces their contracts. The American state in the nineteenth century was a classic example. Protected from European wars by its geographic isolation and blessed with abundant natural resources and a predominantly middle-class population, American society devoted its energies down to World War One largely to its own internal development. Until the 'catastrophic breakdown' of the Great Depression in the 1930s, the American state, gripped by the 'imperatives of ideological liberalism', lacked

> the autonomous power to intervene, control, organize, plan, direct, or in any way significantly affect the course of internal events, or the structure of relationships, or the distribution of wealth and incomes, or the output of industry, or the character of life, or the nature of the economy. (Solo 1982, pp. 57, 59)

As a practical matter, nationalism and liberalism, when transplanted to America, became joint elements of the dominant ideology. The War of Independence both 'asserted a new nationhood' and constituted a 'rebellion of liberalism against state intervention'. The evolution of American law, public policy and ideology proceeded dialectically, through several stages, wherein Congress and the President 'exemplify composite choice, reflecting a balance of pressures and expressing a universe of diverse wants and opinions'. The Supreme Court, by contrast, exemplifies authoritative decision and articulates an ideology (Solo 1974, pp. 33, 40).

> During the first phase of constitutional development, from the birth of the republic through the Civil War, it was the Supreme Court that spearheaded the trend of change and reform in centralizing and rationalizing political authority. In this first phase, the Court expressed the ideology of nationalism and Congress and the President reflected the resistances of the vested [rural and state] power, established governments, and traditional loyalties.
>
> During the second phase of constitutional development, from 1860 to 1935, it was Congress and the President who pressed for reform and change while the Supreme Court was the bastion of status, [the] defender of laissez-faire, [and the shackler of] political authority. (Solo 1974, p. 89)

Down to the Civil War, the Supreme Court, 'acting by reference to the prevailing ideology', forced 'the pace of social change'. The liberal ideology needed 'a solid infrastructural base for a viable market system': a 'sound currency, a national system of banking and credit', enforcement of contracts and the 'claims of creditors', and provision for the security of property. To achieve these goals, a power shift from the states (which were more effective in economic intervention and 'more subject to democratic pressure' to do so) to the national government was needed. Thus, the Court threw its weight 'on the side of the party of property and wealth and against the antagonisms of the rural majority'. It accomplished this feat, under the leadership of Chief Justice John Marshall, through successful development of the process of judicial review (Solo 1974, pp. 57-8).

Over time, with the spread of industrialization, urbanization and large corporate organizations, the Supreme Court increasingly shifted to the defense of an established ideology and practice which became increasingly obsolete in the light of altered circumstances. Eventually, 'it would have to yield' (Solo 1974, p. 90) and, under the pressure of the crisis of the 1930s did so.

Thus, the Great Depression 'broke the grip of ideological liberalism on American thought and policy'. The forces of composite choice – notably, the President and Congress – responded to the catastrophe of the 1930s by adding what Solo calls an 'offset function' to the role of government policy, thereby inaugurating a third stage in the evolution of law and public policy, that of the Welfare State. Under its auspices, beginning with the New Deal and extended after World War Two, the market economy is still accepted as paramount. The political authority as 'offsetter' does not 'replace the market'; it does not 'plan and organize anything'. It simply 'offsets' market processes when their results are considered excessive or inadequate, in the interest of fostering newly established '*welfare* rights' (Solo 1982, pp. 44-5; 1983, p. 51; 1974, p. 388). Prominent examples include:

> offsetting the pools of poverty and the inequities produced by the market distribution of income; offsetting imbalances in the bargaining strength of parties to exchange; offsetting insecurities and vicissitudes of the aged and the sick under the remorseless rigors of the market system; and especially offsetting deviations from that volume of aggregate demand necessary to maintain a normal level of employment. (Solo 1974, p. 391)

The forces of composite choice during the New Deal responded *ad hoc* to overwhelming problems. But an ideology was needed to guide the processes of change. In the United States, the Supreme Court, the 'agency of authoritative choice', as in the pre-Civil War period, became 'again the spearhead in articulating and implementing a new ideological basis for social policy, in the direction of a positive and responsible state'. Keynes and the Keynesians provided an analogous rationale for the economics profession. What was especially persuasive about Keynesian theory was that it appeared to provide a means to enable economists to have their cake and eat it too. In short, Neoclassicism could be retained to explain resource allocation and income distribution, and Keynesian-style theory and policy could be added to explain and resolve problems of insufficient (or excessive) aggregate demand. In principle, therefore, even substantial unemployment could be eradicated by 'simple offsets, transfers and grants, fiscal and monetary manipulations, [and] subsidies and tax incentives'. There was no perceived need 'for the state to control, to regulate, to restructure, to plan ... nor to change the system itself'. The Keynesian 'Revolution' thus 'managed to change the policy prescription without offering any challenge to ideological liberalism' (Solo 1982, pp. 45, 47, 61).[5]

Solo rejects this Neoclassical–Keynesian synthesis. Instead, he posits an 'absolute and fundamental contradiction' between neoclassical theory, rooted in downward wage and price flexibility, and Keynesian theory, which recognizes downward wage and price inflexibility.[6] Suppose that the state raises aggregate spending to reduce unemployment. These demand increases 'are absorbed by higher wages and higher prices raised at the behest of organizational policy' and are based on corporate and labor union power, leaving unemployment 'untouched'.[7] Conversely, suppose that the state reduces aggregate spending in the

---

5. In addition to Chapter 24 of the *General Theory*, traces of this 'Neoclassical–Keynesian' perspective, which focuses on 'equilibrium with less than full employment', looks to government to countervail insufficient (or excessive) private demand, and inspired standard Keynesian analysis after World War Two, can be found in Chapters 1, 3 and 18. Other elements of Keynes's thought, however, notably Chapters 2, 12, parts of 15-17, 19, 21 and 22, together with publications before (1926) and after (1937) the *General Theory*, provide bases for a more radical interpretation of Keynes's argument and have inspired Post Keynesian and other systems of thought. See Elliott (1994a).

6. The statement, however, that 'following the logic of that Keynesian analytic, the Great Depression was the consequence of a downward shift in aggregate spending, producing mass unemployment, *because* price did not move freely' (Solo, 1982, p. 62), while containing an important element of truth, also omits a significant point which Solo discusses elsewhere (1967, 1968). In Chapter 19 of the *General Theory*, Keynes argues in some detail that even if wages and prices were perfectly downward flexible, unemployment would still be the rule and full employment the exception. Therefore, the purely perfectly competitive solution, even if it were not otherwise economically and politically utopic, might well be judged socially undesirable because of its 'extreme [and excessive] price instability' (Solo, 1968, p. 194). See also Elliott (1992).

7. More precisely, if we posit, as Solo does, oligopoly and competitive sectors, under conditions of insufficient aggregate demand to establish full employment, there will be 'relative over-employment and low labor income in the competitive sector, relative over-investment and excess capacity ... in the oligopolistic sector, and pools of unemployment as a part of the latter sector'. Now suppose that government expands aggregate demand sufficiently to eliminate unemployment in the oligopoly sector. That sector can expand output without cost increases because of its excess capacity and its ability to draw on unemployed labor or on workers employed at lower pay in the competitive sector. But as the competitive sector approaches full employment, its prices, factor remunerations, and costs will rise. Higher prices for competitive sector goods will raise costs for the oligopoly sector and decrease real wages for its workers, who then will press for higher money wages. Higher raw

endeavor to offset inflation. Again, Keynesian policy is thwarted by organizational power. Corporate giants typically keep prices more or less stable as demand falls, letting production decrease and unemployment rise. Thus, under conditions of stagflation, the 'Keynesian conceptualization fails as a workable hypothesis for economic control' (Solo 1972, p. 138).

Over time, the dilemmas of stagflation may be reduced or ameliorated by productivity increases, rooted in technological improvements. Keynesian-style policy 'presided' over the 'golden decades' of Western, especially American, capitalism (roughly 1946-68). As long as productivity rose, as it did, sufficiently to satisfy rising expectations of real income, production and employment could expand without significant inflation. But when productivity growth decreased and technological advancement collapsed, as they did in the 1970s and beyond, stagflation and its associated conflicts escalated.[8]

Stagflation and technological eclipse, particularly in the United States,[9] are only two of the most prominent politico-economic failures compelling transformation beyond both the Liberal State and the Welfare State to what Solo calls the Positive State. Such a state is not (or not simply) a quantitatively enlarged version of the Welfare State. The Positive State is qualitatively different from its predecessors. It must 'plan, organize, participate on the inside, initiate, innovate, manage, restructure, control' (Solo 1983, p. 54). The 'planning-programming' function is being added to those of 'housekeeping' and 'offsetting' (Solo 1974, p. 371; ND, Forward, chs. 4-6). The Positive State is thus a politically directed economy. But, unlike the centralized variant of that form of economy (Solo 1967), it must share

---

materials prices and higher wages in the oligopoly sector elicit higher oligopoly prices. If the government stops its expansionary policy, the oligopoly sector maintains prices and cuts production and employments. But sustenance of the government's expansionary policy 'renews the sequence of events that leads us to a further general increase in the price level. Again the dilemma confronts us: an aggregate demand sufficient to maintain full employment is incompatible with general price stability' (Solo 1959, pp. 475, 477).

8. Solo subjects the topic of 'America's technological decline' to careful scrutiny. Among several causes, he focuses on the post-World War Two 'enormous diversion of America's critical resources into the military' and 'change in the internal structure and organization, which has progressively widened the distance between the operation of production and the locus of [financial] decision and control' (Solo 1991a, p. 66). Deterioration in technological progressivity and productivity growth from the 1970s onward in the United States relative to the experience of other countries also should stimulate, he argues, deeper consideration of 'lessons from abroad', for example, those provided by Japan (Solo 1984).

9. Solo notes that 'America's decline' relative to that of other industrialized societies is starkly recorded by Magaziner and Reich (1982). They observe, for instance, that Swiss GNP per capita was 57 percent of that of the US in 1960, but 139 percent in 1979. For Denmark, the figures for these years were 46 and 119 percent. For Japan, the numbers are 16 and 86 percent. These, and other, industrialized economies succeeded in achieving both lower unemployment and higher rates of growth in productivity than the United States in the 1970s.

power with the corporate-industrial sector, in a system of 'dual management'.[10] 'Only the state' can represent the public weal so as to both 'monitor and harness' the arbitrary power of the organizational economy and restore technological progressivity.[11] Ultimately, therefore, the Positive State 'emerges because it must' (Solo 1982, pp. 62-3).

ACKNOWLEDGEMENTS

I would like to thank Professor Solo for providing me with reprints or copies of many of his articles, all of his books, and several unpublished or forthcoming manuscripts. I would also like to thank Professor Warren J. Samuels, editor of this book, for advice and commentary on an earlier version of this chapter. Any remaining errors or misinterpretations are my own.

SOLO'S MAJOR WRITINGS

Books

(1955), *Economics and the Public Interest*. New Brunswick: Rutgers. Republished by Greenwood Press, 1980.

(1959), *Synthetic Rubber, A Case Study in Technological Development under Public Direction*, Washington, DC: US Government Printing Office. Reprinted, with a new Introduction, in Solo (1980).

(1967), *Economic Organizations and Social Systems*, New York: Bobbs Merrill.

---

10. Solo offers numerous examples of policy proposals suitable for a Positive State. Concerning stagflation, he recommends, *inter alia*, interest-free financing of public debt by the Federal Reserve System (mentioned earlier) and 'systematic participation by a public agency', along with corporate and union leaders, in the determination of prices and wages in the 'corporate-industrial sector ... when and if there is a repeat encounter with the phenomenon of stagflation'. Concerning technological progressivity, he proposes such policies as: radical reduction of military spending and conversion to public non-military investment infrastructure; major educational reform; establishment of a MITI-like public agency to '*target* industrial innovation and development' and development banks to foster long-term investment; and the limitation or prohibition of conglomerate mergers (Solo, 1991a, pp. 39, 107).

11. In a developed system of dual management, as in Japan, private management is responsible for 'financial integrity, effective organization, high productivity, consensus, morale, recruitment and training, [and] income distribution at the micro level'. Public management is responsible for 'industrial structure in its evolution and development, infrastructural supports, technological advance and economic growth, distributional equity at the macro level, full employment, price stability, resource conservation and the availability of alternatives to depleting resources, non-discriminatory opportunity, and environmental protection' (Solo 1984, p. 53).

(1974), *The Political Authority and the Market System*, Cincinnati: South-Western.
(1980), *Across the High Technology Threshold: The Case of Synthetic Rubber*, Norwood, PA: Norwood Editions.
(1982), *The Positive State*, Cincinnati: South-Western.
(1991), *The Philosophy of Science and Economics*, London: Macmillan.
(1991a), *Opportunity Knocks: American Economic Policy After Gorbachev*, Armonk: Sharpe.

Articles

(1959), 'Inflation in the Context of the Mixed Economy', *The Canadian Journal of Economics and Political Science*, November.
(1961), 'Intra-Enterprise Conspiracy and the Theory of the Firm', *Journal of Business of the University of Chicago*, April.
(1962), 'Gearing Military R&D to Economic Growth', *Harvard Business Review*, November–December.
(1972), 'Organizational Structure, Technological Advance, and the New Tasks of Government', *Journal of Economic Issues*, December.
(1974a), 'Problems of Modern Technology', *Journal of Economic Issues*, December.
(1975a), 'What is Structuralism: Piaget's Structuralist Epistemology and the Varieties of Structuralist Thought', *Journal of Economic Issues*, December.
(1975), 'Neo-Classical Economics in Perspective', *Journal of Economic Issues*, December.
(1977), 'The Need for a Theory of the State', *Journal of Economic Issues*, June.
(1979), 'The Roots of America's Decline', *Tocqueville Review*, Fall.
(1980), 'The Crisis of Authority', *Review of Social Economy*, December.
(1984a), 'Industrial Policy', *Journal of Economic Issues*, September.
(1991b), 'A Note on Robert Eisner's Debt Thesis', *Journal of Economic Issues*, March.
(1994a), 'A Modest Proposal for a New Technique of Non-Diversionary Public Spending', *Journal of Economic Issues*, September.

Chapters, Other Publications and Unpublished Manuscripts

(1955), 'Economic as Social Philosophy, Moral Philosophy, and Technology', in Robert A. Solo (ed.), *Economics and the Public Interest*, New Brunswick: Rutgers.
(1968), 'Price Theory in Perspective', East Lansing.
(1983), 'The Libertarian State, the Welfare State, the Positive State', in Martin Pfaff (ed.), *Public Transfers and Some Private Alternatives During the Recession*, Berlin: Duncker and Humblot.
(1984), 'Lessons from Elsewhere', in Guy Alperovitz and Roger Skurski (eds), *American Economic Policy: Problems and Prospects*, New York.
(1994), *Autobiographical Narrative*, Okemos, MI: Robert A. Solo.
(ND), *The Political Economics of Public Spending*, Okemos, MI: Xerographed.
(NDa), *Images of Man, and Structures of Thought*, Okemos, MI: Xerographed.
(NDb), *The Paths of Science and the Formation of Policy*, Okemos, MI: Xerographed.
(NDc), *The Works of Michel Foucault: A Clarification*, Okemos, MI: Xerographed.

OTHER REFERENCES

Boulding, Kenneth (1967), '"Review" of *Economic Organizations & Social Systems*', *Science*.

Boulding, Kenneth (1968), *The Image*, Ann Arbor: University of Michigan Press; copyright 1956.

Elliott, John E. (1992), 'Keynes on the Inefficacy of Downward Wage Flexibility as Anti-Depressionary Strategy', in Warren J. Samuels (ed.), *Research on the History of Economic Thought and Methodology*, Greenwich, CT.: JAI Press.

Elliott, John E. (1994), 'Keynes' Theory of Unemployment in the Context of Cyclical Fluctuations', Los Angeles: John E. Elliott.

Elliott, John E. (1994a), 'Keynes's Two Perspectives in the General Theory and After', in Karen Vaughn (ed.), *Contributions to the History of Economic Thought*, Edward Elgar: Brookfield, VT.

Foucault, Michel (1966), *Les Mots and les Choses: Une Archéologie des Sciences Humaines*, Paris: Gallimard. *The Order of Things: An Archeology of the Human Sciences*, London: Tavistock, 1970.

Georgescu-Roegen, Nicholas (1971), *The Entropy Law and the Economic Process*, Cambridge, Mass.: Harvard University Press.

Hicks, John R. (1939), *Value and Capital*, Oxford: Clarendon Press.

Holland, Stuart (1987), *The Market Economy*, New York: St. Martins.

Keynes, John M. (1926), *The End of Laissez Faire*, London: Wolff.

Keynes, John M. (1936), *The General Theory of Employment, Interest and Money*, New York: Harcourt Brace.

Keynes, John M. (1937), 'The General Theory of Employment', *Quarterly Journal of Economics*, February.

Kuhn, Thomas (1962), *The Structure of Scientific Revolutions*, Chicago: University of Chicago Press.

Magaziner, Ira C. and Robert B. Reich (1982), *Minding America's Business: The Decline and Rise of the American Economy*, New York: Harcourt Brace, Jovanovich.

Popper, Karl (1935), *Logic der Forschung*, Berlin. *The Logic of Scientific Discovery*, London: Hutchinson, 1959.

Samuelson, Paul A. (1947), *The Foundations of Economic Analysis*, Cambridge, Mass.: Harvard University Press.

16. Joseph E. Stiglitz

Randall Bausor

Few economists have published as extensively as has Joseph E. Stiglitz. He has addressed issues of imperfect information and the formulation of risk, neoclassical growth theory, the financial structure of firms, moral hazard, principal–agent problems, incentive structures, screening, self-selection and adverse selection, efficiency wages, credit rationing, the optimality of incomplete systems of markets, organizational structures and the micro-foundations of macroeconomics. His contributions to each of these fields would manifest a distinguished career; the combination is truly remarkable.

Common themes run throughout much of this massive program, and link the disparate elements into a coherent image of how an economy operates. Analysis of information and risk glues together the various components of Stiglitz's thought. This, combined with the examination of imperfect competition and incomplete systems of markets, provides the abstract apparatus for exploring a vast array of deviations from the canonical portrayal of perfectly competitive equilibria.

To grasp the broad sweep of this intellectual landscape it is best to start with the most abstract matters, and then to proceed to issues peculiar to particular markets. Consequently, we begin with the treatment of imperfect information and risk, move to matters of market imperfections, and continue by reviewing screening, moral hazard and principal–agent problems. Then we discern how Stiglitz's insight into these phenomena inform his research into the analysis of particular markets, especially those for labor, credit and insurance. From this, we progress to the analysis of incomplete systems of markets, and the microfoundations of macroeconomics. We conclude with a critical appraisal of his methods and results.

CONTRIBUTIONS TO THE ANALYSIS OF MARKETS

The Pure Theory of Risk

The role played by flawless foresight in the classical theorems of existence and optimality of perfectly competitive equilibrium is obvious. Unless people know in advance the outcomes of their decisions, nothing guarantees the infallibility of their choices, and the Fundamental Theorem of Welfare Economics is moot. Consequently, uncertainty is conceived as risk, and the number of markets dilates to incorporate trades in commodities contingent upon possible states of the world. Thus, the analytics of risk, especially in the hands of Arrow (1970), assumes a fundamental position in microeconomics, and the resulting system, as represented in Debreu (1959), rescues the welfare properties of competitive processes. Moreover, incomplete market systems clearly need not generate optimal results (Borch 1968).

Investigating the desirability of risky commodities, especially financial securities, in terms of preferences defined over the first two moments of a probability distribution of possible outcomes typified much of this literature. It allowed separating the attributes of the asset into an average rate of return and a risk premium associated with the variability of the outcome. Until 1970, therefore, economists generally understood 'increased risk' to mean larger variance of a probability distribution.

In a frequently cited sequence of essays in *Journal of Economic Theory* Rothschild and Stiglitz (1970, 1971, 1972) assess the weakness of this definition of increasing risk, and offer alternatives to it. They initially identify four possible definitions of increasing risk. One asserts that one random variable is more variable than another if it equals the latter plus noise. A second holds that one random variable is less risky than a second if it is always preferred to the latter by a risk-averse individual.[1] The third definition notes that the riskier distribution has 'more weight in the tails' and the fourth is the traditional notion that the latter has greater variance than the former (Rothschild and Stiglitz 1970, pp. 225-6). By examining a partial ordering of random variables, they demonstrate the equivalence of the first three, and show that the fourth is not the same. Since the idiosyncratic definition identifies greater risk with larger variance, they conclude that the mean-variance analysis of risk 'may lead to unjustified conclusions' (1970, p. 241).

---

1. A risk-averse individual is defined as a person with a utility function concave in risk.

Their definition of greater risk, that one random variable is distinguished from another by a mean-preserving spread, has been widely used in subsequent neoclassical analysis and has become the foundation of much work on the role of economic information. Rothschild and Stiglitz themselves (1971) applied their definition to the general problem of utility maximizing under risk, from which they conclude 'that the mean-variance approach gives mis-leadingly general results' (1971, p. 68) and that comparisons between random variables separated by a mean-preserving spread is more useful in identifying the risk-averter's preference. Their second employment of mean-preserving spreads was to the conventional portfolio selection problem (1971). By modeling the problem faced by a risk-averse firm facing variable output, they showed that its costs consequently fluctuate, which affects its allocation between capital and labor, so that 'there is always less output under uncertainty than under certainty' (p. 82). The significance of this result, which has become a cornerstone of New Keynesian macroeconomics, is that a firm's optimizing response to increased risk is to curtail production.

Their final paper in this sequence, (Rothschild and Stiglitz 1973) uses an identical argument to compare different distributions of income. The mathematics of comparing distribution functions distinguished only by a mean-preserving spread is here identical to their analytics of risk, but here refers not to informational problems, but to measures of relative equality in the distribution of income.

This early work informs much of Stiglitz's later economics, which utilizes interpretations of imperfect market information as risk in a wide variety of contexts.[2] Indeed, the analysis of risk so pervades his research that one sees his career as the dissemination of fundamental ideas about risk and imperfect information throughout the whole of economics. In one way or another, the mechanics of risk and price distributions inform work on market 'screening' (e.g., Stiglitz 1975) and thus efficiency-wage models of labor markets (e.g., Shapiro and Stiglitz 1984), monopolistic competition (e.g., Salop and Stiglitz 1977), principal–agent problems and moral hazard (e.g., Stiglitz 1987b and Arnott and Stiglitz 1988), optimal taxation (e.g., Arnott and Stiglitz 1986), insurance and financial markets (e.g., Rothschild and Stiglitz 1976 and Stiglitz and Weiss 1981),

---

2. Risk, however, is not uncertainty. The former model's imperfections of knowledge in terms of probability distributions over sample spaces, which must contain all possible outcomes. Uncertainty emphasizes that possible outcomes themselves must be imagined so that sample spaces cannot be known. In particular, one may fail to imagine what proves to happen, and thus be surprised. This distinction between risk and uncertainty has been recognized since Knight (1971). See also Shackle (1969, 1979), Bausor (1982-83) and Vickers (1986).

externalities (e.g., Greenwald and Stiglitz 1986), and competitive price systems (e.g., Grossman and Stiglitz 1976).

Market Screening

If market participants are unsure what it is they are trading, e.g., merchandise quality is ambiguous to at least one of them, then the market outcome itself may signal something about the commodity, thereby affecting the terms on which it is exchanged. Thus, price reveals not simply one's willingness and ability to transact, but also bears admittedly imperfect information about the thing being traded. Although Akerlof (1970) and Spence (1974) initially analyzed market signaling, it is largely in Stiglitz's hand that it becomes a mechanism for market sorting.

As a source of information, market outcomes affect the characteristics of commodities traded as well as their quantities. Stiglitz (1987a) writes

> the uninformed party (the seller of insurance, the used car buyer, etc.) forms rational expectations concerning the quality mix of what is being offered on the market; the price serves as a signal or as a screening device. (p. 2)

and later that

> price serves a function in addition to that usually ascribed to it in economic theory: It conveys information and affects behavior. Quality depends on price. ... one can think of the change in the price as having two effects: a movement along a fixed-information demand curve, and a shift in the demand curve from the change in information (beliefs). (p. 3)

That is, if the consumer is uninformed (as in the market for used cars), then the quantity demanded responds to price not simply as an indicator of availability in the usual sense, but as a signal of what is being offered. The good used car's owner will know it is good, and so requires a higher price than the bad used car's owner. Analogously, if the seller in a market is unsure (in the case of insurance, unsure of a particular customer's propensity to have accidents), then the quantity supplied varies with price in a novel way: insurance customers are 'sorted' by the seller according to what they are willing to pay – those who will pay a higher price inadvertently reveal their greater propensity to have accidents.

Thus, imperfect information about quality freights price offers with ambiguous interpretation, and complicates the economist's analysis of market processes. Although Stiglitz's models of screening, (e.g., 1987a, and 1975) generally require no mathematical sophistication beyond static optimization and the rudiments of probability calculus, the screening literature produces a plethora of particular information assumptions and asymmetries. For example, his landmark essay on screening and education (Stiglitz 1975) identifies the problem of screening labor of unknown quality. Individuals reveal their possible productivity to potential employers by their educational attainment. This endogenous variable (under the control of the worker) is part of the information received by employers. Along with the wage one will accept, it influences the willingness to hire and the wage offered. Not surprisingly, many complications emerge: what are the rents accruing to educational achievement, how can they be collected, and to what extent do educational institutions function as labor-market screening devices? Attaining more-or-less concrete results requires special assumptions on preferences, signals and information asymmetries. Consequently, the analysis embodies a virtual zoo of special cases yielding different possible outcomes. General results are not easily identified. For example, although school systems screen because 'this information is a natural by-product of the principal activity of providing knowledge (skills) and guiding individuals into the right occupations' (Stiglitz 1975, p. 294), when the incentives of school administrators are examined, assumptions about their preferences and even the voting patterns of taxpayers influence schooling's success as a sorting device (pp. 295-7).

Four widespread properties of these models deserve note. First, many of their results depend upon increasing returns to scale (1987b, p. 5). Second, they invariably involve particular informational asymmetries. Whereas one party to a transaction is perfectly informed, the other is not. Thus, one party inadvertently leaks information through the market. Whenever both are equally ignorant then the sorting signal may be so dubious that its information content vanishes, and no screening occurs. Third, when markets screen, equality of supply and demand at the market price may not occur. And fourth, typically a distribution of market prices, rather than a single price, emerges, even for identical commodities (Stiglitz 1987a, pp. 7-9).[3] Therefore, 'screening' models, in which imperfect information generates market failures and dislodges market equilibrium from optimality, assume considerable importance in 'New Keynesian' economics. Their application to labor, credit and insurance markets looms large in the New Keynesian abandonment of *laissez-faire*.

---

3. This property also informs Stiglitz's theory of discriminatory practices in labor markets. Easily identified attributes of a group imperfectly signal economically significant properties, so that productively equivalent workers may receive different wages if employers are imperfectly informed about possible individual workers. See Stiglitz (1973).

Moral Hazard and Principal–Agent Relationships

Imperfect and asymmetric information breed concerns over moral hazard and principal–agent relationships. Moral hazard arises whenever one individual (an agent) ostensibly acts on behalf of another (the principal). The principal's hazard is that the agent's incentives need not coincide with his or her own. Nevertheless, the principal may prefer the agent-facilitated outcome to the payoff with no agent, even if the agent's actions are not fully optimal from the principal's viewpoint. For example, the defendant in a homicide trial may prefer the outcome (conviction of manslaughter) resulting from employment of an agent (an attorney) to that resulting from acting without the agent (execution), even though an outcome more preferred by the principal (no conviction) might have been achieved if the agent had acted differently (bribed the judge).

Stiglitz explains principal–agent relationships in terms of imperfect and asymmetric information. Performance of the agent is unobservable by, and imperfectly inferable from evidence available to the principal. Thus, the principal imperfectly discerns the extent to which the agent's skills are employed on his or her behalf. Stiglitz characterizes the principal–agent relationship as a case of risk on the principal's part compounded with asymmetric information, since the agent knows something of which the principal is ignorant. Stiglitz (1987b) writes:

> Clearly, if an individual's actions are unobservable, then compensation cannot be based on those actions. ... The principal–agent literature focuses on situations where an individual's actions can neither be observed nor be perfectly inferred on the basis of observable variables; thus, for instance, it is usually assumed that output is a function of effort and an unobservable random variable ... (p. 967)

The principal, that is, maximizes a stochastic utility function by selecting his or her most-preferred contract given that the agent accepts it and optimizes as well.

Through the effort function, the contract's provisions indirectly affect preferences and opportunities, thereby complicating market activities. In the context of accident insurance, for example, Arnott and Stiglitz (1988) write

> even when the underlying functions, the expected utility function and the relationship between effort and the accident probability, are extremely well behaved, the indifference curves and feasibility sets are not — indifference curves need not be convex and feasibility sets never are; price- and income-consumption lines may be discontinuous; and effort is not in general a monotonic or continuous function of the parameters of the insurance policies provided or of the prices of goods. (p. 384)

Obviously, discontinuities diminish confidence in market mechanisms. Indeed, they argue (pp. 408-9) that moral hazard renders even 'the appropriate equilibrium concept' context dependent. Subsequently, they hold that nonmarket institutions (such as family members who will help in the event of an accident, thereby discouraging an insurance customer's avoidance of accidents) exacerbates moral hazard. Nonmarket responses to risk may perversely provoke less diligent avoidance of accidents. Thus:

> There is a widespread belief that when significant market failure occurs, there are strong incentives for nonmarket institutions to develop which go at least part of the way toward remedying the deficiency. This paper has provided a counterexample in which a nonmarket institution arises spontaneously (through the uncoordinated actions of atomistic agents), which is completely dysfunctional (has effects opposite to those intended). (Arnott and Stiglitz 1991, pp. 188-9)

Principal–agent and moral-hazard problems occupy a considerable position within New Keynesian economics and are said to be 'pervasive in our economy' (Arnott and Stiglitz 1988, p. 412.). They characterize labor markets (leading to efficiency wages), financial markets (leading to credit rationing) and insurance markets. Moreover, they may separate equilibrium from optimal outcomes in any market.

However, the analytics employed to address them remain remarkably simple, if not unsophisticated. These models are essentially static, and conflicted incentives between principal and agent are cast within a framework little displaced from traditional neoclassical argument. Even when multiple equilibria may occur, the tendency is to invoke comparative statics rather than *bona fide* dynamics. Further, interpreting ignorance as *risk* constricts the conceptual scope of this approach. It neglects anyone's fundamental difficulty of assessing odds in the face of, and adapting to genuine dynamical uncertainty.

Imperfect Competition: Monopolistic Competition

The formal analysis of imperfect competition is another Stiglitz project. This literature models firms as facing risk (outcomes depend upon a random variable), endogenously determines market structure (the number of firms in an industry), and employs game-theoretic ideas (strategies for firm entry and exit and the Nash solution).[4]

---

4. Stiglitz (1986a) is a helpful introduction to the 'new' theory of imperfect competition, and provides a good guide as to how this literature can be coherently read.

In a widely cited essay, Dixit and Stiglitz (1977) present a monopolistically competitive model in which they examine sources of divergence between market and optimal outcomes under increasing returns to scale. Thus,

> A commodity should be produced if the costs can be covered by the sum of revenues and a properly defined measure of consumer's surplus. The optimum amount is then found by equating the demand price and the marginal cost. Such an optimum can be realized in a market if perfectly discriminatory pricing is possible. A competitive market fulfilling the marginal condition would be unsustainable because total profits would be negative. An element of monopoly would allow positive profits, but would violate the marginal condition. (Dixit and Stiglitz 1977, p. 297)

Since convexity of consumer preferences implicitly reveals a preference for diversity (p. 297), there is a tradeoff between variety and the quantity each firm can produce.[5] A monopolistically competitive industry consists of an infinite number of potential commodities over which consumer preferences are defined. When the number of firms is large, each firm can neglect the impact of its actions on its competitors.

In the case of constant elasticities of substitution, Dixit and Stiglitz first derive familiar Chamberlinian dd and DD curves (1977, pp. 298-9). With identical production functions, firms have the same output level, price and zero profits. Next, they construct a constrained optimum, in which lump-sum subsidies to firms are prohibited. However, 'Thus we have a rather surprising case where the monopolistic competition equilibrium is identical with the optimum constrained by the lack of lump sum subsidies' (p. 301), and when the optimum is unconstrained

> The most remarkable result is that the output of each active firm is the same in the two situations. The fact that in a Chamberlinian equilibrium each firm operates to the left of the point of minimum average cost has been conventionally described by saying that there is excess capacity. However, when variety is desirable, i.e., when the different products are not perfect substitutes, it is not in general optimum to push the output of each firm to the point where all economies of scale are exhausted. We have shown in one case that is not an extreme one, that the first best optimum does not exploit economies of scale beyond the extent achieved in the equilibrium. (pp. 301-2)

---

5.   The elasticity of substitution of preferences is closely related to convexity of indifference surfaces, and in this model convexity manifests a preference for variety since the convex combination of two commodities is preferred to consumption of either one alone. Additional discussion of the analytical importance of the particular elasticity assumptions employed in this model are found in Yang and Heijdura (1993) and Dixit and Stiglitz (1993).

That is, the optimum has more active firms (and thereby greater variety produced) than either the equilibrium or the constrained optimum, but no firm is pushed to the lowest point on its average-cost curve. Where elasticities of substitution vary, the situation is more complex:

> Very roughly, the point is that although commodities in inelastic demand have the potential for earning revenues in excess of variable costs, they also have significant consumers' surpluses associated with them. Thus it is not immediately obvious whether the market will be biased in favor of them or against them as compared with an optimum. (p. 306)

These results are summarized by

> In the central case of a constant elasticity utility function, the market solution was constrained Pareto optimal, regardless of the value of that elasticity (and thus the implied elasticity of the demand functions). With variable elasticities, the bias could go either way, and the direction of the bias depended not on how the elasticity of utility changed. ... The general principle behind these results is that a market solution considers profit at the appropriate margin, while a social optimum takes into account the consumer's surplus. (p. 308)

Although the market outcome is suboptimal, its separation from optimality is not, as in textbook presentations of monopolistic competition, because there are too many firms to capture returns to scale, but because markets do not signal the marginal optimizing conditions.

Other discussions of imperfect competition include Salop and Stiglitz (1977), which contains a model in which consumers decide whether or not to purchase market information, and in which a dispersion of prices might emerge. The results depend upon the proportion of agents who choose to become informed, and thus the extent to which 'good' information is transmitted through the market. Dasgupta and Stiglitz (1980) and Stiglitz (1986b) both rely on game-theoretic concepts of strategy selection by firms undertaking research and development. The outcome of investment in innovations is a random variable, and the existence and properties of a symmetric Nash equilibrium in pure strategies is investigated. Principal results are that such equilibria may not exist, and 'that the level of technical progress (but not the level of R&D expenditures) may decline with an increase in competition' (Stiglitz 1986b, p. 430). There is, however, 'no clear presumption' that R&D is greater or lesser in monopolized than in competitive markets. It depends on managerial incentives (p. 440).

These models typify a favored intellectual strategy of Stiglitz. That is, to construct a model and by varying particular assumptions investigate the consequent results. Because one thereby achieves an extensive array of possible results, gleaning general propositions is difficult. Moreover, claims to robustness frequently masquerade as assertions of empirical validity. There is, however, a general theme: markets subject to imperfections do not function as perfect competition suggests. Methodologically, even apparently small deviations from the canonical neoclassical axioms invalidate the canonical neoclassical image of market efficiency and demolish that happy confidence in market results characteristic of neoclassical attitudes.

Economic Organization

In collaboration with Raaj Sah (1985, 1986, 1988, 1991), Stiglitz has recently addressed questions of how the architecture of decision making within an organization affects its choices and efficiency. This work informs both the neoclassical theory of the firm and the New Keynesian understanding of government's appropriate economic activity. Organizations are viewed as networks of decision makers, and the structures within which people interact influence the organization's performance. Individuals screen 'projects', that is, choose which to pursue from a distribution of possible activities. Projects are either good or bad, and each has a known probability of being 'good'. Thus, choice is risky. In a 'polyarchy' if any individual approves a project, it is selected, whereas in a 'hierarchy' a project is screened by a subordinate who recommends 'screened' projects to a supervisor, who must then choose whether or not to recommend it to his or her supervisor. The project is accepted only if the hierarch, or boss, finally selects it. Thus, hierarchy is analogous to a series circuit, whereas a polyarchy resembles a parallel circuit (Sah and Stiglitz 1985, p. 292; and 1986, p. 718.). Organizations can be evaluated in terms of the proportion of good projects which get rejected and of bad projects which are accepted, that is, in terms of Type I and Type II statistical errors committed by each.

Whereas Sah and Stiglitz (1985, 1986) develop the basic structure of these models, 'Committees, Hierarchies and Polyarchies' (1988) generalizes the organization's decision rule to cases between unanimity and single-member approval, including various notions of consensus and majority rule. 'The Quality of Managers in Centralized Versus Decentralized Organizations' (1991) applies the same mechanics to selection of managers. With this background Sah and Stiglitz explore several cases. In (1986), for example, they argue, that

> With a linear screening function, a mean-preserving spread in the initial portfolio leads to a smaller proportion of initial projects being selected in a polyarchy, and a large proportion being selected in a hierarchy. (p. 719)

And in (1988) that 'The optimal size of consensus is large if a committee faces a worse portfolio' (p. 459). Perhaps the most generally applicable result is 'any project (good or bad) has a higher probability of being accepted in a polyarchy than in a ... committee, and the probability of acceptance in a committee is in turn higher than that in a hierarchy' (1988, pp. 463-4). Moreover, this conception of organizations as structured sequences of decision makers informs their attitude towards centralized and decentralized economic systems (Sah and Stiglitz 1991).

This is a truly neoclassical characterization of institutions. Only decisions between 'good' or 'bad' projects transpire. Individuals are all homogeneous, and the distribution of projects from which they choose (and the probabilities that they are 'good') are exogenous to organizational activity. Moreover, people are unchanged by participation in the organization and by exposure to its cultural norms. In addition, there is no creative collective formulation of novel projects emerging through the discussions and deliberations of, for example, a committee.

This is surely a peculiar approach to economic institutions. In the world of Sah and Stiglitz opportunities come to you. In the world of human life in living organizations, opportunities are imagined, collectively shared, and moulded. 'Projects', after all, are not drawn from an urn, but are concocted individually and collectively within a cultural and institutional context of joint activity. The making of possibilities must surely be as important as the architecture of choosing between them.

MARKETS FOR INSURANCE, FINANCE AND LABOR

The tools perused above support an economics of 'rational' decisions undertaken in the context of stochastic events, complex incentive structures and imperfect competition. Stiglitz has repeatedly applied these tools to the markets for insurance, finance and labor, which then form the intellectual foundation for New Keynesian macroeconomics.

Common themes permeate Stiglitz's approach to these markets. First, he characterizes each as subject to stochastic outcomes, so that at least one side of the market faces risk. Second, markets exhibit information asymmetries. Participants on one side of the market are perfectly informed while those on the other are not. Third, principal–agent problems and moral hazard permeate. Consequently, these markets to do not generally clear, and outcomes deviate from optima.

Insurance Markets

Obviously, all insurance contracts are written in the face of uncertainty. If the parties know the consequences of the contract, then at least one party to it would refuse. Reducing uncertainty to risk, models of insurance under competitive assumptions (Rothschild and Stiglitz 1976) and imperfect competition (Stiglitz 1977) typify this literature. They categorize customers for accident insurance as either prone to accident or not, and although no one knows whether or not he or she will have an accident, the customer does know which group he or she occupies. The seller, however, does not know. Thus, the underwriter makes not only price and quantity decisions, but must also design the set of contracts it offers. Market equilibrium

> in a competitive insurance market is a set of contracts such that, when customers choose contracts to maximize expected utility, (i) no contract in the equilibrium set makes negative expected profits; and (ii) there is no contract outside the equilibrium set that, if offered, will make a nonnegative profit. This notion of equilibrium is of the Cournot–Nash type; each firm assumes that the contracts its competitors offer are independent of its own actions. (Rothschild and Stiglitz 1976, p. 633)

Whether or not the market is perfectly competitive, safe and perilous customers are not pooled (p. 634 and Stiglitz 1977) since 'the same contract will never be purchased by both high- and low-risk individuals' (Stiglitz 1977, p. 417). Imperfect competition, however, allows the seller to screen customers on the basis of quantity demanded.[6] Moreover, since customers can take measures to avoid accidents (e.g., drive soberly), insurance markets abound in moral hazard. Arnott and Stiglitz (1988) show that 'nonmarket insurance', for example, help from one's relations while recuperating, can perversely inhibit accident-avoidance resulting in a worse outcome.

Financial Markets

Stiglitz's treatment of finance follows two conflicting threads. The first appears in a series of articles about the financial structure of firms, and the second constructs models of borrowing and lending in the presence of stochastic outcomes and equity constraints. The former approach relates directly to the Modigliani–Miller theorem. Stiglitz (1969a) generalizes the conditions of the theorem to a general equilibrium setting, and avoids the use of risk classes to

---

6.   Note the similarity between an insurance firm which screens customers and a government which screens to select its array of taxes. Compare Stiglitz (1977) with Atkinson and Stiglitz (1976).

demonstrate the irrelevance of corporate financial structure on the value of the firm. Stiglitz (1974) presents a multiperiod one-input, one-output model of firm behavior in a stochastic environment. In the absence of the possibility of bankruptcy, the firm's debt–equity composition is irrelevant (p. 861).

More recent work (Stiglitz 1972, but more pointedly in Stiglitz and Weiss 1981; Blinder and Stiglitz 1983; and Stiglitz 1985) reverses this view. Here, firm financial policy is constrained by equity availability and rationing by lenders. Stiglitz and Weiss (1981) present a model of bank lending in which the borrower knows the risks involved with its activities, but the bank does not. Consequently, banks screen borrowers (just as insurance companies screen customers), and since

> those who are willing to pay high interest rates may, on average, be worse risks; they are willing to borrow at high interest rates because they perceive their probability of repaying the loan to be low. As the interest rate rises, the average 'riskiness' of those who borrow increases, possibly lowering the bank's profits.
>
> Similarly, as the interest rate and other terms of the contract change, the behavior of the borrower is likely to change. ... higher interest rates induce firms to undertake projects with lower probabilities of success but higher payoffs when successful. (Stiglitz and Weiss 1981, p. 393)

That is, in loan markets price not only screens borrowers, but also initiates principal–agent problems between bank and borrower. Relatively prudent firms respond to high interest rates by withdrawing from the market. Those who remain not only were already more risky, but the high interest rate motivates them towards more daring (i.e. risky) activities in order to repay.[7] In the models of Stiglitz and Weiss (1981), Blinder and Stiglitz (1983) and Stiglitz (1985), credit rationing is a common combined consequence of market screening, adverse selection and moral hazard in loan markets. Banks refuse to lend to all the customers desiring to borrow at the going interest rate precisely because it is being used to screen customers. Thus, '*there is no presumption that the market equilibrium allocates credit to those for whom the expected return on their investments is highest*' (Stiglitz and Weiss 1981, p. 407). Once again, markets fail to perform efficiently. Informational inadequacies so burden price signals that optimal adjustments need not transpire. Rather than price flexibility, quantity constraints and rationing emerge as 'rational' responses to imperfect and asymmetric information. These same market attributes support New Keynesian macroeconomic monetary theory.

---

7. Differences in riskiness are identified here with mean-preserving spreads. See, for example, Stiglitz and Weiss (1981, pp. 393-5). This feature forms an analytical link to Rothschild and Stiglitz (1971).

Labor Markets

Stiglitz's analysis of labor markets flows in similar channels. An employer's imperfect and costly information about a worker's productivity provides the basis for both market screening and implicit principal–agent contracts.

Spence's (1974) work on hiring and market signaling was a landmark in economists' understanding of the informational complications when searching is costly. More recently, Arnott, Hosios and Stiglitz (1988), and Greenwald and Stiglitz (1988) employed search behavior to explain labor-market phenomena. In these models, a worker's decision to search for alternative employment is the issue, and the current employer's response may be to differentially encourage search among unproductive workers (Arnott, Hosios and Stiglitz 1988, pp. 1049-53). Further, search activities generate exter-nalities, which Greenwald and Stiglitz (1988) interpret as an additional source of market failure.

Deeper problems concerning screening, moral hazard and efficiency wages emerge. Stiglitz (1975) argued that educational institutions provide important screening services in labor markets when potential employers imperfectly assess the skills of employees. Moreover, the firm must monitor the work and effectively encourage workers to perform. Such models are generally known under the name 'efficiency wages'. Perhaps the simplest description of efficiency wages states 'that the services a labourer renders are a function of the wage he receives' (Stiglitz 1976, p. 186). In terms of implicit contracts, high wages may encourage loyalty and cooperation; they may be a bribe to work, which the firm prefers to costly monitoring. Essentially, it amounts to paying good workers more than the Walrasian wage so that they have something to lose if terminated, and thus have their own incentive to work hard. Obviously, such arguments reflect principal-agent thinking, and used extensively,[8] occupy the focus of Stiglitz's analysis of labor markets.

Although surrounded by a blizzard of special cases and particular combinations of assumptions, some general propositions emerge from this research. First, the hypothesis predicts a market wage higher than the value of marginal product, which results in equilibrium unemployment. This is arguably the most important property of these models. Second, because principal-agent concerns and implicit contracts permeate employer-employee relations,

---

8. For example, Stiglitz (1976) applies efficiency wages to LDCs. Shapiro and Stiglitz (1984) invoke the efficiency-wage hypothesis in a discussion of the firm's threat of unemployment as a tool for disciplining the workforce. Unless they have something to lose, there is no discipline. Stiglitz (1985) contains a model in which multiple equilibrium wages arise from efficiency wages. Arnott, Hosios and Stiglitz (1988) use them to explain wage rigidities. And Greenwald and Stiglitz (1988) explain chronic unemployment with them.

institutional obstructions to wage flexibility characterize labor markets. The cost, in terms of lost work, of lowering wages may exceed the employer's pecuniary gain from the lower wage. Thus, it may be in no one's interest to lower the wage and pressure for price flexibility to clear the market may not be strong.[9] Third, multiple wages may emerge: high-wage firms may pay all their workers generously to attain workplace stability. Fourth, New Keynesians generally view such markets as inconsistent with optimality and Pareto efficiency. Absent the Walrasian wage, market failures tug the system from the perfectly informed, perfectly competitive ideal.[10] Precisely these same features microfound New Keynesian macroeconomics.

All these market failures arise from the simultaneous presence of risk and asymmetric information. Privately motivated actions employ price signals to screen for quality, and to manage moral hazard. Consequently, prices slip from market-clearing equilibrium, and rationing occurs. In insurance markets the terms of contracts are affected, in financial markets credit is rationed, and in labor markets unemployment appears. In each case *laissez-faire* fails to optimize, which raises a potential justification of government intervention in the private sector.

MARKET EFFICIENCY AND MACROECONOMICS

For Joseph Stiglitz, macroeconomics derives from the microeconomics of incomplete and imperfect markets, and reflects the logic of risk, moral hazard, externalities and asymmetric information. These features prompt inefficiencies which justify active government intervention in the economy, and distinguish New Keynesian from New Classical attitudes.

Obviously, if credit rationing prevents loan markets from clearing, the conduct and consequences of monetary policy are affected. Similarly, labor-market failures may produce macroeconomic unemployment. Translating these insights into a *theory* of macroeconomics, however, requires additional attention. In surveying

---

9. This explanation of money-wage inflexibility differs from that of Keynes in *The General Theory*. Keynes argued that individuals in labor markets cope with inescapable uncertainty, as distinct from tradeable risk, by contracting for money wages. Since neither employer nor employee can control the general price level, moreover, there is no institutional mechanism to constantly recontract real wages as prices change. The contracted money wage over a known duration at least allows employers to plan production and employees to plan household consumption. For Keynes the issue was not a partial-equilibrium market failure in the labor market, but a general matter of macroeconomic coordination.

10. Not all authors share the view of Greenwald and Stiglitz (1988) that efficiency wage models yield Pareto inefficiency. Some, for example, see in such models an understanding of a rational and efficient firm's response to the task of organizing its activities. See, for example, Lazear (1991).

this literature, we begin with broad arguments regarding efficiency and optimality. Next we relate this to a sense of the government's ability to 'correct' the deficiencies of markets, and proceed to a more detailed discussion of fiscal and financial policies.

Optimality and Pareto Efficiency of Market Economies

Over the last twenty years Professor Stiglitz and his collaborators have written extensively about the systemic consequences of market imperfections. Grossman and Stiglitz (1976) begin with a model of noisy market signals, in which prices simultaneously clear markets and convey information. The authors argue that 'Although it is easy to show that the market solution is not, in general, efficient, it is difficult to ascertain whether there is too little or too much information acquisition' (p. 251), and conclude that

> Our analysis has suggested that a decentralized economy is likely to be characterized by individuals having differential information, that the separation in the earlier discussion of information and allocative questions is inappropriate, and that alternative informational structures will be characterized by different real allocations. (p. 252)

Similar arguments appear elsewhere. For example, Newbery and Stiglitz (1984) show that, abstracting from comparative advantage and income redistributions, international trade may yield Pareto-inferior outcomes if it increases risk via a mean-preserving spread.[11] Grossman and Stiglitz (1980) produce a 'Noisy rational expectations' (p. 393) model to argue against the informational efficiency of markets. If information is very expensive, no one may gather it. If information is perceived as an externality, then everyone may choose to be a free rider (and all remain uninformed). From this they conclude that

> in general the price system does not reveal all the information about 'the true value' of the risky asset. ... The only way informed traders can earn a return on their activity of information gathering, is if they can use their information to take positions in the market which are 'better' than the positions of uninformed traders. ... when the efficient markets hypothesis is true and information is costly, competitive markets break down. ... thus, we could argue as soon as the assumptions of the conventional perfect capital markets model are modified to allow even a

---

11. Interpretation of results such as this requires caution. Many of the complications of Pareto comparisons explicitly refer to redistributions of real income and welfare. Therefore, arguments in which the distribution is held constant necessarily avoid fundamental issues of Pareto noncomparability, and through simplification, distort. Thus, a policy, such as free trade, which might lead to Pareto noncomparable outcomes when the distribution is allowed to change (remember Stolper–Samuelson), may incorrectly *appear* to generate Pareto improvements or inferiorities when constrained to the case of a given distribution.

slight amount of information imperfection and a slight cost of information, the traditional theory becomes untenable. (p. 404)

Stiglitz (1989) applies analogous arguments to the case of market failures and development. Greenwald and Stiglitz (1986) make similar efficiency arguments in the case of imperfect information, incomplete markets, and externalities. Newbery and Stiglitz (1982) combine imperfect information with rational expectations to yield incomplete markets.

All of these cases exhibit suboptimal outcomes. When markets are complete, reactions to risk may pull the system from the competitive ideal. When a market system is incomplete an additional complexity enters. One consequence of conceptualizing uncertainty as a mean-preserving spread of probability distributions is that it degenerates into risk, which can itself be traded. Persons preferring it accept larger amounts of it and those averse to it pay to shed it. Complete sets of contingency markets, therefore, including contingent financial markets, restore optimality to economies subject to random shocks. This Arrowian result (1970) has been known for decades. If some markets are closed, however, risks associated with the corresponding state of the world cannot be traded since contingent contracts for that state of the world do not exist. Newbery and Stiglitz (1982) and Greenwald and Stiglitz (1986) tackle the welfare consequences of such lacunae.

They establish a 'general equilibrium' model of incomplete sets of active markets. Newbery and Stiglitz do this for a production economy with two distinct classes of identical individuals: consumers and farmers. Farmers plan production given a probability distribution of prices, and consumers act after the price has been announced (Newbery and Stiglitz 1982, pp. 226-7). Thus, farmers face risk, but are Muthian rational, and have utility concave in income and production technique (p. 228). The authors derive the marginal conditions of equilibrium, and then compare this outcome to the solution of a problem maximizing social welfare.

Demonstrating that the two sets of conditions differ renders the market outcome suboptimal.[12] They write

> To do this, we need to compare the welfare of consumers and producers in the market equilibrium with that in some other feasible allocation. In making the comparison, however,

---

12. As in the classical demonstrations of the optimality of perfectly competitive equilibrium, the marginal conditions of the optimum subsume the marginal conditions of Pareto optimality. That is, the equality of marginal rates of technical substitution, which characterizes Pareto optimality, are satisfied at an optimum. Thus, demonstrating coincidence of market outcome with an optimum also demonstrates Pareto optimality of the market outcome. The marginal conditions of a Pareto optimum, however, may also be satisfied away from the social optimum.

we need to take into account the constraints on the set of markets. It is obvious that, except under certain special cases (to be detailed below, the marginal rate of substitution between income in different states of nature will differ for different individuals, so long as there are not markets which enable them to trade income in one state for income in another. Thus, were it costless to establish new markets, clearly there exists a resource allocation which is Pareto superior to the market equilibrium. ... We now wish to know, given the restrictions on the set of markets, whether there exists a Pareto-superior allocation. The answer is that there almost always does. (p. 229)

The task here is first to establish the marginal conditions for the market outcome, for the social optimum, and for the social optimum where the system is constrained such that the only markets are those active in the market equilibrium. In Theorem 2, they demonstrate that 'Sufficient conditions for the constrained optimality of the market equilibrium is the redundancy of risk markets' (p. 232). Theorem 4 goes further: 'A necessary condition for the constrained Pareto optimality of the market equilibrium for all technologies and for all attitudes toward risk by farmers is that risk markets be redundant' (p. 236). Thus,

there is no presumption that market equilibria are efficient; indeed, there is a strong presumption that the market equilibrium is not a constrained Pareto optimum.

In a world of complete markets, insurance markets allocate risk, and goods markets allocate goods; but in the absence of insurance markets, the remaining goods markets have to serve both functions. ... The important point is that it is only under very special circumstances that the market allocation will attain even the weak sense of optimality implicit in our notion of constrained Pareto optimality. (pp. 243-5)

Powerful as these results are, they should be read with care. In particular, one should recall that all consumers are taken as identical and all farmers are taken as identical. While simplifying the analytics, this considerably weakens the theorems. When all individuals are alike, they can be treated as one in Samuelsonian social welfare functions, but the heart of Pareto comparisons lies in determining how diverse individuals interrelate. Thus, for example, if consumers have varying tastes, even if one shows that the market outcome is not socially constrained optimal, one still has not, in general, demonstrated that the social-constrained optimum is Pareto superior to the market outcome. Even though marginal rates of substitution across income in all possible states of the world may not be equated if the market system is incomplete, and they are equated at the constrained optimum, it need not be true that every individual achieves at least as high an indifference curve at the constrained optimum as at the equilibrium: change of the price vector may, in general, adversely affect somebody's consumption plan, and thus reduce his or her welfare. Stiglitz's results abstract from this possibility, and thus should be accepted cautiously. Nevertheless, his results reveal a dreadful fragility of the classical theorems of welfare economics.

These results induce New Keynesian attitudes towards the economic role of government. Stiglitz (1986c) presents one of the most complete articulations of these attitudes. Following a prologue asserting that the state's 'compulsory' nature distinguishes it, he voices the view that foremost among the state's proper functions is correcting market 'failures'.[13] He writes

> whenever information is imperfect and/or markets incomplete – that is, essentially always – then the market is not *constrained* Pareto efficient. (Recall the definition of Pareto efficient: an allocation is Pareto efficient if there is no way by which some individuals can be made better off without making at least one individual worse off. The term 'constrained Pareto efficiency' is used to remind us that, in making the comparison, in ascertaining whether there is some policy of the government which could constitute a Pareto improvement, the government is assumed to be subjected to the same kinds of informational and/or incomplete market constraints that face the private sector.) While traditional literature characterized market failures as exceptions to the general rule that decentralized markets lead to efficient allocation, in this new view, the presumption is reversed. It is only under exceptional circumstances that markets are efficient.
>
> This makes that analysis of the appropriate role of government far more difficult; the issue becomes one not of identifying market failures, for these are pervasive in the economy, but of identifying *large* market failures ... (p. 38)

Later, he admits that the *potential* for beneficent public intervention does not mean that any actual government has the capacity to implement welfare-improving policies, commenting that problems of imperfect information are 'pervasive in the public sector' as well as the private (p. 45). Moreover, 'the lack of competition within the public sector further attenuates incentives' (p. 45).[14] Nevertheless

> some of the market failures are of sufficient importance that some form of government intervention may be desirable. The fact that government intervention is not perfect, that waste and incompetence may – or almost surely will – arise, should only remind us of the importance

---

13. Among the leading policy instruments to 'correct' market failures are tax-subsidy schemes. If market signals inadequately reflect the social costs of an activity (smoking) then a tax (on cigarettes) may generate the 'right' incentive. Similarly, if market signals inadequately promote an activity, then subsidies to its producers may be justified. Some of Stiglitz's most widely cited work has addressed the optimal array of taxes, including wealth, income and excise taxes. Predictably, the analytics of this problem under risk is exactly the same as employed to analyze market screening and principal–agent problems. See, for example, Arnott and Stiglitz (1986), Atkinson and Stiglitz (1976), and Stiglitz (1969b).
14. This view echoes Nalebuff and Stiglitz (1983) and Sah and Stiglitz (1991) which argue that lack of competition (as in the public sector, or in nationalized industries) breeds incentive structures which do not motivate hard work, and that highly centralized economies yield smaller output than decentralized economies.

of human fallibility. Human errors arise in the private sector just as they do in the public. (1986c, p. 56)

and later

> I am advocating here an eclectic position. Doctrinaire positions of the right, saying that government intervention at all times and in all circumstances is welfare-decreasing, that governments are inherently wasteful, that attempts at redistributions simply give rise to rent-seeking activities, are both wrong and unhelpful: governments will intervene when markets fail to meet social needs, and the economists' role is to guide them to understanding when and how government intervention is most likely to be helpful.
>
> Similarly, doctrinaire positions of the left, calling for increased government intervention, idealizing the government, anthropomorphizing it as a single individual (a benevolent despot) and attributing the successive failures of government to correct the market failures to the particulars of the situations (e.g. to the particular leader of the government) without recognizing the limits of government, are also not very helpful. (1986c, p. 57)

Although the state has a role, that is, prudent citizens should recall that politicians, like the rest of us, suffer from imperfect information. Thus, Stiglitz asserts, doctrinal confidence in the preferability of *laissez-faire* should itself be constrained. This attitude towards economic intervention is the sole basis upon which this view might claim to be 'Keynesian'.

Macro from Micro

To assemble macroeconomics from micro components of imperfect information and incomplete markets typifies Stiglitz's thinking. A swarm of microeconomic lessons and impressions explain the whole in terms conceptualized at market and individual levels. Unarguably, his is a macroeconomics of rational, reductionist, neoclassical microfoundations. Greenwald and Stiglitz (1988 and 1993a) make this explicit:

> New Keynesian theories have modified traditional Keynesian assumptions in a number of ways. The different modifications can be grouped by the market on which they have focused. Three broad theoretical approaches have focused on labor markets, concentrating separately on implicit contracts, search, and efficiency wages. Another set of approaches has focused on product markets, seeking to explain price rigidities in terms of menu (adjustment) costs or imperfect competition. Still another set of theories has focused on capital markets and has stressed the roles of credit rationing and equity rationing. (Greenwald and Stiglitz 1988, p. 251)

They also write 'that macroeconomics should be grounded in microeconomic principles, and that understanding macroeconomic behavior requires the construction of a (simple) general equilibrium model' (1993a, p. 24). Their strategy is to understand (imperfect) markets, especially the product, labor and capital markets. As we saw above, analysis of each proceeds without explicit interdependence with the others.[15]

Accordingly, business cycles appear to emerge from actions of risk-averse firms which curtail production in response to adverse shocks in output markets. Fearing bankruptcy as its working capital falls (from lost sales), the firm eschews further production costs, reducing both output and investment until working capital can be restored. Moreover, implicit contracts, especially with workers, limit the ability to reduce prices rather than quantities. Thus, trade cycles arise.

Principal–agent problems, implicit contracts and efficiency wages characterize labor markets. A firm's response to risk and capital-market imperfections yield wage rigidities (Greenwald and Stiglitz 1989). Thus, if the firm seeks to curtail output, employment falls. Greenwald and Stiglitz doubt the efficacy of wage flexibility as a mechanism to restore full employment:

> the fact is that individuals who are observationally indistinguishable from the unemployed individual are being employed at higher wages; that the market equilibrium is inefficient; and that resources which could be productively employed remain idle. (Greenwald and Stiglitz 1987, p. 124)

Since the firm's willingness to produce depends upon its access to working capital, the macroeconomic behavior of labor markets also relates to the financial strength of the firm. Thus,

> In the New Keynesian model ... wages should vary procyclically, as they appear to do, since deterioration in a firm's net asset position reduces the marginal product of labor (taking account of the risk associated with increasing output). Efficiency wage considerations move workers off their supply curves in response to these shifts in demand, inducing more variation in employment and less variation in wage levels than microeconomic labor supply considerations suggest. (Greenwald and Stiglitz 1988, p. 258)

Therefore, New Keynesian macroeconomics returns to capital markets. We have already seen how risk aversion and imperfect information generate credit rationing in these models. Stiglitz (1982) argues that imperfect information and incomplete financial markets misallocate capital across firms and activities, distort investment, and typically yield constrained Pareto inefficiency. Greenwald and Stiglitz (1990 and 1993b) translate these features to macroeconomics. Since

---

15. Lacking interdependence between these markets, this macroeconomics is not truly founded in general equilibrium analysis. Rather, it is founded in a combination of partial-equilibrium descriptions.

rationed working capital and fear of bankruptcy constrict output, they write of aggregate supply that '*in each period output is determined by the level of equity and movements in output over time will be driven by movements in the level of equity*' (1990, p. 324). Thus, financial conditions affect the level of output, not through the interest rate and the marginal efficiency of capital, as Keynes had it, but through equity constraints and rationed capital.[16] Greenwald and Stiglitz (1993b) further tie these arguments to business cycles, *per se*.

Thus, Stiglitz's macroeconomics grows from microeconomic informational imperfections which produce credit rationing, efficiency wages and quantity responses to increased risk. Credit conditions impinge upon the firm's willingness to produce, and thus on aggregate output as well. This reluctance to produce also displaces equilibrium in the labor market, generating unemployment since efficiency wage considerations and implicit contracts discourage wage cuts. Moreover, since the key conduit from financial to real phenomena is firm working capital, the consequences for both output and employment persist through several periods.

This macroeconomics reads strikingly like microeconomics. Whereas neoclassical 'Keynesians' and New Classical economists both seek a macroeconomics that reflects traditional microeconomics, New Keynesians construct a microeconomics that mirrors perceived macroeconomic phenomena (e.g., unemployment). Consequently, macroeconomic policy reduces to microeconomic management. Wise governments intervene to correct market imperfections, and those of greatest concern involve credit and labor markets. Traditional Keynesian macro prescriptions in terms of fiscal and monetary policy simply do not arise within this purview. Neither does the New Classical concern with monetary stability and monetary aggregates. The very concepts have no home in New Keynesian macroeconomics. Aggregate financial conditions matter only as they affect the risky output decisions of firms. Thus we have here a macroeconomics methodologically and stylistically microeconomic in argumentation and conception. Market imperfections displace systemic miscoordination.

---

16. These New Keynesian views contrast sharply with both monetarism and any variant of New Classical economics. For New Keynesians, the effects of shocks persist through depletion of firms' working capital. For New Classical economists, the effects of shocks are dissipated completely in a rational-expectations equilibrium. Moreover, the virtual invisibility of monetary aggregates in New Keynesian monetary theory must shock monetarists.

OF MICRO AND MACRO: A CONCLUDING ASSESSMENT

Joseph E. Stiglitz's career reflects a transformation in neoclassical economics. Accepting the methods of reductionist individualism and economic rationalism, he has repeatedly offered alternative assumptions, especially of asymmetric and imperfect information, and reversed the standard theorems about the existence of equilibria and about the welfare consequences of decentralized market processes. In his hands models contain equilibria in which markets do not clear. Labor is unemployed and credit is rationed. Stiglitz shows that even within relatively simple static models of rational economic behavior, things do not always turn out right. Misallocation of resources occurs, miscoordination of investment is widespread, and moral hazard is ubiquitous. This whole project simultaneously broadens the scope, and reverses the results of neoclassical economics.[17] This New Keynesian approach is methodologically neoclassical without the staunchly unwavering adherence to the desirability of free market processes which characterizes New Classical economists.

By finally divorcing reductionist rationalist economics from the most extreme visions of market optimality and Pareto efficiency, Joseph Stiglitz has forced a new maturity on to economists' thinking. No longer can they presume that markets achieve optimal results. No longer can they complacently invoke assumptions of perfect information and unconcernedly accept arguments which assume complete sets of markets.

This achievement remains, however, primarily prologue. Its image of imperfect information is itself uncompleted since the rich complexities of learning cannot be represented authentically within any essentially static model. Time changes us all, and a *bona fide* economics of uncertainty must be cast inside, not without time. Only then can we address matters arising from the fact that we cannot possibly know the future, and may only imperfectly perceive the past.

In not knowing the future, we cannot know with certainty what all the possible states of the world are. Consequently we cannot concoct sample spaces, since we cannot *know* whether or not we have left unimagined a possibility which may ultimately come to pass. We are, that is, subject to genuine uncertainty, not the pallid rendering of it as risk. Moreover, the psychological sources of confidence

---

17. Also, his approach profoundly departs from the positivist methodology of most neoclassical economists. In particular, the claim that scientific validity resides with agreement between analytical predictions and econometric evidence, and not with the 'realism' of assumptions, is completely disregarded. Virtually his whole strategy has been to develop more 'realistic' assumptions in the belief that patently counterfactual antecedents cannot reliably yield hypotheses concordant with empirical fact. Interestingly, this yields an all but complete neglect of formal econometric tests.

are fluid, making 'rational' decisions vulnerable to sudden and discontinuous change. This constant, dynamic adaptation leads to societies characterized by Shackle as 'Kaleidic' (1969, 1974, 1979).[18] To Post Keynesians and Neo-Austrians, for example, the slip from perfect information to Stiglitz's risk is not much compared to the slide to uncertainty and true economic dynamics.

Since Stiglitz's micro is fundamentally static, its responses to shocks are typically measured by comparative statics. Thus, most of the subtleties of one's acculturation into institutions (e.g., the workplace) are suppressed beneath the formalism of random variables. Although the significance of institutions is recognized, the dynamic processes by which they arise, are sustained and ultimately dissipate, remain invisible here.

Because Stiglitz's macroeconomics is cast within the neoclassical research program and grows from explicit, formal microfoundations, it is more in the tradition of Samuelson than of Keynes. Moreover, this individualistic attitude renders it methodologically closer to New Classical economics (despite their policy differences) than to the economics of Keynes. In Keynes's terminology, Stiglitz pursues an 'atomistic' analysis, whereas in *The General Theory* Keynes adopted an 'organic' approach.[19] Thus, although Keynes may have described macroeconomic behavior in terms of individual motivations, aggregates (for example, the consumption function) are holistically conceived as aggregates and are not directly derived from formal micro models. Keynes did not require an explicit microeconomics of wage rigidity and credit rationing to discuss labor and financial markets. By emphasizing the microeconomics of macroeconomics, on the other hand, Stiglitz derives more from American Keynesians than from Keynes.

Distinguishing 'New Keynesian' economics from the economics of Keynes reveals fundamental policy differences between them. Whereas New Keynesians argue for policies to rectify micro-market failures, Keynes argued for policies explicitly directed at problems of *macroeconomic* miscoordination (e.g., fiscal policy to manage aggregate demand). Similarly, Keynes argued that the demand for money reflects hedging against uncertainty, and integrated the monetary and the real by linking aggregate investment to interest rates. Stiglitz, on the other

---

18. The 'kaleidic' view of the economy arises from social interactions cast in historical time. Thus, it is inseparable from the analytical distinction between risk and uncertainty, a distinction invisible in New Keynesian economics. In addition to Shackle, models grounded in uncertainty and historical time have appeared in Bausor (1982-83, 1984, 1986), Vickers (1978, 1986), and others.

19. Atomistic models tackle their topic via reductionism, initially conceiving components from which wholes are constructed. Organic thought is required when phenomena are sufficiently complicated that the whole cannot be aggregated from its parts, but must be perceived directly. For more on the distinction between atomistic and organic economics, especially in the macroeconomics of Keynes, see Brown-Collier and Bausor (1988).

hand, emphasizes microeconomic credit rationing to firms as the chief mechanism by which monetary policy affects the real. For all these reasons, Stiglitz's work might best be read as a devastating internal critique of neoclassical economics rather than a bold departure from it.

Despite these qualifications, Joseph Stiglitz must be viewed as one of his generation's leaders. For a quarter of a century he has broadened the intellectual base of neoclassical microeconomics by testing the consequences of relaxed axioms. By honing our concepts of risk, of monopolistic competition, and of constrained Pareto efficiency, he has enriched both neoclassical microeconomics and macroeconomics. His insights, however, might themselves be viewed as constrained optima. Although they advance beyond perfect information and perfect competition, the neoclassical methodological anchor nevertheless tethers them. At the very least, however, his work disturbs the quiet complacency with which some economists presume confidence in the power of decentralized systems to flawlessly coordinate activity.

STIGLITZ'S MAJOR WRITINGS

(1969A), 'A Re-Examination of the Modigliani–Miller Theorem', *The American Economic Review*, **59** (5), December, 784-93.

(1969b), 'The Effects of Income, Wealth, and Capital Gains Taxation on Risk-Taking', *The Quarterly Journal of Economics*, **83** (2), May, 263-83.

(1970) (with Michael Rothschild), 'Increasing Risk: I. A Definition', *Journal of Economic Theory*, **2**, 225-43.

(1971) (with Michael Rothschild), 'Increasing Risk II: Its Economic Consequences', *Journal of Economic Theory*, **3**, 66-84.

(1972), 'On the Optimality of the Stock Market Allocation of Investment', *Quarterly Journal of Economics*, **86** (1), February, 25-60.

(1972) (with Michael Rothschild), 'Addendum to "Increasing Risk: I. A Definition"', *Journal of Economic Theory*, **5**, 306.

(1973), 'Approaches to the Economics of Discrimination', *The American Economic Review*, **63** (2), May, 287-95.

(1973) (with Michael Rothschild), 'Some Further Results on the Measurement of Inequality', *Journal of Economic Theory*, **6**, 188-204.

(1974), 'On the Irrelevance of Corporate Financial Policy', *The American Economic Review*, **64** (6), December, 851-66.

(1975), 'The Theory of "Screening", Education, and the Distribution of Income', *The American Economic Review*, **65** (3), June, 283-300.

(1976), 'The Efficiency Wage Hypothesis, Surplus Labour, and the Distribution of Income in L.D.C.s', *Oxford Economic Papers*, **28** (2), July, 185-207.

(1976) (with A.B. Atkinson), 'The Design of Tax Structure: Direct Versus Indirect Taxation', *Journal of Public Economics*, **6** (1, 2), July–August, 55-75.

(1976) (with Sanford J. Grossman), 'Information and Competitive Price Systems', *The American Economic Review*, **66** (2), May, 246-53.

(1976) (with Michael Rothschild), 'Equilibrium in Competitive Insurance Markets: An Essay on the Economics of Imperfect Information', *The Quarterly Journal of Economics*, **90** (4), November, 629-49.

(1977), 'Monopoly, Non-linear Pricing and Imperfect Information: the Insurance Market', *Review of Economic Studies*, **44** (3), October, 407-30.

(1977) (with Avinash K. Dixit), 'Monopolistic Competition and Optimum Product Diversity', *The American Economic Review*, **67** (3), June, 297-308.

(1977) (with Steven Salop), 'Bargains and Ripoffs: A Model of Monopolistically Competitive Price Dispersion', *Review of Economic Studies*, **44** (3), October, 493-510.

(1980) (with Partha Dasgupta), 'Industrial Structure and the Nature of Innovative Activity', *Economic Journal*, **90**, June, 266-93.

(1980) (with Sanford J. Grossman), 'On the Impossibility of Informationally Efficient Markets', *The American Economic Review*, **70** (3), June, 397-408.

(1981) (with Andrew Weiss), 'Credit Rationing in Markets with Imperfect Information', *The American Economic Review*, **71** (3), June, 393-410.

(1982) (with David M.G. Newbery), 'The Choice of Techniques and Optimality of Market Equilibrium with Rational Expectations', *Journal of Political Economy*, **90** (2), April, 223-46.

(1983) (with Alan S. Blinder), 'Money, Credit Constraints, and Economic Activity', *The American Economic Review*, **73** (2), May, 297-302.

(1983) (with Barry J. Nalebuff), 'Information, Competition, and Markets', *The American Economic Review*, **73** (2), May, 278-83.

(1984) (with David M.G. Newbery), 'Pareto Inferior Trade', *Review of Economic Studies*, **51** (1), January, 1-12.

(1984) (with Carl Shapiro), 'Equilibrium Unemployment as a Worker Discipline Device', *The American Economic Review*, **74** (3), June, 433-44.

(1985), 'Credit Markets and the Control of Capital', *Journal of Money, Credit and Banking*, **17** (2), May, 133-52.

(1985) (with Raaj Kumar Sah), 'Human Fallibility and Economic Organization', *The American Economic Review*, **75** (2), May, 292-7.

(1986a), 'Introduction', in Joseph E. Stiglitz and G. Frank Mathewson (eds), *New Developments in the Analysis of Market Structure*, New York: Macmillan, vii-xxiv.

(1986b), 'Theory of Competition, Incentives and Risk', in Joseph E. Stiglitz, and G. Frank Mathewson (eds), *New Developments in the Analysis of Market Structure*, New York: Macmillan, 399-449.

(1986c), *The Economic Role of the State*, Arnold Heertje (ed.), Cambridge, MA: Basil Blackwell.

(1986) (with Richard J. Arnott), 'Moral Hazard and Optimal Commodity Taxation', *Journal of Public Economics*, **29** (1), February, 1-24.

(1986) (with Bruce C. Greenwald), 'Externalities in Economies with Imperfect Information and Incomplete Markets', *The Quarterly Journal of Economics*, **101** (2), May, 229-64.

(1986) (with Raaj Kumar Sah), 'The Architecture of Economic Systems: Hierarchies and Polyarchies', *The American Economic Review*, **76** (4), September, 716-27.

(1987a), 'The Causes and Consequences of the Dependence of Quality on Price', *Journal of Economic Literature*, **25**, March, 1-48.

(1987b), 'Principal and Agent (ii)', in John Eatwell, Murray Milgate and Peter Newman (eds), *The New Palgrave Dictionary of Economics*, Volume 3, New York: The Stockton Press, 966-72.

(1987) (with Bruce C. Greenwald), 'Keynesian, New Keynesian and New Classical Economics', *Oxford Economic Papers*, **39**. Reprinted in P.J.N. Sinclair (ed.), *Prices, Quantities and Expectations*, Oxford: Clarendon Press, 119-33.

(1988) (with Richard J. Arnott), 'The Basic Analytics of Moral Hazard', *Scandinavian Journal of Economics*, **90** (3), 383-413.

(1988) (with Richard J. Arnott and Arthur J. Hosios), 'Implicit Contracts, Labor Mobility, and Unemployment', *The American Economic Review*, **78** (5), December, 1046-66.

(1988a) (with Bruce C. Greenwald), 'Pareto Inefficiency of Market Economies: Search and Efficiency Wage Models', *The American Economic Review*, **78** (2), May, 351-5.

(1988b) (with Bruce C. Greenwald), 'Examining Alternative Macroeconomic Theories', *Brookings Papers on Economic Activity*, **I**, 207-59.

(1988) (with Raaj Kumar Sah), 'Committees, Hierarchies and Polyarchies', *The Economic Journal*, **98**, June, 451-70.

(1989), 'Markets, Market Failures, and Development', *The American Economic Review*, **79** (2), May, 197-203.

(1989) (with Bruce C. Greenwald), 'Toward a Theory of Rigidities', *The American Economic Review*, **79** (2), May, 364-9.

(1990) (with Bruce C. Greenwald), 'Financial Market Imperfections and Productivity Growth', *Journal of Economic Behavior and Organization*, **13**, 321-45.

(1991) (with Richard J. Arnott), 'Moral Hazard and Nonmarket Institutions: Dysfunctional Crowding Out or Peer Monitoring?', *The American Economic Review*, **81** (1), March, 179-90.

(1991) (with Raaj Kumar Sah), 'The Quality of Managers in Centralized Versus Decentralized Organizations', *Quarterly Journal of Economics*, **106** (1), February, 289-95.

(1993) (with Avinash K. Dixit), 'Monopolistic Competition and Optimum Product Diversity: Reply', *The American Economic Review*, **83** (1), March, 302-4.

(1993a) (with Bruce C. Greenwald), 'New and Old Keynesians', *The Journal of Economic Perspectives*, **7** (1), Winter, 23-44.

(1993b) (with Bruce C. Greenwald), 'Financial Market Imperfections and Business Cycles', *The Quarterly Journal of Economics*, **108** (1), February, 77-114.

OTHER REFERENCES

Akerlof, George (1970), 'The Market for Lemons: Quality, Uncertainty, and the Market Mechanism', *Quarterly Journal of Economics*, **84**, 488-500.

Arrow, Kenneth J. (1953), 'le Rôle des Valeurs Boursières Pour la Repartition la Meilleure des Risques', *Econometrie*, Paris: Centre National de la Recherche Scientifique, 41-8. Translated as 'The Role of Securities in the Optimal Allocation of Risk-Bearing', *Review of Economic Studies*, 1963-1964, **31**; reprinted in *Essays in the Theory of Risk-Bearing*, London: North-Holland, 1970.

Bausor, Randall (1982-83), 'Time and the Structure of Economic Analysis', *Journal of Post Keynesian Economics*, **5** (2), Winter, 163-79.

Bausor, Randall (1984), 'Toward a Historically Dynamic Economics: Examples and Illustrations', *Journal of Post Keynesian Economics*, **6** (3), 67-83.

Bausor, Randall (1986), 'Time and Equilibrium', in Philip Mirowski (ed.), *The Reconstruction of Economic Theory*, Boston: Kluwer-Nijhoff, 93-135.

Borch, Karl H. (1968), *The Economics of Uncertainty*. Princeton, NJ: Princeton University Press.

Brown-Collier, Elba and Randall Bausor (1988), 'The Epistemological Foundations of *The General Theory*', *Scottish Journal of Political Economy*, **35** (3), August, 227-41.

Debreu, Gerard (1959), *Theory of Value; An Axiomatic Analysis of Economic Equilibrium*, Cowles Foundation Monograph 17, New Haven: Yale University Press.

Knight, Frank H. (1971), *Risk, Uncertainty and Profit*, Chicago: The University of Chicago Press.

Lazear, Edward P. (1991), 'Labor Economics and the Psychology of Organizations', *Journal of Economic Perspectives*, **5** (2), Spring, 89-110.

Shackle, G.L.S. (1969), *Decision, Order and Time in Human Affairs*, Cambridge: Cambridge University Press.

Shackle, G.L.S. (1974), *Keynesian Kaleidics: The Evolution of a General Political Economy*, Edinburgh: Edinburgh University Press.

Shackle, G.L.S. (1979), *Imagination and the Nature of Choice*, Edinburgh: Edinburgh University Press.

Spence, A. Michael (1974), *Market Signalling: Information Transfer in Hiring and Related Screening Processes*, Cambridge, MA: Harvard University Press.

Vickers, Douglas (1978), *Financial Markets in the Capitalist Process*, Philadelphia: University of Pennsylvania Press.

Vickers, Douglas (1986), 'Time, Ignorance, Surprise, and Economic Decisions', *Journal of Post Keynesian Economics*, **9** (1), Fall, 48-57.

Yang, Xiaokai, and Ben J. Heijdra (1993), 'Monopolistic Competition and Optimum Product Diversity: Comment', *The American Economic Review*, **83** (1), March, 295-301.

17. Richard Thaler

George F. Loewenstein

Where there are predictions, there are anomalies.

Richard Thaler is one of a small number of contemporary economists who are attempting to enrich their field with insights from psychology. Thaler has become something of a leader of guerrilla economists who advocate a new approach (or revival of an old approach) which sees economics as just one approach to social science, and hence obligated – and well-advised – to adopt assumptions that are scientifically certified by other social scientists, particularly psychologists, but including sociologists, anthropologists and others. This approach is not new, but indeed quite old, since earlier more 'literary' economists such as Marshall, Keynes, Edgeworth, Fisher (and even 'Chicago School' thinkers like Knight) often introspected about the likely behavior of everyday folks as inspiration for their ideas. The use of casual introspection as 'evidence' – what most laypersons would call 'intuitive appeal' – was largely replaced post-World War Two by an emphasis on mathematizable results (which many psychological constructs are not) and a deliberate disregard of the realism of underlying assumptions. This lack of concern for the realism of their assumptions freed economists from the burden of familiarizing themselves with sister social sciences, such as psychology, that test assumptions directly. Thus, Thaler can be seen as continuing a tradition of economists beginning with Adam Smith, which was largely interrupted by the rise of mathematics and econometrics.

Although Thaler is not the most famous economist of the late twentieth century, he may well be the most controversial. His controversiality stems largely from his proclivity for arguing by anomaly – that is by highlighting facts that are inconsistent with traditional economic theory. As Kuhn and others have argued, old paradigms are replaced by new ones when they become crushed by the weight of anomalies which a new theory can readily explain. Thaler's role in economics is to accelerate this process.

Thaler's best-known anomalies have been published in the *Journal of Economic Perspectives* and subsequently compiled in his book *The Winner's*

Curse (1992). But most of his prodigious output of anomalies never find their way into print. For example, at a seminar in which Gary Becker presented his model of rational addiction, which views addiction as the outcome of a deliberate long-term plan (as opposed to, for example, weakness of will), Thaler asked Becker whether his theory implied that alcoholics should stock up on large quantities of alcohol to reduce transactions costs and realize the savings of buying in bulk. Becker acknowledged that this was an implication of his theory and lamented the fact that he was unaware of any data addressing the issue. To the best of my knowledge, Becker has not subsequently bothered to collect such data but, in all fairness, neither has Thaler.

Discrediting others' theories is good sport, especially for someone like Thaler who thrives on controversy. However, he cannot be charged with nihilism; in many areas he has proposed new theories or (less grandly) theoretical accounts of behavior that make specific predictions and are thus themselves vulnerable to refutation by anomaly. Thaler's major theoretical contributions have been in the areas of consumer choice, self-control and savings behavior, and finance. These contributions are the major focus of this essay.

Thaler traces his own intellectual odyssey to an unlikely origin, the University of Rochester, where he obtained a PhD in economics in the mid-1970s. The University of Rochester Economics Department was, as Thaler expresses it, a 'University of Chicago farm club' (Thaler 1991) – a bastion of belief in economic rationality and market efficiency. Thaler made his first foray into behavioral economics while doing dissertation research on the monetary value of human life. His dissertation attacked the problem in the manner prescribed by his advisor, Sherwin Rosen – that is, by estimating how much of a wage premium people were paid to engage in risky occupations such as mining and logging. At some point during this research, Thaler took the heretical step of conducting a short survey in which he actually asked people direct questions about the value they placed on their lives. As those who have taken introductory economics know, there are two standard measures of value which are operationalized as 'willingness to pay' and 'willingness to accept compensation'. According to economic theory, these two measures can diverge somewhat, but not by much. (This is due to wealth effects. To sell something one must first own it, which implies a higher level of wealth.) However, when Thaler asked his subjects how much they would need to be paid to accept an extra 0.001 chance of immediate death, the answers they gave were typically thousands of times greater than the amounts specified when asked how much they would pay to eliminate an equivalent preexisting chance of death. Although he put this research aside in the interest of graduating and perhaps, because of the lack of a theory to explain it, this early finding sparked his interest in economic anomalies. From that point on he made a habit of 'collecting' economic anomalies. His professors and colleagues at the University of Rochester were especially amusing sources of such anomalies because, like high-spending revolutionaries, their behavior was at such striking variance to the ideology they preached. For example, many sacrificed present value to get paid on a 12-month rather than 9-month basis (for self-control purposes); they often purchased individual stocks and attempted to time the stock market (despite their espousal of the random walk view of stock prices), and invested the bulk of their retirement funds in bonds (despite historically higher returns on stocks).

If Thaler's value of life survey marked his birth as a behavioral economist (as he calls himself), his discovery of behavioral decision theory in the mid-1970s spelled his coming of age. Behavioral decision theory is a subfield of psychology which seeks a better understanding of human behavior through a mix of cognitive psychology, normative decision theory and economics. Behavioral decision theory was in its heyday in the mid-1970s, marked by the publication of Amos Tversky and Daniel Kahneman's influential paper, 'Judgment Under Uncertainty: Heuristics and Biases' (1974). Thaler obtained a copy of this paper at a fortuitous meeting with Baruch Fischhoff and Paul Slovic, and some time later received a preliminary copy of Kahneman and Tversky's 'Prospect Theory' (1979). In one part of Prospect Theory – the so-called 'value function' – Thaler found what he had lacked until that point: a theoretical explanation for many of his burgeoning list of anomalies. It would be difficult to overestimate the impact that these discoveries had on Thaler's intellectual development; a very large fraction of his subsequent research can be seen as efforts to draw out and test implications that follow from replacing the conventional utility function of economics with the Prospect Theory value function.

The essential characteristics of this value function are:

1. It is defined with respect to gains and losses or departures from a psychologically relevant 'reference point' rather than with respect to levels of wealth. In other words, it assumes that people care about changes in, rather than levels of, wealth.
2. It is steeper for losses than for gains – a property referred to as 'loss aversion'. As Kahneman and Tversky explicate, 'the aggravation that one experiences in losing a sum of money appears to be greater than the pleasure associated with gaining the same amount' (1979, p. 279).
3. It is concave for gains and convex for losses, reflecting diminishing sensitivity to both. In other words, losing $2x$ is less than twice as bad psychologically as losing x, and gaining $2x$ is less than twice as good as gaining x.

Thaler's first paper as a behavioral economist, 'Toward a Positive Theory of Consumer Choice' (1980), presented a variety of economic anomalies, most of which could be explained by the Prospect Theory value function. The first was the tendency to underweight opportunity costs relative to out-of-pocket costs. Economic theory assumes that decision makers should treat opportunity costs as equivalent to out-of-pocket costs. But if people treat out-of-pocket costs as losses, and opportunity costs as forgone gains, then the loss-aversion feature of Prospect Theory implies that out-of-pocket costs will be weighted more heavily in decision making than the opportunity costs. Consider, for example, the case of Mr A who flips hamburgers 40 hours per week, and Mr B who does so for 35. Mr A is given the option of taking 5 hours off without pay, and Mr B is given the option of working 5 extra hours with pay. Economic theory implies that the only relevant distinction between the two men is the hours they work: if Mr B is poorer than Mr A, as a result of working fewer hours, he should be more likely to take on the extra work. However, if Mr A views the reduction in pay as an out-of-pocket cost and Mr B views forgoing the extra pay as an opportunity cost, then underweighting of opportunity costs implies that Mr B will be the one less likely to work 40 hours. Note that the underweighting of opportunity costs produces a strong tendency to stick with the status quo (40 hours for Mr A and 35 for Mr B). To emphasize this implication, Thaler labeled the underweighting of opportunity costs the 'endowment effect'.

The second anomaly discussed in the paper is the widespread failure to ignore sunk costs. As many beginning economics students learn, one of the basic dictates of economic rationality is that sunk costs (costs that cannot be recovered) should be ignored in deciding between options; one should choose only on the basis of expected future costs and benefits. For example, if one has spent $100 on theater tickets, then obtains free tickets to a ball game that one prefers to the play, the $100 is a sunk cost and should not influence one's choice between the two forms of entertainment; one should go to the ball game. Contrary to economic rationality, Thaler argues that people are likely to go to the play because they encode the $100 as a loss that can only be canceled by actually enjoying the consumption it was intended to purchase.

Thaler's next two papers discussed various aspects of intertemporal choice. In 'Some Empirical Evidence on Dynamic Inconsistency' (1981) he reported results from a survey conducted at the University of Oregon in which he estimated individual discount rates by presenting subjects with choices between receipts or payments of different magnitudes at different points in time. This paper was the first to document a series of intertemporal choice anomalies, such as the tendency to discount small amounts more heavily than large amounts, which have stimulated much subsequent research on intertemporal choice. Even more importantly his paper was the first to show (with human subjects) that people do not discount the future exponentially, but instead overweight the present relative to all other periods. In a seminal article, R.H. Strotz (1955) had demonstrated that deviations from exponential discounting would produce dynamically inconsistent behavior (hence the title of Thaler's article). Dynamic inconsistency occurs when one makes plans for the future, but systematically deviates from the plans when the future arrives. One special form of time inconsistency, called 'impulsivity', occurs when people are consistently more shortsighted in the present than called for by their prior plans. Impulsivity is exemplified by resolutions to save more or eat less in the future, accompanied by the failure to save or diet in the present. Impulsive behavior naturally follows from the type of discount function that Thaler had estimated.

When faced with one's own impulsivity, a natural response is to attempt to control one's own future behavior – for example, to force one's future selves to save or diet. Such efforts pose an important anomaly for traditional economic theory, which assumes consumer sovereignty – that is, that people know what they want, that what they want remains relatively stable over time. Thaler and co-author Hersh Shefrin (1981) argued that efforts at self-control are best modeled within a 'multiple self' model – that is, by representing the individual as a series of temporally situated selves with competing interests. Thaler and Shefrin's 'planner–doer' model, which was inspired by principal– agent theory in economics, views the individual as consisting of a series of temporally isolated myopic id-like 'doers' and a unitary and more far-sighted 'planner' who attempts to reconcile the short-sighted demands of the doers. They use the model to account for a wide range of common self-control strategies such as self-binding behavior (for example, giving one's car keys to the host at the beginning of a party), and the self-imposition of rigid rules of behavior.

Thaler's next paper, 'Mental Accounting and Consumer Choice' (1985) initiated three lines of research which he pursued in subsequent years. The first focused on the question of how people judge the fairness of different types of economic transactions. He argued that consumers often derive positive or negative 'transactions utility' from a comparison of the price they pay for a good or service to a fair 'reference' price. For example, Thaler asserted, and later verified by a small survey, that most beach-loungers would be willing to pay more for the same beer purchased from a hotel than from a mom and pop grocery store, even though they were buying the beer for consumption on the beach.

The second line of research focused on the question of when people prefer to aggregate or segregate outcomes from one another. For example, would a race-track visitor who bought one $2.00 losing ticket but won $10.00 on another prefer to keep these two events mentally segregated or to aggregate them, say, into 'racetrack winnings?'. Thaler shows that Prospect Theory makes a number of predictions concerning how people should prefer to aggregate and segregate transactions, including the principle that small losses should be aggregated with large gains (as in the prior example). In a subsequent paper co-authored with Eric Johnson (Thaler and Johnson 1990), Thaler shows that people's intuitions about the hedonics of aggregation and segregation are relatively close to the predictions of Prospect Theory (there is only one major discrepancy). However, people do not seem to encode their own transactions in a utility-maximizing fashion – a proposition that Thaler and Johnson call 'hedonic framing'.

The third line of research introduced in the paper was the notion of mental accounting. Just as businesses keep formal accounts that track receipts and expenses, Thaler postulated that individuals establish mental accounts which serve a variety of purposes – most importantly self-control. For example, a person who wanted to save more might decide to salt away certain income, such as tax rebates and bonus salary, in an 'untouchable' retirement fund that would protect the money and render it free of temptation.

Beginning in the mid-1980s, Thaler concentrated his efforts on several projects aimed at publicizing behavioral economics and at responding to some of the reservations expressed by mainstream economists. These included a number of new data collection initiatives, publication of the anomalies column in the *Journal of Economic Perspectives*, and the establishment of close links to the Russell Sage Foundation and its president Eric Wanner, who has provided behavioral economics with wide-ranging support.

One new line of empirical research was a project on fairness that pursued ideas that Thaler had introduced in the 1985 mental accounting paper. During a year that Thaler spent on sabbatical at the University of British Columbia, he, Daniel Kahneman and Jack Knetsch conducted phone surveys in which Vancouver residents were asked to judge the fairness of various economic transactions (Kahneman, Knetsch and Thaler 1986a and b). The results from these surveys lent support to Thaler's reference price concept. For example, different subjects were asked to evaluate the fairness of the following transactions:

Version 1:

> A shortage has developed for a popular model of automobile, and customers must now wait two months for delivery. A dealer has been selling these cars at list price. Now the dealer prices this model at $200 above list price.

Version 2:

> A shortage has developed for a popular model of automobile, and customers must now wait
> two months for delivery. A dealer has been selling these cars at a discount of $200 below list
> price. Now the dealer sells this model only at list price.

Whereas 71 percent of respondents viewed the first dealer's action as unfair, only 42 percent of respondents viewed the second dealer's action as unfair. This pattern of results is easily assimilated by assuming that respondents view list price as a relevant reference level for matters of fairness. As Thaler notes, these results may help to explain the widespread prevalence of list prices that are far higher than market prices.

Other responses from the same survey, however, told a more complicated story. For example, respondents viewed a much wider range of actions as fair if taken by firms with financial problems; the same actions were viewed as unfair if taken by prosperous firms. If at least one party had to be hurt, survey respondents did not seem to mind if it were consumers; however, they viewed it as unfair for one party to be hurt if the only effect was to enhance another party's already desirable position.

In a second line of research, Thaler pursued his work on mental accounting by connecting it to the earlier work on savings and self-control. The hook for the connection between these two areas of research came from a systematic pattern that Thaler and Shefrin identified in their extensive review of the saving literature. A frequent finding in this research is that consumers have different propensities to save and consume out of income arising from different sources. For example, a consumer whose $200,000 stock portfolio appreciates by $20,000 is unlikely to adjust his/her consumption noticeably in response to the increase in wealth, whereas much smaller gains arising from winnings from gambling, salary bonuses, or tax rebates, are likely to result in significant short-term increases in consumption. This pattern poses a paradox for the standard life-cycle model of consumer choice which, in its most stylized form, assumes that people consume a fixed fraction of their expected lifetime wealth in every time period.

In 'The Behavioral Life-Cycle Hypothesis' (Shefrin and Thaler 1988), Thaler and Shefrin argue that the differences in propensities to consume from different sources arise from mental accounting. They assume that consumers allocate wealth arising from different sources into different mental accounts, each with a different associated marginal propensity to consume. The specific accounting system they propose includes three accounts: the 'current income account', the 'current wealth account', and the 'future wealth account', each with successively lower marginal propensities to consume. The major purpose of such a system is to segregate some money into illiquid accounts that are effectively untouchable, and thus not a source of temptation, while retaining other money in relatively liquid accounts that can be spent without invoking the costs of self-control mechanisms. In two follow-up papers (Kahneman and Thaler 1991; Thaler 1994), Thaler examined a variety of policy implications that follow from such a mental-accounting perspective, such as the possibility that personal savings rates could be increased by encouraging employers to pay a larger fraction of yearly salaries in the form of bonuses.

A third line of research initiated in the mid-1980s focused on the 'endowment effect' that Thaler had first defined as such in his 1980 paper on consumer choice. The endowment effect refers to the tendency for people to value an object more highly if they possess it than they would value the same object if they did not. It is especially controversial because, unlike anomalies that challenge high-level economic theories such as the life-cycle hypothesis of savings, the endowment effect challenges the foundations of the neoclassical economic analysis of consumer choice. A central assumption of the standard account of consumer choice is that utility depends on objective asset positions, but not on how those asset positions were arrived at. The endowment effect challenges this view because it suggests that people value objects much more highly when they are contemplating giving them up than they do when they are thinking about acquiring them.

Because of its controversial nature, there was no shortage of attempts to discredit the endowment effect – that is, to identify methodological flaws in the studies that purportedly demonstrate it, or to argue that it is explicable in terms of standard economic principles. Some critics argued that the effect stemmed from strategic overbidding by sellers and underbidding by buyers, whereas others postulated that the effect would disappear with the right combination of incentives and opportunities for learning. Characteristically, critics expended considerable energy in attempting to discredit the phenomenon, and little energy thinking through its implications for economics. In response to these critiques, Thaler and co-authors Kahneman and Knetsch (Kahneman, Knetsch and Thaler 1990) conducted a series of experiments designed to rule out the artifactual explanations for the effect. The success of the resulting paper is attested to by the fact that subsequent research on the endowment effect has been able to move beyond addressing whether the effect exists, to an analysis of its causes and consequences. Such research is urgently needed since there is still no satisfactory explanation for why certain buying/selling discrepancies (such as the original value-of-life problem Thaler examined as a graduate student) are so much larger than others (such as the purchase and sale of coffee mugs).

Experiments, even those as convincing as the mug experiments, remain to most economists 'mere' experiments. No amount of experimental evidence can move the strong prior belief of many economists that rationality is a good working assumption in 'real markets'. Thaler has addressed this critique in two ways: first by examining theoretically the conditions necessary for markets to eliminate the traces of less than fully rational behavior (what he calls 'quasi rational'), and second through empirical work on financial markets.

In a paper with Thomas Russell (Russell and Thaler 1985), Thaler provides a theoretical analysis of markets comprised of a mix of rational and quasi- rational agents. The question they address is when the outcomes of such markets will resemble those of markets containing only rational agents – that is, the standard economics set up. It turns out that these conditions are quite strict. For example, one needs costless short selling. Short selling is typically impossible (for example, if you buy an American car and I think that you have made a mistake I cannot sell your car short) and rarely costless (in most stock markets there are short-sale restrictions). Even if there is costless short selling, this will improve market efficiency only if the propensity of rational agents to sell short is greater than that of quasi-rational agents. Russell and Thaler conclude that even in financial markets there is no theoretical justification for the a priori belief that quasi rationality by some participants is irrelevant.

This conclusion is strongly supported by Thaler's research on financial market anomalies. Financial markets, like Rochester colleagues, make attractive sources of anomalies because there is such a strong initial presumption of rationality. Mainstream academic finance is dominated by a theoretical perspective called the efficient markets theory which posits that security prices incorporate all available information that is relevant to the security's long-term rate of return.

One implication of this perspective is that detrended stock prices should follow a random walk, since new information, by definition, is unpredictable. In two papers, Thaler and co-author Werner De Bondt (De Bondt and Thaler 1985, 1987) attack this view by showing that stocks that have been big winners in the recent past provide below-market returns in the future, whereas recent losers display the opposite pattern. They attribute this pattern to the tendency of investors to overreact to both good and bad news, and they attempt to rule out a variety of alternative interpretations for their results. A third paper (De Bondt and Thaler 1990) shows that security analysts' estimates of company earnings are similarly characterized by overreaction to good and bad news. As Thaler and De Bondt note, security analysts have a strong incentive for predicting accurately, and also have substantially more information and experience than the typical investor. This finding casts some doubt on the existence of 'smart' money which is sometimes purported to be waiting on the sidelines to arbitrage away any residual wealth left by the irrationality of small investors.

The efficient markets hypothesis assumes not only that security prices incorporate all relevant information, but also that they constitute an unbiased estimate of the long-term-earnings of the underlying assets, appropriately discounted and adjusted for risk. In financial parlance, a firm's stock price should correspond to its *fundamental* value. However, this assumption is difficult to test since objective value is not observable, in part because it depends on myriad present and future variables that are either unmeasurable or not yet resolved.

In 'Investor Sentiment and the Closed-End Fund Puzzle' (Lee, Shleifer and Thaler 1991) Thaler and co-authors Charles Lee and Andrei Shleifer point out that there is one important exception to this rule: the case of closed-end mutual funds. These funds issue a fixed number of shares, then invest the proceeds in other securities. Given that these securities are themselves valued in the market, the fundamental value of a closed-end fund at any time is simply the value of its composite securities. Closed-end funds, however, are rarely priced at this fundamental value. When they are first introduced, they typically sell at a premium above their underlying value, but over time they tend to sell at substantial discounts relative to fundamental value. This pattern not only conflicts with the efficient markets theory; it is difficult to explain why investors would purchase any type of security whose value displayed a systematic downward trend over time. Thaler and his co-authors show that the pattern of price variation over time and across funds is not consistent with a variety of conventional explanations, such as agency costs, and argue that the stylized facts can be explained by a theoretical model that posits the simultaneous existence of two types of traders: noise traders (who trade erratically and are subject to mass shifts in sentiment), and rational investors (who trade based on fundamental values, but are relatively short-sighted) (De Long, Shleifer, Summers and Waldmann 1990).

Thaler's work in progress continues to pursue the anomalies theme and also to trace out implications of the Prospect Theory value function. One major project is looking at the 'equity premium' – the fact that, over almost any moderate length of time, stocks have yielded much higher returns than bonds. This pattern is anomalous since, if stocks produce higher yields, people should transfer their investments out of bonds and into stocks until their risk-adjusted return is equalized. Thaler argues that the equity premium is caused by 'myopic loss aversion' – the tendency for investors to pay too much attention to short-term returns, and their aversion to observing losses when they do so. He argues that the equity premium would be reduced if investors received less information about the short-term returns of their investment portfolios, for example, receiving yearly instead of monthly reports.

Thaler's research has had a profound influence, not only on diverse subfields within economics, but on a wide variety of allied disciplines such as accounting, marketing and law. Moreover, his influences extend well beyond the realm of theory and research. Many people react to Thaler's anomalies by changing their behavior. For example, numerous academics with whom I have spoken have adjusted their investment portfolios in favor of equity as have, it seems, some universities and foundations. It should, therefore, come as no surprise that in scrutinizing his own behavior for fodder for his anomalies columns, and exorcising any anomalous behaviors thereby detected, Thaler's own behavior has been powerfully influenced. Thaler comes closer to satisfying the dictates of economic rationality than the vast majority of economists. He is the ticket scalper's dream – happy to buy scarce tickets at the market-clearing price, unfettered by considerations of fairness. He keeps 100 percent of his retirement funds in stocks, and rigorously attempts to expunge the influence on his own decisions of psychological factors such as regret aversion, attention to sunk costs, or underweighting of opportunity costs. Thus, the master of anomalies may have inadvertently created in himself the most dramatic of all anomalies – a single living example of the legendary 'economic man'.

ACKNOWLEDGEMENTS

I thank Colin Camerer, Donna Harsch, Shane Frederick and Brian Zikmund-Fisher for helpful comments and suggestions.

THALER'S MAJOR WRITINGS

(1980), 'Toward a Positive Theory of Consumer Choice', *Journal of Economic Behavior and Organization*, 1, 39-60.
(1981), 'Some Empirical Evidence on Dynamic Inconsistency', *Economic Letters*, 8, 201-7.
(1981) (with H.M. Shefrin), 'An Economic Theory of Self-Control', *Journal of Political Economy*, 89, 392-406.
(1985), 'Mental Accounting and Consumer Choice', *Management Science*, 4, 199-214.
(1985) (with W.F.M. De Bondt), 'Does the Stock Market Overreact?' *Journal of Finance*, 40, 793-808.
(1986a) (with D. Kahneman and J.L. Knetsch), 'Fairness as a Constraint on Profit Seeking: Entitlement in the Market', *American Economic Review*, 76, 728-41.
(1986b) (with D. Kahneman and J.L. Knetsch), 'Fairness and the Assumption of Economics', *Journal of Business*, 59, s285-s300.

(1987) (with W.F.M. De Bondt), 'Further Evidence on Investor Overreaction and Stock Market Seasonality' *Journal of Finance*, **42**, 557-81.

(1988) (with T. Russell), 'The Relevance of Quasi Rationality in Competitive Markets', in D. Bell, H. Raiffa and A. Tversky (eds), *Decision-Making: Descriptive, Normative and Prescriptive Interactions*, New York: Cambridge University Press.

(1988) (with H.M. Shefrin), 'The Behavioral Life-Cycle Hypothesis', *Economic Inquiry*, 609-43.

(1990) (with W.F.M. De Bondt), 'Do Security Analysts Overreact?,' *American Economic Review*, **80**, 52-7.

(1990) (with E.J. Johnson), 'Gambling with the house money and trying to break even', *Management Science*, **36**, 643-60.

(1990) (with D. Kahneman and J.L. Knetsch), 'Experimental Tests of the Endowment Effect and the Coase Theorem', *Journal of Political Economy*, **98**, 1325-48.

(1991), *Quasi Rational Economics*, New York: Russell Sage Foundation.

(1991) (with D. Kahneman), 'Economic Analysis and The Psychology of Utility: Applications to Compensation Policy', *American Economic Review*, **81**, 341-6.

(1991) (with C.M.C. Lee and A. Schleifer), 'Investor Sentiment and the Closed-End Fund Puzzle', *Journal of Finance*, **46**, 310-52.

(1992), *The Winner's Curse. Paradoxes and Anomalies of Economic Life*, New York: Free Press.

(1994), 'Psychology and Savings Policies', *American Economic Review*, **84**, 186-92.

OTHER REFERENCES

De Long, J.B., A. Shleifer, L.H. Summers and R.J. Waldmann (1990), 'Noise Trader Risk in Financial Markets', *Journal of Political Economy*, **98**, 703-38.

Kahneman, D. and A. Tversky (1979), 'Prospect Theory: An Analysis of Decision Under Risk', *Econometrica*, **47**, 263-91.

Strotz, R.H. (1955/56), 'Myopia and Inconsistency in Dynamic Utility Maximization', *Review of Economic Studies*, **23**, 165-80.

Tversky, A. and D. Kahneman (1974), 'Judgment Under Uncertainty: Heuristics and Biases', *Science*, **185**, 1124-31.

18. Lester C. Thurow

Kathleen Brook and James Peach

INTRODUCTION

Lester C. Thurow is among the most widely known economists (American or otherwise) of the late twentieth century. In one forum or another, he has been involved in nearly every major economic policy debate in the US for more than a quarter of a century. To the general public, he is known for his numerous broadcast media appearances, his contributions to various newspapers and magazines and many public lectures. Within the economics profession, Thurow became widely known early in his career for his analysis of labor markets and the distribution of income. Many of his contributions to economics are innovative and, not surprisingly, controversial.

From our perspective, what makes Thurow particularly fascinating as an economist is not his stature within the profession or his public renown. Instead, what is intriguing about Thurow is the unique combination of conventional (mainstream) and unconventional analysis and conclusions which characterizes his work.

In an era of increasingly narrow specialization among economists, Thurow maintains very wide-ranging interests. Consequently, it is not easy to classify him. His self-identified areas of interest are public finance, macroeconomics and income distribution but many of his written works do not fall neatly into a single field of economics. After a brief biographical sketch, the main body of the chapter is organized around six themes that are found in many of Thurow's works. These themes are: the importance of productivity, the distribution of income, the stochastic nature of the economy, the necessity of tradeoffs, the international economy and the role of government. An additional section titled, 'The Theoretical Thurow', contains a discussion of other aspects of his work that do not fit neatly into the themes identified above. A final section offers a summary assessment of Thurow's contributions. A bibliography of his major works appears at the end. The bibliography includes his books and major journal articles, but we have made no attempt to provide a complete listing of his articles which have appeared in the popular press.

THUROW: BACKGROUND AND BIOGRAPHY

Lester Carl Thurow was born on May 7, 1938 in Livingston, Montana.[1] He received a BA degree in political economy from Williams College in 1960. Subsequently, Thurow was a Rhodes Scholar and was awarded an MA in philosophy, politics and economics (with first class honors) by Oxford University in 1962. In 1964 he received a PhD in economics from Harvard University. He holds eleven honorary degrees and in 1993 served as vice-president of the American Economic Association.

In 1964 and 1965 Thurow held the position of staff economist on Lyndon Johnson's Council of Economic Advisors. In the following three years he served as an assistant professor at Harvard University. Since then he has held several positions at the Massachusetts Institute of Technology, including appointment as Dean of the Sloan School of Management at MIT in 1987. Twice (1975 and 1980) he was a visiting professor at the University of Arizona. Thurow has been an economics columnist for the *New York Times* and was a member of that newpaper's editorial board in 1979. He has been a contributing editor to *Newsweek* and has appeared regularly on various television shows, including the Public Broadcasting System's *Nightly Business Report*.

THE PRODUCTIVITY PRINCIPLE AND THE PRODUCTIVITY PROBLEM

If there is a single unifying focus or theme in virtually all of Thurow's works, it is that 'raising output per unit of input (productivity) is the only long-run technique for raising living standards in every human society' (Thurow 1987c, p. 242). Thurow also makes clear that what he really means is that output per capita must increase in order to sustain increases in the standard of living for the general population. While the productivity principle[2] applies to all economies, Thurow is

---

1. The biographical information provided here was obtained from a short curriculum vitae provided by Professor Thurow.
2. The phrase 'productivity principle' will be used to refer to Thurow's statement that increases in living standards depend on increases in productivity. Thurow does not seem to use this term.

particularly interested in the productivity problem in the United States. According to Thurow,

> Anemic productivity growth stands as America's central economic problem. If productivity growth cannot be reaccelerated, Americans can only look forward to a very slow rise in their standard of living regardless of how successful they are in inflation-proofing the economy, lowering unemployment, restoring a more reasonably valued dollar, eliminating budget deficits, or in dealing with any of their other economic problems. (Thurow 1987d, p. 11)

In all likelihood, few economists, mainstream or not, would disagree with Thurow's statement of the productivity principle.[3] But modern mainstream economists do not, for the most part, regard declining productivity or declining productivity growth rates as a problem for which policy intervention is necessary and they do not make economic growth the central focus of their analysis. In fact, according to the standard model, all that is necessary is to let the market operate efficiently. In this context, government has no direct role in promoting productivity growth rates. For Thurow, however, America's central economic problem is necessarily a central policy problem – to which we return later (see 'The Role of Government' below). For now, Thurow's answers to two fundamental questions concerning productivity will be considered.

First, what evidence exists to suggest that the productivity principle is a meaningful axiom on which to base further analysis? The ultimate truth of the productivity principle may seem intuitively obvious. Simple arithmetic can be used to illustrate its status as a truism and those who are theoretically inclined might argue that it can be derived from economic theory. Thurow (1992, pp. 203-5), however, turns to economic history to support his case, pointing out that no nation has joined the ranks of the world's top-income earners without substantial periods of productivity growth.

Second, what has caused 'anemic productivity growth' in America? Thurow does not attribute the decline to a single cause.

> An autopsy of American productivity growth would record 'death by a thousand cuts' when it came to the line 'cause of death'. No single thing killed American productivity growth; no single thing can revive it. (Thurow 1987d, pp. 11-12)

However, Thurow does at times point to two factors as being critical: the baby-boom (Thurow 1981a) and the policies used to fight inflation (Thurow 1980d, p 42).

---

3. See Thurow's (1987b) discussion for an elaboration of the themes presented in this paragraph.

The post-World War Two baby-boom, perhaps the most significant demographic event in the US during this century, resulted in a large increase in the labor force. In a thoroughly mainstream fashion, Thurow argues that a large increase in the supply of labor means that the price of labor must fall relative to the price of capital. In such a case, firms react by using more of the relatively cheaper input (labor), resulting in diminishing productivity per capita.

Policies used to fight inflation affect productivity growth rates through two main channels. First, to the extent that firms need to borrow to finance new investment, high interest rates associated with restrictive monetary policies raise the cost of capital investment. Second, slow-growth, high-unemployment policies mean that aggregate demand falls and firms have less incentive to make investments in physical or human capital. And, such policies have been used frequently in the thirty-year period in which productivity growth has been falling.

Thurow (1980d, 1984a, 1984c, 1985b, 1985d, 1985e, 1985f, 1989c and 1992) also identifies many of the remaining 998 'cuts' which have killed American productivity growth. Among these are antiquated management practices including a short-term perspective on the part of management, problems in the financial system including the inability of US banks to provide very large sums of risk capital for very long periods of time, difficulties with the antitrust laws which prohibit US firms from acting together in a fashion which is common in other industrial nations, government subsidies to inefficient industries, tariff policies that protect inefficient industries, low savings rates of US citizens, the large federal deficit which means that the federal government is not a reliable source of savings, low profit rates which cause corporations to seek investment capital outside of the firm, problems in the educational system and the lack of political courage to adopt explicit industrial policies.

THE DISTRIBUTION OF INCOME

The second major theme in Thurow's writings is the importance of the distribution of income and wealth to the efficient functioning of the economy. Indeed, very little of what Thurow has written lacks a distributional emphasis.

Thurow (1969a, pp. 10-11) concisely states the case for the importance of the distribution of income in three statements. (1) 'The achievement of efficiency in a market system depends on the prior achievement of an optimum distribution of income. If income is distributed in accordance with society's preferences, individual preferences are properly weighted in the marketplace. If income is not distributed in accordance with society's preferences, the market adjusts to an inequitable set of demands'. However, (2) 'There is nothing in the system that automatically achieves the desired distribution'. And, it is possible that (3) 'the distribution may affect the total amount to be distributed'. In combination, these three statements establish the context for his analysis of income distribution as an important policy issue.

Thurow has been a severe critic of marginal productivity theory as an explanation of the distribution of income. Thurow's critique of marginal productivity theory evolved over a period of only a few years. In 1969 (Thurow 1969a, p. 30), he asserted that '[T]he theoretical equality of earned income and marginal products is based on the hypothesis that all markets are in equilibrium. In a growing dynamic economy, markets are never in equilibrium but are always adjusting to it'. He goes on to argue that (Thurow 1969a, p. 30), '[i]mperfections and monopolies in the product and factor markets are another source of differences between the distribution of earned income and the distribution of marginal productivities'. By the mid-1970s Thurow's dissatisfaction with marginal productivity theory was more complete. He noted (Thurow 1975a, p. 230) that 'Technically, marginal productivity theory is not a theory of distribution until it has been spelled out in sufficient detail to be tested'. And Thurow cited numerous reasons why the theory could not be tested: the level of aggregation, economies and diseconomies of scale, the time period to which the theory applies, the problem of group production, the role of government and measurement problems such as the measurement of so-called psychic income.[4] Thurow is no kinder to marginal productivity theory in his later works.

Shortly after Joan Robinson (1973) told the American Economic Association that '[w]e have not got a theory of distribution', Thurow offered new and separate explanations of the distributions of earnings and wealth.

Thurow (1975a) begins his analysis of earnings with an examination of the existing statistical distribution of earnings rather than with the concept of an equilibrium wage as implied by neoclassical theory. A statistical distribution can be described in simple terms by its mean and variance.[5] If the variance is large, as it is in the US distribution of earnings, there will be a large stochastic element in determining exactly where in the distribution any given individual will fit even if background characteristics such as education and age are taken into consideration.

Thurow does not, however, imply that the distribution of earnings is entirely random. The systematic portion of the distribution of earnings can be explained by the job-competition model.

---

4. Thurow's disdain for the concept of psychic income is more fully explained in Thurow 1978a, 1980c and 1982c.
5. There are distributions without a finite mean or variance and there are many distributions that cannot be described by their first two moments alone. These facts do not affect the current discussion.

> The key ingredient in the job-competition model is the observation that most cognitive skills are not acquired before a worker enters the labor market but after he has found employment through on-the-job training. Thus, the labor market is not primarily a bidding market for selling existing skills but a training market where training slots must be allocated to different workers. (Thurow 1975a, p. 76)

Fundamentally, much of an employee's value to a firm is obtained through on-the-job training (OJT) and, as a consequence, employers have an incentive to minimize training costs. In order to do so, 'employers rank potential workers on the basis of their training costs' (Thurow 1975a, p. 87). This ranking of potential workers is the labor queue in which 'workers compete for position based upon their background characteristics rather than on their willingness to accept low wages' (Thurow 1975a, p. 76). There is no reason, however, why identical workers will have identical jobs. On the contrary, 'Employers have a range of jobs for which they seek trainees and, desirable characteristics may differ across jobs' (Thurow 1975a, p. 91). Further, different employers may rank background characteristics differently. Thus, 'identical individuals do not necessarily earn identical incomes as they do in the wage-competition model' (Thurow 1975a, p. 92).

But the labor queue cannot be considered in isolation from the distribution of job opportunities. Three factors, according to Thurow, are especially important in determining the distribution of jobs. First, the distribution of technical knowledge affects both the quantity and type of jobs. If, for example, there were only one production technology, there would be a fixed distribution of jobs (for any given level of GDP) determined entirely by technology. But given a choice of technologies, the distribution of jobs becomes cor-respondingly complex. Second, the 'sociology of wage determination' affects the distribution of jobs. Here, Thurow suggests that there is more to wage determination than simple supply and demand. In particular, wage determination occurs through a social process conditioned by the fact that relative wages are important. And if, as Thurow suggests, marginal productivity resides in the job rather than the individual, wage determination must occur through a process other than an evaluation of simple marginal productivity considerations. Finally, the shape of the labor queue itself is important in determining the distribution of job opportunities.

In brief, the job-competition model as an explanation of the distribution of earnings consists of three main components: the labor queue, the distribution of job opportunities and a stochastic element. Thurow suggests that the job-competition model holds several advantages over the more traditional wage-competition model. In particular, his model is consistent with the distribution of earnings in the US economy while the wage-competition model is not. Second, it is not necessary to appeal to market imperfections or other mechanisms lying outside the model to explain deviant observations (e.g., persistent unemployment). Third, the job-competition model implicitly contains explanations of some of the most difficult problems of modern economic analysis. For example, while rigid wages cannot be explained within the traditional model, the job-competition model suggests that '[T]he training function of the labor market makes the repression of wage competition profitable' (Thurow 1975a, p. 76). Thurow's model also offers a solution to another tantalizing puzzle: the failure of a more equal distribution of educational attainment to reduce inequality in the distribution of earnings. Since '[T]here are no equilibrium wages that should be paid [to] people based on their personal qualifications' (Thurow 1975a, p. 77), there is no reason to suspect that equalizing the distribution of educational opportunities would result in greater income equality. Finally, we note that Thurow is quick to point out that the job-competition model 'does not imply that wage competition never exists. Wage competition and job competition are not mutually exclusive' (Thurow 1975a, p. 76).

The distribution of wealth requires a different explanation. The neoclassical model attributes wealth to a slow process of accumulation – savings (out of earned income), investment and then wealth. Thurow observes that this sequence of events is empirically false. Inheritance plays a big role in wealth accumulation. 'In addition to inheritance, the distribution of wealth is marked by the rapid accumulation of great wealth, an accumulation so rapid that it cannot come about by a patient process of savings and investment' (Thurow 1975a, p. 130). Thus, like the distribution of earnings, there is a large stochastic element in the accumulation of wealth and Thurow suggests a random-walk model for the distribution of wealth.

Thurow's model has not exactly 'swept the profession' (Thurow 1983a, p. 215), an assessment that may be confirmed by examining any principles of economics text, or for that matter most texts on labor economics. Yet, not only is this Thurow's most imaginative and important work, his alternative explanation of the distribution of earnings and wealth may be the most important contribution to the theory of income distribution in this century.[6]

---

6. This is a strong statement and it deserves some explanation. Marginal productivity theory was a nineteenth-century construct as was the Marxian theory of surplus value. Institutionalists in the tradition of Veblen and Ayres will note that the essential elements of their theory of distribution were outlined by Veblen by the turn of the century or shortly afterwards. The so-called statistical theories of distribution were developed mainly in the twentieth century and are genuinely useful curve-fitting exercises, but they are not really theories of distribution. The post-Keynesians have produced interesting work relating short-run changes in the distribution of income to business-cycle fluctuations but they offer no alternative to marginal productivity theory as a basic explanation of distribution. Dual labor market theories cannot explain why income distributions generated in the 'primary' and 'secondary' labor markets overlap nor do such theories offer any explanation of the

Thurow argues (1971b, 1973a, 1973b, 1973c, 1975a and 1980a) also that all societies must make an ethical decision concerning the distribution of income. Simply relying on market forces to produce a distribution of income without making a value judgement concerning its equity implications is not possible. Such a procedure ignores the fact that the initial (or current) distribution of income determines the current structure of demand and therefore the current distribution of income in a market society. At a minimum, each society must implicitly endorse or condemn the current distribution. Even in the absence of government (also an impossibility), each society must at least decide something about the current distribution of income.

In this context, Thurow also argues (1980a, 1981b, 1985a) that it is possible for economists to analyze equity problems. Thus, the usual dichotomy between analyzing efficiency problems and referring to equity problems as value judgements belonging in the political realm is a false dichotomy. Thurow notes, accurately, that efficiency arguments themselves involve a set of value judgements, for example, 'more is better' or 'Pareto optimality'. Con-sequently, statements about economic efficiency are no more value free than statements about equity. When the value judgements are recognized, Thurow argues, it is possible for economists to make meaningful statements about either equity or efficiency.

Finally, Thurow (e.g., 1969a, 1975a, 1981b, 1985a) advocates a specific distribution of income for the contemporary US economy: the distribution of earnings of full-time employed white males. This distribution is much more equal than the distribution of income for other groups and is also more equal than intergroup (e.g., black versus white) income differentials. While Thurow does not suggest that his recommended distribution is ultimately an optimal distribution, he does argue that such a distribution is consistent with the efficiency (growth) goals of society and he challenges others to justify a greater degree of inequality than the one he proposes.

THE STOCHASTIC NATURE OF THE ECONOMY

A third recurring theme in Thurow's works is that the random or stochastic portion of the economic universe may simply be large relative to the deterministic portion. This conclusion arises largely from his econometric work on production functions (Thurow 1965, 1966b, 1968, 1969e and 1970a), the causes of poverty

---

distribution of wealth.

(Thurow 1967b, 1969a, 1969b), discrimination (Thurow 1969a), income distribution (Thurow 1970d), and macroeconometric models (Thurow 1969d). While such a conclusion leads almost automatically to a critique of econometrics, it also has important implications for mainstream economic theory which is, for the most part, static and deterministic. Perhaps more importantly, if the stochastic portion of the economic universe is large, policies designed on the basis of deterministic models may be inappropriate or self-defeating. In this section, Thurow's critique of econometrics is described. The theoretical and policy implications are considered later.

While it is relatively easy for many economists to dismiss critics of econometrics who have not been involved in econometric work, it is not so easy to dismiss Thurow's critique since much of his early work could be classified as applied econometrics.

Thurow's criticisms of econometrics are explained most concisely in *Dangerous Currents* (Thurow 1983a): (1) macroeconometric models have not and cannot predict 'adverse events' (e.g., the macro disruptions related to the supply shocks of the 1970s); (2) the equations are not stable; (3) economic theory does not tell us the correct functional form of a model; (4) the statistical tests overstate the accuracy of the results because too many degrees of freedom are used in finding the model with the best fit; (5) the error terms which are assumed to be normally distributed and independent over time are not; (6) all time series tend to move together resulting in spurious correlation; (7) the identification problem, though well understood, is not easily solved; (8) it is possible to construct econometric models that are consistent with several theories thus preventing us from having a cutting edge to dismiss stupid theory; (9) most of our theoretical models are static while the economy is dynamic; (10) the macro modelers of the 1970s often confused predictability with controllability; and (11) proxy variables – variables that are not really what we are trying to measure – may be the only ones available.

None of this is particularly new or startling even to econometricians. Indeed, some or all of these criticisms are widely discussed in econometrics textbooks. Nevertheless, these criticisms are not to be taken lightly especially given Thurow's own early use of econometrics. Moreover, Thurow may have made two genuinely new contributions to the growing econometric criticism industry. First, he asserts with good reason that the failure of econometrics is not just a failure of macroeconometric models. If the macro-models have failed, so have the micro-models (Thurow 1983a). For example, the microeconometric models were incapable of predicting sudden price movements such as occurred in the markets for many commodities in the 1970s and 1980s. Second, Thurow's suggestion that the random or stochastic portion of the economic universe may simply be large relative to the deterministic portion is important. It is a logical conclusion from both his own econometric work and from the hundreds of studies in the human capital tradition that fail to explain systematically the variations in earnings of workers with similar characteristics.

In the end, Thurow does not suggest throwing out econometric studies altogether (Thurow 1983a). Robustness (many results that are consistent) offers some hope in some instances. In other cases, there are no alternatives. For example, if you want an estimate of the price elasticity of the demand for oil, there is no other way to get it. Thurow's evolving views on econometrics are another example of his combination of the conventional and the unconventional. While a severe critic of econometrics, his criticism is not so severe that he refuses to consider econometric work when he thinks it is appropriate.

THE NECESSITY OF TRADEOFFS

As a literary and analytical device, Thurow has often described the economic process as a game. The titles of two of his books, *The Zero Sum Society* and *The Zero Sum Solution* reflect both the substance of his arguments and the popularity of game theory among economists[7]. In any game, there are rules and there are winners and losers and Thurow attempts to describe both. In one sense, the game and game theory analogies can be interpreted as a straightforward application of the concept of opportunity cost. Yet, the key to understanding his use of these devices is to understand also that, for Thurow, tradeoffs do not occur in the static deterministic world of economic theory, but in the context of a dynamically changing economic environment.

To better understand Thurow's tradeoffs, we will first summarize his rules of the economic game. The first rule is that the game has already started and we are not given a choice about participation. Second, the game is competitive and there are winners and losers. Third, the rules change as the game is being played and, if you do not recognize that the rules have changed then you probably will not be a winner. Fourth, the rules are not always well enforced. Fifth, different rules sometimes apply to different participants in the game or, stated differently, some individuals and some institutions can set some of the rules for others. Sixth, there is a large stochastic element in the outcome of the game even if you play by what you think are the rules of the game. Seventh, the game is played at different levels:

---

7.   But these books are not the first in which Thurow has likened the economic process to a game. *Generating Inequality* is organized around the sometimes unknown rules of the game as well.

individuals, firms and nations play the economic game. Finally, the economic game is not played in isolation from the political game.

Many of the tradeoffs Thurow describes are of the 'If ... then' variety. If we fail to address the problem of the trade deficit, then eventually US standards of living must fall. If we do not adopt explicit industrial policies, then we are unlikely to promote those industries we need to remain competitive. If we fail to address the distribution problem directly, then inequality will worsen and ultimately, we will be confronted with political instability. Our problems (inflation, environmental, slow growth or whatever) can be solved, but someone or some group will pay a price. To reduce or eliminate the federal budget deficit requires either an increase in taxes or a reduction in expenditures. In either case, some group pays. Nevertheless, Thurow's tradeoffs have a dynamic character. These are not the tradeoffs of a static world in which resources, technology or GDP are fixed at current levels. The dynamic nature of Thurow's tradeoffs may be confirmed by examining his analysis of lifetime consumption expenditures (Thurow 1969c, 1970b, 1975c).

Thurow (1980a, pp. 189-90) describes what may be the ultimate tradeoff in terms of relative income inequality.

> When society has to confront the issue of differences in the relative income of different groups – rich versus poor, black versus white, male versus female, farmers versus urban dwellers – it is addressing the paradigm zero-sum game. Every increase in the relative income of one group is a decrease in the relative income of another group.

For Thurow, such a tradeoff is not mere speculation. Time and again he cites survey data indicating that most people specify a minimum (desirable) income level as a more or less fixed percentage of the average income of a larger group.

The concept of economic tradeoffs is hardly novel to economists. Thurow, however, applies the concept in imaginative ways and, unlike many economists, he is always consistent in asking 'who will pay for a given course of action'.

THE INTERNATIONAL ECONOMY: NEW RULES OF THE GAME

Increasingly, Thurow has turned his attention to the international economy and the dependence of the US economy on international trade. Like many other American economists who had previously concentrated their efforts on domestic economic issues, the rising proportion of international trade (exports or imports) as a percent of GDP, large trade imbalances, changes in the income of Americans relative to the rest of the industrialized world, large differences in growth rates between the US and other nations and the changing structure of international trade and its institutions compelled Thurow to examine the international economy more closely.

Thurow's concentration on international issues did not divert his attention from the themes already described (productivity, distribution, tradeoffs and the stochastic nature of the economy). But, his analysis of these themes in an international context is innovative. As usual, the implications of his analysis are a peculiar mixture of the conventional and unconventional.

Thurow (1992) starts his analysis of the international economy with the assertion that nations, not just individuals and firms, are competitive. And, in any competitive game, there are winners and losers. Moreover, the rules of the international economic game are changing rapidly. The old rules, established after World War Two are either gone (e.g., fixed exchange rates) or not enforceable (e.g., GATT). Further, not only are the rules changing, but those controlling the rules are changing. The US was the dominant economic power at the end of World War Two and could easily establish the rules of international trade. Now, with the European Community and Japan as major industrial powers, the US can no longer establish the rules unilaterally. Thurow argues that there will not be a single dominant economic power in the first half of the twenty-first century but he suggests that 'a manager is needed'.

Thurow (1984c, 1985a, 1987d, 1992; and Thurow and Tyson 1987) argues that the US trade deficit is important and that sooner or later the rest of the world will insist that our accumulating international debt be repaid. Americans simply consume more than they produce and the US, once the world's largest lender, is now the world's largest debtor nation. Thurow (1992) argues rather dramatically that the trade deficit and accumulated interest mean that eventually US standards of living will be damaged. The solution is that consumption must grow at a slower rate than GDP. Exports must increase to offset the trade deficit. He argues that this offset will not come from agriculture or from services. Agricultural exports are limited by our major trading partners and the success of the Green Revolution. Services are not a major net exporter now and cannot be a major source of exports in the future – at least in the absence of a significant manufacturing base. Thus, manufacturing is the only sector capable of providing the needed export revenue.

To avoid the otherwise inevitable decline in American standards of living relative to the rest of the world, Thurow advocates 'building a world-class economy'.[8] While the policies required to build such an economy are described in the next section, two elements of his recommendations are discussed here.

First, Thurow (1981b, 1984c, 1985a and 1992) maintains that building a world-class economy does not require a trickle-down approach involving redistribution of resources to the wealthy. The trickle-down approach suggests that it is necessary to provide both increased savings and greater incentives to the wealthy to stimulate economic growth. Thurow argues that our major competitors have a more equal distribution of income than we do and have recently experienced growth rates higher than in the US. Moreover, our major competitors rely more heavily on teamwork than is the case in the US.

Second, Thurow (1984a, 1985f and 1992) makes a strong case that if the US is to remain competitive in world markets, then explicit industrial policies will be required. All nations, Thurow argues, have an industrial policy. Every tax, government expenditure, tariff, regulation, and subsidy to industry, influences the structure of industry and the rate of growth of productivity. Moreover, Thurow adds to the list education policy, monetary policy, labor legislation and many other items. Currently, these policies are not coordinated or designed to promote those industries that will be most competitive in world markets. Yet, according to Thurow, comparative advantage in the context of a dynamic economic environment is 'man-made' and not a natural phe-nomenon based on the luck of having a particular natural resource endowment. Winners and losers can be picked and can be encouraged. Why not do so?

THE ROLE OF GOVERNMENT

Ultimately, Thurow's focus is always on public policy issues. The importance of the role of government in Thurow's analysis of the economy is reflected also in numerous contributions to the public finance literature (Thurow 1966, 1967a, 1970c, 1971a, 1972b, 1973b, 1974, 1975b, 1980b and 1984b). While his policy focus does not make him unique among economists, his approach is far different from that of the neoclassical mainstream. In the neoclassical world, markets function efficiently while government interference in the system serves mainly to distort prices in a decidedly non-Pareto-optimal fashion. In such a system, economic analysis leads to extremely limited, predetermined policy recommendations. More specifically, *the* neoclassical policy recommendation is

---

8. *Building a World-Class American Economy* is the sub-title of Thurow's 1985 book, *The Zero Sum Solution* and the title of a journal article. But this recommendation is most fully described in *Head to Head.*

to reduce the role of government in the economy.[9] For Thurow, however, it is absurd to suggest that even a predominantly market-oriented economy can function without government. No economy does so. Moreover, no national government can avoid having an impact on the level and rate of growth of productivity or the distribution of income. Appropriate public policies are, therefore, essential to the efficient functioning of the economy.

At the macro level, Thurow (1985f, p. 371) describes himself as 'fundamentally a Keynesian in the sense that I believe it is in fact possible to create a full employment society'. But clearly there is more to Thurow's macro policies than his conviction that full employment is possible. Thurow has been quick to recognize that the increasingly interdependent international economy requires coordination of macro policies among the major industrial nations. Thurow is convinced also that sound macroeconomic policy depends on an equally sound set of microeconomic policies.

What are these microeconomic policies? To understand Thurow's recommendations, recall that he identifies 'anemic productivity growth' as America's central economic problem. Also, recall that Thurow argues that there are many reasons for the decline in productivity growth. Thus, no single policy will solve the problem. As described earlier, Thurow calls for explicit industrial policies, internationally coordinated macro policies, changes in antitrust laws and other policies to address the productivity problem.

All nations, Thurow argues, have policies that influence productivity and economic growth. This is true even if, as in the US, these policies are not explicitly designed to do so. Governments, for example, influence productivity growth rates directly and indirectly through tax and tariff policies, expenditure patterns, investments in human and physical capital and subsidies to various industries.

The actions of government also influence the distribution of income. Yet, we are, as a society, particularly unwilling to directly address the income distribution problem. Indeed, the central thesis of *The Zero Sum Society* is that our economic problems can be solved but that we face political bottlenecks because we are unwilling to decide which group will pay.

In the mid-1960s, Thurow worked for Lyndon Johnson's Council of Economic Advisors. This period was the height of the War on Poverty and Thurow's interest in problems of poverty and discrimination are reflected in a series of books and

---

9.   This description of the neoclassical world is an over-simplification — but not much of an over-simplification. Oddly enough, while the principle of Pareto optimality is often relied upon to recommend against government action, it is rarely suggested that reducing the existing level of government might not be Pareto optimal.

articles. His policy recommendations in this area are far too numerous to repeat here, but one aspect needs comment. Massive expenditures on education were widely viewed at that time as a potentially effective means of reducing poverty and inequality. Thurow's analysis of both the human capital literature and his own econometric work led him to the conclusion that a large portion of the variation in individual earnings cannot be systematically explained. In short, the random part of variations in earnings is large. If that is the case, massive educational expenditures will do little to reduce poverty or inequality (see e.g., Thurow 1982a). That fact does not, however, mean that Thurow favors cuts in education spending. On the contrary, to build a world-class economy requires, in Thurow's words, 'a world-class educational system'.

Whether one agrees or disagrees with Thurow's policy recommendations, several facts are not in dispute. First, Thurow's policy recommendations are a central part of his economic analysis. Second, his policy recommendations are consistent with his analysis. Third, unlike many economists, Thurow is careful to explicitly state both the value judgements and the analysis on which his policy recommendations are based. Fourth, Thurow's major policy recommendations have not been implemented. And, fifth, testing the hypothesis that his policy recommendations are the appropriate course of action may be impossible.

THE THEORETICAL THUROW

In the early stages of his career, Thurow was well within the mainstream of economics. His publications appeared in journals (*The American Economic Review, The Quarterly Journal of Economics* and others) that do not publish work outside of the mainstream. His early work included the estimation of production functions, the construction of macroeconometric models and other statistical efforts – along with a number of contributions to the field of public finance. Although theory is necessary for such efforts, this work was largely empirical and Thurow did not earn his reputation primarily as a theoretician. As most economists do, Thurow borrowed heavily from the theoretical devices that were popular at the time (the 1960s and 1970s).

Yet, Thurow has also contributed to the development of economic theory. His empirical work – especially his work on labor markets – increasingly led him to become a severe critic of modern economic theory, both micro and macro. Although some observers might identify a particular article or particular time at which Thurow began to reject the conventional model, his views on theory more likely developed in an evolutionary fashion. For Thurow, there seems to be no clear break with the conventional wisdom. As early as 1969 in *Poverty and*

Discrimination, he was very critical of the marginal productivity theory as an explanation of how earnings are in fact distributed. By 1975 (*Generating Inequality*), he offered a devastating critique of marginal productivity theory and of conventional explanations of how the labor market worked. Given the critical importance of labor markets, the next logical step was for Thurow to conclude that there was something fundamentally wrong with all of modern microeconomic theory.

Yet, even today, his break with standard theory is far from complete. Thurow, like many economists who have lost their religious zeal for the conventional wisdom, still finds some aspects of the mainstream model to be useful.

Thurow (1983a) suggests that the hypothetical 'average economist' would argue that micro theory is fundamentally sound. If there are any real problems with modern economic theory, the average economist would indicate that the problem is with macro theory, specifically that macro theory is not well grounded in microeconomics. For Thurow, this explanation of the current state of economic theory is backwards.

> Microeconomic theory is not fundamentally sound, and the real problems are to be found in a micro-economic theory that is unsatisfactory. ... Macro problems do exist, but they will not be solved until some fundamental reform occurs in micro-economic theory. (Thurow 1983a, p. 3)

So, what is the problem with the conventional price-auction model? In one sense, Thurow's answer is a simple one: there are too many deviant observations – that is, observations that are inconsistent with the theoretical model. Three examples should suffice. Strictly speaking, the conventional model suggests that there will be no long-term unemployment. With flexible wages, the labor market should clear automatically and if a person is unemployed, this must be voluntary unemployment. Similarly, there is no room in the conventional model for discrimination based on race, age or sex. But, notes Thurow, unemployment at levels that cannot be voluntary does exist for extended time periods and discrimination is an observed fact. Moreover, applied microeconomic theory has a terrible track record in predicting its most important variable, price. No micro model could or did predict, for example, the OPEC-related price increases in oil or the other supply shocks of the 1970s or early 1980s.

Others have noted deviant observations in regard to the price-auction model. Yet, the model has withstood the pressure. Deviant observations have been dismissed as market imperfections or explained away using proxy variables. Thurow suggests another alternative, rebuilding microeconomics so that it is consistent with the facts. He argues that this can be done by noting that most markets are indeed competitive – in the sense that there are few firms that face no real competition – and that markets do clear, but also noting that markets (especially the labor market) do not clear based on price adjustments.

Indeed, suggesting that the labor market clears but that the adjustment occurs through non-price variables is how Thurow handled the labor market problem. In product markets it is also apparent to Thurow that markets sometimes clear on non-price variables. This is a useful contribution. Unfortunately, outside of the labor market, Thurow does not really offer an alternative microeconomics. Moreover, while he recognizes the importance of institutions (see below), he does not really suggest a theory of institutional change.

Thurow (1983) outlined what he thinks must be done to cure the ills of mainstream economic theory. First, the assumption of maximizing behavior must be replaced with something more realistic. Thurow finds little evidence that either producers or consumers are maximizers. He explains the popularity of the maximizing assumption on the basis of its easy mathematical tractability. Second, preferences must not be taken as given – external to the model. That is, we need an adequate theory of preference formation. Third, the profession needs a theory of the labor market that is compatible with the facts that unemployment exists and labor markets do not clear on the basis of price alone. Fourth, we need a theory of the relationship of the individual to society. Fifth, we need a theory of income distribution that explains more than does marginal productivity theory. Sixth, we need an economic theory that incorporates power and power relationships.

Institutionalists will be heartened to note that Thurow has concluded that the institutional environment is an important aspect of the rules of the economic game. Furthermore, the proper design of institutions cannot be derived from economic theory. According to Thurow (1983a, p. 231), the price-auction model indicates that all institutional arrangements are as efficient as they can be.

> Because institutions are nothing but voluntary collections of maximizing individuals, it is reasoned, they exist if and only if they help individuals to maximize. Moreover, because inefficient institutions are driven out of business by efficient economic institutions, no voluntary institution can have an impact on economic output. At all times the market forces institutions to evolve into their most efficient form.

Thurow rejects this view of institutions. Institutions, according to Thurow, do matter. Differences in international savings rates of individuals illustrate this point. The personal saving rate in Japan, for example, is high when compared to the US rate. In Japan, the institutional structure is designed to encourage high savings rates and they do occur. In the US, consumption rather than savings is encouraged and savings rates are correspondingly low. Another example is his case for industrial policies discussed earlier.

SUMMARY AND ASSESSMENT

In his curriculum vitae Lester Thurow describes himself as an 'economics educator'. We interpret this phrase broadly to mean the education of students, policy makers, the economics profession and the public in general. If an economist should be judged on the basis of a self-proclaimed specialty, there can be no doubt about Thurow's success. He is a superb educator. He is thought-provoking and witty and he communicates complex ideas in a straightforward and original fashion. His arguments are buttressed by data and examples which capture the attention of a wide audience, including those whose perspectives are very different from his own. His analyses of economic conditions and problems are eagerly sought by a variety of media.

It is appropriate, however, to judge Thurow as an economics scholar. The earlier sections of this chapter and the bibliography provide ample evidence that Thurow does not suffer from a productivity problem. While his career is far from complete, he has already accomplished more than most economists do in an entire career. His contributions to the analysis of income distribution, productivity and labor markets assure him of a prominent place among contemporary economists.

Thurow's success, in part, is due to his broad macro perspective and his recognition of the interconnections between political and economic issues. Thurow, in this context, is within the best tradition of political economists, acknowledging the political and social aspects of economic issues. For example, he argues that workers are motivated by their real wage relative to those of others in a group and he views the consequences of inflation in psychological terms, not simply in terms of the impact on purchasing power.

Thurow is often explicitly political in his writings and speeches. *The Zero Sum Solution*, published in 1985 was, for example, a blueprint for the revitalization of the Democratic Party in the US. In that book, Thurow explained that the groups which had comprised the New Deal coalition no longer had common interests. He then described the economic issues including high unemployment, low rates of productivity growth and worsening income distribution, that the Democrats should focus on to regain the Presidency. As a professional economist and man of science, Thurow could be criticized for such indiscretions. Yet, as pointed out earlier, Thurow has demonstrated consistently that he knows the difference between value judgements and scientific analysis. In our view, it is far better that the value judgements of an economist are openly stated than hidden.

Because much of his interest in economics is motivated by concern with improving the general standard of living, Thurow views economics as much more than an intellectual activity and he is critical of his profession for building elegant models of a non-existent world characterized by price-auction markets. Critical though he is, Thurow is respectful of his colleagues in the profession and of the strides that have been made in understanding economic activity. He concluded the introduction to *Dangerous Currents* with the following statement.

nothing I have to say will deny the fact that in their 200-year history, economists as a group have advanced our understanding of economic behavior. ... So, even as I criticize the economics profession, let me say at the outset that I am myself proud to be called an economist. (Thurow 1983a, p. xix)

THUROW'S MAJOR WRITINGS

(1965), 'The Changing Structure of Unemployment: An Econometric Study', *The Review of Economics and Statistics*, **XLVII**, 137-49.

(1966a), 'The Theory of Grants-in-Aid', *National Tax Journal*, **19** (4), 373-7.

(1966b) (with L.D. Taylor), 'The Interaction Between the Actual and Potential Rates of Growth', *The Review of Economics and Statistics*, **XLVIII** (4), November, 351-60.

(1967a) (ed.), *American Fiscal Policy: Experiment for Prosperity*, Englewood Cliffs, NJ: Prentice Hall, Inc.

(1967b), 'The Causes of Poverty', *The Quarterly Journal of Economics*, **81**, February, 39-57.

(1968), 'Disequilibrium and the Marginal Productivity of Capital and Labor', *The Review of Economics and Statistics*, **XLX** (1), February, 23-31.

(1969a), *Poverty and Discrimination*, Washington, DC: The Brookings Institution.

(1969) (with Carl Rappaport), 'Law Enforcement and Cost-Benefit Analysis', *Public Finance/Finances Publiques*, **24** (1), 48-64.

(1969b), 'Problems in the Area of Poverty: Discussion', *The American Economic Review*, **LIX** (2), 476-8.

(1969c), 'The Optimum Lifetime Distribution of Consumption Expenditures', *American Economic Review*, **LIX** (3), 324-30.

(1969d), 'A Fiscal Policy Model of the United States', *Survey of Current Business*, **49** (6), June, 45-64.

(1969e), 'A Disequilibrium Neoclassical Investment Function', *The Review of Economics and Statistics*, **51** (4), November, 431-5.

(1970a), *Investment in Human Capital*, Belmont, CA: Wadsworth Publishing Co.

(1970b), 'The Optimum Lifetime Distribution of Consumption Expenditures: Reply', *The American Economic Review*, **LX** (4), 744-5.

(1970c), 'Aid to State and Local Governments', *National Tax Journal*, **XXIII** (1), 23-35.

(1970d), 'Analyzing the American Income Distribution', *The American Economic Review*, **LX** (2), 261-9.

(1971a), *The Impact of Taxes on the American Economy*, New York: Praeger Publishers.

(1971b), 'The Income Distribution as a Pure Public Good', *The Quarterly Journal of Economics*, **LXXXV** (2), 327-36.

(1972a), 'The American Economy in the Year 2000', *The American Economic Review*, **LXII** (2), 439-43.

(1972b), 'Net Worth Taxes', *National Tax Journal*, **XXV** (3), 417-23.

(1973a), 'Toward a Definition of Public Justice', *Public Interest*, **31**, Spring, 56-80.

(1973b), 'The Income Distribution as a Pure Public Good: A Response', *Quarterly Journal of Economics*, **LXXXVII** (2), 316-19.

(1973c), 'The Political Economy of Income Redistribution Policies', *The Annals of the American Academy of Political and Social Science*, **409**, 146-55.

(1974), 'Cash Versus In-Kind Transfers', *The American Economic Review*, **LXIV** (2), 190-95.

(1975a), *Generating Inequality: Mechanisms of Distribution in the U.S. Economy*, New York: Basic Books, Inc.

(1975b), 'The Economics of Public Finance', *National Tax Journal*, **XXVIII** (2), 185-94.

(1975c), 'The Optimum Lifetime Distribution of Consumption Expenditures: Reply', *The American Economic Review*, **LXV** (4), 753-5.

(1976) (with Halbert White), 'Optimum Trade Restrictions and Their Consequences', *Econometrica*, **44** (4), July, 777-86.

(1977), 'Economics 1977', *Daedalus: Journal of the American Academy of Arts and Sciences*, **106** (4), Fall, 79-94.

(1978a), 'Psychic Income: Useful or Useless?', *American Economic Review*, **68** (2), May, 142-5.

(1978b), 'The Carter Economics', *Journal of Post Keynesian Economics*, **1** (1), Fall, 18-23.

(1978c), 'Stagflation and the Distribution of Real Economic Resources', *Data Resources Review*, December, 1.11-1.19.

(1980a), *The Zero Sum Society: Distribution and the Possibilities for Economic Change*, New York: Basic Books, Inc.

(1980b), 'The Indirect Incidence of Government Expenditures' *American Economic Review*, **70** (2), May, 82-7.

(1980c), 'Psychic Income: A Market Failure', *Journal of Post Keynesian Economics*, **3** (2), Winter 1980-81, 183-93.

(1980d), 'The Productivity Problem', *Technology Review*, **83** (2), November-December, 40-51.

(1981) (with Robert Heilbroner), *Five Economic Challenges*, Englewood Cliffs, NJ: Prentice-Hall, Inc.

(1981a), 'Employment and Public Expenditure in the USA in the 1980s', *Giornale degli economisti e annali de economia*, **40** (5-6), 371-8.

(1981b), 'The Illusion of Economic Necessity', in Robert A. Solo and Charles W. Anderson (eds), *Value Judgement and Income Distribution*, New York: Praeger Publishers, 250-75.

(1982) (with Robert Heilbroner), *Economics Explained*, Englewood Cliffs, NJ: Prentice Hall, Inc.

(1982a), 'The Failure of Education as an Economic Strategy', *American Economic Review*, **72** (2), May, 72-6.

(1982b), 'The Missing Mosaic' *Social Science Quarterly*, **63** (2), June, 376-80.

(1982c), 'Reply: Psychic Income A Market Failure', *Journal of Post Keynesian Economics*, **4** (4), Summer, 628.

(1982d), 'Response to Buchanan', *The Journal of Economic Issues*, **16** (3), September, 863-4.

(1982e), 'Reaganomics', *Aussenwirtschaft: Zeitscrift für internationale*, **37** (4), December, 407-15.

(1983a), *Dangerous Currents: The State of Economics*, New York: Random House.

(1983b), 'An International Keynesian Yank', *Challenge*, **26** (1), March/April, 36-9.

(1984a), 'The Need for Industrial Policies', *Annals of Public Co-operation Economics*, **55** (1), January-March, 3-31.

(1984b), 'Public Expenditures and the Elderly', *Eastern Economic Journal*, **XI** (1), January-March, 42-50.

(1984c), 'Building a World-Class Economy', *Society*, **22** (1), 16-29.

(1985a), *The Zero Sum Solution: Building a World-Class American Economy*, New York: Simon & Schuster.

(1985b) (ed.), *The Management Challenge: Japanese Views*, Cambridge, Mass.: The MIT Press.

(1985c), 'Preventing the Next Bank Panic', *Technology Review*, **88** (5), 12-13.

(1985d), 'The Other Deficit', *Resources*, **80**, Spring, 5-9.

(1985e), 'Healing With a Thousand Bandages', *Challenge*, **28** (5), November/December, 22-31.

(1985f), 'Public Intervention in the Industry. The Case of the U.S.A.', *Annals of Public Cooperation Economics*, **56** (1-2), January-June, 41-49.

(1985g), 'The Politics of Deregulation: Evolution of the Major Banks and the Financial Intermediaries in the U.S.A.', *Review of Economic Conditions in Italy*, September-December, 353-62.

(1985h), 'Japan's Economy and Trade with the United States', Selected papers submitted to the Subcommittee on Economic Goals and Policy of the Joint Economic Committee of the United States, 99th Congress 1st Session.

(1987a), 'A Surge in Inequality', *Scientific American*, **256** (5), May, 30-37.

(1987) (with Laura D'Andrea Tyson), 'The Economic Black Hole', *Foreign Policy*, Summer, 3.

(1987b), 'Economic Paradigms and Slow American Productivity Growth', *Eastern Economic Journal*, **XIII** (4), October-December, 333-43.

(1987c), 'Evaluating Economic Performance and Policies', *The Journal of Economic Education*, **18** (2), 237-46.

(1987d), 'Can America Compete in the World Economy', in Y.K. Shetty and Vernon M. Buehler, (eds), *Quality Productivity and Innovation: Strategies for Gaining Comparative Advantage*, Amsterdam: Elsevier, 11-32.

(1989a), *Toward a High-Wage, High-Productivity Service Sector*, Washington, DC: Economic Policy Institute.

(1989b), 'An Establishment or an Oligarchy?', *National Tax Journal*, **62** (4), December, 405-11.

(1989c), 'Regional Transformation and the Service Activities', in Lloyd Rodwin and Hidehiko Sazanami, (eds), *Deindustrialization and Regional Economic Transformation*, Boston: Unwin-Hyman, 179-98.

(1990a), 'GATT is Dead', *Journal of Accountancy*, September, 36-9.

(1990b), 'The End of the Post Industrial Era', *Business in the Contemporary World*, Winter, 21.

(1992c), *Head to Head: The Economic Battle Among Japan, Europe and America*, New York: William Morrow & Company, Inc.

19. Oliver E. Williamson

Scott E. Masten

There is perhaps a little want of the historical spirit which sees the perpetual struggle of mankind to improve institutions so as to confine self interest more and more closely within beneficent channels.

Edwin Cannan (1913, p. 333)

In the history of economic thought, there has been perhaps more than a little want of the spirit of which Cannan spoke. Although a wide variety of institutions and organizational forms influence economic activity, economists have preoccupied themselves primarily with the performance and limitations of markets and, particularly, the role of prices in coordinating production and exchange. The operation and limitations of non-market institutions and, correspondingly the issue of when one institutional arrangement will – or should – be substituted for another had, until quite recently, elicited relatively little systematic attention. Over the last twenty or so years, however, a new science of organization has been emerging in which the determinants and implications of alternative organizational forms are the central concern. Where traditional price theory assumed the institutional structure under which parties exchange – typically individuals transacting with for-profit firms across a market interface – the economics of organization attempts to answer questions like why are some transactions administered within firms rather than mediated through the market, why are there nonprofit organizations, what are the merits of franchise bidding as an alternative to rate-of-return regulation, and what determines the duration and structure of contractual agreements?

Although a number of economists have contributed to the development of the New Institutional Economics, no one has more consistently and steadfastly pursued that inquiry than Oliver Williamson. The approach that Williamson advocates, and with which he has become eponymous, begins with the observation that all organizational forms have drawbacks and that decisions regarding organizational form thus involve choices among variously faulty alternatives. The task, then, becomes one of (i) identifying the features that distinguish governance alternatives, (ii) assessing the differential capacities and hazards of those alternatives, and (iii) matching transactions with governance structures so as to economize on the cost of carrying out the transaction. Williamson's research and prodigious writings over the past two decades have been devoted almost exclusively to making this broad analytical blueprint operational and to refining and applying it to an ever-wider range of governance problems. Those efforts have altered irreversibly the way in which economists perceive and analyze the problem of economic organization.

TRANSACTION-COST ECONOMICS

Williamson's contributions to economics and public policy over the course of his career have been many and diverse, but his crowning professional achievement has been the development of the economics of transaction costs. At the heart of the transaction-cost approach is the proposition, due originally to Ronald Coase (1960), that all potential gains from trade would be realized but for the costs of reaching and enforcing agreements. Hence, in comparing alternative institutional arrangements, the focus of attention becomes the nature and size of the barriers preventing transactors from securing those gains.

Although Coase's insight firmly established the centrality of transaction costs in assessing the merits of organizational alternatives, his original formulation of the theory lacked a basis for determining which institution was preferred other than through the direct comparison of the costs of transacting under each. Because the costs of transacting can, at best, only be observed for institutions actually chosen, claims that observed institutional arrangements minimized transaction costs were easy to make and impossible to refute, a weakness that led economists to disparage early transaction-cost arguments as tautological. In the words of Stanley Fisher, 'Transaction costs have a well-deserved bad name as a theoretical device ... [partly] because there is a suspicion that almost anything can be rationalized by invoking suitably specified transaction costs' (1977, p. 322, as quoted in Williamson 1979a, p. 233).

Williamson rescued transaction-cost reasoning from this state by giving the theory predictive content. The key to operationalizing the theory, Williamson reasoned, was (i) to identify the behavioral traits responsible for the emergence of transactional frictions and (ii) to relate the incidence of those frictions to institutional structures and observable attributes of transactions in a discriminating way, that is, in a way that would permit hypotheses about organizational form to be formulated and tested. Even if transaction costs could not be compared directly, refutable propositions could nevertheless be derived by showing how the details of transactions affected the *differential* efficiency of organizational alternatives.

Setting out to implement this strategy for operationalizing transaction-cost reasoning, Williamson soon discovered that conventional economic as-sumptions regarding human behavior and the economic environment were not conducive to analyzing questions of organizational form. In particular, the high levels of rationality and efficacious enforcement of promises routinely assumed in economic models were incompatible with the existence of organizational failures: interesting institutional choice problems simply do not arise where omniscient administration and comprehensive contracting are feasible options. On the contrary, Williamson argued, organizational form matters only to the extent that individuals are limited in their foresight and cognition and are willing and able to renege on promises. These conditions, encapsulated in the concepts *bounded rationality* and *opportunism*, thus became the critical behavioral attributes to which all organizational ar-rangements must be responsive. In Williamson's conception, self-interest seeking remains the underlying assumption regarding human motivation, but special emphasis is placed on the limitations of human rationality and on the willingness of individuals to conceal or misrepresent facts, skirt rules, exploit loopholes, or otherwise capitalize on strategic advantages. Compared to their neoclassical counterparts, individuals are, on the one hand, less competent optimizers and, on the other, better liars, cheaters and shirkers. (Lest this seem too cynical a view of human nature, Williamson is careful to note that not everyone need be so unprincipled but that bounded rationality makes it difficult to distinguish the trustworthy from the unscrupulous.) Because efforts to control opportunism invariably place additional demands on bounded rationality, the goal of economic organization becomes to '*organize transactions so as to economize on bounded rationality while simultaneously safeguarding them against the hazards of opportunism*' (1985, p. 32; emphasis in original).

Having identified the human factors responsible for organizational failures, it remained to show how the incidence of those failures related to features of the economic environment. Central to this task was Williamson's recognition that even bounded rationality and opportunism pose few organizational problems in a static world. 'Transactions conducted under certainty are relatively uninteresting. Except as they differ in the time required to reach an equilibrium exchange configuration, any governance structure will do' (1979a, pp. 253-4). In the presence of change and uncertainty, however, transactors need to plan, monitor and continually adjust their behavior, activities that demand attention and often cooperation. Thus, for Williamson, as for Hayek, *change* is the pivotal feature of the economic environment and *adaptation* to unfolding events the central problem of economic organization (1975, p. 5; 1991a, pp. 277-8).

Economic institutions represent alternative ways of governing the process of adaptation and differ both in their capacities to effect adaptations and in the costs associated with doing so. Discrete market transactions, for instance, provide transactors considerable autonomy and flexibility in the periods both leading up to and following the actual transaction (1979a, 1991a). In such transactions, parties are generally free to bargain or not bargain as they please and, once the transaction is consummated, have relatively few ongoing obligations. The latitude afforded transactors in simple market transactions provides them both the incentive and the ability to adjust their behavior to unfolding events. But it also furnishes a variety of tactics through which transactors may seek to elicit a more favorable distribution of the gains from trade. Parties to a simple exchange may haggle, stall, or walk away from a deal altogether in hopes of extracting more of the rents accruing to exchange.

Such opportunistic tendencies matter little where the identity of traders is unimportant; the scope for opportunism is limited where transactors can easily turn to alternative trading partners if one seeks to gain at the expense of the other. But realization of cost economies or design benefits often requires investments in relationship-specific assets that isolate the transactors from market alternatives. Relationship-specific investments can take at least four forms: (i) physical-asset specificity, which involves investments in equipment such as tooling or dies specially designed to serve a particular customer; (ii) site or location specificity, which occurs when a buyer or seller locates his or her facilities next to the other to economize on transportation costs; (iii) human-asset specificity, which arises when one or both parties develop skills or knowledge valuable only when dealing with the other; and (iv) dedicated assets, which are investments made to support exchange with a particular customer that, though not specific to that customer, would result in substantial excess capacity were the customer to discontinue purchases (Williamson 1983a, p. 526). Once the die is cast and physical or human capital has been specially designed or located for a particular use or user, continuity in trading relationships becomes important.

This 'Fundamental Transformation' from a situation of *ex ante* competition to small numbers bargaining when relationship-specific investments are made is the dominant force motivating the adoption of specialized governance structures (Williamson 1985, pp. 61-3). Without some form of safeguard against appropriation, parties will be reluctant to invest in relationship-specific assets, despite the gains from doing so, for fear those gains will be dissipated in subsequent contention over their distribution. Securing the terms of trade at the outset through a long-term contract is one such safeguard. But contracting increases the demands on bounded rationality and only imperfectly limits opportunism. To accommodate uncertainty, contractors must either anticipate and devise responses to a large number of contingencies or prescribe a process through which adaptations can be executed. They must do so, moreover, in terms that courts can be expected to understand and implement at reasonable cost. The difficulty of anticipating and defining contractual obligations that avoid the prospect of costly adjudication means that contracts will, on the one hand, tend to be inflexible and, on the other, leave considerable opportunity to cheat on the agreement or otherwise seek to evade performance (1983a, pp. 526-7; 1985, p. 21).

As transactions become more complex and the environment more uncertain, the limitations of contracting as a safeguard against opportunism grow, increasing the attraction of other institutional arrangements that better support adaptive, sequential decision making while circumscribing or redirecting opportunistic tendencies. Naturally, such arrangements also come at a cost. Structures that constrain opportunism inevitably sacrifice some of the high-powered incentives that distinguish market transactions and, consequently, demand greater investments in monitoring and administration (1985, ch. 6; 1991a).

By relating the advantages and liabilities of alternative organizational arrangements to features of the transaction in a discriminating way, Williamson demonstrated that a transaction-cost orientation could indeed generate refutable implications. In doing so, moreover, he provided a systematic conception of the problem of economic organization in which all organizational forms are recognized to be subject to the same fundamental limitations. The aim of transaction-cost economics, as Williamson describes it, is to 'assign transactions (which differ in their attributes) to governance structures (the adaptive capacities and associated costs of which differ) in a discriminating (mainly transaction cost economizing) way' (1989, p. 136).

THE THEORY OF THE FIRM

Williamson first conceived and applied this framework for analyzing economic organization in the context of the problem that had also originally led Coase to focus on transaction costs, namely, the nature and boundaries of the firm. The orthodox portrayal of the firm as a production function that combines inputs purchased from individuals and other firms into outputs that it in turn sells on the market had proved useful for the analysis of market equilibrium. But this abstraction failed to illuminate the purpose or consequences of the vast array of economic activity organized administratively within firms. In the absence of an efficiency rationale, integration of production tended to be seen either as technologically determined or as serving monopoly purposes.

Transaction-cost economics recast the firm as a governance structure, one among several alternative ways in which production and exchange might be organized. By integrating a transaction, transactors alter the rules and processes through which disputes are resolved and adjustments effected. But though a firm-as-governance-structure orientation was a significant step, a complete theory of the firm awaited resolution of three great puzzles. First, what are the properties that distinguish organization within the firm from market exchange? Second, what determines which transactions get integrated? And third, what limits firm size or, as Coase (1991 (1937), p. 23) put it, 'why is not all production carried out in one big firm?'.

Williamson's initial assault on the boundaries of the firm issue, 'The Vertical Integration of Production: Market Failure Considerations' (1971), previewed many of the arguments later to become cornerstones of the comparative institutional framework. In particular, Williamson (i) described the advantages of markets in incentive and bounded-rationality economizing respects; (ii) portrayed the infeasibility of long-term, complete contingent claims contracts; and (iii) identified the hazards of short-term contracting 'if either (1) efficient supply requires investment in special-purpose, long-life equipment, or (2) the winner of the original contract acquires a cost advantage, say by reason of "first mover" advantages (such as unique location or learning, including the acquisition of undisclosed or proprietary technical and managerial procedures and task-specific labor skills)' (1971, p. 116). 'In circumstances ... where protracted bargaining between independent parties to a transaction can reasonably be anticipated', internalization offered 'a wider variety and sensitivity of control instruments' that included 'low-cost access to the requisite data' and 'a comparatively efficient conflict resolution machinery' (1971, p. 113).

It was not until the publication of *Markets and Hierarchies* in 1975, however, that the importance and scope of Williamson's analysis of organization began to be fully appreciated. In this path-breaking book, Williamson organized the components of his earlier analysis into a unified and systematic framework for analyzing the problem of economic organization in comparative terms. Among other things, he categorized the behavioral and environmental attributes responsible for organizational failures, described the distinctive features of market and hierarchical organization, and analyzed the differential effects of idiosyncratic investments and uncertainty on the costs of governing intermediate product transactions internally versus externally. The problems posed by incomplete or 'impacted' information – which Williamson traced to their rudiments in bounded rationality and complexity – also played a central role (1975, pp. 31-7). The publication of *Markets and Hierarchies* was a landmark in the development of transaction-cost reasoning that opened the door to the investigation of a host of organizational problems that had previously resisted economic analysis.

Williamson continued the refinement and extension of transaction-cost reasoning and his analysis of the governance of intermediate product transactions in a series of subsequent articles, the most influential of which has been 'Transaction-Cost Economics: The Governance of Contractual Relations' (1979a). This article offered a refined statement of the logic of matching governance modes with transactions and identified parallels between governance modes and contract law regimes. Williamson also related the choice among governance arrangements to three critical dimensions of transactions: uncertainty, frequency of exchange, and the degree to which investments are transaction specific, the last of which was taking on an increasingly prominent role.

Through his efforts to operationalize transaction-cost theory, Williamson had provided by this point an answer to the question, what determines which transactions get integrated? He had, moreover, as part of that analysis, also described some of the properties that distinguish internal organization from markets (1975, pp. 29-30) and the limits to internal organization (1975, ch. 7). But the basis for the superior auditing and dispute resolution properties Williamson and others ascribed to internal organization remained a matter of controversy. Where does the authority of management to direct production or settle disputes come from, and why are employees less able to hide or distort information than independent contractors? As Alchian and Demsetz had earlier protested, employers have no authority or disciplining power beyond that available in any ordinary contractual relationship; all an employer can do is 'fire or sue' (1972, p. 777). A fully satisfactory accounting of the source of internal organization's distinctive properties and the limits to firm size remained elusive.

Williamson supplied the last two pieces of the integration puzzle with the notions of 'forbearance law' and 'the impossibility of selective intervention'. Building on his earlier association of governance modes and contract regimes (1979a), Williamson proposed that the distinctive feature of the law governing internal organization is forbearance: 'whereas courts routinely grant standing to firms should there be disputes over prices, the damages to be ascribed to delays, failures of quality, and the like, courts will refuse to hear disputes between one internal division and another over identical technical issues' (1991a, p. 274). The decision to make rather than buy thus has substantive implications: while parties to a contract can resort to courts to resolve disputes, top management exercises ultimate authority in disputes between divisions; it is its own court of last resort. Ultimately, termination and legal action are, as Alchian and Demsetz maintained, the only options available, but *when* you can fire and *what* you can sue for depend on the mode of organization adopted. The refusal of courts to intervene in internal disputes affords management flexibility to conduct business and adapt operations as they deem appropriate and thus provides a basis for the control and adaptability advantages of internal organization (1991).

But if internal organization possesses superior control and adaptation properties, why are not all transactions organized with the firm? In principle, a newly integrated firm should be able to operate at least as efficiently as the two independent firms from which it was formed simply by allowing each division of the combined firm to operate independently as it had before and only intervening where net benefits were likely to be realized. As long as managers intervened selectively, combined operations would always dominate independent ones (1985; pp. 131-5).

Williamson's answer to the question, 'what limits firm size?', lay in the impossibility of selective intervention (1985, ch. 6). Unable to use the courts to enforce promises to intervene selectively, management would be drawn to intervening even where joint benefits are not realized. Without effective assurances that owners will not appropriate performance enhancements, the incentives of division managers to innovate, maintain assets, acquire and utilize information, and otherwise invest in the efficient operation of the division are ineluctably compromised. In their place, the firm is forced to substitute weaker, indirect incentives dependent on managerial oversight. The loss of incentive intensity combined with the limited capacity of management to administer additional transactions – which manifest themselves in a variety of bureaucratic inefficiencies – ultimately undermine the efficacy of internal organization and thereby limit firm size.

With the last pieces of the puzzle in place, the tradeoffs between market and internal organization came into still sharper focus. Although the high-powered incentives attainable with market exchange economize on bounded rationality, the dissociation of effort and compensation and resulting loss in incentive intensity resulting from integration is not always to be lamented: high-powered incentives motivate efforts to redistribute as well as increase rents. Where asset specificity is great and uncertainty high – hence the gains to ongoing exchange large and flexibility highly valued – flatter, low-powered incentives supported by enhanced monitoring are likely to be preferred (1988a, 1991a).

A FUNDAMENTAL TRANSFORMATION

Although his name has become synonymous with transaction-cost reasoning, Williamson's approach to analyzing organization was itself the result of a fundamental transformation. Like his work on transaction-cost economics, his early research was marked by brilliance and innovation. But the orientation and methods he brought to this research were more conventional in nature. Entering the doctoral program at Carnegie in 1960 as a transfer from the PhD program in business administration at Stanford, Williamson was attracted to the issues being addressed by the behavioral group led by Herbert Simon, Richard Cyert and James March, but he favored the methods employed by the economists, which included John Muth, Merton Miller and Allan Meltzer. His dissertation combined those interests by addressing the issue of managerial discretion in terms of constrained maximization. In a prelude to later agency treatments, Williamson argued that managers have preferences over such things as staff and emoluments and that costs of detecting and policing managers actions prevented owners from effectively overseeing managers. Modeling the tradeoff between profits and other managerial objectives, he derived a set of testable hypotheses distinguishing profit-maximization and managerial-discretion assumptions and showed, using data from field studies, that observed managerial behavior was consistent with the latter. This research, which was awarded a Ford Foundation Dissertation Prize in 1963 and published as *The Economics of Discretionary Behavior* (1964), introduced the first consistent and economically sound model of firm behavior based explicitly on utility maximization rather than profit maximization and opened for the first time the black box of the firm to the tools of modern economics.

Williamson went on to make a number of important contributions to economics and public policy, including original and influential papers on peak-load pricing (1966), social choice (1967), and the dynamics of interfirm behavior (1965), as well as a pair of articles on barriers to entry, 'Selling Expense as a Barrier to Entry' (1962) and 'Wage Rates as a Barrier to Entry: The Pennington Case in Perspective' (1968a), that were the first to treat entry barriers as a strategic decision and were forerunners to the strategic barriers literature of the 1980s. His primary interest, however, remained issues of organization, and he continued to develop and refine his analysis of the relation between the internal structure and behavior of the firm (1967, 1970).

The transformation of Williamson's perspective and approach appears to have begun during a year at the Justice Department (1966-67) in which he served as special economic assistant to the head of the Antitrust Division. During this experience, Williamson began to suspect that many of the practices antitrust authorities then regarded with hostility actually had efficiency motivations. A prudent antitrust policy, he reasoned, should recognize those motives and distinguish practices that, on net, enhanced efficiency from those that were detrimental to social welfare.

Williamson's concern with the tradeoffs inherent in antitrust policy was first revealed in 'Economies as an Antitrust Defense' (1968b), in which he demonstrated that potential cost economies from horizontal mergers could easily outweigh the dead-weight losses from increased market power and advocated that antitrust policy be modified to recognize demonstrable cost economies as a valid defense in merger cases. The potential for antitrust policy to impede efficient behavior was also evident in his efforts to develop a practical rule for distinguishing competitive from predatory behavior (1977). The resulting quantity-based rule both exhibited superior welfare properties and was easier to implement than previously proposed rules based on the comparison of prices and costs.

Williamson's analyses of horizontal mergers and predatory pricing contributed importantly to the debate over the formulation of a more discriminating antitrust policy. But while both were topics to which existing economic models could be adapted, the same could not be said for the analysis of vertical mergers and restrictions. Among the cases Williamson observed firsthand while in Washington was the Justice Department's successful challenge before the Supreme Court of the Schwinn bicycle company's contractual restraints with its dealers. Williamson was uncomfortable with the Justice Department's position that vertical restrictions had no redeeming features and served only to enhance market power. A conceptual apparatus to support his conjecture that vertical restraints could enhance efficiency had yet to be developed, however.

With antitrust policy as an impetus, Williamson's research began to tilt away from behavior and organization within firms to the structure of relations between them. The first products of those efforts were his 1971 article on vertical integration, which he motivated with references to antitrust policy (1971, p. 112), and *Markets and Hierarchies*, which he subtitled *Analysis and Antitrust Implications*. The necessary apparatus now in place, Williamson returned to the merits of the *Schwinn* decision with an analysis of vertical restrictions in transaction-cost terms (1979b). The economizing orientation of transaction-cost economics as a counter to monopoly and strategic arguments has since been a recurring theme (1985, chs 1 and 14; 1991b, 1992).

APPLICATIONS AND EXTENSIONS

In the meantime, Williamson was discovering the power and generality of the framework he had developed. Indeed, it appeared that any issue that would be posed as a contracting problem could be usefully examined in transaction-cost terms. Two early applications were to the organization of labor and the governance of public utility transactions. In 'Understanding the Employment Relation: The Analysis of Idiosyncratic Exchange' (1975), Williamson (with Michael Wachter and Jeffrey Harris) assessed the role of internal labor markets as solutions to the problems of bounded rationality and opportunism where workers had developed firm-specific skills and, in so doing, developed an efficiency rationale for the promotion ladders and grievance procedures that were common elements of collective labor agreements.

The debate over the prospects for franchise bidding as an alternative to rate-of-return regulation provided another arena in which to demonstrate the value of a transaction-cost orientation. The conventional wisdom in the late 1960s was that public utility regulation was a necessary response to natural monopoly cost conditions. Harold Demsetz (1968) exposed the fallacy in that reasoning by noting that public utility services could be efficiently procured – even where cost conditions dictated a single supplier – simply by awarding a franchise to the firm that offered to serve the market at lowest price. Williamson, who had served on Mayor John Lindsay's task force on cable television in 1969-70, perceived parallels to the theory of vertical integration on which he had been working. In particular, because the supply of public utility services typically requires large, durable, investments in production and distribution facilities that are specialized to a particular market, efficient franchise agreements would have to take the form of long-term contracts to avoid repeated haggling over the terms of trade once those investments were in place. But uncertainty about cost and demand conditions over such long horizons and the complexity of public utility services would leave long-term contracts for public utility services perilously incomplete. To accommodate that uncertainty, franchise contracts would have to employ contract terms and administrative machinery – cost-plus price adjustment, auditing procedures, elaborate and formal dispute resolution processes – that mirrored both in character and in costs the administrative apparatus traditionally associated with rate-of-return regulation (Williamson 1976). While Demsetz had revealed the potential for the efficient supply of public utility services using market arrangements if 'irrelevant complications' were ignored (Demsetz 1968, p. 57), Williamson had shown that it was precisely such complications that underlay the choice between regulation and franchise bidding and that the complications that impeded effective regulation were likely to frustrate franchise bidding solutions as well.

Williamson also showed how the transaction-cost paradigm could be used to provide a fresh perspective on firms' financing decisions (1988b). According to Williamson, debt and equity represent alternative governance structures for the procurement of financial capital analogous to contracting and internal organization for the procurement of intermediate products. For projects involving standardized, redeployable assets, debt, which offers contractual protections for investors, is the low-cost governance arrangement. As asset specificity increases, however, the residual value of the assets and, hence, the value of debtholders' preemptive claims declines. The willingness to supply capital in such cases will be enhanced if management offers investors a safeguard against appropriation or misuse of their investments in the form of a body (the board of directors) that can monitor the use of investors' capital and has the authority to oversee, compensate and replace management. Like internal procurement of intermediate goods and unlike debt, which affords investors the power to intervene only under a set of relatively extreme events (such as bankruptcy), equity financing provides a mechanism for regularized interventions. In contrast to traditional agency treatments, transaction-cost economics 'regards debt and equity principally as governance structures rather than as financial instruments' (1988b, p. 579).

Although the *choice* among organizational forms has been the primary focus of transaction-cost analyses, the *design* of market and firm relations has been another major theme of Williamson's research. Williamson's earliest ex-ploration of organizational design was his analysis of the internal structure of firms. Intrigued by Alfred Chandler's description of the advent of the multidivisional corporation, Williamson set out to analyze how growth in the size and complexity of a firm affected the way tasks and responsibilities are divided within the organization (1970, 1975). Comparing unitary, or U-form, organization, in which operations are grouped along functional lines (sales, finance, manufacturing, and so forth), with multidivisional, or M-form, organization, in which decision-making responsibility was assigned to quasi-autonomous operating divisions organized along product, brand or geographic lines, Williamson argued that the strains on management inherent in large organizations favored M-form organization, which, appropriately ad-ministered, had the properties of a miniature internal capital market. The analysis resulted in the M-form hypothesis: 'the organization and operation of the large enterprise along the lines of the M-form favors goal pursuit and least-cost behavior more nearly associated with the neoclassical profit maximization hypothesis than does the U-form organizational alternative' (1970, p. 134).

Williamson turned to the design of contractual relations with 'Credible Commitments: Using Hostages to Support Exchange' (1983a). Rejecting at the outset the assumption 'common to both law and economics, that the legal system enforces promises in a knowledgeable, sophisticated, and low-cost way' (1983a, p. 519), Williamson argued that the cost and imperfections inherent in court enforcement will lead contracting parties to seek out devices that foster cooperative adaptation to change without the need for recourse to the court system. One such device is the use of economic hostages. As in the days when kings extended their daughters as collateral against breach of their commitments to other monarchs, modern commercial transactors might find it advantageous to make relationship-specific investments whose value would be sacrificed if they failed to perform as promised. Although a unilateral investment in relationship-specific assets exposes the transaction to ap-propriation hazards, a reciprocal investment by a trading partner that balances the parties' exposure to such hazards may strengthen the integrity of a trading relationship. A range of otherwise enigmatic practices, such as reciprocal dealing and aspects of franchise contracts, can thereby be seen to have efficiency motivations (1983a).

RECEPTION AND INFLUENCE

Widely revered for his keen judgement and generous advice, Williamson has been known to summarize his overall assessment of the prospects of a student's research with a statement either that 'I don't see where this is going' or 'I think there might be something there', the latter being understood by all as a signal of approval and encouragement.

Initial reaction of much of the mainstream of the economics profession to Williamson's early writings on the theory of the firm might similarly be described as 'I think there might be something there'. Clearly, Williamson was addressing fundamental questions about the operation of the economic system that had yet to receive a satisfactory treatment. But the analysis developed in *Markets and Hierarchies* involved a significant departure from orthodox assumptions and an investment both in some unfamiliar concepts and in new terminology. To some in a profession increasingly enamored of mathematics and predisposed to skepticism regarding transaction-cost reasoning, Williamson's 'preformal' presentation of the theory seemed vague and unproven. Still, the logic was compelling, and the approach soon developed adherents. Besides Williamson, Victor Goldberg (e.g., 1976a, 1976b) and Benjamin Klein, Robert Crawford and Armen Alchian (1978), among others, began making headway in the development and application of transaction-cost reasoning. Empirical research and formal modeling following soon thereafter fostered further acceptance. By the mid 1980s, *Markets and Hierarchies* rivaled Adam Smith's *The Wealth of Nations* and Keynes's *General Theory* in terms of citations according to the *Social Science Citation Index*. By 1992, *Markets and Hierarchies* and *The Economic Institutions of Capitalism* had surpassed Marx's *Capital* to become the most frequently cited books in the social sciences.

The first empirical studies offering econometric tests of transaction-cost propositions began to appear in the early 1980s. Although Williamsonian transaction-cost economics, unlike earlier transaction-cost arguments, offered a set of testable implications, testing those hypotheses was not without its difficulties. The level of detail at which the theory operates made acquisition of appropriate data difficult; objective measures for factors like asset specificity and uncertainty are hard to devise and, even though variables representing organizational form pose fewer measurement problems, transaction-level data on organization form and contract terms are often not readily accessible. Nevertheless, these impediments gradually gave way to persistent efforts, and the result is a substantial body of evidence supporting the importance of asset specificity and transaction costs more generally in the choice among organizational forms and in the design and duration of contractual relationships (see Joskow 1988; Shelanski 1992; and Crocker and Masten 1994, for recent surveys).

Progress modeling transaction-cost arguments began shortly thereafter. Although economic theorists had developed an enormous body of theoretical work on contracting by the mid-1980s, most of those developments had occurred in the context of agency and asymmetric information models. Gradually, however, awareness was growing that the complete contracts and costless enforcement assumed in these models were inconsistent with contracting as it was observed in practice and did little to explain the variety of terms and duration of contractual agreements (see, e.g., Hart and Holmstrom 1987, pp. 131-3, 147-8). In response, contract theorists began to shift their attention to models of incomplete contracts that permitted, among other things, more rigorous investigation of the tradeoffs involved in the integration decision (see, for instance, Grossman and Hart 1986; Riordan 1990; and the survey by Holmstrom and Tirole 1989).[1] The extent to which Williamson's arguments have held up under these formalizations and their influence on formal theorists is reflected in the extensive and favorable treatments transaction-cost arguments have received in recent textbooks by theorists David Kreps (1990) and Paul Milgrom and John Roberts (1992).

Williamson's influence has also extended beyond economics to law, political science, business strategy and sociology. No doubt, the accessibility of Williamson's analysis to scholars in fields less reliant than economics on formal modeling has contributed to its dissemination. But the more important factors in the adoption and influence of Williamson's ideas have been their immediate relevance to the concerns of scholars in these fields and Williamson's willingness to engage these scholars on their own territory. Williamson has, through his writings on contract, become one of the leading figures in the 'relational contracting' school of legal scholarship. At the same time, Williamson has been a vocal critic of 'legal centralism', the widely held view among legal scholars that governments, and particularly the legal system, represent indispensable and efficacious dispute resolution forums. Instead, Williamson emphasizes the efforts

---

1. Williamson (with Michael Riordan) also published an early model of the integration decision in which the level of investment in specific assets was treated as endogenous (1985).

of contracting parties to '"contract out of and away from" the governance structures of the state by devising private orderings' (1983a, p. 520). Recognition of the ubiquity of bounded rationality and opportunism has important implications for the way courts interpret and enforce contracts and for the design of the legal system more broadly, and has begun to be incorporated in analyses of political institutions as well (see, for instance, Weingast and Marshall, 1988, and the special issue of the *Journal of Law, Economics, and Organization*, 1990).

That transaction-cost economics has become one of the dominant paradigms in strategic management research should not be surprising given the strategic management field's abiding interest in questions of organizational form. By providing a systematic way of analyzing the relative merits of alternative governance arrangements and a set of testable propositions relating those merits to attributes of transactions and the surrounding environment, transaction-cost economics offers strategy a set of normative rules for choosing among alternative organizational arrangements. But where the business strategy literature had been primarily concerned with *strategizing*, that is, efforts to acquire and exploit market power, Williamson advocates an orientation that emphasizes *economizing* (Williamson 1991b). Not only is economizing more fundamental, according to Williamson, but 'emphasis on economizing restores manufacturing and merchandising to a place of importance within the business firm and on the academic research agenda' (1991b, p. 76).

More so than most economists, Williamson has also endeavored both to draw on and contribute to the sociology of organizations. In articles and essays addressed directly to sociologists, Williamson has sought to expand the dialogue between sociologists and economists by laying out the common ground and describing the advantages a transaction-cost economizing orientation offers for analyzing phenomena of long-standing concern to organization theorists (1981, 1990, 1993b, 1993c). At the same time, Williamson has demonstrated an uncommon receptivity to and appreciation of sociological concerns, as is evident from his discussions of the costs of bureaucracy, which trace bureaucratic inefficiencies to sociological phenomena such as the propensities of individuals to manage and forgive (1985, pp. 148-51) and in his references to concepts such as atmosphere and dignity with which economists have yet to come to terms (1985, ch. 10). More broadly, Williamson has repeatedly made the case that economists have potentially a lot to learn from sociologists regarding such matters as the role of process and the dimensions and implications of bounded rationality. This openness notwithstanding, Williamson has been critical of much of the sociological research on organizations, challenging those who would explain organizational structure in terms of power and trust relations to define and operationalize those concepts in a way that allows testable predictions (1990, p. 123; 1993b, 1993c).

Despite the substantial measure of respect and acceptance afforded Williamson's approach by legal scholars, sociologists, and strategic management and organization theorists, transaction-cost reasoning has nevertheless generated its share of disputes and controversies.[2] An example is the debate engendered by Williamson's 1980 article on the organization of work. Williamson's analysis corroborated radical economist Stephen Marglin's verdict that technology alone was not enough to explain hierarchical relations but disputed his claim that the failure of neoclassical economics to supply an efficiency justification for hierarchy supported the Marxian interpretation of hierarchy as a device to exploit workers. Williamson's rejection of both technology- and power-based explanations of the evolution of work organization in favor of an interpretation based on transaction-cost economies prompted a series of replies, to which Williamson offered gracious yet compelling rejoinders (e.g., Williamson 1983b, 1988c).

Through debates of this nature substantive disagreements are aired, mistakes uncovered, arguments clarified, and knowledge ultimately advanced. But transaction-cost economics has occasionally been the target of less constructive criticism as well. Richard Posner's assessment of the contributions of Coase and Williamson at the annual conference on the New Institutional Economics held in Saarbrucken, Germany, in June 1992, is an example of the latter (see Posner 1993, and the responses by Williamson 1993a, and Coase 1993). Posner praised Williamson for helping to correct 'collectivist deformations of theory' (1993, p. 85) and for having invited 'economists' attention to a host of underexplored problems and [for] contributing to their solution by exploring the ways in which businessmen overcome transaction costs by a variety of devices and in a variety of settings' (1993, p. 81). Posner went on, however, to question the novelty of the framework Williamson developed and its contribution to our understanding of the problem of economic organization. The distinctions between transaction-cost economics and other economic analyses of institutional arrangements are, as far as Posner was concerned, mainly terminological, whatever substantive insights transaction-cost economics may once have offered long since superseded by developments elsewhere in economics and particularly in information and game theory (1993, pp. 80-81).

Does transaction-cost economics represent a distinct approach to problems of economic organization? Certainly, parallels can be drawn between the concepts and concerns of transaction-cost economics and those found in neoclassical

---

2. See Zald (1987) for a review of Williamson's *Economic Institutions of Capitalism* from a sociologist's perspective and a summary of the reaction of sociologists to Williamson's work.

treatments. Concerns with the effects of bounded rationality, opportunism and asset specificity in transaction-cost economics overlap more mainstream concerns with information asymmetries, moral hazard and bilateral monopoly. Indeed, given that meaningful institutional choice problems simply do not arise in the absence of bounded rationality and opportunism, it would have been surprising had the critical dimensions underlying the problem of economic organization gone completely unappreciated except by transaction-cost economists.

But to characterize transaction-cost economics solely in terms of a set of isolated concepts and a particular terminology misses the critical features that distinguish a transaction-cost orientation (see Williamson 1993a). First, whereas conventional analyses are content to treat information, bargaining and contracting costs as parameters, transaction-cost economics regards these as consequences of human cognitive limitations and behavior. It is true, for instance, that the complications introduced by bounded rationality can be captured in models of utility maximization constrained by imperfect information. But, without disparaging the contributions of that approach, it is also true that the results of asymmetric information models are extremely sensitive to the particular constraints assumed. Moreover, despite occasional acknowledgements that the roots of market failures lay in transaction costs (Arrow 1969), neoclassical treatments have kept transactional frictions largely hidden in the background, their presence or absence implicit in the behavioral and institutional options assumed available to economic actors. Little effort is made to analyze their determinants and dimensions systematically or to assure that assumptions were employed consistently. By invoking (prohibitive) search and information costs selectively, the literature on asymmetric information risks exposing itself to the sorts of charges of *ex post* rationalization leveled at early transaction-cost arguments.

Transaction-cost economics, by contrast, traces the origins of information costs to bounded rationality, which is omnipresent, and seeks to relate the incidence of information costs to characteristics of transactions and to the informational demands placed on decision makers under alternative organizational forms. Thus, modern transaction-cost economics regards information and other transaction costs as something to be explained rather than assumed, a difference that accounts in large measure for why transaction-cost economics, unlike information and game theories, has generated a substantial body of empirical work using real-world data.

Second, transaction-cost economics contemplates a wider range of behavior than conventional analyses (Williamson 1993d, pp. 100-101). Although both moral hazard and opportunism are motivated by self-interest, moral hazard describes actions taken in response to price signals contained in the contract and thus consists of efforts to effect a de facto adjustment of the distribution of surpluses *within the existing terms of an agreement*. The concept of opportunism, in contrast, encompasses actions designed to force a renegotiation of those terms and thereby to effect a *de jure* modification in the distribution of the gains from trade. Opportunism in contractual settings includes making false claims of dissatisfaction, suing for trivial deviations, and interfering with the other party's performance in hope of inducing a breach of contract (Williamson 1983, pp. 526-7). Such behavior does not benefit an actor directly but is undertaken solely to impose costs on a trading partner in hope of eliciting concessions, the goal being to make the status quo so disagreeable that your partner finds it less costly to accede to a renegotiation than to insist on the current terms. Compared to the types of behavior contemplated in conventional analyses, opportunism is more ingenious, active and likely to provoke strategic responses by other parties.

These differences in the characterization of human behavior, in turn, affect perceptions about the role of contracts. In standard agency models of contract, the primary concern is with aligning incentives to discourage shirking and other forms of moral hazard (Williamson 1985, ch. 1; 1988a). Transaction-cost economics, in contrast, views contracts as means of establishing procedures for adapting exchange and resolving disputes rather than purely as incentive mechanisms. Thus, whereas conventional analyses emphasize the efficiency of *outcomes*, transaction-cost economics focuses on the *processes* through which agreements are reached, modified and implemented (Williamson 1988a). What varies as transactions are relocated from one organizational form to another are the duties, procedures and sanctions available to transactors and, hence, the tactics they can employ and the processes through which adaptations are realized. Since it is the legal system that establishes and supports those distinctions, studying the practical operation and limitations of the legal system becomes an essential element of research on organization.

Most important, while conventional analyses continue to assess the efficiency of organizational arrangements relative to the absolute standard of Pareto optimality, transaction-cost economics is relentlessly comparative, maintaining that the merits of particular organizational arrangements can *only* be assessed relative to the performance of the relevant alternatives constrained by the same human frailties and propensities, technology and information (Williamson 1985, 1993a). A transaction-cost orientation fosters an ap-preciation that problems ascribed to markets, contracts or regulation often inhere in the circumstances. Given the powerful motives to find and adopt organizational forms that increase the available surplus, prudence requires consideration of the remediability of a problem before condemning the performance of a particular arrangement.

CONCLUDING REMARKS

The collapse of central planning and the subsequent problems encountered attempting to establish market economies has contributed to a growing appreciation of the importance of institutions and organization to economic performance. While traditional macroeconomic policy concerns such as fiscal budgets, price-level stabilization and currency convertibility are important to providing an environment conducive to growth, the roots of a successful free-enterprise economy rest in individual competence, sound business organization and the maintenance of a range of supporting institutions to define and protect property rights, facilitate trade and settle disputes (Williamson 1991c).

Simultaneously, awareness has been growing that understanding the economic institutions of capitalism requires an appreciation of the sources and consequences of transaction costs. The two most illustrious figures in the development of transaction-cost reasoning have been Ronald Coase and Oliver Williamson. Coase's contribution, for which he was honored with the 1991 Nobel Prize in Economics, was to show that, in the absence of transaction costs, efficiency could be achieved under any number of institutional arrangements and, hence, that the choice among alternative institutional arrangements, including the choice between firm and market organization, turned on a comparison of the costs of transacting under each. By demonstrating how systematic variations in the incidence of transaction costs across organizational forms and transaction types could be used to explain observed patterns of organization, Williamson elevated Coase's insight from a tautology to a predictive theory, an accomplishment that Coase himself has acknowledged. In a series of lectures celebrating the 50th anniversary of the publication of 'The Nature of the Firm', Coase observed that his 1937 article on the nature of the firm 'had little or no influence for thirty of forty years after it was published' (Coase 1988, p. 33). Referring to Williamson's explanation that this lack of influence resulted from a failure to operationalize the theory, Coase concluded, 'I think it is largely correct' (1988, p. 38; also 1992, p. 718).

On the surface, the operationalization of organizational choice problems might have appeared a natural and straightforward extension of neoclassical methods, the choice among governance arrangements being simply part of an individual's overall optimization problem. But Williamson's efforts to identify and enumerate the factors that lead one transaction to be integrated and another left to market mediation revealed that conventional assumptions regarding human behavior and the economic environment were not conducive to analyzing questions of organizational form. What emerged as a result of those efforts was not merely another extension of price theory and a handful of new insights regarding the decision to integrate but a whole new paradigm for analyzing the structures that govern economic activity. Through his extensive research and prolific writings, Williamson has demonstrated that the issues posed and the factors emphasized in the transaction-cost paradigm are pervasive and, from the point of view of both individual economic actors and society as a whole, of considerable economic importance. In Williamson's words, 'Any attempt to deal seriously with the study of economic organization must come to terms with the *combined* ramifications of bounded rationality and opportunism in conjunction with a condition of asset specificity' (1985, p. 42).

Emphasis on the transaction as the basic unit of analysis is not without its costs, of course. Concentration on individual transactions involves some sacrifice of attention to interactions in the general economy. Moreover, the fact that investments are durable so that the profitability of a current investment is contingent on preceding investment decisions – and recursively, therefore, on all preceding decisions – underscores the need for an evolutionary orientation (or 'historical spirit' as Cannan put it). Nevertheless, Williamson's contributions represent by far the most comprehensive treatment of the issues of economic organization and institutions in the economic literature to date and, given their scope and quality, are likely to remain so for the foreseeable future.

WILLIAMSON'S MAJOR WRITINGS

Williamson, Oliver E. (1962), 'Selling Expense as a Barrier to Entry', *Quarterly Journal of Economics*, 77, 112-28.

(1964), *The Economics of Discretionary Behavior: Managerial Objectives in a Theory of the Firm*. Englewood Cliffs, NJ: Prentice-Hall.

(1966), 'Peak Load Pricing and Optimal Capacity Under Indivisibility Constraints', *American Economic Review*, 56, 810-27.

(1967), 'Hierarchical Control and Optimum Firm Size', *Journal of Political Economy*, 76, 123-38.

(1967) (with Thomas Sargent), 'Social Choice: A Probabilistic Approach', *Economic Journal*, 27, 797-813.

(1968a), 'Wage Rates as a Barrier to Entry: The Pennington Case in Perspective', *Quarterly Journal of Economics*, 82, 85-116.

(1968b), 'Economics as an Antitrust Defense: The Welfare Tradeoffs', *American Economic Review*, 58, 18-35.

(1970), *Corporate Control and Business Behavior*, Englewood Cliffs, NJ: Prentice-Hall.

(1971), 'The Vertical Integration of Production: Market Failure Considerations', *American Economic Review*, 61, 112-23.

(1975), *Markets and Hierarchies: Analysis and Antitrust Implications*. New York: Free Press.

(1975) (with Michael Wachter and Jeffrey Harris), 'Understanding the Employment Relation', *Bell Journal of Economics*, 6, 250-78.

(1976), 'Franchise Bidding for Natural Monopolies – In General and With Respect to CATV', *Bell Journal of Economics*, **7**, 73-104.

(1977), 'Predatory Pricing: A Strategic and Welfare Analysis', *Yale Law Journal*, **87**, 284-340.

(1979a), 'Transaction-Cost Economics: The Governance of Contractual Relations', *Journal of Law and Economics*, **22**, 233-61.

(1979b), 'Assessing Vertical Market Restrictions', *University of Pennsylvania Law Review*, **127**, 953-93.

(1980), 'The Organization of Work', *Journal of Economic Behavior and Organization*, **1**, 5-38.

(1981), 'The Economics of Organization: The Transaction Cost Approach', *American Journal of Sociology*, **87**, 548-77.

(1983a), 'Credible Commitments: Using Hostages To Support Exchange', *American Economic Review*, **73**, 519-40.

(1983b), 'Technology and the Organization of Work: A Rejoinder', *Journal of Economic Behavior and Organization*, **4**, 67-8.

(1985), *The Economic Institutions of Capitalism*, New York: Free Press.

(1985) (with Michael Riordan), 'Asset Specificity and Economic Organization', *International Journal of Industrial Organization*, **3**, 365-78.

(1988a), 'The Logic of Economic Organization', *Journal of Law, Economics, and Organization*, **4**, 65-93. Repr. in O.E. Williamson and S.G. Winter (1991), *The Nature of the Firm: Origins, Evolution, and Development*. New York: Oxford University Press, 90-116.

(1988b), 'Corporate Finance and Corporate Governance', *Journal of Finance*, **43**, 567-91.

(1988c), 'Technology and Transaction Cost Economics: A Reply', *Journal of Economic Behavior and Organization*, **10**, 355-64.

(1989), 'Transaction Cost Economics', in Richard Schmalensee and Robert Willig (eds), *Handbook of Industrial Organization*, New York: North-Holland, 135-82.

(1990), 'Interview with Oliver E. Williamson', in Richard Swedenberg (ed.), *Economics and Sociology*, Princeton, NJ: Princeton University Press, 115-29.

(1991a), 'Comparative Economic Organization: The Analysis of Discrete Structural Alternatives', *Administrative Science Quarterly*, **36**, 269-96.

(1991b), 'Strategizing, Economizing, and Economic Organization', *Strategic Management Journal*, **12**, 75-94.

(1991c), 'Institutional Aspects of Economic Reform: The Transaction Cost Economics Perspective', (mimeo).

(1992), 'Antitrust Lenses and the Uses of Transaction Cost Economics Reasoning', in Thomas Jorde and David Teece (eds), *Antitrust, Innovation, and Competitiveness*, New York: Oxford, 137-64.

(1993a), 'Transaction Cost Economics Meet Posnerian Law and Economics', *Journal of Institutional and Theoretical Economics*, **149**, 99-118.

(1993b), 'Transaction Cost Economics and Organization Theory', *Industrial and Corporate Change*, **2**, 107-56.

(1993c), 'Calculativeness, Trust, and Economic Organization', *Journal of Law and Economics*, **36**, 453-86.

(1993d), 'Opportunism and its Critics', *Managerial and Decision Economics*, **14**, 97-107.

OTHER REFERENCES

Alchian, Armen and Harold Demsetz (1972), 'Production, Information Costs, and Economic Organization', *American Economic Review*, **62**, 777-95.

Arrow, Kenneth J. (1969), 'The Organization of Economic Activity: Issues Pertinent to the Choice of Market vs. Non-Market Allocation', in *The Analysis and Education of Public Expenditure: The PPB System*, Joint Economic Committee, 91st Congress, 59-73.

Cannan, Edwin (1913), 'Review of N.G. Pierson's *Principles of Economics*', *Economic Review*, **23**, 331-3.

Coase, Ronald (1937), 'The Nature of the Firm', *Economica N.S.*, **4**, 386-405. Repr. in O.E. Williamson and S.G. Winter (1991), *The Nature of the Firm: Origins, Evolution, and Development*, New York: Oxford University Press, 18-33.

Coase, Ronald (1960), 'The Problem of Social Cost', *The Journal of Law and Economics*, **3**, 1-44.

Coase, Ronald (1988), 'The Nature of the Firm: Origin, Meaning, Influence', *Journal of Law, Economics, and Organization*, **4**, 3-47. Repr. in O.E. Williamson and S.G. Winter (1991), *The Nature of the Firm: Origins, Evolution, and Development*, New York: Oxford University Press.

Coase, Ronald (1991), 'The Institutional Structure of Production', Alfred Nobel Memorial Prize Lecture in Economic Sciences. Reprinted in *American Economic Review*, **82** (1992), 713-19.

Coase, Ronald (1993), 'Coase on Posner on Coase', *Journal of Institutional and Theoretical Economics*, **149**, 96-98.

Crocker, Keith J. and Scott E. Masten (forthcoming), 'Regulation and Administered Contracts Revisited: Lessons from Transaction-Cost Economics for Public Utility Regulation', *Journal of Regulatory Economics*.

Demsetz, Harold (1968), 'Why Regulate Utilities?', *Journal of Law and Economics*, **11**, 55-66.

Fisher, Stanley (1977), 'Long-Term Contracting, Sticky Prices, and Monetary Policy: Comment', *Journal of Monetary Economics*, **3**, 317-24.

Goldberg, Victor P. (1976a), 'Regulation and Administered Contracts', *Bell Journal of Economics*, **7**, 426-48.

Goldberg, Victor P. (1976b), 'Toward an Expanded Economic Theory of Contract', *Journal of Economic Issues*, **10**, 45-61.

Grossman, Sanford J. and Oliver D. Hart (1986), 'The Costs and Benefits of Ownership: A Theory of Vertical and Lateral Integration', *Journal of Political Economy*, **94**, 691-719.

Hart, Oliver and Bengt Holmstrom (1987), 'The Theory of Contracts', in Truman Bewley (ed.), *Advances in Economic Theory: Fifth World Congress*, Cambridge: Cambridge University Press, 71-155.

Holmstrom, Bengt and Jean Tirole (1989), 'The Theory of the Firm', in Richard Schmalensee and Robert Willig (eds), *Handbook of Industrial Organization*, New York: North-Holland, 61-133.

Joskow, Paul L. (1988), 'Asset Specificity and the Structure of Vertical Relationships: Empirical Evidence', *Journal of Law, Economics, and Organization*, **4**, 95-117.

Klein, Benjamin, Robert Crawford and Armen Alchian (1978), 'Vertical Integration, Appropriable Rents, and the Competitive Contracting Process', *Journal of Law and Economics*, **21**, 297-326.

Kreps, David M. (1990), *A Course in Microeconomic Theory*, Princeton: Princeton University Press.

Marglin, Stephen A. (1974), 'What Do Bosses Do? The Origins and Functions of Hierarchy in Capitalist Production', *Review of Radical Political Economics*, **6**, 33-60.

Masten, Scott E. (1986), 'The Economic Institutions of Capitalism: A Review Article', *Journal of Institutional and Theoretical Economics*, **142**, 445-51.

Milgrom, Paul and John Roberts (1992), *Economics, Organization, and Management*, Englewood Cliffs, NJ: Prentice-Hall.

Posner, Richard A (1993), 'The New Institutional Economics Meets Law and Economics', *Journal of Institutional and Theoretical Economics*, **149**, 73-87.

Riordan, Michael (1990), 'What is Vertical Integration?', in Mashiko Aoki, Bo Gustafsson and Oliver Williamson (eds), *The Firm as a Nexus of Treaties*, London: Sage Publications, 94-111.

Shelanski, Howard (1991), 'Empirical Research in Transaction Cost Economics: A Survey and Assessment', University of California, Department of Economics (mimeo).

Zald, Mayer N. (1987), 'Review Essay: The New Institutional Economics', *American Journal of Sociology*, **93**, 701-8.

Index

anchoring and adjustment, 117-19
anomalies, 351-61

biases, 112-19
Bowles, Samuel, xii-xiv, 1-17

capitalism, critique of, 1-15, 54-62, 96-102, 159-72
change, social, 303-6
Coase, Ronald, 385, 388
coercion, 220-21
collective action, 216-34
Commons, John R., 226
context effects, 119-24

Davidson, Paul, xiv, 18-43
democracy, 6-11
distribution of income, 366-70
domination, systems and structures of, 8-15, 44-65

economic thought, history of, 90-102, 239-52
economics
    philsophy of, 306-8, 312-15
    psychology of, 69-84, 99-102, 111-34, 259-72, 274-87, 351-61
    see *also* rationality
    sociology of, 39-40, 287-8
education, 2-6, 10-11
endowment effect, 125-6, 354, 358

ergodicity, 29-32, 370-72
evolutionary economics, 200-212, 300-322
experimental economics, 111-37, 274-98, 351-61

feminist economics, 44-65
finance motive, 23
firm, theory of the, 195-209, 388-91
Folbre, Nancy, xiv, 44-68
framing effects, 119-24
Frank, Robert, xiv-xv, 69-86

game theory, 259-72
gender, political economy of, 44-65
Gintis, Herbert, xiii-xiv, 1-17
government, economic role of, 315-20, 375-7
group size, 217-20

Heilbroner, Robert, xv, 87-110
heuristics, 112-9
history of economic thought, 90-102, 239-52
household, political economy of, 49-60

income distribution, 366-70
instability, 231-4, 252-6
institutions, 13-15, 69-84, 216-34, 239-51, 282-3, 300-306, 309-12, 379, 385-96